ECONOMICS
OF
DEVELOPMENT

ECONOMICS
OF
DEVELOPMENT

Malcolm Gillis
Dwight H. Perkins
Michael Roemer
Donald R. Snodgrass

HARVARD INSTITUTE FOR
INTERNATIONAL DEVELOPMENT
HARVARD UNIVERSITY

W· W· NORTON & COMPANY
New York London

The text of this book is composed in Times Roman, with display type set
in Optima. Composition by New England Typographic Service, Inc.
Manufacturing by The Maple–Vail Book Manufacturing Group. Book
design by Nancy Dale Muldoon.

FIRST EDITION

Library of Congress Cataloging in Publication Data
Main entry under title:
Economics of development.
  Bibliography: p.
  Includes index.
  1. Underdeveloped areas—Economic policy—Addresses,
essays, lectures. 2. Economic development—Addresses,
essays, lectures. I. Gillis, Malcolm.
HC59.7.E314 1983   338.9   83–4190
ISBN 0–393–95253–3

W. W. Norton & Company, Inc., 500 Fifth Avenue, New York, N.Y. 10110
W. W. Norton & Company, Ltd., 37 Great Russell Street, London WC1B 3NU

1 2 3 4 5 6 7 8 9 0

For Elizabeth, Julie, Linda, and Anne

CONTENTS

PREFACE

This textbook is a product of close to seventy years of experience by its four authors in the field of development, including a quarter century of residence in developing countries. Our involvements have included teaching, research, and especially advisory work on development policy. At one time or another all four of us have taught Harvard's basic undergraduate course on the economics of development, and became convinced of the need for a text with broad and relatively uniform coverage of the wide range of topics that constitute the field of economic development. Our field work, mostly under the auspices of Harvard's Institute for International Development (HIID), persuaded us that a development text ought to have a substantial focus on policy issues, but that these should be imbedded in a historical and theoretical framework to provide perspective.

This book does not take a neutral attitude toward all of the issues pertaining to development. Not every section will begin with "On the one hand there are those who believe . . . while on the other hand there are those who hold the opposite." Where controversy exists we try to point it out. The co-authors of this book differ among ourselves over many questions of development policy, but we do share a common point of view in certain key areas.

First of all, this text makes extensive use of the theoretical tools of classical and neoclassical economics in the belief that these tools contribute substantially to our understanding of development problems and their solution. The text does not rely solely or even primarily on theory, however. For three decades and more development economists and economic historians have been building up an empirical record against which these theories can be tested, and this book draws heavily on many of these empirical studies. We try to give real country examples for virtually all the major points made in this book. In part these examples come from the individual country and cross-country comparative studies of others, but we also draw extensively on our own personal experiences working on development issues around the world. Among the four of us we have been fortunate enough to study and work over long periods of time in Bolivia, Chile,

China, Colombia, Ghana, Indonesia, Kenya, Korea, Malaysia, Peru, Sri Lanka, and Tanzania. At one time or another at least one from this group of nations has exemplified virtually all approaches to development now extant.

While this book draws extensively on the tools of classical and neoclassical economic theory, development involves major issues for which these economic theories do not provide answers, or at best provide only partial answers. In fact economic theory tends to take the *institutional context* (the existence of markets, of a banking system, of international trade, etc.) as given. But development is concerned with how one creates institutions that facilitate development in the first place. How, for example, does a nation acquire a government interested in and capable of promoting economic growth? Can efficiently functioning markets be created in countries that currently lack them, or should the state take over the functions normally left to the market elsewhere? Is a fully developed financial system a precondition for growth, or can a nation do without at least parts of such a system? Is land reform necessary for development, and if so, what kind of land reform? These institutional issues and many others like them are at the heart of the development process and will reappear in different guises in the chapters that follow.

This book is not for readers who are looking for a simple explanation of why some nations are still poor or of how poverty can be overcome. Library shelves are full of studies explaining how development will occur if only a nation will increase the amount it saves and invests, or intensify its efforts to export. For several decades in the mid-twentieth century industrialization through import substitution, the replacement of imports with home-produced goods, was considered by many as the shortest path to development. More recently labor-intensive techniques, income redistribution, and provision of basic human needs to the poor have gained popularity as keys to development. Many economists now counsel governments to depend substantially on unfettered markets to set prices and allocate resources. Another school of thought suggests that development is only possible if preceded by a revolution that eliminates existing elites and replaces the market with central planning. A different theme is that development will only be possible if there is a massive shift of resources, in the form of foreign aid and investment, from the richest nations to the poorest.

No single factor is responsible for underdevelopment, and no single policy or strategy can set in motion the complex process of economic development. A wide variety of explanations and solutions to the development problem make sense if placed in the proper context and make no sense at all outside that set of circumstances. Mobilization of saving is essential for accelerated growth in most cases, but sometimes may come second to a redistribution of income if extreme poverty threatens political stability or forestalls the mobilization of human resources. Import substitution has carried some countries quite far toward economic development, but export promotion has helped others when import substitution bogged down. Prices that are badly distorted from their free market values can stifle initiative and hence growth, but removing those distortions leads to development only where other conditions are met as well. Moreover, some, but certainly not all, centrally planned economies have achieved sustained periods of development with prices that bear little relation to those determined by market forces. Finally, some nations have been ruled by leaders backed by interests hostile to development, or to any change; growth cannot occur in spite of such leadership.

Organization

This book is divided into five parts. In Part I the main issues are what prevents development from taking place and what kinds of structural change occur once growth gets underway. Structural change, of course, does not just happen as a result of impersonal and uncontrolled forces. It is often the result of deliberate planning, and therefore the first part of this book also provides an introduction to the theory and practice of development planning.

Economic development is first and foremost a process involving people. People are the prime movers of development and the main beneficiaries. Part II therefore deals with how human resources are transformed in the process of economic development, and how that transformation contributes to the development process itself. There are chapters on population, labor, education, and health.

The other major physical input in the growth process is capital, and Part III is concerned with how capital is mobilized and allocated for development purposes. Where, for example, do the savings come from, and how are they transformed into investment? What kind of financial system is consistent with rapid capital accumulation? Will inflation enhance or hinder the process, and what role is played by foreign aid and investment?

Economic development, however, is more than a process of mobilizing inputs. One of the most fundamental issues facing a newly developing nation is the degree to which that nation should integrate its economy with the economies of the rest of the world. These international trade and interdependence strategies are the subject of Part IV.

Finally, issues such as technological change and various kinds of institutional reform often differ significantly between sectors of the economy. The problems of agriculture are different from those of industry, and natural resource development is different from either of the other two. In Part V, therefore, problems of economic development are approached from this sectoral point of view.

Acknowledgments

It has taken us four years to translate our concerns and interest in development into a textbook, with a degree of success that must be judged by the reader. The effort spanned a sufficiently long period that the underlying data had to be changed more than once; we have brought the data up to 1980, or as close to that year as reliable sources permit.

In the course of this effort we have been helped in many different ways by a small army of colleagues. Paul Clark, David Singer, and Joseph Stern read the entire manuscript and offered pages of helpful advice that rivaled in length some of our own chapters. Ralph Beals, Richard Bird, Sebastian Edwards, James Duesenberry, Anne Krueger, Charles McLure, Malcolm McPherson, and Louis Wells read one or several chapters and helped transform these into more precise and readable essays. David Dapice, Arnold Harberger, and Sue Horton, along with Clark and Stern, were bold enough to use the draft manuscript in their classes and let us know how it performed under field conditions. We are indebted also to their students, and our own, who had to work through unfinished drafts to help improve the final product. Ricardo Godoy, who probably knows this text as well as any of us, went through the final manuscript with a dedication and competence beyond the ordinary, updating statistics, tracing references with painstaking thoroughness, and ensuring that the text reflected all these changes.

The manuscript has been through many drafts and the capable hands of many typists, including Daphne Crooks, Pauline Holson, Ann MacGowan, Emily Palmer, and Rita Roksoprodjo. Deborah Carroll then put the whole thing on her obsolete but technically appropriate word processor. Fred Bidgood completed the copyediting in what seemed like record time.

We have been encouraged in our work by many people, including the colleagues mentioned above. We are especially grateful to Lester Gordon, former director of HIID, who provided the initial impetus; and to Donald Lamm, president of W. W. Norton & Company, whose enthusiasm for the book and commitment to its authors sustained and prodded us to complete the manuscript in the face of seemingly overwhelming commitments to other projects.

We hope the book lives up to the expectations of all these people, and we thank them for helping us.

Malcolm Gillis
Dwight H. Perkins
Michael Roemer
Donald R. Snodgrass

THEORY
AND
PATTERNS

Chapter 1

INTRODUCTION: WORLDS APART

The people around the village of Jalab, in Senegal, West Africa, and many rural towns of Georgia in the United States live off one essential crop: peanuts.[1] Two of the biggest commercial producers of peanuts are in fact West Africa and the United States. The story of their cultivation and marketing is the story of two very different worlds.

Slave ships carried peanuts to the American South because they needed a high-protein, high-caloric staple to feed their captives. Growing conditions proved ideal, especially in Georgia, where cultivation thrived and where today nearly half the American crop is harvested. Peanuts are the eleventh most valuable crop grown in the United States, worth half a billion dollars a year.

John Johnston, a thirty-four-year-old Georgia peanut farmer, cultivates 540 acres of peanuts and another 650 acres of corn. His ground is prepared for planting by tractor. Government-sponsored research has discovered improved combinations of seed and fertilizer, and the extension service ensures that farmers know how to use them. Pesticides are sprayed on Johnston's crop from airplanes. Combine harvesters pick the ripe plant and separate out the peanuts for drying. Johnston sells his crop to a broker in nearby Blakely, where the peanuts are stored in modern warehouses. The broker sells them to processors through larger brokers in Atlanta, New York, or Chicago. The price received by Johnston is maintained above the world market price by a U.S. government support program which restricts

1. This narrative is adapted from a television film by Otto C. Honegger, *The Nguba Connection,* jointly produced by WGBH Boston, Swiss TV Zurich, and Swedish TV (SK2). We are grateful for permission to use this material. Names have been fictionalized.

imports, limits domestic acreage, and protects the farmer from price fluctuations. Research, mechanization, efficient marketing, government price supports, and hard work enable Johnston to net as much as $100,000 from his peanuts in a good year. At this income the Johnston family lives in comfort, enjoying the wide variety of goods—basics and luxuries—available to affluent Americans.

In Senegal, Cherno Sar grows peanuts on his small farm near Jalab. Like Johnston, Sar inherited his land, which is the sole support for his family of five, plus three relatives. Like Johnston, Sar cultivates relatively good land for peanuts, and he has begun to mechanize what was until recently a hand-picked harvest. But his plows are not as productive as Johnston's combines, while fertilizers and insecticides are either unavailable or too expensive. Sar's yields are about a fifth of Johnston's. And his output must be sold to a government corporation which pays the farmer well below the world market price in order to extract tax revenue for the government. Storage facilities are rudimentary, and much of the harvested crop may be lost to blight, insects, or bad weather. The small size of their farm, poor yields, low prices, and storage losses keep the Sar family very poor. Eight people must live on only $400 of cash income in a good year, much less than John Johnston's field workers, who earn $100 a week when they work, and are extremely poor by American standards. Even though the Sars grow much of their own food their diet is inadequate, consisting mostly of millet made into a gruel. Jalab has no electricity, no school, no clinic, no shops. Cherno's wife draws water from a village well a few hundred yards from their hut, much closer than for most farm families in Senegal. For every 100 children born in his village 20 will probably never see their first birthday.

Not all Senegalese are as poor as Cherno Sar. In Dakar, the modern capital, officials of the government peanut marketing corporation work in air-conditioned offices, own cars, and live in substantial houses, enjoying some of the same comforts as the Johnstons in Georgia. Their children attend the best schools in the country and if necessary can be treated in a nearby modern hospital. Of course these officials are part of a minority group in Senegal, a group favored by birth, education, urban benefits, and income over the vast majority of poor, small farmers. The peanuts the government buys are mostly exported. The resulting government revenues help pay the salaries of government workers, who are much better off than Cherno Sar; and the foreign exchange helps to pay for imports that are consumed largely by people in the cities.

In each country the political process reinforces disparities. John Johnston is represented in Washington by a congressman who is responsive to his needs. Congressmen representing farm states remain powerful enough, even in a predominantly urban country, to perpetuate the government's price supports, agricultural research, and extension system which have been so beneficial to farmers like John Johnston. Cherno Sar has little or no political influence. Although farm families like his make up most of Senegal's population, it is the minority urban dwellers who command most of the government's attention and resources. Sar is virtually helpless to influence the price the groundnut marketing corporation pays for his crop or what services the government provides him and his family.

Nor is there any international mechanism to reduce the vast disparities between people like the Johnstons who live in North America, Europe, and Japan, and the much greater numbers of people like the Sars who live in Africa, Asia, and Latin America. Although national fiscal policy can transfer income from rich to poor within a country, no international fiscal mechanism exists. Foreign aid has been conceived as a method of transfer from rich to poor nations, but it is voluntary and grossly inadequate for the task. Discussions are now going on about international price supports, such as those that exist within many countries, that would raise the incomes poor countries earn from their commodity exports. But differing national interests make agreement on such schemes unlikely. U.S. restriction of peanut imports, which discriminate against the Sars and help the Johnstons, are only one of hundreds of trade restrictions that slow international development.

Why do disparities like these exist? Why are Sengalese farmers—and three billion like them in other countries—so poor while Americans and Europeans are rich? What could be done about it, by Sengalese or Americans? And what is *likely* to happen? These questions, and many others suggested by them, are the subject of this book.

The Third World

The two worlds of the peanut farmer are sharply defined and widely separated by geography, income, standard of living, and economic, social, and political structure. They make it easy to see the differences between "development" and "underdevelopment." But the world is complex, and such simplified, dichotomous examples cannot do justice to the many-dimensional continuum that explains economic development. The bulk of this text is devoted to exploring that continuum, and no single chapter can do the work of an entire book. But it would be useful to orient the reader within the variegated world of developed and underdeveloped countries. Before attempting that, however, we need to sort out some terms.

Terminology: Rich and Poor Countries

The countries with which this book is concerned have been called by many different names. All these terms are intended to contrast their state or rate of change with those of the more modern, advanced, developed countries, so that terms tend to be found in pairs. The starkest distinction is between **backward** and **advanced** economies, or between **traditional** and **modern** ones. The "backward" economy is traditional in its economic relationships and undynamic, in ways that will be described in the next chapter. However precisely and neutrally the term can be defined it retains pejorative connotations, a touch of condescension, and is therefore not much used today. In any case the implication of stagnation is inappropriate because in most countries economic and social relationships are changing in important ways.

The more popular terms of classification implicitly put all countries on a continuum based on their *degree of development.* Thus we speak of the distinctions between *developed and underdeveloped* countries, *more and less developed* ones, or to recognize continuing change, *developed and developing countries.* The degree of optimism implicit in "developing countries" and the handy acronym, *LDCs,* for "less developed countries," make these the two most widely used terms.[2] Developed countries are also frequently called the *industrial countries,* in recognition of the close association between development and industrialization.

A dichotomy based simply on income levels, *the poor versus the rich countries,* has been refined by the World Bank and combined with a second distinction, based on type of economic organization, to yield a five-part classification that is useful for some analytical purposes. The developing countries are divided by income into *low income* (less than $410 per capita in 1980) and *middle income* (between $420 and $4500 in 1980). The third category of developing countries consists of four petroleum exporters (Iraq, Saudi Arabia, Kuwait, and Libya), whose incomes range from $8600 to $27,000 in 1980, but whose economies are more traditional than industrialized; the World Bank calls this anomalous group the "high-income oil exporters." The *industrial economies* are divided into *market* (Western capitalist) and *nonmarket* (Eastern Communist) economies.

The term now in greatest vogue, especially in international forums, is the *third world.* Perhaps the best way to define it is by elimination. Take the industrialized market economies of Western Europe, North America, and the Pacific (the "first" world), and the industrialized but centrally planned economies of Eastern Europe (the "second" world); the rest of the countries constitute the third world. All third world countries are developing countries, and these include all of Latin America and the Caribbean, Africa, the Middle East, and all Asia except Japan. The geographic configuration of this group has led to a parallel distinction—*north* (first and second worlds) *versus south*—that is also in current vogue. But the south or third world encompasses a wide variety of very different nations. The obvious differences between the wealthy (if structurally underdeveloped) oil exporters and the very-low-income, poorly endowed countries have led some to add fourth and fifth worlds to the classification. Political motivations create further exceptions: South Africa and Israel are usually not considered part of the third world; nor are Spain and Portugal, former colonial powers, although in many respects they are less developed countries.

It is necessary to be aware of these various terminologies and classifications, and to recognize their exceptions and inconsistencies. But it is not

2. Recently, the initials "LDC" have been used, especially by the United Nations, to designate the "least developed" countries, those with incomes below $100 per capita (among other characteristics). In this book "LDC" is used to mean "less developed country (or countries)."

wise to dwell too long over them. No system can capture all important dimensions of development and provide a perfectly consistent, manageable framework. The choice of terminology or classification depends on the purpose at hand. As we explore the dynamics of development, still more strategic characteristics will emerge and suggest further classifications. It may seem daunting at first to view the same group of countries from so many different perspectives, but that is the only way to understand both how developing countries differ and what they share in common. Eventually a few clear patterns will emerge.

Because there is no compelling selection of terms, we make none in this book. The less developed countries will be called that, as well as developing or third world countries. The developed countries will also be called industrial countries, and when the difference is important we will distinguish market from centrally planned economies. When one country or several do not fit a general observation, we will name the exceptions and desist from adding new terms to a field that is already awash in classification schemes.

Terminology: Growth and Development

While the labels used to distinguish one set of countries from another can vary, one must be more careful with the terms used to describe the development process itself. The terms *economic growth* and *economic development* are sometimes used interchangeably, but there is a fundamental distinction between them. **Economic growth** refers to a rise in national or per-capita income and product. If the production of goods and services in a nation rises, by whatever means, one can speak of that rise as economic growth. **Economic development** implies more. What happened to the English economy in the eighteenth and nineteenth centuries, for example, was fundamentally different from what has been happening in Libya over the past two decades as a result of the discovery there of petroleum. Both countries experienced a large rise in per-capita income, but in Libya this rise was achieved by foreign corporations staffed largely by foreign technicians who produced a product consumed mainly in the United States and Western Europe. Although the government and people of Libya have received large amounts of income from their oil, that same government and people have had little to do with producing that income. The effect of petroleum development has been much like what would have occurred if a rich nation had decided to give Libya large amounts of grant aid.

What has happened in Libya is not usually described as economic development. Economic development, in addition to a rise in per-capita income, implies fundamental changes in the structure of the economy. Two of the most important of these structural changes are the rising share of industry in national product (and the falling share of agriculture), and an increasing percentage of people who live in cities rather than the countryside. In addition countries that enter into economic development usually pass through periods of accelerating, then decelerating, population growth during which the nation's age structure changes dramatically. Consumption patterns also change as people no longer have to spend all of their income on basic necessities but instead move on to consumer durables and leisure time products and services.

The third key element in economic development is that the people of the country must themselves be major participants in the process that brought these changes in structure about. Foreigners can be and inevitably are involved as well, but they cannot be the whole story. Participation in the process of development implies participation in the enjoyment of the benefits of development as well as the production of those benefits. If growth only benefits a tiny, wealthy minority, whether domestic or foreign, it is not development.

Modern economic growth, the term used by Simon Kuznets, is similar to "economic development" in meaning but even more precise. Kuznets, a Nobel laureate in economics, refers to the "epoch of modern economic growth" as contrasted to, say, the "epoch of merchant capitalism" or "feudalism." Modern economic growth therefore refers to a specific period of world history and to the characteristics that distinguish it from other periods or epochs. The epoch of modern economic growth is still going on so all of its features are not yet clear, but the key element has been the application of science to problems of economic production which in turn has led to industrialization, urbanization, and even an explosive growth in population.

There is also the widely used term *modernization.* Modernization refers to much more than the economy. One can speak of the modernization of a society or of a political system, for example. The main problem with "modernization" is that it is difficult to give the term a precise meaning. Too often there is a tendency to equate modernization with becoming more like the United States or Western Europe. But is it reasonable to say that the Soviet Union is not modern because it is not democratic, or that Japan is not modern because it still maintains certain ways of organizing business based more on its own traditions than on practices in the West? Because of the vague and misleading nature of the term, it will not be used further here.

Finally, it should always be kept in mind that while "economic growth" refers only to a rise in per-capita income or product, "economic development" and "modern economic growth" also involve a rise in per-capita income or product. There is more to development than such a rise, but one cannot have development without it.

A Development Continuum

Much can be learned about the nature of structural change during development and about the many differences within the developing world from a ten-minute perusal of Table 1–1. These data are from the World Bank and use its five-part classification. The wide disparity of per-capita income[3]

3. Income per capita is measured as the gross national product (the value of all goods and services produced by a country's economy) divided by the population. See Chapter 3 for a fuller explanation.

TABLE 1-1 Development Characteristics of Groups[a] and Selected Countries, 1980

	GNP per capita, 1980 (U.S.$)	Energy consumption per capita, 1979 (kg. of coal equivalent)	Labor force: share in agriculture, 1980 (%)	Life expectancy at birth, 1980 (years)	Adult literacy rate, 1980 (%)
Low-Income Countries[b]	260 (230)	421 (87)	71 (73)	57 (48)	50 (34)
Bangladesh	130	40	74	46	26
Ethiopia	140	20	80	40	15
Mali	190	28	73	43	9
India	240	194	69	52	36
Sri Lanka	270	135	54	66	85
Tanzania	280	51	83	52	66
China	290	734	71	64	66
Pakistan	300	209	57	50	24
Middle-Income Countries[c]	1,410	1,976	44	60	66
Ghana	420	258	53	49	NA
Kenya	420	172	78	55	50
Indonesia	430	225	58	53	62
Senegal	450	253	76	43	10
Bolivia	570	447	50	50	63
Egypt	580	539	50	57	44
Philippines	690	329	46	64	75
Nigeria	1,010	80	54	49	30
Guatemala	1,080	229	55	59	NA
Colombia	1,180	914	26	63	NA
Cuba	NA	1,358	23	73	96
Korea (South)	1,520	1,473	34	65	93
Malaysia	1,620	713	50	64	NA
Brazil	2,050	1,018	30	63	76
Mexico	2,090	1,535	36	65	81
Capital-Surplus Oil Exporters[d]	12,630	2,609	46	57	25
Saudi Arabia	11,260	1,984	61	54	16
Industrial Market Economies[e]	10,320	7,293	6	74	99
United Kingdom	7,920	5,272	?	73	99
Japan	9,890	4,048	12	76	99
United States	11,360	11,681	2	74	99
Germany (West)	13,590	6,264	4	73	99
Nonmarket Industrial Economies[f]	4,640	5,822	16	71	100
Soviet Union	4,550	5,793	14	71	100
Germany (East)	7,180	7,136	10	72	NA

Source: World Bank, *World Development Report 1982* (Washington, D.C., 1982), Annex Tables 1, 7, 19, 21, 23. NA = not available.

[a] Average for each group of countries are weighted.

[b] Thirty-three countries with per-capita incomes of $410 or less. China and India, with 77 percent of the population, dominate the statistics for this group. Figures in parentheses exclude China and India.

[c] Sixty-three countries with per-capita incomes of $420 to $4500.

[d] Saudi Arabia, Libya, Kuwait, and United Arab Emirates.

[e] Nineteen countries with per-capita incomes of over $4880. Includes all Western Europe except Greece, plus Canada, U.S., Japan, Australia, and New Zealand.

[f] Six countries in East Europe: Bulgaria, Poland, Hungary, Soviet Union, Czechoslovakia, and East Germany.

among the groups of countries is not surprising because they are classified that way. In Chapter 3 we will discuss the shortcomings of using national income per capita to compare the well-being of country populations, but it remains the most useful single indicator.[4] The industrialized market countries as a group average per-capita GNP over seven times that of the middle-income countries, of which Mexico and the Philippines are typical examples, and *forty* times that of the poorest thirty-three countries, of which India and Tanzania are examples.

A predominant structural characteristic of development is the growing share of both income produced and labor employed in industry. An average 71 percent of the labor force is engaged in agriculture in the low-income countries, contrasted with 44 percent in the middle group and only 6 percent for the industrial market economies. Moreover this characteristic structural shift is taking place more rapidly in the middle-income countries, whose manufacturing growth rates are generally higher than those for the low-income group (or for the industrial countries, except Japan). Thus in India and Tanzania, with over two-thirds of the labor force in agriculture, manufacturing output is growing at under 5 percent a year, while in Mexico and the Philippines with 36 and 46 percent, respectively, of their workers in agriculture, manufacturing has been growing at about 7 percent a year (see Table 1–2).

Rising income is not the only end of development. People aspire to stay healthier and become better educated. Indicators for each of these aspects of well-being are included in Table 1–1, and they are closely correlated with per-capita income. Life expectancy, only fifty-seven years in poor countries (but even lower—forty-eight years—if China is excluded from the average), is seventy-four years in the rich countries. But the most dramatic contrast is in adult literacy: only 50 percent of the adult population can read in low-income countries, compared with 66 percent in the middle group; in industrial countries virtually all adults are functionally literate.

In each category there is considerable variance, and hence some interesting exceptions. China is a low-income country that consumes more energy per capita than most middle-income countries; while Nigeria, which is both a middle-income nation and an oil exporter, has one of the lowest levels of energy consumption in the world. The agricultural labor force share in Kenya and Senegal, middle-income countries, is over 75 percent, more than the average for poor countries, but only about a quarter in Colombia and Cuba, also middle-income countries. Cubans live about as long as British and Americans. And over 60 percent of Sri Lankan, Tanzanian, and Chinese adults have learned to read, more than in middle-income countries like Kenya, Senegal, and Egypt. In Cuba and Korea, however, over 90 percent can read, almost as many as in the industrial countries. Behind these and other variations in development lie many factors: different resource

4. One of the major problems with income comparisons, differences in national price structures, can be overcome by using a physical measure of economic welfare, of which per-capita energy consumption has as much validity as any. The relative levels shown in column 2 of Table 1–1 conform very closely to those of per-capita income.

TABLE 1–2 Growth of Output and Population of Groups[a] and Selected Countries, 1960–1980 (percent per year)

	GNP per capita, 1960–1980	Population 1980[b]	Manufacturing 1960–1980
Low-Income Countries	1.2	1.9 (2.7)	4.9 (4.9)
Bangladesh	NA	2.6	8.9
Ethiopia	1.4	2.5	4.5[c]
Mali	1.4	2.9	NA
India	1.4	2.2	4.8
Sri Lanka	2.4	2.1	3.6
Tanzania	1.9	3.1	3.6[d]
China	NA	1.3	NA
Pakistan	2.8	2.8	6.2
Middle-Income Countries	3.8	2.4	6.7
Ghana	−1.0	3.1	−2.9[e]
Kenya	2.7	3.8	11.4[d]
Indonesia	4.0	2.2	6.7
Senegal	−0.3	2.7	4.9[f]
Bolivia	2.1	2.7	5.7
Egypt	3.4	2.5	6.2[f]
Philippines	2.8	2.7	6.9
Nigeria	4.1	3.3	10.5
Guatemala	2.8	2.9	7.1
Colombia	3.0	2.2	6.0
Cuba	NA	1.2	NA
Korea (South)	7.0	1.7	17.1
Malaysia	4.3	2.4	11.8[e]
Brazil	5.1	2.1	10.3[e]
Mexico	2.6	3.0	7.3
Capital-Surplus Oil Exporters	6.3	3.0	9.2[e]
Saudi Arabia	4.6	3.0	6.5[e]
Industrial Market Economies	3.6	0.6	4.4
Non-market Industrial Economies	4.2	0.7	NA

Source: World Bank, *World Development Report 1982* (Washington, D.C., 1982). NA = not available.
[a] Group definitions are the same as for Table 1–1 (see its notes a–f); group averages are weighted, except for manufacturing growth, which is a median. Figures in parentheses for low-income countries exclude China and India.
[b] Crude birth rate minus crude death rate.
[c] 1961–1980.
[d] 1970–1979.
[e] 1970–1980.
[f] 1960–1979.

endowments, governments' varying ideologies and policies, cultural differences, colonial experience, war, and historical accident. In many cases variations suggest new theories of development, and we will explore some of these in later chapters.

However, development is inherently a dynamic process, not always a predictable one, that cannot be completely captured by the snapshot of Table 1–1. Most less developed countries have experienced growth in incomes since 1960, and many have enjoyed substantial growth, as Table 1–2 shows. Even in the low-income countries, which account for over half the world's population, per-capita GNP grew by 1.2 percent a year (although data for China are omitted from this average), and for some, such as Pakistan and Sri Lanka, growth was fast enough to about double incomes in thirty years. Middle-income countries did much better, with per-capita GNP growing by almost 4 percent a year, which is why some of those countries rose from low- to middle-income status during the period. Brazil and South Korea are the standouts in the table, growing at almost 5 percent and over 7 percent a year, respectively. Nevertheless income growth in the industrial countries exceeded that in the third world, and even the middle-income countries increased their per-capita incomes only slightly relative to the industrial world.

TABLE 1–3   Progress in Social Well-being for Groups[a] and Selected Countries, 1960–1980

	Crude death rate, per 1000		Population per medical professional[b] (1000s)		Percentage of age group enrolled in primary school	
	about 1960	about 1980	about 1960	about 1977	about 1960	about 1979
Low-Income Countries	18 (25)	12 (18)	4 (6)	3 (8)	76 (37)	94 (64)
Bangladesh	28	18	NA	10	47	65
Ethiopia	28	24	13	5	7	36
Mali	27	21	5	2	10	28
India	22	14	3	2	61	78
Sri Lanka	9	7	2	2	95	98
Tanzania	22	15	7	2	25	100[d]
China	14[b]	8	2	0.3	102	118
Pakistan	24	16	4	3	30	56
Middle-Income Countries	17	11	3	1.3	76	97
Ghana	24	17	4	0.6	38	71
Kenya	24	13	2	1.0	47	99
Indonesia	23	13	4	5	71	94
Senegal	27	21	3	1	27	42
Bolivia	22	16	NA	1	64	82
Egypt	19	12	1	0.5	66	75
Philippines	15	7	NA	1	95	98
Nigeria	25	17	4	2	36	79
Guatemala	19	11	3	NA	45	69
Colombia	14	8	2	0.8	77	100[d]
Cuba	9	6	0.5	NA	100[d]	100[d]
Korea (South)	13	7	2	0.4	94	100[d]
Malaysia	16	7	1	0.8	96	93
Brazil	13	9	1	0.6	95	89
Mexico	12	7	1	0.7	80	100[d]
Capital-Surplus Oil Exporters	21	12	4	0.9	28	81
Industrial Market Economies	10	9	0.3	0.2	100[d]	100[d]
Nonmarket Industrial Economies	8	11	0.2	0.1	100[d]	100[d]

Source: World Bank, *World Development Report 1982* (Washington, D.C., 1982) Annex Tables 18 and 23.
[a] Groups are defined as in Table 1–1; figures in parentheses for low-income countries exclude China and India; all group averages are weighted.
[b] 1957.
[c] Medical professional is defined as physicians and nurses.
[d] Actual percentage is over 100, because repeaters who are beyond primary school age are counted as enrollees.

Regardless of income level most developing countries experienced relatively rapid growth in manufacturing (Table 1–2), thus moving through the inevitable structural change that reduces the share of income produced, and labor employed, in agriculture. From 1960 to 1980, a short period in the history of economic development, the share of the labor force in agriculture fell from 77 to 71 percent in low-income countries and, more dramatically, from 61 to 44 percent in middle-income countries.

Perhaps the most remarkable changes in the third world since 1960 have been the virtually universal improvement in health conditions and the wide spread of education, as documented in Table 1–3. The death rate in low-income countries fell from eighteen per thousand in 1960 to twelve per thousand in 1980. For middle-income countries the decline was from seventeen to eleven per thousand, putting this group almost on a par with the industrial countries. Thus although the life expectancies shown in Table 1–1 are low relative to those in industrial countries, they represent increases of six to ten years over the two decades. Moreover these improvements have been enjoyed by every country in our list, regardless of their economic performance. The numbers of physicians and nurses have also increased relative to the population in most countries, although the concentration of these health professionals in urban areas in many countries reduces the impact they might have on health status, especially in the poorest countries. That healthier populations have also meant higher population growth (Table 1–2) is an important consideration, discussed in Chapter 7.

The spread of primary education, which now covers over 90 percent of the population in developing countries, is also shown in Table 1–3. Remarkable strides have been made by countries like Tanzania, which now has virtually all of its eligible students in primary school and has raised its adult literacy rate from 10 percent of the adult population at independence to over two-thirds today; and also by countries such as Ethiopia, Pakistan, Ghana, and Nigeria.

It is sometimes easy to become pessimistic about further progress in developing nations, especially when confronted by gloomy predictions about their future economic growth and by the myriad of problems afflicting LDCs, many of which will be catalogued in this book. As an antidote to discouragement, one needs to keep in mind the considerable economic development that has already taken place and the gratifying improvements in health and education status that mark even the poorest countries. There remains the question of how these benefits have been distributed among the populace, a topic taken up in Chapter 4 and in Part II.

Chapter 2

OBSTACLES TO DEVELOPMENT

The era of modern economic growth is only two centuries old. Before the late eighteenth century there were individuals and families who became rich, but nations as a whole and most of the people in them were poor. An economy was seen as a pie of fixed size. One could cut oneself a bigger piece of the pie, but only by taking away a portion that originally belonged to someone else. Few saw the possibility that the size of the pie itself could be increased so that all could have larger slices.

In the late eighteenth century England began to transform its economy, a process that would later be called the Industrial Revolution. By the middle of the nineteenth century other nations in Europe and North America had begun similar transformations, and toward the end of the century the first non-European population, the Japanese, had begun to industrialize. Two world wars and the Great Depression interrupted industrialization in the already advanced nations and slowed the spread of economic advance to other parts of the globe. The Second World War, however, also undermined the strength of European colonialism and set the stage for a widespread effort to industrialize the large numbers of newly independent nations.

One of the key characteristics of modern economic growth, therefore, is that it did not begin everywhere in the world at the same time. Instead it spread slowly across Europe and North America but did not break out of areas dominated by European culture (except for Japan) until the 1950s and 1960s. In large parts of the world the process has yet to begin. Between those parts of the world that have achieved sustained growth and those that have not a gap in the standard of living has inevitably opened up. The average European, American, or Japanese enjoys a material way of life that is many times richer than that experienced by even large parts of the elites of India or Africa. But there is nothing inevitable or permanent about this gap. In the nineteenth century England was way ahead of the rest of the world, whereas today England is not even in the top ten of the richest nations in terms of per-capita income. In the early 1950s Japan was poorer than such centers of European poverty as Spain or Greece, but by the late 1970s Japanese income per capita was approaching that of such richer Western European nations as France.

In this chapter the main focus is on why these gaps in income between nations open up. Why is it that some nations began developing earlier than others? What has prevented other nations from entering into modern economic growth today? Are the barriers that have inhibited development the result of conditions internal to the country affected or has the lack of development in some nations today been imposed on those nations by outside powers? A related question is whether the barriers to growth in nations are the same everywhere or whether particular conditions in one country act to inhibit growth while similar conditions elsewhere do little harm because the context is different. In much the same spirit, are there "prerequisites" that must be in place, a modern banking system for example, before growth can occur, or are there often substitutes available for particular "prerequisites"?

The Developing Nations: A Glance at History

The one feature common to all traditional societies is a low per-capita income and an absence of modern economic growth. Beyond these simple common features there is a great diversity of national experience about which valid generalizations are difficult to make. The use of terms such as *third world, less developed countries,* or *developing nations* tends to obscure this diversity by implying that all nations other than those already rich have a common experience that transcends any differences in their backgrounds and current conditions. In fact the differences between developing nations are so great that one cannot really understand their development problems without taking these differences into account.

Even within Europe on the eve of industrialization there were great differences between societies, and these differences had much to do with why development began first in the West and spread only gradually to the East. In England, for example, labor was free to change jobs and migrate to distant places, and commerce and banking had reached a high level of sophistication in the centuries preceding the Industrial Revolution. In contrast, in Russia in the middle of the nineteenth century most peasants were serfs tied to their lord's estate for life, while commerce, industry, and transport were still in a very primitive state.

In Asia, Latin America, and Africa the range of premodern experience was far wider than that which existed within Europe. Great empires such as those of China and Japan, for example, had one to two thousand years of experience governing themselves and thinking of themselves as a single unified people rather than as a collection of tribes or regions speaking different languages and frequently at war with each other. China and Japan also had by premodern standards a high level of urbanization and commerce, and Confucian values that placed great importance on education. Long years of comparative stability had also led to a major increase in population that resulted in the great shortage of arable land relative to population that we see in the region today. Because of the comparative sophistication of premodern commerce in East Asia, European and American merchants were never able to play a significant role in the management of domestic commerce in the region. And as Chinese and Japanese merchants gradually acquired an understanding of foreign markets they were able to compete successfully with representatives of the industrialized world in that sphere too.

Colonialism and Independence

At the other end of this spectrum in certain respects were several of the nations of Southeast Asia and Africa. Indonesia, Nigeria, and Pakistan, for example, were really the creations of Dutch and British colonialism that brought together diverse groups of people who spoke dozens of different languages and had no common feeling of nationhood until long after independence. Both Indonesia in 1958 and Nigeria in the late 1960s in fact had to fight a civil war in order to keep their new nations together. Pakistan also fought a civil war in 1971 to hold the eastern and western portions of the nation together, but the effort failed and Bangladesh was formed out of what had been East Pakistan.

Experience with commerce in many parts of Southeast Asia and Africa was also quite limited and illiteracy was often nearly universal. In Indonesia and many parts of Africa south of the Sahara during the colonial era foreign trade and large-scale domestic commerce was almost entirely in the hands of Europeans. Small-scale commerce, particularly that in the countryside, was sometimes in the hands of local people, but more often it was in the hands of minorities who had immigrated from other poor but commercially more advanced nations. Thus local commerce in much of Southeast Asia was in the hands of Chinese, that in East Africa was mainly managed by Indians, while elsewhere in West Africa Lebanese often played a central role. Because of inexperience the local people could not effectively compete with either these immigrant groups or the Europeans. Because they could not compete they did not gain much experience with trade or finance. This was one of the many vicious circles so common to the plight of poor nations.

Not all experiences with colonialism were the same. In India a tiny number of British ruled a subcontinent with a vast population. By necessity the British had to train large numbers of Indians to handle all but the very top jobs in the bureaucracy and army. At the time of independence in 1948 Indians were already largely running their own affairs and had enough trained and experienced personnel to do so. In Indonesia, in contrast, there were fewer than 1000 university or other postsecondary school graduates at the time of independence, and in Zaire there were hardly any (India and China in the 1940s by way of comparison had hundreds of thousands of university graduates). Even the lower levels of the central bureaucracy in Indonesia prior to independence had been manned by Dutchmen and those in Zaire by Belgians.

Latin America's historical heritage was different from that of either Asia or Africa. Independence in most of the region was achieved not after World War II but in the early nineteenth century. Although there were local populations in the region when the Europeans first arrived, these local populations were suppressed or enslaved. To meet growing labor requirements the elites turned increasingly to immigration, partly from Europe but also from Africa. Rule was by the immigrants from Spain and Portugal, the Africans were held in slavery until late in the nineteenth century, and the original population was ignored or pushed aside but continued to exist, often in very large numbers, as in Peru and Bolivia, or largely disappeared as in Chile and Argentina. North America above the Río Grande was also peopled by immigrants who suppressed the local population, and in both North and South America slavery existed in some regions and not in others, but there were important differences between North and South America. In the North the "Indian" population was more thoroughly suppressed, and hence small and isolated and not a factor when economic development began, and European immigration was from the economically most advanced parts of Europe where feudal values and structures had already been partially dismantled. Immigrants from Spain and Portugal, in contrast, came from what by the nineteenth century was one of the more backward parts of Europe. The feudal values and structures that still dominated this region accompanied the immigrants to the New World. Needless to say there were also great differences within Latin America. Argentina, for example, is largely a nation of European immigrants; Mexico, Peru, and Bolivia have large Indian populations but few of African descent; and Haitains are mainly descended from former African slaves.

The Developing Nations: A Brief Taxonomy

It is impossible to summarize all the important differences between nations in the developing world, but those with the greatest bearing on the potential for modern economic growth in the region would include:

Differences between nations with a long tradition of emphasis on education and an elite that was highly educated as contrasted to nations where illiteracy was nearly universal.

Countries with fairly highly developed systems of commerce, finance, and transport mainly run by local people versus countries where these activities were almost entirely in the hands of European or Asian immigrant minorities.

Nations peopled by those who shared a common language, culture, and sense of national identity versus nations where there is a great diversity of language, culture, and no common sense of national identity or shared common goals.

Nations with long traditions of self-government versus those with no experience with even limited self-government until the 1950s or 1960s.

This list could be extended but the point is made. Economic development, as we shall see, requires both a government capable of directing or supporting a major growth effort and a people who can work effectively in and manage the enterprises and other organizations that arise in the course of development. Nations with people who have at least some relevant education and experience in economic affairs and which have governments able to support those people are better positioned for development than nations where the people have little relevant experience and where diverse groups within the nation are still arguing over their shares in what they believe, wrongly for the most part, to be a pie of a fixed size.

The Concept of Substitutes

Given the great diversity in developing-country experience it would be a council of despair to suggest that the way to begin development is first to create the kinds of conditions that existed in Western Europe or North America when those regions entered into modern economic growth. England prior to the Industrial Revolution had centuries of experience with merchant capitalism, but does it follow that Ghana or Indonesia must also acquire long experience with merchant capitalism before economic development would be feasible? If the answer were yes these nations would be doomed to another century or more of poverty.

Fortunately there is no standard list of barriers that must be overcome or prerequisites that must be in place before development is possible. Instead, as the economic historian Alexander Gerschenkron pointed out, for most presumed prerequisites there are usually *substitutes*. The main point of this concept is best illustrated with an example from Gerschenkron's own work.[1]

Capital, like labor, is of course necessary for development, and much more will be said about both in later chapters. But Marx and others have gone a step further and argued that there must be an original or prior accumulation of capital before growth can take place. The basic idea came from looking at the experience of England where, Marx argued, trade, exploitation of colonies, piracy, and other related measures led to the accumulation of great wealth that in the late eighteenth century could be converted into investment in industry. The key question which concerns us here is not whether such an original accumulation of capital did or did not help English development. The issue is instead whether such an accumulation is a *prerequisite* for development everywhere or at least for a large

1. Alexander Gerschenkron, *Economic Backwardness in Historical Perspective* (Cambridge, Mass.: Harvard University Press, 1962), Chap. 2.

number of countries. In the absence of a prior accumulation of capital, did economic development thereby become impossible?

In Europe the answer was clearly no. One did have to find funds that could be invested in industry but they did not have to come out of the accumulated wealth of the past. Germany, for example, had little in the way of an original accumulation of capital when modern economic growth began there. But Germany did have a banking system that could create funds which were then lent to industrialists. How banks create funds is not our concern here—the point is that banks can create accounts that investors can draw upon, and the creation of those accounts in no significant way depends on long years of prior savings and accumulation by merchants or other wealthy individuals.

Russia in the nineteenth century had neither an original accumulation of wealth nor a banking system capable of creating large enough levels of credit. Instead Russia turned to the taxing power of the state. The government could and did tax funds away from people and used this tax revenue for investment in industry. Russia also imported capital from abroad. Thus the government's use of taxation was a *substitute* for an underdeveloped banking system, and elsewhere a modern banking system was a *substitute* for an original accumulation of capital.

Similar examples of substitutes in today's world abound. Latin American countries, for example, rely heavily on financial institutions to mobilize and allocate savings. Sub-Saharan African countries, in contrast, rely more on fiscal institutions (the government budget). Factories in advanced nations with well-developed commercial networks rely on central distributors to supply them with spare parts. Rural industries in China, where commerce is less developed, make spare parts in their own foundries. As already pointed out, a number of nations in the developing world today have substantial numbers of people with training and experience in areas relevant to economic development while the number of such people in other nations is miniscule. The most common substitute for this lack of relevant experience is to import foreigners who have the required experience. For reasons that will become apparent in later chapters, foreigners are frequently a not very good substitute for experienced local talent, but where the latter is missing they can fill the gap until local talent is trained.

In the following discussion of barriers to development and of what is required to get development started, therefore, we shall not be looking for three or four universal causes of poverty or a similar number of prerequisites that must always be in place before growth is possible. Instead we shall attempt to identify some of the more common barriers to development, recognizing that the presence of these barriers or the absence of prerequisites does not guarantee the continuation of poverty. There are usually ways around or substitutes for any single barrier or prerequisite, but the existence of many of these barriers or the absence of a wide variety of desirable preconditions will at least make economic development more difficult and in some cases impossible.

The Central Role of Modern Science

The closest one can come to a single prerequisite without which economic development would be impossible is whether or not a nation has access to the discoveries of modern science and innovators to adapt the lessons of science for the marketplace. The industrial economy of the twentieth century would be inconceivable in the absence of the knowledge arising out of such fields as chemistry, physics, and biology. A high percentage of the products in common use today ranging from electric power to antibiotics did not even exist prior to the advent of modern science.

While science is crucial to economic development, it is also clear that no nation today is really cut off from the main fruits of that science. A lack of modern science probably has a great deal to do with why some of the great civilizations of the past were able to reach a certain level of development but then were stopped and could go no further. It is also the case today that nations with educational and research capacities of their own, such as South Korea and Mexico, can often make more and better use of many scientific discoveries. But even the most poorly endowed nations have access to much of what modern science has contributed since the fruits of scientific discovery are often in products either domestically manufactured using comparatively simple processes or imported as finished goods from more advanced nations. Developing countries do not have to rediscover the basic laws of thermodynamics on their own. For many purposes they only need to understand those laws and how they can be usefully applied, or imitate others' applications of those laws, a much easier task than making the discovery in the first place.

Economic Obstacles to Development

In the eyes of some economists poverty is mainly the result of economic forces within the developing nation. The two most commonly cited economic barriers to development are the vicious circle of poverty and the limited extent of the market in developing nations.

The Vicious Circle of Poverty

The vicious circle of poverty is only one of many "vicious circles" that exist in the less developed world. The idea behind it is that it is easier for rich people to save and invest than it is for poor people. By analogy, therefore, it is more difficult for poor nations to save and invest enough to raise themselves out of poverty. Given that investment is crucial for development, poor nations thus stay poor. To break this vicious circle either one must discover a way of extracting more savings out of very poor people (and poor governments and small businesses), or one must find funds for investment from outside the poor country. The "vicious circle of poverty" argument, not surprisingly, is a frequently heard justification for why foreign aid from advanced nations is essential if the poor nations of the world are ever to achieve substantial progress. (The arguments for aid are examined in detail in Chapter 14.) In effect if developing nations are too poor to save for themselves, richer countries must do part of the job for them.

While the "vicious circle of poverty" argument has a certain intuitive appeal, it is at best only a partial explanation of why savings in poor countries are low. In support of the argument there is the fact that the nations of Western Europe and North America had higher average per-capita levels of income when they began modern economic growth than those of many of the poorer nations of Africa and Asia today. Some of these poor nations, such as Haiti and several Sub-Saharan African nations, have investment rates below 10 percent of national product. But it is also true that some of the poorest nations of the world have managed to achieve quite high rates of savings and investment. Japan when it began developing at the end of the nineteenth century, for example, had an average per-capita income only slightly if any above that of India today. By different means the People's Republic of China raised its rate of savings and investment in the 1950s to nearly 20 percent of national product, a high rate, even though average per-capita income at that time was only around $110 (in 1975 U.S. prices). Even India today has achieved a rate of investment that is not all that much different from the 17 percent figure currently being maintained in the United States.[2]

Part of the reason why intuition is misleading in this situation is that while the majority of people in poor countries are themselves poor, even the poorest of nations usually has a significant minority that range from well-off to fabulously rich. A landless Indian peasant may be unable to save because he needs to consume everything he earns simply to stay alive. But the owners of the Tata Iron and Steel Company in India have no such problem. A second and related reason why savings behavior may not be primarily determined by a nation's average per-capita income is that savings behavior by individuals may have more to do with their relative position, whether they are in the top, middle, or bottom income group in their society, than with the absolute level of their income. Such arguments have been used, for example, to help explain why the rate of savings in the United States has stayed much the same over a century and more of rising average per-capita incomes.

The Limited Extent of the Market

The relationship between the limited extent of the market and economic underdevelopment is based on the idea that economies of scale in industry are a key feature of economic development. If industrial enterprises must be large in order to make most efficient use of modern technology, then the size of the markets on which the goods of those enterprises are to be sold must also be large. But, it is argued, the size of markets in developing countries is small precisely because incomes and hence demand in such countries are low.

2. These figures are for gross fixed capital formation as a percentage of gross domestic product (GDP).

There are several fatal flaws in this argument. To begin with, economies of scale exist in some industrial sectors such as steel and chemical fertilizers, but it is often possible to produce quite efficiently in comparatively small enterprises in sectors such as machinery or textiles. Second, while per-capita incomes in developing countries are low, there are often large numbers of people in these countries so that total income and hence demand can be quite large. Table 2–1 presents data on the share of the developing-country population that lives in nations with over 100 million people, between 30 and 100 million people, and under 30 million. Although the number of nations in the under-30-million-people category is large, the total population in all these nations taken together accounts for only 16 percent of all the people in the developing world.

TABLE 2–1   Developing Country Population by Size of Country[a]

Size of country	No. of countries	Total population
Over 100 million people	4	1,851,573,000
30–100 million people	13	667,031,000
5–30 million people	41	458,118,000
1–5 million people	34	92,601,000

Source: World Bank, *1980 World Bank Atlas* (Washington, D.C., 1980), p. 8.
[a] Excluding nations with under 1 million people; data are for 1978.

If most of the people in the developing world live in comparatively large nations, there is still an important sense in which the domestic markets of these nations are not large. Because of the poor transport and commercial systems that are characteristic of most developing nations, these nations are not one integrated market but a collection of many smaller *fragmented markets.* Thus the scale of cement plants in a less developed country may be small because it costs too much to ship cement long distances over poor or nonexistent roads. But even the existence of fragmented markets does not succeed in completely rehabilitating the notion that the limited size of markets is a major cause (and effect) of underdevelopment. The option of exporting surplus production remains. If the domestic demand for steel is only 500,000 tons a year but the smallest efficient steel plant produces 1,000,000 tons a year, the nation does not necessarily have to buy a smaller, less efficient plant or operate the efficient plant at 50 percent of capacity. It can buy the efficient plant, operate it at full capacity, and unless thwarted by protectionism from developed nations, sell the 500,000-ton surplus abroad. Thus it is possible to argue that the limited size of the market is a problem for some industries in some countries, but only in rare instances is it a major cause of lack of development in a nation as a whole.

The existence of foreign trade also undermines the popularly held belief that a nation must be rich in natural resources in order to be successful in achieving development. As long as a nation can sell what it does produce abroad, it can use the foreign exchange earned to purchase the natural resources it needs. Japan, one of the most natural-resource-poor nations in the world, has done precisely that for nearly a century.[3] More recently South Korea, whose only significant natural resource is farmland, has followed suit with equal success. We shall have much more to say about the relationship between natural resources and economic growth in a later chapter, but from even this brief discussion it is clear that lack of natural resources has not been a major cause of a lack of growth in the past and is not likely to become a major cause in the near future.

Finally, some mention should be made here of the relationship between poverty, malnutrition, and the ability of people to work hard, to show initiative, or even to think clearly. A recent World Bank study has estimated that 434 million people or 25 percent of all the people in the developing world suffer from malnutrition, with by far the largest concentration of these malnourished people in South Asia (see Chapter 10 for a further discussion of these figures). Severe malnutrition can lead to lethargy and disease in adults and permanent brain damage in infants, among other things. Certainly in nations where a high proportion of the population suffers to some degree from such problems the achievement of economic development will be much more difficult. Development depends ultimately on people, and to contribute adequately people must be healthy, vigorous, and mentally alert. While malnutrition is not a major source of underdevelopment in a large number of less developed countries, it could be an important contributing factor in some of the most populated ones such as India and Bangladesh.

While there are economic causes for the prevalence of poverty in large parts of the world, it is apparent that economic explanations alone cannot account for why so many nations are poor. Economists are uncomfortable when they leave the realm of economic explanations in part because the tools of economic analysis are of only limited help outside the sphere for which they were designed. But if one is seriously interested in understanding poverty in nations there is little choice but to explore the relationship between economic development on the one hand and political systems and social values on the other. Political scientists, sociologists, and other social scientists can also contribute to our understanding of these relationships, but economists cannot afford simply to turn the job over to them. A proper understanding of the impact of alternative forms of political behavior on economic development presupposes a knowledge of what economic development entails. Economists may not be particularly well equipped to undertake the task of understanding these relationships, but neither is anyone else, and the issues are far too important to be ignored.

Government Obstacles to Development

Economic development in England in the eighteenth century began with little direct assistance from the government, but since that time the role of

---

3. For example, Japan today imports 99 percent of its crude oil requirements, 100 percent of its tin, nickel, and alumina needs, and over 80 percent of its timber requirements.

government in development has risen steadily to a point where successful growth is not really possible without the active support of a government. In subsequent chapters the roles of many kinds of specific government policies in promoting economic development will be explained in detail. For our purposes here one mainly needs to know that an active positive role for government is essential. It follows that if a government is unwilling or unable to play such a role, then the government itself can be considered a barrier to development or a fundamental cause of poverty.

Political Stability

To begin with, governments must be able to create and maintain a *stable environment* for modern enterprises, whether public or private. At a minimum, civil war, sustained insurrection, or invasion by hostile forces must be avoided. It is an obvious point but one frequently forgotten in discussions of the nature of development. Prolonged instability connected with civil war and foreign invasion go a long way toward explaining why China failed to enter into modern economic growth prior to 1949. By analogy, the creation of a stable environment after 1949 is an important part of any explanation of why growth began after 1949. More recently Vietnam was obviously not in a position to develop its economy on a sustained basis in the 1950s and 1960s. China and Vietnam are extreme cases, but a much longer list of nations that includes Bolivia, Pakistan, Ghana, and many others has experienced prolonged domestic political instability of a kind that has inhibited growth. Bolivia, for example, has had 150 governments since independence. Investors will not put their money into projects that pay off only over the long run if in the short run a change of government could lead to the project's being confiscated or rendered unprofitable by new laws and other restrictions. Where instability is particularly rife, a common solution has been to not invest in the local economy at all but to ship off a large part of one's wealth to banks in Switzerland or to indulge in conspicuous consumption.

Political Independence

A stable environment alone, however, is not enough. Colonial governments, for example, were usually quite stable, often for very long periods of time. There were rebellions against British rule in India, French rule in North Africa, and Japanese rule in Korea, but these rebellions were generally short-lived or on the periphery of the colony. Furthermore most colonial governments had a very specific interest in creating a stable environment for private business and yet few if any European or Japanese colonies experienced anything that could be described as sustained economic development. Part of the explanation is that the stable environment created was often only for the benefit of a small number of traders and investors from the colonizing nation whereas the citizens of the colonies themselves received little such support. Probably a more important part of the explanation, however, is that most colonial governments made only limited investments in training local people, in developing electric power resources, or in promotion of industry. It follows, if not quite automatically, that political independence was in most cases necessary before modern economic growth was possible. Conceivably, colonial governments could have promoted genuine development, but for the most part they did not. We shall return later in this chapter to the question of whether or not relations between rich and poor countries today continue to possess some of the features that characterized the older colonial era.

Government Support of Development

The immediate concern here, however, is not with relations between rich and poor nations but with whether there are many governments of developing countries today that for domestic reasons of their own are not willing to do what is necessary to achieve growth. Since virtually all leaders of developing nations regularly make speeches about the need to grow and appoint commissions to draw up development plans, there would seem to be little point in discussing governments unwilling to do what is necessary to achieve growth. The number of such governments must be miniscule. Nothing could be further from the truth.

The decision to pursue economic development like most other economic decisions involves hard choices or *trade-offs*. While there are many people whose position is improved by economic development, in the early stages at least there are usually people whose position becomes worse off. If those who become worse off in the short run are in a position to topple the government, that government will be unwilling or unable to take the steps necessary to promote growth. The nature of the problem is best illustrated by the experience of a number of developing nations that have attempted either to devalue their currencies, to eliminate excessive staffing of public enterprises, or to remove subsidies on basic consumer goods.

Devaluation of a nation's currency as a policy option for promoting development will be discussed at length in Chapter 17. Here all we need to know is that for some countries growth of the economy requires a more rapid development of those countries' exports and a restriction of imports. Devaluing the currency relative to foreign currencies accomplishes both ends by lowering the prices of the nations' exports (in terms of foreign prices) and raising the prices of imports to the domestic consumer (in terms of local currency). When governments as diverse as those of Ghana and Peru carried out a devaluation (in 1971 and 1968, respectively), however, those governments immediately fell. The reason was very simple. The people most dependent on imported consumer products whose prices had risen were the urban well-to-do, including the military and the civil service elite, who also held most of the political power in these countries. While devaluation made good sense seen in terms of the economic interests of the nation as a whole, it did not make economic sense to the narrower interests of the groups (the bureaucrats and the military) best in a position to prevent it.

Analogous situations are not peculiar to a small number of less developed countries. They are endemic to large parts of the developing world. In Sri Lanka and Bangladesh, for example, political supporters of the government or others who could cause trouble if unemployed have been forced on the managing boards of public enterprises. The result is a large number of overstaffed and hopelessly inefficient enterprises unable either to contribute to national savings mobilization efforts or to deliver goods and services effectively. To fire these unnecessary employees later, however, is not usually politically feasible, but to fail to do so is to settle for little or no growth. In Egypt the problem is both an overvalued currency and large subsidies on food and other basic necessities, subsidies that are a major drain on the government budget, making it difficult for that government to find funds for development purposes. When the Egyptian government started to remove those subsidies in 1977, however, the immediate result was widespread urban rioting contained only by the government's decision to reverse its policy and keep the subsidies.

While problems such as those described in the previous two paragraphs are the most common reasons for governments' being unwilling to take the steps necessary to promote growth, there are other reasons that should at least be mentioned. Some nations, for example, feel that certain international goals should take precedence over domestic developmental goals. President Sukarno in Indonesia, during the period he held real power (1948–1965), was more interested in international affairs such as leadership of the third world or military confrontation with Singapore and Malaysia than in economic development. A number of Arab states have devoted a sizable share of their surplus resources to three decades of confrontation and war with Israel. No doubt both President Sukarno and the leaders of these Arab states would have preferred to have economic development as well as confrontation, but their resources were limited and they had to choose between goals. In choosing they did not opt for economic development.

Other nations have concentrated their energies on achieving what could be termed *social goals* rather than economic development. In the definition used in this book, economic development includes both growth and wide distribution of the benefits of growth. While some nations have pursued growth but not development, there are also several nations that have sacrificed growth at least for a time in order to achieve wider distribution and other social goals. Cuba in the 1960s, for example, experienced little economic growth in large part because energies were concentrated on achieving a major redistribution of income, education, and other benefits in favor of the poorest elements of the society. China's Cultural Revolution (1966–1970) was even more ambitious. There the ultimate goal of at least some of the nation's leaders was to eliminate all class distinctions and to greatly reduce the role of material incentives, and the leaders were willing to sacrifice growth at least temporarily to achieve those objectives. Growth and distributive goals, as will become clear in Chapter 4 need not be in conflict. To the contrary certain kinds of income redistribution can make an important contribution to more rapid growth, but as China's and Cuba's experiences of the 1960s indicate, they can also be in conflict, and when they are in conflict governments do not always choose growth.

From these various examples it should be clear that one of the reasons many nations are still underdeveloped is that the governments of those nations have been unable or unwilling to pursue policies that would achieve development. Governments after all represent various interests in the society and in some cases it has proved impossible to pursue developmental goals and maintain sufficient support from those interests to stay in office, while in other cases government leaders themselves have preferred to pursue objectives that were in conflict with development. An important question is why governments have found themselves in these situations, but the answers to that question would take us deep into the nature of politics and society in developing nations and would divert us from this book's main task of explaining economic development.

Social Values as Obstacles to Economic Development

Whether a society's values and structure lead to political systems that impede or foster modern economic growth, clearly such values have a direct bearing on whether or not development occurs. Much of the analysis of the relationship between values and development has arisen out of concern with how societies create a sufficient number of entrepreneurs to lead the development effort.

Entrepreneurship

The concept of the *entrepreneur* or *entrepreneurship* was developed by Joseph Schumpeter, who put the entrepreneur at the center of his *Theory of Economic Development* originally published (in German) in 1911. The entrepreneur was someone who could take a new technical discovery or a new method of management and make practical use of it in his factory or business. It was one thing to develop a new technique or invention, but unless someone actually put that technique to practical use, to turn it into an *innovation,* it would have little or no impact on economic development. The entrepreneur who played this crucial role was someone who had the imagination to see the potential for profit from the innovation, the initiative actually to carry out the task of introducing the innovation, and a willingness to take a calculated risk that the effort might fail and lead to a loss rather than a profit. An entrepreneur was not necessarily either a manager of the enterprise using the innovation or a supplier of capital (investment funds) to that enterprise. An entrepreneur was an innovator, and while he might manage his own enterprise or supply his own capital, he might also hire a manager or borrow his capital from a bank.

Schumpeter himself raised basic questions about whether entrepreneurship was really necessary once industrial development had reached an advanced level. In advanced industrial economies innovation tends to become routinized. Corporations have their own large research laboratories and managers more or less automatically turn the results of that research into new products or new methods of producing old products. Innovations no longer require the bold imagination of a few unique entrepreneurs. How to introduce innovations can be taught to thousands of future managers at any good business school.

Schumpeter's insight concerning advanced industrial economies is directly relevant to developing countries. If innovation can be routinized in advanced economies, why not in developing economies as well? After all it does not take much imagination or daring to see that a railroad or a chemical fertilizer plant may make a major contribution to a developing country's economy. The value of such innovations is clear to all, and the task for the developing nation is to find the capital and managerial talent to pay for and run the new enterprise. Actually technological transfer is never this simple, as will be amply demonstrated in later chapters, but a case can be made that the role of entrepreneurship in today's world is less essential than it was in nineteenth-century Europe and America.

Still there is some role for entrepreneurship in today's developing world, and the question then becomes—What is it in a society that creates an adequate number of entrepreneurs, or, alternatively, what has blocked the development of entrepreneurship in other societies? One of the best known explanations, that by Everett Hagen of M.I.T., is that entrepreneurs come disproportionately from *blocked minorities*. The basic idea is that certain individuals in a traditional society are prevented from rising to the more conventional sources of prestige, power, and wealth, such as high government office. The reason they are prevented from rising up through the conventional hierarchy may be that they are members of a religious minority subjected to discrimination or because they are immigrants from abroad and not "natives" of the country. If these blocked minorities had previously enjoyed a high status, they have a particularly keen desire to restore themselves to a position of wealth and prestige. Since they cannot join the army or the civil service, the one route open to them is to become wealthy through entrepreneurship.

The examples of blocked minorities that supplied large numbers of entrepreneurs is a long one. The list includes Parsees in India, Jews in Europe, Chinese in Southeast Asia, Indians and Lebanese in Africa, and so on. In looking at the early developing nations of England, northern Europe, and North America, the connection between minority status and entrepreneurs becomes more remote except in a fairly trivial sense. Everyone in the United States is a member of a minority group of some kind, for example, but only a few of those minorities have been blocked from rising up any of the ladders of power and prestige, and those blocked minorities have not yet been the major suppliers of entrepreneurship.

The real question, however, is not whether there is some correlation between minority status and entrepreneurial qualities in certain individuals. In Latin America, for example, most industrialists have been of Lebanese, Arab, Jewish, Basque, German, or Italian origin rather that from the dominant populations of Spanish or Portuguese origin. The logical explanation for this phenomenon, however, has little to do with these people's minority status. Their immigrant background gave these people a greater knowledge of and often access to foreign sources of supply, and hence they often became importers. When the nations of Latin America began to restrict imports in order to promote local industry it was natural for these former importers who already knew the markets to move into manufacturing to preserve their position in those markets.

Similar although slightly different arguments can be made about the Chinese in Southeast Asia or the Indians and Lebanese traders in Africa. The Chinese, Indians, and Lebanese who emigrated to these regions came from societies (described briefly above) where commerce was already highly developed by premodern standards. Commerce in much of Southeast Asia and Africa, in contrast, was much less developed and hence the local populations had little experience as merchants or moneylenders. Is it really surprising under such circumstances that it was the more experienced immigrant populations that, together with the European colonialists, ended up in charge of the commerce that arose during the colonial period?

Motivation for Development

Even if it is difficult, if not impossible, to establish a clear casual connection between certain types of minority-group status and entrepreneurship, there remains the question of whether one can say anything about what causes people to become entrepreneurs whether or not they are members of minorities. One idea first put forward by the Harvard psychologist, David McClelland, is that of *need for achievement,* or *n-achievement* for short. The principal idea behind this term is that certain societies produce a large number of people who have a high level of desire to improve themselves in order to get ahead financially or be recognized as the best at some form of endeavor. Societies where people possessing this kind of motivation are plentiful will produce large numbers of entrepreneurs and hence will experience economic development.

There seems to be little reason to dispute the notion that success in business as in many other activities is somehow connected with a need to achieve. The controversy surrounding the term instead centers around two other issues. There is first of all the question of whether one can come up with plausible and independent methods of measuring n-achievement, levels that can then be compared with economic performance to see if there is a relationship. Proponents of the concept argue that they have developed such measurable concepts and that the correlation clearly exists, whereas the considerable body of skeptics remains to be convinced. A second question is whether n-achievement is something that must exist in adequate amounts before development can occur or whether appropriate motivation is something that arises more or less automatically as economic development creates opportunities for people to exploit.

The nature of this latter issue can be illustrated with an example from history. Malaya had long been known to have rich resources of tin. When European industrialization created a rapidly rising demand for tin, the question arose as to who would develop the Malayan mines. The two main groups in Malaya were the Malays and the Chinese, both possessing rich but very different cultures. Malays lived in villages on the coast, grew rice, fished in surrounding bountiful seas, and showed little inclination to go deep into the jungle where most of the tin was located. Chinese migrants from the extreme poverty of South China possessed little land in Malaya and wanted most of all to accumulate money to send back to their families in China, where they one day hoped to return themselves. The Chinese were willing to go into the jungle to mine tin even though the risk of death from malaria was extremely high. A majority of the first miners to settle in what is now the capital city of Kuala Lumpur, for example, died of malaria. The Chinese who survived these and similar mining camps, at least some of them, however, accumulated funds and started other businesses and soon came to dominate those parts of the colonial commercial economy not in the hands of the British. The Malays remained as fishermen and farmers right into the middle of the twentieth century.

One interpretation of this experience is to say that the Chinese possessed a strong desire to achieve and the Malays did not, and hence the Chinese got ahead economically and the Malays did not. A somewhat different interpretation is to point out that the Malays in the nineteenth century had few rational reasons for wanting to mine tin, since their main wants were met under more favorable conditions on the coast and the risk of going into the jungle was high. By the time the risks had fallen the Chinese and British were in command of virtually the entire mining and commercial network in the country and evinced little interest in making way for Malay participation. Only when a Malay-dominated government came to power after independence were the firms put in a position where they were forced to open up opportunities for Malays. The question then became whether the Malays would respond to the opportunities being created. So far the response has been slow, but it has occurred. Values suitable to the new environment of opportunity do not arise overnight, nor do the skills that come only with experience get created in a year or two. In short, motivation in this case is not just determined by the opportunities of the moment but is rooted in the experience of the past as well.

Clearly the problem of appropriate motivation for economic development exists in some developing societies and for a variety of reasons certain cultures seem more resistant to change than others. It is also clear that the problem of motivation is not confined to the issue of what creates entrepreneurs. Development requires effective managers and a hardworking and disciplined labor force, and motivation presumably has something to do with these people as well. But once one has made these obvious points it is difficult to say much more with any conviction. We have only a general idea of what the appropriate kinds of motivation are for economic development to be successful, and an even hazier notion of how that motivation is created. We suspect, however, that an environment full of economic opportunity eventually brings forth the desired response. At one time it was held by many that only those who believed in the Protestant version of the Christian ethic made successful entrepreneurs. Today as development spreads across the globe the ranks of entrepreneurs include not only Catholics but Hindus, Buddhists, Zoroastrians, and numerous others.

International Obstacles to Development

Up to this point our analysis of the obstacles to development has concentrated on economic conditions, political systems, and social values that are internal to the less developed world. To the extent that these internal conditions are the main causes of poverty, successful development will depend on internal solutions. But many economists and others argue that the main barriers to development today lie not with these internal elements but with conditions external to the developing world. Specifically, the existence of already rich and industrialized nations, it is argued, creates international pressures that hamper the growth efforts of today's poor nations.

Before reviewing the various arguments that stress the negative aspects of the relations between rich and poor countries, it is useful to present a brief synopsis of some of the beneficial aspects for poor nations of existing in a world where some nations are already rich. These positive elements are less controversial and with them in mind one can then ask whether they are outweighed by the negative side of the ledger.

One important part of any argument about the positive side of rich-poor relations is based on the concept of the gains from trade. Since these gains are considered in some detail in a later chapter, only a brief listing of some of these gains will be attempted here.

Gains From Trade: A Preliminary View

To begin with, the ***theory of comparative advantage*** states that nations with different endowments of capital, labor, and natural resources will gain by specializing in those areas where their relative costs are low and importing where their relative costs of production are high. Further, the greater the difference in endowments between countries—and the differences between rich and poor countries are great indeed—the greater are these gains from trade likely to be. In certain extreme cases, but ones that occur in the real world, a nation possesses one resource or factor such as land or oil in such abundance that it is impossible to make effective use of all of that resource internally. Trade makes it possible to use this surplus resource because one can export what is not needed at home for things that are needed. Saudi Arabia could not possibly use all the petroleum it is capable of producing, or Canada all of the wheat from its great plains. Trade thus becomes what is sometimes referred to as a ***vent for surplus.***

Other gains from trade include the fact that real capital goods can only be transferred from rich to poor nations (and vice versa) through trade. In addition there is the fact that some countries' enterprises producing for export are among the most progressive in the nation because they have to be to survive international competition. And the example of these progressive firms influences domestic enterprises as well to follow the progressive example set.

Drawing on Experience

The gains from trade, however, capture only a part of what one means when one talks of the advantage to poor nations of existing in a world where some countries have already achieved sustained development. The term used by Gerschenkron to describe this broader phenomenon is the **advantages of backwardness.** The principal idea behind this term is that developing countries are in a position to learn from the experience of already-advanced nations. The most obvious area in which these advantages exist is the realm of science and technology. As pointed out above, today's developing countries do not have to reinvent processes for producing chemical fertilizer or electric power. That technology is well known and readily available, and all that is required of a developing nation is to acquire and adapt the techniques to its own local conditions, much simpler tasks than inventing the techniques in the first place.

The advantages gained by learning from the experience of industrialized nations, however, are not confined to the area of science and technology. By the middle of the twentieth century advanced nations had acquired a great deal of experience with management of enterprises, with national economic policy-making, and even with widely different kinds of economic systems. In the late eighteenth century laissez-faire capitalism was probably the only system capable of achieving modern economic growth in England. During World War I, however, wartime conditions led Germany and others to experiment with close state management of the economy. In the 1930s the Soviet Union, building on the World War I experience of others, developed what we know today as the Soviet-type or socialist system of planned economy. When China opted for a fully socialized economy in the 1950s Chinese planners were able to draw on Soviet experience, often to the extent of simply translating Soviet planning rules and regulations into Chinese and then putting them into effect. The Chinese later modified the Soviet planning system to make it more suitable to Chinese conditions, but the point is that without prior Soviet experience China would have had to move much more cautiously in setting up a centrally planned economy. In a similar fashion South Korea learned much about how to operate a privately owned but state-managed economy from the experience of Japan.

There are situations, of course, where having a wide range of choices makes it possible for a country to make the wrong choice. Some nations would be better off if they had no range of options and instead had to follow a single optimal or at least feasible development path. But other nations surely have benefited from being able to make choices that took into account their own local economic, political, and social conditions.

Imperialism as an Obstacle

While almost everyone acknowledges the potential advantages of being able to learn from the experience of others, many have argued that this potential is seldom realized in practice because the advanced nations create barriers to the progress of poor nations. Many economists and other scholars have attempted explanations of the nature and sources of these barriers imposed on the less developed world, but the largest group is made up of those who in one way or another owe an intellectual debt to Marx, Hobson, and Lenin.

Marxian Approaches to Development One of the centerpieces of Karl Marx's theory of capitalist development was the view that the rate of profits on capital inevitably declines as growth takes place.[4] These profits were produced by labor out of the *surplus* over and above what was needed to meet the subsistence needs of that labor. Competition in the face of this declining rate of profit leads to the stronger capitalists' swallowing up the weaker, who then join the ranks of the proletariat or workers. Crises or depressions also become more severe as development proceeds, and the wages of workers may actually decline as capitalists squeeze them harder in a desperate attempt to keep profits up. The end result is a revolution that overthrows the rule of the capitalist class.

By the late nineteenth and early twentieth century there was very little evidence to support the view that the rate of profit was declining, and it was clearly evident that real wages were rising. At the same time, however, the capitalist powers of Europe were vigorously expanding their colonial empires. The question then became whether there was a connection between the two phenomena.

Workers in the colonial empire of course also produced a surplus. If the imperial power could drain off enough of that colonial surplus it could maintain profits at home and perhaps have enough left over to raise the wages of workers so that they would not become restless.

Conversely, from the colonial country's point of view development is severely inhibited by the fact that its surplus is being drained off abroad. In the absence of this surplus the colonial nation has little money of its own to invest and at the same time the nation is receiving only small amounts of investment from abroad.

In this simple form the basic propositions of the theory can be tested empirically. The issue is mainly whether the flow of surplus, or profits and tax revenues, from the colonial to the capitalist nation was large enough to keep the profit rate in the capitalist nation high or to keep the rate of investment in the colonial nation low. The issue is not whether this drain of surplus made a few Englishmen and others very rich but whether it accounted for a large share of the total profits of the capitalist world. More important from the point of view of development, was the drain of surplus large enough relative to the national product of the colonial country to

4. Karl Marx, *Das Kapital,* the first volume of which was published in 1867.

have a significant impact on the investment and hence development prospects of that country?

The end of colonialism in much of the world did not by itself necessarily change this situation. Capitalist nations could continue to accomplish much of what was achieved by colonialism through private investment activities abroad. Even many proponents of this basic viewpoint, however, recognized from early on that it was difficult to find quantitative data with which to support the argument in this simplified form. Repatriated profits from foreign investments in developing countries just are not that large when measured against either the total profits of the capitalist world or the national product of the developing nations. J. A. Hobson, writing at the turn of the century, already recognized that repatriated profits were large for individual firms in Europe, but were not large relative to the profits of European enterprises as a whole. Imperialism, he argued, resulted from the ability of the few firms that did benefit to manipulate the government in their interests even though those interests might be against the best interests of the nation as a whole.

A different tack taken by other scholars has been to argue that what was lost was a potential rather than an actual surplus. The drain of profits from the developing world might not be large, but measures taken by the capitalist nations prevented the developing nations from producing the surplus that would have existed in the absence of capitalist pressures from abroad. Some argued, for example, that free-trade policies imposed on the developing world made it impossible to protect infant industries and hence those industries did not develop. The resources that would have gone to produce industrial output and funds for further investment instead lay idle. Free trade, leading to imports of manufactured cloth and the like, also destroyed local handicrafts, it is argued, thereby further contributing to the unemployment of domestic resources. Still other scholars have argued that the drain of profits was real enough but hidden by the way prices are set for goods transferred from the industrial to the developing nation. Multinationals, it is argued, charge much higher prices when they sell to developing countries than when they sell the same product at home.

Modern Theories of Imperialism   Modern theories of imperialism or of the nature of relations between rich and poor nations continue to use many of these older themes, but there has been a definite shift of emphasis. On the question of why capitalist nations are inherently imperialistic, the stress is not so much on a declining rate of profit shored up by returns from abroad. Capitalist firms are interested in protecting their investments abroad and to that end they want a large military force at home and abroad capable of providing that protection. But the workers in capitalist societies also benefit from this large military force even though they gain nothing or less than nothing from foreign investments. In the absence of such military expenditures, scholars like Paul Baran have argued, there would be a great depression and large-scale unemployment in capitalist countries.[5] The reasoning behind this belief cannot be gone into here, but it

5. Paul Baran, *The Political Economy of Growth* (New York: Monthly Review Press, 1957).

is based on a kind of Keynesian analysis of the sources of unemployment. In addition to avoiding unemployment, workers in the large defense industries themselves benefit directly from military expenditures. Thus the presence of democracy in the capitalist world does not prevent imperialism because large numbers of voters in that world see imperialism at least indirectly as being in their interest.

As for what happens to the poor nation attempting to develop, emphasis has shifted away from the role of a direct drain of surplus to collusion between advanced-nation capitalists and antigrowth forces within the developing nation. The issue is not as much the drain of surplus abroad as it is the misuse of that surplus at home.

There are many variations on this basic theme. Some scholars argue that it is in the interest of advanced-nation capitalists to keep developing-nation markets open to their products and to keep cheap supplies of developing-nation raw materials flowing. Industrial growth within the developing nation would be harmful to both goals since local industrial products would compete with imports and would also bid for local raw materials. The old ruling classes made up of landlords and other "feudal" elements also have no interest in promoting the rise of industrial capitalists who would compete with them for power and who might find it in the interest of industry to push such measures as land reform. Although some commercial capitalists exist in such societies, it is argued that they too tend to side with foreign investors and the feudal ruling class because they make their living from the existing pattern of trade and do not want competition from newer patterns. The end result is an alliance of foreign investors backed by their governments, feudal landlord elements, and merchant capitalists who together keep a government in power that does little to promote development.

Income Inequality and the Demand for Luxury Products Another variation on this theme is that put forward by the prominent Brazilian economist Celso Furtado.[6] Furtado starts from the proposition, for which there is much evidence, that poor nations in the early stages of development tend to have a very unequal distribution of income. As a result demand for industrial products in these societies tends to be concentrated on luxury products such as automobiles since the poor have little money left over after purchasing food and housing. It is precisely luxury goods such as automobiles that are usually either imported from abroad or produced domestically by foreign firms. Local enterprises and investors lack the capital or know-how to produce such sophisticated products in the early stages of development. Foreign investors have an interest in keeping the distribution of income unequal because that is what keeps up demand for products only they can produce. The local ruling class has the same interest because they are the beneficiaries of this unequal distribution. Growth is slow because foreign investors only invest the minimum necessary to keep control of the

6. Celso Furtado, "The Brazilian 'Model' of Development," in *The Political Economy of Development and Underdevelopment,* edited by Charles K. Wilber (New York: Random House, 1979), pp. 324–33.

local market. A key link in this argument is the connection between income inequality and the demand for luxury products. It is a link that can and has been tested empirically by seeing what happens to demand in a given country when one redistributes income in a way to achieve greater equality. Although the tests are not conclusive because of the limitations of the data used, the results so far indicate that a major redistribution of income does not lead to large shifts in the structure of demand. The demand for a luxury good such as automobiles might fall but there is little change in the demand for steel, cement, and machine tools, to mention only a few important items.

The common theme of these theories, therefore, is that local elites combine with foreign capitalist powers to maintain a government in power that pursues policies that put obstacles in the way of economic development. The differences among the theories are mainly over the reason why this collusion of antigrowth forces exists, not whether it exists.

The validity of these theories depends to a large degree on the extent to which they claim to be universal explanations for the existence of underdeveloped nations. If the claim is that all or most nations that forge close economic ties with advanced capitalist nations and allow substantial amounts of foreign investment will fail to develop, the claim is easily refuted. Many nations with close economic ties to the United States, Japan, and Western Europe and with substantial amounts of foreign investment have grown rapidly. The list includes countries from South Korea to Singapore, Mexico, and Brazil.

If the claim is that nations that severely restrict foreign involvement will usually develop faster than others, that claim too is easily refuted. Paul Baran, who was writing in the mid-1950s, comes very close to making such a claim when he holds out comparatively bright development prospects for countries such as Egypt, Indonesia, Burma, and even India, which he refers to as having a "New Deal" orientation. The comparison is with the grimmer prospects for such *compradore*[7] nations as South Korea and most of the oil producers. A key difference between New Deal and Compradore nations is precisely the degree to which they restrict or eliminate altogether foreign involvement in their economies. Egypt, Indonesia, Burma, and India were certainly vigorous in the 1950s and early 1960s in their efforts to restrict foreign investment. Burma and Indonesia at that time threw out foreign investors entirely, and Egypt socialized much of its economy. Egypt's economy did poorly thereafter, and national product in Burma and Indonesia probably fell. The contrasting experience of Korea and many of the oil producers is apparent to all.

The point is not the opposite of the Baran argument, that restrictions on foreign investment necessarily lead to economic decline. China after all eliminated foreign investment and grew at a substantial rate. The point instead is that vigorously asserting one's sovereignty by restricting or expell-

---

7. The word *compradore* refers to a merchant in a developing country who works for a company of a foreign, usually industrialized, nation.

ing foreign capitalists does not necessarily lead to conditions conducive to development. Nor does welcoming foreign investors necessarily inhibit the forces of development.

Clearly extreme versions of theories of imperialism that stress the universality of the view that rich capitalist nations are the main cause of a lack of development in today's developing nations do not stand up well to the evidence. If the basic proposition were stated in more modest terms, however, one could find supporting evidence. The more modest version would simply say that some countries are ruled by groups or classes that do not want or support policies that promote development and that these groups or classes sometimes find military and other forms of support abroad. Ethiopia under the rule of Haile Selassie, for example, was afraid of many key development-oriented reforms precisely because they would undermine the government's domestic sources of support. Certainly the Selassie government's ability to stay in power was also reinforced by continuing support from such countries as the United States. Similar situations involving external support from France, Britain, and other nations can be found elsewhere. What cannot be established is that heavy involvement of advanced capitalist nations in the developing world always or even usually has the impact that it may have had in Ethiopia.

Conclusion

The one clear conclusion is that there is no single cause of poverty among today's developing nations. Nor is there any single set of explanations that applies to all countries. Instead there are a wide variety of reasons for the continued poverty of nations, some of which apply in certain cases but not in others.

Although the barriers to development are complex and varied, one can make some generalizations about those barriers. To begin with, extremely poor nations with little experience in self-government and with illiterate populations also lacking in experience with commerce and urbanization are nations that will have great difficulty getting development started. Such countries will have trouble maintaining a stable political environment, difficulty in extracting adequate savings for investment, and will not have the personnel adequately to staff the new modern-sector enterprises and hence will have to rely on foreigners who will be expensive and not available in adequate numbers anyway. For these countries at least some of these missing gaps will have to be filled before economic development can take place.

Even countries with long experience in self-government and with adequate levels of trained or experienced personnel, however, may not succeed in entering the era of modern economic growth. For these nations the most common problem is a government unwilling or unable to make the hard choices needed to get growth started. The source of this incapacity may be either political forces opposed to development that are purely of internal origin or these internal antigrowth forces may be strongly reinforced by powers outside the country.

Mention must also be made of the numerous barriers to development that are peculiar to one country or another. The caste system in India probably limits mobility and hurts development. Other nations are cursed with particularly inept or venal leadership. The list of elements that may have some negative influence on the prospects for development is almost without end. And yet a large number of countries have managed to enter into sustained periods of economic development, and the number of such nations is increasing probably at an increasing rate. The barriers to development are being overcome among an ever-widening proportion of the world's people.

FURTHER Concepts such as the role of substitutes in economic development and the advan-
READINGS tages of backwardness are developed in the various works of Alexander Gerschenkron such as *Economic Backwardness in Historical Perspective* (Cambridge,
Mass.: Harvard University Press, 1962) and *Europe in the Russian Mirror* (Cambridge: Cambridge University Press, 1970). The role and nature of entrepreneurs
was first developed by Joseph Schumpeter in his *Theory of Economic Development*
(Cambridge, Mass.: Harvard University Press, 1934) and receives its most sophisti-
cated treatment in his *Capitalism, Socialism and Democracy* (London: Allen and
Unwin, 1954). Certain obstacles to development have received extensive develop-
ment in the literature while others have received little or none. The role of blocked
minorities in entrepreneurship is analyzed at length by Everett Hagen in *On the
Theory of Social Change: How Economic Growth Begins* (Homewood, Ill.: Richard
Dorsey, 1962) and the need-achievement by David McClelland in *The Achieving
Society* (Princeton: Van Nostrand, 1961). A general study that puts special empha-
sis on social factors is Berthold F. Hoselitz, *Sociological Aspects of Economic
Growth* (Glencoe, Ill.: The Free Press, 1960).

The literature on imperialism is enormous. Classics such as Lenin's *Imperialism,
the Highest Stage of Capitalism* (Moscow: Progress Publishers, 1975) and J. A.
Hobson's *Imperialism—a Study* (Ann Arbor: Univeristy of Michigan Press, 1965)
can still be read by the student with profit. One of the most influential post-1945
books on the subject is Paul Baran's *The Political Economy of Growth* (New York:
Monthly Review Press, 1957). A collection of contemporary essays by Andre
Gunder Frank and others can be found in Robert I. Rhodes, ed., *Imperialism and
Underdevelopment: A Reader* (New York: Monthly Review Press, 1970). A short
study that presents a wide range of points of view toward imperialism is Alan Hod-
gart, *The Economics of European Imperialism* (New York: W. W. Norton, 1977).

The only way to truly appreciate the interaction of historical heritage and economic development is for the student to study the history, politics, and society of
one country or a small number of countries in depth. Examples of this historical
approach to development include D. H. Perkins, ed., *China's Modern Economy in
Historical Perspective* (Stanford: Stanford University Press, 1975); and E. S. Mason
et al., *The Economic and Social Modernization of the Republic of Korea* (Cambridge, Mass.: Harvard University Press, 1980).

There is also a large literature on Latin American development with a historical
perspective. The flavor of some of the most important of this literature can be obtained by reading A. O. Hirschman, "Ideologies of Economic Development in Latin
America," in *A Bias for Hope* (New Haven: Yale University Press, 1971). On
Africa, see, for example, Keith Hart, *The Political Economy of West African Agriculture* (New York: Cambridge University Press, 1982); and Anthony G. Hopkins,
An Economic History of West Africa (New York: Columbia University Press, 1973).

Chapter 3

PATTERNS OF DEVELOPMENT

There is a popularly held view that the main problem of economic development is to get the process started. Once started, the rise to becoming a modern industrial state proceeds more or less automatically. The analogy is to an airplane that requires great energy and skill to get off the ground, but once it has taken off soars easily through the air to its destination.

The concept of a *takeoff* is seen frequently in the development literature and is at the center of Walt Rostow's analysis of the stages of economic growth.[1] When the term means simply that a country has entered into a period of modern economic growth, it causes few problems. Frequently, however, the term has been used in ways that imply much more. Specifically there has often been the implication that development once started proceeds automatically along well-trod paths until the country becomes a modern industrialized nation.

The first problem with the concept is that economic development once started does not necessarily proceed without interruption. Economic development itself, particularly in its early stages, can create enormous social and political tensions that can undermine the stability so necessary for growth. The classic example from the early part of the twentieth century is the case of Argentina. To many observers in the 1910s and 1920s Argentina seemed well on its way to becoming a modern industrial state. At the time it was considered more advanced than Canada. But as urbanization and industrialization progressed, the expanding Argentinian working class

---

1. Walt W. Rostow, *Stages of Economic Growth* (New York: Cambridge University Press, 1960; 2d ed. 1971).

became increasingly alienated from the nation's leadership. Juan Peron was able to use this alienation to build a political organization that brought him to power in 1946, but to keep his support Peron carried out measures such as price control of foodgrains and other necessities and expanded military expenditures that were popular with his constituents but had the effect of stifling or slowing growth and dividing society into sharply contending classes. More important, even with Peron out of office the forces unleashed earlier have prevented the nation from establishing a consensus behind any government that would maintain stability and promote growth.

More recent examples of similar connections between the early stages of economic development and political instability can be found in Pakistan and Iran. Pakistan in the 1960s experienced a decade of fairly rapid industrialization, but most of this industrialization was concentrated in the western half of the country. East Pakistan made few gains and the people there felt that the western section was developing at their expense. It matters little now whether West Pakistan exploited East Pakistan: the people in the east perceived that they were the losers. The result was a civil war, the splitting of the country into two nations with the formation of Bangladesh, and subsequent instability and economic stagnation in both Pakistan and Bangladesh thereafter.

Iran presents a variation on the same theme. Oil revenues in the 1950s and 1960s fueled rapid industrial development, which accelerated even more dramatically after the quadrupling of the price of oil in 1973. Oil revenues, however, were also used extravagantly in the purchase of weapons, in large capital-intensive projects such as the Teheran subway, and in fueling corruption among Iran's elite. Iran's new wealth, far from buying stability, increased the alienation of the great majority of the people who felt that the nation's wealth was being monopolized by a corrupt few. When combined with other deeply felt grievances, such as those of the religious fundamentalists led by Khomeini, the result was a year of rioting and demonstrations culminating in the fall of the shah and his army.

Economic development, once started, therefore, can come to an abrupt halt. Even when a nation's development continues, however, it does not necessarily proceed along a predetermined path. At the same time the possible paths available to any nation are limited. A nation's endowment of resources, when it began to develop, and the policies pursued by its leaders all have an influence on the nature of the growth that takes place, but there are some features of the development process that are common to all nations.

The next sections of this chapter explain what we know about the patterns of development that have occurred in the past and are likely to occur in the future. Attempts to discern these basic patterns have followed two very different approaches—one empirical and the other theoretical. One group of economists, best represented by Simon Kuznets and Hollis Chenery, has attempted to discern patterns of development through an analysis of data on the gross national product and the structure of that product for dozens of nations around the world and through time. The search has been for patterns that are common to all nations or more realistically to a large subgroup of nations.

The second approach has been to construct theories of how the structure of a nation's economy could be expected to change given various assumptions about the conditions facing that nation. This theoretical approach has a long tradition stretching back to Adam Smith and David Ricardo and in more recent decades includes the growth models of Roy Harrod, Evsey Domar, W. Arthur Lewis, John Fei, Gustav Ranis, and many others.

In economics the ultimate objective is to develop theories whose validity can then be tested with the data available. The empirical or data-based approach and the theoretical approach therefore are not two different ways of looking at a given problem, but are two parts of what is really a single approach. In the field of economic development, however, the process being studied is so complex and theorizing is at such an early stage in its own evolution that one can still speak of two quite different approaches to an analysis of the patterns of development.

Estimating Gross National Product

Before we can talk about the empirical approach to patterns of development, however, it is important to understand both the strengths and particularly the weaknesses of the data used to measure those patterns. In essence the analysis of patterns of development involves relating trends in gross national product per capita to trends in the various components of gross national product. *Gross national product (GNP)* is the sum of finished goods and services produced by a society and excludes *intermediate goods* (goods used up in the production of other goods, such as steel used in an automobile or the raw cotton that goes into cotton textiles).

The share of a sector or component of GNP such as manufacturing or agriculture is measured by the value added contributed by that sector. *Value added* refers to the addition to the value of the product at a particular stage of production. Thus the value added of the cotton textile industry is the value of the textiles when they leave the factory minus the value of raw cotton used in their manufacture. This in turn is equal to the payments to factors of production in wages paid to labor plus profits, interest, depreciation of capital, and rents.

The great advantage of the GNP concept is that it encompasses all of a nation's economic activity in a few summary statistics that are mutually consistent. The alternative of describing growth in terms of tons of steel and kilowatt-hours of electricity either leaves out much economic activity or in an effort to be inclusive involves the hopelessly complex discussion of thousands of individual products. Particularly in the measurement of broad economic change over time the analysis of individual products in physical terms can be misleading. Cotton textile output, for example, may fall over time but textiles made from artificial fibers may be increasing by more than enough to offset that fall. Gross national product provides one with a consistent technique for adding these two different trends together.

If the concept of gross national product has certain advantages, it also has certain important limitations, particularly when one is trying to compare patterns of development in a wide variety of developing countries. One difficulty is that poor countries usually have poor statistical services; and data from certain sectors of poor countries, such as agriculture and handicrafts, are the worst of all. Estimates of the gross national products of many developing nations are sometimes based on fairly reliable statistics on modern industrial and mining enterprises combined with estimates of rural sector performance based on small representative samples or outright guesses.

Limitations placed on what we know about economic development by poor data will be a theme to which we shall return often in later chapters. In determining trends in the share breakdown of gross national product, however, there are also basic methodoligical issues that get in the way of reliable estimates.

What Is Included in GNP?

To begin with, there is a problem with the definition of **gross national product.** The proper way to calculate gross national product is to add up all the goods and services produced by a country and then sold on the market. In adding up steel and apples one can use either the prices at which steel and apples were sold on the market **(market prices),** or one can use the cost of all factor inputs (labor, capital, land) used to produce a ton of steel or a bushel of apples. The latter method is referred to as pricing at **factor cost.** Many valuable contributions to society are therefore excluded from gross national product. When housework and child care are performed by paid servants or day-care employees, for example, they are included in GNP but when they are performed by unpaid members of the household they do not enter GNP. And in developing countries a very large number of activities do not enter the market. Much of what is produced by the agricultural sector, to take the most important example, is consumed by the farm household and never reaches the market. Strictly speaking one could not speak meaningfully about the changing share of agriculture in GNP but only of the changing share of the marketed agricultural product in GNP. Because this strict definition of GNP would severely limit the usefulness of comparing structural change among nations where agriculture is the dominant sector, the usual practice is to include farm output consumed by the producer, valuing that produce at the prices of marketed farm produce. While making GNP a more meaningful indicator of the productive capacity of a developing economy, this procedure turns GNP into a somewhat arbitrary concept. If one is to include nonmarketed agricultural produce, for example, why not include household-provided child care services?

Exchange Rate Conversion Problems

A second methodological problem arises when one attempts to convert the GNP of several different countries into a single currency. To compare the changing economic structure of several countries as per-capita income rises one must measure the per-capita income figures in a common currency. The shortcut to accomplishing this goal is to use the official exchange rate between dollars and each national currency. For example, to convert Korean GNP from won into dollars, the official exchange rate between won and dollars (over 700 won per dollar in 1982) is used. One problem with this procedure is that exchange rates, particularly those of developing countries, are frequently highly distorted. Trade restrictions make it possible for an official exchange rate to be substantially different from a rate determined by free trade (see Chapters 15–17).

But even if one could accurately estimate the exchange rate that would prevail under a free-trade regime, that would not eliminate the problem. A significant part of GNP is made up of what are called ***nontraded goods and services,*** that is, goods that do not and often cannot enter into international trade. Electric power, for example, can be imported only in rare cases from an immediate neighbor with a surplus to sell (the U.S. imports some electricity from Canada, for example). For the most part electric power must be provided within a country, and it makes little sense to talk about the international market or the international market price for electric power. Internal transportation cannot by definition be traded, although many transport inputs, such as trucks, can be imported. Wholesale and retail trade or elementary school teachers are nontraded services. The wages of these "nontraded" service workers are little influenced by any international market.

Gross national products converted to dollars by exchange rates that are determined by the flow of traded goods will give misleading comparisons if the ratio of prices of nontraded goods to prices of traded goods is different in the countries being compared. The way around this problem is to pick a set of prices prevailing in one of the countries and use that set of prices to value the goods of all countries being compared. The essence of the procedure can be illustrated with the simple numerical exercise presented in Table 3–1. The two economies in the table are called the United States and India, and each economy produces one traded commodity (steel) and one nontraded service (measured by the number of retail sales people). The price of steel is given in dollars in the United States and rupees in India, and the exchange rate is based on the ratio of the prices of the traded good (in this case, steel). The value of the services of retail sales personnel is estimated in the most commonly used way, which is to assume that the value of the service is equal to the wages of the service personnel. The two methods of converting Indian GNP into U.S. dollars are straightforward, and the reader is referred to the table for the precise figures. As the table makes clear, one gets very different results depending on which method is used.

The calculation in Table 3–1 exaggerates the differences in results obtained from the two methods mainly because the nontraded-services sector is larger relative to total GNP than would normally be the case. Systematic estimates using the two different methods on a select group of countries are

TABLE 3–1 Exchange Rate Versus Individual Price Methods of Converting GNP into a Single Currency

	United States			India		
	quantity	price (in U.S.$)	Value of output (in billion U.S.$)	quantity	price (Rs)	Value of output (in billion Rs)
steel (million tons)	100	200 per ton	20	8	1600 per ton	13
retail sales personnel (millions)	2	5000 per person per year	10	4	400 per person per year	16
Total GNP (in local currency)	—	—	30	—	—	29

Official exchange rate, based on steel prices, = 1600/200 or Rs8 = U.S. $1.
A. Indian GNP in U.S.$ calculated by using the official exchange rate:

$$\frac{29}{8} = \text{U.S. }\$3.6 \text{ billion}$$

B. Indian GNP in U.S.$ calculated by using U.S. prices for each individual product or service and applying that price to Indian quantities:

steel	8 million $\times$ $200	=	$1.6 billion
retail sales personnel	4 million $\times$ $5000	=	$20 billion
GNP		=	$21.6 billion

C. Ratio of B to A:

$$\frac{21.6}{3.6} = 6.0$$

TABLE 3–2 Gross Domestic Product[a] per Capita in 1970 in U.S. Dollars

	Using official exchange rate conversion (1)	Using dollar prices for each individual product (2)	Ratio (2) ÷ (1) (3)
United States	4801	4801	1.00
Germany (Federal Republic)	3080	3585	1.16
France	2902	3599	1.24
Japan	2003	2952	1.47
United Kingdom	2143	2895	1.35
Italy	1699	2198	1.29
Hungary	1037	1935	1.87
Columbia	329	763	2.32
Kenya	144	275	1.91
India	98	342	3.49

Source: I. B. Kravis, Z. Kennessy, A. Heston, and R. Summers, *A System of International Comparisons of Gross Domestic Product and Purchasing Power* (Baltimore and London: Johns Hopkins University Press, 1975), pp. 6–8.
[a] Gross domestic product (GDP) is similar to gross national product (GNP). GDP can be derived from GNP by subtracting payments to a country's own factors (labor and capital) from abroad and adding payments to foreign factors remitted abroad. In brief GDP includes everything produced within a country whoever receives the income, but excludes income received by residents of the country from abroad.

presented in Table 3–2. While the differences in results between the two methods are not as great as in our numerical illustration, they are still substantial. Furthermore there is a reasonably systematic relation between the degree to which the exchange-rate-conversion method understates GNP and the level of development of the country. For Germany and the United States, whose per-capita GNPs were not far apart in 1970, the exchange rate conversion is a reasonable approximation of what one obtains when one converts German GNP into dollars using the better method. For India, however, the ratio between the two results is 3.49 to 1. With differences of that magnitude, exchange rate conversions can only be misleading or worse.

Other Index Number Problems

The issue being discussed here is part of a larger group of issues that are generally referred to as *index number problems.* Index number problems arise not only when one is comparing two countries using two different currencies, but also when one is studying the growth of a single country over a long period of time. As growth occurs it usually happens that relative prices change—that is, the prices of some commodities fall while the prices of others rise. If the country is experiencing inflation all prices are rising, but some rise faster than others so that the relative prices change. To eliminate the impact of inflation so that one is measuring *real* rather than *nominal* increases in GNP, the proper procedure is to recalculate GNP in each year using the prices of only one year. But which year does one pick? Estimates of the growth rate will differ as one uses the prices of different years, just as the ratio of Indian to United States GNP will vary if one uses Indian prices to value both countries' GNP in one case and United States prices in another.

There is no correct answer to the question of which prices give you the best estimate of the real growth in a nation's GNP over time. In certain circumstances prices from an earlier or base year may be better than for a later or current year and vice versa, but the reasons behind these choices would take us too far afield from our main focus. In most cases the only completely "correct" procedure is to calculate GNP in both early and later year prices. A hypothetical illustration of the impact of base year versus current year prices is presented in Table 3–3. In this example a higher growth index is achieved using base year rather than current year prices. The reason for this result is that the relative price of the industrial product (television sets) is higher in the base year than in the current year, and thus

TABLE 3–3   Base Year versus Current Year Price Calculations of GNP

Product per year	Base year (1960)		Current year (1982)	
	quantity	*price (in U.S.$)*	*quantity*	*price (in U.S.$)*
television sets (millions)	1	300	50	100
wheat (million tons)	100	200	200	300

A. GNP index using base year prices:

$$100 \times \frac{(50 \times 300) + (200 \times 200)}{(1 \times 300) + (100 \times 200)} = 271$$

B. GNP index using current year prices:

$$100 \times \frac{(50 \times 100) + (300 \times 200)}{(1 \times 100) + (300 \times 100)} = 216$$

the faster growing industrial product accounts for a larger share of total product when base year prices are used. In most countries the industrial sector is growing faster than the agricultural sector, and hence a set of prices that gives the industrial sector a larger weight in national product will result in a higher GNP growth rate.

Data problems therefore are pervasive whenever one studies the aggregate performance of an economy as it evolves over time or compares the aggregate performance of two different economies. When comparing the steel ingot output of two nations it is possible to say precisely how many more tons of steel one of the nations produces when compared to the other. There is no comparable precision when one compares large aggregates such as GNP. A certain ambiguity is always present, and this ambiguity thus is there when these figures are used to search for similarities in the patterns of development across countries or over time.

The Empirical View of Industry-Agriculture Relations

One clear pattern in the process of economic development shines through these data problems: as per-capita income rises the share of industry in gross national product rises also. While it is possible to conceive of a situation where a nation went from a condition of poverty to one of wealth while concentrating mainly on agriculture, there has never actually been a case in history where this has happened. Every country that has achieved a high per-capita income has also experienced a shift in the majority of its population out of farming into the cities and a rising share of industrial value added in its gross national product.

There are two principal reasons for this. The first is *Engel's law.* In the nineteenth century Ernst Engel discovered that as incomes of families rose, the proportion of their budget spent on food declined. Since the main function of the agricultural sector is to produce food, it follows that demand for agricultural output would not grow as rapidly as demand for industrial products and services, and hence the share of agriculture in national product would decline. This relationship holds for all countries that have experienced sustained development.

A second reason has reinforced the impact of the first: productivity in the agricultural sector has risen as growth has progressed. People require food to survive, and if a household had to devote all of its energies to producing enough food it would have no surplus time to make industrial products or to grow surplus food that could be traded for industrial products. In the course of development, however, increased use of machinery and other new methods of raising crops have made it possible for an individual farmer in the United States, for example, to produce enough food to feed, and feed very well, another seventy to eighty people. As a result only 3 percent of the work force of the United States is in farming while the others have been freed to produce elsewhere.

The rising share of industry also helps to explain why, as incomes rise, an increasing percentage of every country's population lives in cities rather than in the countryside. There are *economies of scale* in the manufacture of many industrial products. The existence of economies of scale implies that output per unit of input rises as the firm size increases, that is, a large industrial enterprise in an industry such as steel will produce more steel per dollar cost (made up from the cost of coal, iron ore, limestone, labor, plant machinery) than will a smaller enterprise. Furthermore it makes sense for many different kinds of industrial enterprises to locate in the same place so that common support facilities, such as electric power stations, transport, and wholesalers, can also operate at an efficient level. The result is that industry leads to the growth of cities, and the growth of cities itself tends to increase the share of manufacturing and some services in gross national product. In the rural economies of most poor countries, for example, food processing is something done in the home and is not usually included in gross national product calculations at all. In urbanized industrial nations, in contrast, food processing is often done in large factories, and the value added produced by these factories is included in the share of the manufacturing sector.

Even though the rising share of manufacturing in gross national product and the declining share of agriculture is a pattern common to all nations, it does not follow that the rates of change are the same in each country. In fact planners around the world have been plagued by the question of how much to emphasize agriculture versus industry during the course of development. The Chinese in the 1950s, for instance, tried to follow the Soviet example of putting most of their investment into industry and hoping that agriculture would somehow take care of itself. Disastrous harvests in 1959–1961 forced the government to put more resources, notably chemical fertilizer, into agriculture, but machinery, steel, and related industries continued to receive the lion's share of investment. Food production grew, but only just fast enough to hold per-capita consumption constant as population grew at 2 percent a year. When wages and farm incomes began to rise in the late 1970s, however, constant per-capita output was not good enough and the government once again greatly increased the share of investment going to agriculture.

For a decade and more after independence some African nations also felt that agriculture required little help. Increased food requirements could be met by the simple expedient of expanding the amount of land under cultivation. But population continued to grow, at rates over 3 percent a year in many countries, and the readily available good land got used up. On the edge of the Sahel desert the overuse of fragile land contributed to severe ecological damage that together with a change in weather patterns brought about widespread famine in the region. Away from the Sahel, even a nation as agriculturally rich as Kenya also found itself facing a food crisis as a result of over a decade of 3 + percent annual population growth.

In fact virtually every government in the developing world has struggled with the question of the proper relationship between agricultural and industrial development. Would a greater awareness of the historical relationship between agriculture and industry in countries undergoing development have improved performance in these countries? If planners knew that the share of agriculture in national product always remained above 40 percent until per-capita income rose above $500, those planners would have a target to aim at. Investment in agriculture could be kept at a level to ensure that the share did not fall below 40 percent. But what if there were no consistent patterns among countries at comparable levels of development?

Hollis Chenery and his co-authors, for example, found that there was no single pattern for the changes in shares and that to talk meaningfully about consistent patterns at all one had to break the nations of the world into three subgroups: large countries, meaning countries with a population over 40 million; small countries which emphasize primary (agriculture plus mining) exports; and small countries which emphasize industrial exports.[2] Even within these subgroups there was enormous variation. Figure 3–1, for example, compares Chenery's large-country pattern, estimated in this case from a sample of nineteen countries, with the actual historical performance of several European countries plus Japan. As is apparent from this figure the average performance of these nine industrialized nations is similar to the trend estimated by Chenery and Taylor, but no single country was on the trend line.

Chenery and his co-authors often speak of the trends they have estimated as being the **normal pattern** of development for large (or small) countries. The term has contributed to a good deal of misunderstanding and misuse of the results. Planners have compared these estimated trends with the actual performance of their country, and if their own industrial share has grown more rapidly than the trend they have congratulated themselves for a good performance. Or if the share has grown at a rate below the general trend line they have concluded that something had to be done to correct a poor performance. In either case a deviation from the trend was seen as a cause for concern. But these patterns are nothing more than the average results obtained from comparing many diverse patterns. They are not a guide to what a country ought to do. Perhaps someday we shall be in a position to say that one trend makes more efficient use of a nation's resources than another trend or leads to a faster overall rate of growth. Today all we have are data and estimates that give us a general idea of the trends to expect as economic development occurs. Under the circumstances it is better to drop the term *normal pattern* from the vocabulary and speak of an **average pattern.** On the average the primary share (agriculture plus mining) of GNP in large countries falls from 32 percent at $200 per capita (in 1960 prices) to 19 percent at $500 per capita, but the variation around that trend is so great that these patterns provide only the crudest of guides to planners.

---

2. H. B. Chenery and M. Syrquin, *Patterns of Development, 1950–1970* (London: Oxford University Press, 1975); and H. B. Chenery and L. J. Taylor, "Development Patterns: Among Countries and over Time," *Review of Economics and Statistics* (November 1968), pp. 391–416.

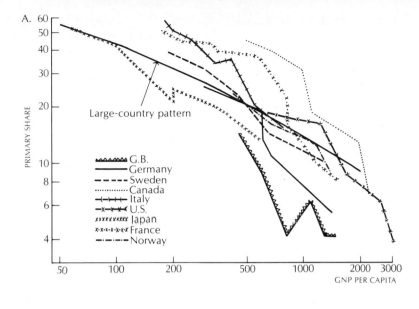

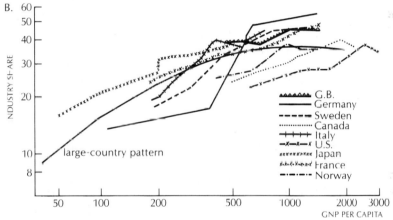

Fig. 3-1 Development Patterns.

A. Share of the Primary Sector in GNP. B. Share of the Industrial Sector in GNP. (*Source:* H. Chenery and L. Taylor, "Development Patterns: Among Countries and over Time" *Review of Economics and Statistics* [November 1968], p. 401.)

The Theoretical View of Industry-Agriculture Relations: The Two-Sector Model

Long before the concept of GNP was invented or economists had many statistics of any kind to work with they recognized the fundamental importance of the relationship between industry and agriculture. To better understand the nature of that relationship they began to design simple models to explain the key connections between the two sectors. The best known of the earlier models appeared in David Ricardo's *The Principles of Political*

Economy and Taxation, published in 1817. Ricardo included two basic as-sumptions in his model that have played an important role in many two-sector models of the relations between agriculture and industry ever since. First, he assumed that the agricultural sector was subject to *diminishing returns,* or steadily decreasing output for a given level of effort. The reason was that crops required land and land was limited. To increase production, Ricardo felt, farmers would have to move onto poorer and poorer land, thus making it more and more costly to produce a ton of grain. Second, Ricardo put forward the concept that today goes under the name *labor surplus.* Britain in the early nineteenth century still had a large agricultural work force, and Ricardo felt that the industrial sector could draw away the surplus labor in the rural sector without normally causing a rise in wages in either the urban or rural areas.

The concept of labor surplus is closely related to concepts such as rural unemployment, underemployment, or disguised unemployment, and these concepts have been refined in recent decades by such economists as W. Ar-thur Lewis, Ragnar Nurkse, John Fei, and Gustav Ranis. *Rural unemploy-ment* is formally much the same as urban unemployment. When there are people who desire work, are actively looking for work, and cannot find work, they are said to be *unemployed.* Very few people in rural areas of de-veloping countries are unemployed in this sense. While most rural people have jobs, those jobs are not very productive. In many cases there is not enough work to employ the entire rural work force full time. Instead members of farm families all work part time, sharing what work there is. Economists call this *underemployment* or *disguised unemployment,* because some members of the rural work force could be removed entirely without a fall in production. Some remaining workers would simply change from part-time to full-time effort.

Underemployment and other features of developing-country labor mar-kets will be discussed at greater length in Chapter 8. Here we are mainly interested in how an agricultural sector with diminishing returns and sur-plus or underemployed labor affects the development of the industrial sec-tor. Put differently, if the industrial sector grows at a certain rate, how fast must the agricultural sector grow in order to avoid a drag on industry and overall economic development? And will accelerated population growth help or make matters worse? To answer these and related questions we shall develop a *simple two-sector model.*

The modern version of the two-sector labor-surplus model was first de-veloped by W. Arthur Lewis.[3] Lewis, like Ricardo before him, pays particu-lar attention to the implications of surplus labor for the distribution of income, and hence it is the Lewis version of that labor-surplus model that is most relevant to the discussion in Chapter 4. The concern in this chapter, however, is with the relationship between industry and agriculture, and that relationship is more completely worked out in a version of the

3. W. Arthur Lewis, *The Theory of Economic Growth* (Homewood, Ill.: Richard Irwin, 1955).

labor-surplus model developed by John Fei and Gustav Ranis.[4] Therefore it is the Fei-Ranis version of the model that is used in the discussion in this chapter.

The Production Function

Our starting point is the agricultural sector and the ***agricultural production function.*** A production function tells us how much output we can get for a given amount of input. In our simple agricultural production function we assume that one input, labor, produces an output, such as grain. Because increases in labor must be combined with either a fixed amount of land or with land of decreasing quality, the production function in Fig. 3–2 is drawn to indicate ***diminishing returns.*** That is, a rise in the labor force from *a* to *b* leads to an increase in output of the amount *dc*, while an increase in labor from *b* to *c* (where the length of *ab* = *bc*) leads to a rise in output of only *ef* (*ef* < *de*). At point *g* further increases in the amount of labor used do not lead to any rise in output at all. Put differently, the ***marginal product of labor*** is falling, which means that each additional unit of labor produces less and less output. Beyond point *g* the marginal product of labor is zero or negative, so additional labor causes no increase or a reduction in output.

The next step in constructing our model is to show how rural wages are determined. The standard assumption in all labor surplus models from Ricardo to the present time so that rural wages will not fall below a minimum level. Thus in its more general form the concept of labor surplus includes not only situations where the marginal product of labor is zero, but also situations where the marginal product of labor is above zero but less than the minimum below which rural wages will not fall. In the Fei

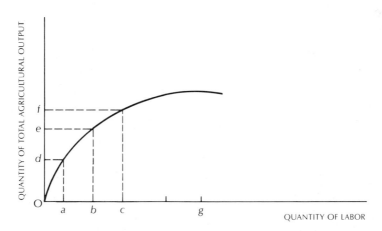

Fig. 3–2 The Production Function.

4. Gustav Ranis and John C. H. Fei, *Development of the Labor Surplus Economy* (Homewood, Ill.: Richard Irwin, 1964).

Ranis model and in other labor-surplus theories the usual assumption is that rural wages do not fall below the *average product* of farm labor in households with a labor surplus. The logic behind this view is that a laborer in a farm household will not look for work outside the household unless he or she can earn at least as much as he would receive by staying at home.

The graph in Fig. 3–3 can be derived directly from Fig. 3–2. The *total* product per unit of labor in Fig. 3–2 was converted into the *marginal product* per unit of labor of Fig. 3–3. The concept of a minimum wage (represented by the dotted line *hi*) was then added to the diagram. The minimum wage is also sometimes called an **institutionally fixed wage** to contrast it with wages determined by market forces. In a perfectly competitive market wages will equal the marginal product of labor for reasons that will be discussed at greater length in Chapter 8. Thus once labor is withdrawn from agriculture to a point where the marginal product rises above the minimum wage (point *h* in Fig. 3–3), wages in agriculture will follow the marginal product curve. To hire away from the farm, factories in the city will have to pay at least as much as the workers are earning on the farm. Thus the line *hij* in Fig. 3–3 can be thought of as the **supply curve of labor** facing the industrial sector. Actually the usual assumption is that the supply curve of labor in industry is a bit above the line *hij* because factories must pay farmers a bit more than they are receiving in agriculture to get them to move.

The key feature of this supply curve of labor is that unlike more common supply curves, it does not rise steadily as one moves from left to right but has a substantial horizontal portion. Formally this means that the sup-

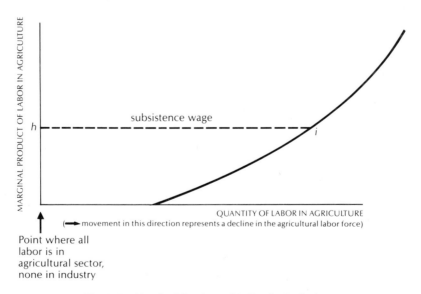

Fig. 3–3 **Marginal Product of Labor in Agriculture.**

ply curve of labor up to point i is *perfectly elastic*. **Elasticity**[5] is a concept used to refer to the percentage change occurring in one variable (in this case, the supply of labor) arising from a given percentage change in another variable (in this case, wages). Perfect elasticity occurs when the ratio of these two percentages equals infinity. From the point of view of the industrial sector this means that that sector can hire as many workers as it wants without having to raise wages until the amount of labor is increased beyond point i.

The final steps are to add a demand curve for labor in the industrial sector (Fig. 3–4) and then to combine the three figures into a single model. The demand curve for labor in industry is determined by the marginal product of labor in industry, and hence the demand curve can be derived from the industrial production function.[6] To simplify our model this step is ignored, and we have simply drawn in the demand curve SS'.

To combine Figs. 3–2, 3–3, and 3–4, one additional piece of information is needed, the size of the nation's labor force. Many models use total population rather than the labor force, and this switch has little effect if the

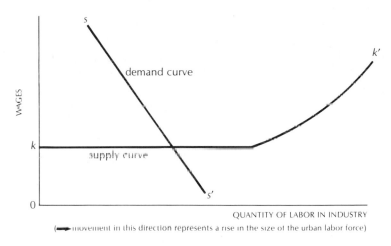

(➡ movement in this direction represents a rise in the size of the urban labor force)

Fig. 3–4 The Supply and Demand for Industrial Labor.

5. The term *elasticity* refers to the percentage change in one variable that results from a percentage change in another variable and is presented as a ratio. In the case discussed here, the elasticity is the ratio of the change in the supply of labor (ΔL) to the total labor supply (L), all over the change in the wage rate (ΔW) divided by the total wage (W). Algebraically,

$$\text{elasticity} = \frac{\Delta L/L}{\Delta W/W} = \frac{\Delta L}{\Delta W} \times \frac{W}{L}$$

In the case of perfect elasticity, this ratio $= \infty$.

6. A factory owner under competitive conditions is willing to pay up to but no more than what a laborer contributes to increase the volume of output of the factory. The increase in output value contributed by the last laborer hired is by definition the marginal revenue product of that laborer.

labor force is always a fixed percentage of total population. Actually this percentage is not fixed, but for certain purposes assuming that it is fixed is an acceptable simplification. All theory is a simplification of reality, and whether or not the simplification is acceptable depends on whether it enhances or distorts our understanding of that reality. The size of the labor force in Fig. 3–5 is represented by the line zero to p. In order to combine the three figures, Fig. 3–2's relation to the others is made clearer if it is flipped so that an increase in labor is represented by moving from right to left rather than the reverse.[7]

If an economy starts with its entire population in agriculture, it can move a large part of that population (pg) to industry or other employment without any reduction in farm output. Industry will have to pay that labor a wage a bit above subsistence (the difference between $p''k$ and $p'h$) to get it to move, but as long as there is some way of moving the food consumed by this labor from the rural to the urban areas, industrialization can proceed without putting any demands on agriculture. Even if agriculture is completely stagnant, industry can grow. As industry continues to grow, however, it will eventually exhaust the supply of surplus labor. Further removals of labor from agriculture will lead to a reduction in farm output. A shift in industrial demand to mm' will force industry to pay more for the food of its workers; that is, the *terms of trade* between industry and agriculture will turn against industry and in favor of agriculture. It is this shift in terms of trade that accounts for the rise in the supply curve of labor between g'' and i''. Industry must pay more to get the same amount of food to feed its workers. Put differently, because the price of agricultural products is rising, the value of the marginal product of workers in agriculture (their **marginal revenue product**), and hence also their wage, are rising as well. For industry to attract workers out of agriculture industrial wages must also rise.

The Fei-Ranis model can be used to explore the implications of population growth and a rise in agricultural productivity, among other things. If, to simplify, one assumes that there is a fixed relationship between population and the labor force, then an increase in population from, say, p to t will not increase output at all. The elastic portion of both the urban and rural labor supply curves will be extended, thus postponing the day when industrialization will cause wages to rise. Most important, if production rises without any increase in food output, the average amount of food available per capita will fall. From the standpoint of everyone but a few employers who want to keep wages low and profits high, population growth is an unqualified disaster. Wages may actually fall in the urban areas, and the welfare of the great mass of farmers will certainly fall. It is a model such as this, even if only imperfectly understood, that people often have in mind when they speak of population growth in wholly negative terms.

7. Fig. 3–2 is reversed so that an increase in the labor force in agriculture will be represented by a movement from right to left rather than the reverse. Handled this way, a movement from left to right represents both a decline in the agricultural labor force and a rise in the industrial labor force, that is, a transfer of labor from agriculture to industry.

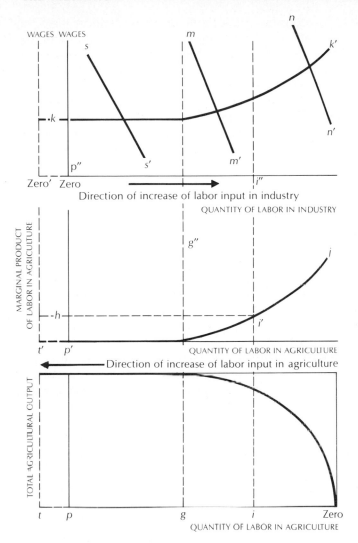

Fig. 3–5 The Two-Sector Labor Surplus Model.

How fast agricultural production[8] must grow depends on what happens to a number of different variables. If industry is growing very rapidly, for example, agricultural productivity must grow rapidly enough to keep the terms of trade from turning sharply against industry, thereby cutting into industrial profits and slowing or halting industrial growth. On the other hand as long as there is a surplus of labor and no population growth, it is possible to ignore agricultural productivity growth and concentrate one's resources on industry.

8. Agricultural productivity in the model presented here refers to a shift in the agricultural production function causing a given amount of labor input in agriculture to produce a larger amount of agricultural output.

David Ricardo, using similar although not identical reasoning, was concerned with keeping population growth down to keep from having to use poorer and poorer land in order to get a sufficient supply of food. He also feared the impact of raising wages because he saw that as leading to a twofold disaster. Higher wages, he argued, following Thomas Malthus, would lead to workers' having more children. And higher wages would cut into profits which provided the funds for investment in capital that made it possible to remove rural surplus labor and employ it in industry. Modern labor-surplus theorists would not agree with Ricardo's harsh policy prescriptions, but they would see the problems facing today's developing countries in a similar light.

The Neoclassical Model

It will be left to the reader to explore the implications of changing many of the assumptions in the labor-surplus model. But the implications of one assumption, the labor-surplus assumption itself, will be explored here. Many economists simply do not agree that a surplus of labor exists in today's developing nations, even in India and China. These economists have developed an alternative two-sector model that is sometimes referred to as a *neoclassical model.*

The framework developed in Fig. 3–5 can also be used to explore the implications of the neoclassical assumptions. A simple neoclassical model is presented in Fig. 3–6. The key difference between Figs. 3–5 and 3–6 is the agricultural production function (Fig. 3–6C). Limited land resources do lead to slightly diminishing returns in the agricultural sector, but the curve never flattens out; that is, the marginal product of labor never falls to a minimum subsistence level so there is no minimum subsistence or *institutionally fixed* wage in Fig. 3–6B. Wages instead are always determined by the marginal product of labor in agriculture. Finally, the supply curve of labor to industry no longer has a horizontal section. Since removal of labor from agriculture increases the marginal product of labor in agriculture, industry must pay an amount equal to that marginal product plus a premium to get labor to migrate to the cities. The supply curve of labor to industry rises for another reason as well. As labor is removed from agriculture farm output falls; and in order to extract enough food from the agricultural sector to pay its workers, industry must pay higher and higher prices for food. Only if industry is in a position to import food from abroad will it be able to avoid these worsening terms of trade. If imports are not available, rising agricultural prices will lead to a higher marginal revenue product, and hence higher wages, for workers in agriculture. As in the labor-surplus case, industry will have to pay correspondingly higher wages to attract a labor force.

The implications of population or labor force growth in the neoclassical model are quite different from what they were in the labor-surplus model. An increase in population and labor in agriculture will itself raise farm output (see dotted lines in Fig. 3–6), and any removal of labor from agri-

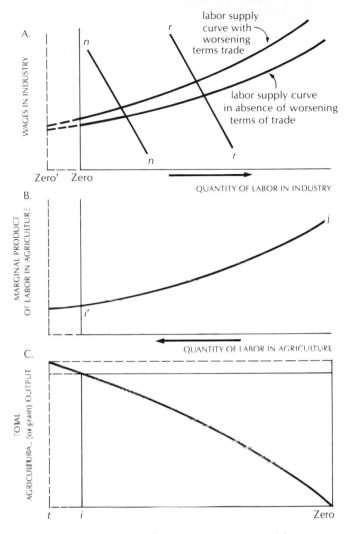

Fig. 3–6 A "Neoclassical" Two-Sector Model.

culture will cause farm output to fall. Thus in a neoclassical model population growth is not such a wholly negative phenomenon. The increase in labor is much less of a drain on the food supply since it is able to produce much or all of its own requirements, and there is no surplus of labor that can be transferred at no cost to agricultural output.

If industry is to develop successfully, simultaneous efforts must be made to ensure that agriculture grows fast enough to feed workers in both the rural and urban sectors at ever-higher levels of consumption and to prevent the terms of trade from turning sharply against industry. A stagnant agricultural sector, that is one with little new investment or technological progress, will cause wages of urban workers to rise rapidly, thereby cutting into profits and the funds available for industrial development. Where in the labor surplus model planners can ignore agriculture until the surplus of labor is exhausted, in the neoclassical model there must be a balance between industry and agriculture from the beginning.

Two-sector models of both the labor-surplus and neoclassical type can become very elaborate with dozens or even hundreds of equations used to describe different features of the economy. These additional equations and assumptions will also have an influence on the kinds of policy recommendations an economist will derive from the model. But at the core of these more elaborate models are the labor-surplus and neoclassical assumptions about the nature of the agricultural production function.

These same points can be made in a less abstract way by returning to the Chinese and African examples with which we began this discussion of the relationship between industry and agriculture during economic development.

Labor Surplus in China   In China by the 1950s most arable land was already under cultivation, and further increases in population and the labor force contributed little if anything to increases in agricultural output. Urban wages rose in the early 1950s, but then leveled off and remained unchanged for twenty years between 1957 and 1977. If allowed to do so, tens of millions of farm laborers would have happily migrated to the cities despite urban wage stagnation. Only legal restrictions on rural-urban migration, backed up by more than a little force, held this migration to levels well below what would have been required to absorb the surplus. Population growth that averaged 2 percent a year up until the mid-1970s continued to swell the ranks of those interested in leaving the countryside. In short, China over the past three decades was a labor-surplus country.

As pointed out earlier China did invest in agriculture, but only enough to maintain, not to raise, pre-capita food production. The rural-urban migration that did occur was not fast enough to eliminate the rural labor surplus, but it was enough to require farmers to sell more of their production to the cities. Thus the prices paid to farmers for their produce were gradually raised, while the prices paid by farmers for urban products remained constant or fell—that is, the rural-urban *terms of trade* shifted slowly but markedly in favor of agriculture.

To get out of this labor-surplus situation Chinese planners in the late 1970s had both to accelerate the transfer of workers from rural to urban employment and to take steps to keep the rural pool of surplus labor from constantly replenishing itself. Accelerating the growth of urban employment was accomplished by encouraging labor-intensive consumer goods (textiles, electronics, etc.) and service industries (restaurants, taxis, etc.). To feed this increase in urban population, the government both increased food imports, shifted more investment funds to agriculture, and allowed a further improvement in the rural-urban terms of trade.

To keep the rural pool of surplus labor from replenishing itself, planners slowed those kinds of farm mechanization that had the effect of reducing the rural demand for labor. Most important, planners attacked the surplus at its source by a massive effort to bring down the birth rate. By 1980 the population growth rate in China had slowed from 2 to 1.2 percent a year. By the early 1980s China was still a labor-surplus country, but the pursuit of similar policies under similar conditions had removed South Korea's labor surplus by the mid-1960s, and much the same thing occurred in Japan at an even earlier date.

Labor Surplus in Africa

Africa, as already pointed out, had low population densities relative to the availability of arable land. In nations such as Kenya increases in population could be readily accommodated in the 1950s and 1960s by opening up new land or by converting land to more intensive uses (for example, from pasture to crops). Increased population therefore was more or less matched by rises in agricultural production. Food output, at least in the richer nations such as Kenya, kept up with the needs of both the expanding rural population and with the even more rapidly growing urban sector. Planners felt little pressure either to improve the rural-urban terms of trade or greatly to increase state investment in agriculture. In short, until recently Kenya fit reasonably well the assumptions of the neoclassical model.

Because Kenya's land resources were not unlimited and because population growth continued at the extraordinarily high rate of well over 3 percent per annum, by the late 1970s Kenya was beginning to acquire some of the characteristics of a labor surplus economy; and planners were having to adjust to the policy implications (more investment and better prices for agriculture, a greater effort to reduce population growth) of these new conditions.

This discussion of the relations between the agricultural and industrial sectors during the process of economic development has gone as far as we can productively go at this stage. Analysis of the patterns of development using data on shares of the two sectors in GNP provided an insight into the patterns that have occurred in the past and might be expected to recur in the future. Two-sector models have made it possible to go a step further and to acquire an understanding of some of the reasons why different patterns of industrial and agricultural development might occur. In later chapters the validity of the labor surplus versus neoclassical assumptions for today's developing world will be explored at greater length. There will also be extended discussions of the nature and problems of industrial and agricultural development that will include further consideration of the nature of relations between the two sectors.

Trade and Industrial Patterns of Growth

Empirical Approaches: Trade

Up to this point the discussion has concentrated on broad aggregate patterns of economic development. GNP has been broken down into only three sectors—industry, agriculture, and services—and the relations between two of these sectors has been explored both empirically and with the use of theoretical models.[9] The search for stable pattern of development and for theories explaining these patterns, however, has also proceeded at a more disaggregated level. A nation's GNP can be disaggregated in many different ways and into smaller and smaller subcategories. Only a few of the more interesting breakdowns will be explored here.

One important pattern, for example, is the relationship between foreign trade's contribution to GNP and a rise in per-capita income. One standard way of looking at this relationship is with the *foreign trade ratio* which adds exports (X) to imports (M) and then divides by GNP:

$$\frac{X + M}{\text{GNP}}$$

The historical experience of the nations of Europe indicates that this ratio rose through the latter half of nineteenth century and up to the beginning of World War I. Since per-capita income in Europe in this period was also rising, simple correlation analysis might suggest that as income per capita rises, that rise leads to or causes or rise in the foreign trade ratio. But a more careful analysis of the European experience suggests that quite different causes were at work. In the latter part of the nineteenth century there was a major revolution in transport technology represented by the introduction of both the steamship and the railroad. These improvements in transport made it possible for Europe to buy its grain from America and Russia at lower prices than it had previously paid for grain much closer to home. In addition the latter half of the nineteenth century was a period when government-imposed barriers to free trade were being rapidly dismantled, largely under the influence of the British. Between the two world wars (1918–1939), in contrast, tariffs, quotas, and other barriers to trade were resurrected and trade ratios fell off.

Using *time series data* derived from the historical experience of particular European nations, therefore, is a treacherous guide or no guide at all to what will happen to the foreign trade ratio as per-capita income rises. An alternative is to use *cross-section data.* Both Kuznets and Chenery, for example, have compared a large number of countries with different per-capita incomes in a single year such as 1965. If the higher income nations also have higher trade ratios, it might indicate that as the incomes of the lower income nations rise their foreign trade ratios will also rise.

---

9. The third sector, services, and its relationship to the other two sectors has only begun to receive systematic treatment by economists. Neither empirical nor theoretical approaches to this subject are sufficiently developed to be presented in a text such as this one.

Unfortunately differences between the foreign trade ratios of nations at a given point of time can also be a treacherous guide to what will happen to today's developing nations as their income rise in the future. A great many forces other than just the differences in per-capita income are at work causing differences in the foreign trade ratios of particular nations. The governments of nations such as South Korea or Denmark have pursued policies designed to promote foreign trade. Others such as North Korea or the Soviet Union have made deliberate efforts to reduce their dependence on foreign trade.

The most important reason for the differing foreign trade ratios between nations with similar per-capita incomes is size. Countries with large populations, whether rich or poor, have lower foreign trade ratios than countries with small populations (see Table 3–4). Not all of the reasons for this relationship between foreign trade and size are well understood. Large countries have larger markets than small countries and hence have less need to specialize on a few products in order to achieve economies of scale in production. Large countries are also more likely to possess all or most of the key raw materials needed by modern industry, such as petroleum or iron ore. Whatever the explanation the relationship clearly exists, and its existence has a major influence on other aspects of the structure of GNP as well.

TABLE 3–4   The Ratio of Exports in GNP by Size of Country and Income

Size of country	Per-capita income		
	$200	$500	$800
Large-country ratio	.123	.131	.140
Small-country ratio	.250	.205	.296

Source: H. Chenery and M. Syrquin, *Patterns of Development, 1950–1970* (Oxford: Oxford University Press, 1975), p. 75.

Clearly neither time series nor cross-section data will always give economists a clear foundation from which to predict future patterns of development. Where both kinds of data give smilar results there is a somewhat stronger basis for speaking of an established pattern of developments, but even then caution must be exercised. The reasons for such caution will become more apparent in the discussion of individual industry patterns that follows.

Empirical Approaches: Industry

If economists knew precisely which industries would develop at each stage in a nation's growth, that would be a very valuable piece of information. Plans could be drawn up that could concentrate a nation's energies on particular industries at particular stages. If all industrial development began with textiles, for example, then planners could focus their attention on getting a textile industry started and worry about other sectors later. Similarly, if only nations with high per-capita incomes could support the efficient production of automobiles, planners in countries beginning development would know that they should avoid investing resources in the automobile industry until a later stage.

Chenery and Taylor[10] have used the terms *early industries, middle industries,* and *late industries.* **Early industries** are those that supply goods essential to the populations of poor countries and are produced with simple technologies so that their manufacture can take place within the poor country. In statistical terms the share of these industries in GNP rises at low levels of per-capita income, but that share stops rising when income is still fairly low and stagnates or falls thereafter. Typically included in this group are food processing and textiles. **Late industries** are those whose share in GNP continues to rise even at high levels of per-capita income. This group includes many consumer durables (refrigerators, cars) as well as other metal products. **Middle industries** are those that fall in between the other two categories.

Unfortunately it is frequently difficult to decide in which category a particular industry belongs. For many industries the nineteenth-century experience of European nations or of the United States is a poor guide because many industries that are important today did not even exist then. The nuclear power industry, for example, did not exist prior to World War II, and even the chemical fertilizer sector as we think of it today did not really begin until well into the twentieth century.

Cross-section data get rid of this particular problem but introduce many others. In several Arab states petroleum accounts for a large share of GNP because these nations have unusually rich underground resources. In Malaysia soil and climate have been favorable to the rise of rubber, palm oil, and timber. Singapore and Hong Kong, which have no natural resources to speak of, have taken advantage of their vast experience in foreign trade to develop textiles, electronics, and other manufactures for export. In short, the share of particular industries in the GNP of individual countries is determined by endowments of natural resources, historical heritages of experience with commerce and trade, and many other factors. There is no single pattern of industrial development, or even two or three patterns, that all nations must follow as they progress out of poverty. Some industries where the techniques used are easier to master, such as textiles, are more likely to get started in the early stages of development than others, such as the manufacture of commercial aircraft. And there is some regularity in the patterns of what people consume as they move from lower to higher incomes. *Engel's law* has already been mentioned as a part of the explanation for the declining share of agriculture in GNP. The same law has much to do with why the share of food processing within industry falls as per-capita income rises. But before planners can decide which industries to push in one country, they must know the particular conditions facing that country as well as these more general patterns.

---

10. Chenery and Taylor, "Development Patterns: Among Countries and Over Time."

Theoretical Approaches to Interindustry Patterns

Economists' debates on balanced and unbalanced growth predate much of the quantitative work on patterns of development. **Balanced growth** advocates such as Ragnar Nurkse or Paul Rosenstein-Rodan[11] argued that countries have to develop a wide range of industries simultaneously if they are to succeed in achieving sustained growth at all. What would happen in the absence of balanced growth has often been illustrated with a story of a hypothetical country that attempted to begin development by building a shoe factory. The factory is built, workers are hired and trained, and the factory begins to turn out shoes. Everything goes well until the factory tries to sell the shoes it is producing. The factory workers themselves use their increased income to buy new factory-made shoes; but of course they are able to produce far more shoes than they need for themselves or their families. As for the rest of the population, they are mainly poor farmers whose income has not risen and hence they cannot afford to buy factory-made shoes. They continue to wear cheap homemade sandals. The factory in turn, unable to sell its product, goes bankrupt and the effort to get development started comes to an end.

The solution to this problem is to build a number of factories simultaneously. If a textile mill, a flour mill, a bicycle plant, and many other enterprises could be started at the same time, the shoe factory could sell its shoes to the workers in these factories as well. Shoe factory workers in turn would use their new income to buy bicycles, clothing, and flour, thus keeping the other new plants solvent. This kind of development is sometimes referred to as **balanced growth on the demand side** because the industries developed are determind by the demand or expenditure patterns of consumers (and investors). **Balanced growth on the supply side** refers to the need to build a number of industries simultaneously to prevent supply bottlenecks from occurring. Thus in building a steel mill planners need to make sure that iron and coal mines and cooking facilities are also developed, unless imports of these inputs are readily available. At a more aggregated level it is also necessary to maintain a balance between the development of industry and agriculture. Otherwise, as pointed out earlier, the terms of trade might turn sharply against industry, thereby bringing growth to a stop.

One problem with the balanced-growth argument is that in its pure form it is a counsel of despair. A poor country with little or no industry was told that it must either start up a wide range of industries simultaneously or resign itself to continuing stagnation. This across-the-board program has sometimes been referred to as a **big push** or a **critical minimum effort.** By whatever name, it was discouraging advice for a poor nation that was tax-

11. Ragnar Nurske, *Problems of Capital Formation in Underdeveloped Countries* (New York: Oxford University Press, 1953); and Paul N. Rosenstein-Rodan, "Problems of Industrialization in Eastern and Southeastern Europe," *Economic Journal* (June-September 1943), reprinted in A. N. Agarwala and S. P. Singh (eds.), *The Economics of Underdevelopment* (New York: Oxford University Press, 1963).

ing its managerial and financial resources to the limit just to get a few factories started.

In the discussion of patterns of industrial development, however, we pointed out that there was litle evidence that all nations had to follow a set pattern. Some nations emphasized one set of industries while other nations concentrated on different ones. Proponents of **unbalanced growth,** especially Albert Hirschman,[12] recognize these differences and use them to suggest a very different pattern of industrial development. Nations, they say, could and did concentrate their energies on a few sectors during the early stages of development. In most cases there was little danger of producing more shoes than could be sold.

Certain industrial products have ready markets, even among the rural poor, in the absence of a big push toward development. A worker in a nineteenth-century factory, for example, could produce forty times as much cotton yarn per day as a peasant with a spinning wheel in a dark rural cottage. From the peasants' point of view, therefore, it made sense to buy factory yarn cheaply and to concentrate his effort on a more productive activity, such as weaving that yarn into cloth. Initially much of this yarn was imported into places like India and China from factories in Britain, but it was not long before entrepreneurs in China and India discovered that cotton yarn could be produced more cheaply at home rather than relying on imports. Thus they substituted domestic production for imports. **Import substitution,** as this process is called, is one way a nation can find a ready market for one of its own industries. The market is already there, and all a country's planners have to do is ensure that the domestic industry can compete effectively with the imported product. How this can be done is a subject to which we shall return in Chapter 16. Here the main point is that import substitution is one way of beginning industrialization on a limited and selective basis rather than with a balanced "big push." Another way is to rely on exports, as England did during the Industrial Revolution. If it is impossible to sell all of a factory's product at home, it is often possible to sell the product abroad, assuming that product could be produced at a cost that is competitive.

Backward and Forward Linkages

Unbalanced growth advocates such as Hirschman, however, did not content themselves with simply pointing out an escape from the dilemma posed by balanced growth proponents. Hirschman developed the unbalanced growth idea into a general interpretation of how development ought to proceed. The central concept in Hirschman's theory is that of *linkages.* Industries are linked to other industries in ways that can be taken into account in deciding on a development strategy. There are both backward linkages and forward linkages. Industries with *backward linkages* make use of inputs from other industries. Automobile manufacturing, for example,

---

12. Albert O. Hirschman, *The Strategy of Economic Development* (New Haven: Yale University Press, 1958).

uses the products of machinery and metal-processing plants, which in turn make use of large amounts of steel. The building of an automobile manufacturing plant, therefore, will create a demand for machinery and steel. Initially this demand may be supplied by imports, but eventually local entrepreneurs will see that they have a ready market for domestically made machinery and steel, and this demand stimulates them to set up such plants. Planners interested in accelerating growth therefore will emphasize industries with strong backward linkages because it is these industries that will stimulate production in the greatest number of additional sectors.

Forward linkages occur in industries which produce goods that then become inputs into other industries. Rather than start with automobiles, planners might prefer to start at the other end by setting up a steel mill. Seeing that they had a ready domestic supply of steel, entrepreneurs might then be stimulated to set up factories that would make use of this steel. In a similar way successful drilling for oil will encourage a nation to set up its own refineries and petrochemical complexes rather than ship its crude oil to other nations for processing.

Both forward and backward linkages set up pressures that lead to the creation of new industries, which in turn create additional pressures, and so on. These pressures can take the form of new profit opportunities for private entrepreneurs, or pressures can build through the political process and force governments to act. Private investors, for example, might decide to build factories in a given location without at the same time providing adequate housing facilities for the inflow of new workers or roads with which to supply the factories and take away their output. In such cases government planners might be forced to construct public housing and roads.

While on the surface the balanced and unbalanced growth arguments appear to be fundamentally inconsistent with each other, when stated in less extreme forms they can be seen as opposite sides of the same coin. Almost everyone would agree that there is no single pattern of industrialization that all nations must follow. On the other hand quantitative analysis suggests that there are patterns that are broadly similar among large groups of nations. While nations with large amounts of foreign trade can follow an unbalanced strategy for some time, a nation cannot pick any industry or group of industries it chooses and then concentrate exclusively on those industries throughout its development, following in effect an extreme form of an unbalanced growth strategy. The very concept of linkages suggests that extreme imbalances of this sort will set up pressures that will force a nation back toward a more balanced path. Thus the ultimate objective is a degree of balance in the development program. But planners have a choice between attempting to maintain balance throughout the development process or first creating imbalances with the knowledge that linkage pressures will eventually force them back toward the balance. In terms of Fig. 3–7 the issue is whether to follow the steady balanced path represented by a solid line or the unbalanced path represented by a dashed line. The solid line is shorter, but under certain conditions a nation might get to any given point faster by following the dashed line.

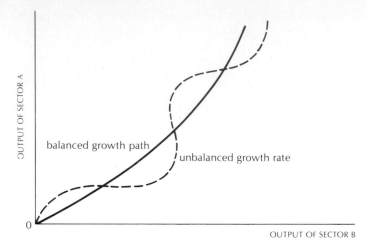

Fig. 3-7 Balanced and Unbalanced Growth Paths.

Conclusion Theory and quantitative analysis both contribute to knowledge of the central relationships that occur throughout the course of economic development. Both approaches separately and together tell something about the nature of the relationship between major sectors such as industry and agriculture, and between industries within these sectors.

There is room for a great deal of improvement in our knowledge of these relationships. Better theories, particularly theories solidly based on empirical evidence, will contribute to this improvement. More and better statistics from the developing nations will also play an important role. But unrealistic prospects should not be held out. Concepts such as gross national product contain ambiguities that no amount of good data or sophisticated theorizing are likely to solve. Techniques of the kind introduced in this chapter therefore are most valuable in providing a general framework into which the more detailed and precise analysis in subsequent chapters can be fitted.

FURTHER The literature on patterns of development is dominated by the works of Simon
READING Kuznets and Hollis Chenery. Although none makes for easy reading, among the works most accessible to the intermediate economics student are Kuznets's *Modern Economic Growth* (New Haven: Yale University Press, 1966) and his *Economic Growth and Structure* (New York: W. W. Norton, 1965); H. B. Chenery's and M. Syrquin's *Patterns of Development, 1950–1970* (London: Oxford University Press, 1975); and Chenery's *Structural Change and Development Policy* (London: Oxford University Press, 1979). The pricing or index number problem as it relates to international comparisons is dealt with by Irving Kravis, Alan Heston, and Robert Summers, *International Comparisons of Real Product and Purchasing Power* (Baltimore and London: Johns Hopkins Universty Press, 1978).

For further development of the two-sector labor surplus model, see J. C. Fei and Gustav Ranis, *Development of the Labor Surplus Economy* (Homewood, Ill.: Richard Irwin, 1964) and W. Arthur Lewis, "Economic Development with Unlimited Supplies of Labor," *The Manchester School* 22 (May 1954): 139–91. For a discussion of the relative merits of labor surplus versus neoclassical models written from a neoclassical point of view, see Dale W. Jorgenson, "Testing Alternative Theories of the Development of a Dual Economy," in I. Adelman and E. Thorbecke (eds.), *The Theory and Design of Development* (Baltimore and London: Johns Hopkins University Press, 1966). The current literature that uses two-sector models to discuss development issues is large and growing, but most of it is only accessible to students with graduate-level training in economic model building.

The best work on balanced versus unbalanced growth remains that of Albert O. Hirschman, *The Strategy of Economic Development* (New Haven: Yale University Press, 1958). The concept of "takeoff" was put forward by W. W. Rostow in *The Stages of Economic Growth: A Non-Communist Manifesto* (Cambridge: Cambrige University Press, 1961). For Kuznets's critique of the concept, see his essay in the above mentioned *Economic Growth and Structure*.

Chapter 4

DEVELOPMENT AND HUMAN WELFARE

In Chapter 1 economic growth was defined simply as a rise in national or per-capita income and product. *Economic development,* it was said, implies more than this: growth *plus* fundamental changes in the structure of the economy, a rise in the share of national product originating in the industrial sector, urbanization, participation by the nationals of the country itself in the process by which these changes are brought about. Despite the many caveats which must be applied to efforts to measure growth and development (Chapter 3), it is evident that most "developing countries" really are growing and developing in the senses implied by these definitions.

The question to be taken up in this chapter is the meaning of that growth and development for the three billion individual citizens of the third world. Are growth and development improving their living conditions as time goes by? If so, to what extent and in what ways? If their welfare is not improving, or not improving very fast, what kinds of changes in development patterns and process could improve this outcome? And how can they be brought about?

Logically speaking, economic growth and development are necessary, but not sufficient, conditions for improving the physical well-being of large numbers of people. If there is no growth, then some people can be made better off only by taking income and assets from others. In poor countries, even if a few people are very rich the potential of this kind of redistribution is severely limited. Even if the metaphorical pie were cut into precisely equal pieces for all, the slices would be very thin indeed.[1]

Economic growth, by contrast, opens up the possibility of making at least

1. There is, however, a view which argues that if assets are redistributed first, faster growth will result. This is taken up in the last section of this chapter.

some people better off without having to make anyone worse off. In metaphorical terms the pie becomes larger; but how is it sliced? Does every piece increase in size or only those received by the fortunate few? Might some people even receive smaller slices despite the large total to be distributed?

There are at least three reasons why we cannot assume that a higher per-capita GNP necessarily means higher incomes for all, or even most, citizens.

First, governments promote economic development not just to improve the welfare of their citizens but also, and sometimes primarily, to augment the power and glory of the state and its rulers. Much of the wealth of ancient Egypt was invested in the pyramids. Some modern LDCs buy ballistic missile systems, develop their own atomic bombs, or construct elaborate capital city complexes in deserts and jungles. The gains from growth can be channeled largely to such expensive projects and thus provide little immediate benefit to the nation's citizens.

Second, resources may be heavily invested in further growth, so that significant consumption gains are put off to a later date. If the process continues indefinitely, that later date never arrives. In extreme cases, such as the Soviet collectivization drive of the 1930s, consumption levels may actually be depressed, even to the point of starvation, so that still faster growth can be achieved. Normally, such extreme measures are within the power only of totalitarian governments.

Third, income and consumption may increase but those who are already relatively well off may get all or most of the benefits. The rich get richer, the old saw says, and the poor get poorer. (In another version, they get children.) This is what poor people often think is happening. Sometimes they are right.

The question of who benefits from economic growth and development is not a new one. In Victorian England, for example, rising inequalities in income and wealth and persistent, even worsening, poverty among the lower classes were widely perceived and frequently debated. Social philosophers such as Karl Marx and novelists like Charles Dickens made these phenomena their major themes. Defenders of the status quo responded either by denying that things were as bad as the critics charged or by arguing that the conditions they deplored were a necessary part of a process of change which would ultimately benefit all strata of society.

Despite the efforts of a few nineteenth-century pioneers in "economic arithmetic" and of subsequent economic historians, we do not know precisely what the dimensions of nineteenth-century inequality and poverty were. It is known, however, that things improved in the developed capitalist countries in the early part of the twentieth century. During this period most governments of industrializing Western states enacted reforms (antitrust legislation, progressive taxation, unemployment insurance, social security, and after 1930, stabilizing monetary and fiscal policies) which helped to mitigate the worst inequalities and assure some minimal living standard for all members of society. Contrary to Marx, who had predicted ever-worsening inequality and instability leading to the collapse of the "bourgeois system" itself, workers in the rich capitalist countries ultimately did reach an era of mass consumption which allowed them to share in the gains from economic development.

But what about the masses of people in Asia, Africa, and Latin America who remain desperately poor by the standards of the ordinary citizen of a rich Western country, or even by those of a worker in an East European socialist state? As industrialization proceeds and their nations' GNPs rise, what happens to their individual economic welfare? When can they hope to reach an era of mass consumption?

The last ten to fifteen years have seen an enormous rise of interest in the problems of inequality and poverty in the less developed countries. This discussion has replayed, with variations, some of the themes heard in the industrial countries a century or more ago. There is no country in which everyone is equally poor, although some exceedingly low-income countries may approach this state of affairs through "shared poverty." As economic growth occurs, inequality is generated because people's incomes rise at varying rates. During the early years of the current period of interest in economic development (c. 1950–1965) it was possible to forget this fact because there were hardly any available statistics on the distribution of income in developing countries. Sometimes people did assume that because per-capita GNP was rising everyone was getting better off. If they were not, it was only a matter of time, some argued, until the benefits of development would "trickle down" to them.

Doubts about whether development was really reaching the poor began in India as early as 1960. By the late 1960s enough income distribution statistics had been complied for India and other LDCs to rock the complacent. These newly gathered data revealed what was for many a shocking reality. Not only was income inequality generally much higher in poor countries than in rich countries, something generally appreciated, but:

1. Inequality was apparently rising in many developing countries.
2. In fact the mass of people in some countries were not benefiting at all from development.
3. Finally, and more controversially, some writers claimed that the poor were actually becoming worse off, at least in certain large and very poor countries such as India and Bangladesh.

Much scholarly work and policy-making concern have resulted from these disclosures. In the following pages we will consider what has been learned, dealing first with *concepts* of economic welfare, then with the *facts* of what has been happening, next with *theories* about the causes and effects of inequality and poverty, and finally with possible *policies.*

Concepts and Measures

Income Distribution

The most common way to evaluate the effect of development on welfare is through the study of income distribution. The two types of income distribution generally cited are the functional distribution and the size distribution. The *functional distribution* refers to the division among the factors of production, traditionally identified as land, labor, and capital. The *size distribution* refers to the distribution of income of all kinds among individuals or families. It is most commonly used as a direct measure of welfare.[2] Since income distribution, according to most theories, is determined largely by ownership patterns of the productive factors and the role each factor plays in the production process, the functional distribution of income is important as a cause of welfare levels. For example, if ownership of land and capital is narrowly distributed, then anything that enhances the returns to these factors will tend to worsen the size distribution of income. Conversely, a higher return to unskilled labor, the most widely distributed resource, will make for a more equal size distribution.

There are many practical problems involved in measuring the size distribution of income. Ideally, average income over several years, or even cumulated lifetime income, should be used since earners in LDCs often experience wide income fluctuations as a result of the vagaries of nature, markets, and their own governments, while earnings also vary systematically with age (see Chapter 9). But such refinements are usually not practical and most studies take income over a particular recent period (a month or year) as their basis. Other practical decisions involve how, precisely, to define income and how to collect data. Usually a sample survey of households is undertaken. Even when considerable care and ingenuity are exercised the resulting statistics are likely to be of questionable accuracy. Respondents may not know what their income is, or they may be afraid to disclose it, perhaps out of fear that their taxes will go up. Generally, reported incomes are understated. If a household income survey is projected over all households, the total ought to equal the household share of national income[3] implied in the national estimates. In practice a shortfall of "only" 15 or 20 percent is regarded as a good result for a household income survey. In general the uncertainties of these statistics require the analyst to tread cautiously when trying to interpret them.

Once the data have been collected, the next step is to analyze them. Respondents (either individuals or households) are first ranked by income size. The best ranking criterion is actualy household income per capita, since family members in LDCs usually pool their incomes and welfare is affected by both the total income received and the number of family members to be supported.

2. One could argue that the distribution of consumption or wealth should be measured instead. Consumption measures the volume of goods and services actually consumed, so it could be equated with material welfare. But income represents *potential consumption,* including a part of the potential which is not realized in the current period because it is saved to yield higher consumption later on. Wealth, finally, defines the potential to earn *and* consume, especially when human capital is included in the definition of wealth (see Chapters 9 and 10). But the distribution of wealth is notoriously hard to measure and statistics on wealth distribution are rare.

3. *National income* equals gross national product less depreciation and indirect taxes; the household share of national income would also exclude profits retained (not distributed as dividends) by corporations.

The data can be arranged in various ways. The most common method is the Lorenz curve, which is illustrated in Fig. 4–1. To draw a Lorenz curve, income recipients are ranked from lowest income to highest along the horizontal axis. The Lorenz curve itself shows the percentage of total income accounted for by any cumulative percentage of recipients. The shape of this curve indicates the degree of inequality in the income distribution. The curve must by definition touch the 45° line at the lower left corner (zero percent of recipients *must* receive zero percent of income) and at the upper right corner (100 percent of recipients *must* receive 100 percent of income). If all recipients had the same income, the Lorenz curve would lie along the 45° line (perfect equality). If only one individual or household received income, it would trace the lower and right-hand borders of the diagram (perfect inequality). In the general case it lies somewhere in between. The farther it bends away from the 45° line of perfect equality, the greater is the inequality of the distribution.

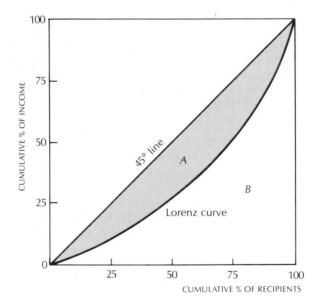

Fig. 4–1 Illustrative Lorenz Curve.

Inequality Measures Statisticians have long been interested in finding a single numerical measure that adequately expresses the degree of overall inequality present in an income distribution. Common statistical measures, such as the range and standard deviation, all have serious faults. The most frequently used measure, the **Gini concentration ratio,** is derived from the Lorenz curve. This ratio is most easily understood as the value of area *A* divided by the sum of area *A* plus area *B* in Fig. 4–1. That is, the larger the share of the area beneath the 45° line that lies above the Lorenz curve, the higher the value of the Gini concentration ratio. One can see from Fig. 4–1 that the theoretical range of the Gini ratio is from 0 (perfect equality) to 1 (perfect inequality). In practice, values measured in national income distributions have a much narrower range—normally from about .20 to .60. Some examples are shown in Table 4–1.

TABLE 4–1 Income Distribution in Selected Countries

Country	Per-capita GNP in U.S.$ (1970 prices)	% of income received by:		Gini concentration ratio
		lowest 40%	highest 20%	
Developing countries				
Pakistan (1963–64)	94	6.5	45.5	.365
Tanzania (1967)	94	5.0	57.0	.458
Sri Lanka (1969–70)	109	6.0	46.0	.370
India (1963–64)	110	5.0	52.0	.418
Kenya (1969)	153	3.8	68.0	.550
Philippines (1965)	224	3.9	55.4	.465
Korea (1970)	269	7.0	45.0	.362
Tunisia (1970)	306	4.1	55.0	.473
Ivory Coast (1970)	329	3.9	57.2	.493
Taiwan (1968)	366	7.8	41.4	.325
Colombia (1970)	388	3.5	59.4	.507
Malaysia (1970)	401	3.4	55.9	.475
Brazil (1970)	457	3.1	62.2	.519
Peru (1970)	546	1.5	60.0	.557
Costa Rica (1971)	617	5.4	50.6	.419
Mexico (1969)	697	4.0	64.0	.526
Uruguay (1967)	721	4.3	47.4	.406
Chile (1968)	904	4.5	56.8	.463
Developed countries				
Japan (1968)	1,713	4.6	43.8	.372
France (1962)	2,303	1.9	53.7	.481
Norway (1963)	2,362	4.5	40.5	.346
United Kingdom (1968)	2,414	6.0	39.2	.322
New Zealand (1970–71)	2,502	4.4	41.0	.346
Australia (1967–68)	2,632	6.6	38.7	.310
West Germany (1970)	3,209	5.9	45.6	.378
Canada (1965)	3,510	6.4	40.2	.322
United States (1970)	5,244	6.7	38.8	.315
Socialist countries				
Yugoslavia (1968)	602	6.5	41.5	.337
Poland (1964)	661	9.8	36.0	.265
Hungary (1967)	873	8.5	33.5	.249
East Germany (1970)	2,046	10.4	30.7	.213

Source: Montek S. Ahluwalia, "Inequality, Poverty and Development," *Journal of Development Economics* 3 (1976). 340–41.

Like all other measures that have been proposed the Gini concentration ratio has its problems. For one thing Lorenz curves can intersect, so that curves of different shapes could generate the same Gini ratio. (This happens because one distribution is very unequal in one part of its range, say, from the bottom to around the middle, while another is unequal in a different part, say, in terms of the income shares of the very richest families.) For another, the extreme nature of the reference standard (perfect equality) makes the measure generally insensitive to changes in distribution. This insensitivity is greatest for changes in the incomes of low-income groups, which may be small in absolute terms but still important in percentage terms to the poor households themselves, and also perhaps an important form of redistribution in policy terms.[4]

Many other inequality measures have been proposed. For example, Simon Kuznets has suggested one (the "Kuznets ratio") which simply sums up the differences (sign disregarded) between the income shares and population shares of all the cells into which a population might be divided. When applied to a size distribution this gives greater weight to inequalities near the center of the distribution than does the Gini ratio, while correspondingly downplaying inequalities at the two extremes.

Any measure which tries to encompass the entire Lorenz curve in a single statistic must contain an element of arbitrariness. One way around this is to look only at a particular part of the curve. Thus if we are interested in how the poor are faring, we might examine the absolute and relative incomes of the poorest 30 or 40 percent of the distribution. Conversely if we are interested in the concentration of wealth at the top of the distribution, the top 5, 10, or 20 percent could be studied. This tells us what we want to know for particular purposes, but at the cost of generality; it ignores what is going on in the rest of the distribution.

TABLE 4-2 Comparisons of Income Distribution in Peru, Kenya, and Malaysia

Country	Income shares of quintiles:					Gini concentration ratio	Kuznets ratio
	Bottom 20%	Second quintile	Third quintile	Fourth quintile	Top 20%		
Peru (1970)	1.5	5.0	12.0	21.5	60.0	.557	.830
Kenya (1969)	3.8	6.2	8.5	13.5	68.0	.550	.960
Malaysia (1970)	3.4	8.0	12.6	20.1	55.9	.475	.720

Source: Montek S. Ahluwalia, "Inequality, Poverty and Development," *Journal of Development Economics* 3 (1976): 340–41.

Some of these points are illustrated in Table 4–2, which compares the income distributions of Peru, Kenya, and Malaysia around 1970. All three countries had relatively unequal income distributions, but which was the most unequal? The Gini concentration ratio says Peru, but according to the different weighting system used in the Kuznets ratio it is Kenya. Yet the bottom 20 percent of the distribution do better in Kenya than in Peru, or even in otherwise more egalitarian Malaysia. The share of high-income families is greater in Kenya than in Peru if we look only at the top 20 percent of the distribution, but exactly the same (81.5 percent) if we look at

4. In India in 1963–1964 the lowest 40 percent of the income distribution received only 5 percent of total income while the top 20 percent of households got 52 percent of total income. Taking 1 percent of total income from the richest of the group and giving it to the lowest 40 percent would raise the income of the poor by 20 percent (one-fifth), a meaningful increase. Yet it would reduce the income of the richest 20 percent of households by less than 2 percent (one fifty-second) and lower the Gini concentration ratio only from .418 to .405 (assuming that the redistributive gain is shared equally by the lowest two deciles).

the top 40 percent of income recipients. So which distribution is really more unequal? In a borderline case like this Peru-Kenya comparison it depends on the measure used. Kenya's distribution was more unequal in some senses, Peru's in others. Malaysia's distribution was less unequal than the other two in most, but not quite all, respects. The crossing Lorenz curves produced by these distributions are shown in Fig. 4–2.

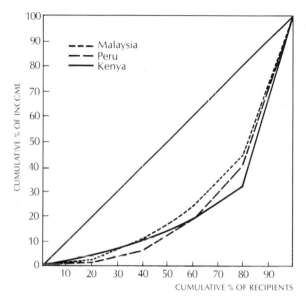

Fig. 4–2   Lorenz Curves for Income Distribution in Peru, Kenya, and Malaysia, c. 1970.

Poverty Measures While inequality is clearly a matter of relative incomes, the concept of ***poverty*** implies that households are poor in some absolute sense. But what absolute standard is there that can be used to distinguish between poor and nonpoor households? One could perhaps identify poverty through its specific manifestations: starvation, severe malnutrition, illiteracy, substandard clothing and housing. But there is more to poverty than that. Fundamentally, poverty is usually defined in *social* terms. "The poor" are those who must live below whatever has been defined as the minimum acceptable standard in a given time and place. It is in this sense that the poor are always with us. Thus while practically everyone in the United States receives a higher income than almost everyone in, say, Chad, there are still poor people in the United States and nonpoor people in Chad. Different standards apply in the two places. So poverty is not entirely a matter of *absolute* levels of living. Its real basis is psychological. The poor are those who feel deprived of what is enjoyed by other people in the society of which they consider themselves to be a part (their "reference group," in psychological terms). Reference groups are probably expanding as education and communication improve. Formerly, peasants might compare their own status to that of the village elites at most. Now they are becoming increasingly aware of the living standards of urban elites in their own countries, and even of standards which prevail in the rich countries. So the sense of deprivation may well be growing.

Measurement of the amount of poverty existing in a country usually begins with the drawing of a *poverty line.* Ideally, this line should be defined in terms of household income per capita. Households with per-capita incomes below the poverty line are defined as poor while those with incomes above the line are not poor. The simplest measure of the extent of poverty is the percentage of poor households in the total. A better measure would take account of the *extent* to which the incomes of the poor fall below the poverty line. Reduction of poverty would therefore be measured through a fall in the percentage of poor households in the total and also through increases in the absolute incomes of the poor.

Table 4–3 illustrates these points using as an example one of the most successful cases of poverty and inequality alleviation. Sri Lanka in 1953 had a low per-capita income, relatively great inequality (as measured by the Gini ratio), and a large population of poor people (defined here as receiving a monthly per-capita income below Rs100 in 1963 prices). Over the succeeding two decades inequality declined and outstanding progress was made in reducing poverty, as can be seen from the rise in the mean income of the bottom 40 percent of the income distribution and from the sharp decline in the percentage of households below the poverty line. Note that this was achieved with only modest growth in average income; according to the statistics, monthly income per capita rose only 28 percent in twenty years, while the average income of households in the lowest four deciles of the distribution rose by 71 percent. Few developing countries have been able to duplicate this achievement.

The poverty analyst can apply similar or different standards across differing times and places. World Bank publications sometimes refer to the quantity and distribution of "absolute poverty" in the world; these calculations are made using a single global poverty line.[5]

Basic Human Needs and Social Indicators

The poverty approach measures purchasing power in the hands of the poor. But some students of development, including many who hail from disciplines other than economics, object to using income as the measure of welfare. Of course, they maintain, higher incomes help *make it possible* for people to live better and longer, but why don't we look to see whether these changes *actually occur?* Efforts to measure a wide variety of *social indicators* have been going on for several years. More recently interest has centered on seeing whether *basic human needs* are being satisfied. Lists of basic human needs can differ, but most versions include minimal levels of

5. For a probing discussion of these measurement problems, see Amartya K. Sen, *On Economic Inequality* (New York: W. W. Norton, 1973). A good short discussion is provided by Richard Szal and Sherman Robinson, "Measuring Income Inequality," in Charles R. Frank and Richard C. Webb (eds.), *Income Distribution and Growth in the Less-Developed Countries* (Washington, D.C.: Brookings Institution, 1977), pp. 491–533.

TABLE 4-3 Changes in Income Distribution and Poverty in Sri Lanka, 1953–1973

Measure	1953	1963	1973
Income shares of quintiles			
Bottom 20%	5.2	4.5	7.2
Second quintile	9.3	9.2	12.1
Third quintile	13.3	13.8	16.3
Fourth quintile	18.4	20.2	21.6
Top 20%	53.8	52.3	42.9
Gini concentration ratio	.46	.45	.35
Mean income per capita, monthly (Rs, constant 1963 prices)	117	134	150
Mean income of bottom 40% (Rs/month)	42	46	72
% of households below Rs100/month (in 1963 prices)	63	59	41

Source: Gary S. Fields, *Poverty, Inequality and Development* (Cambridge: Cambridge University Press, 1980), p. 197.

nutrition, health, clothing, shelter, and opportunities for individual freedom and advancement. Some of these, at least, can be measured.

For some years now the United Nations Research Institute for Social Development (UNRISD), located in Geneva, has been compiling a data bank of social indicators. A selection of its data is shown in Table 4–4. Some of the indicators listed (infant deaths, life expectancy, protein consumption, and adult literacy) reflect the degree to which basic human needs are satisfied in countries at different levels of GNP per capita. Others (newsprint consumption, radios, and motor vehicles) indicate consumption of items that might be regarded as less basic. Remaining indicators are less directly related to welfare. Some, such as fertilizer use and electricity consumption, measure the sophistication of the economy. Finally, a fourth group of indicators, represented in Table 4–4 by densities of physician and hospital services, indicate levels of services which may contribute to basic needs' satisfaction, which is itself measured more directly by other indicators.[6]

Two interesting points come out of an examination of Table 4–4. One is the fact that as a general rule improvement in social indicators goes hand-in-hand with a rise in per-capita GNP. It is striking that in Table 4–4 every time we move to a higher income group *all* the social indicators improve —on average, for those countries represented in UNRISD's data bank. But the second point is that variation among countries within each income class is large. This is demonstrated by the high values for standard deviations shown in the table.[7]

6. Besides being an approach to measuring welfare, basic human needs is also a strategy for welfare-oriented development. This aspect is discussed in the last section of the chapter.

7. The standard deviation is a measure of the average variation among observations. It can be defined as

$$\sqrt{\frac{d^2}{n}}$$

where d is the deviation of each observation from the mean and n is the number of observations. A large standard deviation indicates a wide spread among the observations, while a small one suggests that most observations have values close to the mean.

TABLE 4–4   Illustrative Social Indicators for 1970

Indicator	GNP per capita (1971)									
	< $150		$150–$500		$500–$1000		$1000–2000		> $2000	
Infant deaths/1000 live births	136	(41)	109	(33)	50	(18)	32	(13)	18	(4)
Life expectancy at birth (years)	46	(9)	52	(6)	66	(6)	70	(2)	72	(2)
Thousand inhabitants/ physician	33.4	(24.5)	8.6	(8.5)	2.1	(2.5)	0.9	(0.6)	0.7	(0.2)
Thousand inhabitants/ hospital bed	1.3	(1.1)	0.6	(0.5)	0.4	(0.5)	0.2	(0.1)	0.1	(0)
Protein consumption/ head/day (gms)	55	(11)	61	(13)	75	(16)	90	(16)	92	(8)
Adult literacy (%)	37	(22)	49	(21)	84	(6)	89	(11)	99	(0)
Newsprint consumption (kg/head)	0.3	(0.4)	1.3	(1.2)	5.0	(2.9)	9.8	(12.6)	23.6	(11.3)
Radios/1000 inhabitants	55	(91)	87	(68)	184	(105)	206	(104)	401	(282)
Motor vehicles/1000 inhabitants	5	(3)	16	(11)	45	(25)	106	(67)	250	(117)
Fertilizer use (kg/ha of arable land)	9	(13)	46	(76)	57	(45)	131	(118)	346	(224)
Electricity consumption (kwh/head)	41	(44)	271	(238)	1031	(655)	1675	(834)	5065	(3020)

Source: UNRISD Research Data Bank. Figures in parentheses are standard deviations.

One problem with social indicators is that it is hard to aggregate them to obtain an overall view of a nation's material well-being. An imaginative, if arbitrary, move in this direction has been made by the Washington-based Overseas Development Council (ODC). The ODC's "physical quality of life index" (PQLI) is an aggregation of three widely available indicators of the basic human needs variety: life expectancy at birth, the infant mortality rate, and the rate of literacy.[8] Although easily criticized for its arbitrariness, the PQLI does produce some interesting and intuitively appealing results, which are interpreted by its compilers to suggest that the richest countries do not always enjoy the highest quality of life and that at least a few countries (Sri Lanka, Cuba, Guyana, South Korea) have been able to achieve a comparatively high quality of life at levels of per-capita income well below those of the industrialized nations. Nevertheless the correlation between the PQLI and per-capita GNP is quite high, and the largest deviations are caused by obvious cases such as the oil-exporting countries (which have high GNP and low PQLI). Values of the PQLI for selected countries are shown in Table 4–5.

8. Each indicator is assigned a scaled value from 0 to 100, with the best and worst known cases serving as the limits of the scale. An unweighted average of the three is then taken. See James P. Grant, *Disparity Reduction Rates in Social Indicators* (Washington, D.C.: Overseas Development Council, 1978).

TABLE 4-5 Physical Quality of Life Indicator (PQLI) for Selected Countries, 1974–1975[a]

Country	Life expectancy at birth (years)	Infant mortality (per 1000 live births)	Literacy (%)	PQLI
Bolivia	47	NA	40	39
Brazil	61	70	64	66
Chile	63	79	90	78
Colombia	61	56	74	72
Ghana	44	63	25	39
Kenya	50	51	40	39
Tanzania	45	190	63	27
China	62	NA	NA	69
India	50	122	36	43
Indonesia	48	82	62	48
Korea, Rep. of	61	38	92	80
Malaysia	59	35	60	68
Pakistan	51	113	21	40
Sri Lanka	68	45	78	81

Source: James P. Grant, *Disparity Reduction Rates in Social Indicators* (Washington, D.C.: Overseas Development Council, 1978), pp. 64–69.
[a] NA = not available.

Distribution Weights

A few years ago a study group convened by the World Bank proposed a novel and ingenious way to integrate the study of economic growth and welfare.[9] It involves the use of "distribution weights."

Distribution weights are illustrated in Table 4-6, which compares six countries for which income distribution estimates separated by several years are available. During the periods concerned these countries had average annual GNP growth rates ranging from 9.3 percent (South Korea) down to 4.5 percent (India). Their initial income distributions varied from quite egalitarian (Korea), through moderately egalitarian (India and Sri Lanka), to very unequal (Brazil, Columbia, and Peru). The distribution of amounts added to total income during the periods studied also differed among the six countries. In Colombia and Sri Lanka inequality declined; in the other countries it rose.

TABLE 4-6 Illustration of Distribution Weights

Country	Period	Income growth Upper 20%	Middle 40%	Lowest 40%	Growth rate using Income weights	Population weights	Poverty weights	Initial Gini coefficient
South Korea	1964–70	10.6	7.8	9.3	9.8	9.0	9.0	.34
Brazil	1960–70	8.4	4.8	5.2	6.9	5.7	5.4	.56
Columbia	1964–70	5.6	7.3	7.0	6.2	6.8	7.0	.57
Peru	1961–71	4.7	7.5	3.2	5.4	5.2	4.6	.59
Sri Lanka	1963–70	3.1	6.2	8.3	5.0	6.4	7.2	.45
India	1954–64	5.1	3.9	3.9	4.5	4.1	4.0	.40

Source: Hollis Chenery et al., *Redistribution with Growth* (London: Oxford University Press, 1974), p. 42.

9. Hollis Chenery et al., *Redistribution with Growth* (London: Oxford University Press, 1974).

These varying development experiences can be evaluated using three different weighting schemes:

1. Conventional national accounting uses *base-year income share* as its weighting system. Thus if the top 20 percent of households received half the income, their income growth gets a 50 percent weighting in figuring out the growth rate of society's income (GNP). By this criterion Korea grew more than twice as fast as India and the other countries fell in between.

2. *Population weights* would weight each part of the size distribution of income according to its share in total population. This is an egalitarian approach that weights everyone's income growth equally, neither favoring the rich because they had disproportionately more income originally nor penalizing the poor because they had disproportionately less. Under population weighting Korea remains the country with the best performance, but Colombia and Sri Lanka (in which income distributions improved during the period) begin to look better relative to the others (in which it worsened).

3. *Poverty weights* would go a step further and assign an extra-heavy weight to income growth for the poor. Various weights could be used; the ones employed in Table 4–6 imply a moderately pro-poor bias. Whereas population weights are 0.2, 0.4, and 0.4 respectively for the three income groups, the poverty weights selected were 0.1, 0.3, and 0.6. In other words income gains for the poorest group are valued at one and one-half times as much as under the population weights scheme, gains for the middle group at three-quarters as much, and gains for the richest group at half as much. Under this weighting scheme, as the table shows, Colombia's and Sri Lanka's performances look even better, while Brazil slips from its original position of second to fourth place.

These weighting schemes evaluate the *change in welfare* during the period. They should be read in conjunction with the initial degree of inequality, which is shown in the right-hand column of Table 4–6. Thus while India and Korea showed increases in inequality during the period, evaluation of their performance should be tempered by the fact that they started from relatively equal initial distributions. Brazil and Peru, by contrast, experienced worsening of distributions that were already highly unequal to begin with.

The flexibility of the distribution weights approach is appealing, but there are difficulties with it, both in principle and in practice. Who makes the value judgments implicit in the choice of weights? Those economists who have proposed the reweighting schemes are egalitarian-minded, but do their values coincide with those of poor societies and their governments? Arnold Harberger has demonstrated that seemingly modest reweighting schemes imply that society is willing to accept a large loss in efficiency in return for some redistribution, and he has gone on to argue that by their actions most governments reveal that in fact they are not so interested in redistribution as such.[10] (Harberger believes that governments *do* show commitment to

---

10. Arnold Harberger, "Basic Needs *versus* Distributional Weights in Social Cost-Benefit Analysis," *Economic Development and Cultural Change,* forthcoming.

the satisfaction of "basic human needs" for food, education, health services, and so on.) Yet *not* to reweight also implies a value judgment—namely, in favor of the existing distribution of income.

A practical impediment to widespread use of reweighting schemes is the weakness of statistics on the distribution of income. For most developing countries the analyst is fortunate to have *one* reasonably reliable estimate of the distribution of income. In very few instances are there the two or more comparable estimates required for one to say how the benefits of economic growth have been distributed. Even in a country like Sri Lanka, a pioneer both in the collection of income distribution statistics and in the redistribution of income, questions have been raised about whether the improvement of income distribution thought to have occurred between the early 1960s and the early 1970s actually took place.

We conclude this discussion of concepts and measures of material welfare by observing that universally acceptable measures have not been found and never will be. Development brings about many changes, and any evaluation of its effect on welfare will inevitably depend on how one weighs each type of change. Varying degrees of emphasis on growth, inequality, and poverty will lead to varying assessments. A system of distributive weights can express one evaluator's values, but the values of other observers may well diverge. Agreement is possible only in the loose sense that most people would regard successful development (in welfare terms) as encompassing rising per-capita output, reduced poverty, improved health and longevity, and at least no dramatic worsening of inequality.

Patterns of Inequality and Poverty

In his 1955 presidential address to the American Economic Association, Simon Kuznets put forward the proposition that the relationship between the level of per-capita GNP and inequality in the distribution of income may take the form of an inverted ∪. That is, as per-capita income rises, inequality may initially rise, reach a maximum at an intermediate level of income, and then decline as income levels characteristic of an industrial country are reached. Kuznets based this proposition on mere fragments of data available at the time for estimating income distributions in a few rich and poor countries, and on trends in distribution over time in a very few European countries.

Kuznets's insight has held up well in later years as much larger bodies of data have been amassed. We now have estimates of income distribution in more than seventy countries, although some of these estimates are of dubious quality. One of the more carefully screened data sets, covering sixty countries for which estimates were made in the neighborhood of 1970, is summarized in Table 4–7. Inequality can be measured in this table using any of three measures: the share of total income received by the poorest 40 percent, the share of the top 20 percent, or the Gini concentration ratio. By any of these measures, inequality first rises, then falls, just as Kuznets predicted that it would in 1955. Other studies have obtained similar results.

TABLE 4-7 Estimates of Inequality and Poverty in Relation to GNP per Capita (unweighted averages within groups)

GNP per capita in 1970 ($)	Number of countries included	% of income received by: Lowest 40%	% of income received by: Highest 40%	Gini concentration ratio	Mean income of lowest 40%	GNP per capita ($)
Under $150	10	15.6	51.3	.402	43	109
$150-$500	19	11.2	57.9	.479	84	301
$500-$1500	12	12.2	56.3	.461	230	754
Developed market countries (above $1500)	13	16.1	43.5	.358	1,147	2,849
Socialist countries	6	24.1	34.6	.238	550	913

Source: Based on Montek S. Ahluwalia, "Inequality, Poverty and Development," *Journal of Development Economics* 3 (1976); 340–41.

Most of our evidence on the relationship of inequality to per-capita income comes from this kind of *cross-section data;* that is, from estimates made at approximately the same time for countries at low, middle, and high levels of per-capita income. *Time series data,* comparable estimates at different times for particular countries, are much rarer. For many countries there is only one good estimate of income distribution (at most!), while even where two or more surveys have been made differences in their design and execution may make it hard to compare results. Accordingly the questions of whether low-income countries will necessarily see a rise in inequality as they move to semideveloped status, and whether they can then expect inequality to decline once more as they achieve a high level of development, remain open.

But if, as seems likely, there is a tendency toward the inverted-∪ relationship, two important questions arise. What causes this pattern of changing inequality through the development process? And how predetermined is it? That is, how much latitude is there for differences either in the circumstances of particular countries or in the policies they follow to make a different pattern of inequality consistent with economic growth?

A starting point in answering these questions is the observation that per-capita GDP, using Kuznets's hypothesized curvilinear relationship, "explains" (in statistical terms) only about one-quarter of the intercountry variations in Gini coefficients reflected in the data summarized in Table 4-7. Thus while "Kuznets's law" clearly holds in terms of averages (at least in cross-section data), its application to any particular country is rather limited.

There are many cases in which individual countries depart substantially from the norms. Sri Lanka, South Korea, and Taiwan all have relatively equal income distributions among developing countries. In Latin America, Costa Rica and Uruguay have inequality measures far below the normally high level for the region. Several developed capitalist countries (Norway, the United Kingdom, New Zealand, Australia, Canada, the United States) have less inequality than Yugoslavia, a socialist state. Notable deviations on the other side include a number of African and Latin American countries with unusually high inequality (for example, Kenya, Ivory Coast, Tunisia, Colombia, Brazil, Mexico, and Chile), as well as Malaysia and the Philippines in Asia. Among developed countries, France stands out for its high level of inequality. Statistics for all these countries can be examined by referring back to Table 4–1.

Analysts have tried to increase the percentage of "explained variation" in the degree of inequality among countries by adding more independent variables to the equation. One result which emerges clearly from this effort is that socialist countries have much less inequality than nonsocialist countries with comparable GNP per capita. This fact can be seen in Table 4–7, where the socialist group is represented by Bulgaria, Yugoslavia, Poland, Hungary, Czechoslovakia, and East Germany.[11] Since socialist countries must, for incentive purposes, maintain wage differentials comparable to those existing in nonsocialist countries, their lower inequality must be attributable mainly to the drastic restrictions they maintain on private ownership of land and capital facilities, assets whose ownership is very unequally distributed in nonsocialist countries.

Among the nonsocialist countries much the same factors seem to explain inequality in both low-income and high-income countries. Relatively high enrollment rates in primary and secondary schools and a higher GNP growth rate appear to be associated with reduced inequality, given the level of GNP per capita, while a higher growth rate of population goes with greater inequality. Together these factors can raise the total explained variation in a statistical cross-section analysis to about 50 percent.[12] This still leaves a lot of room for country-to-country variation which has not yet been fit into a general explanatory framework.

There have, however, been attempts to identify the types of societies (in social and political as well as economic terms) in which inequality is likely to be high or low. One such study, which measured incquality in terms of the share of income received by the lowest 60 percent of the income distribution, found that relatively equal income distributions are typically found in two kinds of countries: very poor ones dominated by small-scale or communal (jointly farmed) agriculture and well-developed ones in which major efforts have been made to improve human resources.[13] This conclusion is consistent with the Kuznets hypothesis but more suggestive of the factors that may be associated with the inverted-U pattern. The very poor countries may be quite egalitarian, it says, but only if their economies are dominated by small peasant farms and not by large farms or mines. Rich countries can also be egalitarian, but only if their people have been per-

---

11. It should be stressed that while inequality is low for the socialist countries, absolute income is also relatively low. East Germany, the richest country in this group, had a per-capita income only two-thirds that of its nonsocialist counterpart, West Germany.

12. See Montek S. Ahluwalia, "Income Inequality: Some Dimensions of the Problem," in Hollis Chenery et al., *Redistribution with Growth*, pp. 3-37; "Inequality, Poverty, and Development," *Journal of Development Economics* 3 (1976); 307–42.

13. See Irma Adelman and Cynthia Taft Morris, *Economic Growth and Social Equity in Developing Countries* (Stanford, Calif.: Stanford University Press, 1973).

mitted to share in development by upgrading the productivity of the labor resources that they supply to the economy.

By implication, countries with intermediate income levels are likely to have considerable inequality. This same study found the income share of the poorest 60 percent to be smallest of all where well-entrenched foreign or military elites control the most productive economic sectors and receive most of the benefits of development.

There is a school of thought that is pessimistic about prospects that development will better either the absolute or the relative position of the poor.[14] Much of this pessimism stems from study of South Asian experience. The pessimism does not have strong empirical backing, however, since most studies show that the poor generally do benefit from a rise in GNP, both in terms of absolute income gains and in terms of their share in total income.

Logically speaking, if the *income share* of the poor rises with growth, their *absolute income* must rise by definition, since they are getting an increasing share of an increasing total. But what of the situation, apparently common in the early stages of development, in which their share declines?

The conclusion one reaches will depend on the definition of poverty that one adopts (see earlier discussion), but if we define a single worldwide poverty line it is abundantly clear that economic growth is strongly associated with a reduction in poverty. Based on the data that lie behind Table 4–7, for example, we can ask ourselves how much of the intercountry variation in the absolute mean income of the poor (defined here as the lowest 40 percent of the distribution) can be "explained" statistically using per-capita GNP as the sole explanatory variable. The answer turns out to be a high 94 percent. In other words, while there are many reasons why people may be poor in an absolute sense, the most important one is that they live in poor countries. Other studies have reached similar conclusions.[15]

Another indication of the close association between poverty and low national income per capita is the locational pattern of world poverty. Calculations made by the World Bank in 1975 show that over half the world's poor (defined as per-capita income below $75) lived in the low-income countries of South Asia. Overall, 79 percent of the poor lived in countries with per-capita GNP of less than $265 in 1975 prices.[16] There are of course absolutely poor people in other regions, such as Latin America and the Middle East, but their numbers are much smaller. Most of these poor people live in rural areas.

Is there any need to qualify the strongly indicated conclusion that poverty is associated with low national per-capita income and tends to be eradicated as per-capita income rises? Only, perhaps, in two respects:

14. See Adelman and Morris, *Economic Growth,* as well as International Labour Office, *Poverty and Landlessness in Rural Asia* (Geneva, 1977).

15. See, for example, Ahluwalia, "Income Equality," and his "Inequality, Poverty, and Development."

16. World Bank, *Prospects for Developing Countries, 1978–85* (Washington, D.C., November 1977), p. 8.

1. We have been analyzing absolute poverty using a global poverty line. Relative poverty is far more persistent. There are not many people living on $75 a year in the United States, but there are many who must live on incomes far below a reasonable U.S. standard.

2. Some time series studies for particular countries have shown stagnation or even decline in the incomes of the poor and/or increases in the number of poor people. Many of these findings have been challenged, but they do at least serve to warn us not to assume complacently that economic growth will necessarily eliminate poverty either automatically or rapidly.

None of the global statistics and research that we have been discussing can fully reveal the extent or causes of poverty in particular countries. The four case histories will help to round out the picture. These capsule case studies, if they achieve nothing else, show that one should be cautious in generalizing about development, inequality, and poverty. Much depends on the circumstances of the individual country and the type of development pursued.

South Korea

South Korea has enjoyed a high rate of economic growth, with evident benefits of poverty alleviation and basic needs satisfaction. The Korean development pattern has been highly equitable, relative to virtually all other developing countries, both because assets, especially land, were distributed relatively equally before rapid growth began and because Korea pursued a pattern of development that did not greatly concentrate income or wealth. When Korea emerged from Japanese colonial rule at the end of World War II the many large production units which had been Japanese-owned were either nationalized or broken up and redistributed. Two land reforms subdivided the larger agricultural holdings and virtually eliminated tenancy (in which land is owned by one person but farmed by another, who pays rent for its use). The rapid economic growth which began in the early 1960s emphasized the modernization of small and medium-sized firms. Foreign ownership was held to a minimum. Manufacturing for export boomed, absorbing a larger share of labor force growth than in almost any other country. The Korean educational system, which accommodated all children at its lower levels and then rigorously selected the few best performers for continuation to its higher levels, supported both equity and growth. All these factors contributed to a rapid decline in poverty. Inequality probably rose slightly as development proceeded, especially in the 1970s, when shortages of skilled labor emerged, but it remained low relative to other third world countries and comparable to inequality in the most developed Western countries. Korea, then, is a clear-cut case of rapid growth with equity.

Brazil   Like Korea, Brazil has grown rapidly, but with consequences for human welfare that are more equivocal. Brazil is a large, naturally rich country that has made impressive strides toward creation of a modern, diversified economy. Some of its industries and modern cities bear comparison with those in the rich countries. Besides this urban boom Brazil has also had important areas of agricultural progress, such as the development of soy beans as a major export crop alongside coffee and other traditional items. But Brazilian economic growth has been uneven both in time (it has gone through several stop-and-go phases) and space. Whole sections of the country, most notoriously the northeast, have been largely excluded from development. Even the big, modern cities in the south (Rio de Janeiro, São Paulo, Belo Horizonte) have appalling urban slums, sometimes located side-by-side with luxurious, architecturally impressive, new constructions. Many of the factors that have led to equitable growth in Korea are reversed in Brazil: asset ownership is highly concentrated; there has been no land reform; access to education is uneven and heavily influenced by economic factors; development (in both manufacturing and agriculture) has emphasized large production units; technologies adopted have tended to be capital-intensive. The results: Very high inequality and very little progress toward poverty alleviation, despite rapid growth of the economy and some increases in the real incomes of the poor.

Sri Lanka   Sri Lanka, by contrast to Korea and Brazil, grew at average or low rates until a change of government in 1977 led to a radical shift in economic policies. As a result of the country's open democratic system of government and the articulateness of its well-educated electorate, all Sri Lanka governments since independence in 1948 have had to be populist to survive. A system of social benefits which included cheap staple foods and free schooling and medical services helped to produce a healthy, literate populace. Inequality was kept relatively low, and despite low income levels, the worst manifestations of poverty (premature deaths, malnutrition, illiteracy) have been remarkably absent from Sri Lankan society. The trouble is that economic growth did not occur fast enough either to provide adequate financing for the welfare system or to give employment to the growing labor force, especially of educated youths seeking white-collar jobs. A foreign-exchange crisis in the early 1960s led to many shortages, slower growth, and cutbacks in social services. Chronic popular dissatisfaction led to repeated changes of government at the polls and an unsuccessful youth revolt in 1971. In 1977 a new right-wing government inaugurated an effort to accelerate growth by emphasizing labor-intensive manufacturing, irrigation, and tourism. Sri Lanka is something of an aberration, which tends to be viewed either favorably or unfavorably by development specialists, depending on their biases. Perhaps what it really demonstrates is the interactions between development and a strongly democratic system of government, the latter hardly a common feature in third world countries.

India, like Brazil is a big country which has areas of dynamism and **India** areas of stagnation. Also like Brazil it has emphasized inward-looking development to build a self-sufficient subcontinental economy. Like Sri Lanka, India is a poor country and has not grown very rapidly. Some parts of India, such as Bombay and the Punjab, have in fact grown rapidly, through either industrialization or successful adoption of the Green Revolution in foodgrain production. Others, like Bihar state, remain desperately poor. One state, Kerala, in the south, has a Sri Lanka–like pattern of high basic needs satisfaction together with low income and growth. Overall inequality measures for India come out rather low because there are so many poor people and only relatively small classes of the comfortable or rich. About 50 percent of the population lives below the officially defined poverty line. Whether the poor have gained or lost from development in India has been hotly debated. The most recent analyses suggest that the proportion of people who are poor has changed little since the 1950s.

Theories of Inequality and Poverty

Questions of poverty and inequality and their relationship to economic growth have been emphasized in some periods in the history of economic thought and relegated to the background during other periods. One stage at which they were featured prominently was during the classical period of economic theorizing, particularly in the work of David Ricardo, who wrote in 1817 when England was a developing country.

We saw in Chapter 3 that Ricardo pioneered the two-sector model of development. He analyzed the interplay between economic growth and the distribution of income among the three classical factors of production: land, labor, and capital. Each of these, he believed, was supplied by a distinct social class: land by landlords, labor by workers, and capital by capitalists. Ricardo assumed that capital and labor were each of homogeneous quality; that is, any unit of capital or any laborer could produce the same kind and amount of output. But land, he thought, varied in quality. Economic growth brought less and less fertile lands into use as the demand for food rose. Higher food prices were required to repay the cultivation of the marginal lands, and this generated enormous economic rents for the owners of the more fertile lands. Ricardo assumed, not unreasonably given the British Industrial Revolution environment in which he lived, that development was primarily a matter of industrialization. Rising food prices were bad for industrialization because they raised wages (which were held at the subsistence level, but had to rise if it cost the laborers more to survive) and cut into profits. Since Ricardo also assumed that all saving was done by the capitalists—landlords were spendthrift and laborers too poor to save—these wage increases would gradually eat into profits, eventually bringing growth to a halt in the "stationary state." All of this was an admonition about what would happen if England did not abolish its Corn Laws, which protected grain farmers from foreign competition, and allow imports of cheap food to fuel its Industrial Revolution.

Despite the pioneering features and internal consistency of his model, Ricardo was proven wrong on all his predictions about income distribution and economic growth. Rent has not taken a growing share of national income in industrializing countries, but in fact has remained a rather small share. The profit share has not been squeezed out. And wages have not been held to the subsistence level but have risen, at least in the later stages of industrial development; the share of wages in national income if anything has tended to rise. There are several reasons why actual trends have not matched those predicted in Ricardo's model. One is that England *did* adopt free trade, as Ricardo wanted. But even if it had not, diminishing returns would probably have been largely offset by technological change, which would have made it possible to grow increasing amounts of food on land of given quantity and quality. Ricardo also overestimated the strength of the Malthusian population mechanism, which he thought would hold wages at the subsistence level. (See Chapter 7 for further discussion.)

Karl Marx also believed that capitalist development would create an increasingly unequal distribution of income. Capitalists, he thought, had an incentive to create a "reserve army of the unemployed" whose brooding presence would ensure that the wages of employed laborers stayed at the subsistence level. (He hotly rebutted the Malthusian theory that demographic forces created the labor surplus, calling this line of thinking an insult to the working class.) In Marxian thought, the owners of capital dominate both the economy and the "bourgeois state." But as capitalism develops, the rate of profit falls and crises occur, causing firms to fail and industrial concentration to rise. Eventually, in a final apocalyptic crisis, capitalism itself collapses, to be replaced by socialism. Only then, according to Karl Marx, can the lot of the workers improve.

Marx's theory provided no better guide to the future evolution of income distribution than Ricardo's. Like Ricardo, Marx has been influential not because his theory proved to be prophetic but because of the analytical approach that he used.

During the latter part of the nineteenth century and early part of the twentieth the dominant theory used today to explain income distribution in developing countries was worked out. This is the neoclassical (marginal productivity) theory, which postulates that all factors of production (now more numerous than three, to take account of quality differences) are in scarce supply, and that their rates of return are set equal to their marginal products in competitive factor markets. This theory, although heavily criticized, has yet to be supplanted in analyses of developed countries.

It was W. Arthur Lewis who first observed that conditions in less developed countries are in some ways more similar to those which prevailed in the industrial countries before the Industrial Revolution than they are to conditions in those same countries today. The most useful theory to analyze the workings of the early-stage developing economy, therefore, might be one built on classical rather than neoclassical assumptions. It was this insight that led Lewis to his celebrated model of "economic development with unlimited supplies of labor," which utilized the Ricardo-Marx assumption that labor is avalable in unlimited quantity at a fixed real wage, rather than being a scarce factor of production which has to be bid away from other uses, as in the neoclassical theory. Lewis's surplus-labor model, as pointed out in Chapter 3, was further developed by Fei-Ranis and others. The implications of the surplus-labor model for the importance of agricultural development and the role played by population growth was discussed in the previous chapter. What remains is to bring out the implications of the model for the distribution of income.

The labor-surplus model suggests that inequality will first increase and later diminish as development takes place. In other words its implications are consistent with Kuznets's generalization about what has actually occurred. There are two reasons for expecting the initial rise in inequality to take place. One is that the share of the capitalists (who in the Lewis version of the model could be either private capitalists or governments running state-owned enterprises) rises as the size of the modern, or capitalist, sector increases. The second reason is that inequality in the distribution of labor income also rises during the early period, when increasing but still relatively small numbers of laborers are moving from the subsistence wage level to the capitalist-sector wage level, which Lewis says tends to run about 30 percent higher in real terms.

This tendency toward increasing inequality is finally reversed, as explicitly depicted in the Fei-Ranis extension of the Lewis model (see Chapter 3). When all the surplus labor is finally absorbed into modern-sector employment, labor becomes a scarce factor of production and further increases in demand require increases in real wages to bid labor away from marginal uses. It is the resulting rise in the general wage level, the model suggests, that brings about the eventual downturn in inequality—as well as the long-awaited abolition of poverty, at least by former standards.

In the Lewis version of the labor-surplus model inequality is not only a necessary *effect* of economic growth, it is simultaneously a *cause* of growth. Inequality—that is, a distribution of income that favors high-income groups—contributes to growth because the high-income groups are the elements of society that save, and saving is essential for increasing productive capacity and thus bringing about output growth. In a famous quotation Lewis says that "the central problem in the theory of economic development is to understand the process by which a community which was previously saving and investing 4 or 5 percent of its national income converts itself into an economy where voluntary saving is running about 12 to 15 percent of the national income or more."[17] The answer, he argues, lies with the 10 percent of the population which receives 40 percent or more of na-

17. W. Arthur Lewis, "Economic Development with Unlimited Supplies of Labor," *The Manchester School* 22 (May 1954): 155.

tional income in labor-surplus countries. Growth occurs when they save more, not because their marginal propensity to save increases but because their aggregate income and share in total income go up. This happens because profit's share in income increases with the growth of the modern sector while the wage share remains constant.

Not only does inequality contribute to growth, but attempts to redistribute income "prematurely" run the risk of stifling economic growth. As in Ricardo's theory, anything that raises urban wages cuts into profits, and hence into savings and economic growth. Some of the factors that could have this effect include a rise in the price of food relative to the price of manufactured goods and actions, by trade unions or government, to bargain for or legislate increased modern-sector wages. This would gain little anyway because, as noted earlier, in poor countries there is little to redistribute; everyone will benefit in time, the Lewis model suggests, if they wait for the development process to run its course. A temporary increase in inequality is the price that must be paid for these gains.

The implications of the labor-surplus model have been presented at some length because this has been the dominant model for the past twenty years. It is far from universally accepted, however, and is subject to increasing challenges today. Some of the questions which have been raised about the model include the following. Will the capitalists actually save or will they indulge in luxury consumption? If they do save, will they necessarily invest at home or will they seek higher rates of return abroad? How fast will the capitalist (modern) sector absorb labor, particularly since it may be using capital-intensive technology imported from the developed countries and inappropriate to the factor endowment of a poor labor-surplus economy? (See Chapter 8, below, for discussion of this issue.) Finally, can governments in today's developing countries afford to wait for the accumulation process to work and for the benefits of growth eventually to be distributed throughout the society, or do poverty, population growth, and political instability require interventions to redistribute income sooner?

There are probably no firm, categorical answers to these questions. Some capitalists will save and invest their savings locally, while others will consume their high income or invest abroad. Which they do probably depends on a complex set of factors relating to the characteristics of the upper income group in a particular country and to the local investment climate. Nor does making the government the capitalist necessarily solve the problem. Although a few governments have been able to follow the Soviet model of rapid accumulation under a system of state capitalism, many others have proved unable to evolve the combination of discipline and incentives needed for publicly owned enterprises to generate surpluses (see Chapter 21).

Strategies for Growth with Equity

Countries in Asia, Africa, and Latin America have demonstrated the difficulties of trying to redistribute before growing. "Socialism" has been a popular watchword in many of these countries, connoting immediate redistribution through direct controls on economic activity, elaborate social service networks, consumer subsidies, reliance on cooperatives, and other populist devices. Especially when undertaken by "soft states" which find it difficult to enforce their own mandates on the populace, these measures have generally failed to achieve their redistributive objectives and have often stifled economic growth. Burma, Ghana, and Jamaica are three examples among many. Moreover, even when carried out relatively successfully, they achieve income redistribution only in a rather limited sense. This apears to have been the case, for example, in the Peruvian "national revolution," which redistributed income to the urban working class but left the poorest elements of society (poor peasants, mainly of Indian origin) comparatively untouched. Many similar cases could be cited.

Is there then no alternative to the stern growth-versus-equality trade-off postulated by W. Arthur Lewis? Contemporary development thinking and experience have in fact suggested three alternative models. If Lewis's classical model may be characterized as "grow first then redistribute," the alternatives could be described as a radical "redistribute first then grow" model and two reformist models: "redistribution with growth" and "basic human needs."

The radical model is epitomized by the experience of the Asian socialist economies, especially the People's Republic of China. Socialist development in these countries has begun with the expropriation of capitalists and landlords. Their property has then either been subdivided among small-scale producers, or more often, placed under some system of collective ownership. Confiscation has two kinds of effects on income distribution. The immediate impact is to eliminate the property income of the previous owner and assign this income either to the state or to the new owners of the subdivided property. This immediate effect can have a substantial impact on income distribution if the amount of profit or rent involved is large. In the longer run, however, the second effect of confiscation can be even more important. This effect works through the productivity of the confiscated asset (factory, farm, etc.) under its new ownership and management. If the asset is managed as efficiently, or more efficiently, than under the prior ownership, then the redistributive effect holds up over the long run. If, however, the asset is less productive under the new arrangement then some of the redistributive effect is dissipated. The old owner has lost his property income but the new owners have not benefited proportionately. The management of a confiscated asset is thus an important determinant of its redistributive effect.

Countries which pursue a radical pattern of development are not exempted from the need to amass a surplus and reinvest it productively if they wish to grow. Development in the Soviet Union, which followed a basic-industry strategy, involved a continuous effort to hold down consumption and squeeze a surplus out of the general population, particularly the peasants. Inequality was limited because most property income accrued to the state, but many of the material benefits of economic growth were denied to the population until the Khrushchev reforms of the 1960s provided the first hint of a possible emerging era of mass consumption.

By contrast, the People's Republic of China has tried to follow a more balanced development pattern. By offsetting the emphasis on heavy industry with attention to smaller scale, decentralized, and more labor-intensive production units—by "walking on two legs," as the Chinese say—and by not stinting on basic human services, China has apparently been able to achieve a more equitable pattern of development, and in a much poorer country, than was achieved by the U.S.S.R.

The Chinese Communists contend that their development experience has little to teach other countries which operate under different social systems. It is true that some features of the Chinese approach are probably available only to a strong regime which gained power through a revolution. Yet a modified version of the "redistribute then develop" approach has been used in Taiwan and South Korea, where rural land holdings were redistributed shortly after World War II and development has proceeded rapidly and comparatively equitably despite (or more likely because of) the existence of vigorous groups of private capitalists.

The desire to avoid both the extremes of concentrated industrial development as depicted by the Lewis model and radical restructuring of asset ownership has naturally led to a determined search for a middle way, "redistribution with growth" as a study sponsored by the World Bank called it. Is there, in other words, a way in which the gains from economic growth can be redistributed so that over time the income distribution gradually improves—or at least does not worsen—as growth proceeds?

The basic idea of redistribution with growth (RWG for short) is that government policies should influence the pattern of development in such a way that low-income producers (in most countries, located primarily in agriculture and small-scale urban enterprises) will see improved earning opportunities and simultaneously receive the resources necessary to take advantage of them. According to the World Bank study group, seven types of policy instruments could be employed to this end: (1) measures to alter the prices of labor and capital, to encourage the employment of unskilled labor; (2) "dynamic redistribution" of assets by directing investment to areas in which the poor may be owners of assets, such as land or small shops; (3) greater education to improve literacy, skills, and access to the modern economy; (4) more progressive taxation; (5) public provision of consumption goods, such as basic foods, to the poor; (6) intervention in commodity markets to aid poor producers; and consumers: and (7) development of new technologies that will help make low-income workers more productive. All these policy possibilities are discussed in other chapters of this book.

The way in which these elements could be combined into an effective national policy package will naturally vary with a country's circumstances. A rural-based, equity-oriented, development strategy is often proposed for large, predominantly rural countries such as India.[18] For these countries, it

18. For example, see John Mellor, *The New Economics of Growth: A Strategy for India and the Developing World* (Ithaca, N.Y.: Cornell University Press, 1976).

is argued, the time required for the modern sector to soak up all the surplus labor existing in the traditional sector would be far too long for any reasonable standard of equity to be achieved, or political stability to be maintained. A strategy emphasizing rural development, it is hoped, will bring about a much more equitable pattern of development than could ever be attained through emphasis on urban and industrial growth. (Rural development is discussed in Chapter 18, below.)

On the other hand countries in which the modern sector is large relative to the traditional sector face a less severe trade-off. These countries can hope to have an integrated, modern economy in a much shorter period of time and in the meantime have a much larger surplus available to redistribute to the traditional sector through social services and rural development projects.

The RWG approach has attracted a lot of interest among those who want to see the welfare of the third world poor improve yet wish to avoid violent social revolution. Indeed the reader may note that many of the ideas included in the RWG package are treated sympathetically in this textbook. Yet one must accept that the changes brought about by such a strategy will occur slowly in most countries. Development is usually a gradual business, and even the changes in equality and poverty that were projected by the World Bank's study group (which was of course intellectually and emotionally committed to the approach) struck many readers as disappointingly small and gradual.

Pessimism about how fast economic development, even if it is poverty-focused, can improve the well-being of the poor in most LDCs is one factor contributing to interest in the basic human needs (BHN) approach. Although advocates of RWG and BHN share the same objectives, they differ on the best means of achieving them. Whereas RWG stresses increases in the productivity and purchasing power of the poor, BHN emphasizes the provision of public services, along with "entitlements" to the poor to make sure they receive the services provided.

The BHN strategy is designed to provide several basic commodities and services to the poor: staple foods, water and sanitation, health care, primary and nonformal education, and housing. The strategy includes two important elements. First, it requires finance to ensure that these basic needs can be provided at costs that the poor can afford. Second, the strategy includes service networks to distribute these services in forms appropriate for consumption by the poor, and especially in areas where the poor live.

The possibility of using fiscal policy to ameliorate poverty is discussed in Chapter 12. Redistribution of income through a combination of progressive taxation and public expenditures on social service programs has been an important part of twentieth-century reform movements in Western industrial countries. The potential of this form of redistribution for less developed countries has traditionally been downplayed because the public sector is smaller in these countries and thus has less revenue-raising power; because the government pursues multiple objectives in its tax and expenditure policies and thus cannot devote itself wholeheartedly to redistribution;

and because of the many difficulties of identifying, designing, and implementing public consumption and investment projects which can affect the incomes of the poor. However, there is a more positive side to the picture. Many LDCs now collect 20 percent or more of the GNP in the form of government revenues. Taxes can be made more progressive in developing countries, even when direct (income) taxes are paid by only a small fraction of the population. Such indirect taxes as customs duties, excises, turnover taxes, and sales taxes with exemptions can lend an element of progressivity. Finally, much can be done through the expenditure side of the budget to improve the distribution of benefits from public services. Some of these possibilities will be discussed in Chapters 9 and 10, which deal with education and health.

For BHN programs to redistribute income, services must be offered on a subsidized basis. Otherwise redistribution will not work, either because the poor will spend too much of their meager income on the services offered or because they will be deterred by high user charges and not take advantage of them at all. If these conditions are not met, the income transfer can be perverse (as is the case with government-run universities in many countries, which admit selectively and charge low fees thus subsidizing the well-to-do). For the poor to be reached, appropriate forms of service must be emphasized: primary schools instead of universities, village clinics instead of intensive-care units in urban hospitals. Second, the system must be extended to the poor in their villages and urban slums. There must actually be schools and clinics, teachers and primary health workers, and they must work where the poor live. So far most LDC social service networks have not met this challenge, although there are some honorable exceptions.

Much of the appeal of BHN derives from its link to the notion of investment in human capital. Many kinds of education, health, and other social expenditures can improve the quality of human resources. When such expenditures are directed particularly toward the poor, for instance in primary education or rural community health programs, they become means of poverty reduction by increasing the productivity of the poor. (See Chapters 8–10 for further discussion of this point.)

Conclusions Most observers today would agree that more resources should be devoted to providing basic human needs through public services like education, health, and sanitation. Equally important, attention should be given to redesigning service networks to reach the poor better. In this way BHN services can complement efforts to raise the incomes of the poor and enhance their productivity. However, two other major factors deserve reemphasis as we conclude this chapter: employment and relative prices.

Probably the single most promising way of achieving greater equity during growth under the reformist approach is to give greater emphasis to employment creation. By appropriate price incentives and other measures to absorb more labor in relatively productive forms of employment, the inequality generated by the Lewis-type employment shift can be mitigated and the labor surplus can be eliminated in a shorter time. (This subject is discussed in detail in Chapter 8.)

The other touchstone of equitable growth is the relationship between the prices of rural and urban outputs. If farm prices are held down to depress urban wages and increase the investible surplus, then the majority of the poor who live in the rural areas and depend mainly on agriculture for a living will suffer. (There are also likely to be food supply problems; see Chapter 19.) Of course if agricultural prices rise too high, growth will be choked off. But an equity-focused strategy rules out the squeeze-the-farmer approach that has often been attempted in the past and remains in effect in some LDCs today.

Finally, one can ask whether governments of less developed countries will in fact act to take advantage of these opportunities to reduce inequality arising during the course of economic growth. This is an important question of political economy. Marxists argue that governments are controlled by particular social classes and act in the best interests of those classes. Certainly, many third world governments are heavily influenced by civilian or military elites and for this reason are much less prone to egalitarian reform in their actions than in their verbal pronouncements. But political motivations are perhaps more mixed than the Marxists believe. Some governments may be inclined to make limited reforms for essentially conservative reasons: to forestall upheavals or demands for more radical changes. Others may be motivated toward reform by a different kind of political incentive: in countries where ethnic, tribal, or religious distinctions form an important basis for political activity, it may not be the rich but rather a large but less wealthy social group whose interests are primarily reflected in government policy. In such cases—for example, the Malays of Malaysia—ambitious redistributive programs may be launched even by relatively conservative governments.

Good, wide-ranging reviews of the problems of income distribution, poverty, and development are to be found in Charles R. Frank, Jr., and Richard C. Webb, eds., *Income Distribution and Growth in the Less-Developed Countries* (Washington, D.C.: Brookings Institution, 1977); and Gary S. Fields, *Poverty, Inequality, and Development* (Cambridge: Cambridge University Press, 1980). Amartyn K. Sen's acute theoretical discussion of the problems of measuring inequality (*On Economic Inequality;* New York: W. W. Norton, 1973) has already been recommended. On poverty measurement, see his "Three Notes on the Concept of Poverty," International Labour Office, World Employment Programme Research Paper No. 65 (January 1978). **FURTHER READINGS**

For a challenging critique of conventional views and measures of development, see Dudley Seers, "The Meaning of Development," in *The Political Economy of Development and Underdevelopment,* edited by Charles K. Wilber (New York: Random House, 1973). The use of social indicators and relationships between social and economic development are discussed in various publications of the United Nations Research Institute on Social Development. On the Physical Quality of Life Index, see publications of the Overseas Development Council, particularly Morris David Morris, *Measuring the Condition of the World's Poor: The Physical Quality of Life Index,* Pergamon Policy Studies No.42 (New York: Pergamon Press for the Overseas Development Council, 1979). The distribution weights approach is presented in Hollis Chenery et al., *Redistribution with Growth* (London: Oxford University Press, 1974).

The pioneering empirical works on inequality and development were by Simon Kuznets, who continues to produce important scientific papers. However, the best recent general analysis is Montek S. Ahluwalia, "Inequality, Poverty and Development," *Journal of Development Economics* 3 (1976); 307–42. Irma Adelman and Cynthia Taft Morris, *Economic Growth and Social Equity in Developing Countries* (Stanford: Stanford University Press, 1973), is a stimulating, sometimes controversial study.

Among the modern theories of development that have strong implications for income distribution, see the works of W. Arthur Lewis and John Fei and Gustav Ranis cited at the end of Chapter 3. An excellent review of theoretical as well as policy questions is William R. Cline, "Distribution and Development: A Survey of the Literature," *Journal of Development Economics* 1975; 359–400.

Many writings about the basic human needs and redistribution with growth policy approaches have been produced by the World Bank and International Labour Office. See, for example, Chenery et al., *Redistribution with Growth* (cited above) and International Labour Office, *Employment, Growth and Basic Needs: A One-World Problem* (New York: Praeger Publishers, 1977).

Chapter 5

PLANNING, MARKETS, AND POLITICS

Virtually all developing countries undertake national planning. This wide-spread acceptance was encouraged by a confluence of historical factors. At the end of World War II the Soviet Union emerged as the second world power, having centrally planned and controlled its economy over thirty years to push it from near-backwardness to near-modernity. India's leaders, whose intellectual roots in British socialism encouraged a commitment to national planning, saw lessons for India in the Russian experience. India became a model for other newly independent states that also took up national planning. The United States, then the principal aid donor, and the World Bank, which it dominated, encouraged this tendency. Both donors had been impressed by the success of the Marshall Plan in reconstructing Europe, which was attributed to the ample provision of capital and cooperative planning by the European countries. The widespread influence of Keynesian economics, which encouraged macroeconomic forecasting and fiscal planning, also stimulated development planning.

Plans and Markets

To understand the rationale for national planning in a developing country it is necessary to sort out several concepts that tend to get blurred in debates about planning: **mixed economy,** in which government interventions are superimposed on a market-based system; **socialist economy,** in which direct controls typically predominate over market forms; and **national planning,** which can be helpful in making either system function well, especially in developing countries.

Mixed Economies

Most countries depend largely on the market to allocate goods, services, and factors of production. Three arguments favor market allocation over the alternative, direct controls by government over the quantities produced and sold. First, reliance on markets encourages private economic activity, providing scope for pluralistic societies, hence the potential for democratic government and individual liberties. Second, the market can allocate thousands of different products among consumers, reflecting their preferences, and scores of productive inputs among producers, tasks that if handled by the state would require enormous governmental responsibility for decision-making and control. Third, markets are more flexible than governments and better able to adapt to changing conditions, automatically providing incentives for growth, innovation, and structural change that governments either cannot manage or are slow to achieve. Despite these substantial advantages there are some circumstances in which markets do not perform well on their own. Consequently government intervenes in every market economy. This combination of market allocation and government intervention is called a *mixed economy;* all the nonsocialist countries have mixed economies.

The market failures listed below and the corresponding interventions are not the only ones possible, but include those that seem particularly important for developing countries.

1. Growing concentration and *monopoly power* seem to be features of modern economies. In developing countries, economies of scale may be so large relative to market size that monopoly is inevitable in some industries, while oligopoly (a market with few firms) is probably the rule in most others outside of agriculture, fishing, handicraft industries, transportation, retail trade, and personal services. Monopolistic firms are able to raise their prices, and consequently their profits, by restricting their output. They maximize profits by limiting sales to the level that equates marginal cost with marginal revenue. By contrast, firms in purely competitive markets cannot affect the price they receive and maximize profits by selling enough to equate marginal cost with price. Hence a competitive industry produces more and sells at a lower price than a monopoly or an oligopolistic industry. In large economies, governments can try to limit the exercise of monopoly pricing by regulating the size of firms and breaking up the largest ones. In all economies, the threat of competing imports could be effective but is seldom wielded (see Chapter 16). Price controls are used more frequently in developing countries. If government cannot prevent monopoly pricing, it can capture some of the benefits from monopolists by taxing the resulting profits at high rates.

2. *External economies* are *benefits* of a project, such as a hydroelectric dam, that are enjoyed by people not connected with the project, such as the downstream farmer whose production rises because the dam prevents floods. External economies are important benefits in many economic "overhead" investments, such as dams, roads, railroads, and irrigation

schemes. Although in principle the beneficiaries could be charged for all external benefits, in practice they cannot be: it may be difficult and costly to control access to the facilities and difficult even to identify the beneficiaries or the extent to which they benefit. Hence a private investor would not be able to realize revenue from this aspect of the project's output. Because private investors cannot easily charge for externalities, and because such projects take large investments with long repayment periods, private investors are unlikely to undertake them. Governments do so instead. Another kind of external economy is central to the balanced growth strategy discussed in Chapter 3. If several industries are started at the same time, the resulting labor force may be large enough to create an internal market for the output of all industries, and backward linkages may create adequate markets for producer goods industries. But a single private investor who depended on these newly created markets would not invest without strong assurances that the other investments would take place simultaneously. Government must play a role to ensure that these external benefits can be realized.

3. *External diseconomies,* or *costs* not borne by the firm, are common as well. The pollution of air and water is a widely recognized problem in the industrial world and increasingly so in the developing countries. Since polluters would bear all the costs of reduced emissions and effluents, but benefit only as average members of the population of the affected area, they have little incentive to control pollution on their own. The same situation arises with private access to *common resources,* such as forests or fisheries. Once a certain number of entrants, such as loggers or fishermen, are exploiting the new resource, new entrants cause the cost of logging or fishing to rise per unit output for *all* entrants. Thus the new entrant faces unit costs only slightly greater than the average for all prior entrants, but society as a whole faces a much higher marginal cost, which includes the increases felt by all producers, old and new. In each case, pollution and common resources, some kind of intervention by government—preferably a tax—is ordinarily required to force private producers to bear costs closer to the social cost and consequently to reduce pollution or common resource exploitation to levels closer to the social optimum.

4. Market prices may not reflect the *dynamic effects* of development. The most frequently cited example is the *infant industry,* whose productivity increases, and whose costs fall, over time because managers and workers are "learning by doing" (see Chapter 16). This effect can justify a protective tariff or initial subsidy to protect an infant industry, but only if the tariff or subsidy is reduced as productivity rises. The argument has even greater force for the economy as a whole because experience in all industries creates a more skilled and productive labor force, making all activities more attractive for investors. This "infant economy" phenomenon is closely akin to the balanced growth strategy because it also depends on external economies: as trained, experienced workers leave one employer to work for another, the second firm benefits from the training provided by the first. Sector-wide (or even economy-wide) protective tariffs could be

justified by this effect, although a devalued exchange rate combined with offsetting taxes on traditional exports would be a superior intervention, for reasons explored in Part IV.

5. In developing economies, remoteness, poverty, and illiteracy exclude large numbers of subsistence farmers and their families from large segments of goods and money markets. With an insignificant share of the money "votes," these groups have little influence on the types of goods and services offered. Special efforts are required to bring them into the monetary economy. Even for those in the monetary economy there is inadequate information about markets and products, so many consumers remain ignorant about the goods and services being offered and workers know little about job opportunities.[1] *Institutional underdevelopment* is characteristic and, as explained in Chapter 2, rigidities abound. Perhaps the best example is in banking, which generally remains urban-based and employs standards of service, based on Western banking models, that exclude most of the rural (and much of the poor urban) population (see Chapter 13). In some countries retail and wholesale trade is dominated by racial minorities, such as the Indians and Pakistanis in East Africa, Lebanese in parts of West Africa, and the Chinese in Southeast Asia. Although these entrepreneurially inclined people often do reach out to remote and poor populations, their commercial success engenders suspicion of their prices, practices, and intentions, and governments typically discourage their activities.

With this last point the discussion shades into questions of *national goals and policies.* To a considerable extent market economies require intervention not only because of market failures but also because societies impose on them national goals that even well-functioning markets could not satisfy. Policies to favor poorer majorities over entrepreneurially accomplished minorities are one example. If Malaysian and Indonesian Chinese or Kenyan Indians already dominate the distribution system of those countries, then unguided economic growth is likely to improve their relative position over time. To expand the role of the indigenous majority and allow them to "catch up" requires governmental intervention. More generally, in market economies growth is often led by—and hence favors—people and firms that are already successful, thus concentrating income at least for a period (see Chapter 4's discussion of the Kuznets curve). It is only after growth has been rapid for some time that all groups begin to benefit substantially and the income distribution begins to equalize. But the alleviation of poverty, relative and absolute, is often considered too urgent to await the operation of market forces, and intervention is considered necessary. This may be true for other goals as well, such as greater employment creation or reduced dependence. Even accelerated growth, typically served well by market economies, may require intervention if savings levels are initially low.

---

1. One group, future generations, is necessarily excluded from current decision-making. Parents and governments act for this group by such means as saving, investing, and educating. Public investment may be influenced by use of a social discount rate—explained in the next chapter—which reflects a desire to improve the welfare of future generations.

These are some of the reasons that governments intervene in market economies. The particular interventions chosen are not always ideal. Worse, they often work against the goals they are supposed to achieve. The most egregious examples—minimum wages that concentrate incomes and reduce employment, interest rate ceilings that reduce and bias investment, tariffs and import controls that intensify dependence, food price controls that discourage farm production—will be explored in later chapters. Nevertheless, because markets are imperfect and governments have political goals that markets must serve, intervention is the rule. Usually interventions work best and avoid undesired side effects if they also work through market mechanisms, operating indirectly through prices to alter supply and demand, rather than operating directly through controls. A central role of planning in a mixed economy is to structure these interventions to achieve their aims with minimum incidental costs.

Socialist Economies

Socialism can be defined as government ownership and control of the means of production. Whether a country is socialist or not is a matter of degree. The clear examples are the Communist countries—the Soviet Union, the Eastern European countries, China, North Korea, Vietnam, and Cuba—in which government ownership and control dominate industry and services and strongly influence agriculture. Some Western European countries, such as Sweden and Great Britain, have had socialist governments that nationalized key industries, and many other countries have large state-owned enterprise sectors (see Chapter 21), but these economies retain the market character of mixed economies. Socialism and the market are not inimical. In fact Oscar Lange, an influential socialist economist, proposed a system of market socialism under which publicly owned firms would compete in markets at prices set by a central planning authority to represent real costs to society.[2] The ill-fated economic liberalization of Czechoslovakia during the late 1960s and the more successful reforms of Hungary and Yugoslavia all centered on attempts to employ some of Lange's proposals.

Nevertheless the dominant characteristic of the Soviet and other Communist economies is government control over production. Whereas *in mixed economies the market sets prices* as signals for production and consumption, *in Soviet-type economies central planners control* the quantities produced and consumed. Prices become irrelevant to production or investment decisions. Prices, along with quantity rationing, still regulate demand because no government is able to give directives to each household about its complete consumption basket. Prices also serve an accounting function, determining how much income is transferred from households to government-owned producers (and vice versa, through wage payments), among producers, and from producers to the government.

---

2. The technical term for these costs, *opportunity costs,* is defined in Chapter 6.

The leaders who designed the Soviet economic system began from the premise that market forces, whatever their theoretical merits, were in practice hopelessly chaotic and thus prices determined by the market could not be relied on to guide production. This basic view of the market was reinforced by the pronounced emphasis in the Soviet Union, and later in China, on machinery and steel as leading sectors in their industrialization programs. Since neither economy had much of a steel or machinery industry to begin with, planners were faced with an extreme form of the infant industry problem and with very large external economies, because the main demand for steel was from a machinery sector that did not yet exist. Neither Soviet nor Chinese planners were willing to build a machinery sector first and then wait for the growing demand for steel to accommodate an efficient steel industry. In general the price system is less effective when the change in economic structure being contemplated is rapid and massive. What the Soviet Union desired in the 1930s when it introduced this system, and what China also wanted in the 1950s, was precisely such a rapid and massive restructuring of economies that were fundamentally agricultural into ones that were based on machinery and steel.

The ways in which the Soviet Union and China prior to the 1980s drew up plans were not radically different from the procedures followed in mixed economies described in these chapters. The problems of deciding on goals, the role of bureaucratic politics (described later in this chapter), and even formal planning techniques such as input-output analysis (see Chapter 6) are as much present in the Soviet Union and China as in mixed economies. What separates a centrally planned economy of the Soviet type from the others is the way in which plans are carried out. Once broad goals and targets for individual industries are decided on, planners give direct orders to firms on how much to produce. Firms cannot buy the necessary inputs in a market but must apply to government organizations for the delivery of needed items. The firm must pay money for these items, but willingness to pay does not determine whether or not it gets them. Only if the plan says it should recieve a certain amount of steel will that amount actually be delivered.

In reality the Soviet-type system does not follow the plan quite so rigidly. A variety of devices, both legal and illegal, provide some flexibility. Nevertheless many allocations which in mixed economies are handled by impersonal market forces are decided by government bureaucrats in centrally planned economies. The centrally planned system therefore puts a premium on having large numbers of people trained to manage the complex tasks of deciding which firms ought to get particular inputs. Hundreds and even thousands of different kinds of inputs must be parceled out to tens of thousands of individual enterprises. If the inputs go to the wrong enterprises, those enterprises will have surpluses piling up in their warehouses while other enterprises have to operate below capacity.

The advantage of this system is that it gives central planners a high degree of control over the economy, and with that control the power to restructure key sectors quickly. The system, however, does not put a high premium on the efficiency with which inputs are used. The problems of inefficiency increase if people with skills adequate to managing such a system are in short supply, as is often the case in developing countries. China had sufficient numbers of such people or was able to train them with Soviet help in the 1950s, but by the late 1970s China too had begun to experiment with greater use of market forces in order to reduce waste and other kinds of inefficiency.

Few other developing countries have had the administrative and decision-making capacity to control production through central planning. Among the developing nations only North Korea, Vietnam, Cuba, and China have tried. Tanzania, avowedly socialist, has placed the majority of modern industries under public ownership, nationalized much wholesale and retail trade, and attempted to socialize its agriculture. Nevertheless the government has not tried to set output targets, and most units, public or private, respond to market-determined prices. Interventions in these prices, though substantial, are no greater in Tanzania than in many nonsocialist developing countries such as Bolivia, Ghana, and Indonesia. India based its first development plans on Soviet models that emphasized investment in capital goods and other heavy industries and espoused public ownership of these sectors. Yet its economy remains predominantly market-based, while South Korea, avowedly capitalist, produces more of its output in public enterprises than does India.

National Planning

It should be evident by now that planning is a tool useful in both mixed and socialist economies. In Soviet-type economies planning is essential because production and investment are controlled centrally and the controllers have to balance supplies and demands themselves. Planning must detemine all the basic quantities of an economy for each sector and type of good: consumer demand, government consumption, investment, trade balances, production by commodity and industry, requirements for intermediate goods and raw materials, allocations of labor and finance.

Planning in mixed economies carries less of a burden but still covers a wide range of potential activities. Our discussion of mixed economies suggested a set of market interventions that may be needed either to correct for market failures or to induce markets to achieve social and political ends that govenment imposes on them. Such interventions can be numerous, conflicting, and counterproductive unless they are carefully planned with specific goals and priorities in mind. When government invests directly, as in infrastructure and public enterprises, it needs to select only the most productive projects, because budgetary constraints will limit these investments. Government is also responsible for the macroeconomic guidance of the mixed economy. To satisfy their targets for economic growth, redistribution of income, and stabilization of the economy, governments attempt to manipulate the tools at their disposal: taxation and public spending, control of the money supply and interest rates, management of the foreign exchange regime. To make these tools work, governments require macroeconomic perspectives of the economy, projections of its future course, and predictions of how alternative policy packages might influence that course.

The Planning Process

The Politics of Planning

A rudimentary description of the planning process would include political leaders who set the goals and agree to a final plan of action for achieving them; planners—economists and other technicians—who translate the goals into proposed actions; and technicians, such as engineers and agricultural extension officers, who carry out these actions and thus implement the plan.

But this simple description masks many important qualifications. Who, for instance, are the political leaders, how are they chosen, and for whom do they speak? In democracies like the United States, India, Kenya, and Colombia, the voters select their leaders, presumably choosing among candidates whose views on national goals are known. But election campaigns seldom elicit consistent sets of priorities in the detail needed for national planning, and elected leaders have considerable scope for choice even if they adhere strictly to their campaign promises. More crucially, in pluralistic societies political leaders are influenced by various special interest groups, such as unions, manufacturers, doctors, teachers, and the military. Political leaders' views on national goals must bend to accommodate such constituencies, whether before or after an election, so that development priorities will be influenced at least as much by entrenched interest groups as by electoral majorities.

Authoritarian governments such as the Soviet Union, China, Chile, and Zaire, may appear better able to establish goals based on ideology, national aspirations, or the interests of constituencies that propel them to power. But even governments that are willing to use repression face limits to their freedom of action. Few dictators can defy public opinion indefinitely: in the past two decades popular unrest has toppled authoritarian leaders in places as diverse as Poland, Peru, and South Korea. Special interest groups, especially those with economic or military power, can also influence the actions of authoritarian regimes, either indirectly by swaying public opinion or directly by threatening hostile actions such as strikes or coups.

The planners, who interpret the goals and design plans to achieve them, are not simply technicians. They also participate in the political system. Indeed at high levels planners owe their success as much to their political acumen as to their technical skills and have economic concerns as intense as any interest group. Planners, though removed from the political arena, may still be influenced by their reading of the needs and entreaties of particular constituencies, such as small farmers, factory owners, or civil servants, whether out of conviction or self-interest. And the same is true of technicians who implement plans; their power over the realization of national goals is at least as great as that of the political leaders or planners.

The picture becomes more complex once the several layers of government are introduced: central, regional, and local administration; different departments or ministries within each layer; and semi-autonomous agencies with a variety of missions. Each of these separate bureaucracies may have its own point of view on development issues, yet national plans have somehow to reconcile diverse views if they are to guide the many organs of government. Graham Allison, in a fascinating analysis of decision-making in the United States government during the Cuban missile crisis of 1962, defines the term *bureaucratic politics* to describe the complexity of reaching binding decisions in this environment.[3]

The problem of bureaucratic politics is immediately apparent if we look beyond the central planning unit that provides the macroeconomic framework and has the final word on projects to be included in the plan. In a good planning system the central planners will engage the planning units of sectoral ministries in preparing plans. But the viewpoints of a central planner and a sectoral planner do not generally coincide. Each has a different technical perspective; each works for a different political boss and within a different bureaucracy; each faces the judgment of a different public or interest group; and each tends to identify its own view with the national interest. Conflict between these units on the shape of the plan is likely. Then consider their respective ministers, politicians who are particularly sensitive to their own constituencies. Different segments of the public, pressure groups, other politicians and their own bureaucrats may exert varying influences on ministers. Short-term considerations tend to dominate long-term ones, and economic rationality and efficiency are not of paramount importance.

The plan that emerges from this concatenation of public opinion, special interest groups, political leaders, planners, implementers, and competing bureaucracies is either one of compromise or one that some key party will find difficult to support. The complexities of the planning process need to be borne in mind in the balance of this and the next chapter. The exposition may at times seem to imply the existence of a philosopher-king who expresses national aspirations and of skillful technicians who can manipulate policy instruments to implement such aspirations if they understand the economy well enough. But this is only a device necessary to explain certain points, and the reader should not forget that the planning process is deeply imbedded in an intricate political, economic, social, and bureaucratic system that makes it function very differently from the ideal. Later chapters will elaborate on the interactions of economic policy and pressure group politics in specific contexts, such as trade, taxation, and investment. The same forces that thwart reforms in these areas are also likely to influence planning and implementation.

3. Graham T. Allison, *The Essence of Decision: Explaining the Cuban Missile Crisis* (Boston: Little, Brown, 1971).

Planning as Process

The process of planning can be divided into four elements. Traditionally these have been defined in a sequence that begins when *goals* are set by political leaders and translated into quantitative *targets* for growth, employment creation, income distribution, poverty alleviation, and so forth. Political leaders must also establish goal priorities to guide planners in the likely case that some goals conflict. The result is a *welfare function,* which provides planners with a measure of the extent to which their plans will satisfy national goals. The measure can be expressed mathematically as an arbitrarily weighted sum of specific goal targets in a way described in Chapter 6. This formulation would suggest more precision than is possible in measuring goal achievement; in any case it is rarely employed. It is more common to specify a target increase in one or more of the goals, say, a 6 percent annual increase in GNP and a 4 percent increase in employment, and then to instruct planners to develop programs that achieve these targets. A third alternative would be a welfare function that simply ranks goals, telling planners to consider, for example, both growth and employment, but to give higher priority to employment.

At this point the planner takes over. The second step is to measure the availabilities of scarce resources during the plan period: savings, foreign capital, government revenues, export earnings, skilled workers, and so forth. These, together with administrative and organizational limitations, are the *constraints* that will limit the economy's ability to achieve its targets. Third, most of the planning effort goes into identifying the various *means (activities* or *instruments)* that might be employed to achieve national goals. These include investment projects, such as roads, irrigation schemes, factories, and health centers, to be included in the national plan; policies or price incentives, such as changes in the exchange rate or interest rates, wage targets, tax reforms, or subsidies which may induce private firms and individuals to promote national development goals; and institutional changes, such as the establishment of development banks or the reorganization of agricultural services, which may remove obstacles to change and support other development activities.

Finally, the planner undertakes the mechanical process of selecting from among the possible activities those that will do most to achieve national goals (the welfare function) without violating any of the resource or organizational constraints. The result of this process is a *development strategy or plan* which lays out the activities to be undertaken over the next several years (usually five). The process of selecting activities can be done by formal models, as described in the next chapter, but it is usually done informally, by trial and error.

This traditional sequence of planning works only if political leaders specify national goals and priorities fairly clearly for the planners. Unfortunately political leaders are not always willing to do so. They prefer grand but ambiguous statements of goals, leaving room for inevitable maneuver. Whereas planners think in terms of several years, political considerations dictate much shorter horizons. In any case leaders cannot rationally specify priorities in the abstract without first having at least an approximate notion of the *trade-offs* among goals: for example, how much national growth (if any) would be sacrificed in order to increase employment in a remote region?

A change in sequence can help circumvent this impasse. Planners can start by assuming alternative sets of goals and priorities, then preparing alternative strategies (sets of activities), each designed to perform best under a different set of priorities. This provides the political decision-maker with a measure of the trade-offs among different goals. It also reduces the choice among competing goals to a set of a particular investments and policies, which is easier to grasp than the more abstract concept of goal fulfillment.

Perhaps, after all, it is the *process* of planning that is important, rather than the resulting plan. Recognizing that politicians inevitably have compelling concerns outside economics, the planners can be most constructive by trying to insert economic considerations more firmly into political decision-making, quantifying the elements that can be measured by economists, and identifying those elements that are not quantifiable. This is partly a matter of educating political leaders about economics in general and their own economies in particular. By presenting and explaining the trade-offs involved in choices between alternative projects or strategies, the planner can help the politician trace through the economic implications of planning decisions and highlight both the constraints and opportunities provided by the economic system. Over time, the process of educating politicians through planning may lead to more informed political decisions and consequently to improved economic performance, which is in any case the ultimate goal of development planning.

Decentralization and Participation

In the 1950s and early 1960s planning for the mixed economies of developing countries was focused on the macroeconomics of growth and on broad strategic issues: feasible growth rates, savings targets, strategies for industrialization, and so forth. Consequently efforts were concentrated on establishing national planning agencies that could take a broad view of economic activity and command the respect of sectoral ministries and provincial governments. The precise design has varied, depending on each government's traditions and its seriousness about national planning. These agencies are either planning commissions reporting to a prime minister or president, separate ministries, or divisions of the finance ministry. To help planning agencies become effective coordinators of policy, governments have assigned them some fiscal weapon. All planning agencies write a development plan that includes a long-term, usually five-year, budget for government investment. However, the power of the purse lies in annual development budgets, which allocate government saving and foreign aid to investment projects. The planning agency that shares this power with the finance ministry is usually better able to enforce its views on other ministries and local governments. Central planning agencies have professional staffs, most often trained in economics, that are concerned with macroeconomic analysis, project planning, and annual budgeting.

By the 1960s it had become apparent that planning could not be confined to one central agency. Sectoral ministries, such as agriculture, industry, and transportation, are responsible for proposing and implementing investment projects in their areas. Provincial and local governments have varying degrees of responsibility for smaller, local projects and some services. These entities have a great deal of knowledge necessary for sound planning, and usually a greater awareness of local needs. They are also responsible for implementing development programs, for which their commitment is essential. In order to tap their knowledge and gain their commitment, many governments have assigned relevant planning tasks to ministries and local governments.

These reasons to *decentralize* planning have been reinforced by development strategies that emphasize rural projects, poverty alleviation, and small-scale industry. Programs with these aims require extensive administrative coverage, such as widespread extension services or marketing arrangements, and consequently involve many national agencies and local governments. Central coordination becomes more difficult as the number of agencies increases, and some planning must be done at intermediate levels before the national planning agency tries to digest the constituent parts and coordinate the national plan.

A further argument for decentralization has come from a growing acceptance of the principle that participation is an essential ingredient to development. *Participation* can be defined as sharing of the economic benefits of development by a broad spectrum of people at all levels of society. Rapid growth of employment in all sectors and increased productivity on small farms are two essential ingredients of a participative strategy. But proponents usually go beyond economics and suggest that people ought to have a hand in guiding their own destinies by participating in the planning and design of projects that affect them. For example, the route of a new farm-to-market road ought to be decided in consultation with the villagers and farmers who are affected by the road. Participation is valued for the intrinsic satisfaction it gives to all participants and also because it may promote democratic government at the local level, loosen the grip of local and national elites, and infuse project planning with the practical realities of local attitudes and conditions. Participation can also be viewed as an attempt to enfranchise the economically and politically weak, to give them a chance to influence planning in ways that under centralized planning are possible only for entrenched interest groups.

What emerges from this mélange of national, sectoral, regional, local, and popular planning? Do all the requirements of national coordination, ministry responsibility, local government involvement, and popular participation leave any room for a feasible, let alone an ideal, planning system? In practice there have been a variety of accommodations, with periodic shifts in emphasis and in bureaucratic power. Nevertheless some general principles can be advanced to cope with the competing demands on planning.

Central planning agencies in mixed economies must, at a minimum, provide four functions. First, decisions on *national goals and strategies* need to be drawn from the political process and translated into quantified targets where possible. Next, central planners are responsible for all *macroeconomic, long-term balancing* of the resource constraints on development. Whatever the details of the plan, they must fit within a *consistent* macroeconomic framework in which domestic and foreign saving finances investment, export receipts and foreign capital cover imports, demands for skilled labor can be met, and so on. Third, and really a part of the resource constraints problem, central planners need to indicate the *budget constraints* within which each decentralized planning agency must work. To ensure that decentralized planners come to grips with matters of priority, rather than leave this to the central unit, they must be forced to fit their proposals within a realistic investment budget. Fourth, the central planners need to provide *standards for project design and selection,* so that decentralized planners can identify the activities to be included in the plan. These start with a translation of national strategies and priorities into guidelines for selecting projects, and include a set of rules and national prices for conducting cost-benefit analysis to aid project selection, as described in the next chapter.

Within this framework set by central planning the sectoral ministries, provincial government, and local authorities carry out a similar set of functions at their respective levels. Using project design and appraisal guidelines provided by national authorities the sectoral and regional planners identify potential projects, design them, evaluate them as contributers to national goals, and if they pass the test, propose them to central planning. The investment budget constraint set by central planning is used as a test of priorities. There is ample scope for decentralized planners to exercise judgment about their areas of expertise within the constraints set by central planning, and even to develop a case for increased allocations if enough good projects can be prepared.

Participative planning would be undertaken at the local level within a similar framework. Local planners suggest priority areas for development projects and place budgetary constraints on the projects that could be considered for each locality. In addition, to a greater degree than is true at higher levels of planning, local and ministerial technicians should be available to consult with popular representatives or the people themselves, offering guidance on technical and economic matters, answering questions, and posing alternatives. The essence of planning at this level is the same as elsewhere: those involved should be able to make their own choices, but they must choose within a realistic set of constraints and with knowledge of the costs and benefits of alternative choices.

Development Plans

The end result of the planning processes discussed here is a national (or regional) development plan, a document containing a blueprint for the economy over the next several years. Although development planners are guided by economic analysis and may employ models of the types described in the next chapter, plans are not solely economic documents. They are political statements, buttressed by economic descriptions and projections. What is found in a typical development plan?

The best way to find out, of course, is to read one. Development plans are now written, generally every five years, by most of the hundred-plus developing countries and have found their way into libraries all over the world that specialize in economics, politics, and area studies. A reader sampling these will find a common, though not rigid, pattern. Opening statements by political leaders are followed by an introduction that establishes the national goals which the plan is to serve. Later in the first chapters, some—probably ambitious—targets will be announced for national income, investment, exports, poverty alleviation, education, health, and employment.

National Goals in Two Development Plans

Kenya

Improvements of the well-being of the people remain our dominant aim. The plan focuses sharper attention on measures to deal with the alleviation of poverty through emphasis on continued growth, raising household incomes by creating more income-earning opportunities, increasing the output and quality of services provided by Government, and improving income distribution throughout the nation. . . .

The target set for overall annual growth of the economy is 6.3 percent [per year]. . . . Considering the constraints that we face, it is an ambitious goal. The most severe constraint will be our balance of payments. . . . Two other constraints . . . are the gaps between Government revenue and expenditure, and the gap between the savings that are available within the country and the amount of investment required to meet the goals we have set. . . .

[I]n agriculture, development of arid and semi-arid areas is accorded a high priority. . . . There will also be an emphasis on the promotion of agriculture exports. . . . In manufacturing, our emphasis will shift from producing goods for our domestic use to the more difficult challenge of increasing our exports in highly competitive world markets. . . . The dispersal of industrial activity throughout the country is another important objective. . . .

For the private sector [increased efficiency] entails the promotion of competition and reduction of restrictions. . . . For the public sector, emphasis has been placed on making marketing institutions, local authorities and operating ministries more efficient.

—Republic of Kenya, *Development Plan, 1979–1983*

Indonesia

[T]he Repelita II [Second Plan] goals are: first, to raise the nation's living standard and prosperity, and, second, to lay a firm foundation for the next development stage. . . . Enhancing development means a faster increase in production of goods and services. Production increases must run parallel to and be balanced with equal production dispersion and expansion of employment opportunities, as well as equitable redistribution of the benefits.

In order to achieve [these goals], production in agriculture must increase by around 4.6 percent per year, in industry by around 13.0 percent, in mining by around 10.1 percent. . . . With a population growth rate around 2.3 percent per year, income per capita will increase by around 5.0 percent. . . .

Constant efforts will be directed toward mobilizing forces in the interest of national development by supporting self-reliance in stimulating the initiative and active participation of the entire nation. . . . It is estimated that local savings will increase from 11.6 to 17.8 percent [of national income] . . . [and] that only around 16 percent of development expenditure will be derived from foreign aid [by the end of the plan]. Gross exports will increase by 23.9 percent per year.

—Republic of Indonesia, *The Second Five-Year Development Plan, 1974–75 to 1978–79* (translated from Indonesian)

Somewhere among the early chapters of a plan will be a review of the economy and of progress in achieving the targets of the previous plan, although this may be put in a separate document. Most plans have been based on some macroeconomic analysis of the constraints on achieving economic goals, and often the rough outlines will be presented: target growth requires so much investment and so much saving, and implies import levels that suggest so much export growth and foreign aid; manpower planning shows shortages in the following kinds of skills, which will be imported; and so forth. In many cases it may appear that constraints can be satisfied when in fact they cannot be. The resource needs have been dictated by infeasible targets, but it requires further calculations or a close knowledge of the economy to discover that the resources are not there. This is not necessarily bad. Plans are more than technical documents. They reach a domestic political audience, and leaders want to appear to be offering measurable progress. Ambitious goals may even spur some participants to greater effort, although this incentive can evaporate if the gap between targets and achievement remains large. Plans have also been negotiating documents, particularly during the 1960s, used to support requests for aid from foreign governments, the World Bank, and other aid donors.

Incentives to private investors generally take the forms of tax relief and subsidy schemes. The relative price structure of the economy and its implied incentives are taken as given. To induce private investors to act in ways consistent with national priorities, government may offer tax holidays, accelerated depreciation, export subsidies, and other incentives. Frequently these are catalogued in the plan. Sometimes the scope for private investment is specified for each industry, but not often.

Sectoral chapters provide the bulk of most plans. These cover agriculture, fishing, forestry, mining, manufacturing, power, water supplies, financial institutions, health, and education. Each may begin with general descriptions of the sector and changes in the past five years, perhaps followed by some statements of priorities an policies. Then comes the meat of the plan: public sector investment projects are described, sometimes at length. These are the "shopping lists" of projects the government would like to undertake. Priorities may be implied (though seldom stated), but it is certain that far more is listed than will be implemented. Some of these projects are probably quite far along in their design and financing by the time the plan is published. Some projects have probably been appraised by the techniques described in the next chapter and may have been submitted to an aid donor for consideration. Most others—at various stages of appraisal, design, or imagination—will be sketched only roughly in the plan. A large fraction of these will never see the light of day.

One other section receives considerable attention: the government's long-run development budget. This surfaces in various places depending on the plan, but is essentially an amalgam of those development projects, probably introduced in the sectoral chapters, that are included in the budget for the next five years. Some indication of financing prospects may be included here, or in the chapter(s) on macroeconomic constraints. The development budget is the battleground for financial allocations and implementation. Regardless of what the sectoral project lists show, the crucial task for ministry, regional, or public enterprise planners is to get their projects inserted into the development budget.

The *annual government budget,* though related to the development plan, is a separate document that involves a different process from development planning. The annual budget is under the control of a ministry of finance (often called the treasury). It is typically separated into two parts: the *current or operating budget* and the annual *capital or development budget.* The latter includes government investments and derives from the development plan's long-run budget. In the early years of a development plan the annual capital and long-run development budgets may look quite similar. But as time passes the economic situation most often deviates from the projections in the development plan, and the annual capital budget becomes increasingly divorced from the long-range development plan. The current budget contains expenses, such as the salaries of civil servants, teachers, and the military, and interest paid on the national debt, that recur each year. These items are counted as government consumption in the national accounts. The operating budget also includes transfers, such as subsidies and social security payments, that are not included in the national accounts. Development expenditures frequently have implications for future operating budgets. For example, a program to invest in rural health centers or additional primary schools implies increased wages to health workers and teachers in the future.

Implementation

Taken as a blueprint for development, long-range plans have not worked very well. Although a few countries have had considerable success in carrying out their plans and others have done well over the course of a plan period or two, by and large the record is poor. Most countries over most plan periods do not fulfill their macroeconomic goals nor implement most of their projects. This should not be surprising, nor should it deter countries from continuing to plan. Planning is not a blueprint for detailed development. It has other functions, as we have seen: it stimulates a dialogue between politicians and planners; serves as a domestic political statement and in a few countries as a vehicle for public discussion; and can be an international aid-negotiating tool.

Still, the shortcomings of plans cannot be written off that easily. Even admitting the need for political statements and allowing for the inherent benefits of a plan dialogue, it probably remains true that plans do not fulfill the expectations of politicians, planners, or the populace, not to mention aid donors. What has gone wrong, and what can be done to make planning more meaningful?

Economic Forecasting

Imperfections in economic forecasting and in planning models—both discussed in Chapter 6—create one set of problems. Regardless of the perfection of the model, no country's future can be forecast with great accuracy for as long as five years ahead. This point need not be elaborated for anyone who has been reading a newspaper during the 1970s and 1980s, when commodity price swings, OPEC oil pricing, abrupt shifts in government policies, and persistent inflation have wrecked most economists' forecasts. Add to these worldwide phenomena political crises, floods, drought, earthquakes, extreme heat or cold, and the limitations of forecasting are clear. This is equally true for developed and developing countries, except that the latter generally are not so well insulated from such shocks and suffer more intensely from them. Changing conditions require that multiyear plans be supplemented by annual budgets, periodic reviews, and in extreme cases, early revision. In Soviet-type economies where enterprises must follow plan directives because of the absence of market influences, the key plan is not the widely advertised five-year plan but the annual plan, and even the annual plan must frequently be revised during the course of the year.

Nor are the forecasting models very good. One characteristic of underdevelopment is poor data. Although efforts over the past three decades have improved available data enormously, much remains to be done, and important indicators are simply not measured in many of the poorer countries. The models that are in general use have severe limitations, as discussed in Chapter 6. As predictors of future outcomes based on past data, these models depend critically on continuity and some kind of equilibrium. Yet discontinuity and disequilibrium are the essence of developing economies. It is impossible, for example, to find a valid econometric estimate of a savings supply function in countries where interest rates have been controlled and kept at low levels; or of an import function in countries where the level of imports is determined each year by administrative controls over import licenses. Improvements are being made in these models, but it takes time to adopt newer models for general use in planning and forecasting.

Administrative Capacity

With very few exceptions (e.g., Singapore, South Korea, and China) developing countries must count administrative and organizational capacity among the constraints on development. Their administrative systems lack *absorptive capacity;* they cannot utilize all the resources that could be made available. For the dozens of countries that became independent after World War II local capacity to govern was typically limited by the policies of the departing colonial powers and the new government was barely able to maintain the services already offered. Independence brought enhanced expectations that growth could be accelerated, implying expansion of all sectors, especially government. If investment was to be expanded government had to increase its project formulation and implementation, activities that use managers and administrators intensively, putting an added burden on perhaps the scarcest resource for many of the developing countries.

As all governments expanded their traditional activities to spur development, many governments moved into areas previously left to the private sector. The spread of public enterprise into all phases of the economy is documented in Chapter 21. This expansion further drained government's managerial capacity because the civil service had to provide enterprise managers and technicians as well as informed administrators to supervise the new public corporations. In the fully socialized economy based on the Soviet model the need for informed administrators for supervisory and managerial roles is even greater because so few decisions are governed by market forces.

The suspicions about private enterprise that led many governments to nationalize some industries also led them to intervene in the market, through import controls, investment licensing, and regulation of wages, interest rates, and commodity prices. These and other interventions require large bureaucracies to administer the myriad of regulations that inevitably mushroom under such regimes. The resulting pressures on scarce manpower can be alleviated by phasing out such controls and permitting the market to regulate through prices, something it does well.

A more recent trend in development has intensified the need for trained administrators and technicians. Strategies that emphasize labor-intensive development through small farms and workshops, poverty relief through basic needs provided by government, and participative planning, all feature an administrative structure that reaches more widely and deeply into the countryside and villages than in the past. These strategies are appealing because they try to reach the most deprived members of society. But because such programs draw heavily upon one of society's scarcest resources it may be difficult to implement them effectively or efficiently. One of the pressing problems of the 1980s is to find strategies that can reach the poor without multiplying the demand for administrative skills.

It is not surprising then that even with a will to implement all of the well-designed projects in a development plan the civil service often has been unable to complete the task. In the long run the solution lies in training civil servants with appropriate skills, providing them with material and psychic incentives, and adopting strategies that lean less heavily on direct government involvement. However, education, even in the long run, is no panacea, as Chapter 9 makes clear. It is not always obvious just what the appropriate skills are, how to instill them in students, how to ensure that those students end up in suitable jobs in government, and how to motivate them to serve the interests of the people government is trying to help.

Bureaucratic Politics—Once More

Even if governments had the capacity to implement, would they have the collective will? The concept of bureaucratic politics was introduced earlier in this chapter when we described the way competing bureaucracies force compromises in national plans. Even if plans reflect a strong consensus of interested parties, and especially if they do not, the path toward implementation is strewn with hazards. Implementers are different people from planners. In a ministry of agriculture, for example, the planning unit that works with the central planners on agriculture projects then hands these over to operating divisions—crops or livestock, for example—for implementation. If these programs are innovative, if they shift allocations from one crop or region to another, if they require any kind of change, they are likely to encounter some resistance, both from office heads and field personnel. Officials may resent change because it is threatening to their established way of operating; they may (and likely do) feel pressure from a different constituency, such as local farmers (probably large ones) and traders; and they may have a more realistic view of what can be accomplished. The latter emphasizes the importance of incorporating the views of operating personnel in planning, but this is not easy to arrange for a large ministry and seldom is done effectively. Whatever the locus or causes of resistance, it can obviously endanger any project in the hands of the implementers.

Complexity increases and implementation prospects become dimmer when a project cuts across several agencies. A multipurpose dam, requiring the cooperation of ministries of public works, water, power, and agriculture, involves many politicians, planners, and implementers with potentially conflicting interests. The motives may be petty—a resentment of change that reduces one's control; or large—a genuine belief that, for example, hydroelectric power operations are reducing the potential for needed irrigation. Whatever the case, so long as there are implementers in the long chain of operations who resist the project, it can fail. Obviously this is not inevitable, because some very complex projects have been completed successfully. But the danger is there, and much of the inability to implement can be traced to these conflicts.

Examples can be multiplied at length, but the addition of two more interest groups should illustrate sufficiently. Each of the governmental actors is sensitive to some outside group, such as large farmers, a particular local government, labor unions, manufacturing trade associations, or influential friends. When the interests of these groups are threatened, they can try to act openly by opposing features of the plan they do not like, or they can work against implementation by convincing those in the chain of operation to work against the project. The methods are sometimes obvious and sometimes subtle, as numerous and various as all the ways that well-placed people have for influencing the actions governments take. Even the potential beneficiaries themselves may resist change, either because they do not fully understand the new program or because they have other concerns that would be better served by different policies.

Finally, aid donors enter the picture. They are unlikely to work against any project that they are financing and will try to ensure that needed resources are made available. In a world of scarcity, especially scarce administrative capacity, this often means that some other project goes without the needed resources and may be delayed or may fail. Donors' priorities thus may have considerable influence over which projects are implemented.

There is no easy solution to these problems; they are inherent in government. Participative, consultative planning can help to alleviate some of the dangers. Plans should be responsive to the views of those who must implement them, so that project designs are comfortable to them. However, change is the nature of development and some projects are necessarily radical. Then it is inevitable that implementation will meet resistance on many fronts. Drastic measures may be necessary to make these programs succeed, and it goes without saying that continuing, effective political commitment is essential. Because it is, and because such commitment can be costly to a government, planners cannot lightly suggest such projects, nor try to impose many of them at once.

FURTHER READING Full-length treatments of planning for economic development include Everett E. Hagen (ed.); *Planning Economic Development* (Homewood, Ill.: Richard Irwin, 1963); Louis J. Walinsky, *The Planning and Execution of Economic Development* (New York: McGraw-Hill, 1963); and Albert Waterston, *Development Planning: Lessons of Experience* (Baltimore: Johns Hopkins University Press, 1965). A more advanced treatise is G. M. Heal, *The Theory of Economic Planning* (Amsterdam: North-Holland, 1973). Roy B. Helfgott and Salvatore Schiavo-Campo, "An Introduction to Industrial Planning," in *Industrialization and Productivity* no. 16 (UNIDO, 1970), pp. 5–34, give a detailed but elementary treatment of industrial strategy planning. Articles that discuss alternative strategy planning include an advanced mathematical treatment by Daniel P. Loucks, "Planning for Multiple Goals," in C. R. Blitzer et al. (eds.), *Economy-Wide Models and Development Planning* (London: Oxford University Press, 1975) and a nonmathematical exposition by Michael Roemer, "Planning by Revealed Preference," *World Development* 4, no. 9 (1976): 775–83. Oskar Lange's market socialism is explained in his "On the Economic Theory of

Socialism" in B. Lippincott (ed.), *On the Economic Theory of Socialism* (Minneapolis: University of Minnesota Press, 1938).

Tony Killick presents a perceptive view of the economic planners' role in politically motivated decision-making, in "The Possibilities of Development Planning," *Oxford Economic Papers* 28, no. 2 (1976): 161–84.

Problems of implementing development plans are engagingly discussed, though in an industrial country context, by Jeffrey L. Pressman and Aaron Wildavsky, *Implementation: How Great Expectations in Washington Are Dashed in Oakland* (Berkeley: University of California Press, 1973); reading the balance of the title alone is worth a trip to the library. For a sociologist's view of plan implementation, see Donald Warwick, "Integrating Planning and Implementation: A Transactional Approach," Harvard Institute for International Development Discussion Paper No. 63, June 1979.

Chapter 6

PLANNING MODELS

The national development plan described in Chapter 5 is a product of engineering feasibility studies, economic analysis, and politics. In this chapter we assume that the engineers have done their work, and we abstract from the complexities of bureaucratic and national politics in order to concentrate on economic models that aid national planning. We are now in the unrealistic but instructive world of the philosopher-king who establishes national goals and the economic technicians who determine how to manage the economy to achieve these goals. Five planning models are covered: the basic Harrod-Domar model, a simple Keynesian macroeconomic growth model, interindustry (input-output) analysis, linear programming, and cost-benefit analysis. Before introducing these, we need to make a distinction between two approaches to planning, consistency planning and optimality planning.

Consistency and Optimality

The distinction between consistency and optimality planning can be illustrated with a simple example. If a traveler has a two-week vacation and a budget of $3000 to spend, she may ask whether she has enough time and money to travel to Kenya and see its game parks. Are her plans (to visit Kenya's game parks) *consistent* with her resources (two weeks and $3000)? This consistency problem becomes an optimality problem if asked another way: How far can the traveler go, and how much can she see, in two weeks with only $3000 to spend? How can the traveler make *optimal* use of her resources?

A ***consistent plan*** can be illustrated in terms of the production possibility frontier of Fig. 6–1. The frontier is a heuristic device to illustrate a very simple economy. As its name implies the production frontier defines the

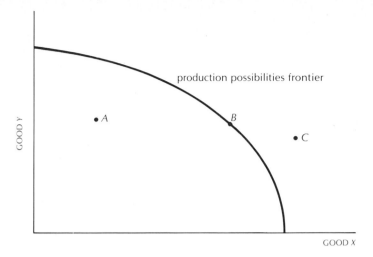

GOOD Y

production possibilities frontier

• A

B

• C

GOOD X

Fig. 6-1   Consistency.

maximum feasible output of two goods, X (say, necessities) and Y (say, luxuries), in an economy with a given endowment of productive resources over a given period, such as one or five years. The more of good Y the economy wants to produce, the less of good X it can produce, because resources (labor, land, capital) must be taken from production of necessities (X) to be used in production of more luxuries (Y). Consistency models ensure that the resulting plan would place the economy *within* its production possibilities frontier, at a point like A in Fig. 6-1, or at best *on* the frontier, at a point like B. A consistent plan cannot, of course, promise output at a point such as C, beyond the frontier which represents the capacity of the nation's resources.

To illustrate an **optimal plan** it is necessary to review the concept of **indifference curves.** Figure 6-2 represents the choices available to a single consumer, who may purchase the two goods available, necessities (X) and luxuries (Y), in various combinations. If the consumer were to purchase quantities X_a and Y_a, he or she would achieve a certain level of satisfaction. Other combinations of purchases, such as X_b and Y_b, may yield the same level of satisfaction to the consumer. If so, then points a and b lie on the same indifference curve, labeled II in the diagram. Indifference curve II is the locus of all combinations of the two goods that give the same satisfaction to the consumer as does the combination X_a and Y_a. Any indifference curve to the northeast of II, such as curve III, contains combinations of the two goods that yield greater satisfaction to the consumer than does any point on curve II. That is, the combination X_c and Y_c is preferred by the consumer to X_a and Y_a (or to X_b and Y_b). Similarly, combinations along curve I, to the southwest of curve II, are inferior to those along curve II.

Introduction of the **budget line** (or *constraint*) completes the picture. The budget line gives the combinations of goods X and Y that can be purchased by the consumer within the limits of the person's income. (The slope of the

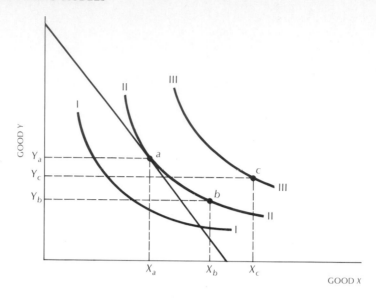

Fig. 6–2   Indifference Curves.

budget line gives the relative price of one good, *Y,* in terms of the other, *X.*) The consumer can maximize his or her level of satisfaction by consuming at point *a,* where the budget line is tangent to indifference curve II. The consumer cannot reach any other point on curve II, such as *b,* and still satisfy the budget constraint. (Nor would he want to, since he is indifferent between combinations *a* and *b.*) Any combination of purchases on higher indifference curves, such as point *c* on curve III, would require more income than the consumer has. And there is no need to accept less satisfaction on a curve such as I, even though it lies partly within the budget constraint, since greater satisfaction is achievable at point *a.*

It takes very restrictive assumptions to use indifference curves, which are valid for individuals, to represent the consumption choices for an entire community. However, the concept of *community indifference curves* is useful—and often used—to illustrate many theories in economics. In Fig. 6–3 a set of indifference curves has been drawn to represent a community's or a country's choices between consumption of goods *X* and *Y.* Just as consumer satisfaction increases as one moves from lower to higher indifference curves, we can imagine that society's welfare increases as we move from community indifference curve I to curve II to curve III. In planning models, society's welfare is represented by an *objective function* that measures the nation's development goals, in a way explained later in this chapter. The community indifference curves of Fig. 6–3 can also represent increasing values of this objective function. The production possibilities frontier in the diagram is analogous to the consumer's budget constraint since it gives the maximum combinations of the two goods that can be produced by the country. The optimal combination of goods *X* and *Y* is given by point *B,* where indifference curve II is tangent to the production

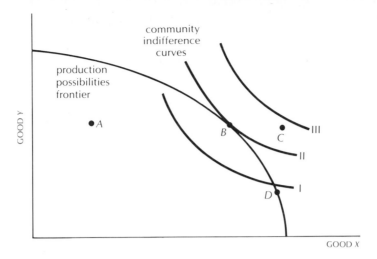

Fig. 6–3 Optimality.

frontier. An optimal planning model seeks solutions like point *B* in Fig. 6–3 for which the value of the objective function is at its maximum given the resource (and hence the production) constraints in the economy.

The method of alternative strategy planning described in Chapter 5 works on the assumption that national plans should be based on social welfare choices made by political leaders. The method essentially seeks to determine feasible output mixes, points along or within the production frontier, and to measure the extent of goal achievement for each. Planners then ask political leaders to indicate their ranking of outcomes, in an attempt to select a strategy that promises a high degree of goal satisfaction, as judged by political leaders. This is analogous to moving from points such as *A* and *D* toward a point such as *B* in Fig. 6–3.

The Harrod-Domar Model

The simplest and best known consistency model for planning is the Harrod-Domar model. It was developed independently during the 1940s by Roy Harrod and Evsey Domar, primarily to explain the relationship between growth and unemployment in advanced capitalist societies. But the Harrod-Domar model has been used extensively in developing countries as a simple way of looking at the relationship between growth and capital requirements.

The underlying assumption of the model is that the output of any economic unit, whether a firm, an industry, or the whole economy, depends on the amount of capital invested in that unit. Thus if we call output Y and the stock of capital K, then output can be related to capital stock by

$$Y = K/k \qquad \text{[6–1]}$$

where k is a constant, called the capital/output ratio. To convert this into a statement about the growth of output, we use the notation Δ to represent increases in output and capital, and write

$$\Delta Y = \Delta K/k \qquad [6-2]$$

The growth rate of output, g, is simply the increment in output divided by the total amount of output, $\Delta Y/Y$. If we divide both sides of equation 6–2 by Y, then

$$g = \frac{\Delta Y}{Y} = \frac{\Delta K/Y}{k} \qquad [6-3]$$

For the whole economy, ΔK is the same as investment, I. In an economy with balanced trade and no net inflow of foreign capital, investment, I, must equal savings, S. Hence $\Delta K/Y$ becomes I/Y, and this in turn is equal to S/Y, which can be designated by the savings rate, s, a percentage of national product. Equation 6–3 can then be converted to

$$g = \frac{s}{k} \qquad [6-4]$$

which is the basic Harrod-Domar relationship for an economy.

Underlying this equation is the view that capital created by investment in plant and equipment is the main determinant of growth and that it is savings by people and corporations that make the investment possible. The *capital/output ratio* is simply a measure of the productivity of capital or investment. If an investment of $3000 in a new plant and new equipment makes it possible for an enterprise to raise its output by $1000 a year for many years into the future, then the capital/output ratio for that particular investment is $3:1$. Economists often use the term *incremental capital/output ratio,* abbreviated **ICOR,** because in studying growth one is mainly interested in the impact on output of additional or incremental capital. The incremental capital/output ratio measures the productivity of additional capital while the (average) capital/output ratio refers to the relationship between a nation's total stock of capital and its total national product.

For economic planners, given this simple equation, the task is a straightforward one. The first step is to try to come up with an estimate of the incremental capital/output ratio (k in equation 6–3) for the nation whose plan is being drawn up. There are two alternatives for the next step. Either planners can decide on the rate of economic growth (g) they wish to achieve, in which case the equation will tell them the level of savings and investment necessary to achieve that growth. Or planners can decide on the rate of savings and investment that is feasible or desirable, in which case the equation will tell planners the rate of growth in national product that can be achieved.

This procedure can be applied to the economy as a whole, or it can be applied to each sector or each industry. Incremental capital/output ratios, for example, can be calculated separately for agriculture and industry. Once planners decide how much investment will be allocated to each sector, the Harrod-Domar equations determine the growth rates to be expected in each of the two sectors.

Fixed-Coefficients Production Functions

At the heart of this kind of analysis is the explicit or implicit assumption that the incremental capital/output ratio is a single fixed number. This assumption is consistent with a production function that employs fixed proportions of capital and labor and constant returns to scale, like that depicted in Fig. 6–4. *Production functions* were introduced in Chapter 3's discussion of two-sector models. they are mathematical expressions that represent the process of production in an industry, a sector, or even the entire economy. A production function gives the quantity of output that can be produced with given amounts of inputs, such as labor, capital, land, and raw materials. In Fig. 6–4 output is represented by *isoquants,* which are combinations of inputs, labor and capital in this case, that produce equal amounts of output. Each level of output is represented by a different isoquant, although only two are shown in the diagram. (In Chapter 3, Figs. 3–2 and 3–5 represented the production function in terms of output and a single input, labor.) Because it is assumed that this production process uses fixed proportions of labor and capital, the isoquants are L-shaped: once the level of capital is known, both output and the minimum amount of labor are also known. For example, it takes capital (plant and equipment) of $10 million and 100 workers to produce 100,000 tons of cement. If more workers are added without investing in more capital, output will not rise above 100,000 tons per year.

If capital in the cement industry is doubled to $20 million and labor is doubled to 200 workers, output also doubles to 200,000 tons per year. This proportional increase in both inputs and output is known as *constant returns to scale.* (If output increases more than proportionally, the production function has increasing returns to scale, also known as economies of scale.) If the price of cement were $50 per ton, then the incremental capi-

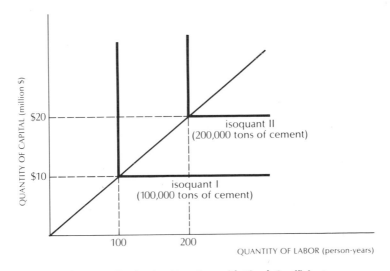

Fig. 6–4 Production Function with Fixed Coefficients.

tal/output ratio would be 2:1 (equivalent to additional investment of $10 million divided by the value of additional output, $50 × 100,000 tons). If there is surplus labor in the economy and available to the cement industry, then it can be assumed that the additional 100 workers will be available and the Harrod-Domar relationship can be used to determine the increase in output with a given investment. But if labor is not in surplus, then the amount of output will also depend on how much labor can be employed in the industry. Similar considerations apply when entire sectors, such as manufacturing, or even the whole economy, are being considered.

Neoclassical Production Functions

Most economists, however, believe that the production function for many industries, and for the economy as a whole, looks more like that depicted in Fig. 6–5. Instead of requiring fixed factor proportions as in Fig. 6–4, output can be achieved with varying combinations of labor and capital. This is called a ***neoclassical production function.*** The isoquants are curved, rather than L-shaped. (The production functions used in Chapter 3, Fig. 3–2 and 3–5, are also neoclassical because they permit varying amounts of labor to combine with a fixed amount of land.) Starting with output of 100,000 tons at point *a,* using $10 million of capital and 100 workers (not shown in the figure), the industry could be expanded in any of three ways. If industry planners decide to expand at constant-factor proportions and move to point *b* on isoquant II, the situation would be identical to the fixed-proportions case of Fig. 6–4. But production of 200,000 tons could be achieved by using more labor and less capital (that is, a more *labor-intensive* method), at a point like *c* on isoquant II. In that case the incremental capital/output ratio falls to 1.4:1 (still assuming the price of cement is $50 a ton). Or if a more capital-intensive method is desired, such

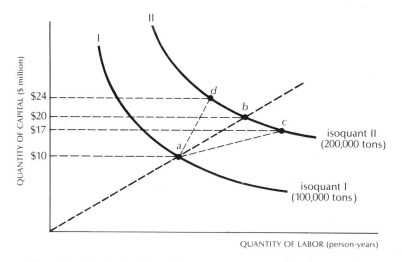

Fig. 6–5 Neoclassical (Variable Proportions) Production Function.

as the production technique given by *d* on isoquant II, the ICOR would rise to 2.8 : 1.

If the production function facing a nation is neoclassical, then the capital/output ratio becomes a variable that is to some extent under the control of the planners. Considering production functions like those in Fig. 6–5 from the industry level, planners in developing countries in which capital is scarce can try to induce manufacturers and farmers to employ more labor-intensive technologies. Then for a given amount of savings and investment both growth and employment can be higher. At the level of the whole economy planners can not only encourage labor-intensive technologies but also encourage investment in the more labor-intensive industries, reducing the demand for investment and saving on both counts. The kinds of tools that planners may use to accomplish this reduction in the capital/output ratio are discussed in depth in several chapters of this text, especially Chapters 8, 13, and 17.

The appropriate incremental capital/output ratio will vary among countries and, for a single country, over time. Poor countries, with low savings rates and surplus (unemployed and underemployed) labor, can achieve higher rates of growth by economizing on capital and utilizing as much labor as possible. As economies grow and per-capita income rises, savings rates tend to increase and the labor surplus diminishes. Thus the ICOR shifts upward. In the more advanced countries it can be higher than in the developing countries without sacrificing growth. And resource-rich developing countries, such as those exporting petroleum, can afford more capital-intensive development than other LDCs. These shifts in the ICORs can come about through market mechanisms as prices of labor and capital change in response to changes in supplies. As growth takes place, savings become relatively more abundant and hence the price of capital falls while employment rises and so do wages. Thus all producers economize increasingly on labor and use more capital. Alternatively, in Soviet-type and other planned economies the planners can allocate investment in ways that move the economy toward an appropriate ICOR. Finally, technological change and "learning by doing" have important roles to play. Both can contribute to increased productivity of all factors of production, which reduces the ICOR. In Fig. 6–4 and 6–5 increased factor productivity can be represented by a shifting inward of each isoquant toward the origin.

Macroeconomic Consistency Models

The Harrod-Domar equation has been described as the simplest kind of consistency model. It is nevertheless the basis of many macroeconomic growth models, some of which can be quite elaborate. To illustrate these models, a still quite simple version would begin by turning the Harrod-Domar investment relationship

$$g = s/k, \qquad\qquad \text{[6–4]}$$

into a more realistic form, such as

$$\Delta Y_t = Y_t - Y_{t-1} = v\Delta K_{t-1} = v(I_{t-1} - \delta K_{t-1}), \qquad [6\text{-}5]$$

which can be written as

$$Y_t = Y_{t-1} + v(I_{t-1} - \delta K_{t-1}) \qquad [6\text{-}6]$$

In Equation 6-5 Y is gross domestic (or national) product, K is the capital stock, I is investment, v is the output/capital ratio (the inverse of the ICOR, k in equation 6-1), and δ is the rate of depreciation of existing capital stock. The subscripts refer to the current year, t, and the previous year, $t-1$. Note that here we simplify by assuming it takes investment just a year before it can produce output. This is the entire supply side of our elementary model, indicating how much the economy can produce. It abstracts from most of the important considerations of production and growth that are the subject of other chapters, and remains a fixed-coefficients production function.

The demand side of the model can be contained in five equations, all in the spirit of Keynesian macroeconomic (multiplier) analysis:

$$S_t = sY_t \qquad [6\text{-}7]$$

$$I_t = S_t + F_t \qquad [6\text{-}8]$$

$$M_t = mY_t \qquad [6\text{-}9]$$

$$M_t = E_t + F_t \qquad [6\text{-}10]$$

$$C_t = Y_t - I_t + F_t \qquad [6\text{-}11]$$

The new variables are S_t = gross domestic saving, F_t = foreign saving (the same as foreign aid plus foreign investment), M_t = imports of goods and services, E_t = exports of goods and services, and C_t = consumption. The parameters are s, the saving rate, and m, the import rate, known as the propensity to import. They, like v, are assumed to be known values. Equation 6-7 is a Keynesian saving function, in which saving is a constant proportion, s, of income. Equation 6-8 says that gross investment must be financed by domestic saving and foreign saving. Equation 6-9 determines imports as a constant fraction, m, of income, while equation 6-10 says that imports must be financed by export earnings and foreign capital (saving). Equation 6-11 determines consumption as a residual between income and saving, but puts it in terms of domestic investment and foreign saving, using equation 6-8.

Any system of equations, such as the six of our model (equations 6-6 through 6-11), can be solved if the number of equations equals the number of unknowns. In this model, however, there are ten variables (Y_t, Y_{t-1}, K_{t-1}, I_t, I_{t-1}, S_t, F_t, M_t, E_t, and C_t), three too many. Three of them, the so-called lagged variables Y_{t-1}, K_{t-1}, and I_{t-1}, are considered to be known because they represent values from an earlier year for which we presumably have data. A fourth, exports, E_t, is usually estimated separately, because it depends on factors outside the model, mainly domestic supply capacity for export goods and the state of the world markets. That leaves just six unknowns to be found from the six equations, and the model can be solved for all variables.

Suppose, however, that another variable, F_t, the flow of foreign saving (aid plus foreign investment), were also estimated independently of the model. This is quite realistic since foreign aid is a matter for negotiation and private foreign investment in LDCs is not closely related to domestic economic variables. Then we have a model with only five unknowns (Y_t, T_t, S_t, M_t, and C_t) but six equations, so the model is *overdetermined:* one of the six equations cannot be satisfied, except by chance. Put another way, one of the equations—and we are not sure yet which one—is not necessary for the model; it is *redundant.* This kind of redundancy is characteristic of planning models.

To see which equations might be redundant let us trace through the working of the model. Potential national income (measured, let us say, as GDP) is already known from the first equation, since it depends only on lagged variables, those determined in the previous year. Thus both saving (equation 6–7) and imports (equation 6–9) can be found directly. However, each of these variables also appears in another equation. Saving helps determine investment from equation 6–8. But what if government has a target income growth rate? Then to make income grow at the target rate in the following year, $t+1$, investment must be

$$I_t = \frac{1}{v}(Y_{t+1} - Y_t) + \delta K_t \qquad [6\text{--}12]$$

This is merely a rearrangement of equation 6–6, with a change of subscripts to the next period, which says that gross investment must be adequate to increase income from Y_t to Y_{t+1} and to cover depreciation of the existing capital stock, K_t. With foreign capital fixed, this target level of investment might require national saving more or less than that forthcoming from equation 6–7. If more, then the economy will not grow at the target rate, because equation 6–7 sets a limit to the level of saving, a level inconsistent with the growth target. Saving becomes a *binding constraint* on investment growth. If equation 6–7 promises more saving than needed, the growth target is consistent with saving behavior and the saving equation is redundant.

Imports might present another problem. Imports include both consumer and producer goods, the requirements of which are determined by national income (equation 6–9). But what if the separately estimated level of exports and foreign capital give a different level of financeable imports from equation 6–10? If more can be financed, then equation 6–10 is redundant and the model is consistent. If, however, the sum of exports plus foreign capital is less than necessary imports, then income cannot reach the target level of Y_t; it would have to be lower to get along with fewer imports. In this case the foreign exchange equation (6–10) becomes a binding constraint on production. Moreover, since most capital goods are imported (an important feature left out of this simple model), the shortage of imports would prevent investment from being high enough to attain the growth target.

This fairly primitive macroeconomic planning model is one version of the *two-gap model* developed by McKinnon, Chenery, and others.[1] The two gaps refer to equation 6–8, which balances investment against domestic and foreign saving, and equation 6–10, which balances imports against export earnings and foreign investment. Under the rigid assumptions of the model only one of these equations will be in balance on the basis of previously determined values of the variables. This becomes the binding constraint, the other being redundant. After the fact both equations will be in balance, but the redundant one will get there because of subsequent adjustments in the variables, for example, a drop in exports or in investments. Targets are consistent with resource constraints (the balance equations) only if both are redundant, in which case higher targets can be achieved; or if one is just balanced and the other redundant, in which case no greater growth can be achieved without some structural change in the economy or a greater influx of foreign resources.

Models like this one can be made much more complicated by *disaggregating* some of the relationships, breaking them into component variables and relationships; by separating the economy and model into sectors, such as agriculture, industry, and services; and by adding factors of production, such as various categories of labor, natural resources, kinds of imports, and so forth. Each new factor of production adds a resource balance or constraint equation, so that these become multigap models. But the basic principles of solution and of planning remain the same.

Interindustry Models

Input-Output Analysis

Macroeconomic models lack detailed information on the many agricultural, industrial, and service industries that make up an economy. The interactions—or *linkages*—between these sectors are of crucial significance for planners, who simultaneously need to keep overall macroeconomic balances in view to ensure consistency. The tool designed to accomplish these tasks is the **input-output or interindustry table.** Its two inventors suggest its flexibility and usefulness. Wassily Leontief developed input-output tables during the 1930s to help understand the workings of a modern economy and later to help with postwar planning in the United States. About the same time, though working independently, Leonid Kantorovich developed the same tool to help Russian planners set quantity targets for Soviet production, allowing both for final demands and for the use of intermediate products within industry. The two economists eventually won Nobel prizes for their efforts.

---

1. Ronald McKinnon, "Foreign Exchange Constraints in Economic Development," *Economic Journal* 74 (1964): 388–409; and Hollis Chenery and Alan Strout, "Foreign Assistance and Economic Development," *American Economic Review* 56 (1966): 679–733.

The essence of an interindustry table is to display the flow of output from one industry to another and to final users (consumers, investors, and exporters). A highly simplified example is shown in Table 6–1, which contains only four sectors: primary products, manufactured consumer goods, manufactured producer goods, and services. Sectors shown in rows are producing industries, while those shown in columns are users. For example, row 1, labeled "Primary industry," indicates that agriculture, forestry, and mining produced $20 (millions, billions, or whatever units are convenient) worth of products used within the sector (e.g., feed for livestock); $75 sold to consumer goods manufacturers (e.g., wheat for bakeries or cotton for textiles); $50 sold to producer goods industries (e.g., wood for pulp or iron ore for steel); and nothing to services. These intermediate uses totaled $145 (column 5). Final products, such as corn for consumption or cocoa for export, were valued at $225, so that total output was $400. Similarly, for example, producer goods manufacturers sold $60 of output (such as chemicals) to consumer good manufacturers (row 3, column 2), and so on.

TABLE 6–1 Simplified Input-Output Table (Flow Matrix), Value in Dollars

	Primary industry (1)	Mfg. consumer goods (2)	Mfg. producer goods (3)	Services (4)	Total inter-mediate use (5)	Final use (6)	Total use (7)
		Using sectors					
1. Primary industry	20	75	50	0	145	255	400
2. Manufactured consumer goods	0	30	0	0	30	270	300
3. Manufactured producer goods	60	60	75	0	195	55	250
4. Services	40	15	50	70	175	175	350
5. Total purchases	120	180	175	70	545		
6. Value added	280	120	75	280		755	
7. Total output	400	300	250	350			1300

Each producer is also a user of intermediate goods, and its purchases are shown in the columns of the input-output table. For example, consumer goods manufacturers brought $75 worth of primary products, which we know from inspecting row 1, and also $30 from within the sector (e.g., textiles used in clothing), $60 from producer goods industries (e.g., chemicals or paper used in printing), and $15 from services (e.g., banking services, transportation of goods). Total purchases for this sector, given in row 5, were $180. These industries added value of $120, including wages, rents, depreciation, interest, and profits, so that total output was valued at $300. This must be equal to the total output shown in row 2 for manufactured consumer goods. The difference is that each row shows output allocated according to uses (including final demand), while each column shows the costs and profit of producing that output. Rules of accounting tell us that these must give the same total. This applies to the total columns (5, 6, and 7) and rows as well. Column 6, "Final use," gives the sum of consumption plus investment plus exports less imports by sector. Add these and the result must be gross national product, $755. Row 6 gives value added by sector, the sum of which must also yield GNP.

National input-output tables are much larger than the example shown here. Small ones may have 15 to 20 sectors, while those developed for the United States economy have close to 500 sectors. Moreover the columns giving final uses and the rows giving value added may be broken down into their components and considerably refined. Quantities of capital, labor, and essential imports (goods not produced in the country) can be added as rows to the bottom of the table, showing the investment, labor, and foreign exchange requirements of expanded output. Some more advanced tables, called social accounting matrices (SAMs), now being applied to a few developing countries, even show value added according to the income group that earns it, making it possible to investigate distributional issues in this large, economy-wide framework.

To turn the input-output flow matrix into a usable tool for planning or analysis, a crucial assumption is required. Interindustry tables are based on observations of a single year's activity for each sector, merely a snapshot of the economy. If it is assumed that the ratio of purchases and value added to total production is fixed for every industry and will prevail in the future, then this accountant's snapshot of costs becomes an economist's production function with fixed coefficients. It says that for any industry, inputs and costs must expand proportionately with output. The flow matrix of Table 6–1 can be converted into a matrix of ratios, called *input-output coefficients*, which is done in Table 6–2. Each column has been divided through by its total, so that the second column, for example, now gives the ratios of inputs to output for consumer goods industries: each unit requires 0.25 of primary goods, 0.10 of consumer goods, 0.20 of producer goods, 0.05 of services, and 0.40 of value added.

TABLE 6–2   Coefficients Matrix[a]

	X_1 (1)	X_2 (2)	X_3 (3)	X_4 (4)
1. Primary (X_1)	.05	.25	.20	.00
2. Consumer goods (X_2)	.00	.10	.00	.00
3. Producer goods (X_3)	.15	.20	.30	.00
4. Services (X_4)	.10	.05	.20	.20
5. Total purchases	.30	.60	.70	.20
6. Value added	.70	.40	.30	.80
7. Total output	1.00	1.00	1.00	1.00

[a] For flow matrix of Table 6–1.

The resulting matrix of coefficients can be seen as a set of production functions for each sector shown in columns. These fixed-coefficient production functions are often called *Leontief production functions,* after the economist who developed this planning device. They are expanded versions of the production function shown in Fig. 6–4, with allowance made both

for additional factor inputs and for inputs of raw materials and intermediate goods. The *elements* (coefficients) of input-output matrices are usually
designated a_{ij}, the subscripts referring to the row (i, for input) and column
(j), in that order. Thus a_{12} is the output of primary products to consumer
goods industries, a value of 0.25, while a_{43} is the 0.20 units of services
needed to produce one unit of manufactured producer goods. The matrix
of coefficients is then called the A-matrix.

The Leontief matrix is particularly suited to solving the following kind of
problem: starting with a target growth rate for an economy over five years,
planners can estimate a bill of "final" goods—those commodities and services purchased by private consumers, investors, government, and foreign
importers—that will be demanded at the higher income level. Approximately how much output will be required from each branch of industry to
produce that set of final goods? If we can estimate the required output,
then it should be possible to determine roughly the amount and kinds of
investment needed to produce it. The latter is of course the heart of a development plan. Interindustry analysis answers these questions at a highly
aggregated level and does not give precise, detailed guidance to planners,
but the results are useful indicators or guidelines to more specific planning
of investment projects.

The answer to the central question, how much of each good, is not immediately obvious. Let us say that 100 units of manufactured consumer
goods will be required. We know from Table 6–2 that this will require, for
example, 20 units of producer goods (coefficient $a_{32} \times 100$). But the story
does not end there, because to manufacture those inputs, producer goods
industries will in turn purchase, for example, 4 units of primary goods (20
units needed for consumer goods times a_{13}, or 20×0.20). To produce this
4 units, primary industries require 0.6 units (4×0.15) of producer goods,
and so on, through an endless chain of outputs and inputs. How can we
solve the problem?

Start by asking a simpler question: For any level of output of the four
products, which we now label X_1 through X_4, how much of one product,
primary goods (X_1) will be required? The answer is

$$X_1 = a_{11}X_1 + a_{12}X_2 + a_{13}X_3 + a_{14}X_4 + F_1 \qquad \text{[6–13]}$$

This says that enough X_1 must be produced to cover the input needs of
each of the producing sectors, given by the input-output coefficient times
the level of output, or $a_{ij}X_j$, plus the amount of X_1 needed for final demand, F_1. The same is true for each of the other products, giving

$$X_1 = a_{11}X_1 + a_{12}X_2 + a_{13}X_3 + a_{14}X_4 + F_1 \qquad \text{[6–13]}$$

$$X_2 = a_{21}X_1 + a_{22}X_2 + a_{23}X_3 + a_{24}X_4 + F_2 \qquad \text{[6–14]}$$

$$X_3 = a_{31}X_1 + a_{32}X_2 + a_{33}X_3 + a_{34}X_4 + F_3 \qquad \text{[6–15]}$$

$$X_4 = a_{41}X_1 + a_{42}X_2 + a_{43}X_3 + a_{44}X_4 + F_4 \qquad \text{[6–16]}$$

We already know the values for F_1 through F_4 because these are the final goods required by our growth targets. Since we have four equations (6–13 through 6–16) and four unknowns (the values of total output, X_1 through X_4), we can solve this set of linear simultaneous equations for each of the outputs and get our answer that way. This is a mechanical process which any student of intermediate algebra (or a computer) can easily complete.

Although the story could end there, much can be gained from going another step which does, however, require rudimentary knowledge of matrix algebra. This further development of the Leontief model is contained in an appendix to this chapter.

This basic calculation, yielding the total production needed for any bill of final goods, is at the heart of planning in the Soviet Union, where it is called the method of *materials balances,* and in China. When the requirements of total production are checked out against the capacity in each sector, it becomes a test of *consistency:* Is present capacity adequate for projected final uses, industry by industry? If not, as is likely in any growing economy, plans must provide enough investment in additional capacity so that each sector can produce the required output. The resulting requirement for investment can then be checked against available savings and foreign investment, one of the constraints of the macroeconomic model. Similarly, requirements for labor of varying skills, for imports (foreign exchange), and for other scarce factors of production can be measured against anticipated supplies. One of these constraints, *manpower requirements,* has received considerable attention from education planners who utilize input-output techniques to project the demands for education implied by growth targets (see Chapter 9).

Thus the input-output table can provide a comprehensive but detailed model of the economy, one capable of tracing through the implications for all resources of any output or growth target. This is the most complete form of consistency planning that is now done, although only a minority of developing countries—including South Korea, Malaysia, India, and Mexico—have used it in this way. Despite its power, the input-output model has some serious drawbacks. First, the assumption of fixed coefficients rules out the real possibility that targets may be met not by proportional growth of all factors of production but through the *substitution* of abundant factors, like unskilled labor, for scarce ones, like capital. This possibility was suggested earlier in this chapter when the Harrod-Domar model was contrasted with a neoclassical production function. The concept of substitution is central not only to neoclassical economic theory but also to much real-world economics. To take only one currently pressing problem, the fuel crisis of the late twentieth century is being solved partly by substitution of more abundant fuels, like coal, and eventually solar energy, for oil.

The fuel crisis also suggests the need for *technological innovations,* another possibility not handled easily by interindustry methods. Any time new technologies appear, new coefficients are required in the Leontief table. If planners anticipate such changes they can make approximate allowances by adjusting the initial coefficients, for example, by reducing petroleum inputs and raising coal inputs as oil prices rise. Nor can tables of fixed coefficients conveniently handle *economies of scale* and *learning by doing*, both of which increase factor productivity with growth. Although some nonlinear methods are available to incorporate these shifts in productivity, they are quite complex and have not been widely used for macroeconomic planning.

Linear Programming

Interindustry analysis is useful for answering the question—Do we have adequate resources to achieve our targets? Planners often ask a different question: Given our resources, how can we use them to achieve our goals to the greatest extent possible? That is, instead of planning a merely consistent use of resources we would like to plan an optimal allocation of resources. Linear programming is a technique used to answer the second question. At the core of a linear programming model is the same input-output table, and its Leontief inverse, used in consistency planning. It also includes a set of resource constraints, as in consistency models. The major difference is in the treatment of goals. Consistency models start with specific values of one or more goals, which we called targets. Linear programming uses a **welfare or objective function** instead.

An objective function is simply an algebraic expression that contains one variable for each of the goals that must be taken into account. To combine these into one formula, each goal must have a *priority weight*, which expresses its importance relative to other goals. Such weights are arbitrary because economics provides no scientific guidance to selecting values for priority weights. Thus, for example, a government may hold three quantifiable economic goals important. (1) increase in national income (G_1); (2) employment creation (G_2); and (3) additional income for the poorest 40 percent of society (G_3). Say the first goal is arbitrarily given a weight of 1. If employment creation—which would have to be measured in terms of wages paid to new jobholders—is considered half as important, then its weight, w_2, would be 0.5; and if redistribution, expressed as increases in income to the poorest 40 percent, is considered 75 percent more valuable than income increases on average, then its weight, w_3, would be 0.75. (Weight w_3 is not 1.75, because increases in income to an average recipient are already counted with a weight of 1 in G_1. Here we only want to count the added weight if the recipient is poor.) Thus the objective function would be

$$W = w_1G_1 + w_2G_2 + w_3G_3 = G_1 + 0.5G_2 + 0.75G_3 \qquad [6\text{--}17]$$

A linear program would choose the activities or quantities of output that would maximize the value of the objective function, subject to two sets of constraints. First, production of each good must satisfy the input-output relationships of the Leontief inverse matrix. In order to obtain high values for equation 6–17 the model will emphasize production in those activities that give rapid growth, high employment, and income for the poor. But whatever activities it selects, it must provide for enough output of each commodity and service to ensure that the required direct and indirect inputs are produced. Second, the production of these goods and services must satisfy the resource constraints and not use more factors of production than the economy has available. In practice, and because this is a model of linear equations, only one of the resources will be used fully, exhausting its supply. Other resources will generally not be fully employed; these are redundant.

The model works, in effect, by trying out a first solution consisting of outputs and resource inputs that are consistent. This set of values results in a trial value for the objective function. The model (or more correctly, the computer program that simulates the model) then searches for a set of variables which, while still consistent, will improve the value of the objective function. Eventually the program will, through this process, find a value of the objective function upon which it cannot improve. This is the solution, the set of outputs and resource inputs that maximizes the welfare function. The process can be viewed in terms of Fig. 6–3 as a search from within the production frontier (a point such as A) to find the point of tangency of the objective function with the production frontier (point B).

Linear programming is a step forward in sophistication from input-output analysis. It depends on the same assumptions, however, and is therefore limited by the same drawbacks. Programming has been widely and effectively used in certain microeconomic applications in agriculture and industry, such as combining nutrients to feed livestock for maximum biological growth or planning industrial processes to minimize costs. Its use as a sectoral or national planning tool has been limited to experiments, principally by academic economists, to apply the technique and draw general lessons about economies such as those of Brazil, Chile, India, Israel, Mexico, and South Korea. These experiments have shown that linear programming is useful not so much for its detailed portrayal of optimal resource allocations, but, perhaps paradoxically, for the macroeconomic picture it provides, based on detailed analysis. Its particular strength is in measuring the trade-offs among different development strategies, precisely the information required for planning by alternative strategies. The financial and manpower costs of building, calibrating, and operating a realistic linear program are large, however, and so far few governments have tried to apply the technique. Nevertheless, as human and computer capacities increase over time, linear programming may find increasing uses in macroeconomic and sectoral planning.

Project Appraisal

Although much attention is, quite correctly, paid to the macroeconomic setting of development plans, the bulk of most published plans consists of descriptions of projects and their costs. Correspondingly, one of the most used tools of development planning is *project appraisal,* also called *cost-benefit analysis.* This technique has its genesis in the kind of analysis done by private firms on their alternative investment prospects. When a firm lays out its investment plans (called capital budgets), it tries to select investments that will yield the highest net income for a given amount of finance. Three basic elements are involved in this calculation.

Present Value

The first is the ***net cash flow*** of an investment, which measures the difference between the cash revenues from the sale of the product and the cash outlays on investment, material inputs, salaries and wages, purchased services, and so forth. Costs which do not deplete the cash resources of the firm, of which depreciation is the most prominent example, are not counted.

The second element involves the observation that cash received in the future is less valuable than cash received immediately, because in the interim the firm could earn interest (or profits) on these funds by investing them in bonds or savings accounts (or in additional revenue-earning production facilities). For example, a firm or individual, asked to choose between $1000 today or $1000 next year, would take the money now and place it in a savings account earning, say, 8 percent a year. Then after one year the interest payment would boost the savings account balance to $1080. So the prospect of $1000 a year from now should be evaluated as equivalent to only $1000 ÷ 1.08 = $926. This process, reducing the value of future flows because funds earn interest over time, is called ***discounting***. Because interest is also earned on previous interest, discounting must allow for *compound interest.* In the second year another 8 percent would be earned on the balance, $1080, increasing it to $1166. The payment of $1000 two years from now would then be discounted to yield a *present value* of only $1000 ÷ 1.166 = $858. A general expression for the present value, *P*, is

$$P = F/(1 + i)^n \qquad [6\text{--}18]$$

where F is the value to be realized in the future ($1000 in our example), i is the interest rate (8 percent), and n is the number of years. As the interest rate and the delay in payment both increase, the present value decreases.

An investment project will result in a series of net cash flows over time: large outflows in the early years, as investments are made, then becoming positive, perhaps gradually, as the new facilities begin to generate revenue in excess of recurrent costs. Such a *time profile* of net cash flow is depicted in Fig. 6–6; it is the most common of several possible profiles. To summarize the value of this net cash flow in a single number, each year's net cash flow is multiplied by the respective discount factor and the resulting present values are added to give the ***net present value (NPV)***. Thus

$$NPV = \sum_{t=0}^{n} \frac{(B_t - C_t)}{(1 + i)^t} \qquad [6\text{--}19]$$

where B_t and C_t are the benefits (revenues) and costs, including investment, in each year, t; i is the discount rate; and n is the life of the project. For a

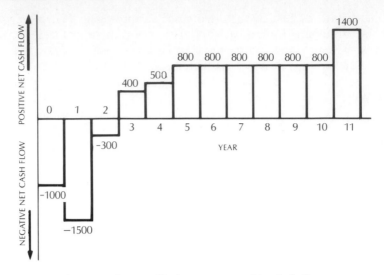

Fig. 6–6   Time Profile for Investment: Net Cash Flow.

Years 0 and 1: Investment in construction and equipment.
Year 2: Start-up period.
Years 3 and 4: Gradually increasing output.
Years 5 through 10: Steady output and cash flow.
Year 11: End of project; higher cash flow due to salvage of some equipment.

firm the correct discount rate is the average cost at which additional funds may be obtained from all sources, the firm's *cost of capital.*

If the net present value of a project, discounted at the firm's average cost of capital, happens to equal zero, this implies that the project will yield a net cash flow just large enough both to repay the principal of all funds invested in the project and to pay the interest and dividends required by lenders and shareholders. In that case, with NPV = 0, the discount rate has a special name, the **internal rate of return (IRR).** If the net present value is positive, then the project can cover all its financial costs with some profit left over for the firm. If negative, the project cannot cover its financial costs and should not be undertaken. Clearly the higher the net present value, the better the project.[2]

2. Another measure of project desirability is the **benefit-cost ratio,**

$$BCR = \frac{\sum_{t=0}^{n} B_t (1 + i)^{-t}}{\sum_{t=0}^{n} C_t (1 + i)^{-t}}$$

which simply rearranges equation 6–19 into ratio form. When NPV = 0, BCR = 1, so that desirable projects have NPV greater than zero or BCR greater than one. Although the BCR can be useful, it has the disadvantage that its precise value depends on sometimes arbitrary decisions about which cash flows to include in the numerator and which in the denominator. Neither the NPV nor the IRR calculation suffers from this ambiguity. However, the IRR has a different problem: there will be more than one IRR for a cash flow if at any time after the initial investment the cash flow again turns negative.

The cash flow of Fig. 6–6 is discounted at a discount rate of 12 percent in Table 6–3, using equation 6–19. The net present value is a positive $518, indicating that the investment project will earn enough to repay the total investment of $2500 with a surplus of $518.

This brings us to the third element in project appraisal, *comparison among projects.* We already know that a project should be considered for investment only if its net present value is positive. But how to choose among many projects, all with positive NPVs? The answer is to select that set of projects which will yield the highest total net present value for the entire investment budget. This assumes that the firm has a set of alternative projects to consider at any one time and an investment budget that can accommodate several but not all of these.

TABLE 6–3   Net Present Value

Year	Cash flow[a] from Fig. 6–2 (dollars)	Discount factor[b] at 12%	Present value[c] (dollars)
0	− 1000	1.000	− 1000
1	− 1500	0.893	− 1340
2	− 300	0.797	− 239
3	400	0.712	285
4	500	0.636	318
5	800	0.567	454
6	800	0.507	406
7	800	0.452	362
8	800	0.404	323
9	800	0.361	289
10	800	0.322	258
11	1400	0.207	402
Net Present Value[d]			+ 518

[a] Cash flow $= (B_t - C_t)$ from equation 6–19

[b] Discount factor $= 1/(1 + i)^t$ from equation 6–19. In this example, $i = 12\%$; t takes the value of each year, 0 to 11. Discount factors for a range of discount rates are readily available in discount tables. (See, for example, the appendix table in Michael Roemer and Joseph J. Stern, *The Appraisal of Development Projects* [New York: Praeger, 1975]).

[c] Present value = cash flow × discount factor.

[d] Net present value = algebraic sum of the present values.

Opportunity Costs

A country wishing to derive the greatest possible future income (or consumption) from the resources available for investment faces the same problem as the investing firm. The only difference is that the country is interested in *resource flows* and their *opportunity costs,* rather than cash flows. When any project in the public or private sector uses goods and services, it denies these to other possible projects. For example, investment in a dam requires utilization of savings that could otherwise be invested in a rural road or a textile factory; cotton used in that factory could otherwise have been exported to earn foreign exchange; or the labor used to build the road might have otherwise been used to build the dam or to grow cotton. To society the cost of undertaking a project is the value of the resources—

goods and services—used to invest in and operate the new facilities. The value of these resources is measured in terms of the net benefits they would have provided if used in some alternative project, the opportunity cost.

A simple illustration should capture this point. A textile factory is built and hires labor away from the rural areas. To the textile firm, the cost of labor is the wages paid. To society, however, the cost is the reduction in the value of production, net of costs, in the rural areas. If ten laborers migrate to take jobs in the new factory, their opportunity cost would be the reduction in agricultural output due to their leaving the farm, net of the nonlabor recurrent costs of producing that output. This reduction in net output is the ***marginal revenue product***[3] of price theory and is the opportunity cost of labor in this situation. Similarly, if the investment in the textile mill means that savings will be drawn away from other projects that would on average have earned a return of 12 percent, then the opportunity cost of capital is 12 percent and this should be used as the discount rate in evaluating the textile mill. Because project appraisals are most conveniently done at *constant prices,* netting out inflation, the discount rate is a *real* rate of interest, also net of inflation. If, in this example, inflation were 10 percent a year, the corresponding nominal interest rate, the rate observed in the market, would be 23 percent.[4]

Foreign exchange plays a special role in cost-benefit analysis. Most developing countries face a shortage of foreign exchange, in the sense that export revenues and foreign investment are not adequate to finance the imports needed to achieve growth and other development targets. When a project requires imports, such as capital equipment or raw materials, it reduces the foreign exchange available to other projects. If it yields additional foreign exchange by exporting its output or by substituting domestic production for imports, it benefits other projects by providing more foreign puchasing power. Thus the opportunity cost or benefit of any good that could be imported or exported should be measured as the net amount of foreign exchange the good represents. For example, the cotton used in the textile mill might have been exported otherwise; if so, its opportunity cost would be the foreign currency it would have earned as an export. If, however, the cloth produced would have been imported in the absence of the mill, its opportunity cost (a benefit in this case) would be the foreign exchange that would otherwise have been spent on cloth imports.

---

3. The marginal revenue product (MRP) of a factor of production can be defined as the revenue earned on the additional physical output which results when one unit of the factor is added to the production process with all other factors held constant.

4. The formula relating these is $1 + i_n = (1 + i_r)(1 + p)$, where i_n is the nominal rate of interest, i_r is the real rate, and p is the rate of inflation. Normally we know the nominal rate and need to calculate the real rate:

$$i_r = \frac{1 + i_n}{1 + p} - 1 = i_n - \frac{p_-}{1 + p_-}$$

For small values of i_n and p, i_r can be approximated by $i_r = i_n - p$.

Shadow Prices

The opportunity costs of goods and services are estimated for the economy as a whole and are called *shadow prices.* The first approximation of a shadow price—for land, labor, capital, foreign exchange—is the price paid by private participants in the market. Many interferences in the market distort market prices from their social opportunity cost: taxes and subsidies of all kinds, monopoly power, minimum wages, interest rate controls, tariffs and import quotas, price controls, and so forth. Prices that are observed in the market need to be adjusted for these effects before a good approximation of shadow prices can be found. A simple example is the wage of textile workers. If the government imposes minimum-wage regulations, the factory will probably have to pay a wage above the opportunity costs of rural migrants and urban workers who are outside the formal, protected urban wage sector.

Estimation of shadow prices is a research task that requires intimate knowledge of the workings of an economy, both its macroeconomic relationships and the microeconomic behavior of its factor markets. It is a task to be undertaken by a central planning agency, which then instructs other planning units—ministries, public enterprises, regional and local governments—in the application of these economy-wide shadow prices to the appraisal of development projects. The use of a single set of shadow prices by all planning agencies and public enterprises is one key to decentralized participative planning, coordinated to achieve national goals. Not only does shadow price estimation help improve the selection of development projects, but the estimation of these opportunity costs teaches the researchers a great deal about the working of the economy, itself an important by-product for a central planning agency.

Although there remains much controversy among economists on the precise estimation of shadow prices, some general results have emerged for a wide range of developing countries. First, and most significant, the shadow foreign exchange rate tends to be higher than the official rate in terms of local currency per dollar, perhaps 10 to 50 percent higher. This reflects the widespread use of import duties and quotas, as well as the reluctance of many countries to devalue their exchange rate despite the inflation of domestic prices. Part IV explores these problems. As a consequence, any export project that earns more foreign exchange than it uses, or any import-substituting project that saves more than it uses, gets a boost from the shadow exchange rate. In terms of the net cash flow profile of Fig. 6–6, application of the shadow rate to such projects will raise the positive net cash flows of years 4 through 12 proportionately more than it raises the negative flows of the first two years, giving the project a higher net present value at the same discount rate.

Although salaries and wages of skilled employees probably require no adjustment from market to shadow prices, it is frequently true that the opportunity cost of unskilled workers is lower than the wage in formal, urban labor markets (Chapter 8). Thus any project using unskilled labor, especially if it is located in a rural area, gets a boost because the shadow wage reduces costs without changing benefits.

The social discount rate can represent either the opportunity cost of investment and saving in the private sector, or the rate at which policy-makers wish to discount future benefits. The first method yields discount rates of 10 to 15 percent for the LDCs. The second approach usually employs a lower discount rate, but entails a shadow price of investment that raises the effective cost of capital. In either case discounting at social rates treats capital as a very scarce factor, discouraging any project with high initial investment costs, long gestation periods, and low net cash flows in the productive years. This system favors projects that generate their net benefits early, because these can be reinvested in other productive projects for continued growth, and projects that use abundant resources, especially labor, instead of scarce ones like capital.

Project Appraisal and National Goals

Project appraisal using social opportunity costs is a simple and powerful device to further certain national goals. Its underlying tenet is that saving should be allocated to investments yielding the greatest future income or consumption, automatically accommodating the goal of efficient resource use to promote maximum growth. This further implies that scarce resources, like foreign exchange, are more highly valued than the market would indicate. The subsidiary goals of improving foreign exchange earnings or reducing dependence on imports are also built in, because any project that efficiently increases exports or reduces imports is given a correspondingly higher net present value by the shadow exchange rate. Once the central planners establish a system of appraisal with shadow prices, then every agency that designs, evaluates, and proposes investment projects is automatically incorporating these national goals in their work.

An illustration of the power of shadow pricing is contained in Table 6–4. It depicts two projects with identical cash flows. However, one project (the textile mill) earns more foreign exchange than the other (a telecommunications system), net of foreign exchange expenditures, and also uses more labor. Because the shadow wage rate is below the market rate, the economic net present value of both projects is raised, but the more labor-intensive textile project benefits more (panel 2). When the shadow exchange rate is applied, the net present value of the exchange-earning textile mill is raised considerably, but that of the telecommunications system, which is a net user of foreign exchange, falls and becomes negative (panel 3).

Not all national goals can be conveniently incorporated into project appraisal, however. Two are of particular concern. The use of low shadow wages for unskilled workers will encourage employment creation but only insofar as this is efficient, in the sense that workers' opportunity cost is below the net benefit they would produce in the project. Government may, however, want to encourage employment beyond this point, because a job

TABLE 6–4   Effects of Shadow Pricing on Cost-Benefit Analysis

1. Take two projects with identical cash flows, but project A earns more net foreign exchange and uses more labor than project B:

Project	Investment (first year)	Net annual cash flow (next 5 years)	Net present value at 10%
A. Textile mill of which:	− 1000	+ 300	+ 137
Net foreign exchange earned	− 500	+ 400	
Wages paid	− 350	− 100	
B. Telecommunications system of which:	− 1000	+ 300	+ 137
Net foreign exchange earned	− 800	0	
Wages paid	− 100	− 50	

2. *Shadow wage* is 75% of market wage, so all wage costs are reduced by 25%. This results in the following net cash flows:

	Investment	Net annual flow	NPV (10%)
A. Textile mill	− 913	+ 325	+ 319
B. Telecommunications system	− 975	+ 313	+ 212

3. *Shadow exchange rate* is 20% above official rate, so net foreign exchange flow is raised by 20%. This results in the following net cash flows:

	Investment	Net annual flow	NPV (10%)
A. Textile mill	− 1100	+ 380	l 340
B. Telecommunications system	− 1160	+ 300	− 23

is the most significant way that people can participate in development and employed workers may be deemed politically more stable (Chapter 8). If projects such as rural public works employ people inefficiently for the sake of employment, then the role of cost-benefit analysis is to estimate the cost of the employment in terms of the greater net benefits that might be earned if investment and labor were allocated to other projects that employ fewer people.

A second class of goals, income redistribution or poverty alleviation, can also be served by project appraisal, because low shadow wages encourage the employment of low-income labor. The impact may be weak, however, because distributional goals are still subordinate to efficient growth in the cost-benefit framework. Situations requiring structural change and large investments to alleviate poverty may not measure up to the high efficiency standard of project analysis in the short run. For this reason some economists have suggested, and some governments have considered, using *welfare weights* in project analysis. These would place a higher value on net additional income to certain target groups, such as families in the lower 40 percent of the income distribution. (We have already seen such a welfare weight: w_3 of the linear programming objective function, equation 6–17, gave an additional value of 75 percent to any income going to the poorest 40 percent of society.) Then projects generating such incomes would have higher NPVs than otherwise and would tend to be selected with greater frequency.

The method is potentially powerful, but has its dangers as well. The welfare premiums are arbitrary weights, subject to planners' or politicians' judgments. This in itself is not bad, but these weights can so overwhelm the other, economically based, shadow prices that project selection comes down to a choice based almost entirely on arbitrary weights. This gives a false sense of precision.

Shadow prices based on existing economic conditions are not value free, either. They imply a welfare weighting scheme that accepts the existing income distribution and the resulting pattern of demand. A compromise is to keep the two goals separate, making measurements of net present values using only the economic variables, then identifying separately the redistributional benefits of projects. The two can be compared, giving the decision-makers a trade-off to consider and the opportunity to make clear choices of goal priorities.

We have skirted an issue of terminology. When a firm undertakes investment analysis, it can be called *commercial project appraisal,* which uses *market* prices. Once *shadow prices* are introduced to reflect the goal of efficient growth and the real scarcities of productive factors, it has been traditional to call this *social project appraisal.* The implication may be too large, however, because only economic, and not other social goals are incorporated. The World Bank, which undertakes a large fraction of the project analysis done in the world, has shifted to a more accurate terminology. It calls the second form *economic project appraisal.* The term *social appraisal* is reserved for a third stage, in which welfare weights are applied to reflect distributional goals. But readers should be wary, because this relatively recent distinction has not yet been widely accepted in the literature.

Transforming Market Prices into Shadow Prices

If governments undertake projects on the basis of economic appraisals, using shadow prices, a problem of implementation arises. A firm, whether a public or private enterprise, can only be financially sound if it covers costs and earns a profit at market prices. The shadow prices of planners exist only on paper; no one pays them or receives them in the marketplace. To take one of many possible examples, consider a public enterprise producing chemicals whose investment is encouraged by the planning ministry because it employs many workers whose opportunity cost is low. However, the enterprise must pay its workers not the low shadow wage, but the higher minimum wage set by the government. If this causes the firm to lose money it could go bankrupt, in which case the economic benefits to the country would be lost. (A private firm, of course, would never undertake such an investment.) Hence if the government wants the project implemented it would have to compensate the enterprise. The most effective compensation would be a direct subsidy to wages, up to the difference between the shadow and minimum wages. Not only would this improve the firm's cash flow, but it would also give the firm an incentive to use more labor because its wage costs would be lower. This is precisely what government wants: to employ more workers, an abundant resource with low opportunity costs, and less of other, relatively scarce factors of production like capital and foreign exchange.

The same holds for any factor of production that is shadow-priced: labor, capital, foreign exchange, and specific commodities. Whenever shadow prices push projects that are commercially unprofitable into the realm of the economically profitable, a subsidy may have to be paid to induce a firm to undertake the project. And, conversely, if economically undesirable projects are nevertheless profitable at market prices, government should consider imposing taxes to discourage firms from undertaking such projects.

This leads to a more general point about shadow prices. They represent the opportunity costs that ideally functioning markets should be generating to give the right price signals to private producers and consumers. If any of the market imperfections, discussed in Chapter 5, intervene to distort market prices from this ideal, then one object of government policy might be to move all market prices toward shadow prices, either by removing imperfections or by imposing compensatory taxes and subsidies. If government can accomplish this, then resources would be used efficiently, that is, according to their relative scarcities. Generally, this would promote economic growth, although some interventions might still be necessary to accommodate externalities, infant industries, and institutional deficiencies.

Policies that move market prices toward shadow prices are at the core of "getting prices right." This implies both a reduction in controls and the movement of prices toward opportunity costs, which may require changes in indirect taxation and other changes in market prices. Government ownership can be consistent with "getting prices right"; indeed this is the essence of Lange's system of market socialism, mentioned in Chapter 5. Later chapters will suggest some of the elements of a price structure that approximates opportunity costs: market-determined wages (Chapter 8), interest rates (Chapter 13), and exchange rates (Part IV). The kinds of market failures covered in Chapter 5 may warrant deviations from market-determined prices, but these need to be carefully designed, moderate, and temporary. Finally, as discussed in Chapter 5, not all national goals are served by enforcing shadow prices on the market, since these accept and tend to perpetuate existing structural conditions, especially the distribution of income. If certain social goals and shadow prices are in conflict, the government must either choose between competing goals or seek compromise solutions. The nature of this choice is explored at many junctures in the rest of this book.

Appendix: The Leontief Inverse Matrix

The set of simultaneous equations derived from the input-output matrix of Table 6–2 was given as:

$$X_1 = \begin{bmatrix} a_{11}X_1 + a_{12}X_2 + a_{13}X_3 + a_{14}X_4 \\ a_{21}X_2 + a_{22}X_2 + a_{23}X_3 + a_{24}X_4 \\ a_{31}X_1 + a_{32}X_2 + a_{33}X_3 + a_{34}X_4 \\ a_{41}X_1 + a_{42}X_2 + a_{43}X_3 + a_{44}X_4 \end{bmatrix}$$

$$X_1 = \begin{bmatrix} a_{11}X_1 + a_{12}X_2 + a_{13}X_3 + a_{14}X_4 \end{bmatrix} + F_1 \qquad \text{[6-13]}$$

$$X_2 = \begin{bmatrix} a_{21}X_2 + a_{22}X_2 + a_{23}X_3 + a_{24}X_4 \end{bmatrix} + F_2 \qquad \text{[6-14]}$$

$$X_3 = \begin{bmatrix} a_{31}X_1 + a_{32}X_2 + a_{33}X_3 + a_{34}X_4 \end{bmatrix} + F_3 \qquad \text{[6-15]}$$

$$X_4 = \begin{bmatrix} a_{41}X_1 + a_{42}X_2 + a_{43}X_3 + a_{44}X_4 \end{bmatrix} + F_4 \qquad \text{[6-16]}$$

These equations can be restated in matrix form as follows:

$$\mathbf{X} = A\mathbf{X} + \mathbf{F} \qquad \text{[6-20]}$$

Here, $\mathbf{X}$ is a *vector* (a column) of the four values of output and $\mathbf{F}$ is a vector of the four values of final demand. The matrix A is the central part of the Leontief matrix in Table 6–2, the sixteen coefficients, a_{ij}, arranged in rows and columns of four each. Thus equation 6–20 represents the four equations 6–13 through 6–16; the term $A\mathbf{X}$ in equation 6–20 stands for the part of equations 6–13 to 6–16 that is shown in brackets, giving the intermediate uses of each product. Another way of expressing equation 6–20 is

$$X_i = \Sigma a_{ij}X_j + F_i \qquad \text{[6-21]}$$

where the sum of terms $a_{ij}X_j$ does the same thing as the matrix term, $A\mathbf{X}$.

Equation 6–20 can be solved as if it were a simple algebraic expression: collect like terms on the left side, giving $\mathbf{X} - A\mathbf{X} = (I - A)\mathbf{X} = \mathbf{F}$; then divide through by $(I - A)$ to get

$$\mathbf{X} = (I - A)^{-1}\mathbf{F} \qquad \text{[6-22]}$$

The term I is not the number one, but the equivalent in matrix algebra, the *indentity matrix.* It consists of a diagonal of ones and zeroes everywhere else; multiply any matrix by the identity matrix and the result is the original matrix. The term $(I - A)^{-1}$ is the *inverse* of the matrix $I - A$, in the same sense that $x^{-1} = 1/x$. Equation 6–21 then says that if we know the bill of final products, we can find the total quantity of each good required, allowing for all intermediate uses, either directly or indirectly. That is, if we know the matrix $(I - A)^{-1}$, we can solve the endless chain of inputs and outputs quite easily for any number of sectors. This matrix manipulation is much easier than the brute-force method of simultaneous equations, especially for a large number of sectors. And some readers will recognize that the matrix method is in fact the one used to solve large systems of simultaneous equations.

The matrix $(I - A)^{-1}$ is called the **Leontief inverse,** and can be easily tabulated by a computer for any Leontief matrix, A, using the rules of matrix inversion which we will not attempt to explain here. The result for our simple A-matrix of Table 6–2 is shown in Table 6–5, which gives the total use of each input per unit of final demand. It shows that, for example, to produce one unit of consumer goods for final use, F_2, requires 0.38 units of primary goods, 1.11 units of consumer goods (including the 1 unit of final goods), 0.40 of producer goods, and 0.22 of services. These coefficients are always higher than the a_{ij}'s, because they account for both the *direct and indirect* uses of any good. All diagonal elements are greater than 1 because they include the final use of output. The direct plus indirect coefficients are sometimes designated r_{ij}, analogous to the a_{ij}.

TABLE 6–5   Leontief Inverse of Direct Plus Indirect Coefficients[a]

	X_1	X_2	X_3	X_4
Primary(X_1)	1.10	0.38	0.31	0
Consumer goods (X_2)	0	1.11	0	0
Producer goods (X_3)	0.24	0.40	1.50	0
Services (X_4)	0.20	0.22	0.41	1.25

[a] From Table 6–2.

The seminal works on the Harrod-Domar model are Roy F. Harrod, "An Essay in Dynamic Theory," *Economic Journal* 49 (1939): 14–33; and Evsey Domar, "Capital Expansion, Rate of Growth and Employment," *Econometrica* 14 (1946): 137–47, and "Expansion and Employment," *American Economic Review* 37 (1947): 34–55. Robert Solow, "A Contribution to the Theory of Economic Growth," *Quarterly Journal of Economics* 70 (1956): 56–94, introduced the neoclassical production function as a model that avoids certain unstable ("knife-edge") properties of the Harrod-Domar approach. For a graduate-level text that treats these growth models, see Hywel Jones, *An Introduction to Modern Theories of Economic Growth* (New York: McGraw-Hill, 1976).

FURTHER READING

The father of econometric policy planning analysis is Jan Tinbergen, who created a system of macroeconomic modeling for this purpose in three works: *Economic Policy: Principles and Design* (Amsterdam: North-Holland, 1956); *On the Theory of Economic Policy* (Amsterdam: North-Holland, 1963); and *Central Planning* (New Haven: Yale University Press, 1976).

On interindustry analysis, the beginning student should consult Hollis Chenery and Paul Clark, *Interindustry Economics* (New York: Wiley, 1959). The standard text on the economic theory of input-output analysis and linear programming is Robert Dorfman, Paul Samuelson, and Robert Solow, *Linear Programming and Economic Analysis* (New York: McGraw-Hill, 1958). Advanced students should read Lance Taylor's tour-de-force of the state of the art in planning models, "Theoretical Foundations and Technical Implications," in C. R. Blitzer et al., (eds.), *Economy-Wide Models and Development Planning* (London: Oxford University Press, 1975), a collection that includes several other articles of interest.

Lance Taylor has also explored various applications of planning models in a recent book, *Macro Models for Developing Countries* (New York: McGraw-Hill, 1979). Another recent collection of model applications is in Jere Behrman and James A. Hanson, *Short-term Macroeconomic Policy in Latin America* (Cambridge, Mass.: National Bureau of Economic Research, 1979). Collections by Irma Adelman and Erik Thorbecke (eds.), *The Theory and Design of Economic Development* (Baltimore: Johns Hopkins University Press, 1966), and Hollis B. Chenery (ed.), *Studies in Development Planning* (Cambridge, Mass.: Harvard University Press, 1971), contain articles on a wide range of applications of the models described in this chapter.

There is a burgeoning literature on benefit-cost analysis which, like macroeconomic planning, is worth a one-semester course in itself. Richard Brealey and Stewart Myers, *Principles of Corporate Finance* (New York: McGraw-Hill, 1981), covers investment analysis for the firm, while Michael Roemer and Joseph J. Stern, *The Appraisal of Development Projects* (New York: Praeger, 1975), provides introductory text and case studies in social (economic) project appraisal. For graduate students, three basic treatises, each proposing a different system of social appraisal, are essential: Arnold C. Harberger, *Project Evaluation: Collected Papers* (Chicago: Markham, 1974); I. M. D. Little and James A. Mirrlees, *Project Appraisal and Planning for Developing Countries* (New York: Basic Books, 1974); and United Nations Industrial Development Organization [P. Dasgupta, S. Margolin, and A. Sen], *Guidelines for Project Evaluation* (New York: United Nations, 1972).

HUMAN
RESOURCES

Chapter 7
POPULATION

The chapters in this part deal with the human factor in economic development. People play a dual role in the development process: on the one hand they are its ultimate beneficiaries; on the other they provide an important input (in the final analysis, *the* most important input) into the process of production growth and transformation which is called economic development.

In view of this dual role, what attitude should one take toward the growth of population at the family, national, and global level? Should population growth be limited on the ground that it creates more mouths to be fed and bodies to be clothed, frequently in households and societies which are having trouble feeding the mouths and clothing the bodies that they already have? World population projections and estimates of resource pressures make frightening reading. Yet each new individual can also bring additional labor power, and even more important, additional human spark and creativity to help solve the many problems which society faces. The argument for some form of population limitation is strong, but agreement is not universal and there are important social, political, and moral issues to be weighed.

The decision of how many children to have is an intimately personal one. Traditionally it has been left to the choice of the couple involved, although all societies condition these individual decisions in many different ways. Arguments *for* conscious policy intervention to limit births must depend either on the rationale that couples do not know what is good for them (for instance, because they lack knowledge on how to limit births) or on the belief that individual reproductive decisions impose excessive social costs at the national and/or international levels. Arguments *against* intervention may appeal either to the value of freedom for the individual or to the alleged advantages of a larger population for a nation or other social grouping. These arguments, and the facts and theories which lie behind them, form the subject matter of this chapter.

Various aspects of the people-as-a-resource concept will be discussed in Chapters 8 through 10. The human resource has quantitative and qualitative dimensions. Often in economic theory the quantitative aspect is emphasized and the qualitative aspect downplayed or ignored. Many economic models assume that labor is homogeneous or undifferentiated and thus can be defined and measured satisfactorily by counting bodies, or hours or days of work. Other models make broad distinctions between skilled and unskilled labor. Such models, although useful for revealing particular truths, are rather extreme simplifications, since the study of economic development clearly demonstrates that the qualitative aspects of the human contribution to production are *at least* as important as the quantitative aspects.

While "labor" is an old way of referring to the human factor of production, newer and more fashionable terms are *human resources* and *human capital.* These phrases embrace qualitative as well as quantitative aspects of the human role in production. Development specialists often talk about "developing human resources" or "investing in human capital." The analogy to natural resources and physical capital is appropriate in many ways. But it can be misleading if it is taken to imply that the nature of "human resources" and the way they contribute to production are understood as fully as the contributions of a lathe, a road, or a ton of bauxite are understood. The role of the human resource is far more complex and mysterious than any of these. To what extent, and in what ways, human resources can be created through an investment-like process are questions addressed in Chapters 8 through 10.

The present chapter lays a foundation for the later discussion by reviewing what is known about population and development. We begin by examining the staggering facts of world population.

The World's Population

History

The demographic history of the world can be divided into several periods, each of which has been characterized by different economic, social, and public health patterns and therefore by different population structures and dynamics. Here four demographic eras will be distinguished.[1]

The Preagricultural Era   During the preagricultural era humankind lived a precarious existence as hunters, gatherers, and at least occasionally, cannibals. Population densities (numbers of people per square kilometer)

1. Based on Lester R. Brown, *In the Human Interest* (New York: W. W. Norton, 1974), pp. 20–21; for an informative and enjoyable longer presentation, see Carlo Cipolla, *The Economic History of World Population* (Harmondsworth, Middlesex, England: Penguin Books, 1962).

were very low. They had to be, since a given population required a vast extent of land to sustain itself. Birth rates were probably high, perhaps thirty-five to fifty births per thousand of population per year.[2] If birth rates were high, death rates must have been high also, since any significant rate of natural increase over this period of perhaps two million years would have produced a total population vastly larger than the one which actually came to be. Archeological evidence suggests that as many as half of all deaths during this first era of the world's demographic history were from violent causes.[3] Female infanticide appears to have been widespread. On the other hand the thinness of the population distribution may have impeded the spread of epidemics.

From Settled Agriculture to the Industrial Revolution   The development of settled agriculture revolutionized the capacity of the earth to sustain human life. The era from the start of settled agriculture up to the Industrial Revolution of the early nineteenth century lasted around 12,000 years. During this era the introduction and gradual improvement of crop cultivation and livestock management enormously expanded the food supply and increased its reliability. The death rate fell, life expectancy increased, and slow but gradually accelerating growth of population began. This growth, however, was set back at intervals by plagues, famines, and wars (often war led to plague or famine), which might wipe out one-fifth, one-third, or even one-half of the population in a given area.

From the Industrial Revolution to World War II   The next major economic event to condition world population growth was the Industrial Revolution. The third demographic era can be defined as beginning with the Industrial Revolution up to World War II. The start of modern economic growth greatly expanded the population-carrying capacity of the earth. Innovations in industry were matched by innovations in agriculture which made it possible to release labor to industry and raise the productivity of the remaining agricultural laborers high enough to feed the growing urban population. Improved transportation, especially transcontinental roads and fast, reliable ocean shipping, further boosted world food output, making it possible to grow more basic foodstuffs in the areas best suited for this activity and to get supplies to food-deficit areas quickly in emergencies. Famines

2. To follow the discussion in this chapter, the reader needs to know a few simple definitions. The *birth rate,* also called the crude birth rate, is births per thousand of population. By the same token the (crude) *death rate* is deaths per thousand of population. The *rate of natural increase* is the difference between the birth rate and the death rate, but it is conventionally measured in percentage terms (that is, per hundred rather than per thousand). Say an LDC has a population of 10,000,000 at the start of a given year. During the year it experiences 400,000 births and 150,000 deaths. If net international migration (immigration minus emigration) is zero, its population at the end of the year is 10,250,000. The mid-year, or average, population is used in calculating the birth rate, death rate, and rate of natural increase, which in this case turn out to be 39.5, 14.8, and 2.47 respectively. A final term used later in the chapter is *infant death rate.* This refers to deaths in the first year of life per thousand live births. Thus if 40,000 of the 400,000 babies born in our hypothetical country died before reaching their first birthdays, the infant death rate would be 100.
3. Cipolla, *Economic History*, p. 79.

declined in frequency and severity. Food prices fell absolutely in many parts of the world. Meanwhile modern medicine, sanitation, and pharmaceutical production began to be developed. All these factors helped to reduce the death rate. Population growth accelerated, reaching about 1 percent per annum by World War II. This third demographic era lasted approximately 100 years.

A feature of the third demographic era was major change in the location of world population. Between 1846 and 1930 more than fifty million people left Europe to settle in other parts of the world. The United States received the bulk of them, while smaller numbers went to Canada, Brazil, Argentina, Chile, South Africa, Australia, and New Zealand. It is estimated that the proportion of world population that was of "European stock" grew from 22 percent in 1846 to 35 percent in 1930, when the Great Depression put an end to the era of mass international migration.[4] During this same period millions of laborers and merchants from overpopulated India and China moved to less densely populated areas in Southeast Asia, Africa, the South Pacific, and elsewhere. The existence of colonial empires facilitated this movement.

The Post–World War II Period The present post–World War II era has seen dramatic further improvements in food supply and disease control. Techniques introduced in the industrialized countries during the preceding era spread throughout the globe. People became more aware of famines and epidemics in "remote" parts of the world and less willing to tolerate them. The result was a veritable revolution in death rates and life expectancy. Plummeting death rates in many areas caused rates of natural increase to rise to 2 or even 3 percent. This latest demographic era is not yet four decades old.

Perhaps the most striking feature of world population growth over the long sweep of history is the dramatic acceleration of change and foreshortening of the demographic eras. By now everyone is familiar with the awesome implications of compound interest, by which seemingly innocuous rates of growth create enormous cumulated totals over the course of time. Although the growth rate of world population never exceeded 1 percent a year before World War II, the total population of the globe has doubled and redoubled through history. It is thought that world population was no more than 250 million at the time of Christ. Not until the early nineteenth century was the 1 billion mark reached. As recently as 1950 world population was "only" 2.5 billion. Now it exceeds 4 billion.

Population growth has not accelerated uniformly in all parts of the globe. All the industrial countries have experienced a *demographic transition.* That is, starting from a pattern of high birth rates and high death rates, they have seen, first, a fall in the death rate which raised the rate of natural increase, and then some years later a fall in the birth rate which brought

4. For discussion, see Cipolla, *Economic History,* pp. 101–4.

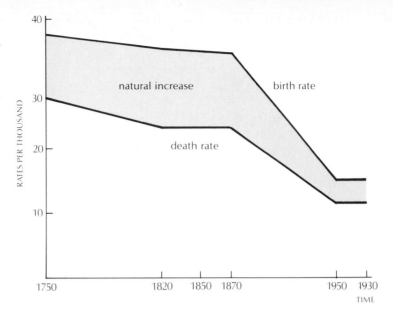

FIG. 7-1   The Demographic Transition in England and Wales, 1750–1950.

[Source: Carlo Cipolla, *The Economic History of World Population* (Harmondworth, Middlesex, England: Penguin Books, 1962), p. 85.]

natural increase back down to the neighborhood of 1 percent. The demographic transition as it occurred in England and Wales is depicted in Fig. 7–1.

During the present demographic era the developing countries have apparently begun to experience a demographic transition of their own. Shortly after World War II death rates began to fall almost everywhere. The causes of this drop in mortality are discussed below in Chapter 10. Here we need only note that death rates in the LDCs began to decline at much lower levels of per-capita income and fell much faster than had those in the developed countries previously. An example is given in Fig. 7–2, which depicts the demographic experience of Ceylon (now Sri Lanka) during the twentieth century. (Note that Figs. 7–1 and 7–2 are drawn to the same scale.) These early and sharp death rate declines, which have now been achieved for practically the entire population of the world, have created rates of natural increase in this last demographic era which far exceed anything witnessed in prior history: around 2 percent for world population as a whole, 3 percent or more in some of the fastest growing countries.

Although most LDCs have experienced a drop in the death rate, not all of them have yet undergone the lagged decline in the birth rate evident in Sri Lanka since 1955 (Fig. 7–2). In some countries the birth rate has fallen little, if at all. Just how the "new demographic transition" will work in the third world is a question to which we will return later on.

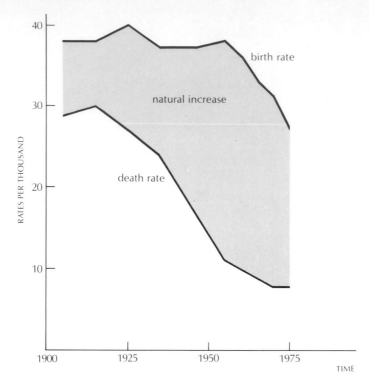

FIG. 7–2   The Demographic Transition in Ceylon (Sri Lanka), 1900–1975.

Present Demographic Situation

The world today exhibits a kind of demographic dualism. The developed countries of Europe and North America are well along on the demographic transition, with birth rates of less than twenty per thousand of population and rates of natural increase below 1 percent. Their population growth is likely to remain low.[5] In some developed countries current fertility is just high enough to replace the existing population. In fact the state of zero population growth (ZPG), promoted by some as a desirable target in view of limitations on natural resources, may not be too far away in industrialized countries.

The developed countries by contrast are at a much earlier stage in the demographic transition—if indeed they are entering a comparable transition process at all. May low-income countries have birth rates of forty or more. Yet their death rates are only ten to twenty, not much higher than those of the rich countries. This means that they are experiencing rates of natural increase of 2–3 percent a year. Since three-fourths of world population is in the developing countries, the average rate of growth of world population is nearly 2 percent (Table 7–1).

5. But demographic behavior does sometimes surprise the experts. They were confounded, for example, by the post–World War II "baby boom" in the United States.

TABLE 7-1   World Population by Region and Development Category, 1980[a]

	Total population		Annual growth rate 1970–1980 (%)	Population density (persons per km²
	Number (millions)	% of total		
By region				
Africa	476	11	2.7	17
Asia	2345	53	2.1	95
Oceania and Indonesia	169	4	2.2	16
Europe	802	8	1.6	29
North and Central America	373	5	2.2	17
South America	238	18	0.8	14
By development category				
Developing countries	3300	75	2.2	46
Low income	2161	49	2.1	70
Middle income	1139	26	2.5	27
High-income oil exporters	14	< 1	5.0	4
Developed countries	1068	24	0.8	20
Market economies	714	16	0.8	23
Nonmarket economies	353	8	0.8	15
World total	4403	100	1.9	34

Source: World Bank, *1981 World Bank Atlas* (Washington, D.C., 1982); World Bank, *World Development Report 1982* (Washington, D.C., 1982), pp. 110–11, 142–43.

[a] The population density column and the entire upper part of the table include countries with population of 1 million or more only. The USSR and Turkey are classified as European countries.

Table 7–2 shows some demographic and population-structure characteristics typical of countries at different levels of GNP per capita. In the Part A of the table one can see something like the "demographic transition" pattern reflected in these cross-section data. After some increase at low income levels, birth rates decline as one moves from countries with per-capita incomes below $500 to countries with higher income levels. Death rates also decline at income rises above $500. Middle-income countries have the highest rates of natural increase. Above $500 per capita (see column 3 in Table 7–2A), the decline of the birth rate causes the rate of natural increase to decline sharply. It is worth noting that many (although not all) of the third world countries that have seen reductions in population growth have also been among the most successful in raising per-capita income. Table 7–3 gives the same information as Table 7–2 for selected countries, providing some idea of the range of intercountry variation.

The infant death rate (see footnote 2, above) is an especially sensitive measure of death rate decline, falling by 84 percent from the poorest group of countries in Table 7–2 to the richest group. This fall in infant deaths causes more children to survive, creating population structures in which children make up very large fractions of the population (see Tables 7–2B and 7–3B). Countries with this age structure are said to have a high ***dependency ratio,*** or ratio of nonworking age population (conventionally measured as zero to fourteen and sixty-five and over) to working age population. A high dependency ratio depresses per-capita income by re-

TABLE 7-2   Demographic and Population Characteristics of Countries by Level of GNP Per Capita, 1980[a]

Income group	A. Demographic Characteristics			
	Crude birth rate (per thousand)	Crude death rate (per thousand)	Rate of natural increase (%)	Infant death rate (per 1000 live births)
Below $200	43	20	2.3	139
$200–$300	43	17	2.6	129
$300–$500	47	18	2.9	127
$500–$1000	41	12	2.9	93
$1000–$2000	35	9	2.6	64
$2000–$5000	24	9	1.5	39
Above $5,000	18	10	0.8	22

Income group	B. Population Characteristics		
	Population below 14 years, 1978 (% of total)	Growth rate of urban population, 1970–1980 (%)	Urban population (% of total)
Below $200	43	5.2	16
$200–$300	41	5.7	16
$300–$500	44	6.1	22
$500–$1000	44	4.9	38
$1000–$2000	43	4.2	49
$2000–$5000	35	2.8	64
Above $5000	26	2.7	74

Source: World Bank, *World Development Report 1982* (Washington, D.C., 1982), pp. 110–11, 142–45; Dorothy L. Nortman and Ellen Hofstatter, *Population and Family Planning Programs: A Compendium of Data through 1978* (New York: Population Council, 1980), pp. 4–16.

quiring that the output of a given number of producers be shared among a large number of consumers.

The *spatial distribution* of the population is another concern in many low-income countries. *Urbanization* is an inevitable concomitant of development (Table 7–2). Many people have argued that the growth of urban areas through migration of people from the countryside is proceeding too fast and is causing serious social problems. Yet third world governments that have tried to staunch the flow have found the task all but impossible. The reason is that people have found that they can better themselves in several ways by moving to the city. Not only do they earn higher incomes than they could have obtained in the rural areas, but they gain better access to schooling for their children and social services of other kinds. This is what people seek in rural-urban migration, and studies have shown that by and large they find it. This raises an important question: if rural-urban migration is good for the people who move, is it really bad for society? It is true that there are external social costs associated with the migration process: congestion may make it harder to provide adequate urban infrastructure and social services. (To some extent these costs arise because governments feel obliged to provide facilities to urban populations which they do not provide to rural populations.) But the common perception of urbanization as a problem also contains an element of class bias. Ruling

TABLE 7-3   Demographic and Population Characteristics of Selected Countries, 1980

A. Demographic Characteristics

Country	Crude birth rate (per thousand)	Crude death rate (per thousand)	Rate of natural increase (%)	Infant death rate (per 1000 live births)
Bolivia	43	16	2.7	131
Brazil	30	9	2.1	77
Chile	22	7	1.5	43
Colombia	30	8	2.2	56
Peru	36	11	2.5	88
Ghana	48	17	3.1	103
Kenya	51	13	3.8	87
Tanzania	46	15	3.1	103
China	21	8	1.3	56
India	36	14	2.2	123
Indonesia	35	13	2.2	93
South Korea	24	7	1.7	34
Malaysia	31	7	2.4	31
Pakistan	44	16	2.8	126
Sri Lanka	28	7	2.1	44

B. Population Characteristics

	Population below 14 years, 1978 (% of total)	Growth rate of urban population, 1970–1980 (%)	Population density per square kilometer	Urban population (% of total)
Bolivia	42	4.1	5	33
Brazil	41	4.1	14	68
Chile	35	2.3	15	80
Colombia	42	3.9	23	70
Peru	43	4.2	14	67
Ghana	46	5.1	49	36
Kenya	47	6.8	27	14
Tanzania	43	8.7	20	12
China	33	NA	102	13
India	41	3.3	205	22
Indonesia	43	4.0	76	20
South Korea	39	4.7	390	55
Malaysia	40	3.3	42	29
Pakistan	47	4.3	102	28
Sri Lanka	39	3.6	223	27

Source: World Bank, World Development Report 1982 (Washington, D.C., 1982), pp. 110–11, 144–45, 148–49; Dorothy L. Nortman and Ellen Hofstatter, Population and Family Planning Programs: A Compendium of Data Through 1978 (New York: Population Council, 1980), pp. 5–12.

elites sometimes feel threatened by rapid growth in the number of poor people who live, so to speak, within marching distance of the palace.

Some third world governments have tried to accelerate the development of secondary towns or backward regions of the country. To the extent that these policies attempt to counteract the existing pattern of incentives affecting the location of population and economic activity, they frequently fail. To make them succeed, governments at least have to commit large amounts of their own resources to the backward areas in the form of infrastructure and public facilities. It may be that nothing less than a radical shift in development strategy to a genuine emphasis on the intensification and diversification of the rural economy will do the job.

The Demographic Future

When extrapolated into the future, a population growth rate of 2 percent, or even 1 percent, fairly quickly generates projected total populations which may strike one as unthinkable. For example, continued growth at 2 percent would bring world population to 6.3 billion in the year 2000 and 17 billion by 2050. Even if population growth were cut to 1 percent the world would still be headed toward 5 billion inhabitants in 2000 and 8.3 billion by 2050.

This type of projection, beloved by popular writers, makes frightening reading for many. It is hard to imagine life in a world with two to four times as many people as there are today. How will this expanded population live? What will be the impact on the globe's finite supplies of space and natural resources? Shouldn't population growth be slowed down? But *can* it be slowed down? What *are* the prospects for population growth in the future? These are obviously vital questions which concern everyone.

The brighter side of the picture is that there are grounds for hope that the developing countries will undergo a demographic transition, as the industrial countries did before them. But it is already evident that there will be some differences in the experiences of the two groups of countries. As has been noted, the decline in death rates in the developing countries has been occurring at much lower levels of per-capita income than in the earlier cases. What is not yet known is how fast birth rates will decline. In the last decade or so the beginnings of birth rate decline have begun to be visible in many, although not yet in all, developing countries. As Table 7–4 shows, the drop in the crude birth rate for the third world as a whole in 1965–1975 was about 15 percent. China, with its population of roughly one billion, made a major contribution to this reduction. A number of much smaller countries (all located in either Latin America or East Asia) have evidenced even sharper birth rate declines. No one can say with any precision how far and fast this trend toward lower birth rates will move. Demographic projections are adjusted up and down as each new census or survey result comes in.

TABLE 7–4   Crude Birth Rate Decline in 94 Developing Countries, 1960–1980

Region	Crude birth rate		% decline 1960–1980	1980 population of included countries (millions)
	1960	1980		
Africa	48	46	4	468
Asia				
China	40	21	48	977
Others	44	36	18	1444
Latin America	42	33	21	352
Total	43	32	26	3237

Source: World Bank, *World Development Report 1982* (Washington, D.C., 1982), pp. 110–11, 144–45.

It is certain, however, that world population will become much bigger in the future than it is now. This is assured by the phenomenon of **demographic momentum.** Even if all couples were to start today to have only enough children to replace themselves in the population, growth would continue into the early part of the twenty-first century. This certainty is based on the age structure of the current population. Because there are so many people in the more fertile age brackets, births will exceed deaths and world population will continue to grow for some time even if fertility drops rapidly to the replacement level. It has been estimated that if the whole world were to achieve the replacement level of fertility by the year 2000, world population would still grow to 8.1 billion by 2050.[6]

Views on World Population Growth

So there will be continuing growth of world population at least over the better part of the next century. Most of this growth will occur in the third world. Viewpoints on this prospect vary, and discussions of world population frequently turn acrimonious, especially when they are conducted on the global or ideological level. Some of the most sensitive aspects involve the questions of whose population is to be limited, and by what means.

Since the highest population densities are to be found in Asia[7] and the highest rates of natural increases are in Africa and Latin America, there is a natural tendency for people to say that responsibility for limiting population growth rests with the countries of those regions. For a number of years international organizations, voluntary groups, and even governments of industrial countries have vigorously urged third world governments to take more decisive action to limit their population growth, and have offered them various forms of assistance for the effort.

It was probably inevitable that this campaign would generate a negative reaction from people in the poor countries. Several influential groups had long denied that population growth was a problem—or at least that it was the *real* problem:

1. The Roman Catholic church, with over half a billion adherents and extensive influence throughout Latin America, in the Philippines, and elsewhere, had long opposed any use of artificial contraception to limit reproduction among its adherents. Although there appears to have been a gradual decline in the strictness with which members follow the teachings of the church in this regard, the official position remains unchanged, and influences both individual actions of church members and public policies in predominantly Catholic countries.

2. Muslim doctrine, although less clear-cut, is also frequently interpreted

6. See Thomas Frejka, *The Future of Population Growth* (New York: Population Council, 1973).

7. Strictly speaking this is true only if the USSR is regarded as wholly European, as in Table 7–1. If the Asian part of the USSR is removed from the European area total, population density in Europe is higher than in Asia. But European population growth is already very slow.

as prohibiting birth control. This influences another half billion or so adherents, mostly in Asia and Africa.

3. Marxist spokesmen argue that population pressure in capitalist countries is merely one more manifestation of class conflict. In a socialist society the problem will disappear because it will be possible to organize society "scientifically," thus providing full employment and fulfillment of everyone's basic needs. In the meantime capitalist efforts to promote family planning are seen as just one more futile attempt to stave off the coming revolution.

4. There have always been countries whose leaders felt that they needed more people, not fewer. For years France worried about how its military-age population cohorts compared in size to those of Germany. Argentina frets about whether its population is large enough to hold its thinly populated border regions. Similarly, some African leaders believe that their countries are underpopulated.

These long-standing sources of pronatalist sentiment, coupled with resentment of the rich countries' attitude toward third world population growth and the weakness of their development aid efforts, have ignited opposition to the push for population control. This opposition was prominent at the United Nations World Population Conference, held in Bucharest in 1974. Participants in that meeting asserted that underdevelopment, not population growth, was the real problem. They argued that substantial economic development, equitably shared, would not only provide for existing population, but would also bring about a gradual decline in fertility. As a popular slogan put it, "Take care of the people and the population will take care of itself." The zeal of the industrialized countries to sell population control to the poor countries was scathingly contrasted to their laggard performance in providing development assistance or agreeing to reforms in the international economic system. National sovereignty, the critics charged, was being trampled on. The right of couples to decide for themselves how many children to have was being infringed. In fact, some participants suggested, the real motivation of the rich countries was to limit the growth of "nonwhite" populations. A few of the most heated speakers went so far as to characterize international support for population programs as a form of genocide.

Things become much calmer when one moves from the arena of international debate to the level of national population policy, although some of the same emotional issues are encountered at the national level as well. According to an authoritative estimate,[8] by the early 1970s thirty-four countries, representing more than three-quarters of the third world's population, had both adopted the limitation of population growth as a policy objective and formulated some kind of policy (usually a family planning program) for attempting to achieve it. Governments of an additional

8. W. Parker Mauldin, "Assessment of National Family Planning Programs in Developing Countries," *Studies in Family Planning* 6, no. 2 (February 1975), pp. 30–36.

thirty-two countries, while not pledged to reduce population growth, offered family planning services for health and humanitarian reasons. Follow-up studies have shown further growth in this kind of interest and commitment during the 1970s.[9]

In regional terms, most of the strongest commitments have come from Asian governments. Latin American governments, when they provide family planning services officially or permit private organizations to do so unofficially, usually justify their actions as promoting the welfare of mothers and children. Some African governments are committed to population growth limitation, while others are indifferent or actively pronatalist. The population policies of Communist regimes have varied among countries and from time to time. China has achieved what is probably the most effective control over population ever attained by any government through its "planned births" campaign.

Some of the political, moral, and religious problems which have been featured in the international debate have also arisen in the national context. As already mentioned, some countries are pronatalist for nationalistic reasons. Sometimes this is caused by a desire to have enough people to hold areas of low population density against external challenges. Other countries (Guyana, Lebanon, Nigeria, Malaysia) have internal racial, tribal, religious, or ethnic divisions which make population policy a sensitive matter, since it involves the balance of power among the various groups. Still other countries have provoked adverse political reactions by pursuing population policies which were regarded as excessively zealous, offensive to local belief, or callous in their disregard of individual rights. Indira Gandhi's surprising defeat in India's 1977 general election was attributed in part to the population policy of her emergency government. Despairing of controlling population growth by conventional means, the government had added male sterilization to its list of promoted family planning methods. Incentives were offered to those who agreed to be sterilized, and quotas were assigned to officials charged with carrying out the program in different parts of the country. The problems arose when force was allegedly used against low-status individuals by overzealous officials anxious to meet their quotas. The result was a setback not only for the Gandhi government but also for Indian family planning.

What should be the program of an LDC which has decided that population growth should be limited? The urgings of the international population control advocates have been directed primarily toward getting countries to implement effective family planning programs. Some of these advocates believe that when contraceptives are widely and cheaply available the "population problem" will be solved. On the other side of the debate, as has been seen, there are those who think that development alone will take care of the problem. Most LDC governments pursue a combination of family

9. B. Maxwell Stamper, *Population and Planning in Developing Nations* (New York: Population Council, 1977).

planning and development approaches. Who is right? We will return to this question in the final section of the chapter. First, it is necessary to review the theory of population.

The Theory of Population

Malthus

The most famous and influential demographic theorist of all time was Thomas R. Malthus (1766–1834). His pessimistic view of the principles underlying human reproduction and the prospects for the betterment of mankind are familiar to nearly everyone, at least in outline. Malthus believed that "the passion between the sexes" would cause population to expand as long as food supplies permitted. People would generally not limit procreation below the biological maximum. Although wages and per-capita food supply might rise over the short run, this would only cause population growth to speed up and wages to fall back to the subsistence level. He did not think that the growth of food supply could stay ahead of population growth in the long run. In a famous example he argued that food supplies grow according to an arithmetic (additive) progression while population follows an explosive geometric (multiplicative) progression.

In these dire circumstances population growth would be limited primarily by factors working through the death rate, what Malthus called "positive checks." By this deceptively mild phrase he meant all the disasters which exterminate people in large numbers: famines, wars, and epidemics. It was these phenomena, he believed, which generally constitute the operative limitation on population growth. Only in later editions of his famous *Essay on the Principle of Population* did he concede the possibility of a second, less drastic, category of limiting factors: "preventive checks" working through the birth rate. What Malthus had in mind here were primarily measures of "restraint," such as a later age of marriage. Unlike latter-day "Malthusians" he was not an advocate of birth control, which as a minister he considered immoral. Even while grudgingly recognizing the possibility that mankind might voluntarily control its own numerical growth, however, Malthus invested little hope in the possibility.

The gloominess of the Malthusian theory is not surprising considering that its author lived during the early years of the Industrial Revolution. In all prior human history (that is, through the first two demographic eras outlined above), population *had* tended to expand in response to economic gains. Now with unprecedented economic growth underway in the world he knew, what could Malthus expect except an acceleration of natural increase as death rates fell? That indeed was happening during his lifetime.

Malthus did not live to witness the rest of the European demographic transition. As it turned out (see Fig. 7–1), the early decline in death rates was followed, with a lag, by a fall in fertility; dramatic increases in wages were eventually recorded. What is less clear is *why* this all happened. It appears that the death rate fell through a combination of the indirect effects of higher incomes (better nutrition and living conditions) and the direct effects of better preventive and curative health measures. (The operation of these factors is examined in Chapter 10.) The fall in the birth rate is harder to understand. Theoretically there is good reason to expect, as Malthus did, that fertility would rise, not fall, as income went up. There are biological and economic reasons for this expectation. Healthier, better fed women are more fecund; that is, they have a greater biological capacity to conceive, carry a child full term, and give birth to a healthy infant. In addition better-off families have the financial capacity to support more children. Why then do increases in income seem to lead to declines in fertility? An answer to this question must be sought in post-Malthusian demographic theory.

Mechanisms for Reducing Birth Rates

By definition three kinds of demographic change can affect the crude birth rate. The first is change in the structure of the population in terms of age groups and sexes. An increase in the share of people of reproductive age (roughly fifteen to forty-five) will increase the birth rate, as was seen earlier in the discussion of demographic momentum. Conversely, if the population gets to have a high proportion of older people, as is happening in many industrial countries now, the birth rate is depressed. Similarly, unbalancing the sex ratio (for example, through migration) will reduce the birth rate, while correcting a previously unbalanced ratio will increase it. However, these structural effects are quantitatively important only in rather special circumstances.

The second kind of demographic mechanism that influences the birth rate is change in the proportion of the adult population that is married. This can be affected both by the number of adults who get married (and stay married) at some time in their lives and by the initial age at which people marry.

The third factor is the marital fertility rate, the number of children born to the average married couple. Most historical birth rate declines are primarily attributable to a fall in marital fertility. However, later age of marriage has also been important in some cases, for example in the fall of the Irish birth rate after the potato famine of the 1840s.

It has been suggested that there are three basic preconditions for a significant decline in marital fertility.

1. Fertility must be subject to conscious choice; it must be socially acceptable for a couple to decide how many children they want to have.

2. Reduced fertility must be seen as advantageous; there must be perceived social and economic benefits of having fewer children.

3. Effective techniques of fertility reduction must be available; couples must know about them and agree to employ them.[10]

10. Michael S. Teitelbaum, "Relevance of Demographic Transition Theory for Developing Countries," *Science* 188 (May 2, 1977); 420–25.

The first and third of these preconditions are believed by some theorists to be only facilitating influences. The active force working for lower birth rates, they argue, is perceived incentives for individuals to have fewer children.

The Theory of Fertility

The first stage of the demographic transition is marked by a decline in the death rate, particularly a fall in the number of deaths among infants and young children (see Chapter 10). This in itself is a very good thing and no humane government would want to reverse the trend. The question of how to bring about a lower rate of population growth therefore narrows down to a matter of reducing the birth rate.

Most governments which have become convinced that the birth rate is too high have initiated, or at least permitted private groups to initiate, programs of "family planning." Typically these programs do two things: they make one or more forms of contraception more widely and/or cheaply available; and they undertake information and propaganda activities to urge people to use them. This kind of program may reduce the birth rate by making it easier for people to regulate the number of births and thus come closer to their desired family size. But the program is likely to have little effect on the number of children that people want to have. This may be affected to some extent by government propaganda, but probably not very much. The motivations which led the government to undertake a family planning program—perceived crowding and strain on national resources, perhaps some pressure from foreign aid organizations—are likely to be very different from the factors which influence individuals. They are unlikely to be moved by appeals based on such general, remote-seeming considerations.

Why then do people have children? Is it because they are affected by Malthus's "passion between the sexes" and do not know how to prevent the resulting births? Or do they have many children because they are tradition-bound, custom-ridden? Or is it perhaps rational in some social settings? There is some merit in all three of these propositions. The case for the first one was stated by a Latin American doctor at an international conference a few years ago. "People don't really want children," he said. "They want sex, and they don't know how to prevent the children that result." This viewpoint captures the element of spontaneity which is inevitably present in the reproductive process. Yet there is strong evidence that human fertility is consciously controlled in all societies. In no known case does the number of children that the average woman has over the course of her childbearing years even approach her biological capacity to bear children. Methods of inhibiting conception, aborting pregnancies, and disposing of unwanted infants are practiced in all societies, including those which have had no contact with modern methods of birth control.

It is sometimes said that many children are the social norm in traditional societies, that society looks askance at couples who have no or few children, that a man who lacks wealth can at least have children, that a woman's principal socially recognized function in a traditional society is to bear and rear children. Such norms and attitudes are important, but they are probably not the dominant factors in human fertility. The determinants of fertility are evidently a complex combination of forces, but social scientists in recent years have been giving increasing credence to the elements of individual rationality in the process. Simply stated, their thesis is that most families in traditional societies have many children because it is rational for them to do so. By the same token people in modern societies have fewer children because that is rational behavior in the circumstances in which they live. It follows that to reduce fertility in developing countries it is necessary to alter the incentives.

Although some would regard it as a cold, inhumane way of looking at the matter, it is nevertheless true that children impose certain costs upon their parents and confer certain benefits in return. To the extent that couples are influenced by these benefits and costs, are able to calculate them, and are capable of carrying out their reproductive plans, it follows that to reduce the birth rate it will be necessary to reduce the net benefits which children provide.

The benefits of having children can be classified as economic and psychic. In the medium term children may supplement family earnings by working. On family farms and in other household enterprises there is usually something that even a very young child can do to increase production. And large numbers of children work for wages outside the home in many poor societies. In the longer run children provide a form of social security in societies which lack institutional programs to assist the elderly. In some cultures it is considered especially important to have a son who survives to adulthood; in view of high infant and child mortality, this can motivate couples to keep having children until two or three sons have been born. Besides these economic benefits, which are probably more important in a low-income society than in an affluent one, children also yield psychic benefits, as all parents know.

The costs of children can also be categorized as economic and psychic. Economic costs can be further divided into explicit (monetary) and implicit (opportunity) costs. Children entail cash outlays for food, clothing, shelter, and sometimes for hired child care services, education, etc. Implicit costs arise when child care by a member of the family (usually but not always the mother) involves a loss of earning time. Psychic costs include such things as anxiety and loss of leisure time activities.

Some of the costs felt by parents parallel costs of population growth experienced at the national level. For example, more children in a family may mean smaller inheritances of agricultural land, an example of a natural resource constraint operating at the family level. Similarly, it may be harder to send all the children in a larger family to school; this reflects the pressures on social investment which are felt when population growth is rapid.

Theorists at the University of Chicago and elsewhere have built models based on the assumption that parents choose their family size so as to maximize the net *economic* benefits of children. This kind of theorizing is sometimes referred to as "the new home economics." Most students of demographic behavior would reject the view that *only* economic considerations matter, but they would agree that they play an important role.

The economic theory of fertility, even in this modified form, has several important implications: (1) Fertility should be higher when children can earn incomes or contribute to household enterprises at a young age than when they cannot. (2) The introduction of an institutionalized social security system should lower fertility. (3) Fertility should be lower when mothers have employment opportunities which are relatively incompatible with childrearing; some forms of employment, especially work in the home, are much easier to reconcile with having and rearing children than others. (4) Fertility should be higher when income is higher because the explicit costs are more easily borne.

The first three theoretical predictions have been pretty well verified in empirical studies. The fourth, however, is in glaring conflict with observed reality. As has been seen, in the real world fertility is usually *negatively* related to income—not positively related, as the theory predicts. The negative relationship shows up both in time-series data (that is, fertility usually declines through time as income rises) and in cross-section data (that is, in most societies middle- and upper-income families have fewer children than the poor).

Population theorists have attempted to explain this anomaly. Gary Becker, a principal formulator of "the new home economics," thinks it is attributable to (1) lack of contraceptive knowledge on the part of low-income groups and (2) a trade-off between "child quantity" and "child quality." He argues that the rich spend *more,* not less, on their children because they invest more in education and other aspects of "child quality." An opposing school of thought, headed by Richard Easterlin, argues that tastes are not given, as Becker and the Chicago school contend, but in fact change, along with the tastes for various types of goods, as one's permanent income changes relative to that of a reference group (essentially, one's parents). Whatever the reason, however, it is clear that a long-term rise in income generally does depress fertility. (A short-term, possibly temporary, rise in income may well have the opposite effect, perhaps because tastes remain unchanged.) This has obvious significance for population policy.

Population and Development

Optimum Population

Two questions are important for population policy. What are the effects of population growth on development and human welfare? And if population growth is thought to have harmful effects, how can these harmful effects best be reduced or eliminated?

The theory reviewed in the preceding section suggests that at the level of the family population finds its optimum, in the sense that people have the number of children that they consider beneficial to their overall welfare. Yet when asked, many parents in LDCs say that they would rather have fewer children than they have. Also, several studies show that rates of sickness and death are higher among children in large families, especially those with a later birth order. So perhaps parents' judgments about an optimal family size change after they have become parents and have formed a more realistic appraisal of the costs and benefits of children.

When the issue of the relationship between population and welfare is transferred from the family level to the national level, the question that arises is whether individual preferences should be allowed to determine how large a population a country has. Is there a case for the state to intervene to curb (or in some instances perhaps to encourage) human reproduction?

We can begin to attack this issue by considering the relationship between per-capita income and the size of the population in a given country. Would per-capita income be higher or lower if the population were larger than it is? In dynamic terms, which are more relevant to policy, the question is whether the future growth of per-capita income would be faster or slower if the rate of population growth were increased (or reduced).

An answer to this question can be approached by means of successive approximations. The oldest and simplest answer is that every mouth comes with a pair of hands. This implies that economic activity is scale-neutral, that per-capita income is unaffected by the size or growth rate of the population. But this ancient piece of folk wisdom is all too obviously an oversimplification. It ignores the role of nonlabor resources and the possibility (which so concerned Ricardo) that diminishing returns will be encountered as population expands.

A somewhat more sophisticated approach that meets this objection is the optimum population theory. According to this notion, for any given country at a particular time, with nonlabor resources fixed in supply, there is a unique population size at which per-capita income is maximized. The idea is that at suboptimal levels of population per-capita income is lower than it could be because there is not enough labor to utilize the available nonlabor resources efficiently, while at population levels above the optimum per-capita income is also lower than it could be because there is too much labor and diminishing returns set in. This relationship is graphed in Fig. 7–3, where the optimum population is OP and the corresponding maximum level of per-capital income is OY.

The optimum population theory is consistent with the intuition that there are underpopulated countries and overpopulated countries. It is not hard to believe that immigration into the United States, Canada, and Australia during the nineteenth century raised per-capita income in these countries. Nor is it implausible to think that Bangladesh's per-capita income would rise if some millions of its population could somehow be made to disappear. The trouble with the approach is that it is a static framework and can take only limited account of dynamic factors.

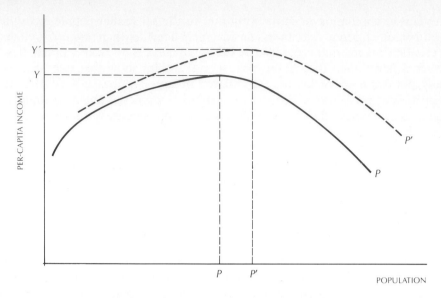

Fig. 7–3　The Theory of Optimum Population.

Capital accumulation, technical change, and natural resource discoveries make it possible simultaneously to raise per-capita income and to increase the optimum population over time. In Fig. 7–3 the broken line depicts a situation in which production possibilities have increased for these reasons. The shapes of the two optimum population curves are similar, but the new line lies entirely above the old one.

Figure 7–3 depicts an exercise in what economic theorists call comparative statics. This "before-and-after" analysis is not an entirely adequate reflection of the dynamic effects on economic growth of different rates of population growth. The pioneering work in developing a truly dynamic model of population's effect on material welfare was done by Coale and Hoover, who published a macroeconomic model of population growth and development in India in 1958.[11] Coale and Hoover concluded that a reduction in the birth rate in India would accelerate growth in per-capita income for two important reasons. First, at the household level slower population growth would reduce the dependency ratio, and this in turn would lower the consumption function and raise the savings function. Second, at the societal level slower population growth would reduce the share of public-sector revenues that must be used to provide social services to the growing population and increase the share than can be invested to raise per-capita income. Subsequent theorists refined their analysis.

There has always been a dissenting minority, however, who doubt that faster population growth retards growth in per-capita income, or who even argue that it is beneficial. For example, Colin Clark, Esther Boserup, and

11. Ansley J. Coale and Edgar M. Hoover, *Population Growth and Economic Development in Low-Income Countries: A Case Study of India's Prospects* (Princeton: Princeton University Press, 1958).

most recently Julian Simon have all maintained that population growth can enhance growth in per-capita income by inducing greater investment demand, thus making it possible to realize economies of scale and stimulating change.[12] While Coale and Hoover argued that population growth depresses the supply of savings, this opposing group of theorists emphasizes the positive efforts of population growth on consumption and investment demand. Recently, Rati Ram and Theodore W. Schultz have pointed out that the longer life spans which accompany falling death rates and faster population growth in the LDCs increase the incentives for investment in human capital (see Chapter 9) and make labor more productive.[13] Several observers of the industrial countries have expressed concern that a slowdown in population growth could have detrimental effects. In the United States in the 1930s Alvin Hansen, who was known as "the American Keynes," evoked the spectre of "secular stagnation," which he feared would result from slower growth of the American population.[14]

Despite these opposing arguments, most analysts would agree that in the circumstances of nearly all LDCs slower population growth would probably permit per-capita income to rise more rapidly. There are two distinct reasons for this belief. First, in many LDCs population density in relation to land and other natural resources is already so high that it is reasonable to believe that it depresses per-capita income. This applies to many Asian countries, to Egypt, to several Caribbean islands, and elsewhere. It does not, however, apply to certain land-rich areas, especially in Sub-Saharan Africa. In addition, however, rapid population growth (as opposed to high existing densities) presses on scarce capital resources and inhibits improvement in productive capital and public services per head. This second point is applicable to nearly all LDCs, including those African nations exempted from the first point. These social costs are not fully reflected in incentives for individuals to get married and have children. For one or both of these reasons therefore, there is good cause for any developing country government to want to slow down population growth.

Before considering how this objective can be achieved, it is worth discussing briefly the arguments for population control at the international level. There are nationalistic reasons, having to do with prestige and sometimes also with military power, why particular nation-states may want to have larger populations. But these motivations can be disruptive to international relations and the welfare of other countries. They may contribute to the likelihood of war by making larger armies possible and by heightening competition for land and other resources. They may create pressures for

12. See Colin Clark, "The 'Population Explosion' Myth," *Bulletin of the Institute of Development Studies,* Sussex, England, May 1969; id., "The Economics of Population Growth and Control: A Comment," *Review of Social Economy* 28, no. 1 (March 1970): 449–66; Ester Boserup, *The Condition of Agricultural Growth* (Chicago: Aldine, 1965); and Julian Simon, *The Ultimate Resource* (Princeton: Princeton University Press, 1981).

13. Rati Ram and Theodore W. Schultz, "Life Span, Savings, and Productivity," *Economic Development and Cultural Change* 27, no. 3 (April 1979): 394–421.

14. Alvin Harvey Hansen, *Full Recovery or Stagnation* (New York: W. W. Norton, 1938).

migration from overpopulated countries to other countries which may have their own population growth under control. For all these reasons there is a case for an international effort to limit world population. The main problem, noted earlier, is to decide whose population is to be limited. Possibilities of doing much about population at the global level are limited by the linkage of the population problem to other issues of international politics.

Although some externalities may thus escape consideration, real population policy is made primarily at the national level.

Population Policy

Our discussion of population policy stems from the main conclusions suggested by the earlier review of demographic theory. First, it seems likely that in the circumstances of most low-income countries a lower rate of population growth will make it easier to raise per-capita income. Second, it seems likely that fertility will fall if incentives change in such a way as to induce couples to have fewer children and if incomes rise in the long run. Various approaches to limiting population growth can be examined in the light of these principles.

The most common approach, as already mentioned, is to have a national *family planning* program. These programs have achieved good results in some cases, but have had little or no discernible effect in others. There appear to be two necessary conditions for such programs to work: they must be well managed (and by no means all of them are); and there must be some preexisting desire for smaller families, at least in some parts of the population. Most of the cases in which family planning programs have been relatively successful in reaching a large number of "acceptors" and retaining a large stock of "current users" over time are to be found in countries which are developing rapidly and where a number of the other factors thought to be favorable to fertility decline (high literacy, reduced infant death rate, widespread female employment outside the home)[15] are also present. In countries where these factors are absent, family planning tends to catch on fairly rapidly among the relatively well-off, the urbanized, and the educated, while spreading only very slowly among the remainder of the population. But the record is not clear-cut. In some parts of rural Indonesia family planning has spread rapidly in recent years and has had a measurable effect on the birth rate, despite comparatively low levels of income, education, and health services.

Population redistribution, a second broad approach to population policy, may help to accommodate a growing total population in limited circumstances, but the magnitude of the effect is not likely to be great. First, there must be empty but habitable space into which people can be moved. Then, particularly if the government is going to organize the movement, a considerable investment of capital and formidable organizational capacity will be

---

15. This list of facilitating factors is based on empirical research. Some of the reasons why these factors should be influential were suggested in earlier discussion.

required. It is hard to move enough people to make a genuine difference, as experience in Indonesia, Brazil, and elsewhere shows. We have already noted that the kind of international population redistribution which was a major factor in the nineteenth century is not likely to be significant in today's world, although smaller movements of people (motivated by political as well as economic considerations) are still taking place.

More drastic methods of population control than contraception, such as abortion and sterilization, have played an important part in the slowdown of population growth in several European, South American, and East Asian countries. These methods are often regarded as objectionable on moral grounds. When forced upon resisting populations, as they were in India during the emergency, they can backfire. Yet when acceptable to local mores they may help to bring about a rapid decline in fertility.

Some people believe that governments should not worry so much about population policy but instead should concentrate on *development,* leaving it to the demographic transition to bring about a decline in fertility. In international conferences verbal wars have been waged between the "family planners" and the "developmentalists." This is an unnecessary debate, since the real issue is not development *or* family planning, but rather the best mix of policies in a particular set of circumstances. Family planning alone is unlikely to reduce the birth rate: we have seen that it seldom works well in settings where there has been little development. Moreover its effects on marital fertility need support from a trend toward a higher age of marriage, and this too is more likely to come about in a more rapidly developing society.

Indonesia is the fifth most populous country in the world. Its 150 million people inhabit a chain of islands stretching some 3000 miles along the equator. Two-thirds of all Indonesians live on Java and Bali, small islands which make up only 7 percent of the land area. In the rural areas of these islands population densities are among the highest in the world, land holdings are small and shrinking, and decent jobs are hard to find.

Population and Family Planning in Indonesia

For many years "transmigration" to the less fertile but relatively uncrowded "outer islands" of Sumatra, Kalimantan, and Sulawesi has been promoted as a way of easing population pressure in Java and Bali. It has never been able to make a dent in population growth in these core islands, let alone lower existing densities. Indeed, while some migrants move toward available agricultural land on the other islands, many others flock to Java's cities, where the best income-earning opportunities are concentrated.

Indonesia's population policy reversed gears in the late 1960s. Sukarno, the ardent nationalist who was president from 1945 to 1966, often proclaimed his belief that Indonesia had too few people, not too many. "We have rich natural resources," he said. "We need more people to exploit them." Yet Sukarno's government failed to develop the country's resources, however rich they might be, and by the mid-1960s Indonesia's masses were desperately short of food, clothing, medical care, and practically everything else.

Suharto, the second president, tried to rebuild the economy. He also declared in favor of population limitation, and in 1970 an official family planning program was launched. Although most people in Indonesia are still poor and ill-educated, and despite the fact that 90 percent are Muslims, this program has succeeded beyond anyone's expectation. Greatest attention was paid to, and greatest success achieved in, the rural parts of Java and Bali. The program was imaginatively conceived, well managed, and implemented largely through existing village institutions. Pills were used as the main method of contraception. By 1980 fertility in key areas had fallen by 15–20 percent. In other areas fertility remained high, while in still others it was low, but only because of low female fecundity resulting from ill-health and malnutrition.

Indonesia's official goal is to cut fertility in half by the year 2000, or even by 1990 if possible. These are ambitious goals and may not be realized, but the fact remains that a determined government has succeeded in improving a critical demographic situation, and has done so under circumstances that the experts considered quite unfavorable for family planning.

Population and Family Planning in Kenya   Kenya is an example of an African country with low current population density but a high growth rate and explosive demographic potential. With a crude birth rate of fifty-one per thousand in 1978 and a crude death rate of thirteen (see Table 7–3), Kenya has one of the highest rates of natural increase observed anywhere. Nor does it show signs of slowing down anytime soon. A survey taken in the late 1970s found that Kenyans regard eight children as an ideal family size, up from six in the 1960s. If things go on like this, Kenya's population will double before the year 2000.

Just why Kenyans are so very fertile is not clear. Although Nairobi, the capital, is a prosperous, modern city, the country is still nearly 90 percent rural. The per-capita GNP of about $400 is very unequally distributed. Water shortages severely restrict the cultivability of much of Kenya's land, while in some of the most fertile areas there are large farms. Many Kenyans therefore must make a living from holdings that are either too small or too poorly watered to ensure an adequate income.

Surprisingly, the Kenyan government adopted a policy of population limitation as early as 1966. Despite substantial international aid, however, the national family planning program has been unable to make much headway. It is said that the late President Jomo Kenyatta, who issued the 1966 statement, subsequently refused to lend public support to family planning. A part of the problem was Kenya's keen tribal rivalries, which made each group fear that if it adopted birth limitation it would only be boosting the power of its competitors.

China has made unique progress toward gaining control over the **Population** growth of its massive population, particularly since 1971. This experience **and Family** has two major kinds of implication for the world at large. First, with a **Planning in** population now estimated (based on the 1982 census) to exceed one **China** billion, population growth in China has a large numerical impact on the total population of the globe. Second, some of the techniques used to reduce the number of births in China are transferable to other developing countries—although others either could not be transferred to other political and cultural settings or would not be widely acceptable because of the loss of personal freedom they involve.

Population policy in China has been anything but constant. After the Communist takeover in 1949 Chairman Mao Zedong repeatedly expressed the view that "revolution plus production" would solve all problems, with no need to limit population growth. China's first census, conducted in 1953, revealed a population total (nearly 600 million) which shook this complacency, but birth control campaigns in 1956–1958 and 1962–1966 had only limited results and were interrupted by Mao's famous policy reversals, the "Great Leap Forward" of 1960 and the "Cultural Revolution" of the late 1960s. Only in 1971 was a serious and sustained effort launched. At that time the crude birth rate, already reduced by the disruptions of the Cultural Revolution, stood at thirty. By 1980 it had been cut to twenty-one.

The "Planned Births" campaign of 1971 was reportedly launched at the personal initiative of Premier Zhou Enlai. It established three reproductive norms: *wan xi shao,* meaning later marriage, longer spacing between births, and fewer children. To implement these norms, the highly committed post-Mao leadership set birth targets for administrative units throughout China (from the province of 2–90 million people down to the production team of 250–800) and placed responsibility for achieving these targets in the hands of the local officials at all levels. The national government conducted information and motivation campaigns to persuade people to have fewer children but it was left to local officials to fill out many details of the program and finance much of its cost. A wide range of contraceptives was offered and family planning was linked closely to efforts to improve child and maternal health care.

Although national officials maintained that participation in the program was voluntary, local officials with targets to fulfill often applied pressure. At the production team level "birth planning" became very personal, as couples were required to seek approval to have a child in a particular year. (The application could be accepted, or they might be asked to wait a year or two.) Such extreme methods seem to have worked and been reasonably well accepted in China, presumably because of its cohesive social structure and strong government authority from the national down to the neighborhood level.

The most popular form of birth limitation in China in the 1970s has been the intrauterine device (IUD). The other two major forms have been abortion and sterilization, both female and male. China has been active in research into contraceptive technologies such as low-cost "paper pills," "morning-after pills," and male contraceptive pills.

Despite the dramatic results of the *wan xi shao* campaign, population projections continued to be a matter for concern, and in 1979 the "One Child" campaign was promulgated. Couples were now told that "only children are better children" and were urged to take a pledge to stop at one. Those who do so often receive special incentives such as an income supplement, extra maternity leave, and preferential treatment when applying for public housing. The success of this newest and most ambitious program, which flies in the face of traditional son-preference by asking half of China's couples to stop reproducing before they have had a male child, remains to be determined. The target now is to stabilize the population at about 1.2 billion early in the twenty-first century.

Although some aspects of China's population program will doubtless remain unique, countries interested in strengthening their own programs could probably learn from China's strong information activities, its use of a wide range of contraceptive methods, and its decentralization of many aspects of planning and implementation to local authorities.

Yet family planning has made its own independent contribution to LDC fertility decline in recent years, as studies have shown.[16] In reality family planning and development are more complements than substitutes. This makes theoretical sense if one thinks of development as influencing desired family size (the demand side of the equation) and family planning as influencing the ability to achieve that desire (the supply side).

Recently there has been growing interest in ways of modifying the development process to increase its impact on fertility. This has been called "population policies beyond family planning," or "the search for selective interventions."[17] Quite a number of "selective interventions" have been proposed: increased education for girls (especially the attainment of basic literacy for all women in countries which have not yet reached this target); increased job opportunities for women outside the home; formal social security systems (a realistic option only for the better-off developing countries); a ban on child labor; compulsory schooling up to a certain age; in general, a rise in the status of women which will give them greater control over their own lives. The use of monetary incentives and disincentives geared to the number of children one has and affecting government services, tax exemptions, and so on has also been advocated. The trouble with these is that while they may discourage parents from having an additional child, they frequently penalize those children who have already been born.

16. W. Parker Mauldin and Bernard Berelson, "Conditions of Fertility Decline in Developing Countries, 1965–75," *Studies in Family Planning* 9, no. 5 (1978).

17. For a thorough discussion, see Ronald G. Ridker (ed.), *Population and Development: The Search for Selective Interventions* (Baltimore and London: Johns Hopkins University Press for Resources for the Future, 1976).

The reduction of infant mortality can be considered another form of "selective intervention." According to the "child replacement thesis," the number of children that a couple has is geared to the number it expects to survive; accordingly, if survival prospects improve, then the birth rate—if not necessarily the rate of natural increase—will fall.

Finally, a rise in the legal minimum age of marriage has been proposed in some countries. It is doubtful that this will have any effect if there are deeply engrained early-marriage norms. More impact is likely from the kinds of "selective interventions" discussed above, since these may affect both marital fertility and age of marriage.

One country which has emphasized non-family planning policies, albeit in rather special circumstances, is Singapore. There 60 percent of the population lives in public housing, and nearly everyone is heavily dependent on the government for a variety of social services. In its campaign to limit population growth the government of Singapore had discriminated among users of public services on the basis of how many children they have. People with large families pay higher maternity fees, get low priority in school selection, and receive no extra income tax deductions or housing space. Abortion and sterilization (male and female) are available on demand at nominal fees. All this is backed up by a determined information campaign. Singapore's tough policy has contributed to a dramatic fall in population growth, although rapid economic and social change in the Southeast Asian city-state has probably had even a greater impact.

A somewhat broader proposition is that *improvement in the distribution of income* will lower the birth rate. (The complementary proposition, that unequal distribution leads to higher fertility, has also been put forward.) This makes sense, since poor households have perhaps three-quarters of the babies in a developing society, and it is their income which must therefore rise if an increase in income is to bring about a decline in fertility. A related idea is that a generally equitable pattern of development, including improving social services for the poor, will induce people to believe that their lives are improving and that they are gaining increasing control over their own destiny, leading to an especially rapid decline in fertility. These are attractive hypotheses and there is some evidence to support them, but it is not conclusive.

Conclusion

This chapter has discussed one of the most complex areas of human behavior, one which is still far from perfectly understood despite extensive study in recent years. Almost any statement made on the subject can be disputed. Yet it seems evident that the phenomenal growth of world population which began after World War II will continue, perhaps somewhat abated, at least into the twenty-first century, and that this growth does constitute a major impediment to economic development in many low-income countries. The situation is to a limited extent subject to modification through public policy measures. Responsibility for taking these measures rests primarily with the governments of the developing countries. Because we live in an interdependent world, the developed countries also have a right, indeed a responsibility, to play a role. Yet if they want that role to be an effective one, they will have to play it less heavy-handedly than in the past. Basically, world population policy is a part of the broader question of relations among the parts of our interdependent world.

FURTHER For a readable presentation of the present world population situation, see Lester R.
READINGS Brown, *In the Human Interest* (New York: W. W. Norton, 1974). A lively historical
account is Carlo Cipolla, *The Economic History of World Population* (Harmondsworth, Middlesex, England: Penguin Books, 1962).

On demographic theory, one could begin by looking at the most influential work
ever written on population, Thomas R. Malthus's *Essay on the Principle of Population* (New York: W. W. Norton, 1976). The application of the more recent demographic transition theory to developing countries is examined in Michael S.
Teitelbaum, "The Relevance of Demographic Transition Theory for Developing
Countries," *Science* 188 (May 2, 1977): 420–25. For a pioneering model of the interactions between population growth and economic development, see Ansley J.
Coale and Edgar M. Hoover, *Population Growth and Economic Development*
(Bombay: Oxford University Press, 1959). Some of the burgeoning literature that
followed from this is surveyed in Nancy Birdsall, "Analytical Approaches to the
Relationship of Population Growth and Development," *Population and Development
Review* 3, no. 1/2 (March–June 1977): 63–103.

For the economic theory of fertility, see Gary S. Becker, "An Economic Analysis
of Fertility," in National Bureau of Economic Research, *Demographic and Economic Change in Developed Countries* (Princeton: Princeton University Press,
1960), and numerous subsequent works by Becker and his followers. For a contrary
view, see Richard A. Easterlin, "An Economic Framework for Population Analysis," *Studies in Family Planning* 6, no. 3 (March 1975): 54–63.

On population policy, W. Parker Mauldin and Bernard Berelson study the respective contributions of family planning programs and other influences on recent
fertility declines in their "Conditions of Fertility Decline in Developing Countries,
1965–75," *Studies in Family Planning* 9, no. 5 (May 1978): 89–147. Ronald G.
Ridker (ed.), *Population and Development: The Search for Selective Interventions*
(Baltimore and London: Johns Hopkins University Press for *Resources for the Future,* 1976), examines a wide range of possible policy influences on population. To
learn more about how the Chinese limit the growth of their enormous population,
see Pi-Chao Chen and Adriene Kols, "Population and Birth Planning in the People's Republic of China," Johns Hopkins University, *Population Reports,* series 1,
no. 25 (January–February 1982). On Indonesia's less spectacular but still impressive
experience with family planning, see Terrence H. Hull, Valerie J. Hull, and Masri
Singarimbun, *Indonesia's Family Planning Story: Success and Challenge,* Population Reference Bureau *Population Bulletin* 32, no. 6 (November 1977).

Chapter 8

LABOR AND GROWTH

The dual role of people in economic development—as both the beneficiaries of development and a major productive resource—is particularly evident in discussing labor and employment. Labor employed in economic activity can be interpreted as both a cost and a benefit. It is a cost—if it has an alternative use and thus a positive marginal product, as discussed below—in the same sense that use of other productive resources represents a cost. But it is also a potential benefit, in two senses. First, in some situations, because of market imperfections, it may be possible to increase production by organizing the available labor better and by adopting technologies more appropriate to the factor endowments of less developed countries. Second, regardless of the impact on aggregate output, increased employment of poor people may be an effective and relatively low-cost way to increase their share of total income.

A perplexing problem is how best to measure the quality of labor used in production. Given the supplies of capital and natural resources available, and given a range of applicable technologies, the level of GNP attainable will depend on the amount of labor available. But what is "the amount of labor available"? We could simply count the number of people potentially available for work—that is, the number of people who are not underage, overage, or infirm—but this could be misleading. In the real world labor productivity, or quality, varies widely, depending on several factors.

One important set of influences is people's *attitudes and values.* How much value is attached to the goods and services that can be earned by working? Are people willing to abandon traditional social settings and take up jobs in unfamiliar environments, such as factories, mines, and plantations? Do they come to work on time? Do they exert themselves on the job? Can they tolerate routinized operations? Is saving for future purposes important to them or do they live for the moment? Although economic theories usually abstract from the effects of values and attitudes on productivity, in the real world they are significant. These values and attitudes are acquired, not inborn. The work of sociologists and psychologists indicates that they are created primarily by experiences in the home, in school, and on the job. In a sense they are thus a *consequence* of economic development, but they are also one of its *causes*. Our understanding of the subject is not yet complete enough for values and attitudes to be readily manipulated as a means of promoting development, although many governments make efforts in this direction.

A second set of factors affecting labor productivity is the *skills* possessed by the population. If values and attitudes refer to the way people look at the world, skills are a matter of what they know how to do. Only some skills are relevant to economic development in a particular environment. One needs to know different things to work effectively in an Asian rice field, a Detroit auto factory, or an Arctic fishing community; skills that are vital in one of these settings may well be useless in another. Compared to attitudes and values, skills are acquired in a more straightforward and easily understood manner. The process can be called education, although this uses the term in a broader sense than is usual. This is taken up in Chapter 9. Here we concentrate on quantitative aspects of the human factor in development.

Characteristics of Labor Markets

Patterns of Employment

One of the best known characteristics of labor in third world countries is that most people work in agriculture and other primary industries. The pattern is most pronounced in the poorest countries and varies systematically with the level of development. As per-capita income rises the share of agricultural workers tends to fall while the shares of both industrial and service workers rise (Table 8–1). Individual countries follow this pattern, with some case-to-case variations (Table 8–2).

TABLE 8–1 **Employment Shares in a Typical Developing Country**

	Level of per-capita GNP in 1978 dollars				
% of employment in:	$200	$600	$1000	$1600	$2000
Primary production	66	49	39	30	25
Industry	9	21	26	30	33
Services	25	30	35	40	42

Source: Based on Hollis Chenery and Moises Syrquin, with the assistance of Hazel Elkington, *Patterns of Development 1950–1970* (London: Oxford University Press for the World Bank, 1975), pp. 20–21.

Another well-known feature of LDC labor is that most workers are paid low wages by the standards of the industrial countries. The main reason for this is that labor in developing countries is generally plentiful relative to the

TABLE 8–2   Employment Shares in Some Representative Countries, 1980

Countries	Agriculture	Industry	Services
Low-income countries			
India	69	13	18
Sri Lanka	54	14	32
China	71	17	12
Pakistan	57	20	23
Tanzania	83	6	11
Middle-income countries			
Ghana	53	20	27
Kenya	78	10	12
Indonesia	58	12	30
Bolivia	50	24	26
Peru	40	19	41
Colombia	26	21	53
South Korea	34	29	37
Malaysia	50	16	34
Brazil	30	24	46
Chile	19	19	62
Industrial market economics			
United Kingdom	2	42	56
Australia	6	33	61
Japan	12	39	49
United States	2	32	66
West Germany	4	46	50
Industrial nonmarket economics			
Poland	31	39	30
USSR	14	45	41
Czechoslovakia	11	48	41

Source: World Bank, *World Development Report 1982* (Washington, D.C., 1982), pp. 146–47.

supplies of complementary resources which could raise labor productivity and permit higher wages to be paid. Nearly all complementary resources are scarce: capital equipment, arable land, foreign exchange, and also those less tangible but important resources, entrepreneurship and managerial capacity. Thus low wages are easily understood from the perspective of an elementary supply-demand analysis.

It is not demeaning to third world workers, however, to note that another cause of low productivity and pay is the characteristics of the workers themselves. Through no fault of their own few of them have the education and experience required for high-productivity labor. In Indonesia in 1971 only 26 percent of adults had completed primary school, a mere 4 percent had gone on to secondary education, and a microscopic 0.2 percent had been to a university. Few indeed had worked in a factory or had other good opportunities for on-the-job training. In many LDCs these proportions are even lower. Often LDC workers lack even the capacity to do sustained physical labor because their health and nutritional status is low (Chapter 10).

Yet LDCs also have in their work forces persons of consummate learning and outstanding abilities. Another characteristic of LDC labor is that differentials among the wages received by different skills and education levels are wider than in developed countries (Table 8–3). In part this is because the rarity of these qualities attracts a larger market premium. Some of the wide differentials, however, may be attributed to a pattern of segmented labor markets, which is discussed in the following section.

TABLE 8–3 Ratio of Skilled Wages to Unskilled Wages Among Manual Workers, Early 1960s

Africa		Latin America	
Algeria	2.01	Brazil	1.84
Ghana	2.40	Chile	2.09
Nigeria	1.57	Colombia	1.81
Tanzania	2.11	Peru	1.71
Asia		Developed countries	
Hong Kong	1.75	United Kingdom	1.18
India	1.68	France	1.39
Pakistan	1.59		
Philippines	1.40		

Source: David Turnham assisted by Ingelies Jaeger, *The Employment Problem in Less Developed Countries: A Review of Evidence* (Paris: Organization for Cooperation and Development, 1971), p. 79.

Besides these structural aspects, the dynamics of labor supply and demand in the LDCs are also important. In most countries the number of people who want to work is currently increasing at around 2 or even 3 percent a year (Table 8–4). Since nearly all adult males and many adult females seek work outside the home, the rise in the number of potential workers is linked closely to the increase in total population. We saw in Chapter 7 that a major component in the post–World War II "population explosion" has been the survival of many more children from infancy to adulthood. This means that accelerated population growth tends to be followed, with a lag of about fifteen years, by a similar acceleration of labor force growth. It also means that a slowdown in population growth will not be reflected immediately in labor force growth. Growth in the LDC labor force speeded up in the 1960s and 1970s, is expected to remain constant in the 1980s, and will begin to decline only in the 1990s as a consequence of the recent moderation in the growth of world population discussed in Chapter 7.

A final characteristic of LDC labor is that often large amounts of it are underutilized. For reasons to be discussed below not all of this underutilization takes the form of visible unemployment as it is known in the industrial countries. Much of it is what has been called *disguised unemployment.* That is, people have some kind of a job, and may even work long hours, but their contribution to output is low. With some reallocation of resources and improvement of institutions their labor could be made much more productive. This is a major challenge for development policy.

To recapitulate, low wages and productivity, large wage differentials, and rapid growth of labor supply combined with underutilization of the existing supply are all characteristic of third world countries. Since hardly any generalizations apply to *all* LDCs, however, there are naturally many intercountry variations. For example, while some countries such as those in East Asia and the Pacific are now entering a period of declining labor force growth, others such as those in Sub-Saharan Africa are still in a period of accelerated growth (see Table 8–4). Similarly, the degree of labor underutilization varies greatly, depending mainly on the supply of arable land and other complementary resources in relation to working-age population.

TABLE 8–4   Growth of Labor Force, 1960–2000

Region	Annual % growth rate			
	1960 70	1970 80	1980–90	1900–2000
East Asia and Pacific	2.4	2.6	2.3	2.0
Low Income Asia	1.7	2.0	2.0	1.9
Latin America and Caribbean	2.4	2.7	3.0	2.7
Middle East and North Africa	1.9	2.6	2.9	2.2
Sub-Saharan Africa	2.2	2.2	2.5	2.6
Southern Europe	0.8	1.3	1.3	1.2
All developing countries	1.8	2.2	2.2	2.1
Industrial countries	1.2	1.2	0.7	0.5

Source: World Bank, *World Development Report, 1979* (Washington, D.C., 1979), p. 47.

The Structure of Labor Markets

It is useful to think of labor services as being bought and sold in markets like other goods and services. However, labor markets everywhere are notoriously imperfect, and none are more so than those of the LDCs. This section will describe a pattern of segmented labor markets which may help to explain wage and employment determination in the LDCs.

A "typical" LDC could be represented by a three-tiered employment structure, consisting of a urban formal sector, an urban informal sector, and rural employment. Figure 8–1 is a schematic representation of these three markets.

The **urban formal sector** is where almost everyone would like to work if they could. It is made up of the government and the large-scale enterprises, such as banks, insurance companies, factories, and trading houses. In some very poor countries or where the growth of the private sector has been held back by public policy, the government makes up almost the entire urban formal sector, all by itself. People welcome the opportunity to work in a modern facility and be associated with a prestigious name, but the main attractions of formal-sector employers are that they pay higher wages and offer steadier employment. One reason they pay more is that they hire virtually all the university- and secondary school-educated labor in the country. But they also tend to pay more for given types of labor, partly because the government presses them to do so, partly because they want to be known as "model employers," and partly no doubt because they can simply afford to do so. With wages held above market-clearing levels by legislation, custom, and other factors (W_F in Fig. 8–1A), there is nearly always a queue of workers ($E_F - L_F$ in Fig. 8–1A) waiting for jobs with urban formal-sector employers. A routine job opening announcement may attract hundreds, or even thousands, of applicants.

Side by side with the large urban formal-sector establishments—or more likely, in the alleys behind them—are the smaller enterprises of the **urban informal sector.** These shops and curbside establishments produce a wide range of goods and services, sometimes competing with the larger enterprises and at other times filling in the gaps that the formal-sector firms do not find it profitable to enter. Sometimes this sector provides jobs for migrants who have come to town from the rural areas seeking work in the urban formal sector but have been unable to find it. However, studies in several third world cities indicate that many of the people who earn their income in this way are long-time urban residents and veterans at their particular lines of work. The urban informal sector is easily entered; one can set oneself up as a street hawker or in dozens of other lines of work with only a tiny amount of capital. For those who lack even the $10 to $100 of capital needed to be self-employed, there is always the opportunity to work for others, albeit at wages far below those offered by the urban formal sector. Domestic servants form one such group, a large and important one in every developing country. The urban informal sector can provide incredible amounts of low-wage employment. In Jakarta, the capital of Indonesia, a few years ago it was estimated that drivers of a tricycle-like form of public transportation called the *becak* numbered between 200,000 and 400,000.

Because of the ease with which it is entered, the urban informal sector labor market tends to be in equilibrium (Fig. 8–1B). New entrants can gen-

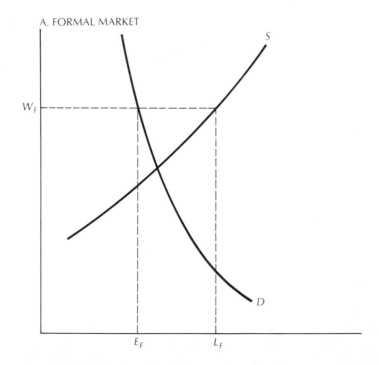

A. FORMAL MARKET

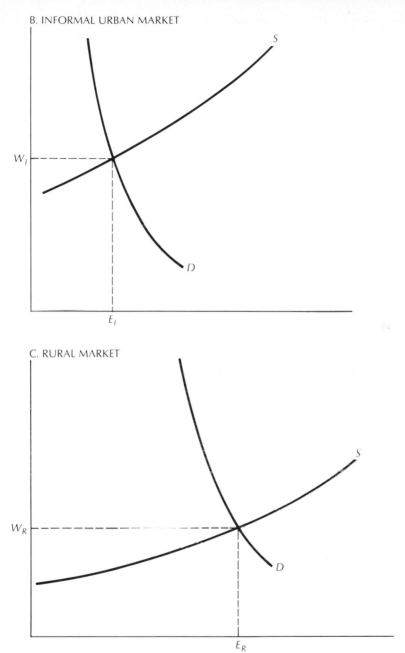

Fig. 8–1 Segmented LDC Labor Market. A. Formal urban market. B. Informal urban market. C. Rural market.

erally find something to do, even if their presence tends to drive down wages a bit for all participants.

Even the urban informal sector is likely to pay higher wages than the **rural labor market.** In part this wage differential is illusory because urbanites have to pay higher prices for food and housing than rural residents and often are forced to buy things (water, fuel, building materials) which are obtainable free in rural areas. But even after allowance has been made for differences in living costs, surveys indicate that practically all urban residents, even recent rural-urban migrants, are better off than all but the wealthiest rural residents.

As assumed by dual-economy models of development (Chapter 3), in rural districts of low-income countries employment commonly means work by family members, not for wages but for a share in the output of a family enterprise. Still there is always a market for hired labor, at least on a seasonal basis. Depending on the amount of population pressure and the prevailing pattern of land tenure, there will be a large or small number of people who must depend on wage employment because they have no land to farm, or not enough to support their families. These agricultural laborers typically make up the very lowest income stratum in a poor country. Even when the number of such unfortunates is small, however, rural households commonly trade labor back and forth at different times of the year, sometimes on a cooperative or barter basis but more often for wages in cash or kind.

Measuring Labor Supply and Utilization

Because of the structural complexity of LDC labor markets, difficulties arise in defining and measuring concepts that are relatively straightforward in developed countries. The two key problems with which policy-makers in both developed and underdeveloped countries are most often concerned are measuring the supply of labor available to the economy and determining how fully the available labor supply is being utilized.

In developed countries labor supply is measured through the *labor force* concept. The labor force consists of everyone who has a job or is actively looking for one. Labor force in developed countries is determined largely by the size of the total population, its composition in terms of age groups and sex, and those social factors (such as educational patterns and the willingness of women to work outside the home) which determine the participation rates of the different segments of the population. There is some short-term responsiveness (elasticity) to the supply of labor. It can be large under unusual circumstances, for example, when women in many countries went to work in factories for the first time during World War II. But normally the short-term elasticity is low. Developed countries experiencing full employment, as did many European nations during the 1950s, can easily have their economic growth constrained by the available supply of labor.

In LDC conditions labor supply is generally not a constraint on development. More people would typically like to work than are working, and many of those who are working are underutilized. Moreover the meaning of "having a job" or "actively looking for work" is often hard to pin down in the LDC context, where multiple job-holding, part-time work, and work for one's own family all tend to be more common than in a developed country. The number of "discouraged workers" (those who have stopped looking for work because they believe none is available) is also likely to be greater in underdeveloped than in developed countries. Using the conventional definitions, women participate increasingly in the labor force as development proceeds and the number of jobs outside the home rises. This suggests that at low levels of development there is a large reserve of female labor not apparent in the statistics, but ready to come forth when reasonably attractive work opportunities open up. (In fact, of course, these women are already working hard in the home, where by convention they are not counted as part of the labor force.)

Labor underutilization in developed countries is measured primarily through the concept of **unemployment.** The unemployed are defined as those who do not have a job but are actively looking for one. The familiar **rate of unemployment** is total unemployment as a percentage of labor force. In industrial countries the rate of unemployment is a closely watched indicator of economic performance.

In developing countries the rate of unemployment understates labor underutilization, often by a large factor. Surveys have indicated that India has a lower rate of unemployment than the United States. Yet most observers would agree that underutilization of labor supply is much greater in India than in the United States. Semideveloped countries with per-capita income levels much higher than India's have also been measured in surveys as having far higher rates of unemployment. One reason for these anomalies is suggested by analysis of the types of people who are reported as unemployed when labor force surveys are carried out in developing countries. Many of them are young, live in urban areas, are far better educated than the population in general, and/or have never worked before. The inference is clear. The unemployed, as measured in these surveys, tend to be those who can afford to remain unemployed while they search for the type of job, undoubtedly in the urban formal sector, that they want and for which they believe their educational attainment qualifies them. They are in fact likely to come from the better-off families in the society and to be supported by their parents through an extended period of search for the "right" job.

The very poor may appear less often in the unemployment statistics, and when they do appear they do not remain unemployed for so long. Because they lack resources, they cannot be without work for more than a brief period or they and their families will starve. They must therefore accept almost any job that becomes available. It has been ironically observed that in a poor country unemployment is a luxury. In other words it is a concomitant of a job-search process which only the relatively privileged can afford to make. LDCs lack unemployment insurance and other forms of social support common in the developed countries, so only the relatively well-off can afford to remain unemployed during an extended job search.

If the standard concept of unemployment is an inadequate measure of labor underutilization in developing countries, what better measure might be devised? This is a complex matter because there are in fact several different kinds of underutilization which are common in LDCs and it is hard to encompass them all in any single measure. These are depicted in Table 8–5.

TABLE 8–5   Types of Labor Underutilization in Developing Countries

Type	Unemployment	Underemployment
Visible	Mostly urban new entrants	Rural labor; seasonal
Invisible	Mostly women ("discouraged workers")	Rural labor + urban informal sector ("disguised unemployment")

The developed country concept of unemployment is characterized here as *visible unemployment.* Many of the people found in this category are urban-dwelling new entrants to the labor force. Rural workers may also be found in this category, but they are more likely to fall into the category labeled *visible underemployment.* That is, in slack seasons they suffer from having insufficient hours of work available to them, although they do continue to work enough hours to escape being classified as unemployed according to the usual definition.

Outright unemployment and underemployment (in the sense of working short hours and wishing to work more) are visible and easily measured. Other important forms of labor underutilization in low-income countries are "invisible" or "disguised." In Table 8–5, "invisible unemployment" represents the "discouraged worker" phenomenon discussed earlier. "Invisible underemployment" represents a category which has featured prominently in theoretical discussions of development.

It has been argued that the major form of labor underutilization in poor countries is "disguised unemployment." Workers in this category are fully, but unproductively, employed in the rural sector or urban informal sector. Standard examples of disguised unemployment include the street vendor who sits for hours just to make one or two trivial sales, the shoeshine boy, and the goatherd. These people, it is argued, contribute little or nothing to production. Like those who are conventionally classified as unemployed, they could be put to work somewhere else in the economy at low or zero opportunity cost. We will discuss the merits of this argument as a guide to development policy later on. The important point here is that while this category of labor underutilization may be large and important, it is exceedingly difficult to define and measure precisely.

One country profile of labor underutilization, based on a framework similar to Table 8–5, was provided by the 1970 International Labour Office (ILO) employment mission to Colombia.[1] Visible unemployment in urban areas was running at 14 percent of labor force, but the mission estimated

1. International Labour Office, *Towards Full Employment* (Geneva, 1970), pp. 13–28.

that when "discouraged workers" and the underemployed (those working involuntarily shortened hours) were taken into account urban labor underutilization rose to at least 25 percent. If "disguised unemployment," as indicated by extremely low income, was added in, then it rose to one-third of the labor force. In rural areas everyone was apparently employed at the peak season, but at least one-sixth of the labor force earned incomes low enough to be characterized as "disguised unemployment."

Other possible approaches to the problem of measuring labor underutilization are the *econometeric estimation of surplus labor,* replacement of a labor-use criterion with an *income criterion,* and the *labor utilization* schema proposed by Philip Hauser.

In the surplus-labor approach estimates are made of two magnitudes: the amount of labor available and the amount needed to produce the current level of output, using some specified technology. The difference between these two is labor surplus. The technique has most frequently been applied to the agricultural sectors of Asian and African countries. Some of the best known estimates are for Indian agriculture. For example, in a well-known 1966 article Mehra reported a surplus equal to 17 percent of available labor.[2] The problem with this approach is that it is difficult to specify either available supply or needs precisely and unambiguously. "Needs" in particular can be defined only in relation to a specific technology. With a different technology a very different quantity of labor may be "needed." Thus the econometric approach can be only a notional indicator of disguised unemployment.

The difficulty of measuring labor underutilization in developing countries has led some analysts to propose abandoning the attempt entirely and substituting an effort to answer a different, if related, question. David Turnham has proposed that unemployment in developing countries should be redefined in terms of earnings.[3] He argues as follows. Low productivity is a more common situation than unemployment and represents a greater waste of resources. Employed workers earning low incomes are a bigger social problem than the unemployed sons of the middle class.[4] A useful definition of unemployment would therefore focus on low productivity regardless of cause. Income differentials provide an objective basis for defining marginal occupations. Under Turnham's alternative scheme, therefore, attention would focus on the measurement of income rather than unemployment or hours of work.

Turnham's emphasis on poverty is welcome in its own right, but it is not an adequate substitute for analysis of degrees and forms of labor utilization

2. S. Mehra, "Surplus Labor in Indian Agriculture," *Indian Economic Review* (April 1966).

3. David Turnham, assisted by Ingelies Jaeger, *The Employment Problem in Less Developed Countries: A Review of Evidence* (Paris: Organization for Economic Cooperation and Development, 1971).

4. The latter, however, may be a bigger *political* problem because the unemployed and their families may be well placed to put pressure on the government. See the discussion of "urban bias" in Chapters 4 and 6, as well as the discussion of employment policy later in this chapter.

as a *cause* of low productivity and income. In other words we cannot focus exclusively on the *result,* low income. We must also look at the causes. What is most needed is measures of the quality or "hardness" of employment, since in poor societies nearly everyone must find *some* kind of employment in order to survive. One of the most ambitious efforts to devise alternative measurement schemes more suited to the environments and needs of the developing countries is the "labor utilization framework" developed by Philip Hauser.[5] It divides the population age ten and over into four categories:

1. Work for wages or profit;
2. Work outside the home without monetary payment (that is, unpaid or for payment in kind; includes sharecroppers, unpaid servants, and labor exchanges);
3. Work inside the home without monetary payment (unpaid family workers);
4. Others (students, the disabled, retirees, inmates, etc).

Data on income, industries, and occupations (including second jobs) are then collected.

Based on these data it is possible to analyze several different forms of labor underutilization: unemployment; underutilization by virtue of short hours; underutilization by virtue of insufficient income and productivity; and underutilization by virtue of doing work which makes insufficient use of one's educational attainment. Studies carried out in six Asian countries provided data which usefully supplemented the information gathered through the usual labor force surveys. They showed underutilization of the male labor force ranging from a low of 11 percent in Malaysia to a high of 42 percent in the Philippines. Underutilization of female labor was greater in almost all cases, running from 15 percent (Malaysia) to 58 percent (Philippines). In all six countries open unemployment was the most important form of underutilization and low income (productivity) the next most important.

Because of the many difficulties of defining and measuring labor utilization, it is not certain just how the overall degree of labor utilization varies with the level of economic development. The highest rates of visible unemployment, often reaching 10 to 20 percent of the labor force, have been measured in the urban areas of low- and middle-income countries. According to broader definitions of underutilization, still larger shares of the labor force are underutilized and overall underutilization is probably greatest in the poorest countries. "Disguised" forms of underutilization are relatively more important in the poorest countries than in the somewhat richer ones. In the semideveloped countries covered by the Hauser and ILO surveys cited above, "disguised unemployment" was significant but quantitatively somewhat less than open unemployment.

5. See Philip M. Hauser, "The Measurement of Labour Utilization," *Malayan Economic Review* 19, no. 1 (April 1974): 16–34, and his "The Measurement of Labour Utilization— More Empirical Results," *Malayan Economic Review* 22, no. 1 (April 1977): 10–25.

Nor is it easy for trends to be established with certainty, but many observers suspect that the degree of labor underutilization in most LDCs increased during the 1970s. On the supply side this reflects faster labor force growth, and on the demand side factors limiting the growth of labor absorption which will be discussed later on.

Labor Reallocation

Costs and Benefits

We cannot talk about employment policy in developing countries without broaching an issue which has been debated extensively by development theorists: how underutilized labor can be used in a development strategy. In theoretical writings of the 1950s it was frequently asserted that large numbers of people engage in work which adds nothing to national output. Two well-known writers who emphasized this idea and made it a cornerstone of their analyses of how development proceeds were Ragnar Nurkse and W. Arthur Lewis.[6] Nurkse saw the reallocation of surplus labor to more productive uses, especially labor-intensive construction projects, as a major source of capital formation and economic growth. Lewis envisaged a similar reallocation process except that he pictured the "capitalist sector," essentially industry, as the principal employer of the surplus labor. (Chapters 3 and 4 discuss Lewis's theory in detail.) Both theorists regarded the labor reallocation process as practically costless, although they did discuss the problem of how to capture from the agricultural sector the food necessary to feed the reallocated laborers.

This approach to development theory instituted a long-running debate on what the marginal product of labor in LDC agriculture actually is and how readily any excess labor can be mobilized in industry or construction projects. The consensus emerging from this debate can be summarized as follows:

1. The marginal product of labor is almost always positive, not zero, although it may be very low, for instance in densely populated Asian countries. At least this is true on a year-round basis. If there is really such a thing as zero-marginal-product labor, the condition is likely to be seasonal.

2. Even if output forgone were zero or negligible, there are other costs associated with the physical movement of labor, often from country to town, likely to be required if it is to be shifted from agricultural pursuits to industry or construction. (This point will be further discussed shortly.)

3. Although growth in the long run consists of reallocating labor to higher productivity uses, there are no free, or even very easy, gains to be had in the short run.

Putting this consensus in more positive terms, it can be said that in almost all countries and times there are opportunities to work, for example,

6. Ragnar Nurkse, *Problems of Capital Formation in Underdeveloped Countries* (Oxford: Basil Blackwell, 1957; first published in 1953); W. Arthur Lewis, "Economic Development with Unlimited Supplies of Labour," *The Manchester School* 22, no. 2 (1954): 139–91.

as an agricultural laborer, at some positive wage and marginal product, even though these may be very low. Some may remain unemployed despite such opportunities; they probably reject the wage offered because it is too low to compensate for their loss of "leisure" and the chance to search for a better paid job.

If this is so, how should an LDC government look at an employment-creating development project? We have already seen (in Chapter 6) that any development project can be evaluated through social cost-benefit analysis. An important part of the social cost of any input is its "opportunity cost"—its value in its next best alternative use. Labor hired for an urban formal-sector project might well be drawn from the urban informal sector. The worker who moves out of the urban informal sector may in turn be replaced by someone from the rural sector. In this example the output lost is that of the worker who was formerly in the rural sector—that is, the one at the end of the employment chain. For this reason some analysts believe that the wage paid to casual agricultural laborers provides a good measure of the social cost of unskilled labor.

However, this measure, while a good indicator of output forgone through labor reallocation, probably understates the true social cost of employing labor, which has other components that are likely to be significant.

One such significant component is *induced migration.* An influential model of rural-urban migration, developed by John Harris and Michael Todaro (see following section), implies that migrating workers are essentially participants in a lottery of relatively high-paid jobs in the towns. When new urban jobs are created, the lottery becomes more attractive to potential migrants. Depending on their responsiveness to this improved opportunity, it is possible that more than one worker will migrate for each job created. If this happens, then the output forgone may be that of two or more agricultural workers, not just one. Familial ties may multiply this effect. If a male worker migrates bringing his family with him, additional output may be forgone because the wife and children find fewer employment opportunities in the town than in the rural areas.

In addition to forgone output, certain *costs of urbanization* should be taken into account in computing the social cost of urban job creation. Some of these costs are internalized by the worker, and presumably taken into account in the migration decision: the higher cost of food, housing, and other items in the town. Other costs are external and must be borne by society as a whole: social services which are provided only to the urban population or are more expensive in the town, pollution, congestion, additional security requirements. It is these costs which make many third world governments frown on urbanization, however much they may desire industrialization.

Finally, there is the possibility of a *reduction in national savings,* which has worried development theorists and Soviet-style economic planners alike. If labor which has been adding little or nothing to agricultural output, but has been consuming a share of that product, is withdrawn from the sector, who controls the food thus freed up? The government's aim is to find a way to remove the food that the worker was consuming in order to feed the same worker in the city. What it fears is that the rural population which remains behind will simply increase its per-capita consumption. Since the urban labor force must be fed—from imports if not from domestic production—the danger is that aggregate national consumption will rise and national savings will fall. During the 1930s this threat moved Soviet planners to drastic measures to extract a surplus from a resistant rural population. Governments of less developed countries generally have neither the means nor the desire to suppress food consumption, so they may indeed experience some decline in savings. This is far from a pure loss, however, because the added consumption is a gain to some members of society. In any case there are other means to increase saving than coercive controls over food consumption.

The primary *benefit* of urban employment is its added output. A highly productive project may easily repay all the costs discussed above. Low productivity, make-work projects in urban areas, by contrast, may incur costs with few offsetting benefits; labor-intensive projects in rural areas (especially those which employ seasonally underutilized labor) are likely to be more beneficial because they do not require workers to migrate. These projects are discussed toward the end of this chapter.

A secondary benefit of urban job creation is the training which it may provide. In LDCs opportunities to learn skills useful in the modern economy are concentrated in urban areas. For example, the ability to operate and repair machinery of all kinds is typically rare. A worker who comes to town can acquire these skills. In doing so he may benefit himself if he can find employment as a skilled worker and obtain higher wages. But he also confers an "external benefit" on society because everyone benefits when bus drivers, auto mechanics, appliance repairmen, and others who work with machinery learn to do their jobs better. This applies to both employers, who can hire labor from a more skilled pool, and consumers, who get better service.

It is evident that developing through the reallocation of low-productivity labor is a more complex business than Nurkse and Lewis imagined in the 1950s. Nevertheless employment expansion remains an important means of both expanding output and redistributing income. A government that can create projects in which the marginal product of labor exceeds its social cost, taking into account all the elements discussed here, can achieve both of these objectives simultaneously. Output goes up and additional income is put in the hands of poor, unskilled workers. Less productive forms of employment creation, in which the social cost of labor exceeds its marginal product, might still be acceptable as redistributive measures, particularly if other ways to achieve the desired amount of redistribution are unavailable. But this would achieve more equity only at the cost of less growth.

Migration

As GNP rises and the structure of employment changes there is bound to be movement of workers and their families from place to place. Most of this *internal migration* is from rural to urban areas. A long succession of theorists has argued that economic factors dominate the decision to migrate. Some early writers distinguished between "pull" and "push" factors. They said that rural-urban migration can result either from favorable economic developments in the town or from adverse developments in the countryside. The Harris-Todaro model integrates these two sets of factors by focusing on the rural-urban wage differential. Yet there is something to the older notion. Just as eighteenth-century English cottagers were pushed into the town by the Enclosure Movement, so peasants in eastern India move to Calcutta primarily because of wretched conditions in the surrounding countryside rather than outstanding income or employment opportunities in Calcutta itself. By contrast the growth of dynamic third world cities such as São Paulo and Nairobi could be attributed at least partly to "pull" factors.

The Harris-Todaro model of rural-urban migration is a recent formulation of the importance of economic incentives in the migration decision.[7] The model assumes that migration depends primarily on a comparison of wages in the rural and urban labor markets. That is,

$$M_t = f(W_U - W_R) \qquad\qquad [8\text{--}1]$$

where M_t = number of rural to urban migrants in time period t, f = a responsive function, W_U = urban wage, and W_R = rural wage. Since there is unemployment in the town (assume that there is none in the countryside) and every migrant cannot expect to find a job there, the model postulates that the *expected* urban wage is compared to the rural wage. The expected urban wage is the actual wage times the probability of finding a job, or

$$W_U^E = pW_U \qquad\qquad [8\text{--}2]$$

where W_U^E = expected urban wage and p = probability of finding a job.

A simple way of defining p is

$$p = \frac{E_U}{E_U + U_U} \qquad\qquad [8\text{--}3]$$

where E_U = urban employment, and U_U = urban unemployment. In this formulation all members of the urban labor force are assumed to have equal chances of obtaining the jobs available, so that W_U^E becomes simply the urban wage times the urban employment rate. Migration in any given time period then depends on three factors: the rural-urban wage gap, the urban employment rate, and the responsiveness of potential migrants to the resulting opportunities.

$$M_t = h(pW_U - W_R) \qquad\qquad [8\text{--}4]$$

where M_t = migration in period t, and h = response rate of potential migrants.

As long as W_U^E exceeds W_R the model predicts that rural-urban migration

7. John R. Harris and Michael P. Todaro, "Migration, Unemployment and Development: A Two-Sector Analysis," *American Economic Review* 60 (March 1960): 126–42.

will continue. It will only stop when migration has forced down the urban wage, or forced up urban unemployment, sufficiently that $W_U^E = W_R$. It is also possible that W_R is greater than W_U^E, in which case there will be a flow of disappointed urban job seekers back to the countryside.

Critics of the Harris-Todaro model point out that the equilibrium condition specified by the model is seldom attained. It is common for urban wages to be, say, 50 or 100 percent higher than rural wages and for urban unemployment to run at 10–20 percent of the labor force. If the figures stay in this range, the expected urban wage (W_U^E) remains above the rural wage (W_R). Migration in practice does not seem to close the gap between W_U^E and W_R as the model predicts. Nor can the theory account fully for "reverse migration" from town to country, which is significant in many countries. Some "reverse migrants" may indeed be disappointed urban job seekers returning home in despair, but even more of this two-way or "circular" migration may be intentional. Workers, especially young, unattached males, often migrate *temporarily* to towns, mines, or plantations, work for a while and amass savings, which they then take back to the rural areas to invest in land, farm improvements, or marriage. This pattern of migration has been especially evident in parts of Africa, perhaps because in many African cultures women normally tend the crops after the men have planted them. The opportunity cost of absent males outside the planting season is thus low.

Economic factors are not the only important influences on migration decisions. Studies have shown that distance and social ties are also significant. Migrants to expanding urban areas tend to come from nearby rural regions, while peasants who have been pushed out of their native districts by some calamity or other are likely to go to the nearest large town. People also tend to migrate to areas where members of their family, village, or ethnic group have gone ahead. Finally, some migrants, especially young males, are attracted by the "bright lights" and excitement of the city. But the view common in the 1950s and earlier that people come for the "bright lights" regardless of the personal economic benefit has been discredited by the work of Harris and Todaro and others.

Although most internal migration in developing countries undoubtedly involves rural-to-urban movement, interregional differences in economic opportunity can bring about substantial rural-to-rural movement as well. Countries fortunate enough to possess lightly settled but cultivable regions often try to bring about such movement as a matter of public policy (see Chapter 7). Unless there are massive physical or legal barriers to settlement of these relatively empty areas, however, these interregional movements tend to occur spontaneously. This has happened in Nepal, for instance, where farmers have moved from the densely packed Katmandu Valley into the southern *terai* region, and in many parts of Africa and South America.

Where internal migration is concerned, it is usually safe to assume that unforced movements of population from one region to another are socially beneficial. People make these moves to benefit themselves and their families. Provided that incentives are not too badly distorted, society is likely to benefit as well from an improved spatial allocation of labor relative to the location of other resources. Even in the most congested slums of major LDC cities (São Paulo, Lagos, Jakarta) migrants report that they are better off than they were in the rural areas and generally do not want to go back.

International migration is frequently regarded as altogether a different matter. To bring a degree of cool rationality to this often heated subject, it is helpful to distinguish between unskilled labor and skilled or educated labor. This distinction may not matter when we look at the problem from the global point of view: it has been argued that world GNP is maximized when everyone works where his salary, and therefore presumably his productivity, is greatest. But it is important when we examine the problem from the viewpoint of the LDCs because skilled and unskilled labor have different opportunity costs.

There are two reasons why the migration of educated, highly skilled labor is abhorrent to most third world countries and has been stigmatized as the "brain drain." One is that such people represent one of the LDCs' scarcest resources. The other is that in most cases their education has been time-consuming, expensive, and heavily subsidized by the state. Their departure for foreign lands can thus be costly. Not only are their services lost, but the cost of training a replacement is likely to be high. Yet if they are so productive at home, why are they not paid enough to keep them there? The answer may be nonmarket influences on the salary structure. For example, if most doctors and engineers work for the government and their salaries are held down to avoid politically embarrassing salary differentials, it is not surprising that many of them seek an opportunity to emigrate. Often international agencies, which recruit in a worldwide labor market, pay far more for the same skills than national governments. This is the reason why one can find Pakistani experts working in Egypt, for example, even as Egyptian experts are employed in Pakistan, despite the likelihood that both groups could work more effectively in their own countries.

International migration of the educated, while it probably raises world GNP, worsens the distribution of income between rich and poor countries. For this reason Jagdish Bhagwati has proposed a "tax on the brain drain," to be collected by the governments of developed countries to which professional and technical personnel from underdeveloped countries have migrated.[8] The proceeds of the tax would be transferred to the poor countries as partial compensation for the loss of talent that they have suffered.

In contrast, international migration of unskilled labor can be beneficial to the country of emigration. Unskilled workers are a more plentiful resource, and their loss is therefore likely to be felt less keenly by the sending economy. There are even significant offsetting benefits. One is remittances: unskilled migrants are less likely to take their families along, and are thus more likely to send money back. This makes labor a kind of national export. For countries such as Turkey, Algeria, and Egypt, worker remittances

---

8. Jagdish Bhagwati and Martin Partington, *Taxing the Brain Drain: A Proposal* (Amsterdam: North-Holland, 1976).

are a major source of foreign exchange earnings. A second potential benefit is training. Unskilled workers who go abroad generally return to their native lands after a few years, bringing back usable skills acquired abroad.

Recently some LDC governments have begun to look more favorably on worker emigration. Despairing of generating enough employment at home, they have begun to encourage their people to go abroad, at least for a while. The South Asian countries, for example, have taken advantage of lucrative employment opportunities in the oil-enriched Middle East. When education is particularly cheap, even the emigration of trained personnel may be encouraged. The Philippines has been exporting doctors and nurses in quantity for years.

Employment Policy

The Employment Problem

By now the main elements of the employment problem in developing countries should be evident. Population and labor force have grown rapidly relative to the natural resource base. Although capital stock has usually risen even faster, it has generally not been deployed in ways that absorb as much labor as might have been possible. It was once thought that industrialization would solve the employment problem in most LDCs. Certainly this was the premise, for example, of India's first two five-year plans. By contrast actual labor absorption by the industrial sector has been disappointing. A simple example will help to explain why this is so.

Industrial sectors in developing countries typically grow rapidly from a low base. Take the example of Malaysia in the 1960s and 1970s. Value added in industry (defined to include manufacturing, utilities, and construction) grew rapidly, about 10 percent a year from 1960 to 1979. Yet employment growth in the sector, as in many other developing countries, was only about half as fast, 5 percent a year. The amount of industrial employment growth expected from a given rate of output growth can be expressed by the following formula:

$$g(E_i) = \eta g(V_i)S_i$$

where $g(E_i)$ = employment growth, expressed as a percentage of total employment; η = an elasticity relating the growth rate of employment to the growth rate of value added; $g(V_i)$ = growth in industrial value added, expressed in percentage points; and S_i = industrial employment as a fraction of total employment. In Malaysia industry accounted for 12 percent of the labor force in 1960, so

$$g(E_i) = 0.5 \times 10\% \times .12 = 0.6\%$$

This means that only six-tenths of 1 percent of the labor force would be absorbed by industrial expansion each year. Yet the labor force grew at 2.7 percent a year from 1960 to 1979. The implication is that less than one-fourth of the workers entering the labor force could find jobs in industry. The rest had to do the best they could in primary production (which was actually expelling rather than absorbing labor on a net basis), or more likely in the service sector.

Is this too pessimistic a depiction of the problem? On the brighter side it can be noted that only *direct employment creation* in industry has been taken into account. Some additional *indirect job creation* can be expected in sectors with either forward or backward linkages to the industrial sector, such as service activities which distribute industry's products and agricultural and mining activities which supply its inputs (linkages within the industrial sector are already accounted for in the model). Indirect job creation can be significant in some circumstances, such as when the capacity to process domestically produced primary commodities is expanded, but it has frequently been weak for the type of import-substituting industrialization experienced by many LDCs, which has few forward or backward linkages. (See Chapter 16 for further discussion.)

Since industrial jobs are often some of the most productive and desirable ones in the economy, it is important to ask what can be done to improve industry's typically weak employment-creation record. In terms of the formula given above, raising $g(E_1)$ requires increasing η, $g(V_i)$, S_i, or some combination of them. Industry's share in employment (S_i) will rise only gradually through time. In the medium term industrial labor absorption can be increased by raising either the growth rate of sectoral value added, $g(V_i)$, or the employment elasticity, η.

The values used in the Malaysian illustration are similar to the experience of many third world countries. There are, however, a few countries that have been able to expand industrial employment much more rapidly. These are also the countries that have achieved greatest success in exporting labor-intensive manufactures. Outstanding among them are South Korea, Taiwan, Hong Kong, and Singapore, sometimes known collectively as the "Gang of Four." There are two separate aspects to their achievement. First, by breaking into the export market they have been able to reach higher growth rates of industrial output, $g(V_i)$, because they have not had to depend on growth of the domestic market for manufactured goods. Second, they have experienced high values of η because the goods they have chosen to export are those which use large amounts of their most plentiful resource, labor. These countries have experienced values of η of around 0.8 instead of the more typical 0.4 to 0.5. Thus Korea after 1963 was able to absorb as much as half of its total labor force growth in manufactured exports alone, at a time when most LDCs were absorbing less than 5 percent of labor force growth in this activity.[9]

The generally poor employment performance of industry is particularly distressing when we remember that the sector should not only be soaking up a good share of labor force growth, but also gradually drawing labor away from less productive forms of employment in peasant agriculture, petty services, and cottage industry. When it fails to achieve either of these

---

9. Susumu Watanabe, "Exports and Employment: The Case of the Republic of Korea," *International Labour Review* 106, no. 6 (December 1972): 495–526.

ends, employment in these less productive sectors will have to rise rather than fall. This can lead to stagnant, or even declining, levels of productivity and income. There is evidence that this is in fact happening, especially in some of the poorest and least rapidly growing countries.

Although the above discussion has been couched in terms of industry, it can easily be extended to cover the entire urban formal sector. Large trading companies, financial organizations, transport and communication facilities, public utilities, and the like may collectively be even more important for intersectoral labor transfer than industry. And they, too, often fail to increase their employment fast enough to satisfy development planners.

Elements of a Solution

In principle the problem of labor underutilization could be attacked on either the supply or the demand side. In practice, however, little can be done to bring about a supply-side adjustment. Labor supply grows steadily from year to year. It is hard to discourage people from seeking work. Nor would most policy-makers wish to do so, given the advantages of employment creation as a means of income redistribution and the psychological and political advantages of enabling everyone to participate in the economy. The only real supply-side potential is to reduce the growth of labor supply in the long run by reducing population growth.

Some years ago it was widely believed that increasing the supply of certain types of skilled labor would produce a strong expansionary effect on employment generally through increased absorption of complementary unskilled labor. Thus India in its early postindependence years moved fast to eliminate a suspected manpower bottleneck by expanding the supply of engineers, thinking that employment in construction and other activities would be increased in this way. The number of Indian engineers increased rapidly. The effect on general employment is hard to determine, but the effect on the engineers was clear-cut: there were soon far too many of them, and many of them were unemployed. The moral is that while skill shortages can constrain employment and output growth, they can sometimes be eliminated relatively quickly and easily through expansion of education and training programs (or through migration). In other countries, where education is less developed, skill formation may be much more difficult and time-consuming.

Since the potential for correcting the labor market disequilibrium by working on the supply side is quite limited, policy must concentrate on the demand side of the equation. Many different kinds of policy affect the economy's ability to create jobs for a growing labor force. Wage, industrial promotion, fiscal, foreign trade, education, and population policies—all have important implications for employment. For this reason other chapters of this book make frequent references to employment, supplementing the discussion in the present chapter.

We have already noted the importance of two different approaches to employment creation. One is to stimulate output, especially in relatively high-productivity and high-wage sectors of the economy. The other is to try to increase the amount of labor used to produce a given amount of output. The first approach is discussed in Chapters 19 and 20, which deal with the growth of the agricultural and industrial sectors. The second will be examined here.

How can production be made more labor-intensive? Two major answers have been suggested by development specialists. One is to alter relative prices and thus create incentives for businesses to substitute labor for capital. The other is to develop technologies more appropriate to the factor proportions prevailing in developing countries.

Factor Pricing

The prices of labor and capital faced by modern-sector firms in less developed countries are frequently distorted in ways that make capital artificially cheap relative to labor. This distortion can inhibit labor absorption at several levels. At the sectoral level it can promote the growth of sectors which are technologically better suited to capital-intensive production (say, basic metals) and hinder the growth of sectors which tend to be more labor-intensive (say, textiles). At the level of interfirm competition it can promote the appearance and growth of plants using relatively capital-intensive technologies (these may be large and/or foreign-owned) and accelerate the decline and disappearance of more labor-intensive units. At the plant level it can promote the use of machines in place of men and women.

Where do these factor price distortions originate? In most cases some sort of government action is involved. Artificially high wages may be imposed on modern-sector firms by minimum-wage laws, by government support of trade union demands, or by pressure on firms (especially foreign- and state-owned enterprises) to be "model employers." Some governments levy payroll or social security taxes on modern-sector payrolls, thus raising the cost of labor to the employer. Another common situation is that when jobs once done by foreigners are taken over by citizens, nationalist pressures cause salaries to be kept at their previously high, internationally competitive levels.

All these policies promote the welfare of one relatively small group at the expense of a much larger group. On the one hand minimum-wage laws and similar measures, if enforced (often they are not effectively enforced), make wages and working conditions better for those workers fortunate enough to get jobs in modern-sector firms. On the other hand by raising the cost of labor they limit the ability of these firms to absorb more workers and inhibit the creation of more enterprises like them. In other words they improve the well-being of the relatively small group of modern-sector employees at the cost of the much larger group that is either unemployed or working in the informal and rural sectors.

Why do governments of countries with serious employment problems enact such measures as minimum-wage laws? The answer lies in points of political economy that have been discussed in earlier chapters. Relatively small but well-organized, vocal, and visible groups of modern-sector workers, nearly always located in urban areas, use their political power to press for enactment of these laws, or for increases in the statutory minimum once a system of minimum wages is established. Under this kind of system the government is typically held directly responsible for the earnings of workers in the protected sectors. If it resists a strongly backed demand for a rise in the minimum wage, it is inviting political trouble. Of course the government is also responsible for the welfare of those who lose from the wage increase because their chances of ever getting a job in the protected high-wage sector are reduced. But their loss is less easily perceived than the wage gain of the protected workers, and the government is less likely to be held accountable for it.

Artificially cheap capital can reinforce the effect of artificially expensive labor. Many LDCs maintain legal ceilings on interest rates. These make capital equipment cheaper for those preferred customers who can obtain the credit necessary to buy it. (For the rest, of course, capital may become more expensive, or even unobtainable, as banks and other financial institutions direct the available funds to their preferred customers.) Overvaluation of the domestic currency in terms of foreign exchange can have a similar effect. It forces the imposition of a licensing system for foreign exchange and/or imports, and this in turn makes artificially cheapened capital goods available to those who can obtain the necessary licenses (see Part III).

Like minimum wages, interest ceilings, foreign exchange control, and import licensing are enacted to serve the interests of influential minorities. In the case of Pakistan, for example, Lawrence White has shown how preferred access to imports and credit led to the increasing concentration of industry and commerce in the hands of an elite group known as "The Twenty Families."[10] Licensing systems also receive strong support from officials of the license-granting authorities, who can earn substantial illicit income from the bestowal of their favors.

Another way governments help to make capital artificially cheap is by gearing investment incentives to the amount of capital invested. Often a firm that invests $50 million is given a longer tax holiday or a shorter write-off period than one that invests only $5 million. This creates incentives for capital-intensive industries to set up in the country and for firms which face a range of possible technologies to select more capital-intensive modes of production.

What can be done to correct these factor price distortions? Certainly the most straightforward approach is for governments to avoid the kinds of price-distorting policies mentioned above, or if they have already instituted them, to deregulate as soon as possible. Often, however, they are reluctant to do so, either because of concern for the welfare of workers already holding modern-sector jobs or because of the political power of those who benefit from artificially high wages or artificially cheap capital and foreign exchange.

When price distortions cannot be changed by direct means it may be

---

10. Lawrence White, *Industrial Concentration and Economic Power in Pakistan* (Princeton: Princeton University Press, 1974).

possible to offset them by taxes or subsidies. Some economists argue that artificially high labor costs faced by modern-sector employers should be offset by a wage subsidy. This advice has been followed rarely if at all, although a few countries have adopted investment incentives that depend in part on the number of jobs an investor creates.

An important question about all these proposals for correcting factor price distortions is how great their employment-creating effect is likely to be. Technically speaking this depends on the *elasticity of substitution,* which can be defined as:

$$\sigma = \frac{d(K/L)}{d(w/r)} \cdot \frac{w/r}{K/L}$$

where K = amount of capital, L = amount of labor, w = wage rate, r = cost of capital, and d = first derivative or difference. The elasticity of substitution is thus the percentage change in the capital/labor ratio, $d(K/L)/(K/L)$, that results from a given percentage change in the ratio of the price of labor to that of capital, $d(w/r)/(w/r)$. (The expression w/r is also called the *wage/ rental ratio.*) Thus if a 10 percent decline in the wage/rental ratio leads to a 5 percent fall in the capital/labor ratio, then the elasticity of substitution is 0.5. In these circumstances a 10 percent decline in the wage/rental ratio would mean that in the future it would take 5 percent less investment (capital) to employ a given amount of labor; alternatively, a given amount of investment would employ 5 percent more workers.

Debates over the efficiency of employment creation through correction of factor price distortions have ranged the "elasticity optimists" against the "elasticity pessimists." The optimists have argued that the employment effects are likely to be large because investors tend to be rational profit maximizers who have a range of possible outputs and technologies open to them. When faced with cheaper labor relative to capital they will therefore make two kinds of adjustment: they will concentrate on goods that can be produced relatively efficiently using a lot of labor relative to capital; and they will tend to use more labor-intensive technologies in all their operations. (The optimists assume that these investors actually have a "shelf" of "appropriate technologies" available to them, an issue which will be explored in the following section.)

The pessimists, on the other hand, argue that the response to a change in the wage/rental ratio may be small or nonexistent. There certainly are modern industries whose technologies permit little substitution of labor for capital. Examples include the "process industries" such as petrochemicals and wood pulp. In such industries highly capital-intensive technologies may be *absolutely* more efficient than any less capital-intensive alternatives. That is, they may use less capital per unit of output *as well as* less labor. In many cases these technical characteristics are linked to economies of scale: a plant must be very large, as well as highly capital-intensive, to be efficient. An LDC government might well think twice before establishing such an industry, but it would be ill-advised to try to make it labor-intensive.

The "elasticity pessimists" also point out that many firms sell in oligopolistic markets and therefore do not necessarily have to maximize profits; that they may prefer the most "modern" (and therefore capital-intensive) technologies for their own sake; and that they may produce goods mainly for middle-class consumption to which capital-intensive technologies are better suited than labor-intensive technologies. For all these reasons the pessimists argue against the policies advocated by the optimists. They would expect, for example, that a wage subsidy would do more to increase business profits than to expand employment.

Figures 8–2 and 8–3 show the difference between what the pessimists and the optimists have in mind. According to the pessimists the elasticity of substitution (σ) is low; factor proportions are relatively fixed, as in Fig. 8–2, which is similar to the fixed-coefficients production function depicted in Fig. 6–4. Isoquants I and II in Fig. 8–2 represent different levels of output (see explanation in Chapter 6). The wage/rental ratio, w/r, is given by the slope of the budget line BB. (The budget line defines combinations of labor and capital that can be purchased with a given monetary outlay.) For a given budget line (say, B_1B_1 in Fig. 8–2) and corresponding wage/rental ratio (w/r_1), the amounts of capital and labor used to produce a given level of output (in this case 100,000 units) are determined. Should the wage/rental ratio fall, say, to (w/r_2), there is relatively little effect on the amounts of labor and capital used to produce 100,000 units of output because the isoquants are nearly L-shaped.

Things are different in the world envisaged by the elasticity optimists. This world is shown in Fig. 8–3, which duplicates the neoclassical production function of Fig. 6–5. Here the technology permits more factor substi-

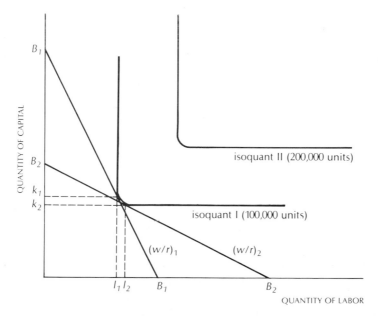

Fig. 8–2   Factor Substitution with Relatively Fixed Factor Proportions (Low Elasticity of Substitution).

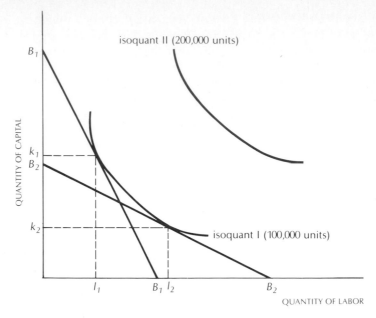

Fig. 8–3 Factor Substitution with Relatively Variable Factor Proportions (High Elasticity of Substitution).

tution (σ is high), so when the wage/rental ratio falls from (w/r_1) to (w/r_2) the amount of capital used is sharply reduced while employment expands significantly.

Which is the better depiction of the real world, Fig. 8–2 or Fig. 8–3? It might seem a simple matter to calculate the elasticity of substitution in developing countries and settle the argument once and for all. And indeed many econometric estimates have been made. Quite a number of these studies have found the value of σ to be from 0.4 to 0.5, not dramatically high values but high enough to encourage the elasticity optimists. But other writers have criticized these estimates on various grounds: they assume labor and capital to be homogeneous—that is, of uniform quality—when in fact they are not; they ignore the roles of other factors of production, such as management; they often deal with industries that are defined so broadly as to encompass a variety of outputs; and so on. Modest changes in assumptions, the critics note, can lead to large differences in conclusions.

Thus the debate between the optimists and the pessimists is not so easily settled, at least not by econometric means. However, there remain good reasons for believing that the relative prices of labor and capital can make a significant difference for employment creation.

1. Whatever the range of technologies available *for producing a particular item,* factor prices can have an important influence on employment by affecting *the choice of goods to be produced.* Recall the example of the successful exporters of labor-intensive manufacturers mentioned earlier.

2. Even if the technology of a core production process is fixed and capi-

tal-intensive, opportunities exist for using large amounts of labor in subsidiary operations such as materials handling. Similarly, in construction some operations are best done by machines at almost any wage/rental ratio, but others lend themselves to labor-intensive methods if "the price is right."

3. Employers are much more responsive to relative factor prices if they are forced to sell their products in competitive markets than if they can sell in oligopolistic markets. An important study conducted in Indonesia by Louis Wells showed that while the nonmaximizing behaviors cited by the elasticity pessimists are real enough, businessmen indulge them much more freely under oligopolistic market conditions.[11] When the competition forces them to seek the most profitable technologies and factor proportions, both domestic and foreign businessmen find ways to economize on capital and substitute more labor in labor-rich, capital-scarce countries.

A broad statement of the conclusion which emerges from these three points is that *openness* promotes appropriate factor choices. Increasing the degree of competition, both within a given economy and among economies (see Chapters 16 and 17), can go a long way toward validating the assumptions of the elasticity optimists and making it possible to promote employment by reducing factor price distortions.

The Role of Technology

For the employment problem to be solved, or even significantly ameliorated, technology appropriate to the factor endowments of the low- and middle-income countries is clearly needed. Does such technology already exist? If not, how can it be brought into existence?

Everyone agrees that much of the technology used in high-income countries is inappropriate to the needs of low- and middle-income countries. Since the beginning of their industrialization processes the United States and Europe have had a scarcity of labor relative to other factors of production. Nearly all their innovations have accordingly aimed at saving labor. The result in almost all sectors of production has been a sequence of increasingly mechanized and automatically controlled technologies, each more appropriate than the last for a country with scarce labor and plentiful capital—but less and less appropriate for a country with the opposite factor endowments.

Excessive capital intensiveness is only one dimension of the inappropriateness of developed-country technology for the LDCs. Since the economies of even the most populous LDCs are generally much smaller than those of most industrial countries, the technology is frequently designed to be efficient at a much larger scale of operation than the developing countries can hope to attain in the foreseeable future. In addition the borrowed technology may necessitate the use of skills which are unavailable in poor

11. Louis T. Wells, "Economic Man and Engineering Man: Choice of Technology in a Low Wage Country," in C. Peter Timmer et al. (eds.), *The Choice of Technology in Developing Countries: Some Cautionary Tales* (Cambridge, Mass.: Harvard University Center for International Affairs, 1975), pp. 69–93.

countries, and thus may require the importation of foreign technicians. Finally, it may be designed to produce the wrong type or grade of product: for example, no-iron synthetic fabrics in countries where cotton is cheaper and there is plenty of labor available to wash and press cotton garments.

Despite the dimensions of inappropriateness, technology developed in rich countries is often transferred intact for use in poor countries. This is not, after all, surprising. Well over 90 percent of the world's expenditure on technology research and development is made in rich countries. Third world countries invite multinational corporations to invest in their leading sectors. They obtain equipment through official aid programs. The investors and aid givers, East or West, can only provide what they know and have available. Hence the transfer of inappropriate technology.

Foreign investments and aid projects often take on the characteristics of their countries of origin. A few years ago four large road-construction projects were being carried out simultaneously in Nepal, financed by aid from the United States, West Germany, the U.S.S.R., and China. The techniques employed varied widely. Predictably, the Chinese project was by far the most labor-intensive, using large work crews brought in from China itself. The German and American projects were far more mechanized. The most capital-intensive project of all, with the largest and heaviest bulldozers and road rollers, was that of the U.S.S.R. Yet the types of road to be built and the terrain over which the roads were to run was much the same in all four project areas.

When technology available from the developed countries is inappropriate, where is more appropriate technology to be obtained? Four possible sources can be distinguished.[12] First, LDCs can use developed-country technologies but make peripheral modifications, for example, in materials handling. Second, they can borrow old technologies from the industrial countries. American technology of twenty, thirty, or even fifty years ago, it has been suggested, may be more appropriate to the setting of, say, India than the methods and machines used in the United States today. A third possible source of appropriate technology is *selective* borrowing from the industrial countries. Former British, French, American, and Dutch colonies in Southeast Asia gradually learned after independence that Japanese equipment was often better suited to their needs than the equipment they had formerly imported from the metropolitan country. Fourth, developing countries can of course do their own research and development work to evolve technologies specifically designed to fit local conditions. It is sometimes said that traditional indigenous technologies which have been developed over the years by local farmers, craftsmen, and fishermen provide a promising basis for this work.

But if these alternative channels of technological development are really open, why does much of the technology used in the third world remain so

---

12. This paragraph and the two which follow are based on Frances Stewart, "Technology and Employment in LDCs," in Edgar O. Edwards (ed.), *Employment in Developing Nations* (New York and London: Columbia University Press, 1974), pp. 83–132.

obviously inappropriate? One important reason has already been suggested: when competitive pressures are absent, incentives to adapt to local conditions are weak. Another barrier is communication difficulties. It is hard for someone sitting in Surabaya or São Paulo to know just what is available in New York or Nagasaki. Communication barriers have been an especially serious impediment to the adoption of older technologies from the industrial countries. Finally, it must be said that most third world governments have not yet fully awakened to the need to promote local research and development. Their universities are usually preoccupied with teaching, and official research institutes in various fields are often either slow to be set up or experience severe staffing difficulties once they open their doors. Sometimes in these circumstances the most useful research and development work is done by foreign firms with a long history of operations in the country.

Frances Stewart has distinguished three schools of thought on technology policies for third world countries. The first group, which she calls "the price incentive school," stresses "getting the prices right," in the belief that factor prices which reflect social costs will not only lead to the selection of the most efficient techniques out of the currently available range, but will also create incentives for more appropriate technologies to be developed. The opposing "technologist school" believes that this mechanism of induced innovation cannot be relied on to do the job, that a conscious decision to invest more in technological development is needed. Finally, there is "the radical reform school," which takes a broader view of the matter. This school argues that both the array of goods produced and the methods used to produce them are inherent features of social systems. One cannot expect anything but capital-intensive methods and products targeted for middle-class consumption from the multinational corporations. Creation of appropriate technologies and use of appropriate factor proportions, this last group argues, requires that production be reoriented toward a multitude of cheap items for mass consumption. This in turn requires a massive redistribution of income, which cannot be achieved without a social revolution. Hence the problem of inappropriate technology and inadequate job creation can only be solved in the context of a radical reform of society.

As Stewart sensibly concludes, elements of all three approaches are probably needed. The best evidence for the efficacy of radical reform comes from China. China has apparently found the social and technological solutions to permit her vast labor force to be employed more fully and productively than ever before. Chinese industry "walks on two legs;" that is, it combines large-scale, relatively capital-intensive production units with smaller, more labor-intensive and decentralized plants. Large-scale public works projects, such as dams and irrigation channels, have been another important form of labor absorption. Finally, intensified agricultural technologies using much larger amounts of fertilizer and other modern inputs have actually managed to absorb more labor productively into China's massive agricultural work force. Appropriate technology is combined with strong production organization at the local level. The rural commune contrives to provide full employment for all its members in a combination of agricultural and nonagricultural activities.

Other socialist developing countries, by contrast, have sometimes had a hard time deciding just which way they want to go. Thus different conceptions of "African socialism" prevalent in Tanzania in the early 1970s stressed decentralized small-scale industry, increased processing of domestic raw materials, and creation of a modern, self-sufficient, state-run economy —not always consistently.

Nonsocialist governments are probably best advised to rely on a mixture of price incentives and judicious investment in research and development. The kind of government-sponsored research, usually adaptive, that most third world countries conduct on peasant crops could well be extended to a wider range of activities. The comparative fortunes of different primary good exporters show what a potent force this kind of research activity can be. Ghanaian cocoa provides a sad example of what can happen when price incentives are wrong (largely because of artificially low producer prices imposed by a government marketing board) and too little is invested in research on improved varieties and planting methods. Ghana, once the supplier of two-thirds of the world's cocoa, has experienced stagnant output for years and has lost its position as the leading exporter to the Ivory Coast and Brazil. A contrast is provided by the work of Malaysia's Rubber Research Institute, which enabled the natural rubber industry to survive the threat of synthetic rubber after World War II and helped Malaysia to become the world's largest and most efficient exporter of the product. Similarly, the Korean Institute of Science and Technology (KIST) has a record of successful innovation in support of South Korea's industrial development.

Other Policies

Some theorists have argued that improvement in *income distribution* would accelerate job creation. According to this argument, goods consumed by poor people tend to be more labor-intensive than items consumed by those who are better off, so redistribution of income in the direction of the poor would create a shift in the pattern of demand which in turn would create employment. A number of simulation studies have tested the probable magnitude of this effect. Unfortunately most of them have concluded that it is not very great. A major stumbling block seems to be that while the *goods* consumed by the middle and upper income groups are indeed more capital-intensive than those consumed by the lower income group, the better-off groups also consume more *services,* many of which are almost pure labor. Another factor is that goods consumed by the rich and poor often use the same intermediate inputs, for example, steel. Thus a shift in the pattern of final demand may have only a limited impact on the structure of production.

An important point for development planners is to look for *investments that complement labor* rather than substitute for it. Such investment opportunities probably exist in every sector of the economy. In agriculture, for example, mechanization of the planting and harvest functions may displace massive quantities of labor, but investments in irrigation may actually create employment by making it possible to cultivate the same land more intensively and through a greater proportion of the year. A different kind of complementary investment, discussed earlier, is training to fill skill bottlenecks.

Despite our perception of low-income countries as capital-scarce, it frequently has been observed that their existing *stocks of capital equipment are underutilized.* Factories produce at only 30 to 60 percent of capacity, shift work is unusual, tractors sit idle in the fields, bulldozers rest by the side of the roads. If all this idle capacity could somehow be put to work, it has been thought, there would be a sharp upswing in the demand for labor, achievable in the short run, without having to wait for new investments to be made and mature. This is an appealing prospect, but we do not yet fully understand how it could be realized. There are many possible explanations for unused capacity, and research now underway is seeking to determine which of them are the most important. It is unlikely that simple Keynesian demand-boosting policies could do the job alone. Insufficient demand is probably only part of the problem. Inappropriate price incentives and a lack of complementary resources, including entrepreneurship and management, are also likely to be involved.

Generally speaking, small informal-sector establishments use less capital and more labor to produce any given type of output than the larger formal-sector firms. An important reason for this is that small firms face prices for labor and capital which are closer to their social opportunity costs. Minimum-wage laws, unionization, and payroll taxation all have little or no application to informal-sector firms. And not being preferred customers of the banks—indeed, often not dealing with banks at all—they have no access to rationed credit at artificially low interest rates. This situation has led many governments and international agencies to advocate special attention to *small-scale industry.*[13]

The employment-creation potentials of small-scale industry are not yet well understood. Normally the importance of small firms declines relative to that of large firms in the course of economic development. The conditions under which small-scale industry could progressively modernize itself and contribute to development as it did in Japan, rather than stagnate and become a continuing drain on the exchequer as in India, have yet to be defined. Most third world governments hamper the ability of small-scale industry to compete with large-scale domestic firms and with imports through a variety of policies and administrative procedures, ranging from exchange rate overvaluation and investment incentives available only to large firms to disruptively selective enforcement of tax and licensing requirements. Even if they are not sure exactly what to do to help small-

---

13. Besides being more labor-intensive, small-scale industry has also been thought to improve income distribution, promote democracy by widening participation in business, mobilize additional grassroots saving, and assist the spread of economic development to outlying areas.

scale, labor-intensive industry, third world governments can at least desist from practices which harm it.

Small-scale industry is linked to the income distribution point made earlier. Since most of the products of small informal-sector units are consumed by the lower-income groups, income redistribution would strengthen the competitive position of these units. The characteristics and problems of small industry are discussed further in Chapter 20.

When all else fails governments may institute *"special" or "emergency" programs* to provide at least part-time or temporary employment to groups which are particularly distressed or in a particularly strong position to give the government trouble if their needs are not looked after. Many of these programs have been financed by foreign food aid, either by paying the participants with food or by selling the food and using the counterpart funds thus earned to help pay the cost of the program.

These programs offer the attractive prospect of combining construction of a socially useful facility with income redistribution to some of the poorest elements in society. It has been discovered, however, that these benefits have been attained only occasionally in the dozens of such programs that have been undertaken so far.[14] Many programs are plagued by bad management, and in some countries local elites have found ways to divert most of the benefits to themselves, sometimes even forcing the peasants to labor at low wages to provide a road or irrigation ditch which only increases the value of the landlord's property. Implementing an effective public works program is a challenging task, best undertaken by governments (such as China's) that possess both a strong commitment to economic and social equity and a capacity to enforce that commitment.

Conclusions   The desirability of accelerating the creation of productive employment, especially in countries which hope to combine a reasonable measure of equity with economic growth, should be evident. The feasibility of doing it is much less straightforward. Many different types of public policy impinge on employment creation. It is really not possible to draw up an "employment plan" for a developing country, only a general development plan which stresses employment as one in a set of interrelated objectives.[15] The importance of employment as an objective of development policy and planning has received full recognition only in the last decade or so. Planners and scholars alike are still learning what is involved in increasing productive employment in developing countries.

It is clear, though, that the context of the particular developing country—its size and economic structure—makes a difference for the kind of employment-creation strategy to be pursued. South Korea and Singapore have been able to solve their employment problems by emulating the Japanese pattern of whirlwind industrialization based largely on the export market. Medium-size, partially industrialized

14. J. W. Thomas *et al.,* "Public Works Programs in Developing Countries: A Comparative Analysis" (World Bank Staff Working Paper No. 224, February 1976).

15. This has not prevented the ILO, under its World Employment Programme, from preparing a series of such plans through the use of visiting missions—for Colombia, Sri Lanka, Iran, Kenya, the Philippines, and the Sudan. While useful as means of publicizing the goal of employment creation and as illustrations of how employment-oriented development planning can be carried out, these plans have not in any literal sense been implemented by the governments concerned.

countries such as Malaysia and the Philippines may be able to follow a similar path, with modifications permitted by their richer natural resource endowments. Larger, more agricultural countries will have to take a more balanced approach. At best they may be able to develop rapidly following a "continental" model, as Brazil seems to be doing. At worst, as in Bangladesh and the other very poor countries, a long period of reliance on job creation in agriculture and other rural activities will be required.

For description and analysis of employment conditions in developing countries, **FURTHER** David Turnham assisted by Ingelies Jaeger, *The Employment Problem in Less De-* **READING** *veloped Countries. A Review of Evidence* (Paris: Organizations for Cooperation and Development, 1971), remains an excellent brief survey. The problems of particular countries are discussed in the series of reports sponsored by the International Labour Office cited above in note 15.

Influential early tracts on development through labor reallocation are Ragnar Nurkse, *Problems of Capital Formation in Underdeveloped Countries* (Oxford: Basil Blackwell, 1957); and W. Arthur Lewis, "Economic Development with Unlimited Supplies of Labour," *The Manchester School* 22, no. 2 (1954): 139–91. Edgar O. Edwards (ed.), *Employment in Developing Countries* (New York and London: Columbia University Press, 1974), is a good collection of more recent articles on various aspects of third world employment policy. Richard Jolly et al., *Third World Employment: Problems and Strategy* (Harmondsworth, Middlesex, England: Penguin Books, 1973), is another. Yet another excellent review is Lyn Squire, *Employment Policy in Developing Countries: A Survey of Issues and Evidence* (New York: Oxford University Press for the World Bank, 1981).

Chapter 9
EDUCATION

The previous chapter discussed labor as a homogenous resource in economic development, as a *quantity* of human power available to produce goods and services. But numbers of workers cannot tell the whole story. Attempts to attribute economic growth to growth in the factors of production, as outlined in the appendix to Chapter 3, always leave an unexplained residual. One important explanation for that residual is the improvement in the *quality* of human resources which leads workers to be more productive. Labor quality may be enhanced by education of either children or adults; by improved health and nutrition for children and working adults; by migration of workers to places with better job opportunities; and by fertility reduction.

Some of these activities are discussed in other chapters. At this point we want to stress their common characteristics. In each case someone—either the community as a whole, employers, the individuals concerned, or their parents—makes a decision to use scarce resources to improve the productivity, present or future, of human beings. In an influential presidential speech to the American Economic Association in 1960, Theodore Schultz suggested that such activities could be considered a process of accumulating capital, which could later be drawn on to increase a worker's productivity and income. He called this ***investment in human capital.*** This form of investment, said Schultz, is every bit as important as investment in physical capital, but until his speech it had been comparatively neglected by academics and policy-makers alike.[1] Subsequent work by Schultz and others elaborated the idea of investment in human capital, applying it to all the

1. See Theodore W. Schultz, "Investment in Human Capital," *American Economic Review* 51 (January 1961): 17.

human resource development activities mentioned above. A much better idea of what the concept implies should emerge from the discussion of it in the context of education later in this chapter.

Recent studies sponsored by the World Bank[2] lend further support to the idea that human resource development has an important bearing on economic growth. There is reason to believe that the relationship is two-way and mutually supporting. On the one hand growing economies can and do devote increasing resources to improvement of educational, health, and nutritional standards. But it is also apparent that investment in human resources helps to accelerate economic growth. It does this by increasing labor productivity, encouraging greater physical investment, and reducing the dependency burden of the population. These contributions to growth are especially evident in the case of education.

Importance of Education

Education can be defined broadly as all forms of human learning, or more narrowly as the process which takes place in specialized institutions called schools. It is unquestionably the most important form of human resource development, in several senses.

First, there is tremendous popular demand for education, particularly for schooling, in virtually all countries, developing and developed alike. Often in LDCs the number of people seeking admittance to schools far exceeds the number of places available. Obviously, people everywhere believe that education is beneficial for themselves and their children.

A second reason for believing that education is important is the frequently observed correlation between education and income at both the individual and the societal level. Figure 9–1 shows some typical patterns relating age, educational attainment, and earnings in two developing countries. The lines in the graphs represent mean earnings at different ages of people with varying amounts of formal education. Although not all high school graduates, for example, earn more than all primary school leavers, the majority do, and on average their earnings are much higher. People the world over intuitively recognize this correlation, and base their desire to obtain the largest possible amount of schooling for their children on it.

Similarly, there is a strong correlation between national income levels and educational attainments. As Table 9–1 demonstrates, illiteracy is rife in the very poorest countries and diminishes steadily as one goes up the income scale. The reason is that mass education is still a relatively recent phenomenon in most parts of the world. When most adults now living were children, schooling was much less prevalent than it is today. Nevertheless all but the very poorest countries are currently educating large frac-

2. See World Bank, *World Development Report 1980* (Washington, D.C., 1980) and the working papers cited therein.

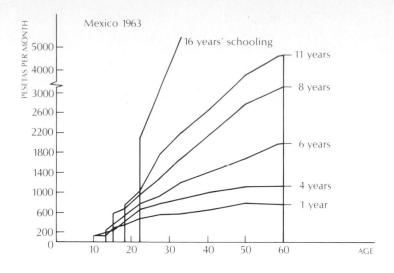

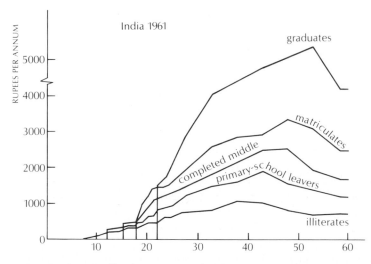

Fig. 9–1   Age-Earnings Profiles in Mexico and India. *Sources:* Martin Carnoy, "Rates of Return to Schooling in Latin America," *Journal of Human Resources,* Summer 1967, pp. 359–74; M. Blaug, R. Layard, and M. Woodhall, *Causes of Graduate Unemployment in India* (Harmondsworth, England: Allen Lane, Penguin Press, 1969), p. 21.

tions of their school-age populations (middle columns of Table 9–1), so the educational attainment of the adult population is rising fast.

It should be emphasized that the relationships shown in Fig. 9–1 and Table 9–1 are averages. There are many contrary cases: of rich individuals and societies which have received little schooling, of well-educated individuals and heavily schooled societies whose incomes are relatively low. Some of the international variations are shown in Table 9–2. On average, however, the correlation between education and income is a strong one. But

TABLE 9-1   Educational Statistics in Relation to GNP Per Capita (1970s)

GNP per capita	% of adults illiterate	Enrollment ratios[b] Primary school Gross	Net	Secondary school gross	Higher education gross	Public expenditure % of GNP	$ per pupil 1st level	2nd level	3rd level
Below $200	77	56	41	15	1.4	2.6	21	268	765
$200–$300	66	69	40	19	1.6	3.3	41	216	2312
$300–$500	73	68	51	15	1.3	4.2	45	264	2037
$500–$1000	45	87	74	33	8.6	4.4	66	167	1165
$1000–$2000	38	100	87	43	11.9	4.5	118	272	1827
$2000–$5000	21	105	93	60	14.7	4.5	280	480	2162
$5000 or more	10[a]	99	92	79	24.9	5.8	1377	1609	4678

Source: UNESCO Statistical Yearbook 1981 (Geneva, 1982).
[a] Rough estimate; many industrial countries with very high literacy rates no longer publish statistics on illiteracy.
[b] Enrollment ratios express enrollment as a percentage of the school-age population. Gross enrollment ratios relate total enrollment of students of all ages to the size of the age group that normally attends that level of schooling; they can exceed 100%. Net enrollment ratios show the percentage of the pertinent age group that is enrolled.

TABLE 9-2   Educational Statistics for Selected Countries[a] (1970s)

Country	% of adults illiterate	Enrollment ratios Primary school Gross	Net	Secondary school gross	Higher education gross	Public expenditure % of GNP	$ per pupil 1st level	2nd level	3rd level
Brazil	24	89	73	32	11.0	3.8	91	277	1325
Colombia	19	128	na	46	10.2	2.3	47	47	280
Bolivia	37	82	74	35	12.6	4.1	96	66	375
Peru	28	112	na	54	16.5	2.1	37	74	na
Chile	11	119	99	55	11.9	3.2	97	156	1216
Kenya	50	99	75	18	0.7	5.5	37	111	2347
Ghana	70	71	na	36	na	2.5	67	194	628
Tanzania	27	104	na	4	0.2	6.4	29	336	7895
Indonesia	43	94	80	22	2.5	2.0	na	na	na
India	67	78	62	27	8.3	2.9	8	43	120
Pakistan	79	56	na	16	2.2	2.0	17	42	311
Sri Lanka	22	98	na	53	1.3	2.2	na	na	46
South Korea	12	111	100	76	12.4	2.7	95	79	173
Malaysia	45	93	na	52	3.0	6.3	156	217	2884
Japan	2	101	98	90	29.3	5.7	1335	1491	1722
Hungary	2	96	94	39	12.3	4.0	928	1817	5325
United Kingdom	na	105	97	83	19.5	6.3	593	979	3631
United States	1	na	na	na	56.0	6.3	na	na	2931

Source: UNESCO Statistical Yearbook 1981 (Geneva, 1982).
[a] na = not available.

does this mean that education really raises a person's, or a nation's, income? Or do richer countries and families simply spend more to acquire greater education? Or, finally, are higher income and education simply the common results of some unidentified third factor? These questions will be explored later in the chapter.

A third reason why education is important in developing countries is that large sums are spent to acquire it. Education is a major item in both household and national budgets. Because their people want it, and to some extent also because they think it will stimulate development, LDC governments devote a substantial fraction of their resources to the creation and operation of school systems. As Table 9–1 (right-hand columns) illustrates, expenditure of 3–5 percent of GNP in public funds is typical; private expenditures on education, which are harder to measure, are left out. Some 15–20 percent of the government budget commonly goes for education. If we looked at education in less conventional terms as an industry, we would see that it is one of the largest industries in all economies, in terms of both value added and employment.

Trends and Patterns

Types of Learning

The preceding discussion treated the terms *education* and *schooling* as if they were synonymous. Indeed this is probably the most common way of using these words in everyday parlance. Modern usage by specialists, however, tends to apply the term *education* to a broader concept, akin to the notion of "learning." The purpose is to stress that there are different forms of learning which are important and can be seen as substitutes for each other in some circumstances. Usually three principal types of learning—education in the broad sense—are identified.

Formal education takes place in institutions called schools. Its participants are usually young people who have not yet begun their working lives.

Nonformal education can be thought of as organized programs of learning which take place outside schools. Often the participants are adults. The programs are usually shorter and more narrowly focused than programs of formal education. Nonformal education may be concerned with occupational skills or with other subjects such as literacy, family life, or citizenship.

Informal education is learning which takes place outside any institutional framework or organized program. People learn many important things in the home, on the job, and in the community generally.

Although other definitions of the three terms can easily be found, these convey a reasonable idea of what is meant. Throughout the remainder of this chapter we will use them in the above senses.

Characteristics of LDC Education

School systems in most third world countries have expanded with extraordinary rapidity over the last three to four decades. Countries which emerged from colonialism after World War II generally inherited narrowly based systems designed to educate only the local elite and a small cadre of literate clerks. Most colonial regimes distrusted the educated "native" and were terrified by the possible consequences of mass education. Even in

Latin America, where most countries had obtained their independence during the nineteenth century, a rigid class structure confined schooling essentially to the better-off urbanites.

After the coming of independence, the political imperatives swung around strongly to favor rapid expansion of schooling. Pledged to change so many things in so short a time, new regimes found that one of the most popular things they could do relatively quickly was to build schools. Whereas a modern economy might be several decades, even a century or more, away, a modern-looking school system could be built in just a few years. The following paragraphs describe some of the most prominent features of third world formal education which emerged during the ensuing period of expansion.

As Table 9–3 shows, school *enrollments* at all levels in developing countries (excluding China and North Korea) doubled during the 1950s, adding some 74 million students. During the succeeding decade growth was nearly 80 percent, and larger yet in absolute terms: 117 million more students were enrolled. The absolute increase in the 1970s was doubtless even larger. Counting China and North Korea, which are excluded from Table 9–3, over 600 million students attended third world schools in 1978.

TABLE 9–3   School Enrollment in Developing Countries,[a] 1950–1978 (millions)

	1950	1960	1965	1970	1975	1978
Primary						
Africa	7	17	24	30	40	50
Asia	43	77	106	129	150	165
Latin America	15	27	34	44	56	62
Total	65	121	164	202	247	278
Secondary						
Africa	—	1	3	4	8	10
Asia	5	17	29	39	51	60
Latin America	2	4	7	11	12	16
Total	7	23	37	54	72	86
Higher						
Africa	—	—	—	—	1	1
Asia	1	2	3	6	7	9
Latin America	—	1	1	2	4	4
Total	1	3	5	8	12	14
All levels						
Total	73	147	205	264	331	378

Source: *UNESCO Yearbook of Educational Statistics 1972* (Geneva, 1973); *UNESCO Statistical Yearbook 1981* (Geneva, 1982).
[a] China and North Korea are excluded from these statistics. South Africa and Japan are regarded as developed countries and are also excluded. Continents may not add to total because of rounding error and exclusion of a few small countries. (— indicates less than 500,000).

In all countries enrollment growth proceeded in waves, hitting the primary schools first, then as applications for secondary schooling swelled, high schools, and finally the universities, technical colleges, and other institutions of higher education. The spread of the system differed from country to country. A relatively Westernized Asian country like Sri Lanka, which adopted a free schooling policy at independence in 1948, was able to achieve practically universal primary schooling in the 1950s and then press on rapidly with expansion of the higher levels until financial difficulties forced a slowdown of enrollment expansion in the 1960s. By contrast some countries in Latin America and elsewhere commenced rapid enrollment expansion at the higher levels long before universal primary schooling was attained. In some countries this pattern resulted from a concentration of political power which allowed the interests of the elite to be raised far above those of the masses. Elsewhere, as in the more conservative Muslim countries, it was a consequence of the low priority attached to education for girls.

Rapid expansion often created *teacher shortages* which led to increasing class sizes and use of less highly trained teachers. In some countries it proved possible to expand teacher training and overcome the worst of the shortages after a few years. In many places, however, teacher shortages persist to this day, particularly in the more remote areas where teachers (like other public servants) are reluctant to go.

As mentioned before, most LDCs were feeling strong *budgetary pressures* from the expansion of schooling by the 1960s, if not before. The most common reaction was to put the brakes on enrollment expansion. Other possible adjustments, such as increasing the efficiency of educational expenditures and asking families to finance a larger share of schooling, were made less frequently. The latter adjustment sometimes took place by default as private secondary schools and colleges sprang up to offer places to disappointed applicants to the public institutions.

A major reason for the inefficiency of educational expenditures has been the high frequencies of *dropouts* (those who withdraw from schooling before completing an academically meaningful course of study) and *repeaters* (those who require more than the prescribed number of years to complete the program). Most educators believe that a child who fails to complete at least five or six years of school gains little from attendance, yet millions fail to do so. In large measure these problems result from poverty. The various costs of keeping a child in school (see below) become too heavy an imposition on the poor household after a while.

With all these problems of educational quality it is not surprising that many of the children who attend LDC schools fail to learn very much. A few years ago the International Association for the Evaluation of Education Achievement (IEA) administered achievement tests to pupils in twenty-three countries, including three developing countries (Chile, Iran, and India). Although there is room for doubt about whether the tests were strictly comparable, it was evident that pupils in poor countries are likely to learn much less than their counterparts in rich countries. For example, final-year secondary school students in Iran and India scored far worse than students from any of the developed countries, and the Chilean students also scored somewhat lower.[3] There is even evidence that those who do master specific skills in school sometimes lose them in later life through lack of use. Functional literacy is likely to be retained only by those who have access to written materials and are faced in their daily lives with incentives to read and write. Many third world people have neither.

Increasing interest in income distribution and equity generally since the late 1960s has caused greater attention to be paid to the *regional and social inequities* which characterize most developing-country school systems. In many countries a child who lives in an urban area or who comes from a favored socioeconomic background is far more likely to receive schooling (and also more likely to receive high-quality schooling) than a student from a rural area or a more ordinary socioeconomic setting. To the (considerable) extent that education leads to a better job and a higher income, this pattern of educational provision worsens the distribution of opportunity and income. Some economists believe that an improved distribution of schooling could be a major force for achieving a more even distribution of income. Governments in the third world are just now beginning to address these problems and potentials.

One reason for the limited learning which seems to take place in third world school systems is, in Ronald Dore's phrase, the *"diploma disease."*[4] According to some analysts these systems are not primarily in the business of conveying knowledge and skills at all, but are principally concerned with "certification" or "credentialing." Dore's studies show that in late-developing countries there is a strong tendency to judge an individual's fitness to work by the academic credentials which he or she possesses. And of course successful completion of a given level of schooling is the main qualification for admittance to the next highest level. In most developing countries there are nationwide examinations which are given at particular stages in the schooling process to determine the student's fitness for educational advancement or employment. These exams take on tremendous importance, causing teachers to bend their classroom efforts to the task of preparing students for them, and often causing students to put in long hours outside of school cramming for the exam. Analysts such as Dore contend that this perverts the true purpose of education and escalates the cost of a selection process which might be carried out more cheaply in other ways.

Many nations which followed the logic of cascading educational expansion during the 1950s and 1960s found they had a problem of *educated unemployment* on their hands after a few years. India and the Philippines,

---

3. The shortfall of the LDCs was more noticeable when average scores were compared than when the scores of the top 9% of students were compared between rich and poor countries. This may reflect the wider quality variations among schools in poor countries as compared to richer ones. For discussion, see John Simmons, "How Effective Is Schooling in Promoting Learning? A Review of the Research" (World Bank Staff Working Paper No. 200, March 1975).

4. See Ronald Dore, *The Diploma Disease: Education, Qualification and Development* (Berkeley and Los Angeles: University of California Press, 1976).

two Asian pioneers in the expansion of secondary and higher education, acquired large pools of job-seeking graduates unable to find "suitable" employment. Sri Lanka, with its long-standing commitment to free schooling, found half its recent university graduates unemployed by the 1970s. A few lucky countries experienced a subsequent upswing in economic growth which soaked up this pool of unemployed labor. Thus South Korea, which had had many frustrated and out-of-work graduates in the late 1950s, moved to a position of shortage of educated workers by the 1970s. Even Sri Lanka, now essaying a growth spurt after years of near-stagnation, should be able to work off some of its backlog in the 1980s. But in many countries educated unemployment seems to have become almost a permanent feature of society.

A *lack of fit* between what is taught in schools and what is needed on the job seems to aggravate the problem. Russell Davis reports that the employment exchange in Calcutta is daily thronged with B.A.s (some of them "firsts"—that is, recipients of top academic honors) in mathematics, English, and physics.[5] Yet employers who approach the same office seeking workers skilled in air conditioning, silkscreen printing, or plumbing come away disappointed. In these circumstances graduates must eventually accept work to which their education bears little relevance (B.A. taxi drivers are said to be common in Manila, as they are in some American cities), while employers most likely will have to use on-the-job training to obtain the skills they need.

Nonformal education played little part in the inherited educational system. Significantly, however, many government departments which required technical skills conducted specialized training programs for their own staffs. This shows that the needed skills were not being supplied by the formal education system. Nor were they available through *informal education,* since the limited experience with modern economic activities meant that accumulated on-the-job learning was necessarily low.

We will return to some of these problems in the concluding section of this chapter. First, however, we consider education's potential contribution to economic development.

Education's Role in Development

Education is different things to different people. Besides the *economic benefits* already mentioned, education up to a certain level has often been thought of as an inherent *right*. Education has also been promoted because it can *socialize* people. Through a common schooling experience, it has often been thought, people from different national, social, ethnic, religious, and linguistic backgrounds can be encouraged to adopt a common outlook on the world. Since many LDCs have diverse populations and must place a high premium on the attainment of greater national unity, this is often an

---

5. Russell Davis, "Planning Education for Employment" (Harvard Institute for International Development, Development Discussion Paper No. 60, June 1979).

important objective for them. Finally, education is also thought to confer *civic benefits*. Some political scientists believe that at least a minimal level of schooling is a prerequisite for political democracy.[6]

Thinking about the way in which education can be used to promote economic development has changed considerably over the years. During the 1950s much of the discussion centered on the need for trained manpower. The manpower-planning approach, outlined below, gained popularity as a way of analyzing a developing country's manpower needs. The emphasis on middle- and high-level trained manpower implies that it is secondary and higher education which are most in need of expansion. As we have seen, however, the 1950s was also a period of rapid growth in primary school enrollments. In 1959 a number of Asian governments subscribed to the "Karachi Plan," which pledged them to provide at least seven years of compulsory, universally, and free schooling by 1980.

As has been noted, disillusionment with this approach followed in the 1960s. Many governments found their budgets overstrained by the attempt to expand all levels of schooling simultaneously. Demand seemed unquenchable; expansion of capacity at one level of schooling only increased the demand for places at the next higher level. Paradoxically, the continuing boom demand for schooling was accompanied by an apparent decline in some of its benefits to the individual. The rise of unemployment among the educated caused politicians and officials to wonder whether more and more resources should be devoted to expansion of the school system, just so people could be unemployed.

This new cost-consciousness fit well with a new method of analyzing educational investments, introduced during the 1960s. Cost-benefit analysis, which was based on human capital theory, looked at both the costs and the benefits of education—unlike manpower analysis, which considered only the benefits. By the 1970s, however, disillusionment had spread still further to include, for many analysts, the human capital approach. A search for alternative conceptions of education's role began, and is still underway. Education remains tremendously important in developing countries. Indeed, larger numbers of people and sums of money are involved than ever before. But there is no definite agreement on how exactly this burgeoning activity should be regarded.

Manpower Planning

In any economy there is a strong tendency for people with certain levels of education to hold certain types of jobs. For example, in developing countries nearly all people who have received a university education work at professional, technical, or managerial jobs, usually either in government or as independent professionals. People whose schooling ended at the sec-

---

6. Education, of course, does not guarantee the existence of democracy, as many examples of countries with educated populations but undemocratic governments attest. And there are examples of democratic systems in countries with relatively little education: India, Jamaica, Guyana, Colombia. So the relationship of education to democracy is not clear-cut.

ondary level tend to hold middle-level jobs in the clerical, sales, and service occupations. Half or more of the labor force in the typical developing country is made up of farmers and agricultural laborers who have received little or no formal education.

It is tempting to jump from these observable facts to the assumption that a certain level of education is *required* if a person is to fill a particular occupational role. If this assumption were valid it would follow that a growing economy, which is expected to undergo a shift in occupational structure toward more professionals, technicians, and industrial workers, must follow a defined pattern of educational development to obtain the kinds of trained people it will need.

Manpower planning is based on this assumption. It presumes that the economy's need for educated labor can be predicted, making it possible to plan the growth of the educational system to avoid both manpower shortages, which may slow down economic growth, and manpower surpluses, which waste educational resouces and may lead to educated unemployment or "brain drain."

The starting point of manpower planning is therefore a prediction of manpower needs. There are various ways of obtaining such a prediction. A simple one is to survey employers, asking how much labor of various kinds they expect to employ, say, five years and ten years in the future. This is not a very good method for several reasons: employers often have no way of estimating future employment; different employers will probably use different assumptions in estimating their future demand for labor, so their replies cannot be aggregated consistently; enterprises to be started up in the coming five to ten years get left out of the calculation; and so on. A second possible method, if data for two historical dates are available, is to calculate past trends and then extrapolate them. A more sophisticated method, based on the work of Jan Tinbergen and Herbert Parnes, involves deducing the future employment pattern from a projection of GNP growth.

The Tinbergen-Parnes methodology involves something like the following sequence of steps. (1) It starts from a target growth rate of GNP during the planning period (which must be at least several years long, since the training of middle- and high-level manpower takes time). (2) It then estimates the structural changes in output by sector of origin needed to achieve that overall growth rate. (3) Employment by sector is estimated, using some set of assumptions about labor productivity growth (or about the elasticity of employment growth relative to output growth, which is its inverse). (4) Next, employment by industry is divided into occupational categories using assumptions about the "required" structure in each industry; these are then summed across industries to get the economy's required occupation mix. (5) Occupational requirements are then translated into educational terms via assumptions about what sorts of education are appropriate for each occupational group.

These five steps lead to an estimate of manpower requirements in some future year. The manpower supply in that year is then matched to the requirements through a stock-and-flow adjustment process. The current stock of manpower is adjusted for expected losses through retirement, death, emigration, and withdrawals from the labor force. The gap between requirements and the supply thus projected must be met primarily through outputs from the school system, although immigration and entry into the labor force by nonworking adults may also help in some cases. Thus, once requirements are established, all that remains is to plan the flow of students through the school system in such a way that the gap between projected needs and the supply from other sources is just closed.

This methodology will sound familiar to anyone who knows input-output analysis, since it involves the use of sets of "fixed coefficients" to derive input needs from output targets (see Chapter 6). The chain of deduction in the calculation of manpower requirements is as follows: GNP → industrial structure → total employment by industry → occupational structure of employment → educational structure of employment. Each arrow represents a set of fixed coefficients.

A major difficulty with the manpower-planning approach is that in the real world these coefficients are often unstable and unpredictable. Labor productivity is affected by many factors, and often changes unexpectedly. The occupational mix also changes, for both exogenous (external) and endogenous (internal) reasons. For example, new technologies may be introduced, bringing a new set of occupational requirements. Or a change in relative wages might induce employers to hire a different mix of workers; such price adjustments are assumed away in the model. In the long run, in fact, changes in the coefficients tend to occur as a direct result of changes in the supply of educated labor. People with more schooling gradually come to be used to do jobs that previously were done by less educated persons. This process can be termed *educational deepening.*

The fact of the matter, which undercuts the logic of manpower planning, is that there is no unique education-occupation linkage. The knowledge required to do virtually any job can be acquired in any of several ways, through formal, nonformal, or informal education. Similarly, only a small fraction of what is learned in most educational programs is unique to a specific occupation; much more of it is applicable to a range of jobs.

Another problem with manpower planning is its failure to take account of the cost of education. Manpower "requirements" are assumed to be absolute, and the conclusion is always that any projected gap should be filled through educational expansion, generally of secondary and higher formal education. Yet these types of schooling are relatively expensive in many LDCs (right-hand columns of Table 9–1), and alternative, possibly cheaper, ways of dealing with the problem, such as nonformal education or on-the-job training, are seldom considered.

These objections, plus the emergence of the competing cost-benefit approach, have doomed manpower planning to limbo as far as most academic specialists are concerned. However, the approach is still used by practical planners to gain at least a rough idea of what a developing country's possible manpower problems are. Often its greatest support comes from politicians who find its apparent (but spurious) precision appealing.

They like to be told, say, that the country needs to train 125 architects by 1990. As a matter of political economy manpower planning is more likely to be influential when it projects deficits than when it projects surpluses. In the former situation it provides an apparently strong rationale for expanding a particular type of education. In many developing countries, however, schooling has expanded so much that few manpower deficits can legitimately be projected. In these circumstances society's demand for education and the political pressures that go along with it generally ensure that the school system continues to expand at a much faster rate than would be indicated by manpower planning.

Cost-Benefit Analysis and the Value of Education

The hypothesis underlying human capital theory is that individuals, or their governments on their behalf, make expenditures on education, health, and other human services primarily for the purpose of raising their incomes and productivity. The added output and income which result in future years then become a return on the investment made. Application of this idea to formal education begins with a set of "lifetime earnings curves," such as those shown in Fig. 9–1. These curves have been calculated for many populations, and nearly all of them show some common characteristics. First, given the amount of schooling defined in terms of either years in school or the highest level attained, earnings increase up to a maximum level which is reached around age forty or later, then level off or decline. Second, for those with larger amounts of schooling the curve is higher, and steeper in its rising phase; although people with more schooling start work a bit later in life they usually begin at a higher earnings level than those with less schooling who are already working. Third, more schooling leads to later attainment of maximum earnings and to higher earnings in retirement. All three of these features can be seen in the curves for Mexico and India shown in Fig. 9–1.

Cost-benefit analysis, introduced in Chapter 6 as a planning tool and used in Chapter 8 to analyze employment, is pertinent to both private and social calculations of the value of education. We can begin by imagining a set of parents faced with a decision on how much schooling to provide a child. They have a rough idea of what the lifetime earnings curves look like and regard them as a prediction of what the child would earn at different levels of educational attainment. Although it may strain one's credulity, it is necessary to think of these parents as calculating the discounted present value of the future earnings stream attached to each level of schooling and comparing it with the cost of attaining that level of school.

The present value of prospective earnings in any future year can be defined as

$$V_o = \frac{E_t}{(1 + r)^t} \qquad\qquad \text{[9–1]}$$

where V_o = present value of earnings in year t, E_t = earnings in year t, and r = the rate of interest (opportunity cost of the parents' capital). The earnings are "discounted" to the present using the rate of interest, r.

The discounted present value of the entire stream of earnings until year n is therefore:

$$V = \sum_{t=1}^{n} \frac{E_t}{(1 + r)^t} \qquad [9-2]$$

This is the *benefit* side of the cost-benefit calculation. The private *costs* of schooling—that is, those costs which are borne by private households—are of two types, *explicit* and *implicit*. Explicit costs are those which involve actual outlays of cash. The most obvious type of explicit cost is tuition fees, but it is important to recognize that even "free"—that is, tuition-free—schooling entails costs, both explicit and implicit. Cash outlays are often required for books, uniforms, transportation, and other purposes. Some type of explicit cost is almost always present, and can serve as an important barrier to school attendance for children from poor families. In addition there are implicit costs in the form of the forgone earnings or opportunity costs of students who if not in school could be working as wage-earners or as unpaid but productive workers in family farms and enterprises. In general these opportunity costs are most significant for older students and higher levels of schooling. But in settings where young children can work productively, they may be a factor even at the primary level, particularly for the poorer households.

The costs of schooling are incurred before its benefits are received. One way to determine whether a particular educational investment is worthwhile is to compare the discounted present values of the benefit and cost streams, as explained in Chapter 6. If the former exceeds the latter, using a relevent rate of interest to discount both streams, then the investment pays off and should be made. If discounted costs exceed discounted benefits, the investment is not worth making.

The more common method, however, involves calculating the *internal rate of return* on the investment. This, you will recall from Chapter 6, is the discount rate which equates the discounted present values of the benefit and cost streams. We can solve for the internal rate of return using the following equations.

$$\sum_{t=1}^{n} \frac{E^t}{(1 + i)^t} = \sum_{t=1}^{n} \frac{C_t}{(1 + i)^t} \qquad [9-3]$$

or

$$\sum_{t=1}^{n} \frac{E_t - C_t}{(1 + i)^t} = 0 \qquad [9-4]$$

where C_t = private costs (explicit and implicit) incurred in year t, and i = internal rate of return. Using this approach the family's rate of return on an investment in education would then be compared to the returns on other investments which might be made. The educational outlay would then be made if it offered the highest return.

What has just been described is the calculation of *private rate of return* to investment in education. There is also a *social rate of return,* which is calculated in exactly the same way except that *all* costs of education, public as well as private, are included on the cost side of the calculation. In other words public-sector outlays that are not reimbursed by tuition are added in here. Since benefits are calculated in the same way in both cases and costs can only be higher in the social cost-benefit calculation, it follows that the private rate of return cannot be lower than the social rate of return.[7]

It should be stressed that social cost-benefit analysis of education is more comprehensive than private cost-benefit analysis only on the cost side. The various social benefits of education, all those which are not reflected in higher earnings, are excluded from both calculations. It would be better to include them, but it is difficult to quantify benefits such as greater social cohesion and enhanced ability to participate in politics.

Many private and social rates of return to investment in education have been estimated for both developed and developing countries. Some representative results are displayed in Table 9–4. All the rates shown in the table are marginal rates. That is, they are rates of return on the *additional* investment needed to move from one level of educational attainment to the next higher level.

Three principal conclusions emerge from Table 9–4 and other similar calculations. First, rates of return to education in developing countries are generally high. In many cases they are higher than the rates of return

TABLE 9–4   Some Estimates of Rates of Return to Education[a]

Country	Year	Social			Private		
		Primary	Secondary	Higher	Primary	Secondary	Higher
Brazil	1970	na	24	13	na	25	14
Colombia	1973	na	na	na	15	15	21
Chile	1959	24	17	12	na	na	na
Ghana	1967	18	13	17	35	23	27
Kenya[b]	—	22	19	9	28	33	31
Ethiopia	1972	20	19	10	35	23	27
India	1965	13	16	10	17	19	16
Indonesia	1977	na	na	na	26	16	na
South Korea	1967	12	9	5	na	na	na
Malaysia	1978	na	na	na	na	33	35
Japan	1973	na	5	6	na	6	8
United Kingdom[c]	1972	na	4	8	na	12	10
United States	1969	na	11	11	na	19	15

Source: George Psacharopoulos, "Returns to Education: An Updated International Comparison," in Timothy King (ed.), *Education and Income* (World Bank, Staff Working Paper No. 402, July 1980), pp. 84–85.
[a] na = not available.
[b] Social rates refer to 1968, private rates to 1971.
[c] Social rates refer to 1966, private rates to 1972.

7. Calculations made for developed countries usually measure income after income taxes in the private cost-benefit calculation and before income taxes in the social cost-benefit calculation. This makes it possible for the social rate of return to exceed the private rate, but this refinement is seldom introduced in analyses for developing countries because personal income taxes are generally much less significant than in developed countries and data on them are harder to obtain.

earned on investments in physical capital. Education therefore looks like a good investment in most LDCs. Second, usually the highest social rates of return are earned on primary schooling. This is particularly true in countries (like Chile, Kenya, and Ethiopia in the table) where primary schooling has not yet approached universality. In countries (like Japan, the United Kingdom, and the United States in the table) where almost everyone has completed primary schooling the rate of return at the primary level becomes indeterminate because there is no lower level with which to compare it. Third, the spread between private rates of return and social rates of return can be large because sometimes the government bears most of the costs. Examples from Table 9–4 are secondary education in the United States and higher education in the three African countries. In other cases most of the costs of schooling are privately financed and the spread between the two rates of return is small.

Of what practical value are these calculations? The idea is that private rates of return can serve as guides to individual educational choices while social rates can inform public investment and policy decisions. But doubts surround the validity of both claims.

From the private point of view the main problem is predicting what the structure of earnings will be in the future. The procedure outlined above implicitly assumes that the current structure provides an accurate guide to the future, but in fact relative earnings can change considerably for reasons originating either on the demand or the supply side of the labor market. In many LDCs in recent years the numbers of people possessing all kinds of academic credentials have increased much faster than the numbers of jobs traditionally held by people with the credentials concerned. The result, also discussed in Chapter 8, is that school leavers tend to be unemployed for a long period of time, following which they may accept lower salaries than their predecessors obtained. This process of educational deepening makes the incomes earned by previous school leavers a poor guide to the future since the rate of return to a particular level of schooling is likely to decline.

Despite this tendency applicants continue to besiege the secondary schools and universities of most developing countries. How is this fact to be explained? Some observers interpret it as evidence that applicants for schooling are not motivated exclusively, or even primarily, by a desire for economic gains, that they want more schooling mainly for social or psychological reasons. A different explanation is that when schooling is heavily subsidized by the government the private rate of return remains reasonably high even as the social rate dips in response to educated unemployment and the continuing devaluation of academic credentials. This latter thesis has been used to explain continuing strong demand for secondary and higher education in countries such as India and Sri Lanka. It suggests that education can be simultaneously a good investment for the individual and a bad investment for society.

In applying the cost-benefit approach to educational planning, the starting point is again data on lifetime earnings by level and type of education, along with information on the costs—explicit and implicit, private and public—of providing each level and type of education. The social rates of return on the various levels of education (primary, secondary, higher) and types of education (academic, vocational, nonformal, on-the-job) can then be calculated and compared. A rational government would expand those forms of education which show high social rates of return and cut back on those which show low rates of return.[8]

There are, however, a number of questions which can be raised about this procedure. As with manpower planning or any other planning methodology its results are only as good as its assumptions, and some of these can be questioned. Like the hypothetical parents discussed earlier, cost-benefit analysts must worry about how the structure of earnings may change in the future. In addition they must make a number of assumptions about things that are of no concern to the private decision-maker.

If education is to be treated as an investment comparable to a road or steel mill, it must be justified in terms of its contribution to national output. Higher earnings are not sufficient justification from the social point of view unless they result from higher productivity. The usual way of linking earnings to productivity is to assume that wages are equated to the marginal product of labor through the workings of a perfectly competitive labor market. But if labor markets are rather imperfect, as we argued that they are in Chapter 8, then wages or earnings are not necessarily equal to marginal product and are thus imperfect indicators of social benefits. In theory this problem could be dealt with by using shadow wages or opportunity costs (estimates of what wages would be under competitive conditions) instead of actual wages, but this adjustment has seldom been attempted.

A second and closely related problem concerns the causal relationship between education and earnings. Up to now we have in effect assumed that average earnings differences *associated with* differences in educational attainments are *caused by* these educational differences. But this is not necessarily the case, since both education and earnings could be the product of some third factor, such as individual ability or socioeconomic origin. Most likely a part of the earnings differential is causally attributable to educational attainment while another part is not.[9] But it is difficult to ascertain what the correct fractions are. Many studies simply assume that an arbitrary fraction of the additional earnings is a direct result of the additional education.

The cost-benefit approach implicitly assumes that educational categories adequately specify the types of labor relevant to the labor market. In other words it assumes that there is perfect substitutability within each educational category. If categories are specified only by level (primary, secondary,

8. More precisely, activities which show a rate of return higher than the opportunity cost of capital (the return thought to be obtainable if the funds were invested outside the education sector) would be expanded and those with lower rates would be contracted.

9. This is a problem for the calculation of individual private rates of return as well. The individual cannot assume that average earnings relationships apply to him/her; the relative importance of schooling, ability, and social status as determinants of earnings may also vary among individuals.

higher) this assumption is obviously crude. Surely there are significant differences between graduates of academic and vocational high schools, or between graduates of medical and legal faculties. Separate calculations should be made for these major different types of education, but even this leaves out the quality dimension. In the real world graduates of the "best" schools (which may be best solely or mainly in terms of popular perceptions) earn far more than graduates of the "inferior" institutions. Finally, alternatives to schooling—nonformal education and on-the-job training—tend to get left out of the comparison altogether. If the Ministry of Education is responsible for educational planning but these programs are provided by other ministries, the tendency to downplay them may be strong.

Despite all these limitations, cost-benefit analysis can tell the planner something about the productivity of the existing pattern of investment in education. For example, the common finding of a high social rate of return to primary schooling suggests past underinvestment at this level and the probable existence of socially remunerative investment opportunities for the future. Similarly, large differences between private and social returns may help explain patterns of educated unemployment, as we have seen. However, the ultimate value of these calculations is limited. Even if we accept the questionable assumptions involved and take the calculations at face value, they still do not tell us how much of different kinds of education to provide because there is no way of telling how fast the social rate of return will decline as a particular variety of education is expanded. To know this we would have to calculate the elasticities relating earnings differentials to the relative supplies of different kinds of labor.

In spite of the attractiveness of its base in human capital theory—at least for those who admire neoclassical economic theory—the cost-benefit approach is of only limited use in practical educational planning. This brings us to the question of what alternatives there might be.

Alternative Viewpoints

Formal Modeling   Most of the time in most developing countries educational policy decisions are made pragmatically, responding to those political pressures which bear most strongly on the decision-makers at any particular moment. Manpower projections and cost-benefit analyses are undertaken from time to time, but they seldom have more than a marginal impact on what actually happens. Because of the intellectual limitations of the two analytical approaches outlined above, more elaborate and formal approaches have sometimes been suggested, but these have had even less influence. For example, several linear programming models (see Chapter 6) of education and its relationship to the economy were constructed a few years back but had little impact. Similarly, efforts have been made to synthesize the manpower and cost-benefit approaches. The latter may be a promising road to take, since polar assumptions of the two well-known methodologies (zero substitutability of different types of labor versus perfect substitutability within broad educational categories) clearly leave reality somewhere in the middle. So far, however, neither effort has had any dramatic influence on how education is planned in developing countries.

The "Left Revisionists" One group of economists and sociologists contends that the idea that education raises productivity is fundamentally erroneous. An element in their critique, mentioned earlier, is that education acts as a screen or sieve to select the fortunate few who are then "credentialed" to hold the elite positions in society. To this the more radical critics add that those who pass through the sieve and receive the prized credentials tend strongly to be the ones who started from privileged positions in life. The school system, they say, essentially reproduces the class structure from generation to generation. Those not destined for elite positions receive a form of education intended to "acculture" them into acceptance of a subservient role in society. They are taught diligence, punctuality, and respect for authority. The solution to all this lies not in any conceivable reform of the school system within the framework of capitalist society, but in the radical reform of the social structure and economic system themselves. Less conventional radical critics argue that efforts should be made to "deschool society" (Ivan Ilych) or to use mass education as a means of raising the consciousness of the poor regarding their oppressed condition (Paolo Freire).

In view of these criticisms and proposals it is of some interest to see how Communist regimes manage their school systems. Very briefly, they put strong emphasis on universal attainment of basic literacy and numeracy, then restrict secondary and higher education rather severely (or just higher education in the richer Communist states), pointing it directly at the attainment of specific vocational skills. In the U.S.S.R. and other East European Communist countries, as in the West, opportunities to obtain the more restricted types of schooling seem to go disproportionately to those with favored positions in society. The Communist regime most noted for radical reform efforts is that of China, especially during the Cultural Revolution of the 1960s, but Chinese educational policy has subsequently returned to something much closer to the Soviet or Western model.

The "Right Revisionists" Meanwhile a diametrically opposed critique and reform proposal argues that educational planning has failed, that all methodologies which have been proposed are inadequate, and that choices about what kinds of schooling to provide and whom to educate should therefore be left much more to the operations of the market. An obvious objection to this proposal is that if the market gives the "wrong" price signal it will only encourage people to respond in the "wrong" ways. As long as education is subsidized people will tend to purchase "too much" of it relative to other goods and services. This problem could be dealt with by reducing the degree of subsidization and charging people something much closer to the actual cost of providing schooling. But this would only serve to strengthen another objection to the market solution: that it takes no account of equity considerations. Proposed means of rectifying this situation include liberal use of scholarships for the poor but deserving, or more far-reaching, creation of *educational vouchers,* a special currency that could be used to purchase any kind of schooling and could be distributed according to any criteria deemed equitable.

Like the radical reform proposals, those coming from the right have been more discussed than implemented. Most LDC governments prefer to retain a much tighter grip on educational activities than this type of reform would permit. The main real-world use of the market in third world education, as noted earlier, is to provide places for those who are unable to gain admittance to public institutions—and even this is permitted only in certain countries.

The "Moderate Reformers" A very old reform proposal is that education should be made more practical. This suggestion has usually led to the creation of agricultural, technical, or vocational schools intended to teach people useful skills. Some of these schools have succeeded and made valuable contributions to development, but many have failed. In a well-known article Philip Foster traced a series of unsuccessful experiments in Ghana going all the way back to the mid-nineteenth century.[10] He attributed the persistent failure to "the vocational school fallacy," a tendency to think of certain types of skilled labor as needed for economic development when in fact the structure of incentives strongly favors "impractical" academic training which opens the door to employment in the urban formal sector. Added to this is the fact that many government-run vocational schools fail to provide the skills that are actually provided by private employers. Yet when planned and administered properly vocational schools can make a real contribution to development.

A more recent reform proposal is to give much greater emphasis to nonformal education.[11] The proponents of this approach argue that nonformal education compares favorably to formal education in terms of practicality, cost, flexibility, and ability to reach lower income groups. The study of nonformal education is still in its infancy and it is not yet clear to what extent these claims are justified. Certainly there have been many successful nonformal education projects—in basic education (literacy and numeracy), family education (health, nutrition, child care, family planning), community education (cooperatives, community projects), and occupational training. It may be, however, that nonformal education is more usefully thought of as a complement to formal education, in terms of the skills taught and audience reached (mainly adults), than as its rival.

A criticism of nonformal education is that, like vocational schools, it perpetuates a two-tiered social system. The favored class gets into the schools while the less favored have to make do with programs of nonformal education.

10. Philip J. Foster, "The Vocational School Fallacy in Development Planning," in C. A. Anderson and M. J. Bowman (eds.), *Education and Economic Development* (Chicago: Aldine, 1966), pp. 142–63.

11. Philip H. Coombs with Manzoor Ahmed, *Attacking Rural Poverty: How Nonformal Education Can Help* (Baltimore and London: Johns Hopkins University Press, 1974).

Conclusion Education in the broad sense—that is, learning—is clearly important for economic development. Differences in learned attitudes and skills account for many of the differentials in levels and rates of development that can be observed in the world. The attitudes and skills which promote economic development have been acquired through education, but by no means always through formal education. People acquired many useful forms of knowledge in the home, the workplace, and the community, long before schools were invented and spread beyond the narrow circle of traditional scholarly communities. Great and ancient civilizations, such as those of China and India, had their traditional schools and attached great prestige to them. But the education which prepared the masses of their populations for survival in a modernizing economic system, and helped them to compete successfully when they migrated to other areas, was not obtained primarily in those schools. Instead it was the result of centuries of struggle and adaptation in the field, in the workshop, and in the marketplace.

Educational systems in the less developed countries have undergone tremendous expansion in the past three decades. Indeed the present educational systems of these countries are virtually the products of this recent historical period. The expansion has brought both benefits and problems. In the process at least a few things have been learned about the role of education in development.

With regard to formal education, most analysts believe that primary schooling is an important contributor to both growth and equity objectives of development. This belief is supported by numerous studies which show significantly higher farmer productivity when the farmers have had at least four to six years of schooling. Literacy, numeracy, and other basic skills acquired in a reasonably well-run primary school are widely useful in economic, social, and political life. Governments which claim to be interested in development yet have not provided basic education to their entire school-age population reveal questionable sincerity. Fortunately most developing countries presently enroll a very high percentage of this population or are moving rapidly in this direction. An example of the latter is Indonesia, which began a fast-moving expansion program in 1973 with the aim of raising primary school enrollment from 55 percent of the age group to 85 percent by 1979 and 100 percent by 1984. After 100 percent enrollment is reached, an LDC's principal remaining problem in primary education is to ensure adequate educational quality so that an acceptable standard of learning actually occurs.

The evaluation of secondary and higher education in the LDCs is more mixed. At these levels schools become deeply concerned with the problem of selecting those members of the coming generation who who will be permitted to take their places among the socially elite and economically privileged. This selection function, vital as it is, can interfere with the learning function. "Educational qualifications" for particular types of work are much more a matter of obtaining the specific piece of paper defined as necessary for those who are to pursue a given occupation than of actually learning the skills needed for the job. In this situation it is important that selection be carried out based on objective ("merit") criteria rather than primarily in terms of factors correlated with socioeconomic origins. In this respect the examination-based systems of Japan and South Korea are outstanding. Although a strain on the students and highly restrictive in terms of the numbers admitted to the highest levels and "best" institutions, they do afford sizable opportunities for the poor but able and hardworking student to rise on the socioeconomic ladder.

A major need of educational development in the third world is to forge a closer relationship between education and work for new labor market entrants. In part this can be achieved through reform of the formal education system. Despite Foster's "vocational fallacy" problem, we have noted that technical and vocational schools can prepare students successfully for employment if their curricula are closely geared to the skills required by employers. This kind of adaptation is the main advantage of traditional apprenticeship schemes. Newer approaches involve a combination of formal and on-the-job training, such as is being attempted by the

National Service for Apprenticeship in Colombia, the National Service for Industrial Apprenticeship in Brazil, and the Industrial Training Board in Singapore, among others. All these programs are financed by a payroll tax which spreads their cost among employers who may benefit from the improved supply of trained labor.

Since it is still uncommon for people in the LDCs to return to the classroom once they have left it and gone to work, efforts to improve the educational endowment of adults must rely mainly on nonformal and informal education. To succeed, nonformal education must provide skills that are usable within the student's environment. Even basic literacy can be lost if it is not used. But many occupational and family life skills have been taught successfully through nonformal education classes. Agricultural extension programs in many countries are a familiar example. More recently courses based on modules of family planning, child health, and nutritional information have been successfully introduced in Indonesia and other countries.

On human resources generally, the influential advocacy of the human capital concept by Theodore W. Schultz is well worth reading. See "Investment in Human Capital," *American Economic Review* 51 (January 1961): 1–17. Several elaborations of Schultz's idea are included in the *Journal of Political Economic* 70 (October 1962), Part 20. A recent review of the state of knowledge on the subject, which argues strongly for investment in human resources as a means of promoting economic development, is included in World Bank, *World Development Report 1980* (Washington, D.C., 1980), pp. 1–104. **FURTHER READING**

On education specifically and its relationship to development, the following works by Mark Blaug are useful: *Economics of Education,* vols. 1 and 2 (London: Penguin Books, 1968, 1969)—these are edited volumes, many of whose papers deal with developing countries; *Introduction to the Economics of Education* (London: Penguin Books, 1970); and *Education and the Employment Problem in Developing Countries* (Geneva: International Labour Office, 1973).

Procedures for estimating returns to education are discussed in George Psacharopoulos, "Returns to Education: An Updated International Comparison," *Comparative Education* 17, no. 3 (1981): 321–42. Psacharopoulos cites earlier works and gives findings for a number of countries. For the rival manpower planning approach, go back to Herbert S. Parnes, *Forecasting Educational Needs for Economic Development,* Mediterranean Regional Project (Paris: Organization for Economic Cooperation and Development, 1962); and Jan Tinbergen and H. C. Bos, "A Planning Model for the Educational Requirements of Economic Development," in *Econometric Models for Education* (Paris: Organization for Economic Cooperation and Development, 1965).

Iconoclastic analyses of education in developing countries include Ivan Ilych, *Deschooling Society* (New York: Harper and Row, 1970); Paolo Freire, *Pedagogy of the Oppressed,* translated from the Portuguese by Myra Bergman Ramos (New York: Seabury Press, 1970); and Ronald Dore, *The Diploma Disease: Education, Qualification and Development* (Berkeley: University of California Press, 1976).

Chapter 10

HEALTH

Improvement of health conditions used to be given a low priority by most LDC governments. It was regarded as something it would be nice to do if possible, but not at the expense of more directly productive expenditure categories. Development specialists generally took a similar view; as far as we know no previous economic development textbook includes a chapter on health. Recently, however, more attention has been devoted to the relationship between health and development. One reason for this is the growing interest in equity-oriented development strategies of the "basic human needs" variety (see Chapter 4) in which provision of basic health services necessarily plays an important part. A second reason is that health expenditures, like education expenditures, are increasingly regarded as investments in human capital.

The health-development relationship is a reciprocal one. As in Chapter 7's discussion of fertility decline, one can ask about the extent to which economic development itself leads to improvements in health status. Proponents of health-sector programs often deny that development alone can or will do the job, arguing that special programs in nutrition, health care, and environmental sanitation are also needed. Sometimes these proponents go so far as to argue that development can be injurious to health, or that provision of appropriate health programs can do the job by themselves, even in the absence of significant overall development. Opponents of this view reply that health status is generally related to income level and specific health measures often fail to have much effect when the surrounding socio-economic and physical environments are unfavorable to health. We will return to this debate later in the chapter.

The other side of the reciprocal relationship between health and development involves the issue of how and to what extent health programs can promote economic development. This will be discussed below, after a presentation of basic facts and concepts.

Health in the Third World

What is "health"? How can one tell whether an individual, or a society, is healthy or sick?

The definition of health is surprisingly elusive. The World Health Organization (WHO), which is the United Nations agency responsible for programs to improve health standards, defines it as "a state of complete physical, mental, and social well-being," but this goes far beyond what is normally meant by health. For most people health is simply the absence of disease and infirmity. But this is not an entirely satisfactory definition either, since it can be highly subjective. Conditions which are seen as disease in countries with high health standards may be so common in countries with lower standards that they are not even recognized as abnormal.

The health status of an individual can be determined through clinical examination by a qualified health professional. Since it is usually not practical to examine large groups of people, definitions of the health status of entire populations must rely on statistics. These are of two kinds: those covering *morbidity* (sickness) and those covering *mortality* (deaths). Morbidity data are much less satisfactory than mortality data. Aside from the lack of a clear-cut definition of sickness, another problem is that many sick people, especially in poor countries, never enter a hospital, or even consult a (Western-style) doctor, as a result of which they often fail to come into contact with the statistical system. Mortality data are considerably better: death seldom goes unnoticed, and most countries now have reasonably complete official systems of death registration, although significant gaps remain in some cases. Death statistics are most useful for assessing the health status of a population when they include detailed information on the person who has died (his or her age, sex, place of residence, and so on) and information on the cause of death. However, data on the cause of death are usually weak in low-income countries.

Patterns and Trends

In Chapter 7 we saw that mortality is negatively related to GNP per capita. The crude death rate is cut in half as one moves up the income scale from countries with less than $150 a year to countries with more than $5000 per capita (Table 7–2). The infant rate falls even more, declining from about 150 per thousand live births to about 20. Another way to look at the relationship between development and mortality is in terms of *life expectancy.* Life expectancy is the average number of years members of a given population are expected to live.[1] As Table 10–1 shows, children born in 1980 in the poorest countries could expect to live only forty-five years on average, while children born in the same period in the richest countries

1. We cannot, of course, know how long any particular individual will actually live. What we can do is predict the average longevity of a class of people (for example, males age five), using the recent mortality experience of the relevant group (in this case, all males) as a guide. Life expectancy at birth is the form of the statistic most often cited (as in Table 10–1), but the concept really refers to expected years of *remaining* life and can thus be applied to people of various ages (as in Table 10–3).

TABLE 10–1 Life Expectancy at Birth, by Income Group, 1980

Income group	Life expectancy
Below $200	45
$200–$300	49
$300–$500	47
$500–$1000	57
$1000–$2000	63
$2000–$5000	69
Above $5000	72

Source: World Bank, *World Development Report 1982* (Washington, D.C., 1982), pp. 150–51.

were likely to live seventy-two years on average. This difference provides one measure of the effect of economic development on health.

The correlation between income level and mortality is high but by no means perfect. Table 10–2 shows life expectancy statistics for selected LDCs in 1960 and 1980. Some of the countries listed in this table have life expectancies far above the average for their income levels. Particularly notable in this regard are China and Sri Lanka, but the populations of India, Kenya, and Colombia also stand out as more long-lived than those other countries in their regions and income classes. Several of the countries listed in Table 10-2 increased life expectancy by ten years or more between 1960 and 1980.

TABLE 10–2 Life Expectancy at Birth, Selected Countries, 1960 and 1980

Country	Life expectancy 1960	1980
Bolivia	43	50
Brazil	55	63
Chile	57	67
Colombia	53	63
Ghana	40	49
Kenya	41	55
Tanzania	42	52
China	na	64
India	43	52
Indonesia	41	53
Korea, Rep. of	54	65
Malaysia	53	64
Pakistan	43	50
Sri Lanka	62	66

Source: World Bank, *World Development Report 1982* (Washington, D.C., 1982), pp. 150–51.

The cross-section data in Table 10–1 reveal a pattern similar to what is believed to have happened through time in the industrial countries. Death rates fall as countries develop. Concurrently life expectancy rises; Fig. 10–1 shows its historical trend in different groups of countries. As can be seen, the early-developing countries have experienced a slow, steady rise in life expectancy since around 1850. Japan, a later developer, was able to extend life more rapidly and reach a level close to that of the early developers by

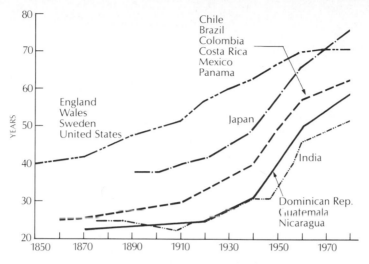

Fig. 10–1 Trends in Life Expectancy in Selected Countries. Source: World Bank, *Health Sector Policy Paper* (2nd ed.; Washington, D.C., February 1980), p. 10.

about 1960. Less developed countries have also been able to achieve rapid increases in life expectancy, particularly over the past forty years. However, their life expectancy remains much less in most cases than life expectancy in the rich countries, as Table 10–1 indicates. In India and other very-low-income countries life expectancy at birth today is about what it was in England in 1910 (see Fig. 10–1).

Most of the reduction in mortality that has been achieved in the developed countries, and most of the difference in life expectancy between rich and poor countries in the world today, affects the very young. This fact is highlighted in Table 10–3, which compares male life expectancy at various ages in Sweden and Bangladesh. It can be seen that these two countries differ enormously in life expectancy at birth. Yet for males who survive the early years of life the differences in remaining life expectancy become much less. Whereas in Sweden and other countries with high health standards the expected years of further life decline steadily as a person ages, in Bangladesh a surviving five-year-old can actually expect to live over seven *additional* years—that is, over thirteen more years in all—than a newborn. This fact is testimony to the terrible extent of infant and child mortality in the

TABLE 10–3 Comparison of Male Life Expectancy in Bangladesh and Sweden

	Additional years a male is expected to live if he is now:				
	Newborn	Age 1	Age 5	Age 15	Age 65
Bangladesh (1974)	45.8	53.5	54.4	46.3	11.6
Sweden (1976)	72.1	71.8	67.9	58.1	13.9
Difference	26.3	18.3	13.5	11.8	2.3

Source: United Nations, *Demographic Yearbook, Historical Supplement* (New York, 1979), pp. 553, 558.

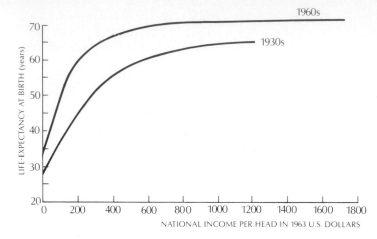

Fig. 10–2 Relationship Between Life Expectancy at Birth and National Income per Head (1930s and 1960s). Source: Samuel H. Preston, "The Changing Relationship Between Mortality and Level of Economic Development," *Population Studies* 29, no. 2 (July 1975): 231–48; adapted from p. 235.

poorest countries. In view of this experience it is not surprising that in some traditional societies children are not regarded as actually having been born until they have survived the first year of life.

Causes of Sickness and Death

Interesting research by Samuel Preston has shown that the cross-section relationship between income and life expectancy is parabolic in form and has been shifting upward during the twentieth century[2] (Fig. 10–2). That is, at any given level of real income per capita people are tending to live longer as time goes by. However, the relationship between income and life expectancy has become looser in recent decades. Preston found that rising income accounted for only 10–25 percent of the rise in life expectancy between the 1930s and 1960s. Other factors accounted for 75–90 percent of the increase.

What could explain this loosening of the relationship between income and life expectancy? Increasing literacy and improved income distribution are possible influences, but the findings of Preston and other researchers are not consistent on this. Most likely, as Preston speculated, the international spread of health technology and a growing similarity of values regarding its application were factors contributing to the loosening of the relationship between income and life expectancy and the tendency for poor countries to acquire statistical life expectancies more similar to those of the rich countries.

Although the international spread of health technology has been a major factor in the worldwide decline in death rates and rise in life expectancy

2. Samuel H. Preston, "The Changing Relationship Between Mortality and Level of Development," *Population Studies* 29, no. 2 (July 1975):

which has occurred since World War II, its effect has sometimes been exaggerated. A debated case is that of Ceylon (Sri Lanka), where a fall in the crude death rate of 43 percent between 1945 and 1949 was originally attributed almost entirely to the control of malaria through the use of DDT. Later it was established that DDT was only part of the story, and that longer-run and more general factors such as rising income, widespread literacy, and the availability of low-priced foodstuffs were also influential.

In some cases the differentials in mortality appear to be attributable to differences both in health policy and in broader social policy. Table 10–4 contrasts two types of poor areas: one (including the Indian state of Kerala) in which a basic human needs strategy emphasizing the attainment of minimum acceptable levels of health services, education, and nutrition was pursued, and another where it was not. Although the first group is no richer than the second—indeed, it is substantially poorer than Iran, a member of the second group—it has achieved a markedly lower level of mortality. We will ponder the lessons of this comparison later in the chapter.

TABLE 10–4   Mortality in Two Groups of Areas, Around 1975

Area	Crude death rate	Infant mortality rate	Life expectancy at birth
Areas with basic needs policies			
China	10	55	62
Sri Lanka	8	45	68
Kerala[a]	9	56	62
Areas without basic needs policies			
Bangladesh	20	132	47
India	15	139	50
Iran	16	139	51
Pakistan	15	124	50

Source: James Kocher and Richard A. Cash, "Achieving Health and Nutritional Objectives Within a Basic Needs Framework" (Harvard Institute for International Development, Development Discussion Paper No. 55, March 1979), p. 19.
[a] A state in southern India.

National statistics on causes of death, although weak, are good enough to permit clear-cut comparisons between rich and poor countries and illuminate the historical pattern of death rate decline by cause. Rich and poor countries as groups have characteristically different cause of death patterns (Table 10–5). In poor countries, infectious, parasitic, and respiratory disease, mainly afflicting the young, account for nearly half of all deaths. Important examples of this category include the "diarrhea-pneumonia complex," malaria, whooping cough, polio, tetanus, and diphtheria. All these diseases are well controlled in rich countries. As Table 10–5 shows, their comparative prevalence accounts for over half the differences in number of deaths between the rich and poor countries. Other causes of death are also less significant in developed than in less developed countries, except for cancer which is more prevalent in rich countries because of the greater longevity of their populations. Again, the time series and cross-section patterns are roughly similar. Diseases which in the twentieth century are known as "tropical diseases" were major killers in temperate Europe in earlier centuries.

TABLE 10–5   Numbers of Deaths by Main Causes in Typical Developed and Less Developed Countries (annual deaths per 100,000 population)

	Typical LDC	Typical developed country	Difference
Infectious, parasitic, and respiratory diseases	874	97	− 777
Cancer	74	137	+ 63
Diseases of circulatory system	296	290	− 6
Traumatic injury	70	61	− 9
All other causes	686	315	− 371
All causes	2000	900	− 1100

Source: Based on World Bank, Health Sector Policy Paper (1st ed.; Washington, D.C., March 1975), p. 13.

Despite the unsatisfactory nature of morbidity statistics it is all too easy to identify a number of endemic and epidemic diseases which affect large populations in the third world. Some of these diseases—tuberculosis, malaria, cholera—are prominent causes of death. Others may not kill large numbers, but they limit people's lives and may contribute to a premature death which is officially ascribed to some other cause. One such category is parasitic conditions, which are all but universal in many areas. (It has been estimated that perhaps one-fourth of the world's population has roundworms.) Another is malnutrition, which is sometimes present in easily recognized clinical form but far more commonly exists at a lower level, where its effects, although destructive, are more subtle and difficult to detect.

Effects of Health on Development

We have considered the effect of development on health. Now it is time to ask what better health can contribute to development. Can health expenditures really be regarded as a form of investment in human capital? Before addressing this question it is important to recognize that the validity of health services as a developmental activity does not entirely rest on our ability to prove that health expenditures increase national output. Better health can also be regarded as an important goal in its own right. It increases the range of human potentialities of all kinds and this is an important aspect of development. Health thus has a good claim to be regarded as a "basic human need." Health is valued for its own sake by all segments of the population. Everyone can benefit from better health in the present, and improved health for the young will lead to a healthier population in the future.

Like education, health services increase the *quality* of human resources, both now and in the future.[3] Better worker health can provide immediate benefits by increasing the workers' strength, stamina, and ability to concentrate while on the job. Better child health and nutrition promote future productivity by helping children develop into stronger, healthier adults. In addition they supplement the acquisition of productive skills and attitudes through schooling. It has been shown that healthy, well-fed children have higher attendance rates and are able to concentrate better while they are in school.

Unlike education, health expenditures also increase the *quantity* of human resources in the future by lengthening the expected working life. In this way too they complement educational investment, since returns to education should be higher if people can be expected to work and earn longer.

The returns to investment in health, however, are even harder to quantify and verify empirically than the returns to investment in education. For one thing there is no simple proxy measure, analogous to years of schooling, of the amount invested in the health of any particular individual. The economic effects of better health are also hard to measure. The *quantitative* effects (extended working life) can be gauged in additional years worked, but what valuation should be put on them? In a private cost-benefit analysis expected additional earnings can be used, but in a social cost-benefit analysis the marginal product of labor should be estimated to determine the value to society of extended working life. This opens up the complex question of what the productivity of the marginal worker really is (Chapter 8). In an economy in which marginal productivity is very low the production benefits of extended working life are necessarily small. The *qualitative* effects of health expenditure (increased worker productivity and earnings) are also hard to measure, in the sense that the amount of any increase in productivity or earnings that is attributable to improvement in health may be difficult to identify.

Studies which have tried to measure the effects of better health on labor productivity have so far yielded varying results. For example, a study of iron supplementation for Indonesian plantation workers was able to measure productivity benefits, but an ambitious attempt to determine the effect of schistosomiasis control on the Caribbean island of St. Lucia had difficulty finding measurable effects.[4] At present therefore one cannot be sure how great these potential productivity gains may be. It is possible that people find ways to adapt to ill-health and malnutrition without greatly reduc-

3. For a comprehensive statement of the case for regarding health expenditures as investment in human capital, along with some U.S. examples, see Selma Mushkin, "Health as an Investment," *Journal of Political Economy* 70, no. 5, part 2 (Supplement, October 1962): 129–57.
4. See S. S. Basta and A. Churchill, "Iron Deficiency Anemia and the Productivity of Adult Males in Indonesia" (World Bank Staff Working Paper No. 175, April 1974); Burton Weisbrod and Robert E. Baldwin, "Disease and Labor Productivity," *Economic Development and Cultural Change* 22, no. 3 (1974): 414–35.

ing their productivity: they may not feel well, but they still can work. In this situation it follows that improving health would not necessarily increase productivity. But it still would be desirable from a humanitarian point of view.

Besides increasing the quantity and quality of the human resource, health expenditures can also make available, or increase the productivity of, non-human resources. The most important example is the situation in which areas of land are rendered uninhabitable, or unusable for particular purposes such as cattle raising, by endemic diseases. Malaria and yellow fever blocked access to many parts of Latin America, Africa, and Asia before these diseases were brought under relatively effective control in the twentieth century. Even today schistosomiasis makes it unsafe for people to enter lakes and streams in sections in Africa, while trypanosomiasis (African sleeping sickness) restricts the range of the livestock industry. So far no chemical means of control has been discovered for either of these diseases. (China, however, has made progress against schistosomiasis through social mobilization, mass campaigns aimed at ridding lakes and streams of the snails that transmit the parasite.)

Improved control of ankylostomiasis (hookworm) and other parasitic conditions would increase resource availabilities in a different way. By cutting the wastage of food through consumption by parasites it would increase the effective productivity of resources devoted to food production.

We have seen that the productive benefits of health expenditures, although easy to hypothesize, have proven difficult to verify empirically. But even the effects on health status are sometimes hard to find. The main reason for this difficulty is the multiplicity of factors that go together to determine health status. For example, a study of the health effects of projects to provide safe water supplies to a number of villages in Lesotho found that, surprisingly, provision of a clean water source failed in many cases to lead to a significant reduction in the prevalence of water-borne and water-related diseases. One explanation was that water-borne diseases are also transmitted by other means, such as contaminated food, and the provision of a safe source of water alone does not prevent villagers from being infected by other sources of disease.[5]

Health improvement has one effect that could be considered a social cost: by reducing the death rate it increases population growth. (Admittedly the decline in the death rate may in turn encourage a drop in fertility, which would reduce the overall positive impact on population growth; but studies indicate that the magnitude of this "replacement effect," if it exists at all, is likely to be small.) At this point, however, we get into a question of ethical values. Even if population growth is acknowledged to be injuriously high, universally espoused values make it unacceptable to reduce that growth by killing people or by allowing persons already born to die

---

5. Richard Feuchem et al., *Water Health and Development: An Interdisciplinary Evaluation* (London: Tri-Med Books, 1974), Chapter 9.

when the means of saving them are at hand. It follows that this "cost" should not be permitted to become an argument against health improvements and that other means should be found to limit population growth if this is considered to be an important social objective.

A more difficult problem is determining just what share of an LDC's national resources should be allocated to health improvement programs. This involves such complex issues as the comparative importance to society of reduced sickness and death versus other benefits that could be obtained using the same scarce resources; the relative claims for better health of various social groups (infants and children, mothers, workers, old people); and the likely productivity of resources devoted to different kinds of health improvement programs (for example, curative versus preventive approaches). Some of these problems will be further considered below.

Causes of LDC Health Problems

The health planner, like the physician, should carefully diagnose before he prescribes. Health planning must address the real health problems found in the less developed countries. One attempt to categorize the fundamental causes of sickness and premature death in the LDCs identifies four major categories: (1) demographic factors; (2) malnutrition; (3) unsanitary living conditions; and (4) lack of medical care of adequate quantity, quality, and type.[6] We will analyze these factors in turn.

Demographic Factors

In the discussion of population growth in Chapter 7, little was said about its relationship to health except to note that the "replacement hypothesis" states that high death rates among infants and children are one cause of high fertility. But there is also a causal linkage leading from high fertility to ill-health and premature death which works both at the familial and at the societal level. Studies have shown that higher rates of maternal, infant, and child mortality are all associated with "high parity"—that is, with having been born into a family in which there are several older siblings. The additional deaths appear to result from the strains which large families impose on various family resources, including income, food supply, and parental time and attention.

Something similar takes place at the societal level. Population pressure can reduce nutritional standards and bring about an insufficiency of publicly provided sanitary and medical facilities. The health effects of rapid population growth and high dependency burdens thus provide an additional rationale for the kinds of population policy measures discussed in Chapter 7.

6. World Bank, *Health Sector Policy Paper* (1st ed.; Washington, D.C., March 1975).

Malnutrition

Malnutrition is a major source of ill-health and premature death in the LDCs. Some data on nutritional standards appear in Tables 10–6 and 10–7. These tables give the most commonly cited nutritional statistic, average daily calorie intake compared to the minimum daily requirement. The actual daily average intake figures are normally compiled from "national food balance sheets," a set of accounts intended to show how much food must have been consumed by human beings, making allowances for supplies from production and imports and for other uses, such as exports; processing, spoilage, and rodent infestation losses; livestock feed; and industrial uses. The resulting quantities of the various foodstuffs are then converted into nutrient values using standard equivalencies for the items concerned. Recommended daily consumption figures derive from an attempt to say how many calories and other nutrients a person would have to consume to maintan good health, given a certain body weight and at least a minimum level of daily activity.

TABLE 10–6 Daily Per-Capita Calorie Supply by Income Class and Region, 1977

Criterion	Total	As % of requirement
Income class		
Below $200	2044	89
$200–$300	2114	92
$300–$500	2165	94
$500–$1000	2296	102
$1000–$2000	2488	105
$2000–$5000	3079	122
$5000 and over	3311	127
Region		
Africa	2219	96
Asia	2411	102
West Asia	2516	97
South Asia	2093	93
East Asia	2413	107
Oceania and Indonesia	2828	110
Europe	3360	131
North and Central America	2531	108
South America	2558	104

Source: World Bank, World Development Report 1982 (Washington, D.C., 1982), pp. 144–45.

According to these statistics there were caloric deficits in 1977 in Africa, West Asia, and South Asia, while in other regions of the world the actual intake was above the minimum required level. Even in the deficit regions things might not seem to be too bad. After all, the deficit was only 3 percent in West Asia, 4 percent in Africa, and 7 percent in South Asia. However, these are tricky averages which understate the actual gravity of the situation for two reasons.

One problem arises from the way the minimum standards themselves are defined. If people do not receive the nutrition needed to maintain a given

TABLE 10-7   Daily Per-Capita Calorie Supply for Selected Countries, 1977

Country	Total	As % of requirement
Bolivia	1974	87
Brazil	2562	111
Chile	2656	110
Colombia	2364	98
Peru	2274	98
Ghana	1983	85
Kenya	2032	96
Tanzania	2063	87
China	2441	103
India	2021	89
Indonesia	2272	102
Korea, Rep. of	2785	117
Malaysia	2610	116
Pakistan	2281	99
Sri Lanka	2126	97

Source: World Bank, *World Development Report 1982* (Washington, D.C., 1982), pp. 144–45.

body weight and activity level, they adapt by weighing, and doing, less. Thus the standards implied for South and East Asia in Table 10–6 are lower than the standards for other regions because Asians tend to be small. But their smallness is at least partially attributable to inadequate nutrition in the past. When Asians regularly get enough to eat, as the Japanese have since World War II and the Chinese and Koreans have more recently, their average weight and height, and thus their caloric requirements, increase rapidly from one generation to the next.

The other problem which causes these averages to be misleading is inequality of food distribution. Even in the least well-fed countries some people receive more than the recommended daily minimum. The difficulty is that their extra consumption, while it raises the average daily intake, in no way diminishes the deficits experienced by those who fail to attain the recommended minimum. Averages computed for large and diverse populations are particularly likely to understate the nutritional problem by offsetting surpluses against deficits in this misleading way.

Because of this problem it may be more revealing to count people than to count calories. According to one estimate, in 1970 one-quarter of the third world's population received insufficient calories for body maintenance, let alone a moderate level of activity.[7] (This estimate excludes China, North Vietnam, and North Korea, for which there were no reliable statistics at the time.) By far the largest number of malnourished people, more than 300 million, were found to be in Asia, where 30 percent of the population received insufficient calories. In Africa 25 percent of the population was malnourished and in Latin America 13 percent.

The prevalance of malnutrition and its injurious effects is greatest among children. The WHO has estimated that 3 percent of third world children

7. Sterling Wortman and Ralph W. Cummings, Jr., *To Feed This World: The Challenge and the Strategy* (Baltimore and London: Johns Hopkins University Press, 1978), p. 23.

are afflicted by severe (third-degree) malnutrition, which gives rise to clinical conditions such as kwashiorkor (a protein-deficiency disease marked by bloated bellies and glassy stares) and marasmus (a condition brought on by shortage of both calories and protein). Another 25 percent suffer from moderate (second-degree) malnutrition and a further 40–45 percent from mild (first-degree) malnutrition.[8] These conditions are indicated by substandard rates of physical development. Malnutrition is said to be present as a primary or contributing factor in more than half of all deaths among children under five in low-income countries. It can turn otherwise mild childhood diseases, such as respiratory problems, gastrointestinal difficulties, and measles, into killers.

Most of the malnutrition in the world today is of the type known as protein-calorie malnutrition (PCM). Conditions caused by deficiencies of specific nutrients—such as rickets, scurvy, and beri-beri—have generally diminished in importance. Among the remaining deficiency diseases the most important are Vitamin A deficiency, which can cause blindness, and iron-deficiency anemia. At one time it was thought that shortage of protein was the principal nutritional problem of the third world, since protein is necessary for physical and mental development. More recently, however, it has been discovered that most of the children whose diets are deficient in protein also suffer from a deficiency of calories, and if protein is added to the diet while calories remain insufficient human development is little affected because the added proteins are used up as energy. Accordingly, calories are now regarded as the limiting factor in nutrition, and most programs attempt to supplement calories first and protein, vitamins, and minerals only secondarily.

Aggregate data (Table 10–8) suggest that the extent of PCM may have lessened in recent decades. Average calorie and protein intakes appear to have increased during the 1960s and 1970s in all third world regions. We must, however, remember the tendency of these averages to mislead. The upper half of Table 10–8 shows how closely average nutritional levels by country are related to income. The same is true within countries: different income groups may have very different consumption levels. Where income distribution worsened during the 1960s and 1970s, the number of malnourished people could have increased at the same time as the average calorie intake went up.

Food Consumption

What causes malnutrition, and how could nutritional improvement contribute to economic development? The determinants of human nutritional levels can be analyzed using microeconomic consumption theory. The consumption of food, like that of other goods and services, can be thought of as determined by three elements: income, relative prices, and tastes.

---

8. See Alan Berg, *The Nutrition Factor: Its Role in National Development* (Washington, D.C.: Brookings Institution, 1973), p. 5.

TABLE 10-8   Daily Per-Capita Calorie Supply by Income Class and Region,
1960 and 1977

	Per-capita calorie supply (% of requirement)	
	1960	1979
GNP per capita (1980)		
Below $200	88	89
$200–$300	86	92
$300–$500	92	94
$500–$1000	87	102
$1000–$2000	95	105
$2000–$5000	106	122
$5000 and over	114	127
Region		
Africa	89	96
Asia	91	102
West Asia	90	97
South Asia	91	93
East Asia	91	107
Oceania and Indonesia	113	110
Europe	106	131
North and Central America	96	108
South America	97	104

Source: World Bank, *World Tables 1976* (Baltimore and London: Johns Hopkins University Press, 1976), pp. 518–21; World Bank, *World Development Report 1982* (Washington, D.C., 1981), pp. 176–77.

Engel's Law, as we saw in Chapter 3, says that households spend an increasing amount, but a decreasing proportion, of income on food as their incomes rise. Very poor households devote more than half their incomes to food and have relatively high income elasticities of demand for food (that is, a significant proportion of any additional income will be used to buy food). At higher levels of income the share of income devoted to purchases of food falls to one-quarter or less, and the income elasticity of demand for food becomes quite low. Thus income is an important determinant of food consumption levels, particularly at lower levels of household income.

Prices are also important, because of both *income effects* and substitution effects. For a poor household, a change in the price of a basic foodstuff, particularly of the staple foodgrain (rice, wheat, corn, or whatever), can have a significant effect on the household's purchasing power. If, say, the household spends 30 percent of its income on rice and the retail price of rice increases by 20 percent, this amounts to a 6 percent cut in the real income of an already-poor household ($0.3 \times 0.20 = 0.06 = 6$ percent). For this reason staple foodgrain prices are a basic indicator of welfare levels among the poor, and of political stability, in many low-income countries.

Substitution effects can also be significant. Even when there are strong preferences for particular foods, large price differences can cause substantial substitution of cheaper foods for more expensive ones, especially among the very poor. By this means it was possible to induce large numbers of people in East Pakistan (now Bangladesh) to consume U.S.-surplus wheat instead of rice, the favored foodgrain, when there was a rice shortage during the 1960s. Similarly, desperately poor families are sometimes forced to "trade down" from the preferred foodgrain to a cheaper source of calories, usually either a hard grain like sorghum or a starchy root crop such as manioc (cassava).

Both income and price influences apply to the consumption of food, not directly to consumption of nutrients. Although nutrition is derived from food, it is food that people consume, not nutrition per se. When people spend more on food they may or may not obtain better nutrition. Some of the additional expenditure goes for a larger *quantity* of food, but much of it, especially above minimal income levels, goes for higher *quality.* Quality is defined in terms of people's tastes. For example, they may prefer a particular variety of rice over other varieties, highly polished rice over brown rice, whole grains over broken ones, and so on. These tastes may have little to do with nutrition. In general, however, people with higher incomes have both a higher calorie intake and a more varied diet which is superior in terms of other nutrients. Every nutritionist can tell "horror stories" about deterioration in nutritional standards as development proceeds: carbonated beverages replace natural drinks, commercial infant foods replace mother's breast milk, various junk foods are increasingly consumed by children and adults. Statistics make it clear, however, that these cases run counter to the general pattern of improved nutrition in relation to increasing income.

Food beliefs and tastes can impede nutritional improvement. In every culture there are beliefs about the health effects of various foods which are not supported by modern nutritional science. Feeding taboos for infants and new mothers are thought to be particularly injurious in many developing countries. In most human environments one can point to nutritional potentials which are underexploited for reasons of taste and habit. For example, soybeans provide a much cheaper source of protein than animal products, yet they are eaten in quantity only in East Asian countries where beancurd is a standard dietary item. Nutritionists can counter the economist's assertion that income is the main influence on nutritional status by demonstrating that even very poor households could eat nutritiously if they had the necessary knowledge and chose to do so.

In conclusion, all three factors—income, prices, and tastes—are significant contributors to the determination of nutritional status. Emphasis on the role of each factor leads to a different approach to nutritional policy, as will be seen shortly.

The distribution of food within a family is another important aspect of individual nutritional status. When food is scarce, children and older adults tend to find their rations disproportionately reduced. It is understandable that in dire circumstances families would channel food to the working adults on whose continued health and strength the survival of all members of the family ultimately depends. This tendency makes it hard to devise programs to improve nutritional status of the more vulnerable members of the family, such as infants and new mothers, since feeding programs aimed at such individuals may set off consumption shifts within the family such that the breadwinner rather than the intended recipient winds up with the extra food.

Nutritional Problems and Health

What is the impact of malnutrition on health status, and thus on economic development? This question can be considered separately for three groups: children and infants; pregnant and nursing women; and working adults.

The greatest nutritional problem in the third world is that of infants and children. Infants are usually adequately fed through the period of breast-feeding, but they may suffer a nutritional decline after weaning. If not corrected this decline will reduce energy levels and physical growth. This in turn may decrease their resistance to disease and impair their ability to learn in school. It has also been argued that malnutrition causes severe, even irreversible, retardation of mental development, but this assertion is now regarded as controversial at best. Even so, nutritional deficiencies among third world children must be regarded as important because they are so widespread and have such serious consequences.

Pregnant and nursing women merit special attention because of their relationship to the child nutritional problem. While she is carrying or nursing a child a woman has especially heavy nutrition requirements because she is, as the saying goes, "eating for two." This is not recognized in all cultures and economic circumstances.

Improved nutrition for working adults could conceivably have the most direct and immediate effect on economic growth if their productivity were increased thereby. There is some evidence, for example from the Indonesian iron deficiency study mentioned earlier, that this potential is a real one. However, it can be asked whether the phenomenon is truly widespread. Since working adults tend to get favored access to whatever food is available, it is not clear to what extent their food supply is reduced when the family as a whole is short of food. Nor is it known what the effects on their productivity might be.

Nutrition Improvement Programs

Nutrition improvement efforts have involved a number of different types of programs. In the 1950s attention focused on the severely malnourished, who required treatment in hospitals. Later the emphasis shifted to treatment of milder cases outside the hospital. Supplementary feeding programs were instituted in a number of countries. Their most severe difficulty turned out to be that of reaching the intended beneficiary group at reasonable cost. School lunch programs can be helpful, but the worst nutritional deficiencies are likely to be among preschool children. Even when the intended beneficiaries are reached and fed, evaluators of feeding programs suspect that substitution frequently takes place in the home, whereby the children are fed less to compensate for the school lunch and the net increase in the family's food supply thus goes to the adults rather than to the children.

The best way to get supplementary food to infants and small children is through a maternal and child health (MCH) program. These programs also provide nutritional surveillance. The food offered can serve as an inducement for mothers to bring their children into an MCH center regularly for weighing, examination, and treatment if necessary. Persuasion and linkage with other services that may be desired, such as family planning, also promote these programs. Without such efforts, very few third world mothers bring their babies in for examination by a health professional unless they are obviously sick.

Other conventional nutrition improvement programs include the promotion of *backyard gardens* to provide dietary supplementation and *nutritional education* conducted in schools, adult education courses, and the like. Since these programs are inherently somewhat limited in scope, there have been attempts to develop broader, more general types of programs. *Food supplementation* (fortification) programs have sometimes had dramatic results in overcoming specific nutritional deficiencies—for example, through the addition of iodine to the salt supply in goiter-prone areas. Fortification of bread and other basic foodstuffs to increase their protein content has been attempted in several areas, with mixed results. Still less successful have been efforts, some of them widely heralded for a time, to develop commercially compounded *new foods* whose exceptional nutritional values would overcome the problem of malnutrition. The main problem with the "new foods" is that their high cost usually puts them beyond the reach of precisely those low-income consumers who are likely to be malnourished.

Growing interest in the problem of malnutrition coupled with the limited success of conventional approaches has led to increasing attention to still broader programs, such as *campaigns to increase national food production* and *food price subsidization* for low-income urban consumers. There is no doubt that food-growing peasants, such as small-scale rice or corn producers, do eat better than when their farms become more productive. Similarly, a price cut for stable food items—made possible by higher farm production and greater supplies—can provide a substantial boost in both real income and nutritional status for the urban poor, as we have seen. The main problem with staple food subsidization programs are how to limit them to the intended beneficiaries and forms of benefit, as well as how to finance them. Recipients of subsidized foodstuffs (or food stamps, as in the U.S. program) may sell them to buy other goods which they prefer. While this practice is consistent with the idea of consumer choice, it may defeat the purpose of nutritional improvement. Subsidy programs can be expensive, especially when their scope is broad. Egypt and Sri Lanka are two countries which have had food subsidy programs extending to nearly the entire population. In both cases subsidization of basic foodstuffs (wheat, beans, lentils, vegetable oil, meat, fish, and tea in Egypt; rice, wheat, and sugar in Sri Lanka) is credited with increasing the real income of the poor and improving their nutritional and health status. But the cost of the program grew to around 15 percent of government expenditure in both countries and came to be regarded as a contributor to fiscal instability. In both cases efforts to cut back on the subsidy bill led to political instability: riots in both countries, and in Sri Lanka the defeat at the polls of more than one government.

The cost-effectiveness of different approaches to nutritional improvement is a subject of current debate. Targeted programs which deliver nutritional services to specific groups of beneficiaries—for instance, school lunch programs or baby-weighing programs—can involve high logistical and supervision costs per beneficiary served. More general programs, such as fortification or food subsidies, may achieve a lower cost per recipient but entail a different kind of cost problem: "leakage" of program benefits to people other than the intended beneficiaries. The extension of nutritional programs (especially food subsidies) to large segments of the population can be costly, as the experience of Egypt and Sri Lanka illustrate.

Environmental Health

The principal problem of environmental sanitation in low-income countries is the contamination of the water supply, and sometimes also of food and soil, with human waste. This occurs in villages and cities alike. Many LDC cities lack safe drinking water because they are unable to protect the public water supply, which may be pure when it leaves the pumping plant, from contamination in the distribution process as the result of a faulty or nonexistent sewage system. The lack of a sufficient water supply for drinking, washing, and sewage disposal is also a serious health problem in some third world environments. Table 10–9 gives some idea of what a small proportion of people in developing countries have reasonable access to water and an adequate system of sewage disposal.

Many of the infectious, parasitic, and respiratory diseases which cause so much sickness and death in poor countries (Table 10–5) are water-borne. Typhoid, dysentery, and cholera are among the leading examples. The results of their prevalence are much sickness among adults and frequent deaths among infants and malnourished children.

A second type of environmental sanitation problem arises from housing which lacks sufficient space, ventilation, and access to sunlight. This situation, which is more likely to arise in urban than in rural areas, promotes the spread of air-borne diseases, such as tuberculosis.

Sanitation improvement programs primarily involve the problems of waste disposal and water supply, particularly the need to keep the one system from contaminating the other. In the village this means safe wells and properly constructed privies. Simple technologies are available for effecting such improvements. In the urban areas matters become more expensive and complex. It will be a very long time before all third world cities have decent sewage disposal and water supply systems, let alone adequate housing for their growing populations.

TABLE 10-9 Access to Water Supply and Sewerage in Developing Countries (c. 1970)[a]

	Per-capita income in 1970 (U.S. $)			
	< $100	$101–$150	$151–$450	> $450
Number of countries	15	17	34	12
% of population with access to water supply				
Rural, with reasonable access	13	8[c]	28	32
Urban, with public standpost	24	31	21	17
Urban, with pipe to house	21	36	58	63
% of population with access to sewage disposal				
Rural, adequate	7	12	26	na
Urban, other disposal methods[b]	54	67	40	na
Urban, sewage system	6	14	24	na

Source: Survey conducted by World Bank and WHO; see World Bank, *Health Sector Policy Paper* (1st ed.; Washington, D.C., March 1975), p. 19.

[a] These estimates are approximate only, since definitions of "reasonable" and "adequate" access differed among countries. na = not available.

[b] Buckets, pit privies, and septic tanks not connected to public sewer system.

[c] This value is dominated by India and Pakistan, which report 6% and 3% coverage respectively.

Historically, improvements in sanitation seem to have been closely associated with the reduction in disease, coming in long before effective means of treatment had been discovered. In the contemporary third world the experience so far has been mixed. Some projects to impove water supply and waste disposal methods have led to dramatic reductions in disease. Others, as noted earlier, have had no discernible effect.

Medical Services

Finally, most LDCs have too few health services, too poorly distributed. Public expenditures on health services are much smaller in developing than in developed countries, even as a percentage of GNP (1–2 percent versus 2–5 percent; see Table 10–10). In terms of dollars per capita these outlays are woefully inadequate. As Table 10–10 shows, governments in the poorest countries typically spent as little as $1 or $2 per capita in the late 1970s.[9] In LDCs, in contrast to the United States, the public sector provides most of the "modern" or Western-style medical and health services. Private doctors and hospitals are typically few and are patronized mainly by well-to-do urban residents. In most countries there are also indigenous practitioners of various kinds: herbalists, exorcists, acupuncturists. Typi-

9. These figures are distorted by the extreme disparity in the pay of medical personnel, especially doctors, between rich and poor countries. A purchasing-power parity adjustment of the sort discussed in Chapter 3 would roughly triple the per-capita expenditure figures for the poorest countries and double those of the somewhat less poor. By any measure, however, the figures would remain abysmally low. See Frederick Golladay, "Health Problems and Policies in Developing Countries" (World Bank Staff Working Paper No. 412, August 1980).

cally the masses of people consult both "modern" and indigenous curers upon occasion, depending on the nature of the ailment and on their access to the various systems of medicine.

TABLE 10–10   Health Personnel, Facilities and Expenditures, 1977

| | Per 100,000 population | | | Public expenditure | |
Income group	Hospital beds	Physicians	Nursing persons	% of GNP	$ per capita
Below $200	67	7	22	1.0	1
$200–$300	144	15	49	1.2	2
$300–$500	144	9	56	1.1	3
$500–$1000	325	45	118	1.7	8
$1000–$2000	240	44	79	1 1	10
$2000–$5000	582	143	254	2.1	48
$5000 and above	955	169	509	4.5	288

Source: World Bank, World Development Report 1981 (Washington, D.C., 1981), pp. 176–77; World Bank, *Health Sector Policy Paper* (2d ed.; Washington, D.C., 1980), pp. 79–82.

Low medical expenditures in the past have led to inadequate stocks of health facilities and manpower in most developing countries, as Table 10–10 indicates. It is easier to make up the deficit in physical facilities than to overcome the backlog in trained health personnel. In Table 10–10 the poorest LDCs ($200 and under) are seen to have about one-fifteenth as many hospital beds per capita as the richest countries ($5000 and over), but only about one-twenty-fifth as many doctors and nurses. Medical training in many of the poorest countries may not benefit society because doctors are highly mobile, and once trained, many emigrate to seek higher income elsewhere. Increasing the supply of nurses and other health auxiliaries may be a better way to improve services in many cases.

Not only are health services in poor countries inadequately supplied but they are also very unevenly distributed among the population. As Table 10–11 indicates, there are usually several times as many doctors in relation to population in the capital city, and in urban areas generally, as in the rest of the country. Similar if slightly smaller disparities exist with respect to hospital beds and primary health workers.

The usual public health service is organized on a referral basis, so that in theory patients in rural areas suffering from acute medical problems are referred on to better facilities in the towns and, if necessary, in the major cities for care. Generally, however, the referral system does not work well in developing countries. For one thing the lower reaches of the system seldom provide easily accessible services to the whole country. For large parts of the population in the typical low-income country event the most rudimentary public health facility may be so far away that, given the poor transportation systems which prevail, it is in effect inaccessible. Those patients who can get to a government clinic or hospital often find that they have to wait many hours before receiving any attention at all. And even then the care they obtain may be slipshod and half-hearted. Managerial and

TABLE 10–11   Ratios of Doctors per 10,000 Population: Capital Cities and Urban Areas Versus Rest of Country, c. 1970[a]

Country	Capital city vs. rest of country	Urban Areas vs. rural areas
Colombia	6.4 : 1	6.4 : 1
Haiti	24.7 : 1	na
Panama	5.8 : 1	3.2 : 1
Ghana	9.5 : 1	na
Kenya	38.1 : 1	62.5 : 1
Senegal	10.4 : 1	na
Iran	6.9 : 1	4.4 : 1
Pakistan	na	6.5 : 1
Thailand	31.3 : 1	na

Source: Based on World Bank, *Health Sector Policy Paper* (1st ed.; Washington, D.C., March 1975), pp. 80–81.
[a]na = not available.

logistical problems overwhelm some third world health systems. Many of the vaccines which they administer, for example, have been rendered ineffective by age and exposure to heat. Sterile fields for medical procedures are all but impossible to maintain under common LDC conditions.

A different aspect of the maldistribution of medical services concerns the relative degree of attention and resources devoted to treating different types of ailments. In many countries large fractions of tight health budgets have been devoted to acquiring state-of-the-art medical technologies for hospitals in the capital city or at the local medical school. Does it make sense for a country which is not providing even rudimentary medical care to sick infants to acquire the capacity to do open-heart surgery? For the cost of a single complicated medical procedure, basic attention could be provided to hundreds of rural patients. Why then do so many countries opt for what appears to be a severe maldistribution of their scant health resources? One reason appears to be "urban bias," which has been defined and analyzed by Michael Lipton.[10] Urban bias has many causes, one of which is the fact that powerful national elites living in urban areas, especially the capital city, want good medical care for themselves and their families. A second reason is nationalism: "our doctors are just as good as doctors in the advanced countries; they can do open-heart surgery too." Yet a third reason is the technology-mindedness which many doctors share with engineers and other professionals; the medical area is often regarded as an outstanding example of the transfer of inappropriate technology from developed to developing countries. These three factors can interact, as when the self-interest of the elites prompts them to indulge the technology-mindedness of the doctors.

10. Michael Lipton, *Why Poor People Stay Poor: Urban Bias in World Development* (Cambridge, Mass.: Harvard University Press, 1977).

We have seen in this chapter that the small South Asian country of Sri **Health in** Lanka enjoys unusually good health and life expectancy compared to **Sri Lanka** other countries at its approximate level of GNP per capita (only $230 in 1979). This favorable experience is attributable to a combination of good fortune and the policies followed in the period since independence (1948).

A small island located on the trade routes between Europe and East Asia, Sri Lanka (formerly called Ceylon) had early contact with Western colonialism. The British, who controlled the island after earlier periods of Portuguese and Dutch domination, began to introduce "modern" (Western) medicine in the early nineteenth century. Campaigns to eradicate smallpox and yaws began in 1802. Later in the century a Civil Medical Department was started in 1858, a Contagious Diseases Ordinance enacted in 1866, and a medical school opened in Colombo, the capital, in 1870. In the early twentieth century Ceylon's tea, rubber, and coconut plantations were required to provide medical care for their workers and their families, and a school health program was started. In the 1940s a network of rural hospitals was built. The compact, self-contained nature of the island supported these efforts, and when it gained its independence in 1948 Ceylon already had unusually high health standards compared to other Asian countries.

Credit for continued improvement since 1948 belongs primarily to the government of Ceylon/Sri Lanka, which has consistently accorded a high priority to improving the health of its people. From the start medical care was free to all. More important, efforts were made to extend the service network to all parts of the island. These efforts were continuously hampered by shortages of funds. Sri Lankan hospitals have always been crowded, and the provision of additional beds ran only marginally ahead of population growth between 1950 and 1980. There was some improvement in the availability of doctors, but efforts to train more doctors were offset in part by the emigration of physicians to countries where much higher incomes could be earned. The only dramatic change was in the supply of nurses and paramedics, which nearly tripled in relation to population between 1950 and 1980. This increase provided essential support for the extension of primary care to the rural areas.

Measures of mortality and morbidity show striking improvement in the past three decades. Epidemics have been eliminated and diseases such as typhoid, tuberculosis, and malaria have declined sharply as causes of death. Crude and infant death rates have fallen and life expectancy has climbed into the upper sixties. Sri Lanka has become, with China, one of the rare examples of a country with a poor but healthy population.

Not all this improvement is attributable to medical services. Sri Lanka is also unusually advanced in education, and its near-universal literacy is thought to have promoted improved health conditions. Another positive factor is the comparative rarity of malnutrition, which results from a relatively equal distribution of income and the policy of subsidizing basic foods. Although the average calorie intake is only average for countries at Sri Lanka's income level (see Tables 10–6 and 10–7), the calories are probably better distributed among the population than in most other countries.

Medical services in Sri Lanka form a colorful mosaic. The indigenous *ayurvedic* system coexists with Western medicine and receives some official support. Psychological disorders are treated by trance-dancers or exorcists in some cases, by Western-trained psychiatrists in others.

Health in Cuba   At the time the Castro forces took over the island in January 1959, Cuba was a middle-income country with reasonably plentiful but poorly distributed health care manpower and facilities. Income levels were higher than in most other Latin American countries, life expectancy at birth was over sixty years, and the population was more than 50 percent urban. But inequalities were marked. For example, the city of Havana, with only 22 percent of the population, had 55 percent of the hospital beds in the country. By contrast Oriente province, one of Cuba's poorest regions, had 35 percent of the population but only 15 percent of the hospital beds. In all there were 6300 doctors to care for a population of eight million.

In the first three years after the revolution 3000 physicians left the country, most of them emigrating to the United States. There is probably no precedent in history for a country's losing such a high percentage of its doctors in such a short time. Massive training efforts were inaugurated to make up this suddenly created deficit. By 1971, 30 percent of all university students were studying medicine. Particularly large numbers of women went into training to become doctors, in the process creating a shortage of nurses. By the late 1970s Cuba was again exporting doctors, this time voluntarily and to such newly "liberated" countries as Angola and Ethiopia. In Cuba itself, however, the result of more than twenty years of massive training efforts was only to restore the ratio of doctors to population to about what it was in 1958. In 1979 Cuba had about 9000 doctors for a population of nearly 9.9 million.

Despite having to cope with this massive problem of medical manpower Cuba has made major strides toward achievement of high health standards for its entire population since 1959. It has done so largely by reorganizing its health services and improving their distribution among social classes and regions of the country. A new system of hospitals and clinics was set up, patterned in part on the national health systems of Britain and Sweden. This system stretched from provincial hospitals serving areas of about one million people down to health centers serving communities of 25,000. A Cuban innovation was to have many of these services provided by specialists (internists, pediatricians, obstetrician-gynecologists), who were required to divide their time between hospitals and clinics, thus providing continuity of care over the various levels of the system. Given the initial disparities, new facilities were constructed primarily in the rural areas. Thus while the number of hospital beds available in Havana increased by only 8 percent in the first postrevolutionary decade, the increases in Camaguey and Oriente provinces were 184 and 147 percent, respectively. Over half of the new health centers built were allocated to rural areas which previously had no such facilities.

Services in the new system were provided virtually free. The increased availability and lower cost of medical services increased their use by the public. In 1963, early in the development of the system, outpatient consultations per person per year averaged 2.0; by 1975 this figure was up to 4.8, not far below the frequency of consultation in the United States.

Medical personnel participated in the planning and management of health services, but the broad guidelines were laid down by the political leadership, dominated by the Communist party. After the introduction of local elections in 1976 community participation in health care planning increased.

Broad social and economic change have supported these improvements in medical services. Economic growth was very slow in the 1960s but has accelerated recently. Public policy has emphasized equitable distribution of basic necessities. Primary foodstuffs are rationed and priced-controlled. Literacy is now estimated at 96 percent and elementary school attendance is universal (uniquely among Latin American countries). Housing problems have been chronic among Cuba's urban population (now 65 percent of the total), but are gradually being remedied by construction of apartment houses.

Mortality indicators for Cuba, always relatively good, are now excellent. The infant death rate is only twenty-five per thousand and the crude death rate is a miniscule six per thousand, thanks in part to the youth of the population structure. Life expectancy at birth is seventy-two years. The birth rate is eighteen per thousand, creating a low 1.2 percent rate of natural increase. Family planning is not officially promoted because the country is perceived as suffering from a labor shortage, but contraceptives are freely available to those who want them.

Still another shortcoming of public health services in most LDCs relates to the balance between preventive and curative services. Since, as we have seen, curing all the sick is a task far beyond the means of many poor countries, it follows that the possibility that sickness and death can be reduced more cheaply through preventive measures deserves careful examination. Preventive actions such as inoculation campaigns, mosquito spraying, and rat killing have produced dramatic improvements in health conditions in some low-income countries, most notably in China. Many LDCs still spend too much on curative services relative to preventive activities.

It is thus evident that inadequate, maldistributed, and inappropriate medical services in poor countries are themselves a contributor to sickness and premature death. What can be done about it?

Improved medical services depend on a better spread of coverage to reach the entire population and on the development of patterns of service more appropriate to the health needs and resource availabilities of a developing country than those which exist at present. The greatest interest now is in reforming the health system along the following lines of emphasis: (1) active and continuous promotion of community health, instead of intermittant treatment of specific conditions in individuals; (2) management of the system by nonphysicians; (3) primary health care provided by a health auxiliary recruited from the community, who has some training and is authorized to diagnose and treat simple ailments; and (4) *limited* referral of difficult cases.

The health care systems evolved by socialist developing countries such as China and Cuba are sometimes taken as models by those interested in such reforms. China in 1976 reported spending over 60 percent of its health care budget in rural areas and sending half its medical school graduates to assignments in the countryside. Like other developing countries it has experienced difficulty in getting health professionals to live in rural areas. It has countered this tendency, however, and provided decent health care for the first time to its enormous mass of peasant population through its well-known system of health auxiliaries. As of 1976 official sources reported that there were 1.5 million "barefoot doctors" working in the country, doing preventive work, treating patients at home and in the fields, assisting with mass health and sanitation campaigns, and disseminating knowledge of family planning and maternal and child health care. In addition there were reported to be some three million part-time health auxiliaries assisting in the same activities. These efforts have contributed to levels of health and life expectancy unusual for a country with China's still-low income level.

Conclusion
There is a strong case for remedying past neglect by giving health care programs a higher priority in the competition for scarce developmental resources, particularly when the programs undertaken genuinely reach the masses of people and provide them with services appropriate to their health needs and socioeconomic circumstances. The case rests firmly on humanitarian grounds. It receives limited support from evidence that health expenditures can lead to higher individual income and national output, at least in some instances. But a balanced reading of the evidence would have to conclude that productive benefits from health expenditures are not yet firmly demonstrated and may be small in many LDCs. This does not in any way detract from the strong equity argument for improved health services.

Health policy must somehow come to grips with the causes of ill-health and premature death discussed earlier: excessive population growth, malnutrition, unsanitary living conditions, and inadequate or inappropriate medical care. There are perhaps three different strategic approaches to the problem.

The *conventional approach* is to loose a separate arrow at each of these targets through a set of target-oriented programs. Thus a typical LDC government would have a family planning program, several different kinds of nutrition improvement programs, common or separate water supply and sewerage programs, a housing program, a health service program, and so on. Many of these programs would be lodged in the Ministry of Health, but others would not. Two problems are typically encountered by this traditional approach. One is a lack of coordination among the various programs, particularly when they come under separate bureaucratic authorities. The second problem is that narrow interventions often fail to have much impact on LDC health problems, which are generally caused by a multiplicity of factors and cannot be significantly ameliorated by any single means.

In response to these problems an *integrated service program approach* has been tried in some countries. Here the idea is to strengthen the various types of health improvement program by providing two or more services together in the same package. For example, family planning advice and services, maternal and child health care, nutritional services, and education might all be offered at the same clinics or by the same mobile fieldworkers. This approach has had somewhat mixed results. Typically the weaker programs are strengthened by being tied in with the better programs or with services for which there is particularly strong demand. Sometimes, however, the enthusiasm and dedication of a program is reduced by making its objectives too multifold and diffuse.

Even the integrated service program approach limits the attack on health problems to a relatively narrow range of policy instruments. As we have seen, many observers believe that health conditions will improve only after more general policies are brought to bear. Thus increases in food supplies, reduction in food prices, improved distribution of income, and growth in average income levels might all be claimed as health policies under a broader *basic needs approach.*

These three approaches have been presented as alternatives to each other as a way of clarifying the differences among them. In fact most specialists today would agree that *both* improved services in the population, nutrition, sanitation, and health care fields *and* an equality-focused development pattern are needed if health conditions in the developing countries are to improve. There are broad hints in the experiences of China, Cuba, Sri Lanka, and the Indian state of Kerala that a generally egalitarian pattern of development which combines broader measures such as improved income distribution, universal literacy, and increased food production with better programs of nutrition, sanitation, and health care provides the best recipe for improving health conditions and reducing morbidity and mortality.

The literature on health and economic development is still relatively thin. Several **FURTHER** useful works have been produced by the World Bank: *Health Sector Policy Paper* **READING** (2nd ed.; Washington, D.C.: World Bank, February 1980); *World Development Report 1980* (Washington, D.C.: World Bank, 1980); and Frederick Golladay and Bernhard Liese, "Health Problems and Policies in the Developing Countries," World Bank Staff Working Paper No. 412 (August 1980). These reports review the results of recent research in the area. For the most recent version of Samuel II. Preston's work on causes of death, referred to earlier, see his *Mortality Patterns in National Populations, with Special Reference to Recorded Causes of Death* (New York: Academic Press, 1976).

Nutrition, as an important aspect of health in less developed countries, has received more attention. The economics student interested in nutrition and food policy might start with Shlomo Reutlinger and Marcelo Selowsky, *Malnutrition and Poverty: Magnitude and Policy Options,* World Bank Staff Occasional Papers No. 23 (Baltimore: Johns Hopkins University Press, 1976); and then proceed to such papers as Shlomo Reutlinger, "Malnutrition: A Poverty or a Food Problem?", *World Development* 5, no. 8 (1977); 715–24; Mohiuddin Alamgir, "The Dimension of Undernutrition and Malnutrition in Developing Countries; Conceptual, Empirical and Policy Issues," Harvard Institute for International Development Discussion Paper No. 82 (February 1980); and C. Peter Timmer, "Food Policy, Food Consumption, and Nutrition," Harvard Institute for International Development Discussion Paper No. 124 (October 1981).

PART

CAPITAL
RESOURCES

Chapter 11

CAPITAL AND SAVINGS: SOURCES AND PATTERNS

Of all of the single-factor approaches to development mentioned in Chapter 2, the concentration on capital formation was perhaps the most influential and durable, for a number of reasons. First, relative to the other approaches it had more respectable theoretical underpinnings: the Harrod-Domar model, discussed in Chapter 6. Properly viewed, the Harrod-Domar model provides insights into vital aspects of the development process, focusing as it does on the difficulties involved in meeting the investment requirements for assuring substantial and steady growth without high rates of inflation or unemployment. However, more mechanistic interpretations of the Harrod-Domar model postulated a lockstep relationship between growth in investment and national income. This view came to be indentified with *capital fundamentalism* as reflected in the development strategies and plans in many countries. The development problem was essentially viewed as one of securing investment resources sufficient to generate some chosen target rate of national income growth. The implications of target rates of income growth for employment and income distribution were rarely examined, as it was widely assumed that faster rates of growth would in and of themselves ameliorate both unemployment and any extremes of income inequality.

Another reason for the wide currency enjoyed by capital fundamentalism in development plans of the 1950s and 1960s was that it resonated with the aims and approaches of foreign aid donors of that era, as it furnished a readily explicable, apparently clear-cut basis for justifying aid "needs." Capital shortage was then widely judged to be the single most important barrier to accelerated economic development, and a heavy premium tended to be placed on framing development plans that reflected this point of view. The best crafted of such plans, for example Pakistan's third five-year plan in the 1960s, were able to show heavy initial capital requirements and a need for large early injections of foreign capital (in the form of aid). Large initial injections of aid would, it was thought, generate new flows of domestic savings, eventually reducing required aid flows in the long run.

Finally, capital fundamentalism was durable because its framework was flexible enough to incorporate new economic ideas of the 1960s, especially the concept of human capital discussed in Part II of this book. The selective imbedding of human capital considerations into the framework made still more plausible the argument that capital formation was the linchpin of development. The incorporation of human capital into the framework was no minor embellishment, for the size of the human capital stock relative to the physical stock can be quite large. For some developed countries the ratio of human to physical capital may be as high as 1 : 1. For example, some recent estimates place the value of the human capital stock in the United States in the mid-1970s at roughly equal to that of the stock of physical capital.

High levels of capital formation made possible by initial abundance of savings matter little for income growth—much less employment creation and improving income distribution—when capital is deployed in projects of low productivity, whether these are the much-ridiculed, large-scale showcase steel mills or tens of thousands of inefficiently small hydroelectric plants, or in expensive higher education or ultramodern cardiac care centers serving small elites in capital cities. Further, massive investment projects financed by foreign savings, however productive, may have little impact on income growth when host country policies are poorly suited for capturing an equitable share of the returns from such projects. As discussed further in Chapter 14, there are several examples, particularly before the mid-1960s, of instances in which host countries, particularly those with sizable natural resource endowments, have ultimately had little to show from major foreign investment projects other than the scrap content of equipment left behind at the end.

Investment Requirements for Growth

One need not be a partisan of capital fundamentalism to recognize the critical role of savings and capital in income growth. The savings–capital-growth nexus has been well established in industrial societies. For example, in a number of studies it has been estimated that expansion in real physical capital inputs alone has been responsible for about half of growth in aggregate income of nine developed countries in the fifteen years prior to 1975. There are abundant studies pointing to the very low investment rate in the United States in the 1970s (at 18 percent of GNP, among the lowest of all major industrial societies) as a prime reason, along with lagging productivity growth, for low rates of per-capita income growth in that country since 1970, relative to Japan and Western Europe. Analyses of the relative contribution of capital to growth in developing countries are neither as numerous nor, owing to data limitations, as conclusive as those for the United States. However, the available evidence suggests that the impact of capital formation on growth is considerable in those countries as well, particularly for the early stages of a country's development; at higher levels of income, productivity growth appears much more important. Studies in such middle-income nations as Korea, the Philippines, and Mexico indicate that in recent years growth in the physical capital stock, quite apart from growth in the stock of human capital, may have contributed from between one-fourth and one-third of income growth, with estimates clustering toward the higher figure, and as much as one-half in poorer countries. None of these studies incorporates the contribution of human capital to income growth, so the results understate the role of capital formation, and therefore savings, in income growth.

In any case while capital accumulation is no longer viewed as a panacea for poor countries, it is nevertheless clear that even mildly robust rates of growth in incomes can be sustained over long periods only when societies are able to maintain investment at a sizable proportion of gross domestic product (GDP). Rarely can this proportion be much less than 15 percent; in some cases it must go as high as 25 percent, depending on the environment in which capital accumulation takes place, and depending on what rate of income growth is deemed essential to allow progress toward basic societal goals. Growth aspirations probably do not vary as widely as did recorded growth performance between low- and middle-income countries from 1960 to 1980, where growth in real per-capita income on the average was only 1.2 percent in the former and 3.8 percent in the latter (see Table 1–2). If LDCs in general seek growth in real per-capita income that at least matches that for the middle-income countries from 1960 onward, then given typical rates of LDC population growth of about 2.4 percent in the past decade, the requisite rate of aggregate income growth would have to be at least 6 percent per annum.

Efficient Use of Scarce Capital

Given a goal of 6 percent growth in real aggregate income, annual investment requirements would then depend not only on the volume of available savings, but on the environment in which capital formation occurs. In developing countries where basic macro or economy-wide prices (exchange rates, interest rates, wage rates) approximate scarcity values for factors of production, there will be a tendency for scarce capital to be deployed in uses where it can be most effectively applied with more abundant labor. In such circumstances a given addition to the capital stock can generate increments to output that exceed those in countries where production is more capital-intensive (see Chapter 6). Depending on the structure of macro prices and the orientation of public sector decision-makers, the incremental capital/output ratio (ICOR) may typically range from 2.0 to 5.0, with a median value for seventy-odd LDCs at between 3.0 and 3.5, as shown in Table 11-1. Consider the investment implications of an ICOR of 2.5 compared with an ICOR half again as high, or 3.75. Countries with an ICOR of 2.5 will find that a necessary, but not sufficient, condition for achieving sustained aggregate growth in output of 6.0 percent per year is that of securing capital resources equivalent to 15 percent of GNP. However, for those countries having an ICOR of 3.75 it is necessary to invest 22.5 percent of GNP to attain the same rate of output growth. Thus efficient deployment of capital can materially reduce the savings effort required for sustained growth.

TABLE 11-1   Average Incremental Capital/Output Ratios, 1968–1973 (66 LDC)

Gross capital-output ratio (ICOR)	Number of countries	Illustrative countries
1.5–1.99	6	Singapore, Indonesia
2.0–2.49	5	Korea, Mali
2.5–2.99	10	Gabon, Ecuador
3.0–3.49	9	Kenya, Colombia, Pakistan
3.5–3.99	9	Thailand, Mauritius, Zaire
4.0–4.5	5	Jamaica, Tanzania
Above 4.5	22	India, Gambia, Guinea, Chile, Guyana, Zambia

Source: World Bank, *World Tables 1976* (Washington, D.C., 1980), Table 13, pp. 488–95.

Efficient use of scarce capital requires in the first instance that it be combined with other productive factors in proportions consonant with an economy's resource availabilities. If all factors of production and all final goods were perfectly mobile throughout the planet, we would not observe very striking differences between countries in the intensity with which capital is used in production of goods and services. However, neither final goods nor productive resources move very freely across national boundaries. Natural resource endowments like land and mineral deposits are completely immobile. Labor is not fully mobile even in the long run, owing to locational preferences as well as immigration barriers. Capital resources tend to be immobile in the short run, locked into their current uses. But with the passage of time capital tends to be mobile, and substantial capital does cross international boundaries. According to one estimate, international mobility of capital is sufficient to cause capital's real after-tax rate of return to converge toward about 7.5 percent in both rich and poor countries, with somewhat lower returns in rich countries reflecting greater relative abundance of this factor.[1] In the absence of moderate mobility, rates of return to capital would be far higher in low-income countries with limited savings than in high-income countries.

1. Arnold C. Harberger, "Perspectives in Capital and Technology in Less-Developed Countries," in M. J. Artis and A. R. Nobay (ed.), *Contemporary Economic Analysis* (London: Croom Held, 1978).

Not even capital, however, is fully mobile across international boundaries in the long run. While potentially great, the mobility of capital resources is significantly impeded by a wide variety of both entry barriers (limits on foreign equity ownership, fear of expropriation) and exit restrictions (exchange controls, taxes on capital outflows) erected both by developing countries and industrial countries.

Capital-Intensive or Labor-Intensive Investment: A Hypothetical Case

In the presence of such immobilities of productive factors a pervasive pattern of capital-intensive production in capital-short countries leads to either lower rates of income growth or strong suppression of consumption, or both. To illustrate, consider two countries that are initially identical in all important respects: per-capita income in 1980 at $200, population of five million, an investment ratio in 1980 of 15 percent, and similar patterns of exports, imports, agriculture, and industry. Both followed, up until 1980, essentially the same development strategies, which resulted in both cases in a historic (1970–1980) incremental capital/output ratio of 3.5. Both experienced real GDP growth rates of about 5 percent over the ten-year period.

In 1980 new governments in both countries altered past development policies. In country A the government opted for a strategy over the coming decade involving heavy outlays on large-scale, capital-intensive investments, such as oil refining, paper mills, and steel mills. As a result of this change, and supported by other government policies, the ICOR is expected to rise from 3.5 to 4. Country B on the other hand decided in 1980 in favor of a shift to a strategy involving emphasis on more labor-intensive investments in agriculture and industry, including textile mills, commercial firewood forests, coastal fisheries, and shoe manufactures. Decision-makers in country B expect the ICOR to decline from 3.5 to 3 as a result. These two capital/output ratios are well within the range for developing countries given in Table 11–1. In this example we overlook contributions of other factors to growth.

We assume that both countries face similar constraints on investment finance over the period 1980–1985. For both, resources available for investment (from both domestic and foreign sources) are most likely to expand at 7.5 percent per year, but certainly at no less than 5.0 percent and no more than 10.0 percent. The implications of these alternative investment availabilities for GDP growth are presented in Table 11–2.

A striking implication can be drawn from Table 11–2. The table shows that the efficiency with which capital is used can be much more important for GDP growth than raising the volume of investment. For the five-year period as a whole, the ICOR of country A is only 25 percent higher than that of country B. But after five years country B has a higher GDP than country A even when investment resources grow at twice the rate in country A as in country B. At 5 percent growth in investment in country B average annual GDP growth is also 5.0 percent, while in country A even 10 percent growth in investment leads to only a 4.2 percent average annual

TABLE 11–2   **GDP and Investment Under Two Different Strategies (millions of U.S.$)**

	1980	Investment growth rate	1981	1982	1983	1984	1985	Average annual growth	1985 % of investment to GDP
Investment availability									
I. Low	150.0	5.0%	157.5	165.4	173.6	182.3	191.4	5.0%	—
II. Medium	150.0	7.5%	161.3	173.3	186.3	200.3	215.3	7.5%	—
III. High	150.0	10.0%	165.0	181.5	199.6	219.6	241.6	10.0%	—
GDP									
Country A:									
Capital-intensive strategy									
(ICOR = 4)[a]									
I. Low	1000	5.0%	1037.5	1076.9	1118.3	1161.7	1207.3	3.8%	15.9
II. Medium	1000	7.5%	1037.5	1077.8	1121.1	1167.7	1217.8	4.0%	17.7
III. High	1000	10.0%	1037.5	1078.8	1124.2	1174.1	1229.0	4.2%	19.7
Country B:									
Labor-intensive strategy									
(ICOR = 3)[a]									
I. Low	1000	5.0%	1050.0	1102.5	1157.6	1215.5	1276.3	5.0%	15.0
II. Medium	1000	7.5%	1050.0	1103.8	1161.6	1223.7	1290.5	5.2%	16.7
III. High	1000	10.0%	1050.0	1105.0	1165.5	1232.0	1305.2	5.5%	18.5

[a] To simplify presentation, the example assumes that all investment resources in any given year are available by the beginning of that year, and that there is only a one-year lag between the time investment resources are available and the time they begin to yield output.

GDP growth; and even to do this, by the fifth year country A must find investment resources equal to 19.7 percent of GDP. With an investment ratio of only 15.0 percent in 1985 country B can still grow faster than the maximum possible for country A.

If on the other hand investment resources available to both countries were to grow at 10 percent per annum, aggregate income in B would be 6 percent higher than in A by 1985, even though they began at the same level. While a 6 percent difference in total income after five years may not seem large, when placed in proper perspective it can be quite significant. There are few developing countries in the world that spend as much as 6 percent of GDP on education, and no LDC that spends as much as 3 percent on public health. Merely because it uses capital more sparingly than country A, country B would, in the extreme, possess the capacity to more than double real outlays for education, or triple expenditures on public health programs. Alternatively, if both countries place a high premium on national autonomy and are therefore apprehensive over foreign participation in their economies, it is much more likely that country B will satisfy this goal since it will have less need to resort to foreign capital to finance a substantial share of its development effort. An investment ratio of 15 percent is clearly much easier to support from domestic resources than the 20 percent required for country A to attain the same level of GDP growth.

Investment Ratios in LDCs

The heavy emphasis on capital-intensive investment often found in developing countries is to some extent the unintended result of government policies. But it may also be attributed to a pervasive belief that only capital-intensive technology is "efficient," and that in any case choice of technology is not sensitive to relative prices of labor and capital. Discussion in Chapter 8 casts significant doubt on the notion that choice of technique of production in LDCs is largely unaffected by price signals. Policies that result in underpricing of capital and overpricing of labor do seem to cause firms and government agencies to adjust by adopting techniques involving more of the former and less of the latter than would be the case in the absence of such policies. However, Chapter 8 also reminds us that wherever found, bias toward capital intensity in investment cannot always, or even usually, be fully explained in terms of distorted price signals, nor is it legitimate to assume that capital intensity always represents vice and that labor-using investment always denotes virtue. For example, those who would advocate a conscious, reverse bias in favor of labor-intensive methods of underground mining of coal or tin have either never visited the hazardous labor-intensive facilities for these activities (for example, in Bolivia and Indonesia), or are unaware of the large surpluses available from capital-intensive mining that can be deployed for labor-intensive investments in other fields. Even in agriculture there are sound arguments, advanced in Chapter 18, for mechanization to increase both productivity and employment.

In the typical labor-surplus situation, 4 percent annual growth in real *per capita* income cannot be sustained over extended periods in the absence of investment ratios of at least 15 percent (in the economies emphasizing more labor-intensive approaches) and 25 percent (in the capital-intensive strategies). Securing investment ratios of even 15 percent has proven a difficult task for many LDCs, and in particular some of the thirty-three nations (other than India and China) falling into the World Bank's category of low-income countries (see Table 11–3, first two columns). Nevertheless all but five of the countries in this group did manage to increase the share

TABLE 11–3 Gross Domestic Investment and Gross Domestic Savings Rates, 1960 and 1980

Category[a]	Gross domestic investment (as % of GDP)[c]		Gross domestic savings (as % of GDP)[d]		Resource gap[e]	
	1960	1980	1960	1980	1960	1980
Low-income nations[b]	19 (11)	25 (15)	17 (9)	22 (7)	−2 (−2)	−3 (−8)
Middle-income nations	20	27	19	25	−1	−2
Capital surplus oil exporters	NA	24	NA	56	NA	+38
Industrial market economies	21	23	22	22	+1	−1
Industrial nonmarket economies	25	24	27	25	+2	+1

Source: World Bank, *World Development Report, 1982* (Washington, D.C., August 1982), Appendix Table 5, pp. 118–19.

[a] For definitions, see notes to Table 1–1.

[b] Figures in parentheses exclude China and India.

[c] *Gross domestic investment* is defined as all public and private sector expenditures for additions to the stock of fixed assets, plus the net value of inventory changes.

[d] *Gross domestic savings* includes both public sector and private sector savings. It indicates the volume of gross domestic investment financed by domestic sources. As given in this table, gross domestic savings is calculated as the residual after subtracting from gross domestic investment the deficit on current international accounts from gross domestic investment.

[e] Gross domestic investment minus gross domestic savings.

of gross domestic investment in gross domestic product over the period 1960–1980. For this set of countries as a whole investment's share rose from 19 percent in 1960 to almost 25 percent in 1980 (but from 11 to 15 percent with China and India excluded). Marked gains were recorded for Bangladesh, Burundi, Upper Volta, Malawi, Rwanda, Haiti, Niger, Madagascar, Lesotho and Togo. The sixty-three countries classed by the World Bank as middle income were on the whole able to attain investment shares of slightly more than one-quarter of GDP by 1980. Investment shares ranged from 5 percent of GDP in Ghana to over 40 percent in Jordan, Singapore, and Algeria. Among the non-oil-exporting middle-income countries, only Singapore, Korea, Jordan, Lesotho, Romania, and Yemen managed to reach or surpass 30 percent levels.

Table 11–3 shows that the middle-income countries had achieved, on the average, higher investment ratios in 1980 than even the advanced industrialized countries.[2] The higher investment ratios in this group are reflected in significantly higher rates of growth in income per capita relative to both the low-income countries and the industrialized countries: annual real rates of per-capita income growth for middle-income countries was 3.8 percent over the 1960–1980 period versus 1.2 percent in the poorest thirty-eight countries, and about 3.6 percent in the industrial countries as a group.[3]

Except for the United States and Britain, where in 1980 gross investment was but 18 and 16 percent of GDP respectively (as compared to 32 percent in Japan) relatively low shares of investment have not been a source of much concern in the industrial countries largely because per-capita incomes there are so high. In any case lower rates of population growth in the industrial countries relative to the rest of the world meant that even at lower real rates of output growth, per-capita income growth rates in rich countries were only just below the middle-income countries from 1960 to 1980, and three times higher than in poorer LDCs. Until such time as population growth rates decline markedly, any significant increases in growth rates of per-capita income in most LDCs will require a loosening of constraints on capital formation, that is, an expansion of available savings.

Sources of Savings

Developing countries were able to finance their higher investment-to-GDP ratios by intensified savings mobilization efforts directed at savings from a variety of sources, both domestic and foreign, public and private. Before turning to an examination of recent patterns of investment finance it will be useful to consider a simplified savings taxonomy.

---

2. The figures given in Table 11–3 have been weighted by the size of countries' GDPs. Thus the average for all industrial countries is dragged down substantially by the low investment rates of such large economies as the United States and the United Kingdom (18 percent over the period 1960–1980).

3. World Bank, *World Development Report 1982* (Washington, D.C., August 1982), Appendix Table 2, p. 112.

Taxonomy of Savings

For a country, the total supply of available savings *(S)* is simply the sum of domestic savings *(S$_D$)* and foreign savings *(S$_F$)*. Domestic savings may be broken down into two components: government, or public-sector, savings *(S$_G$)* and private domestic savings *(S$_P$)*. Government savings consists primarily of budgetary savings *(S$_{GB}$)* which arises from any excess of government revenues over government consumption, where public consumption is defined as all current government expenditure plus all capital outlays for military hardware. Examples of public-sector consumption include expenditure for food subsidies, to meet such recurring costs as salaries for civil servants and police, to purchase stationery and fuel, and for maintenance of roads and bridges, plus interest on the national debt. In focusing on this savings component it is important to note that a country could still have positive public savings even when the overall government budget is in deficit, because budget expenditures include capital outlays, or investment, that represent uses of public savings. In addition in some countries savings of government-owned enterprises *(S$_{GE}$)* have also contributed to public sector savings. Private domestic savings also arise from two sources: corporate savings *(S$_{PC}$)* and household savings *(S$_{PH}$)*. Corporate savings is defined as the retained earnings of corporate enterprises (corporate income after taxes minus dividends paid to shareholders). Household savings *(S$_{PH}$)* is simply that part of household income not consumed. Household savings includes savings from unincorporated enterprises (single proprietorships, partnerships, and other noncorporate forms of business enterprise). In most LDCs unincorporated business enterprise is by far the dominant form of business organization.

Foreign savings also come in two basic forms: official foreign savings *(S$_{FO}$)* or foreign aid, and private foreign savings *(S$_{FP}$)* consisting of direct foreign investment (primarily by multinational enterprises) and external commercial borrowing.

To recapitulate, total available savings may be viewed in the first instance as

$$S = S_D + S_F = (S_G + S_P) + (S_{FO} + S_{FP}) \qquad [11\text{--}1]$$

For purposes of understanding savings patterns and policies, saving may be disaggregated further to

$$S = [(S_{GB} + S_{GE}) + (S_{PC} + S_{PH})] + (S_{FO} + S_{FP}) \qquad [11\text{--}2]$$

Reliance upon different sources of savings differs greatly between developing nations, depending not only on such factors as the level of per-capita income, natural resource endowments, and sectoral composition of GDP, but also on the nature of savings mobilization policies adopted by particular governments. The balance of this chapter identifies the determinants of domestic saving and its various components. We reserve to Chapter 14 a discussion of foreign savings, its patterns, and the controversies surrounding it.

Domestic Savings

Relative to 1960, LDCs as a group had by 1980 greatly intensified their efforts to mobilize domestic savings. Although many relied heavily on foreign savings as a source of investment finance, the rise in investment ratios depicted in Table 11–3 was accompanied by a nearly commensurate increase in the share of gross domestic savings in GDP. While these averages mask some major differences in the savings performances for countries within each category, the general picture is one of some success in mobilizing additional domestic savings since 1960, particularly in the low-income countries. Table 11–4 depicts the evolution of savings and investment ratios for a group of twenty-two LDCs in Asia, Africa, and Latin America, chosen to represent a wide range in per-capita income, natural resource endowments, and ideological orientation. Among countries in this table, domestic savings rates in 1980 ranged from a negative 3 percent to 30 percent. Table 11–4 indicates the significance of income levels for savings mobilization efforts. Among the low-income countries only China,

TABLE 11–4   Domestic Savings Rates of Selected Developing Countries, 1960 and 1980

Country	Gross domestic savings as % of GDP		Gross domestic investment as % of GDP		Domestic savings as % of domestic invest-ment	
	1960	1980	1960	1980	1960	1980
Low-income countries[a,b]	17 (9)	22 (7)	19 (11)	25 (15)	89 (82)	88 (46)
Bangladesh	8	2	7	17	114	12
Ethiopia	11	5	12	10	92	50
Mali	9	3	14	15	64	—
India	14	20	17	23	82	87
Sri Lanka	9	14	14	36	64	39
China	23[c]	30[d]	23[c]	31[d]	100[c]	97[d]
Tanzania	19	8	14	22	136	36
Pakistan	5	6	12	18	42	33
Middle-income countries[b]	19	25	20	27	95	93
Ghana	17	5	24	5	71	100
Kenya	17	15	20	22	85	68
Indonesia	8	30	8	22	100	136
Senegal	15	− 2	16	15	94	—
Bolivia	7	15	14	13	50	115
Egypt	12	16[d]	13	31[d]	92	52
Philippines	16	25	16	30	100	83
Nigeria	7	28	13	24	54	117
Guatemala	8	13	10	16	80	81
Colombia	21	25	21	25	100	100
Korea (South)	1	23	11	31	9	74
Malaysia	27	32	14	29	193	110
Brazil	21	20	22	22	95	91
Mexico	18	26	20	28	90	93

Source: World Bank, *World Development Report 1981* (Washington, D.C., 1981), Table 5.
[a] Figures in parentheses exclude China and India
[b] Countries ranked in ascending order of per-capita income in 1980 (see Table 1–1).
[c] 1961.
[d] 1979.

India, and Niger had savings rates of 20 percent or more in 1980, while among the middle-income group eight of the thirteen in the table have savings rates of over 20 percent. We would ordinarily expect a lower ratio of savings in poor relative to middle-income countries simply because there less is available for savings after subsistence needs are met.

It is also evident from Table 11–4 that the more prosperous LDCs tend to cover a larger share of their investment needs with local savings. Whereas five of the poorer LDCs relied on foreign savings for more than one-third of investment finance by 1980, only one of the middle-income countries in the sample exhibited that much dependence on foreign savings. Indeed in six of the middle-income nations domestic savings rates equaled or exceeded domestic investment rates. The table also shows that over the two decades although domestic savings rates rose appreciably, on the average, in both low- and middle-income countries, the share of domestic savings in total investment finance changed little. But Table 11–4 also indicates that, as usual, experience in individual countries varied greatly.

But even Table 11–4 does not begin to portray adequately the diversity of savings performance across developing countries. While the general pattern for over eighty LDCs was that of moderately strong increases in domestic savings rates from 1960 to 1980, many countries experienced marked increases in savings ratios while several had substantial declines. Table 11–5 arrays these countries, which include a group of twenty-six nations in which domestic savings as a percent of GDP rose by 5 percentage points or more and eighteen nations where the savings/GDP ratio fell by 5 or more percentage points. For several in the latter group of countries, including Tanzania, Nicaragua, Uganda, and Ghana, this meant that the 1980 savings ratio was less than half as high as in 1960; for some in the former group of countries the 1980 savings ratio was considerably more than twice the value attained in 1960 (Nigeria, Tunisia, and Korea among them). There are no generally applicable explanations for the marked difference in domestic savings growth depicted in Table 11–5, but some commonalities can be detected.

For a small group of countries, trends in world prices of their natural resource exports may have been responsible for significant changes in the share of savings. One the one hand such oil exporters as Indonesia and Nigeria were able to more than double their rates of domestic savings; by 1980 consumption in these economies had not adjusted upward as rapidly as had the export income that flowed from much higher oil prices after 1973. On the other hand savings ratios in major copper-dependent exporting countries, especially Zambia and Zaire, declined precipitously over the period as domestic consumption in these economies may hve been slow in adapting to lower incomes from decreased export earnings caused by very weak world copper prices from 1973 through 1980.

Political instability appears to have been loosely associated with poor savings performance over the period under review. In the 1970s the share of savings fell sharply in seven countries that experienced acute or chronic

TABLE 11-5 Developing Countries Experiencing Marked Changes in Domestic Savings Performance (1960–1979)

I. Countries with 5% or greater increase in the ratio savings/GDP	II. Countries with 5% or greater decrease in the ratio savings/GDP

A. Oil exporters
  1. Indonesia[a]
  2. Nigeria[a]
  3. Ecuador[a]
  4. Malaysia
  5. Algeria
  6. Mexico
	A. Copper exporters
	  1. Zaire[b]
	  2. Zambia[c]

B. Others
  1. India
  2. Malawi[a]
  3. Sri Lanka
  4. China
  5. Niger
  6. Madagascar[a]
  7. Togo
  8. Honduras[a]
  9. Thailand
  10. Philippines
  11. People's Republic of Congo[a]
  12. Papua New Guinea[a]
  13. Ivory Coast[a]
  14. Guatemala
  15. Tunisia[a]
  16. Panama
  17. Korea[a]
  18. Argentina[a]
  19. Trinidad-Tobago[a]
  20. Hong Kong
  21. Singapore[a]
	B. Countries experiencing sharp and/or prolonged political disturbances
	  1. Bangladesh
	  2. Ethiopia[c]
	  3. Chad[c]
	  4. Mozambique
	  5. Zaire[b,c]
	  6. Uganda[c]
	  7. Ghana[c]
	  8. Dominican Republic
	  9. Nicaragua
	
	C. Others
	  1. Mali[c]
	  2. Benin[c]
	  3. Tanzania[c]
	  4. Lesotho[c]
	  5. Senegal[c]
	  6. Liberia[c]
	  7. Jamaica[c]

Source: World Bank, *World Development Report 1982* (Washington, D.C., 1982), Table 5.

[a] Domestic savings as a percent of GDP increased by 10 percentage points or more (highest: People's Republic of the Congo, from −21% to 37% of GDP, and South Korea, from −3% to 30% of GDP).

[b] Country found in two categories.

[c] Domestic savings as a percent of GDP decreased by 10 percentage points or more (highest: Lesotho, from −25% to −59% of GDP, and Chad, from 5% to −14%).

sociopolitical disturbances, including revolution (Ethiopia), civil war (Chad), invasion (Uganda and Bangladesh), and coups (Ghana). In eight of these nine countries the domestic savings ratio in 1980 was less than half of its value in 1960, and in two cases (Chad, Ethiopia) savings turned negative. However, political instability appears to be no absolute bar to improved savings performance. Outside the group of oil exporters experiencing sharp increases in savings rates, several countries went through a succession of coups d'états and still experienced improvements in savings rates, including Honduras, Panama, and Bolivia.

It is sometimes held that authoritarian governments are better able to mobilize domestic savings than are more responsive, popularly elected governments, presumably because under the former it is thought easier to impose and enforce discipline of all kinds, including savings discipline. There is little evidence in support of this view. Among the group of countries where savings ratios increased dramatically (again apart from the oil exporters, where savings in any case would have been expected to jump dramatically since 1973), Honduras, Philippines, South Korea, and Argentina in at least some years between 1960 and 1980 would likely be viewed as authoritarian by most, and savings ratios did rise considerably in these countries. But savings rates also increased substantially in India and Sri Lanka, where governments are democratically elected. And authoritarian governments in Zaire, Chile, Ethiopia, Liberia, and Uganda were unable to stem falling savings rates.

Government policies have had a major impact on the ability of developing countries to mobilize domestic savings. We will see in the next three chapters that in some countries governments have actively sought to deploy policies, particularly fiscal and monetary policies, to encourage savings growth, and have utilized instruments well suited for that purpose. In still more countries governments have been no less concerned with the promotion of domestic savings but have relied on policy tools ill-suited for savings mobilization. Finally, in a small group of countries government fiscal and monetary policies appear to have been designed with little or no regard for their implications for domestic savings. As might be expected, savings have generally responded positively to policy initiatives in the first group of countries, less so in the second group, and have tended to stagnate or decline in the third.

Government Savings

Where present, government savings have arisen almost wholly from an excess of total tax revenues over public consumption expenditures (S_{GB}). Chapter 21 shows that in very few cases do savings by government enterprises (S_{GE}) ever materially contribute to aggregate government savings. Given the very minor role for this component of public savings in all but a few countries, the discussion of government savings in this chapter is confined to budgetary savings.

One of the basic tenets of typical development strategies of the 1950s and 1960s was that investment expansion required for sustained income growth could not proceed in the absence of major efforts to increase the share of government savings in GDP. It was commonly held that growth in private savings was inherently constrained by such factors as low per-capita incomes and high private consumption propensities among wealthy families with the greatest capacity for savings. Limited availabilities of foreign savings also led planners as well as aid donors to stress the necessity of programs for mobilizing government savings. In almost all cases the preferred means for achieving this goal was to raise the ratio of tax collections to GNP (the *tax ratio*), through significant reform of the tax structure if possible or via increases in existing tax rates if necessary. Underlying this view was a belief that the propensity to consume out of an additional dollar of income was substantially less in the public sector than in the private sector. In this view diversion of income to the government should increase national savings rates. This engendered a prevailing attitude among many LDC planners that rising tax ratios were associated with "successful" development strategies, a view reinforced by policies of foreign aid donors. In the 1950s and 1960s many donors, including the United States, utilized tax ratios and "tax effort" indices as prime indicators of national commitment to "belt-tightening" in recipient countries. Countries willing to suffer higher domestic taxes were seen as more "deserving" of aid, other things being equal.

It is not easy to increase tax collections in LDCs. Except for those countries blessed with valuable natural resource endowments, developing countries in general would not be expected to have tax ratios nearly as high as is common in the industrial countries, if for no other reason than their much lower per-capita incomes which allow a much smaller margin for taxation after subsistence needs are met. Thus whereas typical tax ratios in LDCs range between 14 and 20 percent, tax ratios in the twenty-one wealthy member countries of the OECD (Organization for Economic Cooperation and Development) ordinarily run about twice that, averaging about 34 percent in 1976.[4]

Despite the difficulties involved, many LDCs have been able to raise shares of taxes in GNP since the 1960s. A recent study by the International Monetary Fund shows small advances in the average tax ratio for a group of 47 developing countries in the past twenty-five years. For these nations as a group the typical share of taxes in GNP hovered at about 11 percent in the 1950s. By 1972–1976 the average tax ratio had risen to 16 percent (see Table 11–6). However, close inspection of this table reveals that the countries where tax ratios were significantly increased in the latter period were not always those that have followed a conscious policy of savings mobilization through higher taxes, but those that have been fortunate enough to benefit from fiscal levies on higher prices for oil and other natural resources after 1973, such as Iran, Venezuela, and Indonesia.

But while higher tax ratios may have in some cases advanced some important goals of development policy, including that of income redistribution, they did not guarantee more than transient success in meeting goals of savings mobilization, except for those countries with substantial export capacity in natural resources, which can easily collect sizable taxes on those exports. Higher taxes lead to higher savings only if the government's marginal propensity to consume (MPC)[5] out of increased taxes is less than the private sector's propensity to consume out of the marginal income from which it pays increased taxes. Without question government savings made possible through budget surpluses did play a major role in the early stages

---

4. The range for 1976 tax ratios in the OECD countries went from a low of just over 21 percent in Spain and Japan to a high of 47 percent for both Sweden and Norway. See Organization for Economic Cooperation and Development, *Public Expenditure Trends* (Paris, 1978), p. 42.

5. The marginal propensity to consume (MPC) refers to the amount of consumption out of each incremental (marginal) unit of income. Thus if a government spends on consumption $80 out of each additional $100 in tax revenue, then the government's MPC is 0.80.

TABLE 11-6 Tax Ratios of Selected Developing Countries, 1969–71 and 1972–76

Country	Taxes as % of GNP 1972–76	1969–71	Country	Taxes as % of GNP 1972–76	1969–71
Iran	32.7	21.6	Thailand	13.9	12.4
Guyana	31.7	23.4	India	13.9	13.4
Zambia	30.8	31.3	Costa Rica	13.6	13.1
Zaire	27.2	29.4	Korea	13.6	15.4
Venezuela	23.1	20.4	Argentina	13.3	13.4
Malaysia	22.5	19.3	Mali	12.9	13.2
Trinidad/Tobago	21.9	17.7	Togo	12.4	11.3
Tunisia	20.7	21.7	Ecuador	12.0	13.4
Ivory Coast	20.6	19.8	Bolivia	11.8	8.2
Senegal	20.2	18.1	Colombia	11.6	12.5
China, Rep. of	19.9	17.8	Honduras	11.5	11.3
Kenya	19.2	14.4	Pakistan	11.4	8.8
Jamaica	19.0	19.4	Upper Volta	11.3	10.3
Tanzania	18.9	13.9	Lebanon	10.2	11.2
Sudan	18.9	18.2	Philippines	10.1	9.1
Morocco	18.6	17.8	Ethiopia	10.1	8.6
Chile	18.4	19.6	Rwanda	10.0	7.9
Egypt	18.1	19.2	Burundi	9.3	11.4
Brazil	18.1	22.9	Paraguay	8.8	10.9
Sri Lanka	17.9	17.7	Mexico	8.6	7.1
Indonesia	16.3	10.0	Guatemala	8.1	7.9
Turkey	16.2	15.6	Nepal	5.4	4.4
Singapore	15.7	13.2			
Ghana	14.2	15.8	Average	16.1	15.1
Peru	14.0	14.2			

Source: Alan A. Tait, Wilfred M. Gratz, and Barry J. Eichengreen, "International Comparisons of Taxation for Selected Developing Countries, 1972–76," *International Monetary Fund Staff Papers* 26, no. 1 (March 1979): 123–56.

of Japan's economic development. But other success stories for savings mobilization through budget policy are difficult to find. Unfortunately there is evidence that for LDCs in general the government's MPC out of taxes has been sufficiently high that increased taxation may easily have resulted in less, not more, total domestic savings. This phenomenon has become known as the "Please effect," after Stanley Please of the World Bank who first brought this phenomenon to widespread attention.[6] Whether or not the "Please effect" is widespread, we will see in Chapter 12 that higher taxes can and do displace some household and business savings in the private sector.[7] And experience over most of the decades of the 1960s and 1970s does show rather high consumption propensities on the part of governments. While tax ratios in LDCs typically rose only marginally over the

6. Stanley Please, "Savings Through Taxation: Reality or Mirage?" *Finance and Development* 4, no. 1 (March 1967): 24–32.

7. Some analysts find a high degree of substitutability between government and private savings; others do not. See, for example, the exhaustive survey in Raymond F. Mikesell and James E. Zinser, "The Nature of the Savings Function in Developing Countries: A Survey of The Theoretical and Empirical Literature," *Journal of Economic Literature* 11, no. 1 (March 1973): 1–26. One article surveyed in this contribution indicated that an additional $1 of government savings is associated with a 57¢ decline in private savings. Another article indicates a positive relationship between public and private savings.

1960s and 1970s, public-sector consumption expenditures expanded at rapid rates over the same period, in general in excess of GDP growth.

As a result the share of public-sector consumption expenditures in GNP rose materially from 1960 to 1980 in both low- and middle-income LDCs, going from an average of 8 to 11 percent in the former and from 11 to 14 percent in the latter.[8] This experience was widespread: in forty-five developing countries the public consumption share in 1980 surpassed that of 1960, even after nearly two decades of intensive efforts in most countries to mobilize savings through the government budget. In only fifteen countries was the share of public consumption in GDP lower in 1980 than in 1960. Still it is worth emphasizing that much of the growth in public sector consumption has been intended to promote development. Some governmental salary adjustments have been meant to keep and attract qualified civil servants, and many governments have strengthened their efforts to maintain roads, schools, health facilities, communications networks, and the like. But when higher government consumption has been traceable to rapid buildup of military purchases (of which more in the next chapter), to waste in government procurement of materials, or to upkeep of a large government vehicle fleet dominated by Mercedes or Bentleys, the effects have been unhelpful to national development.

Nevertheless rapid growth in public-sector consumption in the 1960s and 1970s, coupled with only moderate increases in tax ratios, has meant that growth in government savings has not been a major source of investment finance in most LDCs. And it will be evident from Chapter 14 that foreign saving has been a major source of investment finance in only a few countries, and for limited periods, since 1950. We may wonder, then, what was the source of the additional savings required to cover significantly higher investment ratios (again, see Table 11–3) over that period. To answer that question we must look to the private sector.

Private Domestic Savings

Until relatively recent years economists, aid donors, and many LDC decision-makers tended to view private domestic savings as decidedly secondary to government savings and foreign aid as a source of investment finance. There is, however, some evidence that in many LDCs private saving have come to play a major role in supporting capital formation.

Data compiled by the World Bank, summarized in Table 11–7, indicate that many LDCs have materially restrained growth in private consumption over long periods, thereby expanding the pool of private savings. For 1960–1980 private consumption in both the poorest thirty-three LDCs and the sixty-three middle-income countries grew at significantly slower rates than did GDP, so that by 1980 the share of private consumption in GDP had fallen from 79 to 68 percent in the poorest countries (82 to 76 percent if China and India are excluded) and from 70 to 64 percent in the more prosperous (and more rapidly growing) LDCs.

8. World Bank, *World Development Report 1982,* Appendix Table 5.

TABLE 11-7 Rates of Growth of GDP and Private Consumption, Shares of Private Consumption in Total GDP (96 Countries, 1960–1980)

| | Annual rates of growth (% per year) | | | | % share of private consumption in GDP[b] | |
| | Real GDP[b] | | Real private consumption[c] | | | |
	1960–70	1970–80	1960–70	1970–80	1960	1980
I. Low-income countries[a]	4.4 (4.3)	4.6 (3.5)	3.3 (3.2)	3.6 (3.4)	79 (83)	68 (84)
II. Middle-income countries	6.0	5.9	5.1	5.3	70	64

Source: World Bank, World Development Report 1982 (Washington, D.C., 1982), Tables 2, 4, and 5.
[a] Figures in parentheses exclude China and India.
[b] Weighted average.
[c] Median for the group.

Although data on consumption growth are subject to large errors, other considerations point to the same conclusion: that the share of private consumption in GDP declined significantly over the period for both groups of LDCs. We have seen that the share of taxes in GDP rose only slightly in most LDCs over the 1960s and early 1970s. If higher taxes do not account for the drop in the share of private consumption in GDP, then the share of private savings must have increased. In any case the most plausible source of a large share of finance for the rising investment ratios reported in Table 11–3 was private domestic savings. For LDCs in general, at least one of the components of private domestic savings must have risen at a fairly robust rate. But if so, it is difficult to determine which of the components played the more important role—household savings or business savings.

In approaching an answer to this issue, and to gain further insights into fundamental relationships in the development process, it is useful to consider the economic theory of private-sector savings behavior. We first consider theories of household savings behavior.

Determinants of Private Savings

Household Savings Behavior

All theories of household savings behavior seek to explain the following three observed patterns:

1. Within a particular country at a single time, higher income households tend to save larger fractions of their income than lower income households.

2. Within a particular country over time, household savings ratios tend to be roughly constant.

3. Across countries, household savings ratios vary with no clear relation to income.

To help reconcile these "stylized facts" we will consider four alternative explanations of household savings behavior: the Keynesian absolute income hypothesis; the Duesenberry relative income hypothesis; the Friedman permanent income hypothesis; and the Kaldor class savings hypothesis.

Economists once widely believed in the general applicability of a simple income-savings relationship. Household savings were viewed as directly dependent on current disposable income (household income after direct taxes). The propensity to save out of current disposable income was thought to rise with income. This was known as the **Keynesian absolute income hypothesis,** after the famed British economist who propounded the idea in the 1930s. In this view the savings-income relationship could be expressed as

$$S = a + sY^d \qquad\qquad [11\text{--}3]$$

where S = savings, Y^d = current disposable income, a = a constant (a < 0), and s = the marginal propensity of save (0 < s < 1). Under this formulation savings ratios (savings as a fraction of GDP) should be expected to rise secularly in all countries where income is growing. However, the historical record, both in developed and developing countries, provides very weak support for the Keynesian hypothesis. Rather, we commonly observe that for particular countries household savings ratios tend to remain constant over long periods of time despite significant increases in per-capita income.

At best the Keynesian formulation may depict household savings behavior over the very short term, but breaks down as a long-run proposition. The Keynesian formulation explains only the first household savings pattern, but not patterns 2 and 3. To see why, consider Figs. 11–1 through 11–3. Figure 11–1 illustrates the Keynesian consumption/savings function. It shows what households would consume and save at different levels of income during a period such as a year. The 45° line shows all points at which consumption is equal to income; Z is the familiar "break-even" point. At income levels to the right of Z saving is positive; to the left of Z

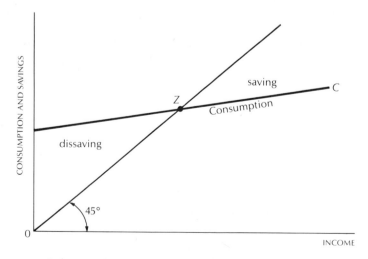

Fig. 11–1   Short-Term Keynesian Consumption Function.

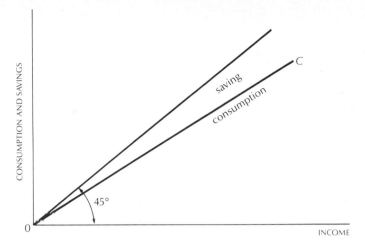

Fig. 11–2 Long-Term Consumption Function.

saving is negative. The graph shows that in the short run we would expect higher and higher ratios of saving to income at higher and higher income levels. However, over the longer run we observe that in most countries the consumption (savings) function appears as in Fig. 11–2: the savings/income ratio tends to remain constant if the consumption function in Fig. 11–1 goes through the origin.

The contradiction between the relationships depicted in Figs. 11–1 and 11–2 is perhaps more apparent than real, once it is recognized that the Keynesian function describes a short-run situation. The apparent conflict may be reconciled by consideration of an alternative view of the income-consumption relationship, the *relative income hypothesis.* In its simplest form this hypothesis holds that consumption (and therefore savings) depends not only on current income but on previous levels of income and past consumption habits. In more formal terms, one form of the relative income hypothesis, called the **Duesenberry hypothesis** after the Harvard economist who originated the concept in the late 1940s,[9] may be expressed as

$$C_1 = a + sY_1^d + bC_H \qquad [11\text{--}4]$$

where C^1 = consumption in period 1, Y_1^d = income in period 1, C^H = previous high level of consumption, $0 < s < 1$, and $0 < b < 1$. Thus under the relative income hypothesis the short-run consumption (savings) function in an economy tends to ratchet upward over time. As income grows over the long term consumers adjust their spending habits to higher levels of consumption. But in the short run they are reluctant to reduce (and slow to raise) consumption levels should income fall (or rise) temporarily. The relationship between the Keynesian absolute income hypothesis and the Duesenberry relative income hypothesis is depicted in Fig. 11–3.

9. James S. Duesenberry, *Income, Savings and the Theory of Consumer Behavior* (Cambridge, Mass.: Harvard University Press, 1949).

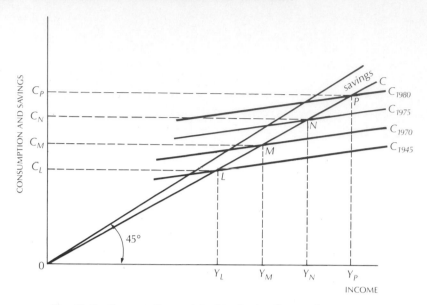

Fig. 11–3   Consumption and Savings in the Short and Long Term.

Four short-run consumption functions are shown for each of the years 1960, 1970, 1975, and 1980, representing what people would have spent at various levels of income in those years. The flatness of these curves reflects consumers' reluctance to change consumption habits in the short run. In each of these years actual (current) income was Y_L, Y_M, Y_N, and Y_P, respectively. Thus actual consumption in each of those years was C_L, C_M, C_N, and C_P. The points L through P trace out a long-tem consumption function, with characteristics matching those of Fig. 11–2: consumption, and thus savings, tend to be a constant proportion of income overtime.

The Duesenberry hypothesis was formulated as an explanation of consmption-savings behavior for the United States. Later researchers argued that it may also be applicable to LDCs as well. Some have suggested that a "demonstration effect" operates to cause consumption in LDCs to ratchet upward as incomes grow. Internationally mobile and worldly-wise upper income groups in LDCs are thought to emulate high consumption patterns of the wealthiest income groups in developed countries; successively lower income groups in LDCs tend to emulate the patterns of higher income groups, such that consumption in the society as a whole tends to be a high and stable function of income. Indeed the British economist Nicholas Kaldor once estimated that if the richest families in Chile had the same consumption propensities as families at the same *relative* income position in developed nations (but at higher absolute levels of income), the Chilean savings rate in the 1950s could have been doubled.[10] The relative income hypothesis helps to explain all three of the observed savings patterns cited earlier.

10. Nicholas Kaldor, "Problemas Economicas de Chile," *El Trimestre Economico* 26, no. 102 (April-June 1959): 193, 211–12.

Other approaches developed to explain consumption and savings behavior in developed countries have been applied to LDCs. The most influential of these has been the *"permanent" income hypothesis,* first formulated by Milton Friedman at Chicago in the 1950s. In the Friedman view income consists of two components: "permanent" income and "transitory" income. The basic idea is simply that because individuals expect to live for many years, they make consumption decisions over a horizon of many years. Permanent income is the yield from wealth, including both physical and human capital assets (education, etc.) at the disposal of the household. Friedman held that individuals can predict with a reasonable degree of assurance the magnitude of these flows over their lifetimes, and that they gear their consumption to what they perceive to be their normal, or "permanent," income, which tends to be stable over time. Furthermore, in the most restrictive variant of the permanent income hypothesis, consumption tends to be a constant proportion of permanent income, approaching 100 percent of permanent income. Thus any savings that occur will primarily be out of "transitory" income: unexpected, nonrecurring income such as those arising from changes in asset values, change in relative prices, lottery winnings, and other unpredictable windfalls. In the most extreme version of the permanent income hypothesis individuals are held to save 100 percent of any transitory income.

The permanent income hypothesis may be expressed as

$$S = a + b_1 Y_p + b_2 Y_t \qquad [11\text{--}5]$$

where S = savings, a = a constant, Y_p = permanent income, and Y_t = transitory income. In the most extreme version $b_1 = 0$ and $b_2 = 1$, so all savings arises from the transitory component of income and all of this component is saved. Modified versions of the permanent income hypothesis hold only that saving out of permanent income is constant over a person's lifetime, but can be positive, and that while the propensity to save out of transitory income is high, all transitory income may not be saved. Equation 11–5 can represent this version with $0 < b_1 < b_2 < 1$.

Several studies have sought to test the applicability of the permanent income hypothesis to a variety of developing countries in Asia and Latin America. The results are far from conclusive, but in toto they do lend some support to the modified versions of the hypothesis: people do tend to save a higher proportion of transitory as opposed to permanent income. In general the permanent income hypothesis explains all three observed savings patterns. Subsequent chapters of this book assess the implications of modified versions of the permanent income hypothesis in understanding the effects of fluctuating export income on growth (Chapter 15) and the impact of foreign aid on domestic savings efforts (Chapter 14).

One further model of household savings behavior merits attention, the "class" theory of the British economist Nicholas Kaldor. This aproach views consumption (savings) habits to be sharply differentiated by economic class. Workers, who receive mainly labor income, are thought to have far weaker savings propensities than do capitalists, who receive primarily property income (profits, interests, rents). The class savings hypothesis is represented as

$$S = s_w L + s_c P \qquad\qquad \textbf{[11–6]}$$

where s_w = workers' savings propensities out of labor income, s_c = capitalists' savings propensities out of property income, L = labor income, P = property income, and $0 < s_w < s_c < 1$.

The class savings hypothesis explains pattern 1, and also explains pattern 3 if factor shares (relative shares of labor and capital income) differ across countries. But the difference between the class savings hypothesis and the permanent income hypothesis may be more apparent than real. It is difficult to see why households, in their spending-saving decisions, treat labor income any differently than property income: a peso is a peso, a rupee of property income is no different from a rupee of labor income. However, propety income of households, particularly that from unincorporated enterprises, tends to fluctuate more than labor income. The permanent income hypothesis suggests that propensities to save out of variable income streams are higher than out of more stable streams. In addition property income is more concentrated in higher income groups. Thus studies of savings behavior based on the class model that show markedly higher savings out of property income may really be recording the effects of higher propensities to save out of higher fluctuating income.

All of the hypotheses discussed above view income, whether current, relative, or "permanent," as the principal determinant of savings behavior. But income is not by any means the only determinant of aggregate private-sector savings behavior, particularly in LDCs. The permanent income hypothesis concedes a role for interest rates in affecting savings behavior. Beyond that, many economists have stressed for years the effects of such explanatory variables as the age structure of a nation's population, location (rural vs. urban families), and, of course, subsistence expenditure as a proportion of per-capita GNP.

Changes in the age structure of a nation's population are often found to have significant effects on private savings in several countries: in general the proportion of any increases in income saved tends to be less in younger households than in older ones. Younger families are rearing children and accumulating belongings, but earn lower incomes. To illustrate, the average ratio of savings to income for older households in Chile in 1964 was found to be twice that of younger households.

There is a strong tendency around the world for rural households to save higher fractions of their incomes than urban households at comparable levels of income, a phenomenon observed in a number of countries, including both Korea and Yugoslavia in the early 1970s. This behavior is also consistent with the permanent income hypothesis, because farmers' incomes are more variable than those of urban wage earners.

A high proportion of income spent on meeting basic subsistence needs implies low capacity for household savings. One recent study of seventeen countries indicates that total subsistence expenditure as a proportion of per-capita GNP falls sharply as GNP per capita increases: from 62 percent at per-capita GNP less than $500, to 46 percent at per-capita GNP of between $1000 and $1500.

The relative income hypothesis and the permanent income hypothesis provide a basis for understanding the lack of strong correlation across LDCs between per-capita income and the ratio of private savings to GDP. The non-income factors (age structure of the population, rural-urban differences, and differences in subsistence ratios) help explain why private saving ratios do vary across countries, even at comparable levels of per-capita income.

Corporate Savings Behavior

We have seen that there is no shortage of hypotheses purporting to explain the determinants of household savings. There is, however, little professional consensus among economists as to the determinants of corporate savings, particularly in developing countries. Indeed there is little general agreement on the determinants of corporate savings even in developed countries. For example, in the United States a major question in research in business finance has been to explain why U.S. corporations pay out such a high proportion of their after-tax income in dividends, despite strong tax and other incentives to retain earnings (save) within the firm.

In developed countries the share of corporate savings in total income is typically less than 5 percent, and the share of corporate savings in gross national savings is commonly less than 20 percent. For example, over the period 1972–1978 the United Nations reported that corporate savings was only 2 percent of gross national savings in Japan, 12 percent in Belgium, 18 percent in Australia, 13 percent in Germany, and 18 percent in Finland.[11] Such data are not available for large numbers of LDCs, but it is known that in only a few countries (Colombia, Pakistan, and Panama in the 1960s) has corporate savings represented a sizable share of total savings over any significant period.

Corporate saving in LDCs is relatively small primarily because the corporate sector is relatively small; for a variety of reasons there are fewer pressures and incentives in LDCs for doing business in the corporate form. The principal reasons for choice of the corporate form of organization are, first, to limit liability of enterprise owners to amounts invested in a business, and second, to facilitate enterprise finance through issue of equity shares (stocks). While these advantages are substantial in developed countries with well-developed commercial codes, civil court systems, and capital markets, they are less so in most LDCs, where collection of commercial claims (e.g., debts of companies) through courts is relatively difficult and where, as shown in Chapter 13, capital markets are poorly developed when they exist at all.

11. United Nations, Department of Economic and Social Affairs, *Yearbook of National Accounts Statistics 1979* (New York, 1979), Table 12.

Nevertheless some large domestic corporations have evolved in a number of middle-income LDCs. Examples include such conglomerates as Bavaria (beverages and food processing) in Colombia and Hyundai (automobiles) in Korea, and enterprises such as Alpargatus (textiles and shoes) in Argentina, Tata in India, and Villares (steel products) in Brazil. But even in middle-income LDCs such large corporations are not numerous, do not ordinarily account for a large share of private-sector farm and nonfarm business activity, and clearly do not provide a high proportion of domestic savings.

The great bulk of private-sector farming, commercial, and manufacturing activity in all but a few of the highest income LDCs is carried on by unincorporated, typically family-owned, enterprises. Some of these fall into the category of medium-scale establishments (from ten to ninety-nine workers). Very few are large-scale enterprises. The great majority are truly small-scale operations (having fewer than ten employees) which, in spite of their numbers, do not account for a sizable share of either value added or savings.[12] Nevertheless the noncorporate sector manages to generate more than 50 percent of domestic savings in LDCs as a group, and this sector is the only consistent source of surplus in the sense that its savings exceed its investment. Even for a high-income country like the United States, with a large corporate sector, income from unincorporated enterprise in 1976 was about double the value of corporate profits (after taxes). For those closely held, largely family-owned and -managed firms, enterprise profits become an important part not of corporate savings, but of gross household income.

The available evidence indicates, and economic theory suggests, that household savings accounts for the overwhelming share of private savings in LDCs, and that the chief source of household savings is probably income from unincorporated enterprises.

Conclusion

In this chapter we have seen that there are a variety of forms of savings that LDCs may tap in order to finance investment in both physical and human capital. Some forms of savings play a much more significant role than others in furnishing the resources necessary to allow income growth. In recent decades different countries have enjoyed differential degrees of success in mobilizing savings: some very poor countries have high savings rates; some relatively prosperous countries have low savings rates. In only a few have public savings provided more than a small share of total savings requirements; the same observation applies with somewhat less force for foreign savings.

Subsequent chapters should make it apparent that the implications of problems in mobilizing savings extend well beyond the national boundaries of individual developing countries; rather, they are of international significance. This will be readily evident when we consider the issues involved in provision of foreign savings to LDCs.

12. One study for twenty-one LDCs in the 1960s shows that small-scale enterprises, while constituting 80 percent of industrial establishments, are responsible for an average of only 13 percent of industrial value added (Randev Banerji, "Small-Scale Production Units in Manufacturing: An International Cross Section Overview," *Weltwirtschafliches Archiv* 114, no. 1 [1978]: 62–82; see also Don Snodgrass, "Small Scale Manufacturing Industries [in Indonesia]: Patterns, Trends and Possible Policies" [Harvard Institute for International Development Discussion Paper No. 54, March 1979]).

The study of the contribution to growth by each factor of production, including **FURTHER**
capital, was pioneered by Edward Denison in two major studies of the United **READING**
States. Denison's *The Sources of Economic Growth in the United States* (New York,
Committee for Economic Development, 1962) and *Why Growth Rates Differ*
(Washington, D.C.: Brookings Institution, 1967) stimulated a series of such studies
for Korea, Mexico, and the Philippines, as well as over a dozen other countries (a
1970 review article by M. Iskah Nediri cites 154 articles and books written on the
subject by then). An instructive application to LDCs of the tools developed in this
extensive literature may be found in Kwang Suk Kim and Michael Roemer,
*Growth and Structural Transformation, Studies in the Modernization of the Repub-
lic of Korea: 1945–1975* (Cambridge, Mass.: Harvard University Press, 1979).

Perils involved in simplistic application of growth models and capital-output
ratios are well depicted in Paul Streeten, "The Uses and Abuses of Models in Development Planning," in *The Teaching of Development Economics* edited by K.
Martin and J. Krapp (London: Cass, 1967), pp. 63–75.

The work of Milton Friedman, *A Theory of the Consumption Function* (Princeton: National Bureau of Economic Research, 1957), helped to stimulate a voluminous amount of work on the determints of saving in developing countries, applying
not only his permanent income hypothesis, but other competing approaches such as
the life-cycle formulation originated by Franco Modigliani and colleagues. See, in
particular, F. Modigliani, R. Brumberg, and A. Ando, "Life Cycle Hypothesis of
Savings: Aggregate Implication and Tests," *American Economic Review* 52, no. 3
(1963). Among the many noteworthy LDC applications of the "new" (as opposed
to Keynesian) approaches to consumption-savings decision, are A. E. Kelley and J.
Williamson, "Household Savings Behavior in the Developing Economies," *Economic Development and Cultural Change* 16, no. 3 (April 1968); J. G. Williamson,
"Personal Savings in Developing Nations: An Intertemporal Cross Section For
Asia," *Economic Record* 29, no. 2 (June 1968). Several studies analyze behavior as
between different types of savers (small-scale entrepreneurs vs. large firms) or different types of income (rural vs. urban). See, for example, Donald F. Huddle, "An
Analysis of the Savings Behavior of a Group of Columbian Artisan Entrepreneurs,"
World Development 4, no. 4 (October, 1978). The former establishes that savings
out of self-employment income, i.e., income from unincorporated enterprise, tends
to be higher than savings out of other sources of income; the latter is another example of research lending credence to the permanent income hypothesis.

Finally, an excellent source of comparative information on savings determinants
and savings patterns in LDCs may be found in Constantino Lluch, Alan Powell,
and Ross Williams, *Patterns in Household Demand and Savings* (Washington,
D.C.: Oxford University Press, 1977).

Chapter 12

FISCAL POLICY

The next two chapters focus on the role of fiscal and financial policies in mobilizing domestic savings and on the immplications of such policies for income distribution, efficiency, employment, and price stability. Policies geared mainly toward foreign savings are discussed in Chapter 14. In mixed economies, fiscal and financial policies are, along with foreign exchange and agricultural policies, the princiapl tools available to governments to influence economic activity and stimulate development. In this chapter we focus on fiscal policy, alternatively called budget policy. Fiscal policy encompasses all measures pertaining to the level and structure of government revenues and expenditures.

As the terms are used here, **government revenues** consist of all tax and nontax revenue flowing to the government treasury, including surpluses of public enterprises and domestic borrowing by the treasury. **Government expenditures** are defined as all outlays from the government budget, including those for such current expenditures as civil service salaries, maintenance, military costs, interest payments, and subsidies to cover public enterprise losses (see Chapter 21), as well as capital expenditures such as outlays for construction of irrigation canals, roads, and schools, and purchase of non-military equipment owned by government.

Although our initial focus is on the role of fiscal and financial policy in the mobilization of domestic savings, it is important to recognize that these policies are generally expected to serve a variety of other important public policy objectives of developing societies. Subsequent discussion can be placed in perspective by a brief examination of Table 12–1, which lists the objectives developing countries commonly establish for both fiscal and financial policy, together with typical instruments employed to secure them. It will be evident from later sections that while these policy tools may be appropriate for promoting some of the objectives listed below, they are less well suited for achieving others.

TABLE 12–1 Objectives and Instruments of Fiscal and Financial Policy in Developing Countries

Objective	Operational objective	Instruments
I. Objectives common to both fiscal and financial policy		
1. Promotion of economic growth	Expanded public- and private-sector savings; greater accessibility of savings	Fiscal: Level of taxes Structure of taxes Restraint on government consumption Financial: Interest rates Development of financial markets, others
2. Equity: reduction of income disparities between households and regions	Lower tax burdens on lower-income households than upper-income households; public provision of basic needs and primary education; promotion of employment	Fiscal: Reliance on progressive taxes, avoiding regressivity Budget subsidies, primary education Revenue sharing Financial: Measures to control inflation Interest rate reform
3. Promotion of economic stability	Reduction of inflation and unemployment	Fiscal: Revenue-elastic taxes Restraint on government consumption Financial: Interest rates Reserve requirements Credit controls
4. Promotion of economic efficiency	Removal of fiscal barriers to efficiency; reduction in costs of tax administration and financial intermediation	Fiscal: Tax reform Training tax officials Financial: Interest rates Financial reform
II. Primarily fiscal policy objectives		
Increased host-country returns from natural resource endowments	Capture of resource rents	Natural resource taxes
III. Primarily financial policy objectives		
Promotion of socioeconomic cohesion	Reduction in fragmentation of national markets; expand opportunities for disadvantaged groups	Financial reform, Special credit programs

Different societies place different weights on these policy objectives; indeed, not all countries pursue all of them. For example, some countries assign heavy importance to equity; for others, little emphasis is given to economic efficiency. Nevertheless the objectives are common enough across such a wide variety of LDCs to merit consideration here. Some objectives are served by both sets of policy instruments; for some purposes fiscal policy is more suitable; for still others financial policy is more germane.

Fiscal policy operates through both the tax and expenditure sides of the government budget. The locus of decision-making on fiscal policy in LDCs is typically split between two agencies: the Ministry of Finance (the Treasury Department) and the Ministry (or Board) of Planning. In most countries the Ministry of Finance is assigned primary responsibility for the design and implementation of tax policy and for decisions concerning current government consumption expenditures. The Ministry of Planning typically holds sway on decisions concerning government capital expenditures. This separation of responsibilities over budget policy is so common, and of such long standing, that many economists and policy-makers tend to reserve the term *fiscal policy* for that which is done by the Ministry of Finance, and to term as *development policy* that under the ultimate control of the Ministry of Planning. This book accepts this convention, with reservations. Therefore this chapter focuses on those aspects of fiscal policy dealing with taxation and government consumption expenditures, while public capital expenditures were considered in Chapters 5 and 6. But the distinction between public "capital" and "consumption" spending is essentially an arbitrary one, both in theory and in practice.

Taxation and Public Savings

Growth in public savings (S_G) can be secured only by measures that expand budget savings (S_{GB}) and the savings of state-owned enterprises (S_{GE}). Because a substantial portion of Chapter 21 focuses on savings mobilization through state-owned enterprises, here we deal only with budget savings, defined as the excess of government revenues over government consumption expenditures.

Until relatively recently, economists and policy-makers alike have viewed the public savings problem as primarily a matter of raising tax collections. This approach has yielded disappointing results, as was seen in the previous chapter. Here we delve more deeply into the reasons why there are severe limits to the contribution taxes can make to increased saving.

Constraints on Taxation

We observed in Chapter 11 that broad patterns of taxation vary widely across developing countries: the share of taxes in GDP varies from as low as 6 percent to upward of 36 percent, with a central tendency about 15 percent. Governments in countries with low tax ratios would ordinarily be expected to be more limited in their abilities to satisfy basic needs such as housing or public health, or to meet goals set for primary education and government investment. Over the past twenty years analysts have sought a basis for explaining why tax shares vary so markedly across countries. By 1980 the literature on this topic was voluminous. The search for determinants of tax shares has led researchers to consider factors ranging from economic explanations, such as differences in per-capita income, the role of natural resources in exports, the degree of industrialization, and the extent of "openness" (share of foreign trade in GDP), to a variety of demographic considerations, such as the dependency ratio, literacy rates, and the degree of urbanization.

An obvious reason for cross-country differences in the share of taxes in GNP would seem to be differences in per-capita income. In the poorest countries the margin between per-capita income and that part of income used for meeting basic subsistence needs is much smaller than in middle-income nations. Thus taxable capacity—and the share of taxes in GDP—should be expected to be greater in countries with higher per-capita income. It is true that the very poorest developing countries tend to have the lowest tax ratios: Bangladesh, Burma, Nepal, Ethiopia, and Mali are all well below the average (see Table 12–2). However, above the group of very poor countries there seems to be very little relationship between per-capita income levels and tax shares, and much of any apparent relationship may be largely explained by factors other than difference in per-capita income. Specifically, many low-income category B countries display tax shares that are strikingly similar to those observed in category E countries, even though per-capita incomes are about four times higher in the latter. Indeed, a number of category B countries, such as Tanzania, Sierra Leone, Sri Lanka, and Kenya, had tax ratios similar to those for several category F countries (Turkey, Costa Rica, and Brazil) where per-capita income was five and six times greater.

Differences in the level and structure of foreign trade appear to have a much more significant impact on tax shares among developing countries. Analysts have long hypothesized that the degree of "openness" in a particular economy would materially affect its ability to collect taxes. Countries with a higher ratio of exports or imports to GDP would be expected, *ceteris paribus,* to have higher tax ratios than those where foreign trade was relatively less important. The reason is that foreign trade, whether exports or imports, must normally pass through a bottleneck—one or more ports— where it can be relatively easily observed and taxed. Therefore import duties and export taxes are imposed on tax bases that are fairly accessible to the tax administration. By way of contrast, taxes on income, wealth, and even domestic consumption depend on bases that are far more easily concealed from tax officials. This holds with particular force for income and wealth taxes: administration of these levies requires administrative resources and skill levels in chronic short supply in developing relative to industrial countries. Even in much of Western Europe outside of Scandinavia

TABLE 12-2 Tax Ratios, Per-Capita Income, and Mineral Exports, 1976

Per-capita income	Exports of minerals and oil less than 20% of total exports[a]		Exports of minerals and oil more than 40% of Exports[b]	
	Country	Tax Ratio[b]	Country	Tax Ratio[b]
A. Under $125	Ethiopia	10.1		
	Mali	12.9		
	Bangladesh	5.8		
	Upper Volta	11.3		
	Burma	7.6		
	Nepal	5.4		
B. $125–250	Benin	16.0	Zaire	27.2
	India	13.9	Indonesia	16.3
	Afghanistan	5.7		
	Pakistan	11.4		
	Tanzania	18.9		
	Sierra Leone	17.0		
	Sri Lanka	17.9		
	Kenya	19.2		
C. $251–$400	Togo	12.4	Bolivia	11.8
	Sudan	18.9		
	Thailand	13.9		
	Honduras	11.5		
	Senegal	20.2		
D. $401–600	Philippines	10.1	Zambia	30.8
	Cameroon	16.2	Liberia	14.4
	El Salvador	11.5	People's Rep. Congo	19.8
	Ghana	14.2	Morocco	18.6
			Nigeria	37.0
E. $601–$1000	Ivory Coast	20.6	Ecuador	12.0
	Dominican Republic	19.3	Syria	11.3
	Colombia	11.6	Peru	14.0
	Guatemala	8.1	Tunisia	20.7
	Paraguay	8.8	Algeria	39.8
	Korea	13.6		
	Nicaragua	11.1		
F. Above $1000	Turkey	16.2	Chile	18.4
	Costa Rica	13.6	Mexico	8.6
	Brazil	18.1	Iraq	37.7
			Venezuela	21.7
Averages:	33 countries with mineral and oil exports less than 20% of total exports	13.4	17 countries with mineral and oil exports greater than 40% of total exports	21.0

[a] Figures for export concentration (mineral and oil exports as percent of total exports) are for 1977. *Source:* World Bank, *World Tables*. Washington, D.C., 1978), Table 5.

[b] Except for Nigeria and Venezuela, tax ratios for any country are averages for 1972–1976 and exclude social security taxes. *Source:* Alan A. Tait, Wilfred M. Gratz, and Barry J. Eichengreen, *International Monetary Fund Staff Papers* 26, no. 1 (March 1979): Table 15, pp. 153–54.

evasion of income taxes is fairly common, and avoidance of taxes is taken for granted.[1]

Perhaps as significant as the degree of "openness" is the relative importance of natural resources in GDP and in exports. Virtually every study on

1. Evasion is distinguished from avoidance of income taxes in the sense that evasion encompasses activities to conceal net income or falsify tax deductions, or other illegal ploys to pay less taxes than due. Avoidance is merely the legal rearrangement of one's affairs to minimize tax obligations. Evasion is illegal, a punishable offense; avoidance is not.

the determinants of tax shares indicates that countries with relatively large production of oil and minerals, and consequently a high share of resources in exports, have substantially greater taxable capacity than countries at the same level of per-capita income and the same degree of "openness," but with relatively small natural resource production and exports. Some confirmation of these phenomena may be derived from the right-hand column of Table 12–2. There it can be seen that countries with the highest tax ratios tend strongly to be those where natural resource exports loom large in total exports. For 1977 the average share of natural resource exports in total exports in LDCs was about 40 percent. For seventeen countries where mineral and oil exports were in excess of 40 percent of total exports the tax ratio averaged 21.0 percent. For thirty-three countries where the share of such natural resources in total exports was less than 20 percent the average tax ratio was but 13.4 percent. Econometric investigations of the influence of mineral and oil exports as well as other factors on taxable capacity and tax shares have been carried out by several analysts. These studies focus not on the share of nonrenewable resources in exports but on their share in GDP, a closely related measure for LDCs, as noted below. All confirm the key role of natural resources in the determination of taxable capacity: countries where mining constitutes a relatively large share of GDP (usually more than 5 percent) find it much easier to collect taxes.

Reasons for higher taxable capacity in such countries are fairly obvious. First, except for countries with large internal markets, such as Brazil, India, and China, over 95 percent of all hard minerals produced in LDCs is exported. And in LDCs with appreciable quantities of oil, upward of 80 percent of annual production is typically exported. For both minerals and oil the tax base is therefore easily accessible to the tax collector. In addition, from 1972 to 1976 oil and a few minerals were the source of high surplus returns, or rents, arising from high world prices. Such rents are not only tempting targets for taxation, but are particularly suitable for tax rates higher than prevailing in the agricultural, industrial, or service sectors of most LDCs. This is true partly because in virtually all LDCs, unlike the United States, property rights in natural resources are constitutionally vested in the state, not in private industry.

Finally, the hard mineral and oil sectors in many, though not all, LDCs are dominated by large multinational enterprises, a fact which also tends to make mineral and oil revenues accessible to domestic tax collectors. It is not that multinationals are inherently more civic-minded in regard to their tax-paying obligations. Indeed we shall see in Chapter 14 that such firms have at their disposal a wide array of devices that can be deployed to avoid LDC taxes. However, the multinationals are large, and being large have an internal need for much more detailed and accurate record-keeping than do small LDC enterprises. Further, substantial evasion of host country taxes is a risky proposition for most multinationals which, after all, owe their presence in LDCs to the sufferance of host governments. Great success in tax evasion in the short run can lead to expropriation in the medium to longer term. By the early 1980s most large mining and oil multinationals had come to perceive that too much is at stake to make wholesale use of devices for escaping host country taxes. This was not always the case for American and British-based firms, the earliest large multinationals, and is sometimes not the case even now for continental multinationals.

Some resource-rich LDCs, such as Algeria, Iraq, and Zambia before 1978, have utilized their high taxable capacity to bring the ratio of taxes collected to over 30 percent of GDP. Other relatively resource-rich nations, such as Indonesia, Mexico, and Bolivia, in the mid-1970s had high taxable capacity but low or average ratios of taxes actually collected to GDP. Countries that intensively utilize their taxable capacity to attain high actual tax ratios are conventionally called "high tax effort" nations. Those that have made little effort fully to tap their taxable capacity are, conversely, termed "low tax effort" countries. There are several countries that, owing to low per-capita income, an absence of mineral and oil exports, and a small industrial sector, have low tax capacity but relatively high tax ratios and thus high tax effort. These include Tanzania, Sri Lanka, Sudan, and Jordan.

By 1980 there was a wide consensus among developmental specialists that high tax ratios were not necessarily a virtue, nor low tax ratios a vice, in mobilizing domestic savings. Tax ratios reflect both opportunity and ideology. African countries, particularly Sub-Saharan nations, tend to tax themselves more heavily relative to their taxable capacities. Ideology may be a factor, but a high tax ratio may also reflect the fact that opportunities for mobilizing other types of savings, especially private savings, are limited because of poorly developed and organized financial systems. Latin American countries tend to dominate any list of countries with low tax effort (low utilization of taxable capacity). This may merely reflect the relatively greater ease with which private savings can be mobilized through the financial system in Latin America. There has been relatively robust growth of organized financial markets in many Latin American countries since 1945, particularly in Mexico, Brazil, Argentina, Chile, and more recently in Colombia and Venezuela.

Tax Measures for Expanding Public Savings

A number of tax measures are available to LDCs for expanding public savings, including (1) periodic increases in rates imposed under existing taxes; (2) enactment of new taxes to tap previously unutilized sources of revenue; (3) improvements in tax administration which allow greater collection under existing taxes at present tax rates, by reducing tax avoidance and evasion; and (4) major reform of the entire tax structure, involving elements of options 1, 2, and 3. For many countries options 1 and 2 offer only slight hopes for increased collections. Options 3 and 4 are perhaps the most difficult to implement, but if feasible are much more likely to achieve the desired results.

Tax Rate Increases The first option, tax rate increases, is often the favored one, owing to a widely prevailing view among finance ministers, their advisors, and often aid donors, that there exists at any given time under-utilized targets of opportunity for heavier taxation. The "slack" in the tax system is thought to make possible, say, a 10 percent increase in tax revenues simply by enacting increases of 10 percent in existing tax rates, with no changes in underlying tax law or tax administration. There are some circumstances in which this approach can achieve the desired results. The potential base for *taxes on natural resources* had been underutilized in many countries prior to the 1970s. In the short term, taxpayers in the natural resource sector, particularly foreign-based multinational firms, are "captive" in the sense that production from *existing* mines and wells will not cease unless after-tax returns are very sharply curtailed. This "slack" in taxable capacity expands when world markets for minerals and oil strengthen rapidly, as in 1973–1974 and again in 1978–1979.

Governments have not in general overlooked this source of higher tax revenues for long, whether in developed or developing countries. Tax increases imposed by Mideast oil nations in 1973–1974 are by now legendary examples. Among less wealthy LDCs, Jamaica in 1974 was able to increase taxes on foreign-mined bauxite by over 700 percent. Indonesia succeeded in nearly doubling its tax collections from multinational oil firms between 1976 and 1978, even as production was beginning to decline and world oil prices had been stagnant for three years. During the 1950s and 1960s Chile began extracting from large copper multinationals a steadily rising share of gross revenues. Gabon enjoyed some success in the early 1970s in extracting higher revenue on uranium from French enterprises.

This strategy works well in the short term, and if carefully applied can be followed with some success in the long run. Possibilities of higher tax collection from this source are not unlimited, however. The usual pattern of company response to very sharp increases in tax rates on their resource earnings is to continue production from existing facilities, but to postpone or cancel new investments in exploration, extraction, and processing. This occurred in both Indonesian oil in 1977–1978 and Jamaican bauxite in 1975–1978. Within three years both countries found it necessary to grant partial rollbacks of the higher tax rates to induce the multinationals to resume investing. The oil firms reinstituted investment in Indonesia; aluminum companies did not immediately do so in Jamaica. But where a developing country has a very strong position in the natural resource market, major rollbacks have not been required. A good example is the case of Indonesian tropical timber. Because of that country's relatively large and rich stands of tropical timber, it is the world's second-largest producer. Indonesia was able to double its export tax rates on logs in 1978, amid little more than perfunctory outcries from international timber firms.

In instances not involving natural resource industries, resort to increased tax rates for existing taxes is usually fraught with problems. Tax structures prevailing in most LDCs are not generally of the type where periodic increases in tax rates alone can be expected to lend to the desired results. Slack is present in virtually all tax systems, but it cannot usually be eliminated merely by enacting higher tax rates on unchanged tax bases.

Import Duties   Tax structures in LDCs have historically depended heavily on *taxes on foreign trade,* particularly import duties. Reliance on import duties (tariffs) as a revenue source is especially heavy in poorer and resource-poor LDCs, relative to middle-income and resource-rich LDCs. Fully twenty such countries rely on import tariffs for more than 40 percent of tax revenue. Dependence on import duties is especially marked in Afghanistan, Benin, Gambia, Ivory Coast, Rwanda, Sudan, Togo, and the Yemen Arab Republic, where over half of total government revenue comes from taxes on imports *versus* less than 30 percent for LDCs as a group.[2] Because imports, like exports, must be funneled through a small number of ports, making them relatively easy to identify and tax, developing countries turned to this revenue source early in the process of development, and most have mined it to the limit. For most countries attempts to raise further revenues through higher duties is often infeasible. Later we will see that it is also usually inadvisable. Higher import duties intensify the incentive on smuggling or evasion of tariffs. Various studies have shown that for countries with already high rates of duty, the incentive to smuggle increases disproportionately with duty rates, so that a 10 percent rise in duty rates can result in an increase in smuggling activity by more than 10 percent (see the example below). And in mountainous countries (Afghanistan and Bolivia) or archipelago nations (Indonesia and the Philippines), borders are especially porous to smuggled imports.

Tax Rates and Smuggling: Colombia   In Colombia before 1969, when the rate of import duty on cigarettes was over 100 percent, it was virtually impossible to purchase duty-paid cigarettes. At such high rates import duty collections on cigarettes were nil and the market was flooded with smuggled foreign brands. In 1969 the duty rate was reduced to 30 percent. Cigarette smuggling on the poorly policed Caribbean coast of that country continued, but duty-paid packages began to appear in the mountainous interior, and duty collections on this product soared. Smuggling profits possible under a 30 percent duty were no longer high enough to compensate smugglers for the risks of arrest. Similar phenomena have been observed in Indonesia, Bolivia, and elsewhere.

Reliance on import duties for additional revenues may be unfeasible for another reason. Except in such open economies as South Korea, Singapore, and Malaysia, the typical structure of import duties in LDCs is, as explained in greater detail in Chapter 16, heavily "cascaded": the highest rates of duty in virtually all countries are imposed on consumer durable goods, particularly "luxury" goods (appliances, cameras, etc.); still lower rates are applied on such intermediate goods as cement and leather, with

---

2. Adapted from Alan A. Tait, Wilfred M. Gratz, and Barry J. Eichengreen, *International Monetary Fund Staff Papers* 26, no. 1 (March 1979): 123–256, Table 14.

the lowest rates of duty on capital goods and imported items viewed as basic "necessities" (foodgrains, fish, kerosene, etc.). When countries sought additional revenues from tariffs, reliance was placed heavily on duty increases on consumer goods already subject to high tariffs. Higher rates on necessities were considered inadvisable for reasons of income distribution. But higher rates on capital goods and intermediate goods were deemed unacceptable because it was believed that this would retard industrialization programs. Enactment of higher duties on consumer goods, and particularly luxury consumer goods, generally did not produce higher revenue. The reason is simple: price elasticity of demand is not zero for any consumer good, and for many already paying very high duties, price elasticity is relatively high, in some cases -2.0 or more. For an import, such as stereos, already subject to a 150 percent duty, with a price elasticity of demand of -2.0, a 10 percent increase in duty rates would actually decrease tax revenue on this item by about 2 percent.[3]

Personal and Corporate Income Taxes Harried ministers of finance utilize other methods to generate greater revenues from tax systems already in place. Perceiving "slack" in personal and corporate income taxes, many resort to rate increases in these taxes, with no change in tax base. The results have usually been disappointing. Even in more prosperous, middle-income LDCs the base of the personal income tax reaches only a very small proportion of the population. In the early 1970s the personal income tax covered no more than 2 percent of the population in Ghana, Peru, and virtually all other developing countries save Burma, Kenya, and Turkey. By way of contrast about 42 percent of the population in the United States filed income tax returns in 1974. Thus few developing countries can rely heavily on the personal income tax for revenues. Whereas the share of the income tax in federal revenues in the United States is about 40 percent, rarely does the personal income tax account for as much as 10 percent of total central government revenues in LDCs. The personal income tax is at least as well developed in Colombia as in any LDC. Yet even though this tax is typically responsible for as much as 15 to 18 percent of national government revenues, a large share of it is paid by a small number of people: in the early 1970s the top 4 percent of households paid two-thirds of the total tax.[4] Furthermore income taxes are largely paid by urban elites in LDCs. Not only are these groups usually the most vocal politically, they

3. This result comes from applying the formula

$$\frac{\frac{dR}{R}}{\frac{dt}{t}} = 1 + \varepsilon \left(\frac{t}{1+t} \right)$$

where R = total duty collections on stereos, t = rate of duty on stereos, and ε = price elasticity of demand.

4. Malcolm Gillis and Charles E. McLure, Jr., "Taxation and Income Distribution: The Colombian Tax Reform of 1974," *Journal of Development Economics* 5, no. 3 (September 1978): 237.

have usually developed over the years such a variety of devices for tax evasion and avoidance that mere rate increases stand little chance of raising additional revenues.

Rate increases for corporate taxes are not usually productive either. Except for several higher income LDCs such as Argentina, Korea, Taiwan, and Mexico, the corporate form of doing business covers but a small portion of the private sector. To be sure, most state-owned firms are corporations, but Chapter 21 shows that few such firms outside the natural resources sector earn sizable taxable profits. Even fewer pay substantial income taxes.

Sales and Excise Taxes A much more promising source of additional government revenue is internal indirect taxes, such as sales and excise taxes. *Sales taxes,* including value-added taxes, are broad-based consumption taxes imposed on all products except those specifically exempted, such as food, farm inputs, and medicine. *Excise taxes* are also taxes on consumption, but these levies are imposed only on specifically enumerated items, typically tobacco, alcoholic beverages, gambling, and motor fuel.

Virtually every developing country imposes some form of sales tax. In most the tax is not applied to retail sales because of the burdensome administrative requirements of collecting from thousands of small retailers. In the past the tax was often (Chile before 1970, some Indian states) imposed as a gross "turnover" tax collected at all levels of production and distribution, with harmful implications for efficiency, income distribution, and virtually every other objective of tax policy cited in Table 12–1. Administrative problems in sales taxation are more tractable when the tax is confined to the manufacturing level: a much smaller number of firms is involved and output of manufacturers is far more homogenous than sales of retailers or wholesalers. For these reasons most LDCs utilize either the single-stage or value-added form of manufacturer's tax (usually exempting very small producers), even though this kind of sales tax involves more economic distortions than either a wholesale or a retail tax.

Governments often resort to general rate increases in the national sales tax as the path of least resistance when public revenue must be increased. Except for those countries where the tax is riddled with exemptions or saddled with unenforceably high rates, this option has on occasion yielded desired results. But repeated resort to sales tax rate increases ultimately leads to strong taxpayer resistance. Once rates of a manufacturer's tax begin to exceed 20 to 30 percent, as in many LDCs, incentives for evasion become irresistible.

Excise taxes might appear to represent an ideal source of additional tax revenue. Such taxes are typically imposed on sumptuary items having relatively inelastic demand in both LDCs and industrial countries: tobacco and alcoholic beverages. When demand elasticity for such products is near zero, as is the case for tobacco products and only slightly less clearly so for alcoholic beverages, an increase in excise tax rates will induce little reduction in consumption of the taxed goods. If price elasticity is as low as -0.2, as is not uncommon for cigarettes, then an additional 10 percent excise tax on this product would yield an 8 percent increase in tax revenues. Moreover it is a hallowed theorem in optimal tax theory that taxes levied on items with inelastic demand and supply involve the smallest losses in economic efficiency (the least "excess burden," where excess burden is defined as loss in private welfare over and above the amount of government revenue collected from a tax). Further, many agree—with much justification—that consumption of both tobacco and alcohol should be discouraged on health grounds.

All three considerations would seem to argue for very heavy reliance on such excise taxes in LDC tax revenue structures. However, it is unfortunately true that in addition to low price elasticity, items such as tobacco and alcoholic beverages have low income elasticity. This means that such goods tend to be more important in the budgets of low-income than high-income households. It follows then that excises on sumptuary items are decidedly regressive in their impact on the distribution of income: poor people pay a higher proportion of their income in excise tax than do rich people, a serious matter when the sumptuary items constitute a substantial proportion of spending by poor people, as in most LDCs. In Indonesia, for example, the poorest 20 percent of Javanese households spent about 5 percent of total income on heavily taxed cigarette consumption in 1976, as opposed to 3.5 percent of income for persons with income more than five times as high. Thus each poorer family pays 60 percent more in cigarette taxes than their richer counterpart. This regressivity conflicts with one of the principal policy aims listed in Table 12–1.

New Sources of Tax Revenues The second option for increasing public savings through taxation is that of tapping entirely new sources of tax revenue. In many LDCs, whether by accident, by design, or simply because of inertia, many sources of tax revenue may have been overlooked entirely. Many countries do not collect taxes on motor vehicle registration, most do not utilize urban property taxes as a significant source of revenue, many do not apply corporation income taxes to income of state-owned enterprises, and a few, such as Indonesia, do not collect personal income taxes on salaries of civil servants. The service sector furnishes another example. Telephone service exists in all but the very poorest countries, and in many is fairly widespread but is often untaxed. Some service establishments such as restaurants and cabarets are commonly taxed, but services of beauty shops, parking lots, tire recapping, photofinishing firms, modern laundries, and foreign travel are among the more common items excluded from the tax base. Not only is taxation of this category of spending attractive from a revenue standpoint, but in LDCs such services are typically characterized by relatively income-elastic demand: because families with higher incomes purchase proportionately more of these items, they would tend to bear the greater burden of taxation, consistent with the equity objectives of fiscal policy. However, these services constitute a small fraction of consumption, even for upper income groups, so their revenue potential is limited.[5]

Changes in Tax Administration   The third and far more significant option for increasing tax revenues is that of implementing changes in tax administration that permit more taxes to be collected from existing tax sources, even at unchanged tax rates. The potential for increased revenues from such action is very large in virtually all LDCs; rarely is this potential even partly realized. Shortages of well-trained tax administrators, excessively complex tax laws, light penalties for tax evasion, corruption, and outdated techniques of tax administration all combine to make tax evasion one of the most intractable problems of economic policy in LDCs. Studies in Colombia indicate that in 1975 as many as 50 percent of small establishments did not file income tax returns, and that underreporting of income among professionals (lawyers, doctors) was as high as 70 percent. Evasion of sales taxes during the same period was between 40 and 50 percent. Still other studies suggest that there remained widespread corruption in the Colombian Tax Service in the mid-1970s even after a decade of intensive effort to curtail such practices: for every peso of bribes paid to tax assessors the state lost about twenty pesos in tax revenue.[6] Similar, if not worse, patterns have been reported in other countries. For Bolivia in the period 1964–1966 it has been estimated that about 60 percent of property income was not reported to the tax administration, while in Argentina in the same period taxpayers succeeded in hiding over 50 percent of total income.[7] In Indonesia estimates suggest that as much as 80 percent of the personal income tax base goes unreported. For comparison, underreporting of total income amounted to about 13 to 15 percent in both the United States and Canada in the 1960s.

Such figures suggest that even modest efforts to collect a greater share of taxes legally due could increase revenues by as much as 50 percent in some countries, without increasing tax rates. Nevertheless there are few cases of even mild success in such undertakings, but many examples of unfulfilled expectations. Korea has been among the more successful. In 1966 it sought to increase tax collections by 40 percent through more effective enforcement alone. This ambitious target was not met, but in five years the Korean revenue service was able to reduce underreporting of nonagricultural personal income from 75 percent to slightly less than 50 percent. In 1974 Colombia, through swiftly implemented administrative changes, was able to make temporary inroads in the evasion problem; but by 1976 taxpayers

---

5. In 1965 Colombia imposed no taxes on any of the services listed above. One of the authors of this text estimated that if that country had enacted rather heavy taxes on these items in that year, total tax revenues would have been increased only by about 2 percent. Nevertheless imposing taxes on them was desirable both from a revenue and an equity standpoint, and some were enacted.

6. Gillis and McLure, "Taxation and Income Distribution," p. 249.

7. Oliver Oldman and Daniel M. Holland, "Measuring Tax Evasion" (Paper presented at the Fifth Annual General Assembly of the Inter-American Center of Tax Administration, Rio de Janiero, May 17, 1971), pp. 33–37.

had crafted several new methods of evasion so that much of the earlier gains in revenue were eroded within three years. Virtually every serious study of the problem indicates that measures to curtail tax evasion in LDCs promise no "quick fixes" to the revenue problem. Rather, capacity for limiting tax evasion, like many other socioeconomic phenomena observable in LDCs, tends to follow a pattern of secular improvement associated with economic development.

Fundamental Tax Reform The final policy option available for increasing tax revenues is the most difficult to implement, but the most effective when it can be done: fundamental tax reform. Tax reform encompasses all of the four prior options: it ordinarily involves increases as well as decreases in tax rates for some existing taxes; the creation of new sources of tax revenue; and adoption of new administrative techniques suitable for improved enforcement of both old and new taxes. Implementation of tax reform engenders enormous technical and informational, not to mention political, difficulties. In general, governments do not resort to genuine efforts to reform the tax structure until fiscal crisis threatens; for only then, if then, can sufficient political consensus be mobilized to allow unpopular tax measures to pass. Tax reform is difficult anywhere. Tax policies that protect favored groups and distort the allocation of resources did not just happen; more likely they were enacted at someone's behest, ordinarily the privileged and the powerful.

It is probably true that tax reform is a topic about which more has been said, to less effect, than almost any topic in economic policy. This is no less true for the United States than for fifty-odd LDCs where major tax reform efforts have been mounted since 1950. That the process is painful and slow is evident from the experience of several countries: in the United States the time lag between birth of ideas for tax innovations (tax credits for child-care expenses, income averaging) and their implementation is usually no less than fifteen years. If anything the lag may be slightly shorter in LDCs.

In spite of the difficulties involved some LDCs have been able to carry through major reforms in tax structure and administration. The classic example is that of Japan in the 1880s, when that society began its transformation to a modern industrial power. Korea implemented a major program of tax reform in the early 1960s, as did Colombia (see the example below) and Chile in the 1970s. But also during the 1970s major tax reform efforts went for naught in many more countries: Bolivia, Ghana, Liberia, and Peru, among others.

Perhaps the most ambitious program of tax structure reform ever undertaken in any developing country was that in Colombia in 1974. The Colombian experience well illustrates both the potential payoffs and the difficulties involved in any serious tax reform effort.

In the last quarter of 1974 the new government of Alfonso Lopez Michelsen, acting in the midst of a national crisis, enacted a tax reform of

Lessons from Comprehensive Tax Reform

very large magnitude. The reform, nearly a decade in the making, was engineered by an extraordinary group of officials as well versed in fiscal economics as in any treasury department in the industrial countries. The reform package was comprehensive, involving nearly all tax sources. It was geared to all the fiscal policy objectives cited in Table 12–1: growth, equity, stability, and efficiency. The instruments employed were well suited to the objectives sought. The reform contained measures to increase progressivity that are still absent in the tax systems of the United States and Canada. Numerous anomalies in the tax system that encouraged waste and inefficiency in the private sector were eliminated. Innovations in tax administration and enforcement were introduced and were allowed to stand for a short time before they were struck down by the Supreme Court.

The most striking initial achievements of the reform were its effects on tax revenue growth and income distribution. In the first year following the reform, tax revenues grew by 45 percent, or more than twice the rate of growth in revenues in the years prior to the reform. The early impact on income distribution was just as striking: in its first year the reform served to shift as much as 1.5 percent of GDP away rom the top 20 percent of the income earners, a rare feat.

Many of the achievements of the reform effort proved short-lived, however. The reform initially caught most powerful economic interests with their defenses down. But by 1976 groups injured by the reform were able to have many key measures watered down or repealed, and taxpayers began to develop defense mechanisms against the new law and to exploit loopholes uncovered by the best legal minds in the country. Also, the reform effort paid far too little attention to practical problems of implementation and to the strengthening of tax-collection procedures. Nevertheless many of the innovations introduced in 1974 survived relatively intact through 1980, such that by that time many revenue-hungry and equity-oriented tax officials in other Latin American countries still viewed much of the 1974 reform package as a model worth detailed study.

Expenditure Policy

The effects of government capital spending on growth were long viewed as unambiguously positive. Although critics of capital fundamentalism later succeeded in demonstrating that not all such investment has contributed to growth, much less development, there is still a pervasive belief that in any trade-offs between government capital spending and recurrent spending, the issue should be resolved in favor of investment, as recurrent outlays are still widely considered unproductive. Indeed recurrent costs of development programs are by usual convention labeled as government consumption, implying that outlays for such purposes have no effect on increasing productive capacity. A number of analysts have sought to correct this misconception. They point out that while most governments focus their attention on new investments, they often do not make adequate provision for the recurrent operational and maintenance costs of previous investments.[8] This gives rise to wasteful underutilization of public-sector capital, and in some cases to its rapid decay.

These observations notwithstanding, it is also true that in many countries there may be some scope for expanding public savings by curbing growth of several types of recurrent expenditure: the "Please effect" discussed in the last chapter is not without empirical support. We will examine the main categories of recurrent, or "consumption," expenditures of government to determine how wide this scope may be.

For many countries, the five most significant categories of recurrent expenditure are:

1. Outlays for wages and salaries of civil servants and the military;
2. Outlays on nondurable goods and services, including those for public sector employees, maintenance, and all spending on military equipment;
3. Interest payments on the government debt;
4. Transfers to subnational governments;
5. Subsidies and other transfers to individuals.

Nondurable Goods and Services

In poorer LDCs, *nondurable goods and services* typically account for between half and three-quarters of total recurrent expenditure (see Table 12–3). The three principal items are: (1) salaries and benefits for civil servants and the military; (2) outlays on maintenance and repair; and (3) other military spending. In most LDCs, salaries and benefits account for considerably more than half of total expenditures for goods and services.

The stereotypical image of public-sector bureaucracies in LDCs is one of bloated payrolls and inefficient, corrupt, even indolent performance. This view is founded essentially on anecdotal, not systematic, evidence; reliable international comparisons of civil service performance are almost nonexistent. It is easy to accumulate anecdotes involving bureaucratic snafus, stupidities, corruption, and short-sightedness in both developing and in developd societies. No firm judgments can be made on the extent of overstaffing of public agencies or overremuneration of officials, or bureaucratic extravagance in LDCs relative to industrial countries: civil service payrolls in Massachusetts and New Jersey may be no less bloated than in many LDCs. And while there are examples of gross venality and blatant use of political patronage in public-sector hiring in segments of the civil service systems of some developing countries, there are also examples of first-rate professionalism and codes of conduct that may rival many found in industrial countries, for example the Indian and Malaysian civil service systems.

While there may be some countries in which the salary bill for civil ser-

8. Pete Heller, "The Under-Financing of Recurrent Development Costs," *Finance and Development* 16, no. 1 (March 1979): 38–41.

TABLE 12-3   Government Recurrent Expenditure, by Type, as % of Total Recurrent Spending in Selected Developing Countries (1978–1980)

Country	(1) (1A) Wages and fsalaries	(1B) Other purchases of goods and services	(2) Interest payments on public debt	(3) Transfers to subnational government	(4) Subsidies and other transfers	(5) Total[b]	Year
Low-income countries							
Ethiopia	43	48	3	5	5	101	1978
India	12	12	11	26	39	100	1980
Indonesia	24	17	6	15	39	101	1980
Kenya	34	36	9	5	16	100	1980
Pakistan	51[a]		13	12	25	101	1980
Sri Lanka	20	30	14	—	36	100	1980
Sudan	15	42	8	35	—	100	1980
Tanzania	44	39	6	—	11	100	1978
Zaire	47	29	10	5	9	100	1979
Middle-income countries							
Argentina	38[a]		11	—	51	100	1980
Bolivia	59	14	4	6	15	98	1979
Brazil	13	8	12	12	55	100	1979
Chile	32	12	3	—	51	98	1980
Colombia	50	17	—	8	24	99	1978
Ghana	23	19	14	22	22	100	1980
Egypt	22	17	10	—	51	100	1979
Korea	73	20	—	—	7	100	1978
Malaysia	42	13	15	3	27	100	1979
Peru	51[a]		26	—	23	100	1980

Source: International Monetary Fund, *Government Finance Statistics Yearbook, 1982* (Washington, D.C., 1982), country tables.
[a] Data not provided for breakdown between categories.
[b] Rows may not add to 100 because of rounding.

vants could be compressed suficiently to materially augment government savings, in others, like Venezuela and Kenya, civil service salaries remain so low relative to those available in the private sector that it has been difficult to attract and hold the type of qualified public-sector managers, secretaries, and technicians essential for efficiency in government operation.

About the only safe generalization that can be made about civil service systems in LDCs is that they apear more or less responsive to the socioeconomic changes that accompany development than any other group in society. In the 1950s it was almost impossible to have a discussion about Latin American development without hearing repeated mention of the "antidevelopmental" effects of the famous *mordida* (bite) then commonly demanded by civil servants there for doing both what they should be doing and what they should not be doing. It was commonly believed then that such behavior was the result of both low civil service salaries and inalterable cultural habits. In the early 1960s many Western as well as Korean social scientists were inclined to believe that widespread corruption and inefficiency in government were immutable owing both to practices that became acceptable under decades of Japanese occupation and to the influence of the Confucian ethic. One hears much less of such claims today, whether for Latin America or Korea. While civil service reformers may not wish to use either the Colombian, Malaysian, Brazilian, or Korean experience as a model for other countries, there can be no mistaking the palpable verve and professionalism displayed by substantial numbers of civil servants in those countries by the 1980s, "cultural habits" notwithstanding.

Excessive public expenditure on nondurable goods and services are often singled out as major reasons for low public sector savings in LDCs. Here again anecdotal evidence, such as the fleet of Rolls-Royces and Mercedes purchased in the 1960s by Nkrumah in Ghana, or the extravagances of Somoza in Nicaragua in the 1970s, forms much of the basis of this view. Such abuses of government are doubtless no less common in LDCs than in the United States or Japan.

But if there is waste in government procurement in some areas, there are others where, for lack of funds, governments have been too miserly in appropriating funds, particularly with regard to provision for maintenance costs for upkeep of the public-sector capital stock and for many vital operating expenses. The phenomenon is aptly characterized by Heller:

> In Colombia, new tarmac roads have suffered rapid and premature deterioration for lack of maintenance. Throughout West Africa, many new schools have opened without qualified teachers, educational materials, or equipment. Agricultural projects are often starved for extension workers, fertilizer, or seeds. In the Sahel, pastoral wells constructed for livestock projects have fallen into disrepair. In Bolivia, doctors are often stranded at rural health centers for lack of gasoline for their vehicles.[9]

Underfinance of such recurrent costs is pervasive across countries. This pattern is exacerbated by policies of aid donors who strongly support capital projects and as a matter of policy are reluctant to support recurrent costs of these projects. As a result, painfully accumulated public-sector capital stock tends to deteriorate rapidly, requiring in the end not incremental maintenance outlays but expensive new public works. Few countries are in a position to expand public savings by further compressing this category of recurrent expenditures.

Many social scientists in industrial countries believe that the potential is great for expanding public savings in LDCs through reduction of military expenditures. Indeed for low-income developing countries as a group, including oil exporters and centrally planned economies, military spending per capita in 1979 was 180 percent higher than per-capita government spending on education and health combined. For middle-income LDCs, however, per-capita military spending was 78 percent of per-capita outlays on education and health.[10] Here we can make no judgments about "appropriate" levels of military spending, whether in developed or developing countries. The fact remains that some countries, including developing countries, do perceive or actually face threats to their national security

9. Heller, "Under-Financing . . . Costs," p. 38.
10. World Bank, *World Development Report 1982* (Washington, D.C. 1982), p. 156.

from time to time: in 1980 alone Thailand, Iran, Afghanistan, Vietnam, Somalia, Ethiopia, Chad, Uganda, and Kampuchea, among others, suffered incursions of foreign troops, for reasons that some might applaud and others dislike. It is also true that many countries, some LDCs included, maintain large, well-equipped military forces even in the absence of any short- or long-term external threats, primarily for domestic political purposes.

In any case it is not so clear that most developing countries could easily achieve significant increases in public savings through reductions in military spending. Table 12–4 furnishes information for 1979 on military spending as a percent of GDP in 122 countries, including over 90 LDCs

TABLE 12–4   Military Expenditures as % of GNP in Developed and Developing Countries, 1979

Military expenditures as % of GNP	GNP per capita				
	Less than $200	$200–$499	$500–$999	$1000–$2999	$3000 and over
10% and over	None	Yemen (Aden) Egypt	Jordan Yemen (Sanaa)	Qatar Israel Saudi Arabia Soviet Union	
5%–9.99%	Ethiopia	China Somalia Zimbabwe Tanzania Zambia Pakistan	Korea, North Morocco	Iraq Korea, South	Bulgaria Singapore Germany, East Greece United Arab Emirates Poland United States
2%–4.99%	Burma Mali Upper Volta Burundi India	Kenya Zaire Madagascar Indonesia Sudan and five others	Congo Peru Thailand Nicaragua Nigeria Bolivia and three others	Turkey Malaysia South Africa Ivory Coast Uruguay Chile Argentina and three others	Czechoslovakia United Kingdom Hungary France Romania Kuwait Netherlands Sweden and nine others
1%–1.99%	Bangladesh Malawi Rwanda	Central African Republic Sierra Leone Cameroon Liberia	Honduras Philippines El Salvador Uganda and three others	Cyprus Ecuador Tunisia Venezuela	Canada Spain Ireland New Zealand and two others
Less than 1%	Nepal Sri Lanka Gambia	Niger Lesotho São Tompé & Principé	Guatemala Colombia Ghana	Brazil Panama Mexico Costa Rica and three others	Japan Luxembourg Trinidad & Tobago Iceland

Source: U.S. Arms Control and Disarmament Agency, World Military Expenditures and Arms Transfers, 1970–1979 (Washington, D.C., 1982), p. 6.

for which recent data is available. Military spending was less than 2 percent of GNP in only a third of the high-income countries, and also about a third of the LDCs. Another third of high-income countries spent more than 5 percent of GNP for military purposes, and a sizable number (seventeen) of LDCs in the table had military spending greater than 5 percent, a heavy burden for any nation to carry. Several countries with a high ratio of military spending, however, are among the poorest LDCs, including Ethiopia, Somalia, Tanzania, and Pakistan. Although there is little a priori basis for concluding that any country could easily reduce its military spending, there are perhaps several in which compression of these outlays may at least represent an option for increasing public savings. Most of these can be found in the category of countries that spend between 2 and 5 percent of GNP for military purposes, and which face no clear external threats to national security. While sharp reductions in the share of GNP spent on military forces may in fact be devoutly sought by the seventeen-odd developing countries spending more than 5 percent of GNP for this purpose, nations in this category may perceive little latitude for doing so, as many have experienced armed conflict with neighboring countries since 1970.

Interest Payments

A major budgetary cost for many LDCs is interest on government debt: in countries included in Table 12–3 this item ranges from no less than 2 percent to as high as 26 percent of total recurrent spending, with a central tendency of about 11 percent. Since outside of OPEC countries recurrent costs run about 80 percent of total government expenditures in both the poorest and the middle-income countries, interest costs are typically about 8 percent of the budget, a figure not materially different from that of the United States in the 1970s.

Interest obligations arise from past government budget deficits that are financed by either (or both) internal or external borrowing. Interest payments on foreign borrowing have grown rapidly in several LDCs since the early 1970s, owing to the surge in external commercial borrowings and to generally higher world interest rates since 1972, both discussed in Chapter 14. Because interest on government debt reflects past decisions, both on deficit finance and external borrowing, this item of expenditure is difficult to reduce: even in the absence of further deficits and a moratorium on external borrowing over a several-year period, outlays for this purpose cannot be easily compressed in the short term. On the contrary, prospects are that through the 1980s a larger number of LDCs will be more heavily involved in external borrowing than in the two previous decades. Interest costs as a proportion of government expenditures are likely to rise in many nations.

Subsidies

A variety of subsidies account for substantial shares of recurrent expenditures in LDCs: the proportion ranges from 5 to 39 percent in the poorer countries included in Table 12–3, and from 7 to 55 percent in middle-income countries, with central tendencies about 25 and 30 percent respectively. These figures do not include subsidies some governments classify, with reason, as capital expenditures.

Recurrent budget subsidies take a variety of forms;[11] the most common are those for consumption of food. Like Indonesia, Sri Lanka provided heavy subsidies on rice consumption from 1960 to 1979; Colombia has at various times given substantial subsidies to consumers of food, as have Egypt and India. The usual mechanism is that of distributing price-controlled foods through state-owned entities and absorbing losses in food distribution through budgetary transfers to these entities. Another subsidy pervasive in oil-producing countries is that on domestic consumption of refined oil products, discussed in a later section. Other items where budgetary subsidies have been common include those provided for rural electrification (Malaysia and Philippines), contraceptive devices (Indonesia), air travel (Pakistan, for travel between East and West Pakistan before 1971), bank interest payments on savings deposits (Indonesia), and urban bus services (Colombia, Indonesia, and perhaps twenty-five other countries.)

In virtually all countries enjoying budgetary subsidies the stated purpose has usually been that of income redistribution. For foods, especially grains, the argument appears plausible, even if the ultimate effect is not always what was intended. The role of many other subsidies in securing goals of income redistribution is less clear, however, as we shall see. Whatever the ultimate impact of budget subsidies on income distribution, it is clear that in many countries substantial sums are involved, and that efforts to remove or reduce them in order to expand public savings meet with strong resistance virtually everywhere. Riots following reduction of food subsidies have occurred in numerous countries, including Sri Lanka, Egypt, and Turkey; severe social disturbances have followed reduction of subsidies on gasoline in Indonesia, Colombia, and Thailand when coupled with increases in urban bus fares. For these reasons governments often tend to view proposals for reducing subsidies with even more reservations than proposals for tax increases.

Intergovernmental Transfers

Transfers from central to subnational governments are conventionally treated as recurrent expenditures, even though subnational governments (provinces, departments, counties, municipalities) may use the proceeds for capital formation. However, some countries, such as Indonesia, classify

---

11. Subsidization of favored activities need not take the form of subsidies provided directly from the government budget. Indeed the prevailing forms of subsidies, in developed and developing countries alike, are those involving no obvious (or visible) budgetary costs. Purchase of capital equipment is subsidized when interest rates are subject to low ceilings; food consumption may be subsidized without such subsidies' appearing in the government budget merely by requiring state-owned enterprises to sell food at below cost and financing the losses through other activities of the enterprise.

some transfers as capital spending and others as consumption. Note again the problem of making international comparisons when classification standards are not uniform across countries.

Table 12–3 shows that transfers to subnational governments (including revenue sharing) constitute a sizable proportion of recurrent spending in some countries (India, Indonesia, Korea) and a very small share in others (Bolivia, Malaysia, Zaire). In a few cases the small share of such transfers is due to the fact that subnational governments have access to very rich sources of revenue. This is true for Bolivia, where oil-producing provinces receive large oil royalties, as well as the Federation of Malaysia, where the East Malaysian governments of Sabah and Sarawak earn substantial tax revenues from the export of tropical timber found there. In most unitary states, such as Argentina and Chile, virtually all government affairs at all levels are run from the capital, and subnational units of government have few responsibilities to go with their small sources of local revenue.

Elsewhere, including many federal states, transfers of funds from the central government to subnational units is essential because the center has monopolized the most productive sources of tax revenue. In most cases this monopoly is due to technical reasons: national governments impose income taxes because subnational governments lack the resources and skills required to administer such a complex tax, and could not do so effectively even given administrative resources because of the ease with which the income tax base can migrate within a country. Similarly, the major source of tax revenue for most countries—import duties—must necessarily remain a central government resource.

Evidently, then, there are few easy ways to reduce most types of recurrent expenditure to achieve higher public savings. Earlier we concluded that there are also few easy ways in which tax revenues can be expanded to serve the same purpose. Finance ministers are responsible for both. Finance ministers who over extended periods have met with some success in holding the line against rising current expenditures and securing robust revenue growth tend to be as unpopular as they are rare. Indeed in some countries over some periods an effective finance minister may have contributed more to income growth than all the development planning apparatus described in Chapters 5 and 6. The far-reaching incentives and distributional and stabilization effects of fiscal policy enhance the finance minister's key role in development.

Taxes and Private Capital Formation

Fiscal policy influences capital formation in the private sector in two main ways: (1) by its effects on both the capacity and the incentive to save in the private sector, and (2) by its effects on incentives to invest in private projects. Taxes impinge more directly, but not necessarily more importantly, on both sets of incentives than do government expenditures, and will be our prime focus here.

Taxes and Private Savings

Taxation of households and businesses is but one of many factors that affect their savings decisions. A proper assessment of the role played by taxes requires an understanding of other determinants of saving, including the level and volatility of household income, the relative share of labor and capital income in private sector income, as well as the role of financial policy. We have already seen that various theories of savings behavior assist in sorting out the prime deteminants of private savings.

An increase in taxes will come partly out of consumption and partly out of savings, but the relative effects of taxes in reducing consumption and savings is a matter of some dispute. Some studies of cross-country savings behavior suggest that increases in taxes in LDCs merely reduce private-sector consumption with little or no effect on savings. Other studies conclude that there is a high degree of substitutability between private savings and taxes: one cited in Chapter 11 found that an additional $1 of public savings in LDCs tends to reduce private savings by at least 50¢. In this case the truth probably lies slightly closer to the latter interpretation. And different taxes will clearly have a differential impact on the capacity to save. While heavy sales or excise taxes on highly price-elastic items of luxury consumption will curtail rates of growth of consumption for such items, heavy taxes on corporate income may come in large part at the expense of business savings that might have been plowed back into company investment.

Where upper-income groups have a high propensity to consume, as has been often argued to hold for elites in many Latin American countries, increased taxes on them may have little impact on private savings. But where the same groups display strong accumulative characteristics, as many argue is true for some ethnic minorities in Southeast Asia, higher taxes may have relatively little effect on consumption and substantial effects on their savings. Further, heavier taxes on foreign natural resource firms will ordinarily have minimal negative impact on availability of private domestic savings unless such firms have local joint-venture partners and cut their dividends to them in response to reduced profitability.

There is less uncertainty concerning the effects of different *forms* of taxes on *incentives to save,* but even here offsetting considerations are present. Taxes on consumption probably impinge less severely on private savings than do taxes on income in most developing societies. Perhaps the only exception to this statement arises when households save primarily for later purchase of items subject to heavy consumption taxes. Some observers have argued that this motivation for savings is common in many low-income LDCs, where the nature of extended-family relationships makes household savings difficult. In some societies households with incomes above subsistence share resources with poorer households within the family group to help them meet subsistence needs. This pattern is characteristic of many African countries and of many parts of rural Asia. Under such circumstances household savings is largely devoted to purchase of prized durable goods, such as transistor radios, bicycles, and sewing machines. In developed countries and middle-income LDCs these are typically viewed as consumer goods that are good candidates for taxation. But it may well be that in some countries heavy taxation of such items primarily reduces incentives to save. It is even questionable whether products such as bicycles, sewing machines, and even small outboard motors should be viewed as consumer goods in many low-income societies. Purchase of a bicycle or a small outboard may allow a rural family to market garden produce and fish more easily; sewing machines are ordinarily bought not for the occasional fashioning of a prom dress or a Halloween costume but to generate extra income for the household.

On balance, consumption-based taxes are probably more favorable for growth in private savings than are income-based taxes. Virtually all LDCs implement aims of consumption taxation through such indirect means as sales and excise taxes. These levies, while not inherently regressive, are often perceived to be so. This perception has led many tax reformers to argue that direct taxes on consumption should instead be employed in LDCs. Under a direct consumption tax, taxpayers would annually report total consumption as well as income. Consumption below that thought minimally necessary for an adequate living standard would be exempt, and any consumption above that level would be taxed at rates that rise progressively with total consumption. If such a levy could be administered it would stimulate savings,[12] since a household could reduce tax liability by not spending. Such taxes have been proposed for India, Guyana, and Sri Lanka, and actually enacted in India in the 1950s. The Indian experiment was short-lived, however, as the tax involved such onerous informational requirements and arbitrary definitions of consumption (recall the sewing machine example) that it proved impossible to administer. Indeed, administrative problems, both real and imaginary, of direct consumption taxes have precluded their adoption even in industrial societies, where the implications for savings and capital formation have made them increasingly attractive to fiscal specialists, most notably in the United States and Britain.

Taxes can affect savings incentives in other ways. To the extent that national savings rates are responsive to the after-tax rate of return on savings (a question examined in the next chapter), heavy taxes on income from capital (dividends, interest) reduce the volume of private savings available for investment. And to the extent that people save mainly to finance retirement, social security taxes can also reduce private and aggregate national savings if the social security system is financed on a pay-as-you-go basis (that is, from current revenues), as in the United States, Colombia, Chile, the Philippines, and India. Under a social security system financed in this manner it is argued that individuals covered by the system will reduce their savings in anticipation of receiving future social security benefits; but there will be no corresponding increase in public savings because the

---

12. The statement that substitution of consumption taxes for income taxes would stimulate private savings is not correct in circumstances where individuals accumulate savings only for the purpose of future consumption within their lifetimes.

social security taxes paid by those covered now are not set aside and invested, but rather are used to pay benefits to those already retired.

This is an important point, because many proposals have been made—and some enacted—for social security systems in Asia and Latin America in order to help *increase* the national savings rate. The argument that social security systems can foster domestic savings is correct only under two circumstances, both relatively uncommon in LDCs. First, social security systems that operate as true retirement funds can clearly help mobilize capital resources provided the funds are invested in projects with an adequate marginal rate of return. Under such systems, called the provident-fund approach, the taxes collected from those covered are invested by the government in assets that earn returns; payments are made to retirees out of these returns rather than (as under the pay-as-you-go system) from taxes collected by those still working. Under this approach, used for some workers in Malaysia and a few other countries, any decline in the private savings of those paying social security taxes is largely offset by a concomitant rise in public savings. But the provident-fund approach is not widespread.

But even the pay-as-you-go system can increase national savings rates in its early years of operation if benefits are denied to those who retired before the system was implemented, and if social security tax rates are set high enough to cover benefit payments for the first decade or so. This is because in the early years after establishment the number of workers covered is large relative to the number of retirees, so that disbursement of benefits is small compared to inflow of revenues. Therefore a government seeking new temporary sources of public savings could enact a pay-as-you-go system for social security that would serve this purpose for a few years. Sooner or later, however, such a system would tend to reduce overall domestic savings, though not necessarily by as much as the social security taxes paid by covered workers.

Taxes and Private Investment

If a country's tax system operates materially to reduce private savings, it will therefore tend to curtail private investment. Beyond that effect, taxes can affect both the amount and allocation of private domestic investment undertaken out of any given volume of private capital available for investment.

In spite of exchange controls and similar restrictions, capital is to some extent mobile across international boundaries. If there are opportunities for earning returns abroad that promise higher after-tax returns than available in a particular developing country, domestic capital will tend to flow to these opportunities. A critical factor determining after-tax returns in a given country is of course the nature of taxes on capital there. Suppose, for example, that owners of capital in the Philippines can secure, on the average, before-tax returns equal to 15 percent of their investments and that capital income is subject in that country to a 50 percent tax. After-tax returns are then 7.5 percent. The same funds invested in well-developed capital markets in Hong Kong might obtain only a 12 percent return there, where capital is less scarce, but are taxed at only, say, 15 percent. The after-tax return in Hong Kong is therefore 10.2 percent. The difference of 2.7 percent in after-tax returns may be large enough to induce movement of Philippines savings to Hong Kong. In general, countries that attempt to impose substantially heavier taxes on capital income may well experience outflows of domestic savings to countries employing lower tax rates on capital, quite apart from the type of "capital flight" from developing to developed countries often observed in countries experiencing severe domestic political turmoil or exchange-rate uncertainties.

Indeed there is no shortage of low-tax foreign opportunities facing domestic savers in LDCs. "Tax havens" such as Panama and the Bahamas in the Caribbean have been attractive to Latin American investors throughout the 1960s and 1970s; Hong Kong and Singapore financial markets garner substantial inflows of savings from other Asian countries. Until Lebanon was first racked by civil war in the 1970s that country offered tax rates and financial services that induced many African and Mideast savers to invest there, rather than at home or in Europe and the United States. Increasingly, enterprises from countries such as India, with relatively high taxes on capital income, have begun to invest in other developing countries where after-tax returns are higher than at home.

Most countries have recognized that capital is fairly mobile across national boundaries and have sought to keep taxes on capital income from reaching levels much above that prevailing worldwide. This is evident from inspection of rates of corporation income tax prevailing in most LDCs. In Latin America corporate tax rates are typically found in a band of from 25 to 40 percent (versus 46 percent in the United States). In Southeast Asia corporate tax rates other than those of Hong Kong cluster in a narrow range of from 35 to 45 percent.

Countries have sought to impede the outward mobility of capital through such devices as controls on movement of foreign exchange, imposition of domestic taxes on worldwide income of residents, and other devices. Flourishing business in "tax haven" countries, coupled with very large investment holdings of LDC citizens in the United States, Switzerland, Hong Kong, and Singapore, are ample testament to the limited effectiveness of such controls.

Partly in order to stem capital outflow, and also to direct private investment into priority areas, such as basic industry, exports, or backward regions, many LDC governments selectively offer substantial tax incentives to domestic investors. The two main types of incentives are income tax "holidays," wherein approved investments are exempted from income tax obligation for specified periods ranging from three to ten years, and tax credits for investment, wherein a government allows an investor to subtract some portion of initial investment—usually 20 to 25 percent—from his income tax liabilities. These types of incentive for domestic investment have on rare occasions led to the desired results, but use of such devices suffers from a number of limitations, discussed more fully in Chapter 14.

Income Distribution

As indicated in Chapter 4, a basic tenet of economic policy in many LDCs has been the mitigation of extreme income inequality. For decades developed and developing countries alike have sought to use the fiscal system, particularly taxation, to redress income inequalities generated by the operation of the private market. Social philosophers from John Stuart Mill and the eminent nineteenth-century Chilean historian Francisco Encino, to John Rawls in the 1970s, have sought to establish a philosophical basis for income redistribution, primarily through progressive taxes. Karl Marx also favored steeply progressive taxes in bourgeois societies, but for reasons other than income redistribution. Rather, in Marx's view, heavy taxes on capitalists were essential for speeding the decline of the capitalist state and its replacement by a socialist order.

There is no scientific basis for determining the "optimal" degree of income redistribution in any society. And across developing countries different views prevail as to the "ideal" distribution of income. But in virtually all countries the notion of "fiscal equity" permeates discussions of budgetary operations. In the overwhelming majority of countries fiscal equity is typically defined materialistically, in terms of the impact of tax and expenditure policy on the distribution of economic well-being. Progressive taxes, those that bear more heavily on better-off citizens than on poor households, and expenditures whose benefits are concentrated on the least advantaged, are viewed as more equitable than regressive taxes and expenditures. However, we shall see that the materialistic view of fiscal equity is not the only one that affects thinking on budget matters in developing societies.

Taxation and Equity

On the tax side of the budget, the materialistic conception of equity requires that most taxes be based on ability to pay. Ability to pay can be measured by income, consumption, wealth, or some combination of all three. Clearly, individuals with higher incomes over their life span have greater ability to pay taxes, quite apart from the moral question of whether they should do so. Indeed the redistributive impact of taxation is almost always expressed in terms of its effects on incomes. However, philosophers from the time of Hobbes have argued that consumption furnishes a better index of ability to pay than income; in this view tax obligations are best geared to what people "take out" of society (consume) rather than what they "put into" society (as measured by income). In addition relative wealth could be employed as a measure of ability to pay: households with large wealth would seem to have higher taxpaying ability than households with the same income but lower wealth.

In practice developing countries have employed all three indices of "ability" in fashioning tax systems. Personal and corporate income taxes employ income as the indicator; sales taxes and customs duties are indirect assessments of taxes on consumption; property taxes are geared to wealth as a measure of ability to pay. But ability to pay is not the exclusive guide to assessment of taxes in all countries. Religious and cultural values often provide other bases for establishing tax liability. Nevertheless most societies do largely define equity in taxation as requiring taxation on the basis of ability to pay, and this is commonly interpreted to mean progressivity. At a minimum equity is usually assumed to require avoidance of regressive taxes whenever possible. There are a number of instruments that have been employed to secure greater progressivity in principle if not in practice; all suffer from limitations to one degree or another.

Tax Equity and the *Zakat*

Consider, for example, the *Zakat*, a form of land tax levied in many Muslim or predominantly Muslim societies, including Pakistan, Malaysia, and formerly parts of Sumatra in Indonesia. According to a materialistic principle of tax equity, a land tax would be imposed on the basis of land value, or the value of income that a given parcel can produce. Therefore for two otherwise identical adjacent parcels, one irrigated and the other unirrigated, the owner of the former would pay more tax as the greater productivity of his land gives him greater ability to pay. But as the *Zakat* is assessed in Pakistan, principles of equity in land taxes call for lower taxes on the irrigated parcel, on the reasoning that the owner of the unirrigated parcel owes directly any prosperity he may enjoy to rain sent by the Almighty, whereas the owner of the irrigated land owes his larger crops to his own labors in constructing irrigation canals and should not on that account be penalized with higher taxes. While by 1980 the *Zakat* was still a relatively minor source of tax revenue even in Pakistan, the above illustration does serve to remind that the philosophical and theological underpinnings of economic policy are not invariant across all societies, particularly those as diverse as those in the developing world.

Personal Income Taxes The most obvious device for securing greater progressivity is that employed most extensively in developed countries: steeply progressive rates under the personal income tax. In some countries in some periods, nominal or legal marginal income tax rates have reached very high levels even at relatively low incomes (less than $1000 per household). Thus, for example, tax rates applicable to any income in excess of $1000 in Indonesia in 1967 reached 75 percent, largely because tax brackets were not indexed to rapid inflation; in Algeria in the 1960s marginal income taxes on all income in excess of $10,000 was subject to marginal tax rates of nearly 100 percent; Tanzania imposed top marginal rates of 95 percent as late as 1981.

While in most LDCs marginal income tax rates are considerably lower than the examples above, some countries do attempt to impose rates that rival those of the United States before 1982, when the maximum marginal tax rate was 70 percent. Although Egypt, Nigeria, and Zambia have progressive income taxes involving top marginal tax rates of about 75 percent, countries such as Brazil, Colombia, Malaysia, Mexico, Panama, Singapore, and Taiwan generally hold maximum marginal rates to 55 percent or slightly less.

If the tax administration machinery functioned well, and if capital were immobile among countries, the pattern of actual tax payments by high-income taxpayers would resemble the legal, or theoretical, patterns described above. In fact taxes actually collected as a percent of income ("effective tax rates") in most countries fall well short of theoretical liabilities for several reasons.

Faced with high income tax rates, taxpayers everywhere tend to react in three ways: (1) they evade taxes by concealing income, particularly capital income not subject to withholding arrangements; (2) they avoid taxes by altering economic behavior to reduce tax liability, whether by supplying fewer labor services, shipping capital to tax havens abroad, or hiring lawyers to find loopholes in the tax law; (3) they bribe tax assessors to accept false returns.

For all of these reasons, achievement of substantial income redistribution through progressive income taxes has proven difficult in all countries, including the United States and Scandinavia, where tax rates are among the world's most progressive. Tax avoidance is the favored avenue for reducing tax liability in the United States, where use of the other methods can result in imprisonment. But where tax enforcement is relatively weak, particularly where criminal penalties for evasion are absent (virtually all LDCs) and tax officials have been deeply underpaid, as in Bolivia, Colombia, Ghana, and Indonesia in the 1970s, to name but a few countries, tax evasion and bribery are more commonly utilized, and the scope for substantial redistribution through the income tax is even more limited.

Notwithstanding these problems, a nontrivial share of the income of the wealthiest members of society is caught in the income tax net in some developing countries. Revenues from personal income tax collections in countries such as Columbia, Korea, and Chile are as high as 15 percent of total taxes, and run between 5 and 10 percent of the total in a few others. In virtually all developing countries the entirety of such taxes is collected from the top 20 percent of the income distribution. This means, of course, that the very presence of an income tax, even one imposed at proportional rather than progressive rates, tends to reduce income inequality. Income taxes, together with taxes on luxury consumption, constitute about the only feasible means of approaching income redistribution goals through the tax side of the budget.

Taxes on Luxury Consumption In view of the difficulties of securing significant redistribution through income taxes, many countries have sought to employ heavy indirect taxes on luxury consumption as a means of enhancing the progressivity of the tax system. Efforts to achieve this goal usually center on internal indirect taxes, such as sales taxes, and on customs duties on imports. For reasons discussed earlier excise taxes on such sumptuary items as tobacco and alcohol are good revenue sources, but tend to be sharply regressive in virtually all countries save the very poorest, where pervasive poverty allows little indulgence in vices of any kind.

Several developing countries have found that, provided tax rates are kept to enforceable levels, high rates of internal sales taxes on luxury goods and services coupled with lower taxes on less income-elastic items can contribute, at least in a small way, to progressivity in the tax system. For revenue purposes countries typically impose basic rates of sales tax on nonluxuries at between 4 and 8 percent of manufacturer's value. This is equivalent to retail taxes of between 2 and 4 percent because taxes imposed at this level exclude wholesale and retail margins. Food (except that consumed in restaurants) is almost always exempted from any sales tax intended to promote redistributive goals. In LDCs exemption of food by itself renders most sales taxes at least faintly progressive, given the high proportion (up to 40 percent in many middle income LDCs) of income of poor households spent on food. Sales taxes involving luxury rates of between 20 and 30 percent at the manufacturer's level have been found to be workable in many LDCs, including Colombia, Chile, Taiwan, and Korea.

The redistributive potential of sales tax rates differentiated in this way is, however, limited by the same administrative and compliance constraints standing in the way of heavier use of income taxation in LDCs. While sales taxes are not as difficult to administer as income taxes, they do not collect themselves. A manufacturer's sales tax system employing three or even four rates may be administratively feasible in most countries, even when the highest rate approaches 40 percent. Rates much higher than that, or reliance on a profusion of rates (over fifteen in Jamaica, over twenty in Chile from 1960 to 1970) in an attempt to "fine-tune" the tax, leads to substantial incentives and opportunities for tax evasion.

While internal indirect taxes, such as sales taxes, can contribute to income redistribution goals without causing serious misallocation of resources, the same cannot be said for use of customs duties for this purpose. Sales taxes are imposed on all taxable goods without regard to origin, including goods produced domestically as well as imported items. Tariffs apply only to imported goods. Virtually all countries, developed and developing, utilize customs duties to protect existing domestic industry. Developing countries in particular employ customs duties as the principal means of encouraging domestic industry to produce goods that were formerly imported. This strategy, called "import substitution," is examined at length in Chapter 16.

Deliberate policies to encourage import substitution through the use of high protective tariffs may, under certain conditions, lead to results sought by policy-makers. But accidental import substitution arises when tariffs are used for purposes other than protection and is unlikely to have positive results, except in rare instances. Many countries use high tariffs to achieve heavier taxation of luxury consumption. Often heavy tariffs are imposed on luxury items that are not only not produced domestically but for which there is no intention of encouraging domestic production. Thus many Latin American and some Asian countries have levied customs tariffs of

100 percent to 150 percent of value on such appliances as electric knives, hair dryers, sporting goods, video-cassette recorders, and mechanical toys. For most countries these items are clearly highly income-elastic, and are apt candidates for luxury taxation.

However, efforts to tax luxuries through high customs duties leads to unintended—and almost irresistible—incentives for domestic production or assembly of such products. In virtually all countries save the very poorest, alert domestic and foreign entrepreneurs have been quick to seize upon such opportunities. By the time that local assembly operations are established, they can usually make a politically convincing case that the duties should be retained to enable local production to continue, even when value added domestically is as low as 10 percent. Such operations, if subject to local sales taxes at all, usually succeed in being taxed at the basic rate of tax, usually 5 to 10 percent. By relying on tariffs for luxury taxation, the government not only ultimately forgoes the revenues it previously collected from duties on luxury goods, but the very aims of luxury taxation are severely undermined as well.

If, instead, higher luxury rates on imports are imposed under a sales tax collected on both imports and any domestic production that may develop, unintended import substitution can be avoided. The use of import tariffs for luxury taxation—indeed for any purpose other than providing protection to domestic industry—is one illustration of the general problem of using one economic policy instrument (tariffs) to achieve more than one purpose (protection, luxury taxation, and revenues). Reliance on import duties for revenue purposes is subject to the same pitfalls just discussed: if it is desired to increase government revenues from imports, a 10 percent sales tax applied both to imports and any future domestic production will yield just as much revenue as a 10 percent import duty, without leading to accidental protection.

Corporate and Property Taxes: The Incidence Problem   Income taxes on domestic corporations and property taxes are often mentioned as possible methods for securing income redistribution through the budget. It is true that corporate income is ultimately received, through dividends and capital gains, almost exclusively by the upper 5–10 percent of the income distribution. It is also true that ownership of wealth, which in LDCs largely takes the form of land, tends to be even more concentrated than income. But efforts to secure significant fiscal redistribution through heavier taxes on domestic corporations and property taxes are, to a greater extent in developing than in developed countries, limited both by administrative and economic realities.

Administrative problems bedevil efforts to collect income taxes from domestic firms to at least as great an extent as for income taxes on individuals. For this reason, in many countries where corporate taxes on local firms have been important, as much as two-thirds to three-fourths of non-oil corporate taxes flow from state-owned firms (Indonesia, Pakistan), not from private firms owned by high-income individuals. Taxes on land should be subject to less severe administrative problems, since this is an asset that cannot be easily hidden. However, valuation of land for tax purposes has proven difficult even in Canada and the United States; it is more difficult in developing countries. Other than Colombia, few LDCs have been able to assess property at anything approaching its true value.

Economic realities hinder efforts to achieve greater progressivity in the tax system through heavier use of corporate and land taxes, because of the tendency of taxes to burden groups other than those intended. This is the incidence problem.

The *incidence* of a tax refers to its ultimate impact: not who actually pays the tax, but whose incomes are finally affected by the tax when all economic agents have adjusted their behavior in response to a tax. The point of incidence is not usually the point of initial impact. Taxes on domestic corporations may reduce the income not only of capitalists, who might shift their investment patterns to reduce taxation, but of workers they employ or consumers as well; taxes on land and improvements may not in the end much reduce the incomes of landholders, but rather may also be reflected in higher prices paid by consumers. Indeed under some plausible conditions higher taxes on luxury consumption may not always be fully reflected in higher prices paid by high-income consumers.

The basic implications of incidence issues may be illuminated by a simple application of incidence analysis to the corporation income tax. Consider a profit-maximizing company that has no significant monopoly power in the domestic market. If taxes on the company's income are increased in 1982, then after-tax returns to its shareholders in 1982 will be reduced by the full amount of the tax. Thus the short-run incidence of the tax is clearly on shareholders. Since everywhere shareholders are concentrated in higher income groups, the tax will be progressive in the short run. If capital were immobile, unable to leave the corporate sector, the long run incidence of the tax would also rest on shareholders and the tax would be progressive in the long run as well. But in the long run capital can move out of the corporate sector. To the extent that capital is mobile domestically, but is not free to cross national boundaries, the corporate tax will still be progressive in the long run. Capital remaining in the corporate sector will have its returns reduced by the tax; untaxed owners of capital employed outside the corporate sector will suffer a reduction in returns as well, because movements of capital from the taxed corporate sector will drive down the rate of return in the nontaxed sector. The corporate tax reduces returns to capital throughout the economy; all capital owners suffer, and the long-run incidence is again progressive.

However, no LDC is a completely closed economy; indeed we have seen that capital tends to be somewhat mobile internationally as well. To the extent that capital is mobile across national borders, and to the extent that higher returns are available in other countries, domestic capital will migrate to escape higher corporate taxes. But as capital leaves an economy, both new investment and replacement investment and, ultimately, output will be curtailed. Prices of products produced with domestic capital will therefore rise. In this way an increase in corporate taxes may be borne by domestic consumers, or by domestic workers whose incomes are reduced when production is curtailed and done with less capital. The corporate tax may therefore be regressive (worsen the income distribution) in the long run. The degree of regressivity will depend on whether consumption of low-income groups is more or less capital-intensive, and on the relative position in the income distribution of workers losing their jobs. In the end capital owners may suffer no significant decline in their incomes. While there are other plausible conditions under which an increase in the corporation income tax may not result in greater relative burdens on capitalists, the scenario outlined above is sufficient to illustrate that the intentions of redistributive tax policy may often be thwarted by the workings of the economy. Clearly a priori assumptions that all taxes intended to burden wealthy households will ultimately be paid by them cannot be easily defended.

Limited Effects of Redistribution Policy   The foregoing discussion suggests that while some tax instruments may achieve income redistribution in LDCs, the opportunities for doing so are limited in most countries. This conclusion is supported by a large number of empirical studies on the question. With few exceptions these show that inability to administer personal income taxes effectively, failure to utilize opportunities for heavier taxes on luxury consumption, overreliance on revenue-productive but regressive excise taxes, and the inclusion of food in sales taxes, all combine to reduce significantly the redistributive impact of LDC tax systems. By and large LDC tax systems tend to produce a tax burden that is roughly proportional across income groups, with some tendency for progressivity at the very top of the income scale. As a result the very wealthy do pay a somewhat greater proportion of their income in taxes than the poor, but the poor still pay substantial taxes: at least 10 percent of their income in many cases studied (Argentina, urban Brazil, Colombia, Jamaica, and a half dozen others).[13] This is the predominant pattern even in those countries (Colombia, Jamaica, Tanzania, Chile before 1970) that have placed strong policy emphasis on use of tax tools to reduce income inequality. One can only conclude that in the absence of such efforts, the after-tax distribution of income may have been even more unequal. This consideration suggests that tax reform intended to reduce income inequality, while difficult to implement and often disappointing in its results, is not a futile exercise in LDCs, and may indeed serve the purpose of at least not having taxes make the poor worse off.

Expenditures and Equity

The limitations of tax policy suggest that if the budget is to serve redistributive purposes the primary emphasis must be on expenditure policy. Indeed where redistribution through expenditures has been a high priority

13. Many of these studies have been summarized in Richard M. Bird and Luc Henry De-Wulf, "Taxation and Income Distribution in Latin America: A Critical View of Empirical Studies," *International Monetary Fund Staff Papers* 20 (November 1975): 639–82.

of governments the results have been generally encouraging. The effects of government expenditure on income distribution are even more difficult to measure than in the case of taxes. But the evidence available—both qualitative and quantitative—strongly indicates that in developing countries budget expenditures may transfer very substantial resources to lower income households, in some cases as much as 50 percent of their income. And the pattern of benefits is progressive, contributing a much higher fraction of income to the poor households than to those in the upper reaches of the income distribution. One of the authors found that in Malaysia in the late 1960s the combined effect of taxes and recurrent government consumption expenditures was to transfer about 5 percent of GNP from the two highest income classes to the two lowest income groups, with more than three-quarters of the transfer going to the poor. This figure understates the actual extent of the redistributive impact of expenditures since they do not include the effects of public investment, which was perhaps the most important tool of fiscal redistribution in Malaysia in 1968.[14] A team headed by another of the authors found that in Indonesia in 1980 the tax system was only slightly progressive. But the expenditure side of the budget, with its emphasis on food subsidies and primary education, was markedly pro-poor: benefits from government expenditure were slightly more than 50 percent of the income of the poorest income group. Similarly, an exhaustive study of the net incidence of the Chilean budget for 1969 shows that while the tax system had virtually no effect on income distribution, government expenditures favored the poor: the lowest income groups received only about 7.5 percent of national income, but about 15–18 percent of the benefits from government expenditure.[15]

Obviously not all items of government expenditure are effective in reducing income inequality. Some, like interest payments on government debt, have the opposite effect because interest income is concentrated in upper income groups. But it is not difficult to identify those categories of budget outlays that tend to have the most marked effects on the incomes of the poor. Public expenditures on primary, but not university, education tend strongly to reduce income inequality (Chapter 9). Government spending for public health programs (particularly water supply, sanitation, nutritional programs, and rural health clinics) also often has a clearly progressive impact (Chapter 10). Although many poor people live in such huge cities as Jakarta, São Paulo, Mexico City, Nairobi, and Calcutta, in most developing countries most of the poorest people tend to live in rural areas and wealthy people tend to live in urban areas. Hence programs that reallocate government spending to rural areas (irrigation programs, secondary roads, erosion control) tend to reduce income inequality overall, although large landlords may be the primary beneficiaries in some cases.

Subsidies for consumption of basic foodstuffs also can result in substantial redistribution, provided subsidy programs for food are not accompa-

---

14. Donald R. Snodgrass, "The Fiscal System as an Income Redistributor in West Malaysia," *Public Finance* 29, no. 1 (January 1974): 56–76.
15. Alejandro Foxley, Eduardo Aninat, and J. P. Arellano, *Redistributive Effects of Government Programs* (Oxford: Pergamon Press, 1980), Chapter 6.

nied by oppressive price controls on production of food by poor farmers. Subsidies to subnational governments are often used to finance provision of basic human needs, such as water, sewerage, education and health services, all of which have benefits concentrated in lower income classes. Housing subsidies favor the poor less frequently since many programs for housing subsidies (Indonesia, Ghana, Pakistan) are in reality largely confined to government employees, a group that in most countries is relatively well-off.

Finally, not all subsidy programs contribute to income redistribution even when redistribution is the announced goal. The most striking example is that of subsidies for the consumption of petroleum products (particularly kerosene) in Bolivia, Colombia, Indonesia, Pakistan, and several other oil-producing countries. In all four cases mentioned a principal justification offered for such subsidies was that of assisting low-income groups. In Bolivia through 1980, and in Colombia through 1974, this argument was extended to cover consumption of gasoline, even though in both countries automobile ownership was largely confined to the upper 5 percent of the income distribution; and in both, urban bus transport was heavily subsidized. In Indonesia gasoline has been only lightly subsidized, but budget subsidies held prices of kerosene and diesel fuel at less than half the cost of production and distribution. While it seems plausible that subsidies to kerosene favor the poor, this turns out not to be the case. The poorest 40 percent of families consumes only 20 percent of the kerosene sold. Therefore for every $1 of subsidy to the poor, relatively high-income families received $4 of benefit. And since substitutability of kerosene for diesel fuel means that consumers would switch to the former if the latter were unsubsidized, the subsidy program included this fuel as well. The result was that subsidies to kerosene and diesel fuel averaged about 5 percent of total tax revenues in Indonesia from 1979 to 1981, a figure in excess of total capital expenditures for education during the same period.

Fiscal policy to redistribute income must be viewed in perspective. It is not the only, and not always the most effective, instrument for redistribution in LDCs. Other chapters, especially Chapter 4, have drawn attention to the pivotal importance for income distribution of land tenure, the terms of trade between rural and urban areas, growth of employment, the relative prices of labor and capital, the openness and market orientation of the economy, and other factors. Taxation and government expenditures can affect most of those factors to some extent, but other, more direct policy instruments may have greater impacts on income distribution. Each of these instruments, some of which force radical changes in the economy, has its economic and political drawbacks. But a government determined to secure a more equitable income distribution probably needs to employ all those measures—including progressive taxation and expenditure policies—to some degree.

Economic Stability

From the publication of Keynes's *General Theory* in 1936 until the 1970s, conventional wisdom in macroeconomics held that active and deft use of fiscal policy in concert with monetary policy was, at least in principle, capable of combating economic instability in the form of inflation and recession. The fiscal policy prescription was simple: when faced with inflation enact tax increases and cut government expenditures to reduce aggregate demand; in recession implement the same set of measures in reverse. Few macroeconomists now believe that the active use of fiscal policy is efficacious in combating moderate inflation or unemployment even in countries such as the United States. Studies of the effects of U.S. fiscal policy since 1960 do not suggest that the public responds to temporary changes in fiscal policy in ways predicted by analysts of an earlier era because such measures do not affect their "permanent income," the income variable on which, many economists believe, households base their spending decisions. In addition, members of an influential school of thought—the "rational expectationists" school—argue that people do not respond in the manner expected because they have learned from past experience that governmental action with the announced goal of stabilization often fails to achieve that purpose.

Although framers of macroeconomic policy in many LDCs briefly flirted with Keynesian ideas of demand management in the early 1950s, active use of fiscal policy for countercyclical purposes has never been common in the developing nations. Macroeconomic budget management has of necessity been focused not on cyclical variations of tax rates but on finding sufficient revenues to finance rapidly rising government expenditures without incurring large deficits. Given that unemployment has been a type not easily remedied by simple demand expansion, and given the persistence of inflationary pressures arising from both the domestic and world economy, the task of macro stabilization policy in LDCs has usually been interpreted as one of restraining inflation. For fiscal policy this ordinarily has meant pursuit of a balanced budget. Adherence to the balanced budget rule is in many circumstances appropriate in light of national objectives. There are, however, three sets of circumstances in which it may be inadvisable to seek balanced budgets. One set of circumstances involves deficit spending; the other two require the overall government budget to be in surplus.

In situations where a society is prepared to accept the income distribution consequences of substantial inflation, and where the tax system has unwanted effects on the income distribution and cannot be easily reformed, a government may conclude that inflation represents a superior means of mobilizing resources for the public sector. Tax collections may be allowed to fall short of government spending; the government then covers the deficit by printing money. This effectuates transfer of resources from the private to the public sector just as surely as government spending out of increased tax collections. Provided the resulting inflation can be held within moderate bounds (see Chapter 13), pursuit of the balanced budget goal under such circumstances may not be consistent with broader national objectives.

Of the two situations requiring surplus in the government budget, one is discussed in this chapter, the other in Chapter 19. In the present case we will assume that any further inflows of foreign savings are unwanted. We also assume that the government is unprepared to accept the ill effects of inflation on income distribution and employs a tax system that results in a distribution of the tax burden consistent with that society's redistributive goals.

In countries with a relatively vibrant private sector but where private savings are insufficient for financing private investment, maintenance of economic stability requires that the overall government budget be in surplus, i.e., government savings must exceed government investment. This can be seen from the use of the national income accounting identity:[16]

$$Y = C_p + I + G + (E - M) \qquad [12\text{--}1]$$

where Y = gross domestic (or national) product, C_p = private consumption, or the demand for domestic goods by domestic residents in the private sector (personal consumption), I = total investment, *including* government investment, G = government consumption expenditures (recurrent expenditures), M = imports (domestic demand for foreign goods and services), and E = exports (foreign demand for domestic goods and services).

Thus income is equal to total spending by domestic residents plus net exports $(E - M)$. Expressed in more detailed form we have

$$Y = (C_p + G) + (I_g + I_p) + (E - M) \qquad [12\text{--}2]$$

where I_g is government investment and I_p is private investment. The first term on the right-hand side of equation 12-2 refers to total consumption, the second refers to total investment. Because our focus in this chapter is on domestic determinants of stability, we will assume that net exports are zero, or $E - M = 0$. From basic macroeconomics we know that if $E = M$, then economic stability requires that total planned investment must equal total planned savings, or $I = S$. Since, with $E - M = 0$, there are two components of savings and two components of investment, we can write

$$I_g + I_p = S_g + S_g \qquad [12\text{--}3]$$

where S_p = private savings and S_g = government savings.

Now suppose the government plans to run a balanced budget for the year, so

$$T = G + I_g \qquad [12\text{--}4]$$

where T = total taxes. Since by definition

$$S_g = T - G \qquad [12\text{--}5]$$

then from equations 12-4 and 12-5

$$I_g = S_g \qquad [12\text{--}6]$$

As long as equation 12-3 holds, stability will obtain. But now suppose

16. These definitions are consistent with those of the macroeconomic consistency model of Chapter 6 (equations 6-7 to 6-11), except that consumption (C in Chapter 6) has been divided into private consumption (C_p) and government consumption (G).

that in the private sector investors plan to invest more than savers plan to save. That is,

$$I_p > S_p \qquad\qquad [12\text{–}7]$$

We will use Z to denote excess demand: the excess of planned investment over planned savings in the private sector. Therefore

$$I_p = S_p + Z \qquad\qquad [12\text{–}8]$$

In this situation maintenance of stability requires an unbalanced budget: T must exceed G by an amount sufficient to offset Z. That is, $I_p > S_p$ is consistent with stability only if $S_g > I_g$ by the amount Z.

The savings shortfall could be made up either by compressing G or I_g by an amount equal to Z, or by increasing T by an amount sufficient to reduce C_p (private consumption) by Z, or some combination of both measures. Because we have seen earlier that a tax increase comes partly out of consumption and partly out of savings, T must ordinarily be increased by more than G to offset Z of any given size. The reduction in G or the increase in T would be taken to the point where once again equation 12–3 is satisfied, i.e., where the excess of S_g over I_g just compensates for the shortfall of S_p needed to finance I_p.

Therefore tax increases or spending cuts may·sometimes be essential even when the government budget is not in deficit. More often LDC governments find that tax increases are essential in order to reduce deficits, because the tax system has failed to generate revenues at a pace consistent with development goals. This consideration implies that a high premium should be placed on building into the tax system features that make it more responsive to economic growth, so that the government does not have to resort to periodic increases in tax rates in order to maintain economic stability and finance growing levels of government spending required for development. Such a tax system would have a high degree of *revenue elasticity* (E_R).

E_R measures the responsiveness of the tax system to growth in GDP. It is defined as the percent change in tax collections divided by the percent change in GDP,[17] or:

$$E_R = \frac{\Delta T/T}{\Delta Y/Y}$$

If $E_R > 1$, then the tax system is revenue-elastic and taxes rise proportionally more than national income. For example, if $E_R = 1.2$, then for every 10 percent increase in GDP tax collections rise by 12 percent. If $E_R < 1$ the

---

17. In actual calculation of E_R, the following formula should be used

$$E_R = \frac{T_1 - T_0}{(T_0 + T_1)/2} \div \frac{Y_1 - Y_0}{(Y_0 + Y_1)/2}$$

when the (0) and (1) subscripts on T and Y refer to the beginning and the end of the time period under consideration (usually one year).

tax system is revenue-inelastic; if $E_R = 0.8$, then with a 10 percent increase in GDP taxes rise by only 8 percent.

Governments are most concerned with fashioning tax systems that will be revenue elastic at unchanged tax rates and with unchanged definition of the tax base. This is termed *ex-ante elasticity* (i.e., the built-in response of the tax system to GDP growth). Few LDCs have been able to secure ex-ante revenue elasticity equal to or greater than 1. Because the observed elasticity of government spending in LDCs is typically greater than 1 (government spending tends to grow at rates faster than GDP), this represents a serious problem.

Some countries, however, have tax systems with *ex-post revenue elasticity* greater than 1. Ex-post elasticity incorporates the built-in responsiveness of the tax system *plus* legislated change in tax policy during the period under review. If ex-ante revenue elasticity is low, periodic tax increases designed to keep ex-post revenue elasticity at acceptable levels rapidly runs into diminishing returns, as we have seen earlier.

A government can enhance the ex-ante revenue elasticity of the tax system by relying on taxes with income-elastic bases, that is, taxes for which the base grows at a rate faster than GDP. The tax bases for excise taxes on tobacco and alcohol are typically income-inelastic, except in very-low-income countries such as Chad, Mali, and Haiti. For countries relying heavily on import substitution as a means of rapid industrialization, the base for customs duties is income-inelastic.

The taxes with the most income-elastic bases are the income tax, sales taxes that exempt food but not services, and luxury consumption taxes. The income taxes have income-elastic bases because as the economy develops, a growing proportion of income is earned in the modern sector and becomes more accessible to the tax collector. Use of progressive rates under the personal income tax accentuates the revenue elasticity of the tax, since with growth more income becomes taxable at the higher rates.

Sales taxes that exempt income-elastic food and tax income-elastic services are moderately revenue-elastic, even at unchanged tax rates. Luxury consumption is by definition income-elastic. It may be noted that virtually all measures taken to enhance the revenue elasticity of the tax system also contribute to the progressivity of the system. This is one of the rare cases in which one policy measure (enhancing ex-ante revenue elasticity) promotes two goals (economic stability and income redistribution).

Economic Efficiency

On the expenditure side of the budget, the tool we earlier called social cost-benefit analysis (Chapter 6) can be deployed to enhance efficiency (reduce waste) in government spending. On the tax side, promotion of economic efficiency is rather more problematic.

All taxes, save lump-sum levies (poll taxes), lead to inefficiencies to one degree or another. Lump-sum taxes are not realistic options for raising government revenues. The objective is therefore one of minimizing tax-induced inefficiencies consistent with other goals of tax policy. In most developing societies this objective largely reduces to the necessity of identifying examples of needless waste engendered by taxes and purging them from the system. If a particular feature of a tax system involves large efficiency losses, and at the same time contributes little or nothing to such other policy goals as income redistribution, then that feature is an obvious candidate for abolition. A full discussion of those elements of tax systems that qualify for such treatment is properly the subject of an extended public finance monograph, not a text in development. We can do little more here than indicate some of the principal examples.

A major source of inefficiency in taxation not counterbalanced by positive gains in revenues, income redistribution, or other objectives of tax policy is excessive costs of tax administration. In some countries and for some taxes these costs have been so high as to call into question the desirability of using certain taxes for any purposes. This is true for certain kinds of narrow-based stamp taxes used widely in Latin America, to collect government revenues on documentation of transfer of assets, rental agreements, checks, and ordinary business transactions. Like a federal tax on playing cards used in the United States until 1964, many stamp taxes cost more to administer than they collect in revenues.

In some countries even broad-based taxes have had inordinately high costs of collection. For example, sales taxes in Chile and Ecuador in the 1960s cost $1 in administration for each $4 collected, as opposed to about $1 per $100 for most state sales taxes in the United States. And because taxes on capital gains are so difficult to administer everywhere—including North America—costs of collecting this component of income taxes often exceed revenues in many LDCs.

Many LDCs, from Ghana in Africa to Colombia in Latin America and Indonesia in Asia, have offered substantial tax incentives to encourage investment in particular activities and regions. Many of these, particularly income tax "holidays" for approved firms, have proven very difficult to administer, and as shown in Chapter 14, few have led to the desired result. Given persistently pressing revenue requirements in most countries, the granting of liberal tax incentives may serve no purpose other than that of requiring higher rates of tax on taxpayers who do not qualify for the incentives. It is a dictum of fiscal theory that any economic wastes (inefficiencies) arising from taxation increases not proportionately with the height of the tax rate employed, but with the *square* of that rate. It is therefore not difficult to see that unsuccessful tax incentive programs involve inefficiencies for the economy as a whole that are not compensated by any significant benefits.

Finally, some features of major tax sources as utilized in many LDCs involve needless waste. From our earlier discussion of the use of import duties for luxury tax purposes it is clear that this is often a major source of inefficiency. The use of progressive tax rates in a corporation income tax (as in Colombia until 1974, Venezuela, Mexico, Brazil, Ghana, and a score of other countries) is another example. Progressive rates of corporate tax, where they cannot be enforced, do little to contribute to income redistribution, and where they can be enforced lead to a variety of wastes. Two of the most important are their effects on fragmentation of business firms and their implication for inefficiency in business operation. The incentive for fragmentation is evident: rather than be subjected to high marginal rates of taxes, firms will tend to split up into smaller units, losing any cost advantages of size. Where progressive rates are employed for company income, the tax will take a high proportion (say, 70 percent) of each additional dollar of earnings; therefore the incentive to control costs within the firm will be reduced. For example, for a firm facing a marginal tax rate of 70 percent an additional outlay of $1000 for materials will involve net costs of only $300, but taxes will be reduced by $700.

FURTHER READING The Anglo-Saxon tradition in fiscal economics, unlike the Italian and other continental traditions, has always shown a preoccupation with the tax side of the government budget. Therefore much of the English-language published material dealing with fiscal issues in both developed and developing countries focuses heavily on taxation rather than expenditure questions. A very useful compilation of forty-one fairly recent contributions on taxation in developing countries may be found in Richard Bird and Oliver Oldman (eds.), *Readings on Taxation in Developing Countries* (3rd ed.; Baltimore: Johns Hopkins University Press, 1975).

Econometric studies of tax ratios, taxable capacity, and tax effort have long enjoyed a prominent place in development finance. One of the earliest and best of these is by Roy W. Bahl, "A Regression Approach to Tax Effort and Tax Ratio Analysis," *International Monetary Fund Staff Papers* 14, no. 4 (1971): 570–608. Caveats in interpreting such studies are well expressed in Richard M. Bird, "Assessing Tax Performance in Developing Countries," *Finanzarchiv,* Band 34, Heff 2, 1975.

A very useful recent example of the growing literature of fiscal reform, in which issues on both the tax and the expenditure side of the budget are given appropriate weight, may be found in Richard A. Musgrave et al., *Fiscal Reform in Bolivia: Final Report and Staff Papers of the Bolivian Mission on Tax Reform* (Cambridge, Mass.: Harvard Law School, International Tax Program, 1981).

On the impact of the budget on income distribution, the work of Charles E. McLure in Jamaica, Colombia, Malaysia, Indonesia, and other countries provides perhaps the best examples of the application of modern incidence analysis to governmental operations. See, for example his "Taxation and the Urban Poor in Developing Countries," *World Development* 5, no. 3 (1977): 169–88. Indeed recent developments in tax incidence theory have proven invaluable in sorting through not only questions of income distribution but of economic efficiency in fiscal policy in open economies. Students with a background in intermediate microtheory may with to consult a recent summary of this work by Arnold C. Harberger, the father of modern general equilibrium incidence analysis. See Arnold C. Harberger, "The Incidence of Taxes on Income from Capital in an Open Economy: A Review of Current Thinking," Harvard Institute for International Development Discussion Paper No. 139, August 1982.

The standard reference on issues of design and implementation of indirect taxes of LDCs is still John F. Due, *Indirect Taxation in Developing Economies* (Baltimore: Johns Hopkins Press, 1970). On the role of fiscal policy in stabilization in open LDC economies, more advanced students will find the recent treatise by Rudiger W. Dornbusch, *Open Economy Macroeconomics* (New York: Basic Books, 1980) will be useful.

Chapter 13

FINANCIAL POLICY

A country's financial system consists of a variety of interconnected financial institutions, both formal (organized) and informal (unorganized). Except in a handful of countries (Liberia, several Francophone African countries), a central bank lies at the core of the organized financial system, responsible for the control of the money supply and the general supervision of organized financial activity. Virtually everywhere, and particularly in developing countries, the commercial banking system is the most visible and vital component of the organized financial system, as acceptor of deposits and grantor of shorter term credit. Other elements of the organized financial system include savings banks, insurance companies, and in a few higher income LDCs, pension funds and investment banks specializing in long-term credit, as well as nascent securities markets. Coexisting with these modern financial institutions are the unorganized and largely unregulated systems of finance, including pawnshops, local moneylenders, trade credit, and other informal arrangements involving the borrowing and lending of money, such as intrafamily transfers and cooperative credit. In very-low-income nations, or even in higher income LDCs with long inflationary histories, the unorganized financial sector may rival the organized system in size.

Financial policy embraces all measures intended to affect the growth, utilization, efficiency, and diversification of the financial system. In North America and Western Europe the term *financial policy* is ordinarily used as a synonym for monetary policy: the use of monetary instruments to reduce instability induced by cyclical fluctuations arising from either internal or external markets. In the United States these instruments include open-market operations,[1] changes in both legal reserve requirements of commercial banks and in central bank (Federal Reserve) lending (rediscount) rates to commercial banks. As typically viewed in LDCs the term *financial policy* has a much broader meaning. Monetary policy is part of financial policy, but so are measures intended to encourage the growth of savings in the form of financial assets, to develop money and capital markets, and to allocate credit between different economic sectors.

Views on the Role of Finance in Development

For the first two decades of the post–World War II era, financial policy was not generally viewed as a significant instrument for promoting economic stability, much less for encouraging growth and development in LDCs. There were a number of reasons for this view. First, until after the Second World War there was a prevailing tradition in economics that monetary changes affected only prices and wages and had little impact on production and employment over the business cycle. The Great Depression served among other things to demonstrate that monetary factors could in fact have significant effects on both output and employment. Nevertheless the tradition died hard; many economists in the industrial countries and in LDCs in the 1940s and 1950s remained convinced that monetary factors had little influence on the business cycle and consequently downplayed the importance of that important subset of financial policy known as monetary policy.

Skepticism over the efficacy of monetary policy was perhaps more pronounced in LDCs, particularly those where a substantial portion of economic activity was conducted through barter and related informal transactions outside the money economy. The **monetization ratio**—the proportion of the total of goods and services in an economy that are purchased with money—was relatively low in many LDCs, particularly low-income nations in Africa. Even by 1980 it is likely that only three-quarters of all economic activity in Africa took place inside the monetized sector, versus 90 to 95 percent in Asia, the Mideast, and in Latin America.[2] The effective use of monetary policy instruments for combating cyclical fluctuations is difficult enough in highly monetized countries such as the United States. In countries where as much as 15 to 25 percent of activity is outside the money economy it was thought that monetary policy would be even less effective in achieving stabilization goals.

---

1. Open-market operations are used as an instrument of monetary policy in countries with well-developed financial markets. When the Federal Reserve System (in the U.S.) or a central bank in Europe wants to curtail the growth of the money supply, it sells government securities (bonds, bills) in the open market. When a buyer pays for the securities the effect is to directly reduce the reserves of the banking system, since the funds are added to the account of the Federal Reserve. When the Federal Reserve wants to expand the money supply it buys securities on the open market, directly adding to bank reserves.

2. Anand G. Chandavarkar, "Monetization of Developing Economies," *International Monetary Fund Staff Papers* 24, no. 3 (November 1977): 678–79.

Finally, postwar economic history to 1972 was a period in which fixed exchange rates prevailed virtually everywhere, including LDCs. It is well established in the literature on money and international trade that, given perfect capital mobility and fixed exchange rates, small countries will find monetary policy ineffective. Through the 1970s policy commitments to fixed exchange rates were relaxed in a few countries. Also, by the end of the decade there were few countries outside the twelve to fifteen poorest where the monetization ratio stood at less than 85 percent. And as we have noted in Chapters 11 and 12, the international mobility of capital is far from perfect. In light of these considerations there was by the early 1980s a growing number of adherents to the view that financial policy, when deftly applied, can contribute something to maintenance of short-term economic stability.

Less widely accepted, however, is the contention that financial policy can have an important influence over the long-term course of economic development. Earlier views of the role of finance in development held that the effect of financial policies on growth was benign at best and mildly restrictive at worst; financial policies were not thought to make much difference for higher living standards in any case. More recently, analysts such as Edward Shaw and Ronald McKinnon at Stanford have argued that financial policies have important implications both for the accessibility of domestic savings to domestic investors and for the efficiency with which these savings are allocated to competing investment purposes. In the McKinnon-Shaw framework financial policy can have potent effects on growth and development. "Shallow" financial policy (financial repression) is considered inimical to growth, serves to worsen unemployment and income distribution, and to reduce national economic independence. On the other hand financial "deepening," or liberalization, is viewed as favorable for growth, employment, equity, and national economic independence in developing countries.

We will identify the major elements of policies geared to "shallow" finance and "deep" finance as the discussion proceeds. For the moment it is sufficient to note that the hallmark of shallow finance is the presence of sharply negative real rates of interest on financial assets such as demand and time deposits; the essence of deep finance is avoidance of negative real rates of interest, where the real rate of interest is defined as the nominal interest rate adjusted, as explained below, for anticipated inflation.

The Functions of a Financial System

The financial system provides four basic services essential for the smooth functioning of an economy: (1) it provides a medium of exchange and a "store of value" called "money," which also serves as a "unit of account" to measure the value of the transactions; (2) it furnishes a vessel for mobilizing and allocating funds, gathering savings from numerous savers and channeling them to investors; this process is called "financial intermediation"; (3) it provides a means of transferring and distributing risk across the economy; (4) it provides a set of policy instruments for stabilization of economic activity.

Money and the Money Supply

An economy without money as a *medium of exchange* is perforce a primitive economy. Trade between individuals must take the form of high-cost, inefficient, barter transactions. In a barter economy goods have prices, but they are expressed in relative prices of physical commodities: so many kilos of rice for so many liters of kerosene, so many meters of rope for so many pairs of sandals, and so on. To exchange commodities and services in a barter system an individual would need to know a large number of these relative prices, which will change from week to week as relative supplies change (in response to, say, weather conditions) or relative demands shift (in response to seasonal influences or to changes in tastes, for example). Trading under such circumstances involves onerous information costs. Time and effort that could have been spent in other activities (more production, more leisure) must be devoted to acquiring price information. Thus costs of making transactions are high. Furthermore, with no widely accepted medium of exchange individuals must store sizable stocks of commodities to meet future transactions' needs, at substantial cost.

Few societies have ever relied heavily on barter precisely because of the high costs implicit in this means of exchange. At some point prices of goods and services begin to be expressed in terms of one or more universally accepted and durable commodities, like gold and silver, or even beads and cowrie shells. The rise of commodity money diminishes transaction and storage costs of trade, but still involves problems of making exchanges across space and time. Gold and silver prices do fluctuate, and the commodities are thus not fully reliable as *units of account.* As specialization within an economy increases, financial instruments backed by commodities appear. In the last century, with the rise of central banking all over the world, currency has evolved into *fiat* money: debt issued by central banks that is legal tender. It is backed not be commodities of equivalent value, but only by the full faith and credit of the central bank. As markets widen and specialization proceeds apace, a need for still another financial instrument—*transferable deposits*—arises. In the normal course of development checking deposits appear first: deposits that may be transferred to any economic agent at the demand of the depositor. These are liabilities (debts) of commercial banks and ordinarily bear no interest. With further monetization still another financial instrument begins to grow in importance: *time deposits* which are not legally transferable on demand, but only after stated periods. Rising levels of economic activity require increasing needs for transaction balances; individuals will always maintain some balances in demand deposits to meet these needs, but will tend to economize on levels of such deposits if no interest is paid on them. Time deposits, however, do involve contractural interest payments; higher interest induces people to hold greater amounts of deposits in this form.

While checking (demand) and time deposits are *liabilities* (or debts) of commercial banks, they are *financial assets* to the persons who hold them. Both demand and time deposits are known as **liquid financial assets.** Unlike **nonfinancial assets** that can also be held by households and businesses (inventories, gold, land), demand and time deposits can be quickly and conveniently converted into their currency equivalents. Currency is, of course, the most liquid of all assets.

The concept of liquid financial assets is an important one in any discussion of financial policy in developing countries. For most LDCs, movement of savers in and out of liquid financial assets may be the prime factor behind the success or failure of financial policy. We will see that secular shifts from tangible, or nonfinancial, physical assets to financial assets, particularly liquid assets, bodes well not only for economic growth but for economic stability as well.

But more important, a country's **money supply** may be defined as the sum of all liquid assets in the financial system. While not all economists agree about what constitutes a liquid financial asset, most vastly prefer this money supply concept to those commonly employed in early postwar monetary analysis. Formerly the money supply was conventionally defined as the sum of only two liquid financial assets: currency in circulation outside banks (C) plus demand deposits (D), which together are known as M_1 (narrow money). However, it has become clear that because depositors tend to view time deposits (T) as almost as liquid as demand deposits, the former should also be included in any workable concept of money supply, called M_2 (broad money). Thus

$$M_1 = C + D \qquad\qquad [13\text{--}1]$$

$$M_2 = M_1 + T \qquad\qquad [13\text{--}2]$$

For most low-income LDCs and many middle-income countries liquid financial assets constitute by far the greatest share of financial assets outstanding. But as income growth continues and the financial system matures, financial assets other than liquid assets assume progressively greater importance. These include primary securities such as stocks, bonds (issued both by government and firms), and other financial claims on tangible (physical) assets that are convertible into currency equivalents only with some risk of loss to the asset-holder, and are hence less liquid than demand or time deposits.

The evolution of financial activity follows no set patterns across countries. Differing economic conditions and policy emphases may result in widely divergent patterns of financial growth. Nevertheless the level of financial activity tends to increase relative to economic activity as per-capita income rises over time. M_1, the narrowly defined money supply, may be as low as 10 percent of GDP in very-low-income countries, and tends to rise more or less steadily to between 25 and 30 percent of GDP in high-income LDCs and industrial countries. As income rises from very low levels, much of the growth in liquid assets tends to take the form first of growth in demand and then of time deposits. The ratio of M_2 to GDP can be taken as a measure of the real size of the banking system, a rough gauge of the flow of loanable funds in LDCs. This ratio during the 1970s has been typically no more than 12 to 15 percent in very poor countries, rising to an average of about 30 to 40 percent in middle-income nations and between 70 and 100 percent of GDP in such industrial countries as the United States, Canada, France, and Japan (see Table 13-1). But diversity in financial development is well exemplified by the fact that in some relatively high-income LDCs (Taiwan and Malaysia), the share of liquid assets in GDP is higher than in some industrial countries.

Liquid assets are not, however, the only source of financial growth. As financial markets widen with the spread of the money economy, they also tend to deepen as a greater variety of financial assets begins to appear. With rising incomes, a growing proportion of financial growth tends to come in

TABLE 13-1   Liquid Assets[a] (M_2) as a Percent of Gross Domestic Product: Selected Countries, 1960-1979

	1960	1970	1979
I. Developed countries			
Canada	33.8	52.2	71.6
France	47.6	62.6	85.6[b]
Italy	59.9	86.8	100.6
Japan	66.6	92.8	87.2[b]
United Kingdom	52.4	55.1	33.7
United States	63.5	70.0	72.6
II. Developing countries			
A. Latin America			
Argentina	—	30.6	—
Brazil	26.4	23.1	17.3
Chile	—	17.5	14.3[c]
Colombia	17.6	19.8	20.3[b]
Mexico	74.3	33.1	35.8[b]
Peru	21.1	22.8	22.4
Uruguay	31.6	21.5	36.0
B. Asia			
Indonesia	—	10.0	17.6
India	27.8	27.3	40.4
Korea	10.7	37.1	35.8
Malaysia	26.4	39.8	59.6[b]
Philippines	20.0	23.4	24.9
Sri Lanka	29.5	29.3	36.5
Thailand	23.7	30.7	36.4
Taiwan	17.0	44.9	98.2[b]
C. Africa			
Ghana	17.8	19.3	17.8[b]
Kenya	—	31.4	36.9
Nigeria	12.6	17.5	—
Tanzania	—	24.8	37.1

Source: International Monetary Fund, International Financial Statistics (various issues, 1970–1981).
[a] Liquid   assets = money + quasi   money + all   deposits   outside   commercial   banks   (Lines 34 + 35 + 44 + 45 of IMF tables).
[b] For 1978.
[c] For 1977.
[d] For 1976.

the form of nonliquid financial assets, such as primary securities, suitable as a basis for the type of longer term finance that commercial banking systems cannot easily provide. The *financialization ratio* (the ratio of all financial assets to GDP) tends to rise steadily from less than 20 percent of GDP in very poor countries (such as Haiti or Chad) to between 50 and 60 percent in higher income LDCs, such as Brazil, Korea, and Venezuela. In very-high-income developed countries, including Japan, Canada, and the United States, total financial assets are nearly twice as large as GDP. Here again, however, there is no evidence of immutable "laws" of financial development. Many very-high-income industrial countries, including France and Holland, have financialization ratios that are less than half those of Japan and the United States. And many higher income LDCs, particularly those with long traditions of inflationary history (Uruguay, Chile, Argentina), display a lower ratio of financial assets to GDP than such poorer countries as India and Thailand.

Financial Intermediation

As financial structures become increasingly rich and diversified in terms of financial assets, institutions, and markets, the function of money as a medium of exchange, store of value, and unit of account, tends to be taken for granted except in the context of hyperinflation situations discussed late in the chapter. As financial development proceeds, the ability of the financial system to perform its second major function—*financial intermediation* —grows as well. The process of financial intermediation involves the gathering of savings from multitudinous savers and channeling them to a smaller but still sizable number of investors. At early stages of economic development a preponderant share of intermediation activities tends to be concentrated in one type of institution: commercial banks. As development proceeds, new forms of financial intermediaries begin to appear and gradually assume a growing share of the intermediation function. These include investment banks, insurance companies, and securities markets. Plentiful intermediaries, however, do not always guarantee successful intermediation.

Financial intermediation activities are best measured through use of flow-of-funds accounts, which display the uses of finance by different economic sectors together with the sources of savings by sectors. These are akin to the flow matrix of input-output tables (see Chapter 6). Unfortunately, reliable flow-of-funds tables are available for only a few LDCs at present; therefore cross-country generalization about intermediation based on such tables is not yet possible. In the absence of information of the type available from flow-of-funds accounts we will employ the liquid asset/GDP ratio as an approximate measure of financial intermediation.

Financial intermediation is best seen as one of several alternative technologies for mobilizing and allocating savings. The fiscal system discussed in Chapter 12 furnishes another alternative, and we will see in the next chapter that reliance on foreign savings constitutes still another. Further, we will observe in this chapter that inflation has also been employed as a means of mobilizing public sector savings. Indeed a decision to rely more heavily on financial intermediation as a means of investment finance is tantamount to a decision to rely less heavily on the government budget, foreign aid and foreign investment, and inflation to achieve the same purpose.

Transformation and Distribution of Risk

Another major service provided by a well-functioning financial system is the transformation and distribution of risk. All economic activities involve risk-taking, but some undertakings involve more risks than others. Individual savers and investors tend to be risk-adverse, i.e., the marginal loss of a dollar appears more important to them than the marginal gain of a dollar. But the degree of risk aversion differs across individuals. When risk cannot be diversified, or "pooled," across a large number of individuals, savers and investors will demand greater returns, or premiums, for bearing risk, and activities involving high risk will tend not to be undertaken. But high-risk activities may well offer the greatest returns to the economy as a whole. A well-functioning financial system furnishes a means for diversifying, or pooling, risks among a large number of savers and investors. The system may offer assets with differing degrees of risks. Financial institutions that specialize in assessing and managing risks can assign them to individuals having different attitudes toward, and perceptions of, risk. Indeed a perfectly functioning financial system can reduce all risk premiums to zero, except for those *systematic* risks that can never be diversified away from the domestic economy such as those arising from natural disasters and recessions in the world economy.

Stabilization

Finally, the financial system provides instruments for stabilization of economic activity in addition to those available under fiscal policy and direct controls. All economies experience cyclical changes in production, employment, and prices. Governments often attempt to compensate for such fluctuations through policies affecting the money supply. Because unemployment in LDCs is rarely of the type that can be readily cured by monetary expansion, use of financial policy for purposes of stabilization generally focuses, as we shall see, on efforts to control inflation.

Inflation and Savings Mobilization

By the 1980s price inflation was generally regarded as a malady which in its milder forms was annoying but tolerable, and in its moderate form corrosive but not fatal. Acute inflation, also known as hyperinflation, however, is always recognized as severely destructive of economic processes, with few offsetting benefits. Whereas a number of influential thinkers in the 1950s and 1960s advocated some degree of moderate inflation (e.g., inflation rates of between 8 and 12 percent) as a tool for promoting growth, few adherents of this view remain, for reasons discussed below. Many others did not actively advocate inflation, but tended to have a higher threshold of tolerance for a steadily rising general price level than is now common, on grounds that development inevitably involved trade-offs between inflation and unemployment, and that the wise course was to resolve the trade-off in favor of less unemployment and more inflation. Today few economists still believe in a fixed, long-term relation between inflation and unemployment; and many believe that restraint of inflation may enhance, rather than retard, prospects for long-run growth.

Inflation in the LDCs: The Recent Record

Generalizations about inflation in developing countries are difficult to make. Inflationary experiences across countries are as diverse as their experiences in the fields of literacy, nutrition, and tax collection. Nevertheless postwar economic history offers some interesting country and regional contrasts in both susceptibilities to and tolerances for different levels of inflation.

Except for several inflation-prone countries in Latin America and intermittent outbursts of acute inflation in Asia and Africa, the period prior to the early 1970s was one of relative price stability in most developing countries. Nevertheless 11 developing countries have experienced "acute" inflation (here defined as inflation in excess of 50 percent over a period of three years or more) since 1950, with the worst examples in Indonesia from 1962 to 1967 and Argentina and Chile in the years before 1976. All of these countries had inflation rates close to 300 percent over different three-year periods (see Table 13–2). Eight other countries as diverse as Ghana, South

TABLE 13-2   Chronic and Acute Inflation Among Developing Countries, 1950-1979

Country	Years of chronic inflation[a] and average annual rate		Years of acute inflation[c] and average annual rate	
	year[b]	rate (%)	year	rate (%)
Argentina	1950–74	27	1974–76	293
Bolivia	na		1952–59	117
Brazil	1957–76	35	1978–80	72
Chile	1952–70	32	1971–76	273
Ghana	1973–76	34	1976–81	73
Indonesia	1954–60	25	1962–67	330
Paraguay	na		1951–53	81
Peru	1974–78	34	1978–81	68
South Korea	na		1950–55	102
Uruguay	1958–65	26	1965–68	95
			1971–74	83
Zaire	1973–76	46	1977–80	63

Source: Except for Indonesia, Ghana, Peru, and Zaire: adapted from Arnold C. Harberger, "A Primer on Inflation," *Journal of Money, Credit and Banking* 10, no. 4 (November 1978): 505–21. For Ghana, Peru, and Zaire: *International Financial Statistics,* various issues; for Indonesia, Central Bank Reports.

[a] "Chronic" inflation: annual inflation rates between 25 and 50%.

[b] na = not applicable.

[c] "Acute" inflation: annual inflation of 50% or more for three or more years.

Korea, and Chile also experienced acute inflation. In a majority of cases for countries in Table 13–2, episodes of "acute" inflation were preceded by long periods of "chronic" inflation (inflation rates between 25 and 50 percent).

This group of eleven countries is best viewed as falling into two special cases. In one group a succession of very large fiscal deficits (large relative to GDP) were financed by recourse to the banking system's resources (Chile, Indonesia, Ghana). In another group massive expansion of credit to the private sector beyond rates compatible with price stability was the major factor (Brazil and Uruguay before 1974, and Paraguay in the early 1950s). Causes of inflation in these countries are not difficult to identify for the periods in question.

But this group of eleven countries constitutes only a small minority of LDCs. Through most of the postwar era most have restrained budgetary deficits to more manageable proportions, and few have allowed rates of credit expansion to the private sector to reach uncontrollable levels. Indeed aside from the countries listed in Table 13–2, the period 1952–1979 was one in which there were more years when inflation was marginally greater in developed than in developing countries. Only since 1973, after the first oil price shock in that year, have inflation rates in LDCs (again, apart from the "outliers" in Table 13–2) tended to exceed those in developed countries. This pattern has been documented by Harberger in a comparison of twenth-eight developing and sixteen industrial countries for the period 1952–1976,[3] and also in Table 13–3 for a comparison of twenty-two developing countries and the twenty-three member countries of the Organization for Economic Cooperation and Development (OECD), embracing Europe, Australia, Japan, and North America above the Río Grande (compare Groups F and G).

Another interesting observation can be drawn from Table 13–3. It is clear from the last row that world inflationary history from 1952 to 1979 was characterized by three distinct periods. For convenience we will take the weighted inflation rates in industrial countries of the OECD as our measure of "world" inflation. In the first period (from 1952 to 1966) annual inflation both in industrial countries and most LDCs was held to little more than 2 percent. In the second period (1967–1972) inflation almost everywhere surged to nearly 6 percent. In the third (after 1972) the pace of world inflation had accelerated strongly, rising to almost 10 percent by 1979. Inflation tended to be somewhat less in LDCs relative to industrial nations in the first two periods and somewhat more in the last. However, what is more striking is the similarity of rates of inflation within each period between the more "typical" LDCs and the industrial countries, as well as the significant change in the rhythm of inflation between the three periods. It seems reasonable to conclude from these patterns that all countries were coparticipants in a common process of world inflation, made possible

3. Arnold C. Harberger, "A Primer on Inflation," *Journal of Money, Credit and Banking* 10, no. 4 (November 1978): 505–21.

TABLE 13-3 Average Annual Rates of Inflation (%) Since 1952—Selected Developing Countries Excluding Those with Histories of Chronic[a] or Acute[b] Inflation

	1952–66	1967–72	1973–79
A. South America			
Colombia	10.5	8.9	23.8
Costa Rica	1.8	3.8	11.3
Mexico	4.3	4.4	19.8
Panama	0.3	2.7	7.1
B. Africa			
Egypt	1.4	3.3	10.8
Ivory Coast	(1960–66) 3.1	3.6	16.3
Kenya	(1959–66) 10.6	2.4	14.7
Morocco	2.7	2.5	10.8
Nigeria	3.4	8.3	20.9
Senegal		3.4	12.4
C. South Asia			
India	4.8	3.7	7.2
Pakistan	3.8	4.0	13.5
Sri Lanka	0.9	5.6	7.4
D. East Asia			
Malaysia	− 0.2	3.2	6.2
Philippines	2.7	8.5	13.7
Singapore	(1969–66) 1.1	0.96	5.9
Thailand	2.7	2.2	9.7
Taiwan	6.7	4.4	(1973–78) 5.1
E. Middle East			
Iraq	0.5	4.2	6.8
Jordan		(1964–72) 6.1	10.7
Syria	0.9	2.7	12.9
F. Range encompassing			
80% of observation	0.5 to 4.8	2.4 to 8.3	6.2 to 11.8
G. World inflation			
(OECD countries)	2.1	5.7	9.9

Source: Group A–F: *International Financial Statistics* (various issues), Consumer Price Index; Group G: OECD, *Economic Outlook* (various issues), Consumer Price Index.
[a] *Chronic inflation: inflation in excess of 25% for ten years or more, but less than 50%.*
[b] *Acute inflation: inflation in excess of 50% for more than three years.*

by a significant acceleration in the growth of the world money supply (a weighted average of the growth rates of money supply in different nations)[4] in a world of largely fixed exchanged rates, or at best intermittent "dirty" floating rates.[5]

4. The International Monetary Fund now computes and publishes figures on the "world money supply," with weights assigned to different countries on the basis of relative size of economies. The growth in the world money stock rose from less than 3 percent in the fifteen years before 1967 (when world inflation was but 2 percent) to 12.5 percent in the period 1972–1976, when world inflation accelerated to nearly 10 percent.

5. Countries employing floating exchange rates allow the value of their currency to fluctuate according to relative supply and demand for that currency in world markets. Countries employing a fixed exchange rate system establish a set value for their currency in terms of one of the major currencies used in world trade, usually the U.S. dollar. Thus Mexico's currency was defined as 22 pesos to one U.S. dollar at the beginning of 1982. A fixed exchange rate will usually be maintained for as long as a country can defend the rate. When that is no longer possible, a new exchange rate is chosen and fixed to some higher (or lower) value. For example, the Mexican peso was devalued to a new fixed rate of P.29 to U.S. $1 in February 1982, and later (September 1982) to P.60 to U.S. $1.

Given the openness of virtually all LDC economies, and given the acceleration of inflation in the industrial countries after 1973, we shall see that it is also reasonable to conclude that no small part of the responsibility for more marked price level instability in LDCs as a group since 1973 is attributable to imported inflation, in addition to the home-grown variety.

Forced Mobilization of Savings

Chapter 12 identified a number of problems involved in the use of conventional taxes, such as income and sales taxes, for mobilizing public sector revenues. One significant form of taxation available for this purpose was discussed only briefly: inflation. Governments from the time of the Roman Empire have recognized inflation as an alternative means of securing resources for the state. All that is required is that the stock of money be expanded at a sufficiently rapid rate to result in increases in the general price level, and that people be willing to hold some money balances even as the value of these holdings decline. Inflation then acts as a tax on holdings of money. At 15 percent inflation the annual tax on currency is 13 percent, and at 40 percent inflation the tax is 29 percent.[6] These are higher annual tax rates than any country has ever managed to impose successfully on any physical asset, such as housing, automobiles, or equipment. Under infinitely high rates of inflation, as in the German hyperinflation in 1922–1923, households attempt to reduce holdings of money balances to virtually nothing. However, because money is so convenient as a means of exchange and unit of account, people will always hold some money balances even if they must pay fairly heavy inflation taxes for the convenience.

Difficulties in collecting conventional taxes, the apparent ease of collecting inflation taxes, the convenience properties of money balances, and the view that inflation taxes are progressive (richer people hold higher money balances) have led many policy-makers and economists to view inflation as a desirable means of development finance. During the 1950s and 1960s the influential United Nations Economic Commission for Latin America saw moderate inflation as a means of "greasing the wheels" of development, forcing savings from holders of money balances and transferring such savings to governments that were strapped for investment resources. Accordingly, much effort was expended in the search for what was viewed as an "optimal" rate of inflation for developing societies: the rate that maximized tax collections, including both conventional taxes and inflation taxes.

---

6. Say the nominal value of money balances at the beginning of a year is M_n^o, equal to the real value, M_r^o. Now if price inflation proceeds at a rate p per year, then after one year the real value of money balances would be

$$M_r' = M_r^o/(1 + p)$$

The tax on these balances is $T = M_r' - M_r^o$ and the tax rate is $t = T/M_r'$. So

$$t = (M_r' - M_r^o)/M_r^o = \frac{1}{1+p} - 1 = p/(1 + p)$$

If $p = 40$ percent, $t = p/(1 + p) = 29$ percent.

Clearly implementation of such a forced-savings strategy will tend to curtail some private investment, since some of the inflation tax will come out of money balances that would have been used for investment in the private sector. However, proponents of tax maximization through inflation assumed explicitly that the government's marginal propensity to invest out of inflation taxes exceeded that of the private sector, and that the government would invest in real assets as productive as the private investment it displaced. Therefore, it was thought, forced-savings strategies would never reduce total investment.

Two other implicit assumptions lay behind the argument that the forced-savings strategy would improve economic welfare in LDCs. Collections of conventional taxes were believed to be highly responsive to inflationary growth, i.e., the revenue elasticity of the conventional tax system with respect to nominal income growth is greater than 1. And efficiency losses from inflation taxes were thought to be less than efficiency losses from use of conventional taxes to increase government revenues.

Indeed, it can be shown that under circumstances where (1) a government's marginal propensity to invest out of inflation taxes is unity or greater, (2) the revenue elasticity of the tax system is also unity or greater, and (3) the marginal efficiency costs of inflation taxes are less than those for explicit taxes, the growth-maximizing rate of inflation may be as high as 30 percent. However, a number of analysts have argued that these assumptions are so far divorced from economic realities in LDCs as to undermine severely, if not demolish, the case for forced savings through inflation. First, there is little evidence that governments anywhere have a marginal propensity to invest out of inflation taxes that is near unity. In Chapter 12 we noted that, owing to the "Please effect," LDC governments typically have a marginal propensity to save and invest out of additional revenue that is well below unity. In order for tax maximization through inflation to stimulate growth, governments' marginal propensity to invest would have to rise with inflation. Research by von Furstenberg and others finds no support at all for even the weakest form of this hypothesis.

In addition the net result of inflation, even moderate inflation, on a government's total revenues (conventional taxes plus inflation taxes) may actually be to decrease the government's ability to expand total investment. This may easily occur if the revenue elasticity of the tax structure is less than unity, as is the case in many, but not all, LDCs (see Chapter 12). In such cases growth in collections from conventional taxes lag well behind nominal GNP growth. Particularly in the early stages of an inflationary process, part of the higher inflation tax collections will therefore be offset by a decline in the real value of conventional tax collections.

Third, available evidence suggests that once inflation exceeds 2 percent per annum the incremental efficiency losses from inflation taxes tend strongly to outweigh those from conventional taxes.[7] And it is well to note that since 1973 typical rates of inflation in LDCs have been far above 2 percent (Table 13–2).

7. George M. Von Furstenberg, "Inflation, Taxes, and Welfare in LDCs," *Public Finance* 35, no. 2 (1980): 200–1.

At best, then, government mobilization of resources through inflation is a knife-edged strategy. Inflation rates must be kept high enough to yield substantial inflation taxes, but not so high as to cause holders of liquid assets to undertake wholesale shifts into real assets in order to escape the tax. Inflation rates must be kept low enough so that both collections from conventional taxes do not lag well behind growth in nominal income and efficiency losses from inflation do not greatly exceed efficiency losses from higher conventional tax revenues. Paradoxically, then, the inflation tax device can work best where it is needed the least: in those countries having tax systems that are most responsive to growth in overall GNP and which involve low efficiency costs. Countries with revenue-elastic tax systems do not need to resort to inflation in an attempt to finance expanded government investment. In this sense tax reform can be seen as a substitute for inflationary finance, but not the other way around.

Inflation as a Stimulus to Investment

The forced-savings doctrine was not the only argument employed in favor of purposeful inflation. For more than fifty years some economists have argued that even in industrial countries rising prices can act as a stimulus to private business enterprise, as inflation was thought helpful in drawing labor and capital out of declining sectors of the economy and into dynamic ones. If true for industrial societies then, it was reasoned, the argument might apply with special force in developing countries, where rigidities, bottlenecks, and immobilities were such that resources were particularly likely to be trapped in low productivity uses. Inflation, it was argued, would help to speed up the reallocation of labor and capital out of traditional or subsistence sectors into the modern sectors with the greatest development potential. Thus moderate inflation was not only seen as inevitable, but desirable: a progressive government would actively seek some target rate of inflation, perhaps as high as 10 percent, in order to spur development.

Experience with development since 1950 strongly suggests that some inflation is indeed inevitable in developing societies seeking rapid growth in per-capita income: factors of production are relatively immobile in the short run, and imbalances and bottlenecks in supply do develop in spite of the most careful planning. However, deliberate use of sustained inflation to spur development is likely to achieve the desired results only under a limited set of circumstances.

First, if inflation is the result of deliberate policy or can otherwise be anticipated, then in a sustained inflationary process the approaching rise in prices will cause individuals and firms to adjust their expectations of inflation. To the extent that the inflation is anticipated the supposed beneficial effects will never occur; people will have already taken them into account in their decision-making.[8] For industrial societies it would be difficult, at

---

8. This observation dates at least as far back as the early 1930s, to the Swedish economist Knut Wicksell. It contains the germ of the idea behind the rational-expectations school of thought of the 1970s and 1980s.

least for an economist, to accept the idea that behavior does not ultimately adjust to expectations of inflation. In developing countries, where all markets, including that for information, tend to be more imperfect than in developed countries, it might be argued that firms and individuals are less efficient in collecting and using information, including that pertinent to formation of price expectations. Thus inflation may not be fully foreseen throughout the economy, and consequently rising prices may result in some stimulus to development, but only in the early stages of an inflationary process. Over the longer run it should be recognized that a successful policy of deliberate inflation depends on people's not understanding the policy.

Second, the argument that deliberate inflation enhances private-sector performance overlooks the effects of inflation on risk-taking. Inflation increases the riskiness of all investment decisions. Suppose that businesses can anticipate inflation with a margin of error of plus or minus 20 percent of the actual rate of return. (If the margin of error is wider the effects about to be described will be more pronounced.) If inflation has been running at 5 percent per year there may be a general level of expectation that over the near future it will settle within the range of 4 to 6 percent. But if inflation has been running at substantially higher rates, say, 30 percent, then expectations of future inflation may rationally be in the much broader range of 24 to 36 percent. The entrepreneur therefore faces far higher levels of uncertainty in planning investments and production. The more unsure he is concerning future returns and future uncertainties, the more likely he is to reduce his risks. Investments with long lives (long gestation periods) tend to be more risky than those with short lives. Thus inflation tends to reduce private-sector investment in projects with a long-term horizon, with the inhibiting effects rising with the rate of inflation. Unfortunately these are often precisely the types of investment most likely to involve high payoffs in terms of income growth for society as a whole.

Finally, inflation may severely curtail private-sector investment by constricting the flow of funds to the organized financial system if nominal interest rates are not allowed to rise with the expected rate of inflation. As we shall see in the next sections, such situations are typical under strategies of "shallow' financial development.

In any case many of the arguments developed in favor of deliberate inflation may have been little more than efforts to rationalize failure of many governments (particularly in Latin America from 1950 to 1975) to bring inflation under control. In most cases inflation in developed and developing countries more often than not has been a consequence of policy miscalculation or economic dislocations (oil price shocks, agricultural disasters, etc.) than a consciously chosen instrument of economic growth. Some reflective observers of inflationary dynamics, such as Albert Hirschman, have maintained that inflation, in Latin America at least, is *not* usually the outcome of a systematic set of choices designed to promote growth and other policy objectives. Rather, inflation usually represents the consequences of governmental temporizing, of postponing difficult decisions that might shatter fragile consensus in governments with sharply divided constituencies.[9] Measures to increase collections from conventional taxes, or measures to reduce spending (particularly government consumption spending) on programs enacted in the first place at the behest of powerful vested interests, are examples of such difficult decisions. Avoiding increases in the former and reductions in the latter is tantamount to choosing inflation in the hopes that at some point in the future a more enduring coalition of constituencies could be assembled to confront directly difficult issues. Seen this way, inflation thus results not by design but by default, from postponing painful remedies. If so, then many of the formal arguments presented in favor of inflation as an engine of growth might be viewed not as an outgrowth of systematic analysis but as an apologia for inflation.

Inflation and Interest Rates: Nominal and Real

The concept of real interest rates is central to the understanding of the implications of financial policy for growth and development. Interest rates may be viewed as prices of financial assets. Currency, which is debt of the central bank but a financial asset for currency-holders, bears a *nominal* interest rate of zero.[10] In some countries, such as Indonesia, Turkey, and Korea, interest is paid on demand deposits, but typically this asset receives a nominal return of zero. Time deposits (including savings accounts) always bear positive nominal rates of interest, ranging from as high as 30 percent in Indonesia in 1974 (for deposits committed for a two-year term) to as low as 4 percent in Ghana in the early 1970s. When an enterprise borrows from a commercial bank in an LDC the interest rate it agrees to pay is quoted in nominal terms, that is, independent of any changes in the general level of prices. Because costs are incurred in intermediating between savers and investors, the nominal lending rates must exceed nominal deposit rates or financial intermediaries will operate at a loss. However, in some countries governments have, as a part of broader anti-inflationary programs, deliberately set lending rates below deposit rates and have subsidized banks to cover their losses, as in Korea (1960s) and Indonesia (1968–1980).

Levels of nominal interest rates—those quoted by banks on loans and deposits—are often subjected to maximum ceilings imposed by governments. For example, usury laws and conventions throughout much of the history of the United States limited nominal interest rates that could be charged on loans both to private citizens and the government. Similar laws have operated in many, perhaps most, developing countries. Also, several organized religions support limitations on nominal rates to limit usury, adding moral force to usury conventions.

9. Albert O. Hirschman, *Journeys Toward Progress: Studies of Economic Policy-Making in Latin America* (New York: Twentieth Century Fund, 1963), pp. 208–9.
10. The **nominal interest rate** on loans is the stated rate agreed between lender and borrower at the time of contracting a loan. The nominal rate of interest on deposits is the rate offered to savers at the time the deposit is made. The nominal rate is defined as an obligation to pay (on loans) or a right to receive (on deposits) interest at a fixed rate regardless of the rate of inflation.

Nominal interest rates are significant for financial development because the nominal rate governs the height of the *real* interest rate. The *real interest rate* is the nominal interest rate adjusted for inflation, or more precisely, the inflation rate expected by the public. Consider two depositors in different countries in otherwise identical circumstances, except that in one country the inflation rate is expected to be 5 percent and in the other 10 percent. If both receive nominal interest rates of 6 percent, then the real rate of interest in the first case is a positive 1 percent, and in the second case a minus 4 percent. The prospective value of the deposit will rise in the first and fall in the second.

Borrowers as well as depositors respond ultimately to real, not nominal, rates of interest. At sustained high rates of inflation, say, 30 percent per year, borrowers will be quite willing, indeed eager, to pay nominal interest rates of 30 percent per year, for loans then are costless: they can be repaid in money with purchasing power well below that at the time of borrowing.

Where legal ceilings do not apply on nominal interest rates they will tend to adjust as expected inflation rises and falls. However, because ceilings on nominal interest rates are widespread and infrequently changed to reflect inflation, the inflation rate in many countries exceeds the nominal interest rate, and negative real rates of interest result.

When expected inflation rates are relatively low the real interest rate can be calculated merely by subtracting the expected rise in prices from the nominal interest rate. Thus for annual inflation (p) below, say, 10 percent,

$$r = i - p \qquad\qquad [13\text{--}3]$$

where r = real interest rate, i = nominal interest rate, and p = expected inflation (all expressed in percent per annum).

Reference to *the* real rate of interest on deposits or other financial instruments can be misleading. At any given time there will be a number of different nominal deposit rates in force in any economy. Nominal rates of interest on shorter term (say, three-month) deposits will generally be lower than those on longer term (say one- or two-year) deposits. The real rate can of course be computed for any class of deposit. In this chapter it will be convenient to speak of "the" real rate, meaning the one rate that has been selected as an indicator of the structure of deposit rates. And because of difficulties in quantifying the expected rate of inflation, the typical surrogate for the expected rate is a weighted average of inflation rates over the recent past (two to four years). "The" real rate of interest on loans is determined in similar fashion: a representative nominal rate on loans is chosen from the multitude of loan rates, and expected inflation is deducted to determine the real rate.

In economies experiencing very high inflation and expectations of continued high rates of price increase equation 13–3 does not provide a reliable measure of real rates of interest. It then becomes necessary to employ a formula that more accurately recognizes that the corrosive power of inflation on nominal asset values works not instantaneously, but throughout a year:

$$r = \frac{(1+i)}{(1+p)} - 1 \qquad \text{[13-4]}$$

For example, inflation in Brazil in 1980 was near 100 percent but the nominal interest rate on one-year time deposits through most of the year was held to no more than 50 percent. Use of equation 13–3 would indicate a real rate of interest on deposits of a minus 50 percent, assuming that inflation was expected to continue at near 100 percent rates. However, correctly measured to reflect the steady, not precipitous action of inflation on nominal values, the real rate was a minus 25 percent, as calculated below:

$$r = \frac{1 + 0.50}{1 + 1.00} - 1$$

$$r = -25\%$$

This means that depositors who placed their money in a time deposit on January 1, 1980, would by the end of the year have suffered a decline in asset value of 25 percent even though the nominal rate was a positive 50 percent. Put another way, depositors paid a tax of 25 percent on their interest-bearing money balances even if they paid no conventional taxes on their nominal interest income on bank deposits.

In cases where conventional income taxes are collected on interest income, the tax (at rate t) must also be deducted from the nominal rate in order to arrive at the real deposit rate net of taxes, r_n:

$$r = \frac{[1 + i(1 - t)]}{1 + p} - 1 \qquad \text{[13–5]}$$

Thus with only a 20 percent income tax on interest, the real rate of deposit interest in Brazil would be a minus 30 percent. A few countries, for example Indonesia and Chile (for some types of interest), do not impose taxes on such income. But most others do, including Colombia, Thailand, Philippines, and Korea.

The discussion of inflation and real interest rates brings us to the point where we may evaluate the role of financial policy in systematic fashion. We shall see that the real interest rate is critical in determing the extent to which the financial system will be able to *mobilize and allocate* savings for development finance. It is important to note that this is not the same thing as saying that higher real interest rates will induce households to save much higher proportions of their income than would be the case at lower real interest rates. This would imply that the interest elasticity of savings is greater than zero. But if savings and consumption decisions are responsive to the real rate of interest, the effects of financial policy on income growth will be magnified.

Interest Rates and Savings

Savings Decisions and Channels

In evaluating the impact of financial policy on economic growth it is important to distinguish between the implications of real interest rates for consumption-savings decisions on the one hand and for decisions about the uses of savings—including the channels through which savings flow—on the other. Debate over the first issue revolves around estimates of the interest elasticity of savings (E_{sr}); debate over the second is couched in terms of the elasticity of demand for liquid assets with respect to the real interest rate (E_{lr}).

Where both elasticities are zero, then financial policy can only have a minimal role in the development process. Where both elasticities are high and positive, then the scope for growth-oriented financial policy can be substantial. Where E_{sr} is small or zero but E_{lr} is positive and large, financial policy may still have significant impacts on savings mobilization through the financial system. Virtually all economists can agree that the real interest rate has a significant impact on the demand for liquid assets; that is, with higher real rates, a higher proportion of savings will be channeled through the financial system. But as of the early 1980s there was no real consensus on the responsiveness of domestic savings to real interest rates, that is, on the extent to which higher real rates may stimulate an increase in the ratio of savings to GNP.

Interest Rates and Savings Decisions

Many economists remain skeptical that interest rates, whether nominal or real, have any significant impact on private-sector consumption behavior in either developed or developing countries. Since savings is defined as not consuming, economists of this persuasion conclude that interest rates have little impact on private-sector decisions to allocate income between consumption and savings: the interest elasticity of savings is held to be zero or insignificantly small.

Economists in the Keynesian tradition, both in industrial and developing countries, have been the leading elasticity pessimists. The standard Keynesian short-run consumption function was given in Chapter 11 (equation 11–4) as

$$S = a + sY^d \qquad\qquad [13\text{--}6]$$

where $S =$ savings, $Y^d =$ current disposable income, $a =$ a constant $(a < 1)$, and $s =$ the marginal propensity to save $(0 < s < 1)$. Neither this absolute income hypothesis, nor the closely related relative income hypothesis of Chapter 11 (equation 11–5), provides any role for the interest rate as a variable affecting savings behavior. (However, Keynes himself, in Chapters 8 and 9 of his influential *General Theory*, did assign a minor role to the interest rate as well as to such demographic variables as the age structure of the population.) It was not until the 1950s that hypotheses of private-sector savings began to appear in which interest rates figured as determinants of savings behavior. These hypotheses were the life-cycle hypothesis and the closely related permanent income hypothesis, both of which by the 1980s had been extensively applied in studies of savings in developing countries.

The life-cycle hypothesis, associated with Franco Modigliani and James Tobin, is founded on the proposition that individuals save in their working years in order to maintain a stable stream of consumption during retire-ment years. According to the theory net lifetime savings of individuals will be zero in static economies and positive in growing economies. Under sev-eral variants of the life-cycle hypothesis the interest rate is given a positive role in affecting savings decisions. It is interesting to note that in virtually all versions of the life-cycle hypothesis the level of absolute income *(Y)* plays no role in explaining the ratio of savings *(S)* to income *(Y)*. The life-cycle hypothesis may be represented as

$$\frac{S}{Y} = a + b_1 H + b_2 U + b_3 W + b_4 D + b_5 r \qquad [13\text{--}7]$$

where a = a constant, H = rate of growth of productivity, U = life expec-tancy of older people, W = the real stock of nonhuman wealth, D = the dependency ratio (proportion of minors and aged persons in the total pop-ulation), and r = the real rate of interest. We expect that b_1, b_2, and b_5 are positive, and b_3 and b_4 are negative. Thus rising productivity growth, life expectancy, and interest rates would all increase the savings ratio, while a rise in the stock of real wealth and a rise in the dependency ratio would decrease it.

The permanent income hypothesis, first formalized by Milton Friedman, was introduced in Chapter 11 (equation 11–6).

$$S = a + b_1 Y_p + b_2 Y_t \qquad [13\text{--}8]$$

where Y_p = permanent income, Y_t = transitory income, and we expect that b_1 is positive but close to zero, and b_2 is less than, but close to, one. Thus most savings that do occur in an economy will come out of transitory in-come, such as might arise from an unforeseen boom in markets for ex-ported goods.

The parameter b_1, which governs the (small) fraction of savings out of permanent income, is in turn a function of several variables, including the real interest rate:

$$b_1 = c_1 \left(\frac{W}{Y_p} \right) + c_2 N + c_3 r \qquad [13\text{--}9]$$

Where W/Y_p = wealth as a porportion of permanent income, N = socioeco-nomic variables such as family size, life expectancy, etc., and r = real inter-est rate. The coefficients c_1 and c_2 are presumed negative, and c_3 is positive. Thus a rise in the real interest rate is hypothesized to raise the fraction b_1 of saving out of permanent income.

Research on consumption and savings in both industrial and developing countries has increasingly relied on variants of the permanent income and life-cycle hypotheses. The results of these studies have conditioned many economists in both developing and developed countries to accept the no-tion of at least some positive interest elasticity of savings. In particular studies by Boskin and Wright using U.S. data indicate sizable elasticities of savings with respect to real interest rates, between 0.2 and 0.4.[11] However, even if these estimates ultimately gain wide acceptance for the United States, confirmation of similar relationships in the LDC context must await results of further econometric research.

We are left with the conclusion that real interest rates may be expected to have some positive effect on national savings ratios, but credible empirical estimates have yet to be made for developing countries. Positive real interest rates result in somewhat higher savings ratios than negative ones, but perhaps not by very much.

Interest Rates and Liquid Assets

Whereas the role of the real interest rate in savings-consumption decisions is a matter of some dispute, the role of real interest rates in influencing the demand for liquid assets is rarely questioned, whether in developed or developing countries, by Keynesians or monetarists. Indeed there is evidence that the real interest rate paid on deposits plays an even greater role in liquid asset demand in LDCs than in industrial countries. Furthermore, experience with marked adjustments in real interest rates in Korea (1965), Indonesia (1968–1969, and again in 1974), Taiwan (1962), and a host of Latin American countries strongly indicates the significance of real interest rates for growth in money holdings demand and time deposits (M_2).

Liquid assets, or financial assets in general, represent one channel of savings open to those who have already saved out of past or current income. The demand for liquid assets in economies where nominal interest rates are not allowed to adjust fully to expected rates of inflation, as is true for virtually all LDCs, is typically represented as a function of income, the real interest rate, and the real rate of return available on nonfinancial assets:

$$\frac{L}{P} = f(Y, e, r) \qquad\qquad \textbf{[13–10]}$$

where L = liquid asset holdings, Y = real income, i.e., money income deflated by the price level, P = price level, e = real return on nonfinancial assets, and r = the real rate of deposit interest. Equation 13–10 can be expressed by a linear relationship

$$\frac{L}{P} = d + d_1 Y + d_2 e + d_3 r \qquad\qquad \textbf{[13–11]}$$

11. Wright's work in 1975 concluded that the interest elasticity of savings was about 0.2, suggesting that a 50 percent increase in interest rates (say, from 6 percent to 9 percent) would provoke an increase in savings of about 10 percent. Boskin's results, strongly challenged by some economists, suggest an interest elasticity of savings of twice as high, at 0.4. See Colin Wright, "Savings and the Rate of Interest" in Arnold C. Harberger and Martin Bailey (eds.), *The Taxation of Income from Capital* (Washington, D.C.: Brookings Institution, 1969); and Michael J. Boskin, "Taxation, Savings and the Rate of Interest," *Journal of Political Economy* 8b, no. 2, part 2 (April 1978): 3–27.

where d = a constant, d_1 and d_3 are expected to be positive, and d_2 negative.

The values for the parameters in equation 13–11 are readily understandable. As real income (Y) grows, the public will desire to hold more purchasing power in the form of cash, demand, and time deposits, the principal forms of financial assets available in LDCs. In particular, d_1 is positive because at higher levels of real income there will be greater need for higher real levels of liquid balances to carry out transactions and meet contingencies. Clearly, liquid asset balances furnish a convenience service to asset-holders. In industrial societies with highly developed financial systems and securities markets it might be reasonable to expect something like a proportional relationship between growth in income and growth in demand for liquid assets. However, in developing countries the demand for liquid assets may, given relative price stability, rise at a faster rate than income because of the paucity of other financial assets in which to hold savings. That is, in developing countries the income elasticity of demand for liquid assets may be expected to exceed unity. Indeed even for such fairly wealthy countries as Malaysia in the 1970s the demand for liquid assets grew 1.6 times as fast as did real income. For many Latin American countries the long-run income elasticity of money demand is also often above unity. In such circumstances the rate of increase in the supply of liquid assets (M_2) can exceed the rate of income growth by a substantial margin and price stability can still be maintained.

The sign for d_2, the coefficient of the return on nonfinancial assets, is negative since liquid assets are not the only repository for domestic savings. A range of assets, including nonfinancial assets and (in higher income LDCs) nonliquid financial assets such as securities, is available to savers. Higher returns on these nonliquid assets relative to liquid assets will induce a shift of savings out of the latter.

The coefficient of the real deposit rate, d_3, has a positive sign, for at higher levels of real interest rates the public will be willing to hold larger liquid balances. Where r is negative, holders of all liquid assets pay hidden inflation taxes on their balances, with the higher rates of tax imposed on non-interest-bearing assets (cash and demand deposits) than on interest-bearing time deposits; savers will therefore be less willing to hold liquid assets.

There have been numerous studies of the demand for liquid assets in a variety of LDCs over the period 1965–1980. In these studies estimates of the elasticity of demand for liquid assets with respect to real interest rates vary according to differing economic conditions across countries. However, in country after country the real interest rate has been found to be a powerful factor in affecting liquid asset demand. In Colombia, Indonesia, Taiwan, and Korea, sharp increases in the real interest rate on time deposits (from negative to positive levels) have resulted in dramatic growth in the volume of such deposits. Marked increases in real interest rates (through increases in nominal rates) were undertaken in the mid-1960s in Korea and Taiwan, and in the late 1960s and again in 1974 in Indonesia, and in Colombia in 1974. In all cases the share of liquid assets in GNP rose strikingly.

On the other hand most Latin American countries through 1975 and West African countries through 1980 allowed real interest rates to remain negative over long periods (see Tables 13–4 and 13–5). Consequently growth in demand for liquid assets was minimal in the countries, and the share of liquid assets in GDP either declined or remained constant (see Table 13–1).

Financial Development

Shallow Finance and Deep Finance

Policies for financial "deepening" seek to promote growth in the real size of the financial system: the growth of financial assets at a pace faster than income growth. In all but the highest income LDCs private sector financial savings predominantly take the form of currency and deposits in commercial banks, savings and loan associations, postal savings accounts, and in some countries, mortgage banks. Thus for most LDCs growth in the real size of the financial system is primarily reflected in growth in the share of liquid assets in GDP. By contrast, under shallow finance the ratio of liquid assets to GDP grows slowly or not at all over time, and typically will fall: the real size of the financial system shrinks. Countries able to mobilize large volumes of government savings or foreign savings can sustain high growth rates even under shallow finance policies, although even these countries may find deepening attractive for reasons of employment and income distribution. But for countries where mobilization of government savings is difficult and foreign savings scarce or unwanted, deep finance may be essential for sustained income growth. This is because growth in the share of liquid assets in GDP provides an approximate indication of the banking system's ability to increase its lending for investment purposes.

Growth in the real size of the financial system enhances its capacity for *intermediation*: the gathering of savings from diverse sources and the channeling of these savings into productive investment. The need for financial intermediation arises because savings endowments do not necessarily correspond to investment opportunities. Individuals with the greatest capacity to save are not necessarily or usually those with the entrepreneurial talents required for mounting new investment projects. Except in very simple, rudimentary economies, mechanisms are required to channel savings efficiently from the former to the latter. In rudimentary economies, production in farming, industry, and other activities is small scale, involving traditional technologies. Producers can ordinarily finance most of their modest investment requirements from their current savings or those of their families, that is, by self-finance. Small-scale enterprises employing traditional technologies have an important role to play in development (see Chapter 20). Yet at some stage improvement in productivity (and therefore living standards) in any economy requires adoption of newer technologies.

These typically involve lumpy investments that are ordinarily well beyond the financial capacity of all but the wealthiest of families. Where enterprise finance is restricted to current family savings only very wealthy groups can adopt such innovations. Thus heavy reliance on self-finance tends to be associated both with low productivity generally and, usually, persistent income inequality.

Restriction to self-finance also guarantees that many productive opportunities involving high private and social payoffs will never be seized, because even the resources of the small number of very wealthy are not unlimited. Innovating, smaller scale investors are not the only groups who fare poorly where financial intermediation is poorly developed; savers are penalized as well. Let us first examine the case where even the most basic financial intermediaries—commercial banks—are absent. Under each circumstances the domestic options open to savers are limited to such forms of savings as acquisition of gold and jewelry, purchase of land and consumer durable goods, or other relatively sterile forms of investment in physical assets. Alternatively, wealthier savers may ship their savings abroad. The common feature of all such investments is that the resources devoted to them are inaccessible to those domestic entrepreneurs who would adopt new technology, begin new firms, or expand production in existing enterprises. Savings in the form of physical assets such as gold may be plentiful, as in France or India, but this type of savings is effectively locked away from investors, or at a minimum may be trapped in declining sectors of the economy, unable to flow to sectors with the brightest investment prospects.

However, even where financial intermediation is poorly developed, individuals have the option of holding some of their savings in the form of currency. Additions to cash hoards are superior to investment in unproductive physical assets from an economy-wide point of view, since at least this serves to curtail the demand for physical assets, reducing upward pressure on their prices, and thus moderating domestic inflation. Nevertheless savings held in this form are still relatively inaccessible to investors.

There are now virtually no societies where financial systems are as rudimentary as those sketched above. All LDCs have financial institutions, however embryonic, to serve as intermediaries between savers and investors, even where these intermediaries are limited to commercial banks that accept checking (demand) and time (savings) deposits from savers, for purposes of relending to prospective investors at short term. Intermediation flourishes under deep finance, but under strategies of shallow finance intermediation is constricted and the financial system can contribute little to furtherance of goals of economic growth. Later we will see that shallow finance may have unintended effects on employment and income distribution as well.

Shallow Financial Strategy

Shallow financial policies have a number of earmarks: high legal reserve requirements on commercial banks, pervasive nonprice rationing of credit, and most of all, sharply negative real rates of interest. Countries rarely if ever have consciously and deliberately adopted strategies of shallow finance. Rather, the repression of the financial system flows logically from certain policies intended to encourage, not hinder, investment.

In developed and developing countries alike, policy-makers have often viewed low nominal rates of interest as essential for expansion of investment. Indeed, so long as the supply of investible funds is unlimited, low interest rates will foster all types of investment activities as even projects with low returns will appear more attractive to investors. In accordance with that observation, and in the belief that low interest rates are particularly essential to assist small enterprises and small farmers, governments have often placed low ceilings on nominal interest rates charged on all types of loans, quite apart from special credit programs involving subsidized credit for special classes of borrowers. Because financial institutions must ultimately cover costs (or else be subsidized by governments), low legal ceilings on nominal loan rates mean low nominal rates of interest on deposits as well.

As long as inflation is held in check, low ceilings on nominal loan and deposit interest rates may not retard growth, even when these ceilings are set below the opportunity cost of capital. Indeed the United States over the period 1800–1979 managed rather respectable rates of income growth even in the presence of a set of archaic usury laws and other interest rate controls that (particularly before 1970) often involved artificially low, administered ceilings on interest rates. Even so, throughout most of the 170 years before 1979 real interest rates in the U.S. remained positive; periods in which real interest rates were sharply negative were intermittent and confined to wartime (1812, 1861, 1917–1918, and 1940–1946).[12]

Usury laws and other forms of interest rate ceilings have been common in developing countries as well, for all the reasons given above plus one more: in many LDCs financial officials, observing gross imperfections in financial markets, have concluded that the market should not be permitted to determine interest rates. Monopoly (or oligopoly) power in financial markets—particularly in commercial banking—does in fact provide substantial scope for the banks and other lenders to exercise monopoly power in setting interest rates on loans at levels higher than the opportunity cost of capital.

There are ample observations of gross imperfections in financial systems in LDCs. Barriers to entry into banking and finance often allow a few large banks and other financial institutions to possess an inordinate degree of control over financial markets. Often these barriers are a direct result of government policies, as governments have either prohibited new entrants into the field, adopted such stringent financial requirements for entry that only the very wealthy could amass the needed capital, or reserved permis-

---

12. Steven C. Leuthold, "Interest Rates, Inflation and Deflation," *Financial Analysis Journal* 37 (January-February 1981): 28–51.

sion for entry to political favorites who were attracted to banking and finance largely by the monopoly returns available when entry is restricted.

In this way one set of government policies—entry restrictions—helps give rise later to the need for extensive controls on prices charged by financial institutions. Given imperfections in financial markets, for whatever reason, as long as banks and other financial institutions remain in private hands policy-makers are loath to allow interest rates to be determined in the market. Interest rate ceilings are then imposed to limit the scope for exercise of monopoly power in the financial system. Controls on nominal interest rates therefore may often be justified. Controls do not by themselves necessarily lead to shallow finance. It is the combination of rigid ceilings on nominal interest rates and inflation that impedes financial development and ultimately retards income growth.

Few economists believe that steeply positive real interest rates are essential for healthy growth in the real size of the financial system. Indeed there is no widely accepted answer to the question—What level of real interest rates is required for steady development of the financial system? Clearly the required real rate will differ across countries in different circumstances. In some, financial growth may continue even at zero or mildly negative real rates of interest; for others, moderately high positive real rates at between 3 and 5 percent may be essential.

We have seen in an earlier section that apart from a few Latin American countries and Indonesia, most LDCs were able to keep rates of inflation at or below 5–6 percent prior to 1973. Inasmuch as nominal deposit rates were typically between 3 and 5 percent, real interest rates tended to be slightly positive or only mildly negative. After 1973 inflation accelerated in all countries, including those accustomed to relative price stability, with typical rates (again except for several Latin American countries experiencing acute economic instability) varying from 8 to 16 percent. Because few countries made more than marginal adjustments in nominal deposit rates, real interest rates after the early 1970s turned significantly negative in many Asian and Latin American nations (see Table 13–4) and sharply negative in several, i.e., those with inflation rates in excess of 25 percent. Negative real rates of interest were even more common and enduring in some African countries in the period after 1975. Table 13–5 displays real interest rates for eight countries in West Africa. Of this group only Senegal recorded positive real rates of interest over the period 1976–1980, and that was only for two years. And in Ghana the real rate was never more than a minus 42 percent in any year.

When real interest rates turn materially negative—e.g., much more than a minus 3–6 percent—then maintenance of low nominal rates for purposes of promoting investment and income growth becomes counterproductive. Inflation taxes on liquid financial assets will bring real growth in the financial system to a halt. Sharply negative real rates lead to shrinkage in the system, as the demand for liquid assets will contract. This tendency is evident from a comparison of Tables 13–1 and 13–4. Countries where real interest rates were only mildly negative, or sharply negative for short periods

TABLE 13-4   Nominal and Real Interest Rates[a] in Selected Asian and Latin American Countries During 1968–1978 (in percent)

	1968	1970	1972	1974	1976	1978
Asia						
1. Korea	27.6	22.8	15.6	14.8	15.5	16.7
	(17.7)	(12.6)	(1.6)	(19.2)	(3.1)	(4.5)
2. Malaysia		3.5	3.5	6.5	5.0	5.0
		(1.6)	(0.3)	(− 10.9)	(2.4)	(0.1)
3. Philippines	5.8	6.0	6.0	6.0	7.0	7.0
	(3.6)	(− 8.3)	(− 4.3)	(− 28.5)	(0.9)	(0.6)
4. Thailand		6.0	6.0	7.0	7.0	7.0
		(6.1)	(1.1)	(− 14.7)	(1.7)	(− 2.2)
Latin America						
1. Argentina	8.0	8.0	17.5	14.8	45.0	215.0
	(− 6.9)	(− 4.8)	(− 25.8)	(− 7.0)	(73.3)	(− 84.0)
2. Brazil		26.4	24.6	23.8	24.0	27.0
		(3.0)	(7.0)	(− 3.0)	(− 12.0)	(− 9.3)
3. Chile	3.0	3.0	3.0	117.9	n.a.	42.0
	(− 18.3)	(− 22.7)	(− 41.9)	(64.0)		(2.1)
4. Colombia	4.1	4.1	7.2	9.0	14.0	20.0
	(− 1.7)	(− 2.5)	(− 6.2)	(− 12.4)	(− 2.9)	(2.1)
5. Mexico	4.5	4.8	4.8	4.0	4.0	4.5
	(2.3)	(− 0.4)	(− 0.2)	(− 16.0)	(− 10.4)	(− 10.3)
6. Panama	5.0	5.0	5.0	5.0	5.0	n.a.
	3.3	1.4	(− 0.3)	(− 10.1)	(2.5)	
7. Uruguay	6.0	6.0	6.0	10.5	51.0	n.a.
	(− 52.9)	(− 9.9)	(− 39.9)	(− 37.6)	(0.3)	

Sources: Korea before 1978—David Cole and Yung Chul Park, *Financial Development in Korea, 1945–78* (Cambridge, Mass.: Harvard University Press, 1983); Malaysia—Hans Rhoden, "Formulation of Monetary Policy: Case Study of Malaysia" (unpublished manuscript; Jakarta, 1980); Philippines before 1978—World Bank / International Monetary Fund, *The Philippines: Aspects of the Financial Sector* (Washington, D.C., 1980), p. 60, Thailand—World Bank, *Thailand: Industrial Development Strategy* (Washington, D.C., 1980), p. 57; Latin American countries before 1978—Vicente Gablis, "Inflation and Interest Rate Policies in Latin America," *International Monetary Fund Staff Papers* 26, no. 2 (June 1977), Tables 1, 4, and 6; all countries after 1978—U.S. Department of Commerce, *Foreign Exchange Trends and Their Implications for the United States* (Washington, D.C., various issues).

[a] Deposit rates on savings deposits, or where rates on savings deposits are unavailable, rates on shortest term time deposits. Real rates are in parentheses; n.a. = not available.

TABLE 13-5   Real Interest Rates:[a] Eight West African Countries, 1976–1980[b] (in %, end of period)

	Year				
Country	1976	1977	1978	1979	1980
Cape Verde	− 1.3	− 4.7	− 6.8	− 0.4	− 3.5
Gambia	− 13.8	− 8.9	− 5.2	− 2.6	− 1.8
Ghana	− 48.6	− 108.9	− 61.1	− 42.4	− 38.1
Ivory Coast	− 6.6	− 21.9	− 7.5	− 11.1	− 7.1
Liberia	− 0.6	− 1.3	− 0.3	− 3.6	− 5.8
Mali	− 4.8	− 21.0	− 29.2	NA	NA
Senegal	4.4	− 5.8	2.0	− 4.1	− 1.3
Sierra Leone	− 10.2	− 1.4	− 3.9	− 13.2	− 1.1

Source: Sergio Pereira Leite, "Interest Rate Policies in West Africa," *International Monetary Fund Staff Papers* 29, no. 1 (March 1982): 48–76.

[a] Deposit rates.
[b] NA = Not available

of time, experienced little or no growth in the real size of their financial systems as measured by the ratio of liquid assets to GDP. These include the Philippines, Colombia, Turkey, Kenya, and India and Sri Lanka before 1977. But where real interest rates have been sharply negative over extended periods of time, as in Argentina, Brazil, Chile, Ghana, and Uruguay through much of the 1970s, the real size of the financial system has shrunk. Contraction in the real size of the financial system results in a reduction in the real supply of credit, and thus constricts investment in productive assets.

Under such circumstances nonprice rationing of investible resources must occur. Nonprice rationing can take many forms. In most LDCs only those borrowers with either the highest quality collateral, the "soundest" social and political connections, or those willing to pay the largest under-the-table inducements to bank officers, will be successful in securing finance from the organized financial system. These criteria do not yield allocations of credit to the most productive investment opportunities.

Negative real rates of interest make marginal, low-yielding investment of traditional types appear attractive to investors. Banks and financial institutions find such projects attractive as well, since they may be the safest and the simplest to finance and involve the most "credit-worthy" borrowers. Thus such undertakings tend strongly to move to the head of the queue of borrowers. Satisfaction of financial requirements of such investors constricts the pool or resources available to firms having riskier projects offering greater possibilities for high yields. In addition, interest rate ceilings in the presence of substantial inflation discourages risk-taking by the financial institutions themselves, since under such circumstances they cannot charge higher interest rates (risk premia) on promising but risky projects. Also, negative real interest rates are inimical to employment growth, as they make projects with relatively high capital output ratios appear more attractive than if real interest rates were positive. This implicit subsidy to capital-intensive methods of production reduces the jobs created for each dollar of investment, even as the ability of the financial system to finance investment is shrinking.

In all of the ways described above negative real rates of interest tend to lower the marginal efficiency of investment. In terms of the Harrod-Domar model described in Chapter 6, shallow financial strategies cause higher capital/output ratios. Consequently growth in national income, and therefore growth in savings, tend to be lower than when real rates are positive. Therefore shallow finance retards income and employment growth even if the interest elasticity of savings is zero. And if savings decisions are responsive to real interest rates, then shallow finance will have even more serious implications for income growth, as the ratio of private savings to GDP will also contract.

Deep Financial Strategies

Deep finance as a strategy has several objectives: (1) mobilizing a larger volume of savings from the domestic economy, that is, increasing the ratio of national savings to GDP (where the interest elasticity of savings is thought to be positive and significant); (2) enhancing the accessibility of savings for all types of domestic investors; (3) securing a more efficient allocation of investment throughout the economy; (4) permitting the financial process to mobilize and allocate savings to reduce reliance on the fiscal process, foreign aid, and inflation.

A permanent move toward policies involving positive real interest rates, or at a minimum, avoidance of sharply negative real rates, is the essence of deep finance. In turn this requires either financial liberalization that allows higher nominal rates on deposits and loans, or curbing the rate of inflation, or some combination of both.

Given the difficulties involved in securing quick results in reducing inflation to levels consistent with positive real rates of interest, the first step involved in a shift from shallow to deep financial strategies is ordinarily that of raising ceilings on nominal rates for both deposits and loans. In some cases this has required nominal interest rates as high as 30 percent per annum on time deposits (Korea in 1966, Indonesia in 1969 and 1974).[13] In extreme cases of acute inflation the initial step has involved raising ceilings on nominal deposit rates to as much as 50 percent in Argentina and Uruguay in 1976 and to nearly 200 percent in Chile in 1974 (where real interest rates nevertheless remained negative). As the real rate moves toward positive levels, savers strongly tend to increase their holdings of liquid assets, allowing a real expansion in the supply of credit to investors. Marked responses of savers have been observed when nominal rates were increased substantialy, as in Uruguay in 1976, Indonesia in 1968–1969, Taiwan and Korea in 1965 (see Tables 13–1 and 13–4). Notable responses have also occurred in countries where mildly negative real rates were moved closer to positive levels through increases in nominal rates: these include India and Sri Lanka after 1977, and Turkey after 1980.

Available evidence suggests that countries that attempt to maintain positive real rates of interest over long periods tend to be among those with the highest rates of financial growth. Malaysia and Thailand both experienced steady increases in the real sizes of their financial systems over the period 1960–1979. For the entire period real interest rates have been positive in both countries, save for 1973 and 1974 when world inflation unexpectedly surged to double-digit numbers. Real rates have been positive in Taiwan almost every year since 1965, and over that span the ratio of liquid assets to GDP has risen to levels characteristic of industrial countries.

Where finance is deep, inflation tends to be moderate; therefore savers are not subject to persistently high inflation taxes on liquid asset holdings. That being the case they will be less inclined to shift their savings into much more lightly taxed domestic assets such as gold, land, or durable

13. Ceilings need rarely be increased to the point where they match the *current* rate of inflation. For example, in Indonesia in 1974 the nominal ceiling on two-year time deposits was raised to only 30 percent, even though inflation over the previous twelve months was 42 percent. The increase in nominal rates, coupled with a battery of other measures, convinced depositors that real rates would soon be positive. All that is required is that inflation expected by savers be reduced to levels closer to the nominal deposit rate.

goods, and such foreign assets as dollars, Deutschemarks, or overseas land and securities. Rather, financial resources that otherwise may have been utilized for these purposes flow to the financial system, where they are more accessible to prospective investors. Nonprice rationing of credit, inevitable under shallow finance, will diminish as well. As a result the capacity of the financial system to identify and support socially profitable investment opportunities expands: higher risk, higher yielding investment projects stand a far better chance of securing finance under deep rather than shallow finance. Growth prospects are accordingly enhanced.

The preceding discussion represents but a sketch of policies designed to promote financial deepening. The focus has been on the real interest rate on deposits and loans when in fact a variety of other policies may be involved. These include central bank payment of interest on commercial bank reserves, and avoidance of high legal reserve requirements on commercial banks. That positive real rates of interest tend to lead to growth in the real size of banking systems is now rarely questioned. Such a development materially enlarges the real flow of short-term credit, the stock-in-trade of commercial banks. However, problems of investment finance do not end with provision of a growing real flow of short-term credit. As economies move to higher levels of per-capita income the pattern of investment shifts toward longer horizons. Longer term investment requires longer term finance. Commercial banks are everywhere ill-suited for providing substantial amounts of long-term finance, given that their deposits are primarily of a short-term nature.

Therefore as financial and economic development proceeds the need for institutions specializing in longer term finance rises accordingly: insurance companies, investment banks, and ultimately equity markets (stock exchanges) become important elements in financial intermediation. Nevertheless the type of well-functioning commercial bank system that tends to develop under deep finance is almost always a necessary condition for the successful emergence and long-term vitality of institutions specializing in longer term investment finance. Where entry into financial activities is only lightly restricted, longer term financial institutions may appear spontaneously. But earlier we observed that entry into the financial field is rarely easy, and other factors also often lead to gross imperfections in financial markets. In such circumstances many LDC governments have found intervention essential in order to develop financial institutions specializing in longer term finance. Intervention may take the form of establishment of government-owned development banks and other specialized institutions, to act as distributors of government funds intended as a source of longer term finance, as in Indonesia and Pakistan. In other cases, as in Mexico, Colombia, and Venezuela, governments have provided strong incentives for private-sector establishment of long-term financial institutions. Finally, in other countries governments have sought to create conditions favorable for the emergence of primary securities (stocks and bonds) markets, the source par excellence for long-term finance. In cases where these measures have been undertaken in the context of financial markets with strong systems of commercial banking (Korea, Thailand, Brazil, Mexico), efforts to encourage long-term finance have met with some success. In cases where commercial banking has been poorly developed as a consequence of shallow finance (Ghana, Uruguay before 1976), or where government has sought to "force-feed" embryonic securities markets (Indonesia, Kenya), the promotional policies have been less effective.

Monetary Policy and Price Stability

We have seen that apart from a limited number of cases in Asia, prior to the 1970s double-digit inflation was largely confined to a few developing countries in Latin America. But by the 1980s inflation had become a serious problem across a wide variety of countries, not only in Latin America but in Africa and Asia as well.

Sources of Inflation

The acceleration of world inflation in the 1970s, coupled with widespread use of fixed exchange rates in LDCs, meant that sooner or later the pace of inflation in LDCs would quicken as well, to rates at least as high as in the industrial countries. LDCs could have avoided "importing" substantial world inflation only by shifting to floating exchange rate regimes. But while the currencies of the major industrial countries have all floated vis-à-vis one another since 1973, LDCs in general have wisely avoided floating exchange rate regimens and instead have attempted, with a few exceptions, to maintain their currencies in a fixed relation to one or a basket of major currencies. Note, however, that statements on the suitability of fixed exchange rate regimes for LDCs do not in any sense imply that any given fixed rate should be maintained at all costs. Maintenance of fixed rates in countries with inflation rates persistently higher than world inflation is not only impossible but inadvisable, as shown in Chapters 15 and 16.

For countries operating under fixed exchange rates financial policies cannot be divorced from the balance-of-payments situation. Open economies that attempt to maintain a fixed exchange rate cannot for long have a domestic inflation rate that is different from the world inflation rate. This point is best understood in the context of a truth known for centuries: monetary expansion is ultimately required to fuel inflation. This statement is often misunderstood, as it is taken to imply that nonmonetary factors have no effect on inflation. This is not so, but the mechanism whereby nonmonetary factors may initiate or worsen inflation needs to be clearly portrayed. An external shock such as a drastic increase in imported oil prices, or an internal event such as widespread crop failure, may indeed precipitate government policy reactions that lead to a monetary expansion large enough to accommodate higher relative prices of oil or food, and also large enough to cause inflation. In the absence of accommodating monetary expansion in the face of such shocks, inflation can be contained, but at some cost. In practice failure to allow the money supply to expand to accommodate higher relative prices of such important goods as oil or food leads to increases in unemployment that most governments find unacceptable. Therefore as a matter of course governments in such cases usually do attempt to allow monetary expansion sufficient to avoid unwanted consequences for employment. But it is important to remember that however advisable monetary accommodation may be on social and employment grounds, expansion in the money stock is required to fuel inflation, whatever may be the factor or factors that precipitated the expansion.

This is as true for a completely closed economy as for very open economies characteristic of the developing world. In a completely closed economy isolated from international capital markets and with no exports or imports, creation of money at a rate that is in excess of what people are willing to hold (as given by the demand for liquid assets) will ultimately lead to inflation. If the central bank restricts monetary expansion to a pace that just matches the public's willingness to hold money, the price level will remain stable. Thus in a closed economy the price level is determined solely by domestic developments: the country can have any rate of inflation it chooses. In open economies that make up the real world the same essential truth also holds: inflation requires monetary expansion. But in open LDC economies with fixed exchange rates, monetary expansion is no longer under the complete control of domestic monetary authorities. Rather, countries with fixed rates may be viewed as essentially sharing the same money supply, because the money of each can be converted into that of the others at a fixed parity.[14]

For any particular LDC on fixed exchange rates, the stock of money *(M)* is definitionally the sum of two components: the amount of domestic credit of the banking system that is outstanding *(DC)*, and the stock on international reserves of that country *(IR)*, measured in terms of domestic currency. There is therefore a domestic and an international component of the money supply. Thus we have

$$M = DC + IR \qquad [13\text{--}12]$$

Changes in the domestic money stock can occur either through expansion of domestic credit or by monetary movements that lead to changes in international reserves. That is,

$$\Delta M = \Delta DC + \Delta IR \qquad [13\text{--}13]$$

Under fixed exchange rates a central bank of any small country can control ΔDC, the domestic component, but it has only very limited control over ΔIR, the international component. Under such circumstances LDCs that attempt to keep the rate of domestic inflation below the world inflation rate (through restrictive policies on domestic credit) will be unable to realize the goal. If, fueled by monetary expansion abroad (growth in the

14. This section draws substantially on recent syntheses of monetary and international economics by Arnold C. Harberger. See his "A Primer on Inflation," *Journal of Money Credit and Banking* 10, no. 4 (November 1978): 505–21; and his "The Inflation Syndrome" (Paper presented in the Political Economy Lecture Series, Harvard University, March 19, 1981).

world money supply), world inflation initially is running in excess of domestic inflation, the prices of internationally traded goods will rise relative to those of domestic nontraded goods.[15] Imports of foreign goods will fall, exports will rise, and the balance of payments of the LDC will move toward surplus, causing a rise in international reserves. Thus the foreign component of the money stock will rise. This is tantamount to "importation of money" and will eventually undo the effort to prevent importation of world inflation. Again, a small country on fixed exchange rates can do little to maintain its inflation rate below that of the rest of the world. For very open LDCs with few restrictions on the movement of goods and capital into and out of the country, the adjustment to world inflation can be very rapid (less than a year). For less open countries with substantial restrictions on international trade and payments the process takes longer, but the outcome is inevitable under fixed exchange rates.

However, the fact that financial policy for stabilization in LDCs under fixed exchange rates is heavily constrained by international developments does not mean that changes in the domestic component of the money stock have no impact on prices in LDCs adhering to fixed rates of exchange. On the contrary excessive expansion in money and credit in a small economy attempting to maintain a fixed exchange rate will result in domestically generated inflation that, depending on the rate of such expansion, can for a time be well in excess of world inflation rates. However, such a situation cannot continue for long, as excess money creation will spill over into the balance of payments via increased imports, leading to a drain on international reserves and ultimately inability to maintain the fixed exchange rate. As reserves dwindle the country can no longer defend its exchange rate and devaluation becomes inevitable.[16] Inflation can therefore be transmitted to LDCs through the working of the world economy or can be generated by domestic developments.

Domestically generated inflation may result from excessive increases in domestic credit from the banking system to either the public or the private sector. Budgetary deficits of the central government must be financed by borrowing.[17] The embryonic nature of money and capital markets in most LDCs generally means that governments facing deficits must ordinarily resort to borrowing from the central bank, a process equivalent to direct money creation via the printing press. The result is a direct addition to the reserve base of the monetary system, an increase in so-called high-powered money. It is important to recognize that not all budgetary deficits are inflationary. We have seen that a growing economy will be characterized by a growing demand for liquid assets, including money. Moderate budgetary

15. The above is but one of several mechanisms that lead to changes in international reserves sufficient to thwart efforts by LDCs to insulate themselves from world inflation. See Harberger, ibid.

16. Controls on imports are frequently used to stem the drain of reserves and avoid devaluation for a time. But import controls engender another set of distortions and inefficiencies—explored in Chapter 16—that eventually require more drastic measures, including devaluation.

17. We will see in Chapter 19 that in resource-rich countries, inflation can occur even with a budgetary surplus, or an excess of receipts over expenditures.

deficits year after year, financed by the central bank, can help to satisfy this requirement without leading to inflation. In general the money stock may expand by at least as fast as the growth in real income, with little or no inflationary consequences.[18]

For a country like Colombia where the money supply is around 20 percent of GDP (see Table 13–1), even a small deficit can result in substantial inflation. For a country such as Malaysia where the money stock is close to 60 percent of GDP, a much larger deficit would be consistent with price stability. In Colombia a noninflationary deficit might be as low as 0.5 percent of GDP; for Malaysia a budgetary deficit financed by bank credit might be as high as 1.5 percent of GDP with little inflationary consequence.[19] In general, deficits of around 1 percent of GDP or less are not inconsistent with price level stability in most LDCs. But given a stable demand for liquid assets, much larger deficits will clearly be inflationary.

Use of bank credit to finance government deficits has not been the only source of inflationary monetary expansion in LDCs. Sometimes excessive growth of credit to the private sector has played the most significant role in domestically generated inflationary processes. Nevertheless, as a general rule inflation rates for a particular LDC that are much in excess of world inflation have usually been traceable to budgetary deficits.

It is evident then that for LDCs attempting to maintain fixed exchange rates, efforts to avoid inflation rates in excess of world inflation must primarily be a matter of fiscal policy, not monetary policy. If budget deficits are not held to levels consistent with world inflation, even very deft deployment of monetary policy instruments will be unable to prevent rapid inflation, devaluation, or both. There is still a role for monetary policy in LDCs, but that role must be largely passive in nature. Resourceful use of monetary policy can help by not making things worse, and also by moderating strong inflationary pressures until the budget can be brought under control, provided the latter is done fairly quickly.

Controlling Inflation Through Monetary Policy

The array of available instruments of anti-inflationary monetary policy in developed countries include: (1) open-market operations, wherein the central bank can directly contract bank reserves by sales of government secur-

18. Earlier we saw that liquid assets are normally between 25 and 40 percent of GDP in most LDCs, or equivalent to roughly three to four months of income. Thus the public is generally willing to hold this much in money balances. A deficit of 3 percent of GDP financed by money creation would add only marginally to the supply of money, and may easily be accepted by the public. But a deficit of 8 percent of GDP would increase the stock of money by an amount equal to one more month of income, or by an amount more than the public would be willing to hold (unless nominal interest rates on deposits are greatly inreased). The excess would spill over into higher prices.

19. A deficit of 0.5 percent of GDP in Colombia would, if financed by the central bank, cause the stock of money to grow by 2.5 percent, a rate well below the rate of real income growth in that country since 1960. A deficit of that size could be financed, while still allowing substantial growth (5–6 percent) in credit to the private sector. A deficit of 1.5 percent of GDP in Malaysia, financed also by credit to the government, would also lead to growth in the money stock of only 2.5 percent, clearly well below expansion required to fuel inflation.

ities; (2) increases in legal reserve requirements of banks, so that a given volume of reserves will support a lower stock of money (and reduce the credit expansion multiplier as well); (3) increases in rediscount rates, so that commercial bank borrowing from the central bank becomes less attractive; and (4) moral suasion, wherein the exhortations of monetary authorities are expected to lead to restraint in bank lending policies.

For virtually all developing countries the first instrument—open-market operations—is not an available tool for inflation control. Securities markets are typically absent or not sufficiently well developed to allow exercise of this powerful and flexible instrument, although some countries, including the Philippines and Brazil, have utilized this tool to a limited degree. The other three instruments of monetary policy are employed, with varying degrees of success, in developing countries as well. In addition developing countries often resort to two other tools employed only infrequently in developed countries: (5) credit ceilings imposed by the central bank on the banking system; and (6) adjustments in allowable nominal rates of interest on deposits and loans. Governments attempting to control inflation usually resort to all of these instruments, often together but sometimes separately.

Reserve Requirements   All central banks require commercial banks to immobilize a portion of their deposits in the form of legal reserves that may not be lent to prospective customers. For example, legal reserve requirements for Indonesian and Malaysian banks in the late 1970s were expressed as 30 percent of deposits in domestic currency in the former and 20 percent of all deposits in the latter. Thus in Malaysia, for example, banks were required to add 20 units of currency to reserves for every 100 units of deposits. These figures are not too far out of line with legal reserve requirements in most industrial nations, where reserve ratios of 15 percent for demand deposits and 5 percent for time deposits are not uncommon. Increases in reserve requirements can be used to help moderate inflation. An upward adjustment in reserve requirements works in two ways: it reduces the stock of money that can be supported by a given amount of reserves; and it reduces the money multiplier. The first effect induces banks to contract credit outstanding; the second reduces the growth in the money stock possible from any increment to reserves.[20] Changes in legal reserve requirements are usually employed only as a last-ditch measure. Even small changes in the required ratio of reserves to deposits can have a very disruptive impact on commercial bank operations unless banks are given sufficient time to adjust.

In addition increases in reserve requirements increase the costs of financial intermediation, especially since central banks rarely pay interest on re-

20. In its simplest form the money multiplier *(m)* can be expressed as:

$$m = \frac{c+1}{c+r}$$

where c = the ratio of currency outside banks to deposits and r = the ratio of reserves to deposits.

quired reserves held with the central bank. Higher costs must be reflected either in higher interest on loans to borrowers or lower interest paid to depositors, or both. Since most developing countries impose legal ceilings on interest rates charged on loans, higher costs arising from increased legal reserve requirements must usually be passed on in the form of lower interest rates on deposits. For example, some countries (such as Chile in the mid-1970s), in the effort to bring acute inflation under control, have resorted to increases in reserve requirements that have propelled the ratio to 50 percent or more. Banking (intermediation) costs—exclusive of costs implicit in holding idle reserves—may be as high as 3 percent of deposits in many LDCs. With a legal reserve requirement of 50 percent for all classes of deposits, the nominal rate of interest on deposits can be only half that of the nominal rate charged on loans, minus intermediation costs. Thus if nominal rates on loans are set at a maximum of 20 percent, then the nominal rate of interest received by depositors can be at most 7 percent, unless the central bank pays interest on reserves held with it, a practice found rarely in LDCs (Chile) in the early 1980s. Therefore increases in legal reserve requirements inevitably mean a decrease in real interest rates received on deposits. Indeed since upward adjustments in legal reserve requirements are undertaken only in the presence of very strong inflation, the result is often that of converting mildly negative real deposit rates into sharply negative ones, with all that that implies for financial development.

Credit Ceilings In some countries, particularly Indonesia since 1974 and at various times Malaysia, Sri Lanka, and Chile, credit ceilings have been used as supplementary instruments of inflation control. Indeed the International Monetary Fund often has required countries seeking balance-of-payments support to adopt credit ceilings as a prerequisite for IMF assistance. General ceilings on domestic credit expansion represents a useful method of controlling growth in domestic components of the money supply. However, credit ceilings do not allow full control of money supply growth in the overwhelming majority of LDCs operating under fixed exchange rate regimes, since the monetary authorities have no control over foreign components of the money supply. Nevertheless general credit ceilings can be usefully deployed in combating inflation in countries not experiencing major imbalances in external payments. Unfortunately ceilings work best where they are needed the least, since countries attempting to deal with chronic inflation are usually the same countries that are experiencing the most destabilizing changes in the international reserve positions. Finally, general credit ceilings are unlikely to have much effect on inflation unless the government at the same time takes steps to reduce the budgetary deficits that are—except in major oil-exporting LDCs—typically the root causes of chronic and acute inflation.

For example, consider the case of a country with a money supply/GDP ratio of 25 percent, in which inflation has recently surged to 30 percent per annum. In such a country the monetary authorities may have calculated that restriction of domestic credit expansion to 15 percent may be required to push the inflation rate down to 12 percent (the exact limit will depend on the income and interest elasticity of the demand for liquid assets, the projected growth in real income, and other factors). But suppose that for the coming year the budget deficit is projected at 3 percent of GDP, a level typical of countries experiencing chronic inflation. In order to finance this deficit, credit from the banking system to the government would have to increase by 3 percent of GDP. But an increase of credit to the government of 3 percent of GDP would, with a money/GNP ratio of 25 percent, translate into credit growth of 12 percent. Thus of the 15 percent limit on credit expansion the government would take 80 percent of allowable credit expansion, leaving little for the private sector. In such instances government deficits are said to "crowd out" the private sector from sources of credit. Initially the monetary authorities may be able to resist private-sector demands to increase the ceiling, but 3 percent growth in private credit in the face of even 12 percent inflation translates into a decline of nearly 9 percent in the level of real credit available. The consequences of adhering to a 15 percent ceiling would therefore be severe disruption in the private sector, including rising unemployment and low real income growth. Few governments anywhere are able to withstand such pressures for long, and inevitably the ceiling is raised to accommodate some or all of private-sector credit requirements. Therefore successful use of ceilings on credit expansion ultimately depends primarily on fiscal, not monetary, policy.

Interest Rate Regulation and Moral Suasion   In most industrial countries the central bank can influence interest rates through market forces, by variations in the rate of interest (the rediscount rate) charged on central bank lending to commercial banks. Otherwise interest rates on deposits and loans are largely left to market forces. Among developing countries only Singapore and Chile (both since 1975) have left interest rate determination to market forces, although in 1981 both Brazil and Turkey experimented with freeing most interest rates from government controls. However, for reasons discussed earlier few LDCs are willing to allow interest rates to be determined in the market, largely because money markets are not competitive.

In the large majority of LDCs where loan and deposit rates are regulated the monetary authorities have sometimes enacted upward adjustments in regulated interest rates as part of an overall anti-inflationary package. Since 1973 use of such interest rate adjustments has been common in Latin America,[21] and increases in deposit rates and loan rates were major elements in stabilization programs in Korea and Taiwan in the mid-1960s, and in Indonesia in both 1968 and 1974. The objective in each case is twofold: to stimulate the demand for liquid assets and to discourage loan demand on the part of private-sector borrowers. The extent to which such measures can be successful depends on the interest elasticity of the demand

21. See Vicente Gablis, "Inflation and Interest Rate Policies in Latin America, 1967–76," *International Monetary Fund Staff Papers* 26, no. 2 (June 1979): 334–65.

for liquid assets and the interest elasticity of the demand for loans. In most of the cases cited above, and particularly in the three Asian countries, both sets of elasticities were evidently sufficiently high, as the stabilization packages did succeed to a large degree.

Moral suasion by the monetary authorities, sometimes called "open-mouth operations" or "jawbone control," is practiced no less extensively in LDCs than in developed countries and with much the same effect: minimal. Warnings and exhortation to commercial banks to restrict lending or to encourage them to focus lending on particular activities have been quite common in Ghana and were used at various times in Malaysia, Singapore, Brazil, and elsewhere, sometimes prior to imposition of credit ceilings and often to reinforce pressures on banks to adhere to ceilings.

FURTHER READING Before 1970 systematic discussions of the role of money and finance in development were virtually impossible to find. That situation changed for the better beginning in 1973, with the almost simultaneous publication of two influential, though not universally accepted, treatises on money and development. Edward Shaw's *Financial Deepening and Economic Development* (New York: Oxford University Press, 1973) represented the forceful views of a lifetime of thinking on the subject, and together with the next book mentioned, awakened many economists to the possibilities of deploying financial policy in support of the goals of income growth, employment, and economic stability. Ronald MacKinnon's equally forceful and, to many, no less persuasive *Money and Capital in Economic Development* (Washington, D.C.: Brookings Institution, 1973) employed a somewhat different perspective, but reached essentially similar conclusions. Furthermore, new textbooks on the topic have appeared, offering a wider menu of interpretations on the role of money and financial policy in development. For example, see Subrata Ghatak, *Monetary Economics in Developing Countries* (London: MacMillan Press, 1981); and P. J. Drake, *Money Finance and Economic Development* (New York: John Wiley and Sons, 1980).

Turning to more specific issues, a thorough treatment of the impact of world inflation on LDCs may be found in several articles in the book by William R. Cline and associates, *World Inflation and the Developing Countries* (Washington, D.C.: Brookings Institution, 1981). No student of money and finance in development can afford to overlook several contributions by Arnold C. Harberger over the period 1950–1982. Other than the articles cited in the footnotes to this chapter, an early representative example of his work is his "Dynamics of Inflation in Chile," in *Measurement in Economics: Studies in Mathematical Economics in Honor of Yehuda Grunfeld,* edited by Carl Christ (Palo Alto, Calif.: Stanford University Press, 1963).

Space limitations in this book have meant that many important topics in finance were given less attention than many would prefer. This is particularly true regarding agricultural credit. Fortunately this topic is exhaustively covered in many publications by economists at Ohio State and elsewhere, particularly Dale W. Adams, Robert Vogel, and Millard Long. See, for example, Dale W. Adams, "Mobilizing Household Savings Through Rural Financial Markets," *Economic Development and Cultural Change* 26, no. 3 (April 1978): 547–60. Those interested in a rigorous demonstration of the constraints on monetary policy in open LDC economies under fixed and flexible exchange rates would do well to consult Rudiger Dornbusch, *Open Economy Macroeconomics* (New York: Basic Books, 1980).

Finally, for a cohesive discussion of one country's experience with active financial policies over several decades, see David Cole and Yung Chul Park, *Financial Development in Korea, 1945–1978* (Cambridge, Mass.: Harvard University Press, forthcoming).

Chapter 14

FOREIGN SAVINGS: AID AND INVESTMENT

Countries that are unable to generate sufficient domestic savings to fuel their aspirations for economic growth have historically sought finance from other countries. The United States relied heavily on foreign saving, particularly during the period from 1835 to 1860, as did Russia, to help propel its development spurt in the three decades before World War I. Yet Japan, which has actively discouraged inflows of foreign saving and investment throughout its history, nevertheless became a prosperous modern nation during the period after the Meiji Restoration of 1868. Foreign saving can help development but is not essential for it.

It is helpful to keep these examples in mind at a time when a majority of developing countries consider foreign saving to be an important ingredient in their development efforts, and when controversy surrounds both foreign aid and investment. This chapter examines the roles of foreign saving in development and explores some of these controversies.

Concepts and Magnitudes

Definitions

Before proceeding, we offer some definitions. *Foreign saving* includes both official saving and private saving. Most *official saving* is on *concessional* (or "soft") terms; that is, it is made available either as outright gifts *(grants)* or as loans bearing lower interest rates and longer repayment periods than would be available in private international capital markets. Governments also make some loans on commercial terms, including export credits, equity investments, and "hard" loans from the World Bank and regional development banks. Concessional flows are technically called official development assistance (ODA), but popularly called foreign aid. Aid can be further divided into bilateral aid, given directly by one government to another, and multilateral aid, in which the funds flow to an international agency like the United Nations, the World Bank, and the regional development banks (described below), which in turn grant or lend the funds to recipient developing countries. Finally, aid can be in the form of *technical assistance,* the provision of skilled individuals to augment national expertise; or *capital assistance,* the provision of finance or commodities for a variety of purposes discussed later in this chapter.

Foreign private saving consists of four elements. *Foreign direct investment* is made by nonresidents, typically but not always by multinational corporations, in the enterprises located in host countries; direct investment implies full or partial control of the enterprise and physical presence by foreign firms or individuals. *Portfolio investment* is the purchase of host country bonds or stocks by foreigners, without managerial control. This was a very important form of foreign investment in the nineteenth and early twentieth centuries, but is no longer so. *Commercial bank lending* to developing-country governments and enterprises has supplanted portfolio investment in importance. Finally, exporting firms and their commercial banks offer *export credits* to importing countries as a way of promoting sales by permitting delayed payment for imports, often at commercial rates of interest.

Recent Trends

Trends in the net flows of foreign saving (resources) by category are summarized in Table 14–1 for the two decades from 1960 to 1980. Total net resource flows in nominal terms in 1980 were eleven times the level in 1960. As world prices increased by factor of 3.4, according to the World Bank, real net resource flows more than tripled during those twenty years.

Although no precise estimates are available, it can be roughly estimated that the $89 billion of net resource flows in 1980 was equivalent to about 4.5 percent of gross domestic product for the low- and middle-income countries taken together, excluding China (which probably received a very small portion of the resources listed in Table 14–1). This compares to roughly 3.7 percent in 1960. Foreign saving per capita in LDCs was roughly $39 in 1980. Although individual country experience differs, all but one of the low-income countries listed by the World Bank and half of the middle-income countries increased the amount of foreign saving they accepted relative to GDP. Table 14–2 presents the figures for a representative sample of LDCs. It shows some dramatic increases in the share of foreign saving in 1980, compared to 1960, including GDP shares of 12–22 percent for Bangladesh, Mali, Sri Lanka, Pakistan, Tanzania, Senegal, and Egypt. Of the four countries in the table with negative flows in 1980, which were themselves net investors abroad, three were oil exporters: Indonesia, Nigeria, and Malaysia.

TABLE 14-1 Total Net Resource Flows (Disbursements) to Developing Countries from All Foreign Sources (billion U.S. $)

	1960[f]	1970	1980[i]
A. Official flows: aid	4.94[g]	8.05	33.46[j]
1. Bilateral: DAC[a] countries	4.27	5.66	17.64
2. Bilateral: OPEC[b] countries	—	0.36	6.11
3. Bilateral: CMEA[c] countries	na	0.96	1.80
4. Multilateral agencies[d]	0.67	1.07	7.71
B. Official flows: nonaid[e]	na[g]	1.85	13.60
1. Bilateral: DAC countries		0.74	4.70
2. Bilateral: all others		0.41	4.10
3. Multilateral agencies[d]		0.70	4.80
C. Private flows	3.01	9.08	41.89
1 Direct investment	1.88	3.69	9.69
2. Bond lending (portfolio investment)	0.67	0.30	2.00
3. Commercial bank lending	na[h]	3.00	18.00
4. Export credits	0.46	2.09	12.20
D. Total net resource flows	7.95	18.98	88.95

Source: Organization for Economic Cooperation and Development (OECD), *Development Coopera-tion: 1981 Review* (Paris 1981), Table A.1; and OECD, *The Flow of Financial Resources to Developing Countries in 1961* (Paris, undated), Table 1.

[a] Development Assistance Committee of the OECD, consisting of 17 industrialized aid donors of Europe, North America, Japan, Australia, and New Zealand.

[b] Organization of Petroleum Exporting Countries.

[c] Council for Mutual Economic Assistance, including the Soviet Union and the countries of Eastern Europe.

[d] The World Bank and affiliates, plus the regional development banks.

[e] Loans and equity investments on commercial terms.

[f] DAC countries only.

[g] For 1960 nonaid official flows are included with aid flows under Part A.

[h] Included under bond lending.

[i] Estimated.

[j] Totals do not add up because of the omission of $0.20 billion of aid from other bilateral sources.

Private flows contributed more to the growth of foreign saving to developing countries than did official flows: the share of private saving in the total flow rose from 37 to 47 percent over the twenty-year period. Within foreign private saving commercial bank lending and export credits contributed the most to growth. Direct investment, which is the most discussed category of foreign private investment, did not keep pace and dropped to less than a fourth of all private flows. Thus the tendency has been for capital on fixed, hard commercial terms to finance an increasing share of developing countries' net foreign resource flows.

This tendency has been intensified by the trends within official flow categories, because official finance on nonconcessional terms has grown more rapidly than aid (foreign aid in general). Although the nominal value of aid from all sources increased about sixfold from 1960 to 1980 (see Table 14-1), the real value rose by only 75 percent. Aid as a fraction of GDP in the third world actually fell slightly during the two decades, and was about 2 percent in 1980, or roughly $15 per person.

TABLE 14–2 Foreign Saving as a Share of GDP for Selected Developing Countries, 1960 and 1980

	Foreign saving[b] as a % of GDP	
	1960	1980
Low income countries[a]	? (?)	3 (8)
Bangladesh	− 1	15
Ethiopia	1	5
Mali	5	18
India	3	3
Sri Lanka	5	22
Tanzania	− 5	14
China	0	1
Pakistan	7	12
Middle-income countries[a]	1	2
Ghana	7	0
Kenya	3	7
Indonesia	0	− 8
Senegal	1	17
Bolivia	7	− 2
Egypt	1	15
Philippines	0	5
Nigeria	6	− 4
Guatemala	2	3
Colombia	0	0
Korea (South)	10	8
Malaysia	− 13	− 3
Brazil	1	2
Mexico	2	2

Source: World Bank, *World Development Report 1982* (Washington, D.C., 1982), Table 5.

[a] Definitions are the same as for Table 1–1. Figures in parentheses exclude China and India.

[b] Measured as the difference between gross domestic investment and gross domestic saving. Negative numbers mean the country was itself a net foreign investor.

Foreign Aid

Historical Role

Foreign aid as now conceived is a product of the post–World War II era. Its roots are in the Marshall Plan, under which the United States transferred $17 billion over four years—equivalent to about 1.5 percent of U.S. GNP—to help rebuild Europe after the war. Two elements of the Marshall Plan were believed at the time to have been crucial for its success: an influx of financial capital from the United States and coordinated plans to employ it productively to rebuild Europe's devastated physical capital stock. This early manifestation of capital fundamentalism was reinforced by the Harrod-Domar view of growth economics, which emerged during the 1940s and perceived capital and its productivity to be the critical factor responsible for growth (see Chapter 6).

The two decades after World War II saw the emergence of independent nations from Europe's colonies, especially in Asia and Africa. Encouraged by its role in rebuilding Europe, the United States took the lead in trying to help the newly emerging nations by providing that same element, capital, in the form of foreign aid, especially to countries that had development plans for investing the aid they received. Early aid programs also recognized that developing countries lacked certain kinds of skills and expertise, so technical assistance programs, which supplied foreign experts in fields from economic planning to engineering to construction, were also offered.

The motives behind the American aid programs of the postwar years were complex, and ranged from the selfish to the generous. The security of the United States was the center of Congress's concerns in approving both the Marshall Plan and the "Point IV" program, under which President Truman began to shift U.S. attention and resources toward the less developed countries. This meant "containing communism" around the perimeter of the Soviet bloc as well as trying to ensure access to raw materials needed for U.S. industry. Prosperity of both the United States and its allies required expanding trade and investment, also promoted by aid. It was believed that development would serve both security and economic interests by reducing instability and giving the emerging nations a stake in the capitalist world order. U.S. aid policy was also intended to encourage the new countries to maintain or adopt democratic political institutions and private-enterprise-based economies in the U.S. image. But it has been argued that there was also a core of humanitarian concern for the welfare of the world's poor. Indeed the strength of the early aid programs depended on this mixture of nationalistic and altruistic motivations, which drew political support from a wide spectrum of opinion. Although the context has changed over thirty-five years and, as we shall see, the number of major donors has increased, the mixture of aims for all donors remains much the same in the 1980s: security, economic leverage, economic health, political evangelism, and humanitarianism.

Over time the size and composition of aid programs changed in important ways. Most of the growth in real aid flows did not come from the bilateral programs of the traditional donors of Western Europe and the United States. The real value of bilateral aid from these countries, which are grouped into the Development Assistance Committee (DAC) of the Organization for Economic Cooperation and Development (OECD), increased only by about one third. Rather, Table 14–1 shows that the large new infusion of aid came from the Organization of Petroleum Exporting Countries (OPEC) and the multilateral development agencies, led by the World Bank. However, most of the capital of the World Bank and the regional development banks originated in the DAC countries.

The DAC countries as a group disbursed $26.8 billion in aid in 1980, including both direct (bilateral) programs and their contributions to the multilateral aid agencies. This is less than a sixfold increase since 1960 and represents a 70 percent increase in real terms (Table 14–3). The United States, which in 1960 accounted for well over half of the DAC total, was responsible for only 27 percent in 1980. In that year U.S. aid represented just 0.27 percent of its GNP; only four DAC countries—all small donors —had lower shares. All the other large contributors of the DAC, shown in Table 14–3, increased their nominal aid flows by at least fourfold over the

TABLE 14-3   Net Official Development Assistance (Disbursements) from DAC Countries to LDCs and Multilateral Agencies, 1970–1980

Source	1960 (million U.S. $)	% of GNP	1970 (million U.S. $)	% of GNP	1980 (million U.S. $)	% of GNP
Canada	75	0.19	337	0.41	1,036	0.42
France	823	1.35	971	0.66	4,053	0.62
Germany (West)	223	0.31	599	0.32	3,517	0.43
Japan	105	0.24	458	0.23	3,304	0.32
Netherlands	35	0.31	196	0.61	1,577	0.99
Sweden	7	0.05	117	0.38	923	0.76
United Kingdom	407	0.56	500	0.41	1,781	0.34
United States	2,702	0.53	3,153	0.32	7,138	0.27
Total DAC	4,628	0.51	6,967	0.34	26,776	0.37
Indexes						
Nominal value	100		150		578	
Real value	100		114		169	

Source: OECD, *Development Cooperation: 1981 Review* (Paris, 1981), Tables A.3 and A.8 (1980); World Bank, *World Development Report 1981* (Washington, D.C., 1981), Table 16 (for 1960, 1970).

twenty years, and some by much more. In 1980 France, Germany, and Japan together contributed 50 percent more than the United States; in 1960 the U.S. program had been double that of the other three combined. And six countries—Belgium, Denmark, Netherlands, Norway, Sweden, and France—gave aid worth more than 0.6 percent of their GNP.

As aid flows and the number of donors expanded, the economic development rationale for aid changed as well. During the 1950s the main economic goal was rapid growth of output and incomes, to be achieved by increasing the amount of domestic and foreign saving available for investment. By the 1960s the two-gap model augmented the Harrod-Domar perspective, and foreign exchange became as important as capital (see Chapter 6). Human capital received emphasis beyond the recognized role of technical assistance, and aid programs spread into education, health, and other human services. During the late 1960s and the 1970s aid programs began to incorporate goals other than promotion of economic growth: income redistribution, poverty alleviation, supply of basic needs, and rural development became motivators for the aid programs of most donors.

We said earlier that in 1980 developing countries on average received aid equivalent to 2 percent of their GDP. However, there are major and moderately systematic variations around this rather low average, as Table 14-4 reveals. First, there is a strong tendency for aid to represent a higher fraction of GDP for poorer countries. All countries with GDP shares over 5 percent—and aid per capita levels over $10—have incomes per capita below $600 in 1980, while those with incomes over $600 generally have negligible flows of aid. This was not always true. In the early 1960s relatively prosperous Brazil and Colombia, for example, had large shares of the U.S. aid program. But the increasing scarcity of concessional resource flows, combined with growing emphasis on the relief of poverty, have probably intensified the tendency to aid very poor countries more than others.

TABLE 14-4   Net Receipts of Official Development Assistance from All Sources by Selected LDCs, 1980[a]

Country	GNP per capita ($) 1980	Net official development assistance		
		U.S. $ (millions)	% GDP	Per capita ($)
Low-income countries				
Bangladesh	130	1220	11	14
Ethiopia	140	178	5	6
Mali	190	210	15	30
India	240	2161	2	3
Sri Lanka	270	431	11	29
Tanzania	280	625	14	33
China	290	55	0	0
Pakistan	300	1037	5	13
Middle-income countries				
Ghana	420	183	1	16
Kenya	420	380	6	24
Indonesia	430	939	1	6
Senegal	440	237	9	42
Bolivia	570	169	3	30
Egypt	580	1354	6	34
Philippines	690	294	1	6
Nigeria	930	34	0	0
Guatemala	1080	73	1	10
Colombia	1180	90	0	3
Korea (South)	1520	139	0	4
Malaysia	1620	122	1	9
Brazil	1870	85	0	1
Mexico	2090	56	0	1

Sources: OECD, Development Cooperation: 1981 Review (Paris, 1981), Table D.2 (for aid receipts); World Bank, World Development Report 1982 (Washington, D.C., 1982), Tables 1 and 3 (for GDP and population).

[a] Definitions are the same as for Table 1-1.

The exceptions to this rule point to a second strong tendency. Among the countries with incomes below $600 per capita in the table only the very large ones—China, India, and Indonesia—have low aid levels relative to GDP or population. The dollar amounts going to these countries are quite large, except for China. Donors, faced with a choice of spreading their aid proportionally (to GDP or population) and having scant impact anywhere, or concentrating it where they can make a larger impact, choose the latter. Small countries thus get greater relative amounts of aid, but also become more dependent on the donors who provide it, than is true for large countries.

Finally, Table 14-4 includes some examples of countries that are favored for political and strategic reasons. Mali and Senegal benefit disproportionately, as do all Francophone African states—former French colonies—from France's generous aid program. Egypt, along with Israel, has been favored by United States' efforts to reduce tensions in the Middle East. During the 1950s South Korea, Taiwan, Pakistan, Turkey, and other military-dominated governments were favored recipients of U.S. aid. Although the manifestations of politically inspired aid are strongest in these cases, they are present to some extent in many other countries.

Aid Institutions and Instruments

Bilateral aid donors usually plan and dispense loans and grants through an aid agency, such as the United States Agency for International Development (USAID), Britain's Overseas Development Ministry (ODM), the International Development Agencies of Canada (CIDA) and Sweden (SIDA), and others. Most development assistance agencies deal with a wide range of aid instruments, both technical and capital assistance. Most of the capital aid is disbursed against specific projects, such as a hydroelectric dam, a road, or a rural development project, and is called *project aid.* However, some bilateral agencies, including USAID, have made *program loans,* which finance general categories of imports and are conceived as broad support for the balance of payments, in the spirit of closing the foreign exchange gap of the two-gap model. Program loans were more important during the 1960s when large amounts went to countries like India, Pakistan, and Brazil, than during the 1970s, but have made a comeback—largely as "structural adjustment loans" by the World Bank—during the period of extreme resource scarcity following the second oil price increase in 1979. *Food aid* is a kind of bilateral program loan since it provides commodities, mostly grains, that would otherwise have to be purchased with a country's own foreign exchange earnings.

The full range of motives of the donor countries, discussed above, is given fullest expression in bilateral programs, which can easily be treated as extensions of donors' foreign policy. Establishment of multilateral institutions to dispense aid, and providing these international agencies with a growing share of aid resources, indicates that the donor countries give aid for reasons other than simple self-interest. Nevertheless it is true that the largest donors exercise greatest control over the World Bank and other multilateral agencies (though not over the United Nations' agencies). Still the multilateral organizations are focused almost exclusively on development and shield recipients to a considerable extent from the foreign policy concerns of the industrial countries.

The main multilateral aid agencies and the amounts they disbursed in 1970 and 1980 are given in Table 14–5. The largest and most influential of these is the World Bank (International Bank for Reconstruction and Development, or IBRD), together with its affiliates, the International Development Association (IDA) and International Finance Corporation (IFC). Despite its leading role in the aid community, most of the capital supplied by the World Bank is not aid. The IBRD obtains its funds by borrowing on world capital markets at prevailing prime interest rates and relends to developing countries at slightly higher rates. It makes more capital available, and at lower interest rates, than could be obtained by the developing countries on their own. Its affiliate, the IFC, lends on commercial terms and takes small equity positions in support of private foreign investments. Only the IDA, which channels contributions from the richer member countries to the poorer LDCs at very soft terms, dispenses aid in the strict sense. Most of the World Bank's and IDA's loans are for projects, but program loans are also made. During the 1970s the World Bank became the

TABLE 14-5 Net Disbursements by Multilateral Aid Agencies, 1970–1980 (million U.S. $)

Agency	Concessional flows		Nonconcessional flows	
	1970	1980	1970	1980
World Bank and related institutions[a]	163	1650	576	3461
Interamerican Development Bank (IDB)	224	326	84	567
African Development Bank	—	96	2	97
Asian Development Bank	1	149	15	328
Caribbean Development Bank	—	43	—	11
EEC/European Invest. Bank	210	1013	11	257
IMF Trust Fund	—	1636	—	—
United Nations	498	2512	—	—
Arab OPEC	—	263	—	142
Total	1096	7688	688	4863

Source: OECD, *Development Cooperation: 1981 Review* (Paris, 1981), Table C.2.

[a] The World Bank group includes, besides the World Bank, the International Development Association (IDA) which dispenses heavily concessionary aid, and the International Finance Corporation (IFC), oriented toward lending to the private sector.

world's leading center for research, information, and policy advice on economic development. In 1980 the World Bank group disbursed over $5 billion, 40 percent of the total for all multilateral agencies.

The word "Reconstruction" in the bank's title stems from its origin, at the Bretton Woods (New Hampshire) conference in 1944, when its first task was to help finance the reconstruction of wartorn European countries. The other institution founded at the conference was the International Monetary Fund (IMF), whose main charge was to reestablish an international system of national currencies in stable relation to each other, in support of a rejuvenated world trade system. The IMF played a significant role in the unprecedented expansion of world trade during the 1950s and 1960s. Although not primarily concerned with promoting development, IMF practices and resources have had a major effect on developing countries and the fund is increasingly turning its attention toward assisting LDCs by offering balance-of-payments support in a variety of ways, sometimes on easier terms than obtained by more developed countries. The IMF's lending policies, which focus on programs of economic stabilization to control inflation, have come under attack from critics in the developing countries who would like to see fewer economic conditions attached to IMF loans.

Each of the third world's continents—Asia, Africa, and Latin America—has its own regional development bank. These each have separate "windows," or programs, that dispense hard and soft loans to member countries. Regional members and the major aid donors contribute to the capital of these banks, which also borrow on private capital markets to finance hard loans, and receive contributions from aid donors for their soft loan windows. Virtually all finance from the regional banks is for projects.

Two regional organizations are aid donors: the European Economic Community and the Arab OPEC states. The EEC originally concentrated its aid on former French colonies in Africa, but now spreads its assistance more widely, especially in Africa. OPEC, a new arrival on the aid scene, uses a part of its oil wealth to aid developing countries, with a concentration on Islamic states.

Finally, the United Nations has the largest concessional program of the multilaterals, $2.5 billion of mostly technical assistance in 1980. The focus of this effort is the United Nations Development Programme (UNDP), which makes grants to member countries. However, the "specialized agencies" of the U.N., such as the U.N. Industrial Development Organization (UNIDO), International Labor Organization (ILO), and World Health Organization (WHO), among others, execute the technical assistance projects financed by UNDP.

Impacts on Development

In a Harrod-Domar world it would be easy to measure the contribution of aid and other foreign saving to development. In this model the role of foreign saving of all kinds is to augment domestic saving to increase investment and thus accelerate growth. If aid and other foreign saving added, say, 6 percent to GDP, all of it went to additional investment, and the capital/output ratio were 3.0, then the growth rate would be increased by 2 percentage points.[1] A glance back at Table 14–2 shows that for some countries—Bangladesh, Mali, Sri Lanka, Tanzania, Pakistan, Senegal, and Egypt—foreign saving is a large fraction of GDP and could be contributing 4–6 percentage points to the growth rate. For countries like India, China, Ghana, Mexico, and Brazil, foreign saving is a small fraction of GDP and cannot have much impact on growth.

In the slightly more complex world of the two-gap model, where aid and other foreign saving contribute either to greater investment or to greater imports (by supplying more foreign exchange), the story is essentially the same. If foreign exchange is the scarce factor, then aid's contribution to growth would be proportional to its contribution to additional imports. These contributions have been quite large for the more favored recipients of foreign saving shown in Table 14–2.

The fact that growth rates in the large aid-recipient countries have not been very high is one indication that the Harrod-Domar approach is faulty. Developing countries may of course lack some important complementary inputs to development, such as human skills, administrative capacity, infrastructure, economic institutions, and political stability, without which even high savings rates may not stimulate growth. But even if these barriers to growth were overcome, some economists have argued that foreign saving, especially aid, may not contribute much to additional saving or imports. Rather, they suggest, foreign saving may substitute for (not add to) domes-

---

1. From equation 6–4 of Chapter 6, $g = s/k$. Here, additional foreign saving adds a fraction, f, to GDP, all of which is saved, so $\Delta s = f$. Hence, $\Delta g = \Delta s/k = f/k = 0.06/3.0 = 0.02$ or 2%.

tic saving, permitting increases in consumption (instead of increases in investment) and decreases in exports (rather than additional imports).

A debate has been waged between economists who claim that aid merely substitutes for domestic saving and others who say it adds to domestic saving and thus to growth. As with most such debates the answer lies somewhere between, and Fig. 14–1 helps us to understand why.[2] It depicts a developing country that, before it obtains aid, can produce consumption goods and capital goods along the production possibilities frontier *PP*. To simplify, the diagram ignores international trade. Community tastes are defined by a set of indifference curves, of which two, labeled I and II, are shown. Without aid the country's welfare is maximized if it produces and consumes at point *A*, where indifference curve I is tangent to frontier *PP*, with consumption at C_1 and investment at I_1.

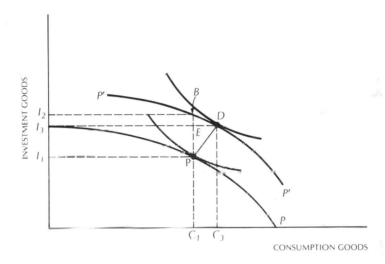

Fig. 14–1 Impact of Aid on Investment and Consumption.

Now donor countries contribute an amount, *AB*, of aid. They intend that the full amount should be invested, raising total investment to I_2. However, for reasons explained below, recipients have considerable freedom to convert aid into either investment or consumption. In this case the offer of aid *AB* in effect moves the production frontier outward from *PP* to *P'P'*. With these added resources the country maximizes its welfare by producing at point *D*, the tangency between *P'P'* and indifference curve II. It consumes C_3 and invests I_3. Of the aid amount *AB*, *AE* (equal to $I_3 - I_1$) has been invested, as intended by the donors, but *BE* (equal to $I_2 - I_3$) has been consumed. If the country's tastes favored consumption over investment even more, then it would reach equilibrium at a point along *P'P'* to the

2. The figure is adapted from Paul Mosley, "Aid, Savings and Growth Revisited," *Oxford Bulletin of Economics and Statistics* 42 (May 1980): 79–91. The article summarizes and extends the debate on aid as a substitute for domestic saving.

southeast of D, and would convert even more of its aid into consumption. Thus the amount of aid actually used to increase investment will depend on production possibilities, community tastes, and other variables, such as trade, left out of the diagram.

How can a country convert aid and other foreign saving, which is intended to be used for investment, into consumption? Some forms of foreign saving, such as program aid or commercial bank loans, are designed to provide finance for general purposes and thus deliberately give the recipient the kinds of choices demonstrated in Fig. 14–1. Food aid, of course, is intended to increase or maintain consumption rather than investment. But even if all foreign saving were dispensed as project aid and targeted to specific investment projects, substitution would be possible. Project aid might, for example, be used for investments that the government or its private investors would have made even without aid. In that case resources are freed up for other purposes, including consumption. When aid finances projects that might not otherwise be implemented, government may simply cut back on its preferred projects because it wants to raise the share of consumption, for economic or political reasons. When substitutions of these kinds are possible, aid is called "fungible."

Perhaps more important, a host of subtle influences of foreign saving on relative prices may also contribute to substitution. More capital in general could conceivably mean a lower return on investments and hence a greater tendency to consume in the recipient countries, although this has never been documented. More foreign exchange tends to lower its price (i.e., to revalue the exchange rate; see Chapter 15) and cause greater demand for imports, as intended by donors, but would also create a reduced incentive to produce for export, which is not intended. And food aid has a similar effect, lowering food prices because it satisfies part of domestic demand, hence reducing the incentive for domestic farmers to produce foods. These influences could be overcome by countervailing government policies, but governments may not undertake such measures for a variety of reasons discussed in other chapters. In sum the contribution of aid and other foreign saving to development is not that it provides specific amounts of additional investment, imports, or food. Rather, foreign saving provides additional purchasing power for the country and hence the *possibility* of increasing investment, imports, or food. Recipient countries will take advantage of such possibilities to varying degrees.

Considered in terms of substitution possibilities, aid is probably not very different from other sources of foreign saving, official or private. But in two respects aid makes a different kind of contribution to development. Obviously it comes on softer terms, thus reducing the burden of repayment in the future and increasing future net inflows of foreign resources, other things equal. A measure of this is the **grant equivalent** of aid. The grant equivalent of a loan is the difference between the loan amount and the discounted present value of loan repayments—principal and interest—expressed as a percentage of the loan's face value. The discount rate would be the interest rate obtainable in commercial markets. Thus the grant element of a commercial loan would be zero and that of a grant would be 100 percent. Soft loans, such as those made by the International Development Association, have grant elements over 90 percent. The grant elements for bilateral aid programs of the major DAC donors are all 90 percent or more, except for Japan.

The second difference between aid and private flows is that aid donors and other official sources of capital often try to use their assistance as a lever to obtain their own policy goals. Donors offer aid to reward political friends and military allies, and withhold it from those perceived as enemies. They tie aid funds to the purchase of goods and services in their own countries as a way of increasing their own markets for exports and of dampening the impact of aid on their own balance of payments. They channel it toward countries and institutions within countries that adhere most closely to the donor's own views of economics and politics. These are perhaps the crassest uses of aid, and they are generally confined to bilateral donors.

Donors, both bilateral and multilateral, also use aid to induce LDC governments to change their development policies in what donors believe to be the country's own best interests. For reasons discussed in Part IV, donors offer aid in support of currency devaluation and liberalization programs. They make loans contingent upon changes in tax systems, adoption of new wage and income policies, adjustments in food and other agricultural prices, and many other policy actions. They change aid allocations to match shifts in development thinking, for example toward rural development and away from industrial development during the 1970s. Donors supply technical assistance, much of which is truly technical in a narrow sense, but some of which involves foreign advisers whose aim is to change government policies in various ways or to alter budget and other resource allocations. To the extent that host governments acquiesce to such changes (and in many cases they may want to undertake them in any event), policy leverage may be as important a contribution of aid programs to development as the resource flows they finance. However, governments have ways of appearing to accept conditions, then not implementing them fully; and donors have reasons to continue offering their aid even if conditions are not met. A summary judgment is that aid leverage generally is a weak and somewhat clumsy instrument, not difficult for host governments to evade if they choose.

Foreign Investment and the Multinationals

Foreign direct investment accounted for only 11 percent of the total foreign saving entering developing countries in 1980, a sharp drop from its 23 percent share in 1960 (Table 14–1). Yet direct investment still receives most of the attention, and attracts most of the controversy, when foreign resources flows are discussed in the literature or by LDC officials. There are two reasons for this. First, foreign investment comes in a package that may include not only equity finance, but often much larger amounts of loan finance, management expertise, modern technologies, technical skills, and access to world markets. The other elements of the package are perceived to be as important as the equity finance itself. Second, this package is controlled by multinational corporations, whose size and economic influence often match and sometimes outstrip that of the recipient country governments. An invitation to a multinational corporation raises the spectre of interference by, and dependence on, foreign economic powers that seem beholden to no government. We shall examine the reality of these fears, and the potential benefits of foreign investment, in this section.

Multinationals' Investment Patterns

The overwhelming proportion of direct foreign investment in third world nations is done by multinational corporations (MNCs). A multinational is an enterprise that has significant productive operations in more than one nation and considers production abroad to be a central, rather than a peripheral, concern. Multinational enterprises come in all sizes and from all regions of the world, but a relatively small number are dominant. In 1978 roughly 10,000 MNCs were in existence, exercising control over nearly 83,000 foreign affiliates.[3] But only 430 firms accounted for 80 percent of the world's stock of direct foreign investment in that year.

A common misconception is that most foreign direct investment from industrial nations is located in developing nations. However, except for Japan, rich countries tend strongly to invest in one another, not in LDCs. Fully three-fourths of the MNC affiliates are located in the European Economic Community (EEC), Switzerland, and North America. Over the period of most rapid expansion by United States–based multinationals, 1950–1970, United States direct foreign investment grew from about $19 billion to $140 billion. Only 30 percent of this new investment went to developing countries. By the mid-1970s only 14 percent of total U.S. direct investment was in developing countries.[4] Foreign investment by multinationals based in Britain, Germany, and France has followed a similar pattern over the period 1966–1976. The developing country share in total flows of foreign investment from these countries was only 19 percent for Britain and barely 30 percent for West Germany and France. Only Japan ran counter to this pattern: 60 percent of Japanese direct foreign investment from 1960 to 1976 went to developing countries. Overall, the share of the stock of investment by all developed-country MNCs in developing countries fell from 30 percent to 25 percent from 1967 to 1977.[5] From Table 14–6 it is evident that foreign investment in most LDCs, except for

---

3. John Stopford, John Dunning, and Klaus Haberich, *The World Directory of Multinational Enterprises* (London: Facts on File, 1980), p. xiv.

4. Figures on foreign investment flows by country come from K. Billerbeck and Y. Yasugi, "Private Direct Foreign Investment in Developing Countries" (World Bank Staff Working Paper No. 348, 1979), Table II–1.

5. Stopford, Dunning, and Haberich, *World Directory*, p. xvii.

TABLE 14-6   Stock of Direct Foreign Investment, in Developed and Developing Countries, 1975 (U.S. billions in current prices)

I. Total foreign direct investment in host countries		$263.0
II. Total foreign direct investment in developed market economies		$193.5
1. Canada	36.6	
2. United States	26.7	
3. United Kingdom	22.3	
4. West Germany	19.6	
5. Italy	5.8	
6. Japan	1.5	
7. All other developed countries	81.5	
III. Total foreign direct investment in developing economies		$69.5
1. Brazil	9.1	
2. Mexico	4.8	
3. Venezuela	4.0	
4. Indonesia	3.5	
5. Nigeria	2.9	
6. India	2.4	
7. Malaysia	2.3	
8. Argentina	2.0	
9. Singapore	1.7	
10. Peru	1.7	
11. Hong Kong	1.3	
12. Iran	1.2	
13. All other LDCs	31.6	

Source: Derived from Tables 2, 3, and 4 in John Stopford, John Dunning, and Klaus Haberich, *The World Directory of Multinational Enterprises* (London: Facts on File, 1980), pp. x–xviii.

Brazil, is a small proportion of that undertaken in most of the largest industrial country recipients (Canada and the United states).

Another common misconception is that most direct foreign investment from rich to poor countries reflects an attempt by multinationals to shift manufacturing activities to LDCs to take advantage of "cheap" foreign labor. Some foreign investment in manufacturing is motivated by this consideration, and employment generation by MNCs is actively sought in many LDCs. However, from 1965 to 1978 manufacturing investments were only 38 percent of total foreign investment flows from rich countries. Historically a very sizable proportion of the flow of MNC capital to LDCs has been concentrated in the extraction and processing of natural resources, a highly capital-intensive activity which depends very little on the availability of low-cost labor but very much on the presence of natural resource deposits. Far more MNC investment goes to relatively high-income, high-wage LDCs than to very poor countries with "cheap" labor. By 1975 countries with per-capita income in excess of $1000 had received half of all direct foreign investment.

Finally, investment activities of MNCs are not evenly distributed among different regions in the developing world. Latin America and the Caribbean have received about half the flow in recent years. Asia, principally Southeast and East Asia, received about a quarter of the total, followed by Africa with about 12 percent.

Characteristics of Multinationals

The stereotypical image of a multinational enterprise is that of a very large, U.S.-based, private sector enterprise. Moden multinational (MNCs) are indeed typically very large, but they are no longer essentially American creatures, nor do all trace their lineage to the private sector. Indeed Chapter 21 identifies several state-owned MNCs that have in recent years begun to play a major role in international investments. Many multinationals have worldwide sales or assets that are large compared to the GDPs of some host country LDCs (see Table 14–7). Comparisons of MNC sales with GDP of LDCs are not, however, particularly instructive since GDP measures not total sales, but value-added. Comparisons of the relative size of MNC assets to those of LDCs would be revealing if data on the latter were available.

TABLE 14–7 Comparison of Relative Size of Multinational Corporations and LDC Host Country Economies, 1979 (billions of 1979 $)

	Total GDP	
I. Largest LDC Market Economies		
A. Largest (Brazil)	$204.5	
B. Fifth largest (Nigeria)	75.2	
C. Tenth largest (Malaysia)	20.3	
D. Fifteenth largest (Pakistan)	17.9	
E. Twentieth largest (Zaire)	6.0	
	Sales	*Assets*
II. Largest MNCs in Fortune 500 (U.S.)		
A. Largest (Exxon)	$79.1	$49.5
B. Tenth largest (Std. Indiana)	18.6	17.2
C. Twenty-fifth largest (Union Carbide)	9.1	8.8
D. Hundredth largest (Textron)	3.4	2.1
E. Smallest MNC in Fortune 500 (Dow Jones)	0.5	0.4
	Sales	*Assets*
III. Largest MNCs in Fortune 500 (outside U.S.)		
A. Largest (Royal-Dutch Shell-Br., Holland)	$59.4	$59.6
B. Tenth largest (Siemens-Germany)	15.1	17.0
C. Twenty-fifth largest (Petrobas-Brazil)	10.3	11.1
D. Hundredth largest (Alusuisse-Switz.)	3.5	5.0
E. Smallest (Fuji Kosan-Japan)	0.8	0.7

Sources: Section I: World Bank, *World Development Report 1981* (Washington, D.C., 1981), Table 3; section II: *Fortune* magazine, May 5, 1980, pp. 280–90; section III: *Fortune* magazine, August 11, 1980, pp. 489–500.

The perception that modern MNCs are essentially American creatures carries over from the early postwar period when European firms were preoccupied with rebuilding war damage and domestic markets. By 1971 U.S.-based firms accounted for about 57 percent of the total stock of foreign investment in the world (see Table 14–8). By 1978, the share of U.S.-based firms had fallen to 46 percent, owing to very rapid growth of Japanese- and German-based MNCs. U.S. and to a lesser extent British

TABLE 14–8   Stock of Direct Foreign Investment from Developed Market Countries: 1967, 1978 (U.S. $ billions in current prices)

	1967		1978	
Country of origin	Amount	%	Amount	%
1. United States	56.6	49.3	168.1	45.5
2. United Kingdom	17.5	14.1	41.1	11.1
3. West Germany	3.0	4.3	31.8	8.6
4. Japan	1.5	2.6	26.8	7.3
5. Switzerland	5.0	5.7	24.6	6.7
6. Netherlands	11.0	8.2	23.7	6.4
7. France	6.0	4.3	14.9	4.0
8. Canada	3.7	3.9	13.6	3.7
9. Sweden	1.7	1.4	6.0	1.6
10. Belgium-Luxemburg	2.0	1.4	4.5	1.5
11. Italy	2.1	1.8	3.3	0.9
12. All other LDCs (est.)	4.0	3.0	10.0	2.7
Total	114.1	100.0	369.3	100.0

Source: John Stopford, John Dunning, and Klaus Haberich, *The World Directory of Multinational Enterprises* (London: Facts on File, 1980), Table 2, p. xv.

domination of foreign investments in LDCs has diminished as well. Over the period 1960–1976 U.S.-based MNCs accounted for barely 50 percent of total flows of foreign investment to LDCs. British and French firms were responsible for 10 and 8 percent, respectively, while French and Japanese MNCs accounted for about 9 percent each.[6] The remaining 15 percent of foreign direct investment in LDCs was carried out by enterprises based in other Western European countries and—increasingly since 1970—over 1000 multinational enterprises from developing countries such as India, Brazil, and Argentina.

Multinationals from developing countries have been investing in other LDCs for decades. Three Argentine-based firms had foreign subsidiaries before 1940. By the late 1970s MNCs from such Asian countries as Korea, Hong Kong, India, Philippines, and Malaysia operated nearly 700 foreign investment projects, primarily in labor-intensive manufacturing investments and logging. Many of these are quite small, both in terms of total investment and in sales. But a few, such as India's Birla, Malaysia's Sime Darby, or Argentina's Bunge y Born, are among the largest privately owned firms in LDCs.

In sum, multinationals are now so varied in nationalities, production, ownership, and size that generalizations about their characteristics, much less their objectives and conduct, have become increasingly more difficult to make.

The Multinational Investment "Package"

Today, foreign investment is valued, where it *is* valued, not so much for the additional capital it makes available but for other reasons. The successful multinationals have been able to assemble a distinctive "package" of

6. Billerbeck and Yasugi, "Private Direct Foreign Investment," pp. 4–5.

resources attractive to host countries, developing and otherwise. Capital is an important part of the package, because the MNCs possess prodigious capacities for raising it. But MNCs have been able to bundle within the package other elements that are even more difficult for LDCs to secure: technology, management expertise, technical skills, and access to markets, all viewed as vital not merely for the process of industrialization but for coping with an increasingly complex, rapidly changing world society.

Technology often constitutes the core of the package, and is the element most jealously guarded by the MNCs because the maintenance of technological advantages increasingly determines the long-run survival of the firms. In some cases such advantages can vanish almost overnight, as in the early 1980s in the electronics industry when Japanese firms outraced U.S. enterprises in implementing successive innovations. The technological component of the multinational package is embodied in processes (such as in metallurgy or textile manufacture) and equipment (as in steelmaking and communications). But it also encompasses the information and technological skills required to adapt, install, operate, and maintain processes and equipment. Occasionally these skills, but rarely ever the processes, can be lured away from the multinationals, or can be home-grown by developing countries, as Mexico has shown in certain lines of metallurgy and Hong Kong in textiles.

Another prime component of the package is managerial ability, without which access to technology is largely ornamental. To be sure, many LDCs have gifted indigenous entrepreneurs and innovators. The market women in West African countries such as Ghana and Nigeria are prime illustrations, as are many representatives of such ethnic groups as the Batak and Minangkabau in Indonesia, or regional clusters of adaptive industrialists in such Latin American cities as Monterrey, Medellin, and São Paulo. Nevertheless few third world countries possess sufficient numbers of managers capable of organizing and operating large industrial projects such as those undertaken by MNCs, and virtually all are short of people with advanced training in management. For example, in 1980 Indonesia, with 147 million people, had fewer than 30 resident indigenous M.B.A.s, and Ecuador, with 8 million people, had but 5; whereas IBM alone has perhaps 1000 M.B.A.s. While an M.B.A. diploma is not a guarantee of managerial competence, other trained personnel with technical backgrounds capable of assuming management tasks are also typically in short supply.

The final major component of the multinationals' package is access to world markets. LDCs capable of producing at competitive costs often find it difficult to penetrate foreign markets. Many MNCs, particularly in natural resources, are part of vertically integrated, oligopolistic industries in which marketing is primarily a matter of intrafirm transactions. In the mid-1970s around half of all imports into and exports from the United States were intrafirm sales, while in both Canada and Sweden about 30 percent of MNC exports were from parent multinationals to their affiliates.[7] In other cases MNCs have been able to develop preferential access to

---

7. Stopford, Dunning, and Haberich, *World Directory,* p. xxiii.

customers by fashioning and adhering to long-term contracts in standardized products, such as petroleum, or by acquiring a reputation for delivering a specialized product of satisfactory quality on a reliable schedule, as in construction and engineering. LDC efforts to overcome the marketing advantages of the multinationals often require years before a breakthrough is made, although Asian LDC textile firms have shown that it can be done.

For much of the post-war era LDCs were generally forced to accept the entire multinational package or get none of it. The multinationals have been loath to allow any "unbundling" of the key ingredients, in the probably correct belief that the package as a whole is more profitable than the sum of its separate elements. Unbundling is also resisted because technological secrets might thereby be made more easily accessible to competitors, and because in some cases various elements of the package may have been inextricably linked, unable to stand alone.

The international oil industry illustrates the widespread resistance to unbundling. Large MNCs in petroleum have ordinarily preferred direct investment in overseas oil sectors, with equity funds forming a substantial part of the total investment. LDCs with prospective oil deposits face not only very large capital requirements in mounting exploration on their own but even more fundamental technical and marketing barriers. Yet some host governments are reluctant to allow international petroleum companies to enter as equity investors, both because they reject any implication of foreign "ownership" of oil deposits and because equity investment entitles the oil companies to a portion of any future windfall gains from discovery and export of particularly attractive deposits. Consequently host governments, particularly in Latin America, have sought to induce oil companies to unbundle the package of resources at their disposal. Contractual devices such as service contracts are designed to limit MNC capital to debt, not equity, and to strip the companies of marketing functions, but at the same time to attract the technological and managerial skills held so closely by the MNCs. The companies would in effect perform a banking function on the one hand and act as vendors of technology and skills on the other.

The companies, however, do not perceive themselves as bankers, or as retailers of technological information, and tend strongly to resist any such efforts toward unbundling. Although these and most other LDC efforts to break down the MNC package in oil and other fields have not been particularly successful to date, the potential benefits have appeared large to many governments. Nevertheless some knowledgeable observers of MNCs doubt whether the gains from unbundling would prove to be very great.[8] Although the Japanese have had some success in licensing technologies from multinationals without buying the whole package, they have also met stubborn resistance from the multinationals. But the large size of the Japanese market gives them greater bargaining power. Also, the Japanese possess greater technical skills for adapting technologies to local conditions than do most, if not all, of the developing countries.

8. See, for example, Raymond Vernon, *Storm Over the Multinationals: The Real Issues* (Cambridge, Mass.: Harvard University Press, 1977), pp. 159–61.

Benefits of Foreign Investment

Host country legislation toward foreign investment reveals that those LDCs that do actively seek foreign investment expect a variety of tangible and intangible benefits from infusion of the package of resources provided by MNCs. Perhaps the most commonly stated objectives are those of job creation, transfer of usable technology and skills, and saving or earning foreign exchange. In addition many host countries seek foreign investment, particularly in natural resources, to help promote regional development objectives and to increase domestic tax revenues.

Employment Expansion   The spotty empirical evidence on employment expansion from foreign investment is hardly convincing one way or another. Some observers maintain that displacement of local firms by multinationals may actually reduce local employment.[9] The argument hinges on the labor intensity of production techniques selected by foreign firms, a matter discussed below. The available evidence seems to indicate that host country hopes for significant employment gains from MNC investments are seldom realized. In very few LDCs has employment in MNC projects exceeded 1 percent on the labor force. Prominent exceptions include Brazil and Mexico, in which foreign-controlled affiliates compose half of the industrial sector,[10] and Spain before 1970, when that nation was generally regarded as a developing country. Other exceptions include such relatively small countries as Singapore (manufacturing and tourism), Jamaica (tourism and bauxite), and perhaps Cuba before Castro.

One reason for limited employment growth from MNC investments is that LDCs frequently limit entry of foreign firms to sectors, such as minerals, petroleum, and chemicals, that are typically very capital-intensive. A $500-million oil refinery may employ fewer than 400 people, and a $1-billion natural gas liquefication plant ordinarily operates with even fewer workers. The share of multinational investments in LDCs devoted to natural resource extraction and processing has been placed as high as 42 percent for the period 1965–1972.[11] In these industries investment costs per job created can be quite high. In 1976 it took $220,000 of investment to create one job in nickel mining in Indonesia, and $467,000 per job in pulp and paper in 1980, both sectors in which foreign companies are welcome. Yet in textiles, where they are no longer welcome, a job could be created for only $10,000 of investment.

Critics of multinationals allege that not only do these firms tend to invest in capital-intensive sectors (where the host governments usually want them to invest), but they also tend to utilize more capital-intensive technologies than host country firms in the same industry. But there is little if any empirical support for this claim. One recent study found that subsidiaries of U.S.-based firms appeared to use technologies similar to those of locally

9. Osvaldo Sunkel, "Big Business and Dependencies," *Foreign Affairs* 50 (1972): 518–19.

10. C. Fred Bergston, Thomas Horst, and Theodore H. Moran, *American Multinationals and American Interests* (Washington, D.C: Brookings Institution, 1978), p. 355.

11. Billerbeck and Yasugi, "Private Direct Foreign Investment," Table SI–6.

owned firms, but to operate in a more capital-intensive manner because as foreign investors they faced higher labor costs than local firms. The study found that U.S. and Swedish multinationals do adapt to lower labor costs in LDCs by using more labor-intensive methods than the same firms use in industrial countries.[12] White cites a number of studies showing mixed results, but concludes that although MNCs may not be heroes of "appropriate" technology, they are far from the villains painted by many critics.[13]

Estimates of employment created in LDCs by American multinationals range over a wide span,[14] but a 1975 figure of between 1.0 and 1.7 million jobs appears plausible, with about 80 percent of these jobs in Latin America and the Caribbean. These jobs were associated with about $29.1 billion in U.S.-based MNC investments in LDCs. Even the higher estimate suggests that U.S. multinationals employed only about 1 percent of the combined labor force in all Latin America. For LDCs outside of Latin America the proportion was less than one-twentieth of 1 percent. There are no reasons for believing that the investment of U.S.-based firms tends to be any more or less capital-intensive than for MNCs from other industrial countries.

MNCs from other developing countries tend to be more effective job creators, even though the volume of their investments remains relatively small. There is a growing body of evidence that developing-country multinationals employ markedly more labor-intensive practices than their developed-country counterparts.[15] Their investments are more heavily concentrated in relatively labor-intensive industrial undertakings like textiles and simple consumer goods, such as umbrellas, kerosene lanterns, utensils, and several types of machinery. And the majority of the LDC firms depend on special production abilities on a small scale, attributes that are inherently labor-intensive.

Technology Transfer   The second major benefit expected from foreign investment is the transfer of technology, skills, and know-how. The issue is best seen as only peripherally involving exotic processes and sophisticated equipment, but as a fundamental problem in the market for information, a market characterized by severe imperfections. Because much of the world's research and development activities has been undertaken by firms in North

12. Robert E. Lipsey, Irving B. Kraus, and Romualdo A. Roldan, "Do Multinational Firms Adapt Factor Proportions to Relative Factor Prices?" (Cambridge, Mass.: National Bureau of Economic Research Working Paper #293, October 1978). For supporting evidence, see Byung Soo Chung and Chung H. Lee, "The Choice of Production Techniques by Foreign Firms in Korea," *Economic Development and Cultural Change* 29 (1980): 135–40.

13. Lawrence J. White, "The Evidence on Appropriate Factor Proportions," *Economic Development and Cultural Change* 27 (October 1978): 27–59.

14. Results from several methodologies estimated a low of 871,000 and a high of 1.5 million in 1973. For 1975 the lower estimate was about 971,000, and the same methodologies as used in the high estimate would result in a figure of about 1.68 million. See Bergston, Horst, and Moran, *American Multinationals,* p. 368.

15. Prof. L. T. Wells of Harvard University had conducted a number of studies on LDC MNCs. See, among other examples of his work, "The Internationalization of Firms from LDC," in Tamir Agmon and C. P. Kindleberger (eds.), *Multinationals from Small Countries* (Cambridge, Mass.: MIT Press, 1977).

America, Europe, and Japan, these firms are a potentially rich source of valuable information on new technology, new processes, new marketing methods and managerial approaches. Smaller MNCs, particularly those from other LDCs, offer another kind of technological benefit: successful adaptation to LDC conditions of older technology from developed countries, and new, cost-saving innovations in small-scale manufacture. If this information can be transplanted to host countries, material increases in growth and productivity can result over the long term. The ability of an LDC to capitalize on such opportunities depends primarily on three factors: (1) the host country's capacity to absorb new information as defined by the skills of its people; (2) the willingness of MNCs to accommodate host country desires for technological transfer; and (3) host country policies toward technological transfer and information generation and dissemination in general, which is discussed in a later section.

The type of absorptive capacity required for successful transfer of technology from MNCs depends on the nature of the investment project. For some operations, such as logging, many manufacturing activities, and open-pit hard minerals mining, acquisition of new information and methods by host country workers requires only a basic educational background and a willingness to work in a modern, structured enterprise with clear standards for work schedules and workpace. But in other activites, particularly in natural-resource-based industries such as steelmaking, copper smelting, and chemical manufacturing, absorptive capacity depends on a locally available stock of more highly trained technical personnel such as chemical engineers, metallurgists, geologists, biologists, and industrial economists.

Some developing countries, such as India and Mexico, have trained relatively large numbers of technical industrial personnel and are capable of relatively rapid absorption of new technologies. Other countries, though not so well endowed with technical personnel, have made strong efforts to train them in order to take over important foreign-owned industries. For example, Venezuela has trained petroleum engineers and managers who now successfully run that sector; South Korea used its first chemical fertilizer plant, built and operated by a foreign firm, to train Koreans who now operate several other nationally owned fertilizer plants; and Malaysia has made itself capable not only of managing its own rubber industry, but of conducting its own research on new species and methods of cultivation. But for the most part developing countries do not have sufficient cadres of technically educated people to manage technologically complex industries. And as Chapter 9 suggested, it may be difficult to justify the large capital investments involved to train such personnel in sufficient numbers when substantial fractions of the population have not even completed primary school. Further, many countries that have tried to educate a technical cadre have suffered from a "brain drain," as those with advanced educations are attracted by salaries and work conditions to emigrate to the industrial countries.

Perspectives on technology transfer clearly differ markedly between multinationals and developing countries. The former view their investments in production of technology as a continuing process which should earn financial returns just as any investment would. Host countries, however, are concerned primarily with access to existing knowledge, and with some justification regard past MNC investments in the generation of technology as sunk costs not requiring reimbursement. Public goods theory, as well as casual observation, tell us that MNCs will withhold information on technologies when they would not otherwise be able to appropriate the returns. This is, according to some analysts, likely to be particularly true for the types of simple product technologies and unskilled-labor-using production techniques of most interest to LDCs.

Foreign Exchange Benefits   A third objective of LDCs which seek foreign investment has been to save and earn foreign exchange. The impact of multinational investments on LDC balance of payments has been a source of some controversy. One study, published in 1973 and covering over 100 MNCs, concludes that in the late 1960s net positive effects of MNCs on the balance of payments was negligible; indeed in perhaps half the cases firms were found to export more foreign exchange (through imports from abroad and profit repatriation) than they earned.[16] Whether these results can be generalized to include most MNCs in most LDCs is a matter for further empirical work. However, this finding does serve to underline a critical point concerning interpretation of foreign exchange benefits from any MNC project: the emphasis must be on *net*, rather than gross, foreign exchange earnings, in recognition of the fact that a sizable share of gross export earnings does not represent "retained value" to host countries. As this issue—as well as the objectives of regional development and an increased tax base—are of central importance of natural resources investments, we will postpone detailed consideration of such benefits until Chapter 19.

LDC Policies Toward Foreign Investment

LDC governments use a wide range of policy tools intended to elicit desired behavior from multinational corporations. Of the four policy tools discussed here, three are restrictions: (1) performance requirements, (2) "saturation" laws, and (3) controls over profit repatriation. The fourth tool is tax incentives. Performance requirements are generally tailored to fit each industry. MNCs entering the automobile assembly industry are often forced to increase the local content of vehicles progressively, for example, while those entering hard minerals extraction may be required to commit themselves to future investments in domestic minerals processing. Performance requirements are most commonly established to serve the same LDC objectives already discussed: employment, transfer of technology, and for export-oriented activities, foreign exchange earnings.

---

16. Paul Streeten and Sanjaya Lall, *The Flow of Financial Resources: Private Foreign Investment, Main Findings of a Study on Selected Developing Countries* (New York: United Nations Document TD/B/C–3 III, May 1973).

Restrictions   Policies requiring MNCs to utilize local personnel are common both in labor-intensive and capital-intensive undertakings. These measures are aimed not only at job creation but also at increasing absorptive capacity for the transfer of technology from multinationals. Provisions generally involve a time schedule with specific targets for employment of local labor and managers, with different targets established for different types of skills. For example, Indonesia typically requires MNCs in natural resources to fill all unskilled jobs with Indonesians after three years, but only 75 percent of skilled and supervisory jobs and 50 percent of technical and managerial personnel. Many countries provide strong incentives for training local personnel and often, as in the petroleum sectors in Indonesia, Liberia, Trinidad-Tobago, and Bangladesh, some attempt to reinforce these incentives by requiring firms to mount specific training programs.

LDCs have utilized a number of requirements intended to promote technology transfer apart from the encouragement of training programs. Many developing countries have imposed standards requiring MNCs to import only the most advanced capital equipment, and what amounts to the same thing, have prohibited the importation of used machinery. Such measures work against other LDC goals, however, because older used equipment is likely to be more labor-using, quite apart from being cheaper. This is but one example of a widespread tendency to associate technological transfer with importation of equipment, rather than of information.

In addition some governments have imposed special taxes on MNCs to finance government research and development (Ecuador) or have required the firms to invest in local R&D labs (India), or have otherwise pressured companies to undertake local R&D activity. One study cites eleven instances, primarily in Brazil and India, in which firms responded by establishing R&D labs in the host country.[17]

A more widely used policy, intended in part to yield greater transfer of technology, has been LDC insistence that foreign investors acquire local partners by forming joint ventures with local firms. These requirements are usually contained in what has become known as **saturation laws,** which make it mandatory for MNCs to sell a specified percent of equity in each project to host country citizens. The idea has been that the local joint-venture partners could by virtue of their internal positions somehow monitor incoming technology, appropriate it, and permanently imbed it in the host economy. However, many local joint-venture partnerships are pro forma arrangements involving local elites close to centers of political power with little interest in business matters. And parent MNCs often show even greater reluctance to allow diffusion of technology to joint ventures than to wholly owned subsidiaries.

Saturation laws have also been intended to increase host country capital income by reducing the future flow of dividends to foreigners. While saturation laws are becoming increasingly common throughout the developing

17. Jack N. Behrman and William A. Fischer, *Overseas R&D Activities of Transnational Corporations* (Cambridge, Mass.: Oelgeschlager, Gunn and Hain, 1980), pp. 107–9.

world, they are particularly well established in Latin America and South-east Asia. For example, foreign enterprises may only enter the Philippine timber industry as minority partners, and in Indonesia MNCs in all fields must offer 51 percent of total shares for sale to local investors within a specified period, usually ten years.

Saturation laws requiring investment in the form of joint ventures clearly involve greater national presence and greater potential for host country control over activities of foreign investors. Whether these devices also serve on balance to increase income of local owners of equity capital and whether they involve net economic benefits to the host country are somewhat less certain. Indeed some analysts argue that such requirements may have little, if any, positive effects on national income of the host country because they divert scarce local resources to the multinational's sector, and also reduce the inflow of foreign capital.[18]

Other restrictions commonly applied to LDCs to the behavior of MNCs include ceilings on repatriation of profits to the parent corporation and measures to increase reinvestment of profits in the host country, including stiff taxes on profits remitted to the parent firm abroad. Ceilings on profit repatriation are, like saturation laws, designed to reduce future outflows of resources from LDCs. Such limitations have been widely used by LDCs, particularly in Latin America and in India. In Colombia profits remitted by a firm to a parent abroad were limited to 14 percent of the firm's Colombian investments; Brazil has at times limited remittances to 10 percent of registered capital. In other countries, such as Argentina and Ghana, although no explicit percentage ceilings on profit repatriation may be established, repatriation is limited through the administration of the system of foreign exchange controls (see Chapter 16).

Tax Incentives　For foreign investors able to meet performance requirements, most LDCs offer positive inducements: tax holidays and other tax incentives, monopoly rights in the local market, and guarantees that investors will be allowed to repatriate profits. The latter inducement is rarely important in influencing investment decisions, since such guarantees represent only good intentions on the part of the government. Monopoly rights in the local market to a foreign investor do increase the incentive to invest, and such rights have long been sought by many miltinationals wanting to invest in import-substituting industries in LDCs. Several countries have granted them. Zambia and Indonesia, for example, awarded monopoly rights to two of the world's largest tire manufacturers. Monopoly positions, however, reduce pressure on MNCs to hold prices down and keep quality up. Moreover, because they create higher domestic prices, monopoly rights result in direct transfers from LDC consumers to the foreign stockholders of the multinational.

Tax incentives are by far the most widely used inducements offered to

---

18. For example, Vernon stresses that if local buyers pay a price fully commensurate with the earnings they receive, all they will have done is export scarce capital to a foreign seller (Vernon, *Storm Over the Multinationals,* p. 168).

multinationals. While the variety of such incentives is almost limitless, we will focus on the most common one, income *tax holidays* or exemption. Tax rates on corporate income in LDCs are typically between 40 and 50 percent. To attract foreign investment, LDC governments often offer to exempt income of newly entering MNCs from corporate taxes for the first several years of operation, usually three to six years. During the heyday of these tax holidays, the postwar period through 1970, most MNCs investing in the third world received exemptions, usually for five-year periods. By 1980 tax holidays had virtually vanished for natural resource investments, except in some former French colonies in Africa, and were becoming less common in other sectors as well. But there are still enough recent examples of tax holidays to arouse wonderment, if not dismay, among economists. Increasingly host countries have learned that where such incentives are not valueless to MNCs they usually serve little purpose other than enrichment of foreign shareholders at the expense of local treasuries.

Tax holidays have been ineffective instruments of public policy for several reasons. First, for most of the postwar era tax holidays were of very limited value to multinationals from many of the major capital-exporting countries, including the United States, Japan, and West Germany. These and most other developed countries, excluding France, employ a "global" income concept: they tax all income of corporations based in their borders, whatever its source. If the income is earned abroad, the home country income tax applies when the earnings are remitted. A multinational whose home country taxes global income can, except in Sweden, credit (offset), within limits, taxes paid on foreign income against income taxes due in the home country. Thus if the company pays zero or reduced taxes in the host country, it simply pays more taxes at home. For these investors the effect of tax holidays offered by developing countries is to transfer tax revenues from host LDCs to the treasuries of the industrial home country, a kind of reverse foreign aid. With no host country income taxes to credit against home country taxes, the only benefit received by an MNC subsidiary is the deferral of home country taxes, since these are not due until income is repatriated. Figure 14–2 illustrates how tax holidays, alone and when coupled with such other incentives as *monopoly rights* have resulted in large benefits to foreigners with little gain to host countries.

Consider a multinational firm that has received monopoly rights to manufacture automobile tires for an LDC market and has also received a five-year tax holiday. For simplicity we shall assume that the monopolist can produce at constant marginal cost (MC) and hence constant average costs ($AC = MC$). If the tire industry were a competitive industry consisting of many firms, then the supply curve of that industry would be identical to $MC = AC$. The price of tires would then be P_c, and the output of tires would be Q_c; equilibrium would occur at point E, where demand and supply schedules intersect.

A profit-maximizing monopolist, however, does not equate demand and supply: rather, a monopolist determines the level of output (Q_m) where

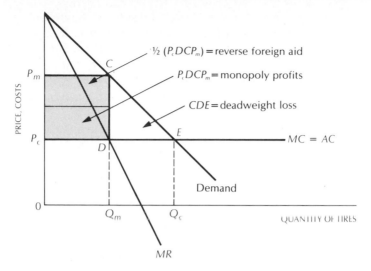

Fig. 14–2 Interaction of Incentive Policies: The Case of Tax Holidays with Award of Monopoly Rights to Foreign Enterprises, Monopoly Costs, and Reverse Foreign Aid.

MC = marginal cost of tire production under competition and monopoly; AC = average cost of tire production under competition and monopoly; MR = marginal revenue of monopolist; P_c = price of tires to consumers under competition; P_m = price of tires to consumers under monopoly; rectangle P_cDCP_m = monopoly profits to foreign tire firm; one-half rectangle P_cDCP_m = reverse foreign aid, taxes transferred from LDC treasury to treasury of capital-exporting firm (where foreign income tax rates are 50%); triangle CDE = deadweight loss from granting monopoly privileges to tire company (losses in consumer satisfaction over and above monopoly profits); and area P_cECP_m = total loss to host country consumers from granting of monopoly rights.

marginal cost and marginal revenue are equal. Q_m, being smaller than Q_c, can be sold at a price of P_m, well above P_c. As a result monopoly profits (rectangle P_cDCP_m) are generated over and above "normal" (competitive) returns to capital. Consumers in the host country pay higher prices for fewer tires, and there is substantial economic waste (area CDE). When the monopolist repatriates his profits to the home country, the home country treasury will take a proportion equal to the income tax rate (50 percent in the diagram). The monopolist is no better off with the tax holiday from the host country than without. But for the five years of the tax holiday host country consumers will not only pay dearly for tires, they will send contributions to governments in rich countries. After the tax holiday expires tire consumers will continue to subsidize waste, but the host country treasury will at least receive some taxes.

As the existence of "reverse foreign aid" began to be more widely recognized in the 1960s, LDC governments began demanding adjustments in home country treatment of foreign-source income of MNCs. Eventually many LDCs concluded tax treaties with industrial countries in which multinationals receiving tax holidays were in effect allowed to credit income taxes forgiven by LDCs (due to tax holidays) against income taxes due in the home country. These arrangements, known as "tax-sparing" clauses, have been granted by most capital-exporting countries, though not by the United States. Under tax sparing, income taxes given up by LDCs that award tax holidays benefit the foreign investor, not the home country government. However, tax holidays granted by LDCs to U.S. firms still result in "reverse foreign aid" to the U.S. government and are of little value to U.S. multinationals.

Even though MNCs from certain developed countries other than the United States do now receive the full benefits from LDC tax holidays, there remains substantial doubt that the availability of such incentives causes multinationals to alter their investment decisions in ways desired by LDCs. First, a tax holiday benefits a multinational subsidiary only to the extent that it has taxable profits. But in many cases foreign investment projects do not begin to show profits until the third or fourth year of production, when the tax holiday has almost expired. Second, income tax holidays are often conditioned on the requirement that an MNC locate operations in a particular region within a country, usually a depressed area. An investor would locate in the depressed region without the incentive if that were the most profitable thing to do. If tax incentives are required to induce investors to choose such a location, then their profits will be lower; consequently the value of the tax holiday will be lower. And if they would have located in the depressed region anyway, then the tax holiday merely provides them with a windfall. Indeed study after study from locations around the world indicates that income tax holidays of virtually all types more often than not have only marginal effects on MNC investment decisions, rewarding them for what they would have done in any case.

One possible exception to this general rule is the location of export-oriented, labor-intensive industries that make little use of domestic raw materials. A prominent example is the electronics industry, which utilizes large amounts of unskilled labor to manufacture chips, make integrated circuits, and assemble parts of such products as electronics calculators and computers. These firms operate largely in export processing zones in such countries as Malaysia, Thailand, Indonesia, and Ecuador. Electronics firms are primarily concerned with a stable source of low-cost, unskilled, and unorganized labor. They appear sensitive to differences in incentives offered by host countries, and LDCs have competed with one another in offering investment incentives and privileges to them. But even in this case inducements like tax holidays may play a secondary role in investment decisions. Malaysia and Indonesia, for example, have both offered similar tax incentives to semiconductor firms since 1970. But even though wage rates for unskilled labor were much higher in Malaysia, that country has been able to attract more than a dozen plants employing 80,000 people, while in Indonesia, with a labor force three times as large, only 5000 people were employed in the two semiconductor firms that have located there. Clearly factors other than tax incentives were more important in influencing investment decisions, even in an industry where inducements should be expected to matter.

Objectives of Multinational Firms

Although the objectives of multinational enterprises may vary across firms even within the same industry, these various goals can perhaps be subsumed under two broad, related categories: the search for global profit and the drive for stability. The profit objective speaks for itself. Stability is sought because it moderates the risks and uncertainties that threaten long-term profits essential for enterprise survival. Uncertainty, whether stemming from the activities of competitors or from political instability in host countries, is anathema to enterprise managers.

The interplay between profit and stability goals is perhaps best depicted by reference to insights offered by an important field in economics: industrial organization. There, theory shows that even within one national market large firms in an oligopolistic industry do not necessarily seek to maximize profits at the level of the individual enterprise. Rather, firms may attempt to maximize the joint profits of the industry as a whole while maintaining stability to the extent possible. This is possible only when market power is concentrated in the hands of a few firms. Maintenance of stability requires above all discouraging new entrants into the industry, as well as any actions within the industry that might erode the market share of the firms in the oligopoly. New entrants are attracted by high profits; thus the existing firms in the oligopoly may not attempt to maximize profits in order to maintain stability in the industry. Therefore investment within a national market does not necessarily flow to the place where returns, as conventionally defined, are highest.

Similar observations apply at the level of international markets. There are thousands of MNCs. Although concentration of economic power in global markets has been declining in many international markets since 1945, direct foreign investment is still dominated by firms in oligopolistic industries controlling a large share of the market for their products. Multinationals in international markets pursue profits as intensely as oligopolists in national markets, with one important difference. A project in a particular host country is evaluated not so much in terms of the potential profitability of the project viewed in isolation, but in terms of the effects of the investment on the global profitability of the MNC and on the implications of that investment for enterprise stability. LDC policies that take into account this central aspect of MNC strategy are far more likely to yield desired results than those formulated on the assumption that the enterprises are involved in a single-minded, project-by-project hunt for profits as conventionally defined.

Balancing the goals of global profit and stability has led multinationals to undertake projects in LDCs that would otherwise appear inexplicable. Oil multinationals with reserves concentrated in one or two LDCs have accepted contractual arrangements from a host country involving lower returns than received by multinational competitors because they wanted to diversify reserves. A large tire manufacturer may agree to operate rubber plantations in a country not particularly suited to rubber cultivation simply to assure itself of adequate sources of raw material in times of market scarcity. A U.S.-based sulfur firm might enter copper mining in an LDC because it offers an opportunity to diversify activity and thereby better insulate the firm from vagaries of the sulfur business. Another MNC in copper might respond to the sulfur firm's threat in the copper industry by accepting less favorable terms to mine copper in the same country, merely to protect its existing market share. Japanese firms often establish subsidiaries for producing in developing countries simply to protect the export markets they already have.

Such investments point to a fairly coherent pattern of defensive behavior by multinationals. Increasingly LDC negotiators have recognized the importance of stability and other strategic considerations in MNC planning, which in turn has enhanced their abilities to play off one firm against others. In the process many host countries have been able to curtail, if not abandon, use of generous inducements to invest, particularly tax incentives.

Conflict and Conflict Resolution

The previous two sections make clear that objectives of multinational investors and host LDCs often are not well matched, nor are their bargaining and administrative capacities.

The reality, or even the perception, of poorly matched interests inevitably leads to conflicts between multinationals and host country governments. Settlements of conflict range from the relatively amicable (Zambia's takeover of foreign-owned copper mines in the early 1970s) to the acrimonious (nationalization of the International Petroleum Company in Peru in the 1960s). Amicable resolution, or at least resolution without rupture, is the predominant pattern. Expropriation of MNC properties, particularly without compensation, is, contrary to popular stereotypes, now relatively rare. It was more widespread in the late 1950s and early 1960s after many LDCs in Asia and Africa first gained their independence. For the period 1960–1979 one periodical was able to identify 563 acts of expropriation in developing countries involving nearly 1700 companies. But these companies represented only about 5 percent of the total value of MNC investments around the world.[19]

In an earlier era threat of expropriation was one of the few devices available to host countries dissatisfied with a multinational's performance. Leverage in conflict resolution, as well as prevailing philosophies concerning sanctity of contracts, was primarily on the side of the multinationals. MNCs were unaccustomed to dealing with LDC demands for redress, and orderly mechanisms for resolving conflict were lacking. Over time several factors have led to fundamental alterations in LDC–MNC relations, including those involving conflict resolution. First, the so-called sanctity doctrine has been steadily undermined around the world, especially as industrial country governments began in the 1960s to abrogate or modify

19. *Business Week*, Sept. 14, 1961, pp. 49–50.

their own large contracts, as happened with wool and dairy products in Japanese-Australian trade. Increasingly there developed a consensus, with reluctance by the multinationals, that some investment contracts in LDCs were too much the product of unequal bargaining positions and skills. By the 1980s there was a widespread view, less evident among European than American firms, that changes in underlying conditions could justify changes in contract terms.

Second, the demonstration of market power by OPEC countries in 1973 suggested to other developing countries that more aggressive behavior in dealing with multinationals, short of expropriation, could on occasion succeed. Third, bitter memories of expropriation, rising "fiscal militancy" of host countries in general, together with the near-universal spread of joint ventures among LDCs, has served to convince many MNC managers of the tenuousness of their involvement in many developing countries. Many began to seek ways to moderate the scope for harsh conflict with host country officials.

As a result, whereas even the word *renegotiation* was inadmissable in the MNC lexicon two decades ago, laws, contracts, and regulations governing MNC participation in LDCs now commonly contain provisions for periodic review of investors' activities to allow for orderly renegotiation of the original terms of entry. Further, new methods of arbitration have been devised for those conflicts that cannot be resolved by mutual agreement between host country and MNC. Earlier, multinationals were generally unwilling to accept any provisions for arbitration other than those calling for ultimate settlement in the International Court for the Settlement of Industrial Disputes (ICSID) in The Hague. Increasingly host countries came to view this arbitration mechanism as an infringement of their sovereign powers and, particularly in Latin America, began to require MNCs to accept arbitration as prescribed by host country laws.

By the 1980s the principal threat to MNC control over foreign subsidiaries was no longer that of forcible seizure of assets through outright expropriation, but what MNCs view as "creeping expropriation." This is said to result from stiffening requirements for local participation in joint ventures, growing restrictions on profit repatriation, and steadily rising host country taxes on MNC operations. Both outright and "creeping" expropriation are important considerations affecting MNC views of "political" risks of investing in LDCs. Multinational concern is reflected in growing efforts to insure themselves against political risk. One study indicates that in 1980 alone MNCs worldwide paid as much as $700 million in political risk premiums to insuring agencies.

One of the major sources of conflict in MNC–LDC relations has been over the problem of **transfer pricing.** Because a substantial proportion of transactions by multinationals are internal to the firm (between affiliates of the same firm), such transactions may be assigned an arbitrary value to suit the interests of the enterprise. Unlike transactions between unaffiliated firms there are often no objective, market-determined, or "arm's length" values that can be used to verify prices recorded in intrafirm and interaffiliate transactions. This being the case, MNCs can use transfer-pricing devices to change the location of reported income from countries with high taxes to countries with lower taxes, thereby maximizing after-tax profits of their global operations, or in some cases evading foreign exchange controls of host countries. For example, a multinational in cosmetics, headquartered in London with a subsidiary in Nairobi, could understate profits of its operations in Kenya by billing its Kenyan subsidiary for facial cream ingredients at twice the price it charges its affiliate in Hong Kong. Or an American MNC in forest products might attempt to underdeclare profits in the Philippines by overstating the costs of logging equipment it ships to its Philippine subsidiary or by understating the per-unit value of logs exported from the subsidiary to still another subsidiary in Korea.

Critics of multinationals have long maintained that the companies have used intrafirm pricing as a means of reducing LDC shares of gains from foreign investment for the benefit of the MNCs and home country treasuries. Transfer-pricing devices can clearly be used to evade host country income taxes. MNCs also have strong incentives to underreport profits of subsidiaries in host countries that impose ceilings on profit remittances to the parent. Even without such ceilings, and even when taxes on the LDC subsidiary are lower than in the home country of the multinational, transfer-pricing devices may still be employed for political reasons if the parent MNC believes that high reported profits in LDC subsidiaries increases the risk of contract renegotiation or expropriation.

The scope for transfer-pricing abuses is clearly substantial, and some analysts believe it has grown in recent years. One study indicates that in 1977 fully one third of all exports of developed-country MNCs from their home country was to their own affiliates in other countries. There are, however, important differences between firms. The incidence of intrafirm transactions tends to be higher, the greater the proportion of sales of foreign subsidiaries to total sales of the enterprise. Further, firms in high-technology, high-research fields, such as electronics and chemicals, engage in intrafirm transactions to a greater degree than do firms in industries producing standardized products like textiles and food processing. U.S. firms, being generally more multinational in nature and more concentrated in high-research-intensity fields, engage more frequently in intrafirm transactions than their counterparts in Europe.[20]

LDCs have responded to transfer-pricing abuses by attempting to tighten preexisting controls and by intensive investigation of industries reputed to be notorious for transfer-price manipulations, such as the pharmaceutical industry. Given sufficient vigilance by host countries, transfer-pricing abuses can be curtailed easily enough in cases where intrafirm trade in standardized products is involved. Products such as copper concentrates, ammonium nitrate, plywood, and crumb rubber have well-established

---

20. Stopford, Dunning, and Haberich, *World Directory,* p. xxiii. For a summary of studies portraying transfer-pricing abuses, see Lewis D. Solomon, *Multinational Corporations and the Emerging World Order* (London: Kennikat Press, 1978), pp. 79–83.

world market prices that can be used to determine whether an intrafirm transaction has been valued at "arm's-length." However, much of the intrafirm transactions of MNCs involve nonstandardized products and services, for which arm's-length prices are not readily available. This is particularly true for goods shipped largely within vertically integrated MNCs (bauxite), and for payments made to parents by subsidiaries for technology, research, and overhead. Full resolution of the transfer-pricing issue to the satisfaction of LDCs appears unlikely in the near future.

Commercial Borrowing

The most rapidly growing types of foreign saving inflow to LDCs have been private loans from three sources: bond lending, commercial bank lending, and export credits. *Bond lending* is one form of portfolio investment. The other form, foreign purchases of equities (stocks) in LDC enterprises, never really was important in most LDCs, except during certain periods of Argentine, Brazilian, and Chilean history. The international bond market has been used from time to time by such relatively prosperous LDCs as Mexico, Turkey, and Algeria. In this market LDC governments (rarely private firms) borrow at long term (five to twenty-five years) by issuing bonds backed by the full faith and credit of the issuing government. Bonds are purchased by a variety of investors, normally from developed countries, operating through large brokers such as Kuhn-Loeb and Morgan Stanley (U.S.) or the Rothschild group (France, Britain).

The second, much newer, channel for capital transfers is *commercial bank lending,* particularly from the Eurocurrency market, also a market for debt. The *Eurocurrency market* dates from the early 1960s, when it developed in response to measures by the United States government to protect the American dollar. By 1979 the total net size of this financial market was on the order of $475 billion. Eurocurrencies are simply currencies on deposit at banks outside the country that issues the currency. Thus there are Eurodollars, Euromarks, Eurofrancs, etc. Eurocurrency credits or loans are typcially made not by one bank but by syndicates of banks, each of which provides a share of the loan. Eurocurrency loans are typically granted for much shorter terms than those available from bond issues, at interest rates geared to rates charged by banks when they lend to other banks. The traditional rate employed for this purpose is the London interbank borrowing rate (LIBOR), which fluctuates from period to period. In 1979 and 1980 LIBOR ranged from 13 to 16 percent, but was as low as 6.5 percent in 1977. Borrowers pay a premium on LIBOR depending on the market's assessment of risk; since loans to LDCs are typically considered riskier propositions, the premium is usually higher for them than for developed-country borrowers. In recent years the premium was as low as five-eighths of 1 percent for some borrowers (Colombia in 1981) and as high as 2.5 percent for others (Panama in 1978, at the time of the canal negotiations).

Until the 1960s commercial borrowing by LDCs was small relative to total capital inflows, and the predominant share of such borrowing was in the form of international bond issues, which rarely exceeded $2.0 billion in gross value in the years prior to 1970. While this form of borrowing expanded rapidly after 1975, reaching a peak gross value of about $6.0 billion in 1978,[21] this development pales in comparison to the explosion in Eurocurrency borrowing by LDCs after 1970.

Prior to 1970 only a few developing countries partook on any significant scale in commercial borrowings in the Eurocurrency market. Reported, or publicized, gross Eurocurrency credits (between a quarter and a third of such transactions are not publicized) to LDCs rose from virtually nothing in 1967 to almost $7 billion in 1973, and to over $42 billion by 1979, representing a compound rate of interest of over 40 percent per year in just that latter five-year period.

In some respects the rise of the Eurocurrency market as a source of foreign savings from LDCs has been a beneficial development, particularly for the middle-income LDCs that accounted for over 80 percent of such debt. Prior to the emergence of this market many LDC governments with an attractive list of domestic investment projects could secure financing for them only through requests for foreign aid from industrial country governments. Many countries found this to be unsatisfactory, not only because aid was often subject to conditions imposed by the donor country, but because procedures of many aid donors were so involved that even good projects were sometimes delayed for several years. The Eurocurrency market provides an alternative source of finance that involves no supplication to aid donors, and in the eyes of many LDC officials, a channel of finance that is both more flexible and less intrusive on LDC economic independence.

Eurocurrency borrowing is, however, very expensive relative to official aid from industrial countries. Throughout most of the 1970s the weighted average interest rate on all foreign aid to LDCs was never greater than 3 percent.[22] Interest rates faced by LDC borrowers in the Eurocurrency market through the 1970s were, on the other hand, never less than 8 percent (1976), usually greater than 10 percent, and between 13 and 16 percent in 1979 and 1980.

Further, the very rapid buildup of external commercial debt of LDCs from 1970 onward has resulted in serious debt service problems for many, as their export earnings available for paying interest and principal on debt have not grown at anything approaching the 40 percent rate of annual increase in commercial debt obligations.

Prior to 1979 most countries, particularly the five major LDCs which together owed about half of total Eurocurrency debt in 1979 (Brazil, Mexico, Venezuela, Spain, Argentina), encountered no serious problems in meeting debt service requirements. However, by 1980 a number of LDCs, including Peru, Sudan, Turkey, Zaire, and Zambia, had experienced serious difficulties in coping with their debts, and both Turkey and Zaire avoided

21. World Bank, *World Development Report 1980*, p. 28.
22. World Bank, *Annual Report 1978*, Appendix Table 3.

default only through massive reschedulings. More ominously, there were indications by the early 1980s that at least one of the large borrowers (Brazil) had reached or surpassed its capacity to service further debt, as a combination of a doubling of import prices for oil, obligations from past external borrowings, and rising protectionism in the industrial countries left little foreign exchange to pay for imports.

The Brazilian experience illustrates the crux of the debt problem for LDCs. External borrowings are essential both for finance of new investment and ordinary imports, as well as for amortization (repayment of principal) and interest on previous external debt. In 1970 for each $1 borrowed abroad LDCs as a group utilized about 55¢ for amortization and interest payments. By 1980 70¢ of each borrowed dollar went for amortization and interest, and this is expected to rise above 80¢ by 1985.[23]

That portion of foreign borrowing that must be used for debt service cannot be used to finance internal investments in LDCs. Thus if the explosion in foreign borrowing by LDCs does not lead to widespread default or massive reschedulings, as some observers predict, it will surely lead to a need for greater reliance on domestic sources of savings within LDCs, or measures to expand availabilities of foreign aid and curb protectionism in industrial countries, or some combination of all three. Otherwise rates of GDP growth in LDCs in general, and oil-importing countries in particular, could be lower than those experienced even in the 1970s, much less in the 1960s. For low-income countries in particular this could translate into real per-capita income growth rates of not more than 1.3 percent (versus 1.6 percent from 1960 to 1978). At that rate Bangladesh would be at the same level of income per capita by the year 2030 as that of Sri Lanka in 1980, Sri Lanka in 2030 would have reached Egypt's 1980 level, and Egyptians would enjoy an income level in 2030 comparable to that of Peru in 1980, where per-capita income then was but one-twelfth that of the United States.

For many developing countries a point may soon be reached where virtually all proceeds of new external borrowings will be required merely to service past borrowings. At that point national self-interest of host countries may be served by decisions to default on external debt; at the very least the option will be tempting. The international economy would probably survive a series of major defaults by LDCs, even given the potentially large sums involved. But the experience would be painful for both debtor and creditor countries, a sharp and costly reminder of the interdependence of the industrial and third worlds. Moreover massive default is avoidable. In a basic sense the need, especially of the rapidly industrializing LDCs, to borrow heavily on commercial markets is partly due to their inability to sell more textiles, plywood, steel, or rubber products to the industrial countries in Europe and America, who increasingly protect high-cost domestic industries from LDC competition (see Chapter 17). Without a relaxation of protectionism in the industrial countries, many LDCs may be unable to

---

23. World Bank, *World Development Report 1980,* p. 25.

generate sufficient foreign exchange earnings to continue servicing external debt. They would then lose a significant source of potential savings required for continued growth, to the detriment of both developing and industrial countries.

FURTHER READING

There have been two global reviews of international aid programs in the past fifteen years: Lester B. Pearson, chairman, *Partners in Development* (New York: Praeger, 1969), and Willy Brandt, chairman, *North-South: A Program for Survival* (Cambridge, Mass.: MIT Press, 1980). Current data and commentary on aid programs are available from the Organization for Economic Cooperation and Development, *Development Cooperation,* a review published annually in Paris. Each of the development banks mentioned in the chapter publishes annual reports that contain' detailed data on its own lending programs, while the annual *Congressional Presentation* of the United States Agency for International Development goes into depth for each country program of the agency. The literature on the impact of aid on economic development is summarized in the article by Paul Mosely, cited in footnote 2.

There are few topics in international trade and development that have generated more controversy than the role of multinational enterprises in development. A sample of contending views can be found in the following five volumes. First, Raymond W. Vernon, *Storm Over the Multinationals: The Real Issues* (Cambridge, Mass.: Harvard University Press, 1975), especially Chapter 4. A volume that attempts to present several sides to the problem is Thomas J. Bierstaker, *Distortion on Development: Perspectives on the Multinational Corporation* (Cambridge, Mass.: MIT Press, 1978). An assessment of multinationals' impact on both host and home countries may be found in C. Fred Bergsten, Thomas P. Horst, and Theodore H. Moran, *American Multinationals and American Interests* (Washington, D.C.: Brookings Institution, 1978). A book on multinationals that was widely quoted in the popular press in the mid-1970s was R. J. Barnet and R. E. Muller, *Global Reach* (New York: Simon and Schuster, 1974). Several articles attempt to place in perspective the role of commercial debt in development. See particularly Helen Hughes, "Debt and Development: The Role of Foreign Capital in Foreign Growth," *World Development* F, no. 1 (1979): 95–112.

PART V

TRADE AND DEVELOPMENT

Chapter 15

INTERNATIONAL TRADE: PRIMARY CONSIDERATIONS

This and the following two chapters examine the interactions between developing countries and the world economy. This chapter begins by offering a perspective on international payments, trade, and comparative advantage. It then focuses on the dominant means by which developing countries earn foreign exchange, the export of primary commodities, which include food crops, agricultural raw materials, and minerals. Chapters 16 and 17 explore two industrialization strategies that turn on a country's trading posture: import substitution and the outward-looking development of manufactured exports. A fourth chapter—Chapter 19—returns to international trade issues as they bear on the role of natural resources in development.

The Structure of Foreign Payments

Foreign exchange, like capital, is a concept that can be understood on several levels. Most simply it is foreign money that a country uses to conduct transactions overseas, a cash flow. Like any economic unit, the country must be careful to balance its payments of foreign currency against its income. To protect against shortfalls, countries keep stocks of foreign money in the form of international reserves. At another level foreign exchange represents purchasing power over foreign resources of all kinds: goods (imports), transportation and other services, skilled manpower, and assets (investments) in foreign countries. Thus a country's ability to earn foreign exchange, by exporting goods and services and by attracting foreign capital, determines its command over the goods and services produced in the world economy.

Finally, foreign exchange can represent a factor of production. Many countries, and especially those less developed, are unable to produce, at acceptable cost, certain goods or services that contribute to well-being and growth. In some countries consumers demand more food than can be produced; in other countries certain raw materials are not available; and most LDCs seek capital equipment and some technical and managerial skills from the industrial countries. These imports contribute as much to production and growth as do supplies of labor and capital, and like them are primary factors of production. Thus because foreign exchange represents purchasing power over factors of production, it can itself be considered in that light.

The availability of this resource is usually measured in terms of foreign currency. A country's *balance of payments,* like an accountant's ledger, measures the anual flows of receipts of foreign currency and compares these to annual payments, as shown in Table 15–1. To help keep items on the correct side of the ledger, remember that any payment to a country's government or its citizens is considered a receipt or credit, while any payment by the country's government or citizens to any foreign person or

TABLE 15–1 Balance of Payments—Developing Country

Payments (debits)	Receipts (credits)
Import purchases (including freight)	Export earnings
National's travel abroad	Foreigners' travel in country
Remittances of income on foreign investment	Income on overseas investments (e.g., foreign reserves)
Interest on foreign debt	Remittances by nationals working abroad
Remittances by foreigners working in country	Grants from foreign governments

(−) Balance on Current Account (+)
(typically negative)

Investment abroad by nationals	Investment by foreign firms
	Long-term loans from foreign individuals
Repayments of principal on foreign long-term debt	Long-term loans by foreign govenments

(−) Balance on Long-Term Capital Account (+)
(typically positive)

Basic Balance

= balance on current account + balance on long-term capital account

Short-term loans abroad by nationals	Short-term loans from abroad (e.g., trade credits)

(−) Balance of Payments (+)

= decrease or increase in foreign reserves

agency is a payment or debit. Thus although exports send goods out of the country, they earn revenues from overseas and are thus credits; while imports, which bring goods to the country, are debits. A loan from overseas, such as foreign aid or a line of credit with a foreign bank, is a receipt when the proceeds of the loan are given to a country, but is reflected on the debit side in later years when interest is paid and the principal is repaid.

All flows of goods and services, such as exports, imports, freight, interest, and so forth, are considered part of the *current account;* investment and loan flows—the foreign aid and private investment discussed in Chapter 14—are part of the *capital account.* The sum of these two is the balance of payments which if positive equals the addition to foreign reserves, and if negative is covered by drawing down reserves accumulated in the past. Once changes in reserves are included, the balance of payments must always balance: credits (including any fall in reserves used to finance a deficit) must equal debits (including any rise in reserves, the reflection of a surplus).

Governments do not have inexhaustible foreign reserves, so deficits cannot be run indefinitely. However, most developing countries, with the major exception of the mideast petroleum exporters and some others, run chronic deficits on current account. Essentially they import more than they export. Ordinarily the difference is financed by foreign investments and loans. The sum of these long-term capital inflows and the current account balance is often called the *basic balance.* As long as foreign investors and lenders, including aid donors, are willing to invest enough to cover the current account deficit, the country's foreign payments can be considered in balance. Indeed, standing the problem on its head, if a developing country is able to add to its resources by attracting foreign capital on favorable terms, then it should do so (see Chapter 14). To convert foreign capital into real resources—goods and services—for development, a country must import goods and services from abroad. Then the country necessarily runs a deficit on current account because imports exceed exports. But if a country runs a current account deficit that is not matched by an inflow of foreign capital, the country will eventually have to take steps to curb its imports or increase its exports, probably both.

Table 15–2 gives a broad view of the structure of foreign payments of the developing countries that are members of the International Monetary Fund; several socialist developing countries, China, North Korea, Vietnam, and Cuba, are not included in these data. The table shows that merchandise exports (measured "freight on board"—f.o.b.—at the country's border) are responsible for over 70 percent of total receipts, while imports (measured with costs, insurance, and freight—c.i.f.—also at the country's border) cover almost the same proportion of payments. Clearly merchandise trade is the dominant source of foreign payments. Of the other items that receive most attention, private investment and aid (long-term capital in the table) contribute about 10 percent to receipts, while the returns on past capital inflows—profits and interest on debt—constitute 8 percent of total payments. The non-OPEC countries are relatively more dependent on

TABLE 15–2 Developing Countries[a]—Aggregate Balance of Payments, 1977 (billion U.S. $)

	All developing countries		Non-OPEC developing countries	
	Receipts	Payments	Receipts	Payments
Current Account				
Merchandise exports, f.o.b.	237.7		114.2	
Merchandise imports, c.i.f.		219.8		135.5
Transport and travel	18.6	16.3	14.6	9.9
Investment income	9.6		3.4	
Profits remitted or reinvested		11.4		4.0
Debt service (interest payments)		13.0		11.8
Other services and transfers	31.8	35.6	27.9	15.2
Total current receipts/payments	297.7	296.1	160.1	176.4
Balance on current account	1.6			16.3
Long-term capital				
Direct investment	7.0	0.4	4.8	0.2
Private loans	10.9	0.7	9.1	0.5
Official loans	15.8	11.6	13.7	0.1
Total long-term capital	33.7	12.7	27.6	0.8
Basic balance[b]	22.6		10.5	
Short-term Capital (net)[c]		8.7		1.6
Total receipts/payments	333.3	319.4	187.7	178.8
Balance of payments[d]	13.9		8.9	
As a percentage of world[a] total				
Exports/imports	24.9	21.2	12.0	13.3
Total receipts/payments	23.7	22.9	13.3	12.8

Source: International Monetary Fund, *Balance of Payments Yearbook,* Supplement to vol. 29 (Washington, D.C., December 1978).

[a] Coverage includes members of the International Monetary Fund.
[b] Equals balance on current account plus balance of long-term capital items.
[c] Includes errors and omissions.
[d] Surplus of receipts equals the gain in reserves.

foreign capital, which contributes 15 percent to total receipts, but exports still account for over 60 percent of receipts.

The table also helps to place the developing nations in the world economy. By virtually any measure, such as export receipts, import payments, or total receipts and payments, developing countries are responsible for between one-fifth and one-fourth of world totals (again, including only IMF members). For the non-OPEC countries the shares are much lower, converging on one-eighth of world totals. For all developing countries this share of trade and payments exceeds their share of world GNP (about 17 percent, counting only the same IMF member countries), but for the non-petroleum-exporting countries the payments share falls short of their 14 percent share of world income.

Comparative Advantage

Every country, regardless of size, ideology, or state of development, participates in international trade. Trade theorists have tried to explain why nations trade and how they benefit from it largely under assumptions of *static conditions* which hold all domestic factors of production (land, other natural resources, labor, and capital) in fixed supply. The resulting **theory of comparative advantage** is rich in its implications about the gains from trade, the following among them:

1. Any country can increase its income by trading, because the world market provides an opportunity to buy some goods at relative prices that are lower than those which would prevail at home in the absence of trade.

2. The smaller the country, the greater this potential gain from trade, but all countries are likely to benefit to some extent.

3. A country will gain most by exporting commodities that it produces using its abundant factors of production most intensively, while importing those goods whose production would require relatively more of the scarcer factors of production.

The first implication is a subtle one that requires elaboration. To simplify greatly, assume that two countries, which can be called Mexico and the United States, both produce only two products, vegetables and automobiles, and use only one factor of production, labor. Table 15–3 shows the labor days required to produce these products in each country. Notice that in this example it takes more labor days to produce either product in Mexico. Despite this, it is to the advantage of the United States to buy vegetables in Mexico, even though they can be produced at home with less labor, and to sell cars to Mexico in return. In the United States labor costs dictate that an automobile sells for the equivalent of five tons of vegetables.[1] But if the United States sells one automobile in Mexico, it can buy six tons of vegetables for consumption. So if labor is shifted from farming to manufacturing automobiles, American consumers can eat more vegetables than if there is no trade with Mexico, while driving the same number of cars. At the same time Mexico, which has to produce six tons of vegetables to buy one car in the home market without trade, is better off to switch its labor into producing more vegetables and selling them to the United States, where it only needs to trade five tons of vegetables for a car, saving the other ton for its own consumption.

The important point of this example, and the core of comparative advantage, is that *both* countries can gain from trade whenever the *relative* prices of commodities in each country differ in the absence of trade. If the two countries do trade, then the relative price of vegetables in terms of automobiles would settle between five and six, the two relative prices prevailing before trade. The final trade price, which can be called the world price, will settle closer to the initial price in the market of the country whose economy is larger. Thus small countries benefit more from trade because the gains are greater the more the pretrade relative price differs from the

---

1. If each ton of vegetables requires four labor-days to produce, then it takes five tons of vegetables to absorb the same labor as one car, which uses twenty labor-days. This formula for calculating relative prices works in this oversimplified example because labor is the only input into production.

TABLE 15-3 Production Costs and Comparative Advantage

	Mexico	United States
Labor-days to produce:		
Vegetables (one ton)	5	4
Automobiles (one)	30	20
Relative price (tons of vegetables per auto)	6	5

posttrade world price. To see this, consider an extreme case in which the United States economy is so large that the posttrade price settles at the U.S. price before trade. Then the United States cannot gain from trade (nor can it lose), while Mexico would gain to the full extent of the price difference.

The theory of comparative advantage is posed here in the very simple form developed by David Ricardo during the nineteenth century: two countries, two goods, and only one factor of production, labor. Some of the complexities of the real world can be incorporated into the theory, however. A trading world of many countries can be handled by taking the home country, say, Kenya, and treating the rest of the world as its trading partner. The complexities of many goods will be addressed in the next chapter. The theory was expanded to deal with two factors, such as labor and capital, by the Swedish economists Heckscher and Ohlin during the first half of the twentieth century. Under certain conditions the Heckscher-Ohlin theory can be extended to include more factors of production and to yield the third implication, that a country exports products which use its abundant factors of production more intensively and imports products which require relatively more of its scarce factors.

The implications of comparative advantage are encapsulated in Fig. 15-1. It depicts a country that has considerable potential to produce a good, such as rice, that uses labor and land, both abundant, but whose consumers' preferences favor the consumption of, say, cloth, which it produces in more limited quantities with labor and scarce capital. The production frontier gives the maximum quantities of each good that can be produced with available capital, labor, and land. Community indifference curves, which were introduced in Chapter 6, show the combinations of goods that the country would consume with equal levels of satisfaction. *Before trade,* the country would achieve its greatest utility by producing and consuming at point *A*, the tangency of indifference curve I with the production frontier. The slope of the production frontier at this point (equal to that of the indifference curve) determines the relative price at which rice would trade domestically for cloth if international trade were not permitted. On world markets it is likely that land-intensive rice would command a higher price relative to capital-intensive cloth, since the world as a whole has more capital relative to other factors than does this capital-poor country. That is, in the rest of the world for any given relative price demand for cloth is smaller relative to supply than is true within the developing country at the same relative price; for rice, the opposite is true.

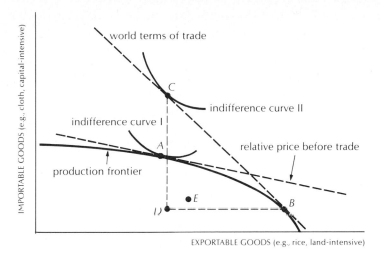

Fig. 15–1   Gains from Trade.

After trade, the country can sell its rice and import cloth at the relative price of rice and cloth prevailing on world markets. A shorthand term for this price is the world **terms of trade.** A country with relatively small supplies of rice to export would not influence the world price and hence would sell at fixed terms of trade; we call this country a "price-taker." A country with larger rice supplies would, by exporting, drive the world relative price of rice down somewhat, though it would remain above the relative domestic price prevailing before trade. In either case the country can produce more of its abundant commodity, rice, and less cloth, settling at point *B*, the tangency of the world terms of trade and its production frontier. By exporting rice and importing cloth, it can consume *more of both* goods, at point *C* in Fig. 15–1, the tangency of the world price and community indifference curve II. Because the second indifference curve is to the northeast of curve I, both consumer satisfaction and national income are higher after trade. The quantities of rice exports, *BD*, and of cloth imports, *DC*, are given by the *trade triangle, BCD.*

The situation depicted in Fig. 15–1 is generalizable to every country in the world, whatever its size and stage of development, from small countries like Ghana or Belgium to large ones like China, India, and the United States. Any country gains from trade if only relative domestic prices, in the absence of trade, differ from relative world prices.

Export Characteristics of Developing Countries

When Chenery and Syrquin looked at cross-country patterns (see Chapter 3), they found that as incomes per capita rose from the neighborhood of $200 to $2000 (in 1978 prices), the average export share of gross domestic product rose from 19 to 25 percent.[2] Size makes a considerable difference, however: for an average "small" country with a population of five million and income per capita of $400, exports of goods and services constituted about 24 percent of GDP, compared with half that level for an average "large" country with forty million people at the same income.

Some sense of the wide variety of individual country characteristics can be had from column 3 of Table 15–4, which shows the expected low export share of domestic product, 7–12 percent, for very large countries like Brazil, India, Mexico, and Pakistan; rather high ratios for the oil-rich countries of any size (including an extreme of 65 percent for Saudi Arabia); and a wide range for the smaller, non-petroleum-exporters, from 13 percent for Ethiopia and 17 percent for Colombia to over 30 percent for such different countries as South Korea, an exporter of manufactures, Malaysia, a diversified primary exporter, and Zambia, which exports little other than copper.

The advantages of trade are so compelling that even countries with a strong ideology favoring *autarky,* the absence of trade, participate in world markets. Despite their size both the Soviet Union and China, whose Communist governments place a high value on self-reliance and independence from capitalist-dominated world markets, export in order to obtain food, sophisticated capital goods, and other commodities that are scarce in their economies. And since 1976 China has moved dramatically to increase its trade as a means of stimulating development. Cuba broke sharply with its former trading partners after 1959, but is no less dependent on its exports of sugar than before its Communist revolution; now those exports go to the Soviet Union.

Knowing the factor endowments of developing countries helps us explain the kinds of goods they export and import. Natural resources provide an obvious case and evoke images of the oil-rich countries of the Middle East and elsewhere; the copper exporters, Zambia, Zaire, Chile, and Peru; or timber exporters, such as Indonesia, the Philippines, and Ghana. Tropical climate may be considered a factor of production that helps to explain the exports of foods such as coffee, cocoa, bananas, and vegetable oils, and raw materials like rubber and cotton. Finally, abundant labor suggests the export of crops that can be produced efficiently with labor-intensive methods such as coffee, tea, rice, and tobacco, and of labor-intensive manufactures such as textiles, clothing, and electronic components. The relative lack of both physical and human capital in developing countries indicates that they would gain by importing goods that use these factors intensively; such goods include most capital equipment and many intermediate products from the chemical, petroleum, and metals industries.

As expected from their factor endowments, developing countries are overwhelmingly characterized by primary-product exports. In all countries

2. Hollis Chenery and Moises Syrquin, *Patterns of Development, 1950–1970* (London: Oxford University Press, 1975). Their work used data from the mid-1960s in prices of 1964. We have converted per-capita incomes to 1978 prices by using a factor of 2.0, which is approximately the ratio of 1978 to 1964 price levels in the United States, to reflect world inflation during that fourteen-year span.

TABLE 15-4 Export Characteristics of Selected Developing Countries, 1980

Country	1 Population, 1980 (millions)	2 GNP per capita, 1980 (U.S. $)	3 Export share of GDP 1977-80 (%)	4 Primary share of merchandise exports, 1980 (%)	5 Major commodity exports[i]	6 Share of Col. 5 in merchandise exports, 1977-80 (%)
Large countries						
Brazil	119	2,050	7[c]	61	Coffee, soybeans, iron ore	36
India	673	240	7[d]	39[h]	Jute fabrics, tea	11[f]
Indonesia[a]	147	430	27	97	Petroleum, rubber, wood[c]	78
Mexico[a]	70	2,090	12[c]	61	Petroleum, coffee	47
Nigeria[a]	85	1,010	29[e]	99[h]	Petroleum	93
Pakistan	82	300	11	44	Rice	19
Petroleum exporters						
Iran	39	2,160[b]	38[d]	97[h]	Petroleum	97
Saudi Arabia	9	11,260	65	100	Petroleum	100
Venezuela	15	3,630	29[c]	99	Petroleum	95
Other countries						
Bolivia	6	570	19	97	Tin, gas, silver, petroleum, zinc	85
Chile	11	2,150	20[c]	80	Copper	50
Colombia	27	1,180	17	78	Coffee	62[c]
Cuba	10	810[b]	NA	99[h]	Sugar	high
Egypt	40	580	21[c]	80	Cotton	22[c]
Ethiopia	31	140	13[f]	100	Coffee, hides	85
Ghana	12	420	19[g]	99[h]	Cocoa, wood	64[d]
Guatemala	7	1,080	22[c]	77	Coffee, cotton, sugar	56
Ivory Coast	8	1,150	41[h]	92	Coffee, cocoa, wood	67[c]
Jamaica	2	1,040	43	48	Alumina, bauxite, sugar	78
Kenya	16	420	29[c]	86	Coffee, tea	45
Korea (South)	38	1,520	34	11		—
Malaysia	14	1,620	53[c]	82	Rubber, wood, tin, petroleum, palm oil	73
Peru	17	930	24	89[h]	Copper, fishmeal, lead, silver, zinc, coffee	55[c]
Philippines	49	690	19	65	Sugar, coconut, copper, wood	48
Sri Lanka	15	270	34	88	Tea, rubber	59
Tanzania	19	280	19[c]	83	Coffee, cotton, sisal, cashew nuts	54
Thailand	47	670	23	75	Rice, rubber, corn, tin, tapioca, sugar	55
Zambia	6	560	40[c]	87	Copper	88[c]

Sources: Columns 3, 5, and 6—International Monetary Fund, *International Financial Statistics Yearbook 1980, 1981* (Washington, D.C., 1980, 1981); columns 1, 2, and 4—World Bank, *World Development Report 1982* (Washington, D.C., 1982), Table 1.

NA = not available.

[a] Could also be classified as petroleum exporters.

[b] 1978.

[c] 1977-1979.

[d] 1975-1977.

[e] 1976-1978.

[f] 1974-1976.

[g] 1974-1977.

[h] 1979.

[i] Commodities accounting for at least 5% of total export revenue.

shown in Table 15–4, primary commodities accounted for at least 70 percent of merchandise exports, with the notable exceptions of India and Pakistan, large countries whose internal markets are broad enough to enable the efficient production of manufactures that can be exported; South Korea, whose export success story is featured in Chapter 17; Mexico; and Jamaica.

A standard description of a developing country would add that only one or a few primary commodities are responsible for most export earnings, and many countries in Table 15–4 exhibit that characteristic. Ghana is perhaps typical. Almost all of its exports are primary products and one of these, cocoa, earns over half its commodity export revenues. Two coffee exporters, Colombia and Ethiopia, two copper exporters, Chile and Zambia, as well as all the major petroleum exporters, are extreme cases of primary export concentration. Not surprisingly the very large countries show a much more diversified pattern. What may be surprising is that many of the primary-product exporters are highly diversified. In five of the cases shown —Malaysia, Peru, Philippines, Tanzania, and Thailand—no one product dominates, and at least four commodities each account for 5 percent or more of total earnings.

However suggestive the theory of comparative advantage may be for developing countries, it is not at the heart of development. The theory fails to explain growth and structural change because it excludes growth in the stocks of productive factors, as well as improvements in the quality or productivity of those factors. The theory thus provides no mechanism to explain how economies evolve over time and change the composition of their output, their consumption, and their trade. Extensions of the theory have been used to explain some facets of growth, but even these leave much unexplained.[3]

In order to understand how trade and development interact, one affecting the other, it is preferable to adopt an eclectic approach, using trade theory where it is useful but reverting frequently to other kinds of analysis. The unifying theme is trade strategies: how different approaches to trade, favoring different types of exports and imports, lead to different kinds of economic development. The first such strategy, growth fueled by primary exports, is examined in this chapter. As indicated by the summary balance of payments and the discussion of export characteristics, food and raw material exports remain the principal means by which developing countries gain purchasing power over the imports that are essential to their development.

Primary Exports as an Engine of Growth

Before the 1950s, it was conventional wisdom that the road to development could be traversed most rapidly by following comparative advantage, exporting foods and raw materials, raising per-capita income, and permitting structural change to take place as a consequence. The United States, Can-

3. Gerald M. Meier summarizes these approaches in *The International Economics of Development* (New York: Harper & Row, 1968), Chapter 2.

ada, Australia, and Denmark had become developed countries at least partly by following this path, and Argentina had gone quite far in that direction. Some countries in the third world, such as Colombia, Mexico, Ghana, Nigeria, Malaysia, and the Philippines, have undergone significant structural change as a consequence of primary exports, although these changes have propelled them only part of the way to development. Students of development, observing such cases, have noted three kinds of benefits to primary-export-led growth: improved utilization of existing factors, expanded factor endowments, and linkage effects.

Improved Factor Utilization

Static models of the gains from trade start with a country that is not trading and show what happens when it is opened to trade. An isolated country, shut off from world markets, might have substantial amounts of land that is either idle or used in relatively unproductive ways. Recall the land-abundant, capital-short country of Fig. 15–1. In that case all factors of production are fully employed without trade. However, by reallocating resources—producing and exporting more land-intensive goods such as rice or cocoa, and importing more manufactures such as cloth or chemicals—the country can consume more of both kinds of commodities and increase its welfare. The country moves along its production frontier, from A to B in Fig. 15–1. Land, the abundant factor of production, is utilized more intensively with trade in the sense that its productivity (the yield per hectare) has risen as labor shifts from handicraft industries to agriculture or mining.

If instead before trade the country has idle resources, it can gain even more substantially from trade. This case is represented in Fig. 15–1 by points D and E, within the production frontier. Trade may stimulate the economy so that all factors of production are utilized and the country moves toward its frontier, able to produce more of both goods.

This static model of the gains from trade can, with imagination and some judicious simplification, be applied to the development of several countries. In the nineteenth century the United States and Canada had abundant land in relation to their endowments of labor and capital. Much of this land was idle, so both countries produced at points within their production frontiers. British demand for cotton and wheat enabled North America to bring this land into production and move toward the production frontier by growing cotton and wheat for export, while importing the manufactured goods it could not produce as efficiently as Britain.

Hla Myint has observed that when parts of Africa and Asia came under European colonization, the consequent expansion of their international trade enabled those areas to utilize their land or labor more intensively to produce tropical foodstuffs such as rice, cocoa, and oil palm for export. Myint applies Adam Smith's term, "vent for surplus," to these cases (as well as the cases of surplus land in the Americas and Australia).[4] The con-

---

4. Hla Myint, "The 'Classical Theory' of International Trade and the Underdeveloped Countries," *Economic Journal* 68 (1959): 317–37.

cept implies that some land or labor is idle before trade and that trade enables these economies to employ either land or labor more fully.

However, when underutilized land or labor was "vented" as a result of colonization, as was typical during the nineteenth century, the gains from trade were often purchased at high cost to the indigenous population. Land which may have been idle or utilized at low productivity was frequently alienated from its occupiers, whether these were American Indians, the Kikuyu and other peoples of East Africa, or Javanese farmers. Colonizers also used taxation and coercion to keep plantations and mines supplied with low-cost labor in many parts of Africa and Asia. And especially in British India, the movement along a production frontier toward greater production for export often resulted in cheap imports to compete with traditional handicraft industries, displacing artisans and workers. The question about colonization is whether the distribution of gains from trade favored native populations enough to compensate them for the losses they bore, and whether colonial economies propelled indigenous people toward development or retarded their eventual progress. We cannot answer these complex historical questions in this text, but it is well to remember, when evaluating the static and dynamic gains from entering world trade, that much depends on who gains and who loses.

Expanded Factor Endowments

Once the profitable opportunities in tropical agriculture or natural resources become apparent, foreign investment is likely to be attracted to the country, first to exploit the country's comparative advantage and, perhaps eventually, to invest in other sectors. The influx of foreign investors has been the familiar story in all mineral exporting industries and in many tropical products industries in which plantation agriculture was the rule: Standard Oil in Venezuela, British Petroleum in Iran, Anaconda in Chile, Alcoa in Jamaica, Lever Brothers and Firestone in West Africa, and United Fruit in Central America are only some of the more visible of scores of examples. Capital has frequently brought migrant labor to the mines and plantations, as occurred in Southern and West Africa, Malaysia, Sri Lanka, and many other places. Both foreign investment and migrant labor were of course prominent features in the development in the 'new lands" of the Americas and Australia in the nineteenth century. The emergence of new lines of export production is also likely to open up many new profitable outlets for investment that foreign capital will not completely satisfy, whether in the export sector itself or in related industries. These opportunities represent an outward shift of the demand for domestic savings and should induce some supply response, further increasing investment in the economy.

Thus the expansion of potential markets for primary products can lead to expanded supplies of foreign investment, domestic saving, labor, and skilled manpower to complement the fixed factors of production, land, and natural resources. Not only does trade help an economy move toward its production frontier and then along it, but trade can also expand the frontier outward, enabling the economy to produce more of all goods than before.

Linkage Effects

The notion of export-led growth implies some stimulus to other industries that would not otherwise expand. When the growth of one industry, such as textiles, creates sufficient demand for some input, such as cotton or dyestuffs, it may stimulate domestic production of that input. Hirschman coined the phrase *backward linkage* for this stimulus.[5] Backward linkages, which were described in Chapter 3, are particularly effective when the using industry becomes so large that supplying industries can achieve economies of scale of their own, thus lowering their costs of production and becoming more competitive in domestic or even export markets. The wheat industry worked this way in North America in the nineteenth century, creating sufficient demand for transportation equipment (especially railway rolling stock) and farm machinery that these industries became established in the United States. In Peru the rapid expansion of the fishmeal industry during the 1950s and 1960s led directly to the production of fishing boats and processing equipment. The boatbuilding industry became efficient enough to export fishing craft to neighboring countries, while the processing equipment industry gave Peru a start on one kind of capital goods production that can supply a wide range of food-processing industries.[6]

The linkage between food processing for export (rice, vegetable oils, tea) and a processing equipment industry might well be repeated in other developing countries over time. Three conditions would contribute to such linkages. Production should initially take place in small units that use simple technology, giving the fledgling equipment industry a chance to master production techniques and learn its trade by repetitive production. The export industry should grow steadily over time, promising a continuing market for its suppliers. And the export sector should be large enough to enable equipment manufacturers eventually to achieve scale economics. These conditions were met in fishmeal and can be met in several agricultural fields. But they are generally not satisfied in mining, which typically requires complex equipment for large-scale investments that must be implemented in the shortest time possible, conditions under which domestic infant industries are unlikely to thrive.

Linkages may also develop indirectly through the demand by income recipients for consumption goods. The *consumption linkage* is most likely to operate if a large labor force is paid wages above previous levels, creating a demand for mass-produced consumer goods like processed foods, clothing, footwear, furniture, radios, packaging materials, and so forth. The North

---

5. Albert O. Hirschman, *The Strategy of Economic Development* (New Haven: Yale University Press, 1958), Chapter 6.

6. Michael Roemer, *Fishing for Growth: Export-Led Development in Peru, 1950–1967* (Cambridge, Mass.: Harvard University Press, 1970).

American wheat industry, with its extensive endowment of land, high labor productivity, and egalitarian income distribution based on family farms, successfully stimulated local consumer goods industries. Neither plantation agriculture in Africa, with its large labor force but low wages, nor mining industries, which pay high wages but employ relatively few workers, are able to generate adequate demand to stimulate local consumer goods industries.

The provision of overhead capital—roads, railroads, power, water, telecommunications—for the export industry can lower costs and otherwise open opportunities for other industries. The classic example is the railroad in the nineteenth-century United States, built to connect the East Coast with the grain-producing states of the Midwest, which lowered costs of transporting both inputs and outputs for manufacturing industry in the wheat-exporting region.[7] Harbors, and rail and road networks built to facilitate the export of copper in Southern Africa, cocoa and timber in Ghana, tea in India, and beef in Argentina have had similar effects on domestic manufacturing industry. Power projects that are made economically feasible by export industries, such as the Akosombo Dam in Ghana and the Guri Dam in Venezuela, provide cheap power that may encourage domestic manufacturing industry.

Primary export sectors may also encourage the development of local entrepreneurs and skilled laborers. The growth of the Peruvian fishmeal industry, with its many small plants, encouraged scores of new entrepreneurs and trained many skilled workers to operate and maintain equipment. These resources then became available for subsequent development. Rubber, palm oil, and tin production for export have encouraged entrepreneurs in Malaysia, and small-scale farming for export has proved to be an outlet for entrepreneurial talent in several African countries.

The best case for petroleum, mining, and some traditional agricultural crops is the fiscal linkage, which means simply that the large government revenues typically derived from these exports (as taxes or dividends) can be used to finance development in other sectors. Although a government is obviously better off with than without such a revenue source, its effectiveness in stimulating self-sustaining development in the rest of the economy depends critically on the kinds of programs and interventions that government undertakes.[8]

---

7. It is an interesting question whether wheat production induced railroad construction or vice versa. Whatever the answer, it seems certain that one linkage reinforces the other in a "virtuous circle"—wheat production makes rail transport more profitable, but the railroad then lowers the cost of producing wheat. See Albert Fishlow, *American Railroads and the Transformation of the Antebellum Economy* (Cambridge, Mass.: Harvard University Press, 1965); and Robert W. Fogel, "Railroads as an Analogy of the Space Effort: Some Economic Aspects," in Bruce Mazlish (ed.), *Space Program: An Exploration in Historical Analogy* (Cambridge, Mass.: MIT Press, 1965).

8. The impact of export industries on economic development through various forms of linkages is the focus of a body of literature called *staple theory,* which tries to explain differing impacts by differing characteristics of production technologies. For examples of the genre, see Robert E. Baldwin, *Economic Development and Export Growth: A Study of Northern Rhodesia, 1920–1960* (Los Angeles: University of California Press, 1966); Douglas C. North, "Loca-

Barriers to Primary Export-Led Growth

Since the late 1950s conventional wisdom has argued that primary exports other than petroleum cannot effectively lead the way to economic development: markets for primary products grow too slowly to fuel growth; the prices received for these commodities have been declining; earnings are too unstable; and linkages do not work. We examine each of these arguments in turn.

Sluggish Demand Growth

In a world of balanced growth exporters of primary products could expect their exports to expand at the same pace as national incomes of the countries that import primary products and could also expect their own incomes to grow at that rate. Faster income growth for primary exporters would require structural changes such as import substitution. The world is not balanced in this way, however, and economists skeptical of primary export potential have cited structural shifts in the industrial world that seem to condemn third world primary exports to slower growth than industrial world incomes.[9] It is a common observation, known as Engel's law, that the demand for staple foods and beverages grows more slowly than income (see Chapter 3). For the industrial world the income elasticity of demand for foods is probably below one-half. Thus even if the growth in production of foodstuffs in the industrial world fell short of income growth, there is a prima facie case that its imports of foods would lag behind income growth. Technological change in manufacturing may also be working against the consumption of raw materials, as producers attempt to reduce costs by reducing wastage and otherwise raising the yield of finished products from a given input of raw material. Metal cans contain less tin, modern looms waste less cotton yarn, sawmills turn wood shavings into boards, and so forth. Concurrently, in affluent societies expenditures are expected to shift away from goods and toward services, further reducing the expected growth of material imports relative to income.

The outlook for primary commodity exports may not be so bleak as the skeptics suggest, however. The impact of Engel's law in LDC exports seems incontrovertible, except perhaps for meat and dairy products. However, it is not clear that technological change has been uniformly materials-saving. A study of structural change in the United States economy from 1949 to 1958 showed that for ten final goods-producing sectors, the total require-

tion Theory and Regional Economic Growth," *Journal of Political Economy* 63 (1955): 243–58; Michael Roemer, *Fishing for Growth;* and Melville H. Watkins, "A Staple Theory of Economic Growth," *Canadian Journal of Economics and Political Science* 29 (1963): 141–58. Perhaps the ultimate expression of production characteristics and linkages as determinants of development patterns is the essay by Albert O. Hirschman, "A Generalized Linkage Approach to Development, with Special Reference to Staples," in Manning Nash (ed.), *Essays on Economic Development and Cultural Change* (Chicago: University of Chicago Press, 1977), pp. 67–98.

9. An early and articulate proponent of this view is Ragnar Nurkse, *Equilibrium Growth in the World Economy* (Cambridge, Mass.: Harvard University Press, 1961), Chapters 10 and 11.

ments for inputs of metals and wood fell significantly per unit output. But the picture was mixed for agricultural, glass, rubber, and plastic products, while the unit requirements for stone products, plastics, and basic chemicals all rose.[10] Furthermore there is no discernible trend in the ratio of expenditures on services to national income for advanced economies.

World Bank data show that the share of nonfuel raw material and food imports in total industrial country imports fell substantially, from 42 percent in 1960 to about 30 percent in 1973, just before the oil price rises.[11] Yet this took place during a period when the import growth in the industrial world was so rapid (over 8 percent a year) that imports of nonfuel raw materials and foodstuffs, valued in constant prices, appear to have grown about as fast as GDP in the industrial world, about 5 percent a year from 1960 to 1973. Over this period, admittedly one of extraordinary growth of trade and income in the industrial world, the balanced growth model seems to have prevailed. In the late 1970s, however, the growth of industrial countries' GDP slowed to about 3 percent a year, and their real imports of nonfuel raw materials and foods grew very slowly, under 1 percent a year.

Whatever the broad trends, there are likely to be encouraging prospects for some primary commodities and some primary-exporting countries. Many of the raw materials now prominent in world trade were hardly on the scene at the turn of this century and thus have undergone substantial growth. The demands for petroleum, rubber, copper, aluminum, newsprint, plywood, and vegetable oils received substantial boosts from technological innovation or from high income elasticities of demand, the very factors cited against raw material exports. Several commodities have experienced substantial export growth rates since 1960: exports of soybean products, coconut and palm oil, logs and sawnwood, aluminum, iron ore, phosphate rock, and petroleum all grew by at least 5 percent a year from 1961 to 1977, valued at constant prices.[12] Among the countries producing these commodities several experienced moderately rapid economic growth, especially during the 1960s, including Malaysia, Jamaica, Liberia, Mauritania, and Jordan. Of course many petroleum-exporting countries grew rapidly during the 1970s (see Chapter 19). In addition several countries—including Kenya, Ivory Coast, Thailand, Guatemala, Nicaragua, and Panama—have used a diversified group of other traditional exports to stimulate growth.

The lesson is not that demand for primary imports in the industrial world will grow sufficiently to support rapid development in the third world. It is rather than some commodities will face brisk demand growth and some countries will benefit substantially from producing such exports. A prudent forecast of demand growth for primary commodities as a whole would, however, be lower than the postwar experience until the mid-1970s.

10. Anne P. Carter, "Change in the Structure of the American Economy, 1949 to 1958 and 1962," *Review of Economics and Statistics* 49 (1967): 209–24.

11. World Bank, *World Tables 1976* and *1980* (Baltimore: Johns Hopkins University Press, 1976 and 1980).

12. World Bank, *Commodity Price Forecasts* (Washington, D.C.; May 1979).

With slower growth in industrial countries, the impact of Engel's law, and materials-saving innovations, it seems unlikely that the developed countries will import enough tropical foods and raw materials to fuel an era of rapid development for the third world as a whole during the rest of this century.

Declining Terms of Trade

An influential school of thought, led by Raul Prebisch and Hans Singer,[13] has argued that not only will primary exports face sluggish growth of demand, but prices received for these commodities will fall on world markets relative to the prices of LDC imports of manufactures from developed countries. The most commonly used measure of these relative prices is the commodity or ***net barter terms of trade*** (T_n). T_n is a ratio of two indexes: (1) the average price of a country's exports (P_x), which can be approximated by dividing an index of export volume into an index of export revenue, and (2) the average price of its imports (P_m), determined for imports by the same method as P_x. The commodity terms of trade rise if export prices rise relative to import prices.

Prebisch based his prediction of declining relative export prices on his observations of the terms of trade for the United Kingdom over the period 1870–1936 when the net barter terms of trade rose by 36 percent. On the apparently reasonable assumption that Britain exported manufactures and imported foods and raw materials, this rise in British terms of trade must mirror a fall in those of primary exporters. But the data can be faulted. Over the long period from 1870 to 1936 the nature of the products in world trade, especially manufactures, changed dramatically; indeed many products exported from England in 1936 did not exist in 1870. Under those conditions some or all of the increase in British export prices could be attributed to improved productivity or otherwise enhanced quality of the goods exported. Much of the apparent fall in British import prices can be attributed to dramatically falling shipping costs, as steamships replaced sailing vessels. Since the shippers were industrial countries, this fraction of the export price decline did not affect the net revenues of the primary exporters. Postwar data on the terms of trade of the less developed countries, perhaps somewhat less susceptible to these problems, is summarized in Fig. 15–2. The figure illustrates what a regression analysis can prove: there has been a very slight downward trend in the terms of trade of non-petroleum-exporting LDCs since the early 1950s, no more than 0.3 percent a year; and probably no significant trend at all since 1960. Of course, petroleum exporters enjoyed substantial improvements in their terms of trade, which doubled for middle-income oil exporters and rose by a factor of six for the high-income exporters of the Middle East from 1960 to 1980.

13. United Nations (Raul Prebisch), *The Economic Development of Latin America and Its Principal Problems* (Lake Success, N.Y., 1950); Hans W. Singer, "The Distribution of Trade Between Investing and Borrowing Countries," *American Economic Review* 40 (May 1950): 473–85. An excellent review of these arguments appears in Meier, *International Economics of Development,* Chapter 3.

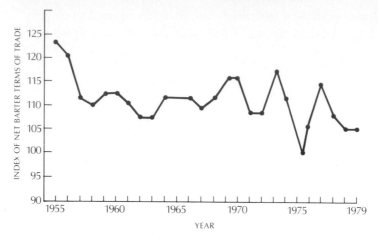

Fig. 15–2   Commodity Terms of Trade for Non-Petroleum-Exporting Developing Countries, 1956–1979 (1975 = 100).

Source: International Monetary Fund, *International Financial Statistics Yearbook* (Washington, D.C., 1981), pp. 66–76.

Not only are the long-term data inconclusive, but the measurement concept is also in doubt. The net barter terms of trade tells us little about income or welfare, which ought to be the basis for judging changes in world trade conditions. A better measure of the income effect of price changes would be the ***income terms of trade***, T_i, which measures the purchasing power of exports by comparing an index of export revenues to an index of import prices. This is equivalent to the net barter terms of trade multiplied by the volume of exports (Q_x), or $T_i = P_x Q_x / P_m = T_n Q_x$. If, for example, Zambia increases its copper exports and causes the world price to fall, but less than proportionately to the volume increase (that is, the absolute value of the demand elasticity for Zambian copper is greater than 1), then copper revenue would increase and, in the absence of import price changes, the income terms of trade would rise. Assuming the resources shifted into copper production could not have produced goods or services of equal value in other sectors, Zambia would be unambiguously better off than before. For any *single* country, the elasticity of demand for a particular export is likely to exceed 1, even if the elasticity of *world* demand for this export is below 1.

Similarly, an increase in Zambia's production of copper due to higher productivity may cause world copper prices to fall. But if the price decline is less than the percentage rise in the productivity (Z_x) of all factors engaged in production for export, the factors engaged in copper mining would be better off than before. The ***single factoral terms of trade***, T_s, measures factor income relative to factor inputs and import prices, or $T_s = (P_x/P_m)Z_x = T_n Z_x$. Note that a rise in either the income or single factoral terms of trade implies an improvement in income or welfare relative to that country's previous situation. But if, as is often the case, either index rises less than export volume, this also implies that exporting countries are sharing part of the potential gains with importing countries, as Prebisch and Singer suggest.

Fluctuating Export Earnings

Even if the net barter terms of trade show little or no sign of secular decline, they do fluctuate considerably, as is evident in Fig. 15–2. If the underlying source of instability is export supplies there is likely to be considerably less variation in export revenues than if the problem is unstable world demand for a country's exports. If export *supply* is unstable, as for most agricultural exports, then the supply curve shifts, as shown in Fig. 15–3. While output falls from Q_1 (good weather) to Q_2 (drought), price *rises* from P_1 to P_2. Consequently the change in export revenues (PQ) is dampened. If export *demand* is unstable, a condition typical of the markets for metals such as copper, then as demand falls in Fig. 15–4, both price and quantity fall (P_1 to P_2 and Q_1 to Q_2). The variation in export revenues is then greater than the change in either price or quantity. (Note that this argument holds even if the country is a "price-taker," i.e., faces a perfectly elastic demand for its export.) We have some indirect evidence to suggest that most export instability is due to shifts in supply. MacBean has found that for forty-five developing countries over a period from 1946 to 1958 the instability in export prices was not correlated with that in export revenues, while there was a highly significant correlation between variance in quantities and variance in revenues,[14] consistent with the situation depicted in Fig. 15–3.

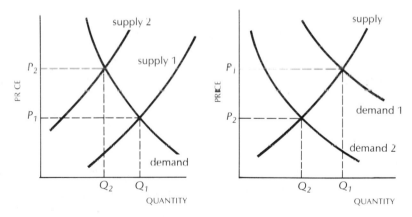

Fig. 15–3 Variable Export Supply.   **Fig. 15–4 Variable Export Demand.**

Whether the principal source of instability is demand or supply, or a combination of both, a second question remains: What kinds of exporting countries suffer most from instability? The usual expectation is that export instability will be most serious among less developed countries whose export earnings are concentrated in one or a few products, especially if those products are primary commodities, and especially if its markets are concentrated in a few importing countries. However, not all of this specifica-

14. Alasdair I. MacBean, *Export Instability and Economic Development* (London: George Allen and Unwin, 1966), pp. 46–48.

tion stands up to empirical testing. Two thorough studies, one by MacBean using data from the 1950s and a second by Knudson and Parnes that extends the data through the mid-1960s, come to several conclusions. First, developing countries as a group do have more unstable export earnings than industrial countries, although the difference between the two groups is not great. Second, although not all studies agree, commodity concentration does seem to be a significant cause of fluctuations in export earnings. However, there appears to be little or no association between export instability and the geographic concentration of export markets or the fraction of a country's export that consists of primary commodities. In fact manufactured goods may be subject to earnings instability as great as primary commodities.[15]

The truly surprising empirical result in these studies is that even if developing countries suffer more export instability, their investment and economic growth may not be hurt by it. Conventional wisdom has generally held that the instabilities of export earnings would be transmitted to the domestic economy, making domestic demand unstable and rendering investment more risky. Uncertain access to imported materials, caused by fluctuating export earnings, intensifies investors' risks. Consequently, investment is discouraged and economic growth retarded. The econometric tests of these propositions either fail to support them or prove the opposite: export instability seems positively correlated with investment and growth. However, there is some controversy over the validity of these findings, and observations on the structural characteristics of nonfuel minerals exporters —especially their heavy dependence on one or two mineral exports for government revenue—suggest that these countries may be severely hampered by earnings fluctuations.[16]

Knudsen and Parnes have advanced the permanent income hypothesis to explain why fluctuating earnings might not retard development. Income earners (and by extension, countries) count on some level of relatively certain annual income and try to maintain consumption patterns based largely on that "permanent" income. More of the uncertain, fluctuating component of income tends to be saved than is true for the "permanent" component. The more unstable total income is likely to be, then the larger the fraction that income earners will save. Under this hypothesis about behavior, greater export instability forces residents (and governments) to save more than they otherwise would, hence to invest more.[17]

---

15. Ibid., pp. 34–52; Odin Knudsen and Andrew Parnes, *Trade Instability and Economic Development* (Lexington, Mass.: Heath Lexington Books, 1975), pp. 19–30.

16. The work of F. G. Adams and J. R. Behrman, *Commodity Exports and Ecnomic Development: The Commodity Problem and Policy in Developing Countries: An Integrated Econometric Investigation* (Lexington, Mass.: D. C. Heath, 1982), points to a negligible effect of export instability on growth. Gobind Nankani, "Development Problems of Non-fuel Mineral Exporting Countries," *Finance and Development* 17, no. 1 (March 1980): 6–10, provides structural reasons for believing that fluctuating export earnings do harm the development efforts of these countries.

17. Knudsen and Parnes, *Trade Instability,* pp. 81–128. Chapter 13 of this text has a fuller treatment of savings and the permanent income hypothesis.

Most individuals and presumably most governments prefer situations of greater stability, other things equal. If, as suggested by the permanent income hypothesis, greater variance of export economies leads to faster growth, then the preference for stable earnings (reduced variance) may force governments to choose slower growth as well. In Fig. 15–5 the curve *RR* represents the trade-off between export stability and economic growth in a particular economy. It is analogous to a production possibilities frontier in which the two "goods" are stability and growth. The indifference curves reflect preferences for lower variability and higher growth and are typical of risk-avoiding individuals or governments. A typical primary-exporting country might be in position *A,* with high growth and high variability of export earnings. By reducing both risk and growth, shown as a move from *A* to *B,* the country could achieve a higher indifference curve and thus would consider itself better off. Something like this model could explain the efforts expended by many developing-country governments to stabilize export earnings through producer price controls, international buffer stocks, or compensatory payments schemes, despite the implications of the permanent income hypothesis.

Commodity Agreements to Raise Prices

Developing countries have made several attempts over the past two decades to raise the prices of specific export commodities. One of the proposals of the 1974 United Nations resolution on a "New International Economic Order" (NIEO) called for international *commodity agreements* which would both stabilize commodity prices and raise them. In order to raise export prices it is necessary either to restrict output (that is, to shift the supply curve to the left) or to impose a common export tax. If world

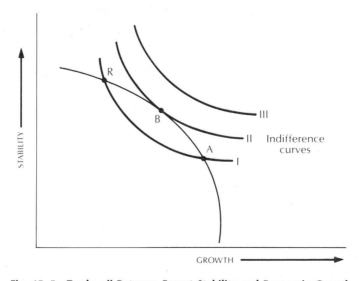

Fig. 15–5 Trade-off Between Export Stability and Economic Growth.

demand for the commodity is inelastic (i.e., the price elasticity is between 0 and -1), as is true for most tropical food exports, then restricting supply causes a more than proportional increase in price and an increase in total revenues to exporters. If, however, world demand is elastic, as may be true for meat and for many manufactured goods, then supply restrictions raise prices less than proportionately and revenues fall.

Output restriction works best when large majorities of both producing and consuming nations participate. The International Coffee Agreement, negotiated in 1960, was a notably successful example for about a decade. Export quotas were allocated to all producers, while most Western consuming nations agreed to buy only from producing members of the agreement. Exporters could sell to nonquota markets, such as Eastern Europe and most developing countries, but at market prices that were generally lower than in participating countries.

However, under certain conditions producers may be able to restrict demand and raise prices without consumer agreement. Among many unsuccessful attempts to accomplish this there looms the one dramatic success, the Organization of Petroleum Exporting Countries, known by the household acronym OPEC. Every reader of this book has seen clear evidence of OPEC's ability to raise oil prices severalfold for almost a decade since 1973. This example has stimulated exporters of other commodities—especially minerals—to form their own *cartels,* as price-raising commodity agreements among producers may be called. The ability of mineral cartels to achieve their aim is assessed in Chapter 19.

Attempts to raise world prices for primary exports are akin to a "zero-sum game" in which the gains of one group of countries (producers) are offset by the losses of other groups (consumers and the foreign owners of capital). There has been little consumer country support for the price-raising features of the NIEO and the debate has instead centered on price stabilization, which can benefit both exporting and importing countries.

Commodity Agreements to Stabilize Prices

Following the 1974 United Nations resolution on the New International Economic Order, the United Nations Conference on Trade and Development (UNCTAD) developed an "Integrated Programme for Commodities," which became the pivotal proposal in NIEO discussions. Under this integrated program a common fund was to be established by agreement among both exporters and importers. The fund would be used to purchase stocks of commodities, called *buffer stocks,* that would be used to stabilize the prices of eighteen commodities that are among the most important LDC exports: bananas, bauxite, cocoa, coffee, copper, cotton, hard fibers, iron ore, jute, manganese, meat, phosphates, rubber, sugar, tea, timber, tin, and vegetable oils.

To stabilize commodity prices in world trade it is necessary for some central authority—a large company, a private cartel, a single government, a cartel of producing countries, or an international agency—to intervene in the market, buying the commodity when prices are falling and selling from their stocks when prices are rising. To do this the authority must control a buffer stock and must have access to funds that can be used to increase that stock when necessary. The principle of stabilization is easy, but the application is fraught with difficulty. First, the buffer stock authority must have a reliable forecast of the commodity's price trend over a long period, because intervention is intended to reduce fluctuations about that trend. If predictions of future prices are too high, the authority will on balance buy more for the buffer stock than it sells and may eventually be unable to finance further purchases. Conversely a low prediction results in excessive sales, depleting the buffer stock.

Second, even if price forecasts are accurate the authority must set floor and ceiling prices that it can maintain, given available finance and the size of the buffer stock. Once speculators sense that the authority's resources are too limited they can bid the price up or down, depending on whether stocks or finance are in short supply, to break through the ceiling or floor and make a certain profit. Finally, if buffer stocks lead to higher inventories of a commodity than would otherwise be held, this represents a real resource cost to someone. In the NIEO proposals the industrial nations were to finance the stocks and would thus have borne this cost.

Discussions continue under United Nations auspices on the establishment of commodity agreements and a common fund. Because of the large resource costs involved—probably $10 billion or more—the success of negotiations will depend not only on whether the technical problems can be overcome, but also on the assessment of consuming nations about the costs to them of continued price fluctuations.

Stabilizing world commodity prices is not necessarily the same thing as stabilizing a particular country's export earnings. As suggested above, if production is itself unstable because of variable weather, strikes, or other disruptions, then a stable world price can increase the variability of earnings, although studies by Jere Behrman suggest that this would not be a serious problem in the UNCTAD scheme.[18] An alternative with considerable appeal is to compensate directly for earnings fluctuations rather than to stabilize prices. Two such schemes are in existence: the Compensatory Financing Facility of the International Monetary Fund and the Stabex scheme operated by the European Economic Community under the Lome Convention. Under the IMF facility countries can borrow to finance balance-of-paments deficits which are partially caused by a drop in export revenues below a five-year moving average. The EEC scheme permits borrowing if a country's particular commodity export revenues, earned

18. Jere R. Behrman, *Development, the International Economic Order and Commodity Agreements* (Reading, Mass.: Addison-Wesley, 1978), Chapter 3, provides an analytical treatment of commodity agreements and summarizes the conditions under which stable prices will stabilize or destabilize revenues. On pages 87–90 he reports his conclusions that UNCTAD's scheme would either stabilize revenues or have no impact on their variability.

from the Community, fall below a four-year average. During 1980 the IMF lent $996 million under its facility.

Ineffective Linkages

An export sector may grow satisfactorily, enjoying favorable and steady prices, yet still fail to stimulate development if linkages fail to materialize. From the previous discussion of linkages it would appear that the petroleum industry and, with a few exceptions, the mining industry generally remain *enclaves,* remote from other centers of production and ill-adapted to link with them economically. Neither backward linkages to suppliers of production materials and equipment nor consumption linkages are likely to work. In some instances railroads and ports built for the mines do aid other industries by lowering costs and stimulating investment, but examples of remote or specialized overhead capital can also be found: Liberia's rail and harbor link with its iron mines is ill-placed to stimulate agriculture or other industry, and the pipelines and tanker ports of the petroleum industry have no uses outside that sector. Some agricultural export sectors, particularly plantations in colonial Africa, also had few effective linkages. But generally the smaller scale and greater labor intensity of agriculture make possible more linked development than is true for minerals.

The *fiscal linkage,* which can channel resource wealth to finance development in other sectors, is too often used to avoid the difficult choices required to launch development. A typical pattern is represented by Zambia, whose copper wealth has allowed it to invest in highly protected, inefficient industries with no potential market outside the country and to avoid the difficult problem of stimulating small-scale African agriculture in a sector dominated by large-scale European farmers. The petroleum exporters face similar choices: whether to use oil revenues in employment and welfare programs, unrelated to increased productivity among its farmers and industrial workers, or to resist this temptation and invest in agriculture and industry that will eventually be able to compete in world markets, thus diversifying the economy.

The choice is made more difficult by the high wages typically paid in capital-intensive petroleum and mining sectors, which often provide high wage standards for union bargaining and government minimum wagesetting in other sectors. As wages rise the prospects for development based on abundant low-cost labor diminish. The dualistic structure (see Chapter 3) is perpetuated, with a small but relatively high-income work force in modern employment and a large, low-productivity work force of farmers and marginal urban workers, the latter mostly in casual employment and petty services.

An even more pervasive bar to generating linkages from mineral enclaves and certain other primary export sectors is the impact of abundant export revenues on the exchange rate. Figure 15–6 shows what happens when minerals or tree crops like cocoa and coffee dominate the supply of foreign exchange revenues for a country. In this diagram of a foreign exchange

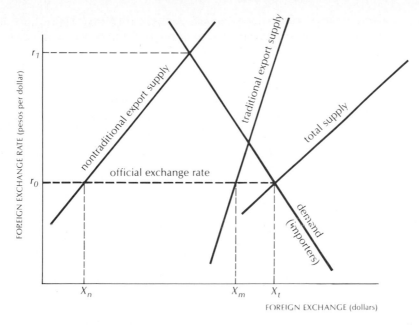

Fig. 15–6   Foreign Exchange Market in a Resource-Rich Country.

market the quantity along the horizontal axis is the amount of foreign exchange while the price along the vertical axis is the exchange rate, expressed as units of local currency per unit of foreign currency, e.g., pesos
per dollar. The demand curve is a *total revenue curve,* giving the amount of
foreign exchange (price in dollars per ton times quantity in tons) that importers would spend at any given exchange rate. The supply curves are also
total revenue curves and three are shown: (1) a traditional mineral or agricultural export supply, abundant but fairly inelastic, either because the resource is being fully exploited or because it takes a long time to explore
and bring new supplies into production; as shown here, the country's traditional export faces elastic world demand; (2) supplies of nontraditional
exports; and (3) total supply, a horizontal summation of the first two. The
supply of nontraditional exports has been shown as if, at a given amount of
revenue, unit costs would be considerably higher than for traditional exports, a realistic assumption for resource-rich countries. For a major petroleum or hard-mineral exporter the traditional export supply curve might be
even less elastic and farther to the right, completely dominating total export
supply.

If the market is permitted to determine the exchange rate it would settle
at r_0, where the total supply and demand curves intersect. At that exchange
rate traditional exports (X_m) would dominate total exports (X_t). Nontraditional export revenues (X_n) would be relatively small because the local currency yield for a dollar's worth of export (the exchange rate, r_0) would be
too low to make it profitable for most nontraditional industries to produce
for export or for import substitution, given their high costs. For these in-

dustries the exchange rate is *overvalued,* because the dollar price of the currency is too high (and the local currency price of the dollar is too low).[19] If the country represented in Fig. 15–6 suddenly lost its supply of traditional exports, the foreign exchange market would eventually come into balance at the much higher peso-dollar exchange rate, r_1, where import demand equals the supply of nontraditional exports. This high rate would not only discourage imports, but also provide a large stimulus to the production of new nontraditional exports. Overvalued exchange rates together with high wages discourage the development of new industries and thus prevent diversification of the economy. These adverse impacts of rich natural resource deposits are not confined to developing countries. The exploitation of offshore oil and natural gas reserves has had a similar effect in the Netherlands, damaging once-competitive export industries, from which observers coined the term "Dutch disease." In its most extreme developing-country manifestation this has also been termed the "Kuwait effect." (In Chapter 19 we explore these issues and some country cases in more detail.)

Several policy interventions have been used to raise the effective price to nontraditional industries and thus encourage their development. *Taxes on primary exports,* whether for fiscal revenue or to restrict supply and thus raise world prices, have the effect of devaluing the exchange rate. Figure 15–7 repeats Fig. 15–6. Before a tax is imposed on traditional primary exports the exchange rate is r_0; export revenue is X_t^0, of which X_n^0 comes from nontraditional exports. A tax on the traditional export (assumed to face an elastic demand) has the effect of shifting the export supply upward, since exporters must now obtain a higher price to pay the taxes and cover costs. In the new equilibrium the exchange rate is devalued to r_1 and traditional exporters receive only r_2 net of the export tax. Although traditional and total export revenues are lower (X_m^1 and X_t^1), the greater stimulus to nontraditional industries causes a rise in nontraditional exports, from X_n^0 to X_n^1. For a rich mineral resource, especially petroleum, with large profits (rents), the supply curve could be almost completely inelastic and even a large tax might not have the effect shown in Fig. 15–7. Also, if the country faced an inelastic demand for its traditional export, the traditional export supply curve would bend backward and a tax would have the opposite effect, increasing the total quantity of foreign exchange and lowering the exchange rate in local currency, thus reducing the supply of nontraditional exports.

The same effect could be obtained by maintaining a *split exchange rate.* The central bank would pay r_1 pesos per dollar of receipts for nontraditional exports (and require importers to pay this rate also) but pay only r_2 pesos per dollar for traditional export receipts. To accomplish this, however, authorities must prevent exporters of traditional commodities from selling foreign exchange to importers or other exporters, who would pay more than the official rate on traditional exports. This may be virtually impossible to police, especially over the long term. Finally, *import tariffs and quotas* are used in most countries to raise the local price of imports, thus

---

19. For a more complete definition of an overvalued exchange rate, see Chapter 16.

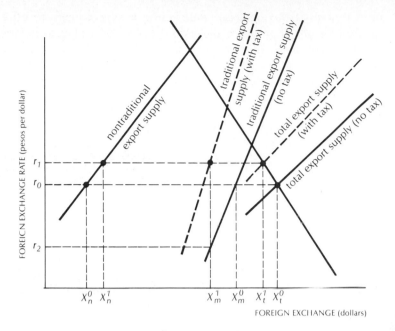

Fig. 15–7   Export Taxes and Split Exchange Rates.

protecting import-competing industries and stimulating their development. This policy is explored at length in Chapter 16.

Natural resource exporters, recognizing the need to diversify their economies and raise productivity, have begun to turn toward the processing of their exports as a vehicle for development. If petroleum and mining industries create few backward linkages, they can generate *forward linkages* to industries whose principal input is the export sector's output. Thus Venezuela is using its iron ore, natural gas, and hydroelectric power to produce steel, part of which is to be exported in place of the iron ore and part of which is to be used domestically. If and only if the domestic steel is cheaper than imported steel, it may stimulate further forward linkages to steel-using industries like construction, transport equipment, processing equipment, and even oil derricks, one of those undeveloped linkages to the petroleum industry. Other mineral and timber exporters are trying to exploit forward linkages and either substitute processed exports for raw materials or divert part of their raw materials into inputs for domestic industry.

These *resource-based industrialization strategies* may succeed in expanding the industrial base and increasing the economic benefits derived from a natural resource. However, resource processing is no panacea for development. Most of the mineral-processing industries share with mining the characteristics of large scale, capital intensity, sophisticated technology, and high wages, so they tend to be extensions of the export enclave, generating little employment and realizing few linkages to the rest of the economy. Nor would they represent much diversification if the processed product is mostly exported in place of the raw material.

We are left with the conclusion that primary exports can be effective leading sectors for development if the nature of the natural resource and of the production process is conducive to linkages. Where these characteristics are absent, the task is more difficult and requires enlightened, forceful, and sustained government intervention to channel revenues into productivity-raising investments elsewhere in the economy.

FURTHER READING   Three books that deal in depth with the impact of international trade on economic development, at a level similar to this textbook, are Gerald M. Meier, *The International Economics of Development* (New York: Harper & Row, 1968), especially Chapters 2, 3, and 8; Charles P. Kindleberger, *Foreign Trade and the National Economy* (New Haven: Yale University Press, 1962), especially Chapters 7, 11, and 12–14; and Gerald K. Helleiner, *International Trade and Economic Development* (Baltimore: Penguin Books, 1972), especially the first six chapters. The reader wishing to brush up on comparative advantage should consult any of several standard textbooks in international trade, too numerous to list here.

The impact of export industries on economic development through various linkages is the focus of a body of literature called staple theory. For examples of this literature, see footnote 8. Edward J. Chambers and Donald F. Gordon, "Primary Products and Economic Growth," *Journal of Political Economy* 74 (1966): 315–32, are critical of the explanatory power of staple theory. A useful collection of case studies measuring the impact of export industries on growth is contained in Scott R. Pearson and J. Cownie, *Commodity Exports and African Development* (Lexington, Mass.: D. C. Heath, 1974).

The opening rounds in the case against primary export-led growth were fired by Raul Prebisch and Hans W. Singer, in works cited in the footnotes. Other influential works include those by Ragnar Nurkse (see footnote 9) and Jagdish Bhagwati, "Immiserizing Growth: A Geometrical Note," *Review of Economic Studies* 25 (1958): 201–5. Charles P. Kindleberger, *The Terms of Trade: A European Case Study* (New Haven: Yale University Press, 1962), presents counterarguments to Prebisch's pessimism about the developing countries' terms of trade.

A comprehensive, analytical, and generally sympathetic study of commodity agreements in the context of the New International Economic Order is contained in Jere R. Behrman's work cited in footnote 18. Less sympathetic views are offered by Harry G. Johnson, "Commodities: Less Developed Country Demands and Developed Countries' Response," in Jagdish N. Bhagwati (ed.), *The North-South Debate* (Cambridge, Mass.: MIT Press, 1977), pp. 240–51; and by Rachel McCulloch, "Economic and Political Issues in the New International Economic Order" (Harvard Institute of Economic Research Original Paper No. 22, July 1979).

On resource-based industrialization, see Michael Roemer, "Resource-based Industrialization: A Survey," *Journal of Development Economics* 6 (June 1979): 163–202.

Chapter 16

TRADE STRATEGIES: IMPORT SUBSTITUTION

Whatever the relative merits and drawbacks of primary-export-led growth, most governments have pushed their economies full-speed in other directions. There have been exceptions: Malaysia, Thailand, Kenya, and Ivory Coast have diversified their primary exporting base and prospered, while the petroleum exporters simply followed their overwhelming comparative advantage. For most of the rest, development has become synonymous with industrialization, which has been pursued by substituting domestic production for imports of manufactures. A few countries have followed a very different path, emphasizing the export of labor-intensive manufactures. This chapter examines the first of these strategies and Chapter 17 describes the second, then attempts a synthesis among the various trade-and-industrialization approaches to development.

The Strategy of Protection

Import substitution is a well-trod path to industrialization. It was followed during the nineteenth century by most of the currently industrial countries as they followed the pathbreaker, England, into the Industrial Revolution. In the newly independent United States, Alexander Hamilton's 1791 Report on Manufactures argued for tariffs to protect American manufacturers from cheap British imports, and President Jefferson unintentionally boosted American manufacturing by the politically inspired Embargo of 1807. Friedrich Liszt, the German economist, espoused protective tariffs as an instrument to industrialize Germany in mid-nineteenth century, and all the major European powers, followed most successfully by Japan, marched down the road of protectionism to develop manufacturing as it became apparent that military strength depended on industrial strength.

In the third world, import substitution was first explored by Latin American countries when their primary export markets were severely disrupted, first by the Depression and subsequently by the breakdown of commercial shipping during World War II. Emerging from the war with fledgling industries, countries like Argentina, Brazil, Colombia, and Mexico began systematically to sustain these manufacturers by erecting tariffs and other barriers to competing imports from the United States. The export pessimism chronicled by Prebisch, Singer, and others reinforced protectionist sentiment, and Latin America developed import substitution regimes with a multitude of protective techniques that were later emulated by other developing countries. A few Asian countries, such as India and Turkey, also began to industrialize before World War II. But in most of Asia and Africa independence was the stimulus that induced countries to embark on the path of import substitution. By the 1960s import substitution had become the dominant strategy of economic development.

The underlying concept of import substitution is simple. First, identify large domestic markets, as indicated by substantial imports over the years. Then ensure that the technologies of production can be mastered by local manufacturers or that foreign investors are willing to supply technology, management, and capital. Finally, erect protective barriers, either tariffs or quotas on imports, to overcome the probably high initial cost of local production and make it profitable for potential investors in the target industries. This approach has generally meant that consumer goods industries—especially processed foods, beverages, textiles, clothing, and footwear—became the first targets for investment. Not only are these products manufactured with relatively standardized technologies easily accessible to LDC producers, but it was also believed that consumers could bear the higher costs of local production without disrupting development. The only other major category of manufactured import before industrialization began was capital goods. Increased investment was essential to development, however, and it was believed that higher costs of capital equipment would discourage investors.

At the core of import substitution have been two policy instruments, the protective tariff and the import quota. To understand how import substitution works, and why it may ultimately fail, it is necessary to explore these two instruments in some depth, together with a third element, the overvalued exchange rate, that imparts a detrimental bias to the system.

Infant Industries

Economists find much to criticize in the protective structures of both developing and industrial countries, as this chapter will make clear. But there are some valid arguments in favor of protective tariffs as a tool of development, centering on the concept of an infant industry. A country wishing to develop through industrialization may see opportunities in several lines of manufacturing to begin the process. (A similar argument could be made in terms of diversifying agriculture by introducing new crops.) With little experience in these new lines of production, domestic capitalists, managers, technicians, workers (and farmers) are likely to be relatively inefficient compared to producers in more advanced industrial countries, and are likely to remain so for several years. Eventually as the new industries "learn by doing" the productivity of all factors of production will rise, and eventually the new enterprises may be competitive in world markets. That is, they may be able to compete at home with imported goods without tariff protection, or may even be able to export. Until these producers gain the necessary experience, however, they are unable to manufacture (or grow new crops) profitably and sell at the price of competing imports. So unless the government either subsidizes these fledgling industries, or protects them by imposing tariffs on or limiting the quantity of competing imports, the infant industries have little chance of being born, let alone maturing into efficient competitors.

To justify protection or a subsidy, an infant industry must eventually be capable of competing against imports in the home market or, a stronger condition, as an export sector. This suggests a temporary tariff, one that declines toward zero as productivity increases and costs fall, or a declining subsidy. The subsidy has the advantage of clearly identifying the costs of starting the new industry but the disadvantage of an additional burden on the government's revenue system. Most governments find it easier to impose tariffs, which make domestic consumers bear the cost instead. Even a temporary tariff or subsidy may not be justified if the eventual benefits to society of establishing the new industry, suitably discounted as explained in Chapter 6, do not exceed the costs of protection.[1] All too often these conditions are not met. The industrial landscape is littered with infants that never grew up and require protection indefinitely, from the petrochemical industry of Colombia to the textile industry of Ghana.

The infant industry argument can be extended to include several industries at once, and even to include all manufacturing. For example, a balanced growth strategy of developing many industries simultaneously (see Chapter 3) might be started with a uniform protective tariff, declining over time. This is a third approach to the problem discussed at the end of Chapter 15, diversification of the economy away from dependence on a few primary-product exports. There we discussed taxing the primary exports or imposing a split exchange rate in order to raise the prices facing other industries. A uniform protective duty on competing imports would have the same effect on nontraditional industries, although the costs of protection would be distributed differently. Ideally all these interventions in the market share three characteristics: they are intended to diversify the economy toward a new but efficient structure; they are necessary because the market,

---

1. For a complete specification of the infant industry argument, see Harry G. Johnson, "Optimal Trade Interventions in the Presence of Domestic Distortions," in R. E. Caves et al., *Trade Growth and the Balance of Payments* (Amsterdam: North Holland, 1965), pp. 3–34.

left alone, would not achieve this desirable result in a reasonable time; and they should be temporary measures with declining impacts if the diversification strategy is successful. As we will see, the protective structures used to promote import substitution deviate from this ideal in crucial ways.

Protective Structure

In the early stages of import substitution, when a protective tariff is placed on competing consumer good imports, not one but two significant aids are provided simultaneously to the potential manufacturer. First and obviously, the domestic price of the good, say, cloth, will be raised above the world price. For the importing country the world price of imported cloth is the cost of the cloth landed at the port of entry, the c.i.f. or "border" price. With no tariff, the domestic price of cloth would settle at the world price. When a tariff is imposed the domestic price must rise above the world price. If the home country's demand for imports does not affect world prices (i.e., the world supply is perfectly elastic), and if the tariff does not preclude imports altogether, then the domestic price will rise by the full extent of the tariff. Any potential manufacturer can charge anything up to the tariff-supported domestic price and still compete with imports, assuming his quality is comparable and that domestic consumers do not prefer imports simply because they are foreign.

This effect of increased domestic price is called **nominal protection** and is depicted in Fig. 16–1. At a world price P_w (equal to the border price, c.i.f.), consumers demand Q_1 of, say, cloth, and local producers find it profitable

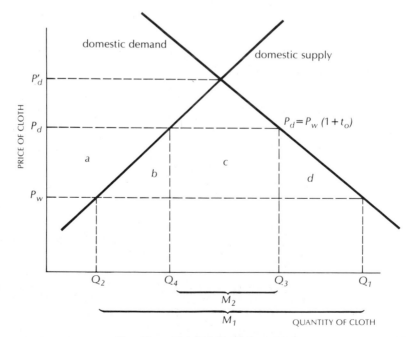

Fig. 16–1 Nominal Tariff Protection.

to produce only Q_2; the balance, $M_1 = Q_1 - Q_2$, is imported. If an *ad valorem*[2] tariff t_o is imposed on imports competing with domestic cloth and if world supply is perfectly elastic, then the domestic price rises to P_d, reducing demand to Q_3 and increasing domestic production to Q_4. Imports are thus reduced to $M_2 = Q_3 - Q_4$. The *protective effect*, given by the increase in domestic output from Q_2 to Q_4, entails a rent or *producers' surplus,* given by trapezoid *a;* and a *resource cost*, given by triangle *b*, because factors of production are diverted from more productive uses into import substitution for imported cloth. Government's tariff revenue is represented by rectangle $c = t_o P_w (Q_3 - Q_4)$. Consumers pay for protection by the loss of *consumer surplus,* equal to area $a + b + c + d$, generated by both the higher price and reduced consumption. Area $b + d$, two triangles representing welfare losses that are not compensated by gains to anyone, is called the *deadweight loss.* A prohibitive tariff would raise the domestic price to P'_d, at which point domestic demand equals domestic supply and no cloth is imported.

The second aid to domestic manufacture is that tariffs are typically *not* raised on the imported inputs required for production. If the textile manufacturer is to import cotton which he will spin into yarn and weave into cloth, then his concern is not only with the price of the cloth but with the margin between the cost of imported cotton (and other imported inputs, such as chemicals and dyes) and the sale price of finished cloth. It is within this margin that he must pay wages, rents, and interest on borrowed capital and from which he must extract his profit. The greater that margin, the more room there is to accommodate higher factor costs and/or the higher the potential profit. This margin is the *value added* measured in *domestic prices.* It can be increased either by raising tariffs on competing imports of finished products, lowering tariffs on imported inputs, or both. This dual effect of the tariff structure is called **effective protection.**

To measure this concept of effective protection it is necessary to compare two margins: first, the margin between the domestic, tariff-determined prices of inputs and outputs, or the domestic value added; second, the same margin, but measured at world or c.i.f. prices, which is called value added at world prices. The fraction by which the first margin exceeds the second is called the **effective rate of protection,** abbreviated ERP:

$$\text{ERP} = \frac{\text{value added at domestic prices}}{\text{value added at world prices}} - 1 \qquad \textbf{[16–1]}$$

To refine this further, note that value added at domestic prices (V_d) is the difference between the potential domestic price (P_d) and the potential domestic cost of material inputs per unit of output (C_d). Further, the potential domestic price is equivalent to the world price (P_w) plus the increase permitted by the percentage (or *ad valorem*) tariff on competing imports (t_o),

2. Tariff rates can be expressed as a fraction of import value *(ad valorem* tariff) or as a price per unit (specific tariff, given for example, in cents per kilogram). In this book we follow the general practice and use *ad valorem* tariffs for convenience.

while potential domestic cost equals the cost at world prices (C_w) plus any increase permitted by the *ad valorem* tariff on imported inputs (t_i). The denominator, value added at world prices (V_w), is the difference between the world price of competing imports and the cost of inputs, also valued at world prices (C_w). Given this, then[3]

$$ \text{ERP} = \frac{P_d - C_d}{P_w - C_w} - 1 = \frac{P_w(1 + t_o) - C_w(1 + t_i)}{P_w - C_w} - 1 \qquad \text{[16–2]} $$

$$ \text{ERP} = \frac{P_w t_o - C_w t_i}{P_w - C_w} \qquad \text{[16–3]} $$

To illustrate the workings of effective protection, assume, using equation 16–3, that $100 of cloth, valued at world prices, would require $60 of material inputs, such as cotton and chemicals, also valued at world prices. Value added is $40 at world prices. If the government has imposed a uniform duty of 20 percent on both competing imports and imported inputs, then

$$ \text{ERP} = \frac{100(.20) - 60(.20)}{100 - 60} = 0.20 $$

A uniform tariff, 20 percent in this case, yields an effective rate of protection of the same amount. If, however, in order to encourage investment in the textile industry the government were to permit textile firms to import cotton and chemicals duty-free, then $t_i = 0$ and

$$ \text{ERP} = \frac{100(.20)}{40} = 0.50. $$

Effective protection is 50 percent, or 2.5 times the nominal rate of 20 percent. Similarly, if the input duty stayed at 20 percent but competing cloth imports were taxed at 32 percent, the ERP would also be 50 percent.

The implication in the second and third examples is that even though modest nominal protection is provided, the domestic manufacturer enjoys a large margin of 50 percent over value added at world prices. If the local manufacturer takes advantage of the effective protection afforded by the tariff structure, he can earn extremely high profits, pay high wages, and/or simply accommodate inefficiencies and high costs substantially above those of foreign competitors. The higher the effective protection, the greater the

---

3. As a last refinement, equation 16–3 can be put in terms of a dollar of output by dividing the fraction through by (P_w). The cost of an input for a dollar's worth of output, C_w/P_w, can then be designated a, an input coefficient. If we then allow for several inputs, each with its own input coefficient, a_i, and its own tariff, t_i, then the formula can be writen:

$$ \text{ERP} = (t_o - \Sigma a_i t_i)/(1 - \Sigma a_i) \qquad \text{[16–4]} $$

This formula can also accommodate subsidies on competing outputs and on inputs by treating them as negative tariffs. For a complete, although advanced, treatment of effective protection, see W. M. Corden, *The Theory of Protection* (London: Oxford University Press, 1971), especially Chapters 2 and 3.

potential for inefficiencies, high input costs, or profits, and hence the greater the likelihood that the industry will be established in the country.

Tariff structures in most countries, including most industrial countries, are like those in the latter two textile examples: duties tend to escalate from low rates on imported industrial inputs to higher rates on imports of finished goods that compete with domestic manufactures. In fact the levels of protection in this hypothetical example are modest by world standards. It is common to observe effective protection of 100 percent or more in several industries in countries strongly pursuing import substitution. Not only is the level high, but there is a wide range of protective rates that result in severe discrimination against particular kinds of investment. A study by Bela Balassa and others reveals the fairly typical pattern of protection, illustrated by the data in Table 16–1 for Brazil, Pakistan, and the Philippines in the mid-1960s.[4]

TABLE 16–1   Effective Rates of Protection

Sector	Brazil (1966)	Pakistan (1963–64)	Philippines (1965)	Norway (1954)
Agriculture	46	− 19	33	34
Mining	− 16	29	− 9	− 7
Manufacturing	127	188	53	9
Consumer goods[a]	198	348	72	29
Intermediate goods[a]	151	160	45	9
Machinery	93	110	24	18
Transport equipment	− 26	—	− 3	− 6

Source: Bela Balassa et al., *The Structure of Protection in the Developing Countries*, (Baltimore: Johns Hopkins University Press, 1971), p. 55.

[a] Aggregates for consumer goods and intermediate goods are simple, unweighted averages of constituent data from Balassa. ERPs are based on input coefficients (the a_i's of equation 16–4) calculated as if tariffs were zero (so-called "free-trade coefficients").

The average level of effective protection is quite high for manufacturing as a whole in Brazil and Pakistan, though only modest for the Philippines. However, the structure within manufacturing is widely skewed. Consumer goods are highly protected, at considerable cost to consumers of manufactures, and intermediate goods are comfortably protected, though at lower rates. The capital goods industries, however, receive less protection because tariffs on capital goods are thought to discourage investors; rates are especially low for transport equipment (which does not include automobiles, a consumer durable). As a consequence the incentive to invest in capital goods production is less than in other manufacturing, and the development of this sector typically lags behind the others. More damaging in terms of many development objectives, manufacturing as a whole enjoys a substantial advantage over agriculture, which faces effective rates of protection ranging downward from 46 percent to a negative 19 percent in these exam-

4. Bela Balassa et al., *The Structure of Protection in the Developing Countries* (Baltimore: Johns Hopkins University Press, 1971).

ples.[5] These biases against investment in agriculture and in capital goods industries are characteristic of import substitution regimes and have been partly responsible for the failure of import substitution to stimulate self-sustaining development. This biased protective structure is not unique to developing countries, as demonstrated by the figures for Norway in Table 16–1. However, extremes like the Pakistan structure, especially the severe bias against agriculture, do seem confined to the third world.

A closely related measure, the **domestic resource cost** (DRC), also compares value added in domestic and world prices. However, it measures domestic value added as the *actual* payments to factors of production—wages, rent, interest, depreciation, and profit—in local currency units such as pesos or rupees. This contrasts with the ERP measure, which is usually (though not necessarily) based on the *potential* domestic value added created by the tariff structure, as measured in equation 16–3. The denominator of the DRC, value added at world prices, is the same as that for the ERP, only it is designated in foreign currency. Thus

$$DRC = \frac{\text{value added at domestic prices in local currency}}{\text{value added at world prices in foreign currency}} \qquad [16–5]$$

This measure has some potential wrinkles that make it useful. First, domestic value added can be measured not at the private costs paid by firms for factors of production, but at the actual value to society, the opportunity cost or shadow price of these factors (see Chapter 6). Second, the denominator can allow for payments to foreign capital and other foreign currency costs, so that the DRC becomes a measure of the domestic cost of earning or saving foreign exchange. Third, linked industries can be incorporated into this measure, which can therefore cover either the textile industry or the textile industry and cotton farming together. (The ERP can also be adjusted to incorporate actual value added at domestic prices and to allow shadow prices and linkages. However, in that form the ratio no longer measures the impact of the tariff and subsidy structure, as it was designed to do.)

The DRC has dimensions of local currency per unit of foreign exchange, for example, rupees per dollar. If for a particular investment this ratio is below the official exchange rate it implies that the country could save or earn foreign exchange through this project, convert the dollars into rupees at the official rate, pay the factors of production, and still retain a surplus in local currency. Such a project is obviously desirable. In order to reach its development goals a country may have to undertake projects for which the DRC is above the official exchange rate. This indicates that the official rate is not set at a level consistent with development goals; it is "overvalued,"

---

5. A negative effective rate of production can have two meanings. If the rate is small it means that the industry faces high taxes on either its inputs or its own outputs, as is likely to be true for many primary-exporting industries. Alternatively a very high negative ERP usually indicates that the industry is so inefficient that its inputs cost more in foreign exchange than its outputs are worth at c.i.f. prices; i.e., value added is negative if measured at world prices! Then the denominator of equation 16–3 or 16–4 becomes a small negative number.

in a sense explained below.[6] Projects can be ranked in ascending order of DRC and this ranking used to select the most efficient projects for investment.[7]

A sample of Indian industries ranked by their DRCs is shown in Table 16–2. At a time when the official exchange rate was 7.50 rupees per dollar, all industries except foodgrain production required at least 10 rupees to save $1 of foreign exchange. Without considerable protection these sectors could not compete with imports. Note the wide range of estimates: the DRC for petroleum products is over six times that for foodgrains. The pattern is consistent with the tendency toward escalating tariff rates. Industries with low DRCs are agricultural products and capital goods, while manufacturers of consumer goods and producers of intermediate goods have high resource costs.

TABLE 16–2   Efficiency Indicators for Selected Industries, India, 1968–1969

Rank	Industry	Domestic resource cost (rupees/dollar)[a]
1	Foodgrains	7.5
2	Timber	10.7
3	Cement	10.8
4	Cotton	11.5
5	Transport equipment	12.1
6	Wood products	14.2
7	Electrical equipment	16.5
8	Leather footwear	16.9
9	Leather	17.1
10	Metal products	17.5
11	Vegetable oils	18.0
12	Iron and steel	18.9
13	Paper and products	20.4
14	Cotton textiles	24.3
15	Fertilizer	42.1
16	Mill products	46.6
17	Petroleum products	47.6

Source: Jagdish N. Bhagwati and T. N. Srinivasan, *Foreign Trade Regimes and Economic Development: India* (New York: Columbia University Press, 1975), pp. 179–81.
[a] Official exchange rate, 1968–69, was 7.50 rupees per dollar.

Import Quotas

The protective effects of tariffs can also be achieved through restrictions on imports, known as quantitative restrictions (QRs), quotas, or import licensing. For both the government and the domestic manufacturers it is trying to protect from foreign competition, import quotas have the advan-

6. If these are infant industries whose domestic resource costs may be expected to fall over time, a temporary protective tariff may be indicated rather than a change in the exchange rate.
7. For a comparison of the DRC and ERP as measures of efficiency, see Michael Bruno, "Domestic Resource Costs and Effective Protection: Clarification and Syntheses," *Journal of Political Economy* 80 (1972):16–33; and Bela Balassa and Daniel M. Schydlowsky, "Domestic Resource Costs and Effective Protection Once Again," *Journal of Political Economy* 80 (1972): 63–69.

tage of permitting a known quantity of imports. With tariffs the quantity of imports depends on the elasticities of supply and demand, which are generally not known in advance. A quota that limits imports to the same quantity as a tariff would have most of the same effects. To see this, refer back to Fig. 16–1. Instead of the tariff t_o, assume that the government limits imports of cloth to the quantity $M_2 = Q_3 - Q_4$. As with the tariff the domestic price would still rise to P_d; domestic production would rise from Q_2 to Q_4, causing a resource cost measured by triangle b; and consumption would fall from Q_1 to Q_3, adding the area of triangle d to the deadweight loss. But in two important respects the effects of import quotas differ from those of tariffs.

The first difference is that the govenment no longer collects tariff revenues. Instead the government issues licenses to a limited number of importers, giving them the right to purchase imports of cloth up to a total of M_2 in Fig. 16–1. If government were to sell these import licenses at auction, potential importers would be willing to buy these licenses for as much as $P_d - P_w$ per unit of imports. Then they could purchase each unit of imported cloth for P_w, the world price, and break even by selling it at the domestic price, P_d. In that case the auction price for import licenses would just equal the tariff, t_o, that would have led to the same quantity of imports. Also, government would collect the same revenue as under a tariff, rectangle c in Fig. 16–1, in the form of fees for import licenses.

However, most governments do not auction import licenses, but give them free to a limited number of those importers who apply for them. Then although the importers pay only P_w for their imports, they can sell them at the domestic price, P_d in Fig. 16–1, and keep for themselves a windfall profit, or rent, of $P_d - P_w = t_o$. These rents—often called a "quota premium"—can be substantial, so import licenses are valuable to their recipients. With such high stakes it often pays importers to offer bribes to officials who control licensing. The greater the restrictiveness of import controls, the greater the value of a license and the greater the tendency for corruption. Bribery aside, administrative allocation of imports can lead to favoritism in which large producers, the wealthy and the powerful, especially those who support the government, get preferred access to licenses. Competitive forces are stifled and the system tends to entrench the powerful.

The second difference between quotas and tariffs is that quotas can convert a single domestic manufacturer into a monopolist who can charge whatever price maximizes his profits. Fig. 16–2 depicts the market for a single domestic producer who is protected by a tariff, t. Imports are available at the world price, P_w, plus the tariff, tP_w. With infinitely elastic world supply, domestic consumers can buy all they want at world price plus tariff, $P_d = P_w(1 + t)$. The domestic producer, despite being the only local supplier, must compete with this price, which becomes his marginal revenue. Consumers purchase Q_c while the domestic producer offers Q_p, an output that equates his marginal revenue and marginal cost (point A). The balance, $Q_c - Q_p$, is imported.

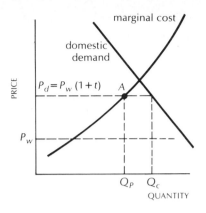

Fig. 16–2 Domestic Monopoly
Protected by Tariff.

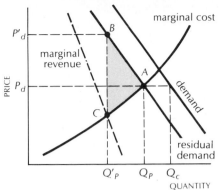

Fig. 16–3 Domestic Monopoly
Protected by Equivalent Quota.

With a quota (Fig. 16–3) the government uses licensing to hold imports to the previous level, $Q_c - Q_p$, leaving the domestic manufacturer with a residual demand (which must be drawn through the same point A) that can only be met from domestic production. With no further competition from imports, the firm now faces a marginal revenue curve that is below the residual demand curve. It equates marginal revenue with marginal cost at point C, producing only Q_p and charging P'_d in the captive residual domestic market. Hence, output and consumption fall, prices rise, and society faces a deadweight loss (reduction of consumers' plus producer's surplus) given by shaded area ABC. It clearly matters a great deal whether protection is granted through tariffs that are not prohibitive or through equivalent import quotas.

Overvalued Exchange Rates

The third prop of the import substitution regime, the one that clarifies the biases of the entire system, is the overvalued exchange rate. There have been several definitions of the term *overvalued* in this context, but for purposes of understanding import substitution a simple explanation will do, and it is provided in Fig. 16–4. The curves representing exporters' supply of and importers' demand for foreign exchange were explained in Chapter 15. In the absence of tariffs or quotas an exchange rate of r_e in the diagram would just clear the market and thus be an equilibrium. If tariffs are imposed on imports (but not on exports) it would take a lower rate, r_t, for equilibrium. Often, however, the official exchange rate, r_0, is below both those levels. Because the peso price of the dollar is so low, import demand is high (M_d) and export supply is low (X_s), creating a potential deficit in the current account of the balance of payments. To reduce this deficit governments typically resort to import quotas. The rate, r_0, is considered *overvalued* in the sense that the dollar price of pesos (the reciprocal of that shown in the diagram) is too high; the peso rate, r_0, is therefore too low.

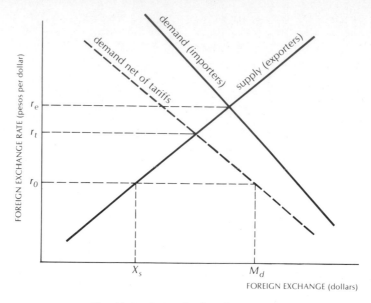

Fig. 16–4 Overvalued Exchange Rate.

Exchange rates become overvalued for a variety of reasons. The genesis of the problem is sometimes an abundant supply of primary exports, which tends to support local (peso-dollar) exchange rates and thus to discourage investment in nontraditional industries (see Chapter 15). As incomes rise and import demand increases at any exchange rate, devaluation is required to stimulate the production of import substitutes and exports, and thus to maintain equilibrium in the balance of payments. Domestic inflation, which causes domestic prices and costs to rise faster than the world average, also requires devaluation to maintain exports and restrain imports. Until recently, however, most governments have maintained fixed exchange rates and have been reluctant to risk the destabilizing political effects of devaluation. The exchange rate is one of the most pervasive prices in the economy, perhaps affecting more transactions than any other single price. To change it, especially by the large amounts sometimes required, means changing the relative wealth of influential segments of the population. Not only are the relative prices of imports raised, but in order to prevent domestic prices from rising as much as the currency is devalued, wages and other incomes must be restrained by government policy. Frequently it is the politically powerful who would lose by these measures, especially urban workers, middle-class professionals, civil servants, the upper classes, and others whose consumption depends substantially on imports. For these reasons governments resist devaluation, and when they do undertake it, often devalue by too little in the face of growing demand and continuing inflation. Hence there has been a tendency for exchange rates to remain overvalued in the third world (and in many countries of the industrial world, at least before the recent experience with flexible exchange rates).[8] This tendency has been alleviated to some extent by the greater flexibility in exchange rates since 1971, but controlled rates at overvalued levels remain the rule in the third world.

A glance at Figure 16–4 shows that the overvalued exchange rate discourages exports. It does so by reducing the local currency payment for any given dollar amount of exports, hence reducing revenues to domestic exporters in the currency that matters to them, the home currency. But overvalued rates also encourage imports by keeping the peso payments lower than they should be, and this in turn is detrimental to import-substituting industries. How then is the overvalued rate consistent with import substitution regimes?

The answer lies in the triumvirate of exchange rates, tariffs, and quotas. Because the exchange rate is so low, import-competing industries depend heavily on high effective tariff protection and on quotas to shield them from cheap imports. Industries without such protection are unlikely to find it profitable to produce for either the home or foreign market. Recall, then, the highly skewed protective structure presented in Table 16–1: consumer goods and intermediate goods manufacturing can overcome the overvalued exchange rate with their high effective rates of protection, or with additional help from import licensing. But agricultural and capital goods manufacturing are exposed to import competition at the low local currency prices engendered by the overvalued exchange rate. Even import quotas on capital goods do not help much because these tend to be variable, depending on the state of the balance of payments.

Outcomes and Problems

Import Substitution in General Equilibrium

The process of import substitution is represented in Figs. 16–5, 16–6, and 16–7. The first figure shows the situation before the imposition of protective tariffs, say, in 1960 when the country produces (at point A) and consumes (at C) under world terms of trade favorable to its export. Imposition of the tariff, presumed here to be a uniform one on all imports, swings domestic relative prices in favor of importable goods. Production moves toward point B where more of the importable and less of the exportable are produced. If the country is relatively small and does not affect relative world prices, trade can take place at the same terms of trade as before, so that consumption settles somewhere, such as point E, along line BD drawn parallel to the terms-of-trade line. Consumption of both goods is lower than before the tariff, so consumers' well-being has been reduced. Both imports and exports have also fallen, as indicated by the line segment

8. The economic and political difficulties of devaluation make selective tariffs and quota restrictions even more appealing to governments, despite the allocative inefficiencies such measures entail.

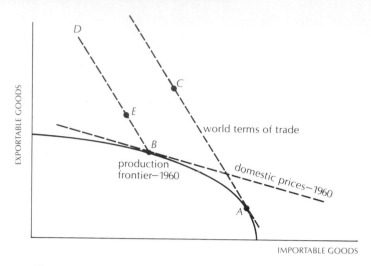

Fig. 16–5   Imposition of Protective Tariff—Situation in 1960.

BE, which is shorter than *AC*. (The reader should draw the resulting trade triangles—see Fig. 15–1—and demonstrate this.)

If that were the end of the story the reduction in imports, however much it served the goal of self-reliance, would be achieved at considerable cost to the welfare of consumers in general. However, the prime motivation of import substitution is not a static shift of resources, as shown in Fig. 16–5, but rather a desire to increase both production and consumption, to shift the production frontier outward as shown in the next two figures. If the strategy is able to stimulate infant industries that would not attract investors without protection, the production frontier will be pushed strongly toward greater potential production of importables, the situation depicted in Fig. 15–6. Because more import substitutes are available their relative domestic price is likely to fall even if the protective tariff is maintained, so the 1980 domestic price line in Fig. 16–6 is drawn with a steeper slope than the 1960 line in Fig. 16–5. In 1980, then, production takes place at a point like *F*, where the domestic price line is tangent to the new frontier, and consumption can take place at a point like *H*, somewhere along line *FG*, drawn parallel to the original world terms of trade (which are presumed not to have changed since 1960). In 1980 consumers are better off at *H* than they had been in 1960 at *C* since they are on a higher indifference curve, and there is also less trade than in 1960 (*FH* is shorter than *AC*). However, once the production frontier has been expanded, consumers' welfare could be improved still more by removing tariffs and reverting to the world terms of trade. Producers would then move along the 1980 frontier to point *I*, permitting consumption at a point to the northeast of *H* on a still higher indifference curve. Trade would be increased compared to the situation at point *F*, and the country would reap the gains from trade at world prices. But it took a move away from trade, the protective tariff, to stimulate in-

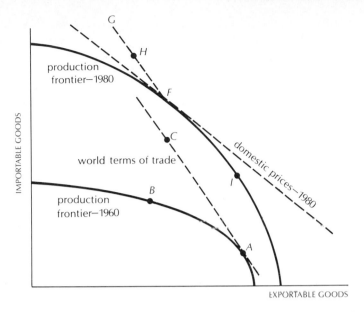

Fig. 16-6   Import Substitution After 20 Years of Rapid Growth, 1980.

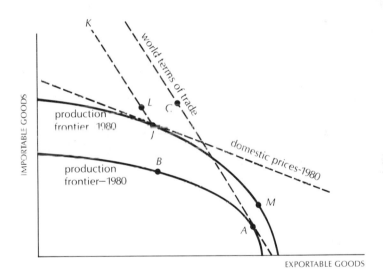

Fig. 16-7   Import Substitution After 20 Years of Slow Growth, 1980.

fant industries and make it possible to achieve greater production at points like *F* and *I*.

If, however, import substitution is less successful and investment only moves the production frontier a small distance outwards (though still favoring production of importables), then consumption may not achieve its former level. Figure 16-7 pictures such a case, in which producers reach point *J* on the 1980 frontier, but consumption, at a point like *L*, remains below the original point C. Trade is reduced from its 1960 level. Unfortunately, as we shall see, slow or arrested growth is one likely outcome of import substitution as typically practiced. Here again consumption of both goods could be increased if the country reverted to world prices and moved production from J to M on the new frontier.

Import Levels and Structure

In both Figs. 16–6 and 16–7 the *ratio of imports to national product* declines from 1960, before the tariff is imposed, to 1980.[9] This suggests that we use the ratio of imports to national product as an indicator of import substitution. But Table 16–3 shows how ambiguous such an indicator can be. The table reveals only six cases among the twenty-four countries listed in which the import share of GDP declined over an extended period, from 1955 or 1960 to 1970 or 1977: Bolivia, Ghana, India, Kenya, Mexico, and

TABLE 16–3   Ratios of Imports to Gross Domestic Product, 1960–1980

	Imports to GDP (%) in				Annual growth of GDP (% per year) 1960–1980
	1955	1960	1970	1980	
Bolivia	—	20	20	15	5.0
Brazil	6	6	7	11	6.8
Chile	8	17	14	23	3.3
Colombia	14	16	16	17	5.5
Egypt	—	20	19	47[a]	5.7[c]
Ethiopia	—	10	11	20	3.0[d]
Ghana	31	35	23	12[a]	0.7
Guatemala	14	15	18	25	5.6
India	8	8	5	7[b]	3.4
Indonesia	—	13	16	23	5.5
Ivory Coast	—	35	38	38	7.3
Jamaica	37	38	38	54	1.6
Kenya	44	34	31	33[a]	6.2
Korea (South)	10	13	24	45	9.0
Malaysia	35	41	39	57	7.1
Mexico	16	13	10	16	6.1
Nigeria	17	20	17	22	4.5
Pakistan	—	15	15	26	5.6
Peru	23	21	16	21	3.9
Philippines	13	10	19	25	5.7
Tanzania	—	26	28	28	5.4
Thailand	22	19	22	30	7.8
Turkey	8	5	9	16	5.9
Zambia	40	41	37	43	2.2

Sources: Imports to GDP—World Bank, *World Tables* (2d ed.; Washington, D.C., 1980), pp. 384–89; growth rates—World Bank, *World Development Report, 1982* (Washington, D.C., 1982), pp. 112–13.
[a] 1979.
[b] 1977.
[c] 1960–1979.
[d] 1961–1980.

9. For this to be unambiguously true national product must be measured at domestic (rather than world) prices. Since measures of national product are virtually always in domestic prices, this presents no problems in what follows.

Peru. Of these Mexico seems a clear example of import substitution leading to rapid income growth, at least until the mid-1970s, as in Fig. 16–6, while Ghana conforms to the low-growth case depicted in Fig. 16–7. For Chile, Pakistan, Philippines, and Turkey, which had determinedly followed import substitution policies, the import/GDP ratio rose, while it changed little for several other import substituters, such as Brazil (whose main spurt of import substitution probably came before 1960), Colombia, and Tanzania.

These results do not necessarily mean that import substitution has failed to replace imports with domestic production. The level of imports is probably determined more by the levels of exports and capital inflows than by any other factors. Thus import ratios may rise despite import substitution if a country is fortunate in expanding its primary exports (despite the adverse incentives of import substitution regimes) or in obtaining rising export prices. Chile, Indonesia, Ivory Coast, Malaysia, Nigeria, and the Philippines are countries that may have import substituted in several sectors while increasing their primary export earnings and thus their capacity to import. If import substitution in some industries stimulates rising incomes that are biased toward imported goods, or if import-substituting industries require imported inputs themselves, then part of the reduction in the import ratio would in any case be cancelled. Chenery and Syrquin observe that as incomes rise (in 1978 prices) from $200 per capita to $2000, there is a gradual but steady tendency for the import ratio to rise, from 22 to 26 percent, apparently despite import substitution in manufacturing.[10]

Whatever happens to imports as a whole, one trend is clear: as import substitution proceeds through finished consumer goods toward producer intermediates, the *composition of imports* shifts noticeably. Table 16–4 presents indicative data from four countries that underwent substantial import substitution. All show a marked decline in imports of nonfood consumer goods, accompanied by a marked increase in the share of intermediate goods. There is no clear trend for capital goods, although given the protective bias against their production we would not expect to find the sharp declines in share evident in Brazil and Turkey. The marked increase in foodgrain imports in Pakistan is testimony to the bias against agriculture inherent in the exchange rate structure and evident in Table 16–1.

Once the structure of imports has been transformed from a concentration on consumer goods and capital goods to a greater share of materials and intermediate goods, the economy is in some ways more vulnerable to disruptions in trade. In times of drought, falling export production, or falling export prices, nonfood imports must be reduced. Whereas these cuts would primarily affect the less essential consumer goods in the past, they must now be absorbed by intermediate and capital goods. Because industrial production and employment depend on imported inputs, and continued growth depends on imported investment goods, swings in export

10. Hollis Chenery and Moises Syrquin, *Patterns of Development, 1950–1970* (Baltimore: Johns Hopkins University Press, 1975), p. 37.

TABLE 16–4   Composition of Imports: Brazil, Ghana, Pakistan, and Turkey

Country	Category of import	Share of total imports (%)	
Brazil		*1946–48*	*1960–62*
	Wheat	6	13
	Other consumer goods	15	9
	Intermediate goods	41	49
	Capital goods	38	29
Ghana		*1956*	*1969*
	Consumer goods	54	30
	Intermediate goods	31	47
	Capital equipment	15	23
Pakistan		*1951–52*	*1964–65*
	Grains and flour	0	13
	Cotton yarn and cloth	29	0
	Iron and steel products	7	17
	Capital equipment	9	33
Turkey		*1961*	*1970*
	Consumer goods	23	15
	Raw materials	41	62
	Investment goods	36	23

Sources: Brazil—Joel Bergsman, *Brazil: Industrialization and Trade Policies* (London: Oxford University Press, 1970); Ghana—J. Clark Leith, *Foreign Trade Regimes and Economic Development: Ghana* (New York: Columbia University Press, 1974), p. 176; Pakistan—Stephen Lewis, *Economic Policy and Industrial Growth in Pakistan* (London: George Allen and Unwin, p. 6; Turkey—Anne O. Krueger, *Foreign Trade Regimes and Economic Development: Turkey* (New York: Columbia University Press, 1974), p. 127.

earnings have a direct impact on output, employment, and growth. *Import dependence* has not been reduced, although its form has been changed.

Dynamic Consequences

Import substitution regimes establish a series of interrelated effects that over the long run reinforce dependence and retard structural changes required for self-sustaining development. Underlying the regime is a set of incentives that reward political astuteness more than economic competitiveness. Probably the most important determinants of a manufacturer's profit rate are the tariff and quota treatment bestowed upon him by government. Protective duties and access to low-cost inputs create the import-substituting firm. Should costs of production rise or world prices of competitive imports fall, the natural reaction is to return to government for enhanced protection. This blunts the competitive instincts of entrepreneurs, who might otherwise work to raise productivity to increase or protect their profits in the face of changing conditions. Thus the most effective restraints on increased costs operate in muted fashion and industry tends to become and remain high cost by world standards. The infant industry argument, which could justify a protective tariff, fails to hold. Instead of facing reduced protection over time the entrepreneur can look forward to rising protection, as needed, if he minds his political fences.

In this environment of government intervention the most successful managers are those who have political skills, who can bargain effectively with those who administer quotas or control tariff rates, or who have close ties with the political and bureaucratic elite. It is no accident that manufacturers usually have their top executive, if not the plant itself, located in the capital city, nor that he spends much if not most of his time seeing government officials. Thus the wealthy and powerful succeed best and become reentrenched in their wealth and power. These tendencies exist in most political-economic regimes, but the adverse economic impacts seem accentuated in many import substitution regimes.

Because import-substituting industry typically produces at high cost, it has little potential to penetrate export markets in the absence of large subsidies. Export subsidies have been part of several import substitution regimes: in Pakistan bonus vouchers were paid to exporters of nontraditional goods, giving them access to licensed imports that carried large quota premiums; in Colombia exporters were granted certificates entitling them to income tax reductions; in Ghana cash subsidy payments were offered; and in several countries exporters of nontraditional products received access to controlled imports, tariff reductions on inputs, access to cheap credit, and so forth. In a few cases, notably Pakistan and Colombia, manufactured exports did respond to incentives. But for the most part these were weak measures. In the face of much stronger incentives to produce for the domestic market and of bureaucratic requirements that made it difficult to realize the proffered export incentives, such incentives often had only a marginal impact on exports. Moreover the price incentives that work against agriculture discourage that potentially important source of new exports. Export diversification and growth are really not consistent with the biases of an import substitution regime, but represent a very different approach to development, as will be seen in the next chapter.

Import substitution regimes also have a tendency to limit backward-linked industrialization. Once consumer goods industries have been started it is natural to seek further import substitution by producing at home the intermediate goods used by consumer industry. Because the domestic market for such intermediate goods as chemicals and metal products is frequently smaller than for consumer goods, and for some producer goods industries economies of scale are large (see Chapter 20), there is a natural barrier to investment in these sectors. This could be overcome by protection, but that would drive up the costs of inputs to already established manufacturers whose profits depend both on protection for their products and on low duties on their inputs. Since established manufacturers have already proven their political adeptness in establishing their industries and keeping them profitable, they now turn these skills toward preventing tariff increases on their imported materials, effectively discouraging investment in backward-linked industries.[11] This is not an absolute barrier to backward

---

11. This phenomenon is described by Albert O. Hirschman, "The Political Economy of Import Substitution," *Quarterly Journal of Economics* 82 (1968); 1–32, who also notes that if the owners of initial import-substituting industries are capable of running the backward-linked industries themselves, the barriers to backward integration may be lower.

integration, as attested by casual observation of many chemical, fertilizer, and steel plants in the third world. And in large countries such as Brazil and India, the ability to achieve scale economies can mitigate to some extent the high costs of backward integration. However, especially for small economies, these barriers do exert a tendency to slow down industrial development once most consumer industries have been established.

The *foreign exchange gap,* introduced in Chapter 6, has evolved from these characteristics of import substitution. The bias against agriculture that prevents food supplies from keeping pace with population and income growth; the shift toward imported inputs for industrial production; continued dependence on imported capital goods for investment; and the blockages, or at least retardation, of backward integration in manufacturing—all combine to make it essential that import levels continue to grow about as rapidly as the national product. Yet the rapid growth of nontraditional exports required to finance growing import bills is stifled by price incentives that condone inefficiency, favor industrial production for the home market, and frequently work against agriculture (see Chapter 18). Any attempt to accelerate growth thus faces increased imports beyond the likely growth of exports. The country then must either borrow abroad or restrain its ambitions to develop. The level of foreign investment and aid then determines how fast the economy can grow.

In addition to these structural problems, import substitution incentives also lead to potentially severe misallocations of national resources. The most serious of these is foreign exchange. The overvalued exchange rate encourages use of imported inputs, expecially those on which duties are also low, further widening the foreign exchange gap. If imported materials are cheap, users have less incentive to adopt practices or technologies that conserve their use, and in this sense scarce foreign exchange may be wasted. When the imports in question are capital equipment, on which duties are typically very low, investment is encouraged to be more capital-intensive than is desirable, hence raising capital/output ratios and reducing the growth realizable from a given amount of saving. This effect is reinforced by the habit of constraining interest rates, discussed in Chapter 13. The motivation for low interest rates has little to do with trade strategy. However, the combined effect of low rates and relatively cheap capital equipment imports, typical of import-substituting regimes, can reduce the cost of capital substantially below its relative scarcity in most developing countries.

Concomitant with excessive use of imports and capital, labor is not used intensively in import-substituting manufacturing and hence employment does not grow as rapidly as it might. One characteristic of these regimes has been high labor costs, as governments legislate minimum wages, add social benefits to these wages, and protect the employed worker by limiting firms' freedom to dismiss workers. As explained in Chapter 8, these measures have been legislated or decreed to protect workers' incomes and not for any purpose of trade policy. But they happen to reinforce the anti-employment bias of protectionist policies. Facing high wages and relatively inexpensive capital, investors—who are in any case insulated from competitive forces by protection—have little incentive to seek and use labor-intensive technologies, even though labor is relatively abundant. Domestic policies are not alone to blame for this. The capital goods readily available on world markets were mostly developed for use in labor-scarce economies, and third world investors often have to make special efforts to obtain labor-intensive technologies. But such technologies do exist and domestic policies discourage the effort needed to find them. Furthermore, to the extent that agriculture is more labor-intensive than industry and export sectors more labor-intensive than others, the price biases against these kinds of activity further reduce the potential employment generated by economic growth. It is too much to say that the employment problem endemic to developing countries can be blamed entirely on import substitution strategies, but they have certainly contributed to it.

Several of these characteristics combine to suggest that import substitution strategies may intensify the tendency, noted in Chapter 4, for income distribution to worsen in the early stages of development. Two effects are probably critical in this respect. First, limited employment generation reduces access to two of the poorest groups in society, landless rural workers and the urban unemployed. Policies such as minimum-wage legislation, intended to protect workers' incomes, typically worsen income distributions because they protect only employed workers and exclude others. Second, in economies characterized by small-holder agriculture, as in much of Asia and Africa, one of the most effective instruments for equalizing incomes is to improve the prices facing farmers, who tend to be among the poorest groups in society, relative to the prices of goods produced in urban industry. Yet protection does just the opposite. The problems of income distribution canot be solved by a choice of trade strategy alone. Land and other asset distribution, the ethnic composition of society, access to education, and other factors are probably more important than the trade regime. But the tendency of import substitution is in the wrong direction.

This catalogue of woes has become a familiar one, shared by economists and many policy-makers in the third world. Import substitution, though still widely practiced, is viewed more skeptically now than twenty years ago, and disillusioned policy-makers are seeking alternative paths to development. Export substitution, described in the next chapter, is the most promising of these. However, to preview the concluding lessons from Chapter 17, it has not been import substitution as such that has been responsible for the disappointing performance of manufacturing in many countries. Rather it has been the distortionary policies that accompanied and promoted it. A less doctrinaire form of import substitution, promoted by more moderate, market-oriented pricing policies, could well be a successful mode of development in the future.[12]

12. Two excellent articles summarizing the experience of import substitution are John H. Power, "Import Substitution as an Industrialization Strategy," *The Philippine Economic Journal* 5 (1966): 167–204; and Henry J. Bruton, "The Import Substitution Strategy of Economic Development," *The Pakistan Development Review* 10 (1970): 123–46 (excerpts reprinted in G. M. Meier, *Leading Issues in Economic Development* [3d ed.; New York: Oxford University Press, 1976], pp. 747–52).

FURTHER READING There is now a rich literature on foreign trade regimes and economic development headed by a coordinated set of studies under the auspices of the National Bureau of Economic Research (NBER). The two summary volumes are Jagdish Bhagwati, *Foreign Exchange Regimes and Economic Development: Anatomy and Consequences of Exchange Control Regimes* (Cambridge, Mass.: Ballinger Press, 1978); and Anne O. Krueger, *Foreign Trade Regimes and Economic Development: Liberalization Attempts and Consequences* (Cambridge, Mass.: Ballinger Press, 1978). Ten companion country studies detail the experiences of Colombia, Chile, Egypt, Ghana, India, the Philippines, South Korea, and Turkey. An earlier set of case studies is summarized in I. M. D. Little, Tibor Scitovsky, and Maurice Scott, *Industry and Trade in Some Developing Countries* (London: Oxford University Press, 1970). The developing countries' experience is placed in the context of trade theory by Charles P. Kindleberger, "The Disequilibrium System of Foreign Trade and Developing Countries," in James E. Theberge (ed.), *Economics of Trade and Development* (New York: John Wiley, 1968).

Chapter 17

OUTWARD-LOOKING DEVELOPMENT

For countries that are resource-poor and have relatively small domestic markets the trade strategies based on primary exports or on import substitution provide scant hope for sustained development. Four countries in Asia—Taiwan, South Korea, Hong Kong, and Singapore, popularly called the "Gang of Four"—have pursued an alternative strategy that has gone by different names, but is basically to export manufactures that use intensively their most abundant resource, labor. Gustav Ranis has termed this strategy, "export substitution," in the sense that exports of labor-intensive manufactures replace exports of labor-intensive agricultural products.[1] Other authors have called this an "outward-looking" strategy, in contrast to the "inward-looking" strategy of import substitution.

The Strategy of Export Substitution

Although the Asian model of export substitution has hinged on labor-intensive manufactures and services (construction, tourism, finance, etc.), a more general specification would be the promotion of nontraditional exports, whether these happen to be labor- or land-intensive, manufactured or agricultural products, or services. The common denominator is the pursuit of any exports in which the country has a potential comparative advantage, that is, whose production costs are or could become relatively low by world standards. The distinguishing characteristic is a thoroughgoing application of pricing policies that closely reflect both world commodity prices and the

---

1. Gustav Ranis, "Industrial Sector Labor Absorption," *Economic Development and Cultural Change* 21 (1973): 387–408.

scarcities of domestic factors of production. This definition would exclude several countries, such as Pakistan, Ghana, and Colombia, for which export promotion has been a limited part of a trade regime that remained overwhelmingly protectionist.[2]

The Exchange Rate and Related Policy Instruments

To oversimplify only a little, a useful prescription for export substitution policies is to do everything that the import substitution regime avoids. First, to promote the growth of new exports a necessary condition is to maintain an exchange rate that helps make it profitable for domestic producers to sell their crops, manufactures, and services on world markets. The export-substituting country must undertake periodic devaluations, initially to approach an equilibrium, market-clearing rate, and subsequently to maintain that rate relative to inflating domestic prices and costs. South Korea entered its phase of export substitution in the early 1960s with two large devaluations, of 104 and 65 percent, respectively, and maintained the resulting rate relative to domestic prices by continuing devaluations in the succeeding year. Brazil began to emerge from its postwar import-substitution phase with a massive 100 percent devaluation in 1964, then continued to devalue over the next several years to overcome the effects of rapid domestic inflation.

Second, it may be necessary to subsidize some exports to induce manufacturers and farmers to invest in capacity for the export market. Breaking into export markets entails more risk than producing behind protective barriers for the domestic market. Cost competitiveness is greater, quality standards are higher, and marketing is more demanding. Once a producer learns how to cope with these factors, however, he may enjoy a large, profitable market. Compensation in the form of tax relief, import duty rebates, reduced interest rates, cash payments, or a variety of other means can help make it more attractive for a potential exporter to overcome these barriers to entry. This case for export subsidies is completely analogous to the infant industry argument for a protective tariff. One advantage of the subsidy over a tariff is that, except for preferential interest rates, the cost is borne by the government's budget, and fiscal pressures sometimes limit the size and duration of the subsidy, more closely approximating the desirable phase-out of an infant industry tariff.

Third, if governments want producers to turn toward world markets they must enhance the relative attractiveness of production for the world market. This implies reduction of high protective tariffs for favored industries and the avoidance of quantitative restrictions on imports. Because the strategy, to be successful, needs domestic firms that produce efficiently by world

---

2. For a recent, detailed study of the trade regimes of ten countries, see the volumes by Anne O. Krueger, *Foreign Trade Regimes and Economic Development: Liberalization Attempts and Consequences,* and Jagdish N. Bhagwati, *Foreign Trade Regimes and Economic Development: Anatomy and Consequences of Exchange Control Regimes* (Cambridge, Mass.: Ballinger, 1978), and the companion country studies.

standards, it is not consistent with the establishment or expansion of industries on the basis of high tariffs or quota protection. Also, because investors are likely to seek the most profitable opportunities, profits in import substitution must be kept in line with those in exporting. This means that tariff protection should be no higher than export subsidization and should also be fairly uniform for all commodities. The biases in effective protection, illustrated in Table 16–1, must be reduced if not eliminated. South Korea's protective regime provides a contrast to those shown in the table. The effective rate of protection for agriculture (18 percent) was not only modest during the late 1960s but *higher* than for manufacturing (− 1 percent). And the bias between exports and domestic sales was reversed: allowing for subsidies, exports had an effective rate of protection-cum-subsidy of 12 percent, compared with a − 9 percent for domestic sales.[3]

Effective Exchange Rates

The combined incentive effect of the exchange rate, subsidies, tariffs, and quota premiums can be captured by a very useful concept, the ***effective exchange rate*** (EER). The EER corrects the nominal (i.e., official) exchange rate to measure the actual amount of local currency paid for a dollar's worth of imports, or received for a dollar's worth of exports, by allowing for average duties, subsidies, and quota premiums. There may be as many EERs in an economy as there are goods traded. Generally, however, two effective exchange rates are measured: one for exports,

$$EER_x = r_o \left(1 - t_x + s_x\right) \qquad\qquad [17\text{--}1]$$

and another for imports,

$$EER_m = r_o \left(1 + t_m - s_m + q_m\right) \qquad\qquad [17\text{--}2]$$

In these equations r_o is the official exchange rate, t is the average duty or tax rate on exports (subscript $_x$) or imports $_{(m)}$, s is the average level of subsidy, and q_m is the quota premium (see Chapter 16) averaged over all imports.

One way to differentiate an outward-looking regime from an inward-looking one is to compare the EERs for exports and imports within each country. Table 17–1 does this for eight countries studied by the National Bureau of Economic Research. Only in South Korea, which has had the most thoroughgoing export substitution policy of all countries listed, does an exporter receive more local currency (won in this case) per dollar of foreign exchange than an importer must pay. That is, in Korea the bias favors production for export over import substitution. In Egypt the ex-

3. Charles R. Frank, Jr., Kwang Suk Kim, and Larry E. Westphal, *Foreign Trade Regimes and Economic Development: South Korea* (New York: Columbia University Press, 1975), pp. 195–200. Note, however, that the effective rate of subsidy was exceptionally high for two important export sectors, plywood and cotton fabrics, indicating inefficiencies in the export sector. See Anne O. Krueger, *Studies in the Modernization of the Republic of Korea, 1945–1975: The Developmental Role of the Foreign Sector and Aid* (Cambridge, Mass.: Harvard University, Press, 1979), Chapter 5.

TABLE 17–1   Effective Exchange Rates[a] (local currency per U.S. $)

Country	Year	EER_x	EER_m
1. Pro-export bias:			
South Korea	1964	281	247
2. Negligible bias:			
Egypt	1962	43.5	42.9
3. Pro-import bias:			
Chile	1965	3.31	3.85
Brazil	1964	1874	2253
India	1966	6.79	9.23
Philippines	1970	5.15	8.70
Ghana	1967	0.84	1.50
Turkey	1970	12.9	24.0

Source: Anne O. Krueger, *Foreign Trade Regimes and Economic Development: Liberalization Attempts and Consequences* (Cambridge, Mass.: Ballinger, 1978), p. 73.
[a] Following devaluation in year shown.

TABLE 17–2   Effects of Inflation and Devaluation on Exporters' Profits

Year 1: Exchange rate = 12 pesos (P) per dollar	
1. Exporter sells goods worth	$ 100,000
2. For which exporter receives local currency of	P1,200,000
3. If exporter's costs—all domestic—are	P1,000,000
4. Then exporter's profits are	P 200,000
Year 2: Domestic inflation has been 20% a year	
1. Exporter sells same goods, still worth	$ 100,000
2. For which exporter receives	P1,200,000
3. But exporters costs are now 20% higher	P1,200,000
4. So exporter now earns no profit	P 0
Year 2: If currency were devalued by 20%, to P 14.40 per dollar, then	
1. Exporter sells goods worth	$ 100,000
2. For which exporter now receives	P1,440,000
3. With costs of	P1,200,000
4. Profits are	P 240,000
5. Which, deflated by 20% to year 1 prices, have been restored to	P 200,000

change regime was neutral, while all other countries showed a bias in favor of import substitution, listed in ascending order in the table. None of the countries with a bias favoring import substitution was able to diversify its exports substantially in favor of manufactured goods. (Brazil began to export manufactures only after it changed its trade regime; see below.)

It is not enough, however, to offer a pro-export bias in the effective exchange rate for short periods. Investment for export will depend on government's demonstrated willingness to maintain the incentive in favor of exporting over long periods despite domestic inflation. To the extent that domestic prices (and costs) rise more rapidly than foreign prices the exchange rate is eroded and becomes increasingly overvalued. As demonstrated in Table 17–2, devaluation is then necessary to restore exporters' profits. Thus to measure the effective exchange rate over time, index numbers are substituted for actual values in equations 17–1 and 17–2 and price indexes are added, as follows:

$$IEER = R_oTP_w/P_d, \qquad [17–3]$$

where IEER is the index of the *price-deflated EER*, R_o is an index of the official exchange rate, T is an index of 1 plus the average tariff rate (net of subsidies),[4] and P_w and P_d are indices of world and domestic prices, respectively. The formula can be used for either exports or imports, with appropriate substitutions, and can be calculated separately for specific commodities or groups of commodities. If domestic prices rise more rapidly than world prices the index falls, indicating that the exchange rate has become overvalued; that is, the peso-dollar rate is now too low, or the dollar peso rate too high.

One element in South Korea's rapid growth of manufactured exports, detailed later in this chapter, has been the government's willingness and ability to adjust the exchange rate, tariffs, and subsidies, both to maintain the effective exchange rate for exports over time and to prevent the import rate from slipping above the export rate. Table 17–3 shows the movement of EERs from 1960 to 1975, with the export value in 1964 taken as 100 and the import index adjusted to show its level relative to exports. Notice the fairly steady level of the export rate, which was also maintained above the import rate throughout the period. This performance has required a series of devaluations and subsidy adjustments, as Korean domestic inflation was considerable throughout the period.

Brazil, which also promoted manufactured exports successfully, shows a similar pattern (Table 17–3). From 1968 onward Brazil adopted a policy of small, regular currency devaluations that for a time kept pace with domestic inflation. Concurrently tax relief and other export incentives were increased from an average of about 18 percent of domestic prices for equivalent goods sold in Brazil to 40 percent in 1973. The combined effect

TABLE 17–3   Index of Effective Exchange Rates, South Korea and Brazil

	South Korea			Brazil	
Year	IEER$_x$	IEER$_m$		Year	IEER$_x$ (mfgs)
1960	104.9	71.2		1963	73.2
1964[a]	100.0	87.9		1964	100.0
1965	99.9	96.2		1967	85.0
1970	101.1	85.4		1970	98.0
1975	94.9	85.8		1972–3	107.9

Source: Kwang Suk Kim and Michael Roemer, *Studies in the Modernization of South Korea, 1945–75: Growth and Structural Transformation* (Cambridge, Mass.: Harvard University Press, 1979), p. 73; William G. Tyler, *Manufactured Export Expansion and Industrialization in Brazil* (Tubingen, W. Germany: J. C. B. Mohr, 1976), p. 220.
   [a] All indexes, for exports and imports, based on IEER$_x$ = 100 in 1964.

4. That is, $T_m = (1 + t_m - s_m + q_m)/(1 + t^o_m - s^o_m + q^o_m)$, where the the superscript, ^{o}, denotes the base year.

was to raise the effective exchange rate for manufactured exports substantially after 1967. Also, effective tariff protection for import-competing manufactures was reduced from 180 percent in 1966 to only 47 percent in 1973, narrowing or eliminating the differential between the import and export effective exchange rates.

Factor Prices and Government Support

To work effectively, outward-looking regimes must also maintain the relative prices of domestic factors of production at levels reflecting their scarcity. The underlying principle is to export those products that use most intensively the productive factors that are most abundant in the economy. To ensure that enterprises, whether private or public, make investment and production decisions consistent with this principle, the relative prices they pay for labor, capital, and land should not be very different from the prices that would be established by competitive market forces, given the supplies of and demands for these resources. If labor is abundant its wage and other costs should be low, while scarce capital should be costly to investors. Then not only will firms and farms substitute labor for capital where possible, but those lines of production that use labor more intensively will be more profitable than capital-intensive ones. The four Asian exporters all avoided artificially high wages. Their interest rate policies were not so exemplary, although South Korea and Taiwan did undertake monetary reforms that raised interest rates to scarcity levels for a period.

Governments determined to diversify their exports do not depend on market prices to accomplish the task alone. The successful ones are, like governments pursuing import substitution, interventionist. But they intervene by helping fledgling exporters to find markets and pushing reluctant producers toward world markets. These governments provide market information, and to some extent market access, by establishing trade offices overseas, sometimes attached to diplomatic missions. They place a high priority on port facilities, transport networks, and communications infrastructure. Commercial and government banks are encouraged to favor exporters in their lending policies and credits may be offered to foreign customers if necessary to help exporters compete. Political favors are part of life in every country, but in export substitution regimes they are used to encourage exporting. In South Korea, for example, tax authorities bear less heavily on those who export successfully. Market inducements and political power, both working obviously in the direction of export growth and diversification, can be an irresistible combination.

Outcomes and Limitations

Export Achievers

Only a handful of countries have followed the export substitution path to industrialization. The five most prominent of these—Asia's Gang of Four, plus Brazil—are featured in Table 17–4. In all five, GNP per capita and manufacturing output grew significantly faster than for the average middle-income country, and Hong Kong, South Korea, and Taiwan also had much faster export growth. (Korea's exceptional performance and Brazil's more limited experience are described in case studies.)

TABLE 17–4   Growth in Five Outward-Looking Economies, 1960–1979

Country	Average annual growth (% per year), 1960–1979, in			Manufactured exports[d] as share of commodity exports 1978
	GNP per capita	Manufacturing value added	Exports	
Hong Kong	7.0	9.3[b]	10.5	97
Singapore	7.4	11.2	7.3	46[d]
South Korea	7.1	17.7	30.1	89
Taiwan	6.6[a]	14.8[a]	17.1[a]	85[e]
Brazil	4.8	10.1[c]	6.0	34
Average for all middle income countries	3.8	6.8	5.8	36

Source: World Bank, *World Development Report 1981* (Washington, D.C., 1981); World Bank, *World Tables 1980* (Washington, D.C., 1980).
[a] 1960–1978.
[b] 1964–1977.
[c] 1965–1977.
[d] Excludes processing of minerals and fuels, which accounts for close to 30% of Singapore's exports.
[e] 1977.

The market incentives and political support of the South Korean government from 1961 onward led to a remarkable sustained growth in exports that averaged 28 percent a year for twenty years, from 1960 to 1980. During the same period Korean GNP per capita grew by 7.1 percent a year, one of the highest rates in the world. It has been estimated that, allowing for both the direct effects of export industries and the indirect effects of other industries stimulated by exporters' demands for inputs, exports were responsible for from a third to 40 percent of the growth in national product from 1955 to 1973. During that interval exports rose from only 3 percent of GNP to 28 percent, almost three times the average for a "typical" country of Korea's characteristics (according to Chenery and Syrquin's regressions). To achieve this Korea depended almost entirely on its manufacturing sector, whose share of exports grew from 17 percent to over 80 percent by the mid-1970s. Diversification and structural change accompanied growth. All sectors of manufacturing developed rapidly. The producer goods industries, which accounted for only 15 percent of manufacturing value added in the early 1960s, grew sufficiently rapidly to account for 39 percent by the mid-1970s, indicating industrial diversification as backward linkages were developed.[5] Since this

Export-Led Growth in Two Countries

South Korea

5. Kwang Suk Kim and Michael Roemer, *Studies in the Modernization of the Republic of Korea, 1945–75: Growth and Structural Transformation* (Cambridge, Mass.: Harvard University Press, 1979), p. 114–15.

occurred under competitive conditions, some of the new producer goods industries were later able to export.

Although exports were mostly labor-intensive manufactures in the early years of growth, principally clothing, textiles, and footwear, by the mid-1970s South Korea was also exporting steel plate, electrical machinery, ships, and construction services. International competitiveness and the realization of backward linkages were further enhanced because, by depending on the world market rather than the limited domestic market, firms could achieve economies of scale without creating domestic monopolies. The benefits of this developing capacity to produce a variety of products efficiently were realized with the petroleum price increase of 1974. Despite a temporary setback as imports of petroleum caused a balance-of-payments deficit in 1974, the Korean economy rebounded quickly, began to sell goods and especially construction services to the booming Middle East market, and achieved a small current account surplus by 1976.

New employment was created rapidly enough—12 percent a year in manufacturing—so that by the late 1960s rising Korean real wages indicated a probable end to the labor surplus condition that had characterized the economy until then. Credit for this performance is due to several factors, including the rapid growth of labor-intensive manufactured exports and the policy toward wages and interest rates which made it attractive to utilize more labor and less capital wherever possible.

Both South Korea and Taiwan, another successful export substituter, enjoy relatively equal income distributions, especially by third world standards. The principal causes of equality are thorough land reforms, equal access to education, and at least in Korea, homogeneity of the population. However, a case can be made that rapid export growth based on labor-intensive industries, and the resulting employment creation, played a role in stimulating development without substantially worsening the distribution. As the labor surplus became absorbed and real wages began to rise, it was also possible to raise farm prices so that all elements of the population benefited from growth.[6]

Brazil   Brazil provides a less dramatic story of manufactured export-led growth. After the military took power in 1964 the government went through a stabilization process to control inflation. The ensuing reduction in domestic demand, helped by a devaluation, induced manufacturers to seek export markets for their output. Although Brazil had protected its manufacturing as heavily as most import substitution regimes, many firms had costs low enough to make export feasible. Brazil's relatively large domestic market, which in many industries permitted several firms to at-

6. For full treatments of South Korea's modernization, see Frank, Kim, and Westphal, *Foreign Trade Regimes and Economic Development;* Paul W. Kuznets, *Economic Growth and Structure in the Republic of Korea* (New Haven: Yale University Press, 1977); Kim and Roemer, *Studies in the Modernization of the Republic of Korea;* and Krueger, *Studies in the Modernization of the Republic of Korea.*

tain economies of scale, undoubtedly worked to reduce costs, as did the long period during which Brazil had undergone import substitution. From 1968 to the early 1970s a policy of small but regular devaluations and larger incentives for exports, together with reduced import protection, steadily improved the relative incentive to export (recall Table 17–3).

In response the volume of exports grew by almost 9 percent a year from 1964 to 1977. The share of manufactured exports in the total tripled from 1965 to 1977, but still reached only 26 percent in 1977, testimony to the predominantly agricultural base of Brazil's exports. Because Brazil's economy is much larger than Korea's, the contribution of exports to growth was less dramatic. Exports rose only modestly, from 6 to almost 8 percent of GNP, from 1964 to 1977. Manufactured exports accounted for under 5 percent of manufacturing output in 1972, compared with 24 percent in Korea. By 1971 exports accounted for about 6 percent of employment in manufacturing. Thus the picture in Brazil is one of rapid export growth, but within a small segment of a large economy. Because the impact of exports on income growth and employment creation was inevitably limited, and contained within the advanced sectors of the economy, it did not contribute noticeably to ameliorating Brazil's sharply unequal income distribution. Indeed it has been argued that the wage-containment policies required by this strategy may have contributed to a worsening income distribution since 1964.[7]

Thus in smaller economies the outward-looking policies of export substitution can have remarkable success in stimulating the growth of new export products and thus diversifying the economy; in stimulating industrialization and growth of national income, and in distributing the benefits of growth widely through employment creation, rising real wages, and rising agricultural prices. In large economies like Brazil, however, export substitution is unlikely to have such widespread, structural effects. Given its success in Asia, is export substitution a strategy for all countries? Probably not, for reasons both domestic and international.

The four Asian countries promoted manufactured exports because they had no place else to go. Lacking abundant natural resources, unable to feed themselves (except Taiwan), and recognizing the limitations of their domestic markets, these countries had to turn outward to generate self-sustaining growth. Resource- and land-rich countries, with opportunities to sell raw materials and foods on world markets, may still find it advantageous to do so and relatively costly to develop manufactured export industries. If agriculture can be organized on small-holder principles, primary-export activity can be at least as egalitarian as industrially oriented export promotion. Although lacking natural resources the Asian exporters

7. For full treatments of Brazil's export promotion strategy, see William G. Tyler, *Manufactured Export Expansion and Industrialization in Brazil* (Tubingen, West Germany: J. C. B. Mohr, 1976); Albert Fishlow, "Foreign Trade Regimes and Economic Development: Brazil," and Richard Weisskoff, "The Growth and Decline of Import Substitution in Brazil—Revisited," *World Development* 8 (September 1980): 647–76.

were relatively richly endowed with human resources, especially entrepreneurs and a large, relatively well-educated labor force. Countries with lesser endowments of these resources will find Korea's kind of diverse, small-unit, internationally competitive manufacturing sector very difficult to develop, even with the right incentives; in other words, the supply elasticities may be too low.

The Political Costs of Transition

A final caution is the potentially great cost—economic, social, and political—of the transition from an entrenched regime of import substitution to one of export promotion. The shift in relative prices of imports versus exports and of agricultural goods versus manufactures; the broadened access to imports and credits; rises in real interest rates; and reduced growth of real wages—all hit groups in society that have been most successful in realizing their claims on rising incomes: successful manufacturers and traders, strong labor unions, civil servants, and most critically, the officer corps of the army. Any change, but most especially liberalizing change, will be resisted by these groups, which have the most to lose from them. The potential beneficiaries—small farmers, rural laborers, small manufacturers, the unemployed—are generally politically impotent and count for little in the urban-based struggle to maintain existing income shares.

Compounding these difficulties, there is likely to be a lag of several months to a few years before the clear advantages of liberalized, outward-looking policies become evident. Those investors waiting in the wings have based plans on the old prices; it takes time for them to adjust their expectations and their investment plans to fit the new conditions. Some existing producers may respond immediately by shifting to export markets, but the needed massive growth of exports is likely to take a year or more to develop in some economies. Until that happens it may be necessary to maintain some controls on imports, restricting supplies. Furthermore the initially higher prices of imports due to devaluation, which can only ease after quotas can be removed and imports increased, will fuel an inflationary psychology.

This kind of fundamental transition in which the powerful are hurt and the beneficiaries, weak to start with, do not realize their gains for some time is a passage of great danger for any government. In Ghana such a transition was attempted by a democratic government in late 1971, followed by a military coup early the next year. In Korea, despite some rocky passages in the early 1960s, and in Brazil, successful transition was accomplished by strong regimes, backed by the military, which repressed political opposition. Colombia went through a moderate transition (though not to a completely outward-looking regime) with a democratic government, but a popular one that shared power with the opposition. And Sri Lanka has been attempting one under a democratic government since 1977.[8]

---

8. John Sheahan discusses the connection between outward-looking strategies and political repression and suggests some compromises that might avoid repression, in "Market-oriented Economic Policies and Political Repression in Latin America," *Economic Development and Cultural Change* 28 (January 1980): 267–92.

Whatever the government, it is safer to navigate this passage when economic conditions are favorable, harvests good, unemployment low, and the balance of payments strong. Paradoxically, that is the least likely occasion to induce governments to change things. But if a crisis is awaited, the government's position is likely to be weakened and its prospects for success dimmed.

Access to Industrial Country Markets

As a group the developing countries have become significant suppliers of manufactured goods to consumers in the industrial world. In 1978 the developing market economies exported $45 billion of manufactures to the industrial market economies, representing a sixfold expansion in export volume (i.e., at constant prices) from the 1960 level (see Table 17–5). Although almost a third of these exports were concentrated in textiles and clothing, products such as wood paneling, machinery, electronics, and chemicals were also exported to industrial countries. Asian exporters, led by the Gang of Four, were responsible for over 70 percent of these manufactured exports. And although in the aggregate LDC exports of manufactures to industrial countries accounted for only 9 percent of the industrial countries' imports of manufactures, in textiles the share was 17 percent and in clothing the share was 40 percent in 1978.

TABLE 17–5   Exports of Manufactures from Developing Countries to Industrial Countries[a]

	1960	1978
A. *Value* of exports (billion dollars)		
1. All exports (0–9)[b]	20.0	212.5
2. Manufactures (5–8)	2.6	44.6
a. Chemicals (5)	0.2	2.0
b. Machinery[c] (7)	0.1	8.8
c. Other (6 + 8)	2.3	33.7
1) Textiles (65)	NA	4.4
2) Clothing (84)	NA	8.9
B. *Quantity index* of exports (1970 = 100)		
1. All exports (0–9)	52	139
2. Manufactures (5–8)	37	225
C. *Share* of industrial country imports (%)		
1. All commodities (0–9)	25.0	25.6
2. Manufactures (5–8)	6.5	8.7
a. Chemicals (5)	4.5	3.4
b. Machinery[c] (7)	0.7	4.0
c. Other (6 + 8)	10.7	15.0
1) Textiles (65)	NA	16.6
2) Clothing (84)	NA	39.6

Source: United Nations, *Yearbook of International Trade Statistics 1979*, vol. 1 (New York, 1981), Special Table C.

[a] Market economies only, excluding socialist Asian and Eastern European countries and Cuba. NA = not available.

[b] Figures in parentheses give the standard industrial trade classification (SITC) for each group of commodities.

[c] Includes transport vehicles.

The success, particularly of the Asian exporters, in penetrating industrial-country markets for several labor-intensive manufactures has been met
with increasing protectionism from the importing countries. The United
States and European Economic Community have erected quotas against
textiles, clothing, and footwear (although the United States recently withdrew its restrictions on footwear imports). Moreover the expansion of third
world manufactured exports during the 1960s and early 1970s took place
in an environment of unprecedented prosperity and growth of both income
and trade in the industrial world. By the early 1980s economic growth had
slowed markedly in the developed economies, and LDC exporters have to
compete even more intensively with industrial country manufacturers to
extend their market penetration. To some extent the Gang of Four will be
moving out of textiles, clothing, and other labor-intensive exports into new
lines, leaving room for more recent entrants, especially in Asia and Latin
America. But many developing countries are poised to increase manufactured exports, and the question of access to industrial markets has become
a troublesome issue for countries that are considering outward-looking
strategies.

Trade Preferences

One response to this problem has been the drive, begun by the United
Nations Conference on Trade and Development (UNCTAD) in 1964, toward a Generalized System of Preferences, or GSP. Under GSP, all LDC
manufactures would be permitted to enter developed-country markets duty
free while competing imports from developed countries would be subject to
whatever tariff was then in force. Tariff preferences have two implications.
First, they cause a transfer of resources from the importing government,
which no longer collects the duty, to the exporter, permitting the latter to
charge a higher price and remain competitive with manufacturers in industrial countries. Second, because this transfer raises the return on capital in
LDC export manufacturing, it creates an additional stimulus to investment
and helps developing countries to diversify further into manufacturing for
export.

By 1976, after more than a decade of discussion and resistance, all industrial countries had adopted some form of generalized preferences. But these
schemes were far from the broadly based system originally contemplated by
UNCTAD. The system legislated in the United States, the last country to
offer preferences, is illustrative of the kinds of restrictions that most countries imposed on their schemes. The U.S. excludes from preferences several
commodities in which LDCs have a strong comparative advantage, including textiles and footwear. Further, preferential treatment is withdrawn for
any export of a country that supplies 50 percent of the U.S. market for that
manufactured good or which exports more than $25 million of the good to
the U.S. The U.S. also applies rules to ensure that a certain fraction of the
good is actually manufactured in the LDC. The EEC imposes a systematic
"tariff quota," under which imports from all LDCs enter duty free up to a

specified limit, after which the full duty is applied. And any one country is limited to a share of the quota, 50 percent or less, to ensure that no one country obtains all the benefit. Finally, some countries, such as Spain, Portugal, Greece, Hong Kong, and Taiwan, are excluded from at least one of the GSP schemes.

These restrictive preference schemes provide only modest benefits to the developing countries. Baldwin and Murray have estimated that the GSP schemes finally put into effect would have increased exports of LDC manufactures by $480 million in 1971.[9] This is less than 4 percent of the gross value of LDC manufactured exports in 1971. And the benefits tend to be gained by the more advanced of the developing countries. Three-fourths of the GDP benefits estimated by Baldwin and Murray are earned by only a dozen countries, such as Taiwan, South Korea, India, Brazil, Mexico, and Yugoslavia, that have already made great strides in exporting manufactures and have shown that they are able to compete without preferences in any case.

Trade Reform

Some observers of preference schemes have suggested that LDCs would be better served in the future by general tariff reductions for all commodities under the *most favored nation principle* (MFN), which ensures that a tariff reduction to any one country is offered to all countries.[10] The successful LDC exporters of manufactures have proved already that they do not need preferences to compete. And the less advanced countries, which might begin to compete in simple labor-intensive manufactures, find these commodities barred from preferences anyway. In the long run both the middle-income and low-income countries would probably benefit more from trade reforms that accomplished three goals.

First, and perhaps most important, industrial countries need to make greater progress toward adjusting their own economies away from those industries, principally textiles, clothing, footwear, and for many countries, steel, in which the developing countries have a comparative advantage. Tariffs are already low on many of the products in these categories, but quotas and marketing agreements limit the quantity of goods that may be imported. This issue goes to the heart of North-South relations because domestic politics intervene to make it difficult for industrial countries to adjust to greater volumes of labor-intensive manufactures. Many workers in the affected industries will lose their jobs and may remain unemployed for some time. Eventually, as new industries, in which the industrial countries have comparative advantage, grow and employ more workers, much or all of the job loss will be recovered. And in the long run as resources are reallocated to more efficient industries in both the North and the South, all

9. R. E. Baldwin and T. Murray, "MFN Tariff Reductions and LDC Benefits under GSP," *The Economic Journal* 87 (March 1977): 30–46.
10. See, for example, ibid., and Mordechai E. Kreinen and J. M. Finger, "A Critical Survey of the New International Economic Order," *Journal of World Trade Law* 10 (1976): 493–512.

countries will benefit. But in the short run adjustment means unemployment in the declining industries of the North and creates political pressure for protection, rather than liberalization.

A second goal of trade reform is to reduce tariffs on the processed forms of LDC raw material and food exports. Although these tariffs are not very high for the most part, ranging from 5 to 20 percent, there is often a much lower duty, or no duty, on the raw material import. Hence the effective protection is high and discourages exporting countries from processing their own raw materials and foods. Such a tariff reduction would of course help countries to undertake resource-based industrialization, described in Chapter 15. Finally, LDCs and many industrial exporters would gain from a general reduction in nontariff barriers to trade, such as quotas, packaging and labeling requirements, health provisions, customs delays, and high warehousing charges. These often appear to be innocuous enough, but are sometimes retained, or even instituted, primarily to protect domestic manufacturers. In Japan, for example, nontariff barriers are often as powerful as tariffs in restricting competitive imports.

Integration Among Developing Countries

The developing countries, frustrated by their inability to gain wider access to industrial-country markets or to improve their terms of trade with these markets, have exhorted each other to form larger and more meaningful regional trade groups. In essence groups of developing countries would try to stimulate development by granting preferential access to each other's exports, placing relatively less emphasis on access to industrial country markets. Table 17-6 shows that although trade among developing countries grew threefold from 1960 to 1978, intra-LDC trade increased only modestly as a share of total LDC exports in that period. In 1978 developing countries sold about a quarter of their exports to other third world countries; for manufactures the share was one third. Proponents of regional trade groups hope that greater economic integration among developing countries would increase the importance of intra-LDC trade to the benefit of all participants.

Three systems of trade arrangements can be defined, in increasing degree of economic integration. *Free-trade areas* eliminate tariffs among member countries, but each member is permitted to set its own external tariff for imports from the outside world. The European Free Trade Association was a prominent example before the broadening of the European Economic Community. The Latin American Free Trade Association is the largest current example. Because members are typically free to set their own external tariffs, free-trade associations represent minimal cooperation and integration and have generally not been very effective. *Customs unions* eliminate tariffs among members, but go beyond free-trade areas by erecting a common external tariff against imports from the rest of the world. This is sometimes a stated aim of trade groupings, such as the Andean Pact among countries along the west coast of Latin America, but is often difficult to achieve.

TABLE 17-6 Trade Among Developing Market[a] Countries

	1960	1978
1. *Value* of exports (billion dollars)		
A. All exports (0–9)[b]	6.1	73.3
B. Manufactures (5–8)	1.1	23.2
2 *Quantity index* of exports (1970 = 100)		
A. All exports (0–9)	57	183
B. Manufactures (5–8)	35	275
3. *Share* of intra-LDC in total LDC exports[c] (%)		
A. All exports (0–9)	23	26
B. Manufactures (5–8)	31	34

Source: United Nations, *Yearbook of International Trade Statistics 1979* (New York, 1981).
[a] Excludes Cuba and socialist countries in Asia.
[b] Figures in parentheses are SITC numbers for each group of commodities.
[c] Exports by current market value.

Common markets move several steps closer to full integration. In addition to free trade among members and a common external tariff, common markets either eliminate or materially reduce restrictions on the movements of labor and capital among member states. They may go further to promote coordinated fiscal, monetary, and exchange rate policies and may cooperate in many other ways. The European Economic Community (EEC) is the most integrated group in the world today. Both the Central American and the East African Common Markets had achieved important elements of economic integration until each fell afoul of political differences among members that effectively destroyed these groupings.

Static Gains

Customs unions (which we use here as a shorthand for all regional preferential trading arrangements) may benefit their members by conveying **static gains** in the form of a one-time improvement in resource allocation and/or by offering **dynamic gains,** stimulating investment in production for export and linked industries. The traditional analysis of the static gains from customs unions makes the distinction between *trade creation* and *trade diversion.*

Trade is created when a new customs union, which lowers the duty on imports from all member countries, permits some member, say, country A, to export more to another, country B, by displacing production of country B's own industries. The import-competing industry in country B was presumably able to sell in the home market because the protective duty shielded it from the exports of more efficient, lower cost industries in other countries. When the customs union lowers the duty on exports from other member countries, more efficient industries in those countries can then compete with country B's firms in their own markets. More is traded than before, hence the term *trade creation.* Although some producers in country B are disadvantaged by the change, presumably there are others that benefit from the lower duties in other member countries' markets, and of course consumers benefit from lower prices and wider selection. Gains from trade creation are analogous to gains from the opening of trade (see Chapter 15) except that they take place in the limited world of the customs union.

Because customs unions also discriminate against outside countries, they may *divert trade* by permitting member country A to export more to country B by displacing imports previously bought from a nonmember country. If country B had a most favored nation tariff before the union, then the outside country's exports must have been cheaper than those of country A (or else country B would have imported from country A in the first place). Once the union is formed, consumers in country B will buy from producers in country A at a lower cost to the consumers but at a higher cost to the country as a whole. Part of the revenue previously earned on imports from nonmember countries is now paid to exporters in country A, who are less efficient producers than their outside competitors.

From each member country's standpoint the customs union is beneficial if trade creation outweighs trade diversion. This is more likely to be the case if customs union partners have different relative resource endowments or their consumers have different tastes, so that the members have a comparative advantage in the export of different commodities. For example, if Mexico, with a comparative advantage in vegetables and petroleum, were to join in a customs union with Colombia, with a comparative advantage in coffee and textiles (to oversimplify greatly), trade is likely to be created and both countries would benefit. But on the whole neighboring developing countries tend to export goods that are more similar than different, and there is a presumption that trade diversion would be large. In the East African Common Market, for example, much of the trade in manufactured goods came from industries, such as tire manufacturing in Kenya, that could not compete with the outside world and for which Tanzania and Uganda had to pay higher c.i.f. prices than if they had purchased from outside the market. Note that even if, on balance, trade creation within the union exceeds trade diversion, so long as there is some diversion nonmember countries are losers.

Dynamic Gains and Risks

Most advocates of customs unions among developing countries would argue that the major gains are not static, but dynamic. Customs unions widen the market for industries in all member countries, with the attendant benefits noted by Adam Smith. Economies of scale may be realized by some industries whose output would be too small if confined to the home market. This broader market especially benefits infant industries which are not ready to compete in world markets. If the larger protected market helps them achieve scale economies, they may reduce the time it takes to learn to become competitive in world terms. One potentially important, if largely unimplemented, feature of the Andean Pact and the Association of Southeast Asian Nations (ASEAN) is the *complementation agreement,* under which large-scale infant industries are allocated to member countries so that each can benefit from, while each shares the costs of, starting industries such as petrochemicals, fertilizer, pulp and paper, vehicle manufacture, and basic metals.

Customs unions also increase competition among producers in the member countries and reduce the perverse effects of protection, discussed in Chapter 16. This effect can be especially important for large-scale industries which would otherwise monopolize home markets at efficient levels of output. But it can have a much more pervasive effect, sharpening entrepreneurial and managerial performance in all industries. The bracing winds of competition are thought to have played a major role in stimulating European growth after the formation of the EEC and may have contributed to the temporary success of the Central American Common Market as well. One manifestation of increased competition is a characteristic pattern of trade in customs unions: much increased trade is in similar or even identical products. Members will export shoes, clothing, or canned foods to each other. To some extent this represents specialization in fine detail, one textile firm narrowing its products to concentrate on the few things it does especially well. To some extent it may represent more efficient subregional patterns of trade, a realignment to reduce transport costs once borders no longer serve as barriers. But a lot of the trade in similar goods may just reflect greater competition and a wider range of choice for consumers. In any event it certainly belies the trade creation approach, which predicts that countries will gain only if they export dissimilar goods. Trade in similar goods is good evidence that dynamic gains are more important than static ones.

These dynamic effects act over the long run to induce greater investment within the customs union, stimulating accelerated growth, and to restructure the economy toward exports of all kinds and toward industries that might otherwise have a difficult time getting started. Given these advantages, why are there so few examples of successful customs unions in the third world? One major problem has been the distribution of the gains, whether static or dynamic. The East African Common Market illustrated this point. When it was functioning well, both Tanzania and Uganda believed that Kenya benefited most from the resulting development of manufacturing. Kenya, which had moved fast to industrialize, was better able to take advantage of the customs union and exported more to its neighbors than it imported. (Indeed, Kenya kept its trade close to balance primarily because of this; it generally ran a deficit with the outside world.) Once Kenyan industries began to export, more investment flowed into Kenya to take advantage of the industrial infrastructure and the central location of Nairobi. Thus Kenya, and in particular Nairobi, acted as a growth pole for the whole East African market. Growth poles are often considered desirable in developing countries, but not when the pole is outside one's own borders. The increasing concentration of gains in the more advanced members of common markets causes the less advanced partners to resist integration, to avoid becoming "backwaters." This contributed to the demise of the East African experiment and has helped to dampen the ardor of countries like Bolivia and Ecuador for the Andean Pact.

The concentration of gains—real or perceived—in the more advanced member countries leads to political tensions that sometimes exacerbate the political problems among neighboring countries. Conversely, political disagreements among neighbors, which are probably inevitable, become much more dangerous when those neighbors are tied together in customs unions or other economic arrangements. Each partner, but especially the economically less advanced one, can use participation as a whip to threaten partners if decisions are not taken in its favor. The rise of Idi Amin and the tensions between Tanzania and Kenya eventually destroyed the East African Common Market. Chile withdrew from the Andean Pact over political disagreements with Peru and other countries. The potential for such schisms always exists, and increases substantially the risk that a country takes when it enters an integration scheme. Certainly the country can reap substantial economic benefits from integration with its neighbors. But to achieve these gains it must develop its economy in ways that do not make much sense outside the customs unions. Malaysia might invest in a fertilizer plant intended to serve the ASEAN countries. But if the free-trade area does not develop, or if political arguments make it ineffective, Malaysia has considerably more fertilizer capacity than it can use, especially if it remains a high-cost producer. This kind of example, multiplied over several industries, could lead to severe dislocation and stagnation if the customs union breaks up.

Will the developing countries move toward greater trade with each other? The potential advantages are great, but so are the risks. To be successful any integration plan must bring the promise of substantial additional investment in the foreseeable future and must provide for a broad and equitable distribution of the benefits of union. Member countries will have to be governed by strong leaders who recognize common interests and work harmoniously together. Even this cannot rule out the risk of political change and future disagreements that cripple the union. It would seem that the conditions for successful integration schemes are no less stringent than those for successful outward-looking strategies of development. The political risks are reduced, however, the wider the membership of any union, so that no one country can destroy the arrangement by withdrawing.

Trade Strategies: A Synthesis

What general rules can be derived from experience with the three major trade strategies—primary-export-led growth, import substitution, export substitution—since World War II? First, pragmatism and eclecticism should rule over any doctrinaire, single-purpose approach. Although it is comfortable to think in terms of import substitution or export substitution, our understanding of these strategies has been enhanced by identifying and analyzing their components. It would be better in the future to avoid labels and to construct strategies from the components that seem to have worked. Whether the resulting product mix is import-substituting or export-led should not matter if the strategy leads the country effectively toward its development goals.

What elements seem to work best? Import substitution has gone awry in its excessive protection and its divorce of production decisions from market conditions, while an orientation toward world markets has been crucial for successful export substitution. If, for whatever reason, one or several import-substituting industries appear advantageous at a particular stage of development, they should be encouraged, not with high and continuing tariffs or restrictive quotas, but with moderate tariffs or subsidies. And either of these should be phased down on a predetermined schedule to force the infant industries to mature into efficient adulthood. Some long-standing tariffs are part of every trade regime. In most developing countries tariffs are a necessary source of government revenue (see Chapter 12), and in some resource-rich LDCs tariffs may support diversification away from dominant primary exports (see Chapter 15). But permanent tariff protection should be modest and uniform, covering all imports, including capital goods, and avoiding the disincentives to backward linkages mentioned above. Import-substituting industries that grow up under these conditions are likely to avoid the worst excesses of protracted inefficiency and eventually become capable of exporting.

Resource-rich countries should, of course, exploit their natural advantage by exporting primary products. The task for them is to avoid the sharp dualism that infects such economies. Export taxes on primary products can be used to control profits and supplies, while the exchange rate supported by modest protective tariffs can be used as an incentive for efficient import substitution and export diversification. The tendency for rising wages in the nonresource sectors needs to be resisted so that these can be developed in labor-intensive ways.

To the extent that investment is left to private, market forces, then the price signals generated in reasonably open economies should lead to efficient investments that promote development goals. If governments prefer to plan industrial and agricultural investment, then cost-benefit analysis or linear programming models (explained in Chapter 6) can be used to select projects for implementation, not according to some predetermined criterion such as import substitution, but for their ability to satisfy national development goals. In some situations these may yield a preponderance of import substitution industries; in others primary or manufactured exports could predominate. The nature of this outcome should be secondary to the ability of the package to propel a desirable kind of development. Once the investment package is set, the market environment must be carefully designed, avoiding large distortions and exposing producers to the discipline of competition. This outcome holds for private or public companies. "Getting prices right" is not a panacea for development, but getting them wrong has been a proven formula for failure.

These prescriptions apply with less force to large countries than to small. The distinguishing characteristic is the size of the potential domestic market. The massively populated countries, China and India, qualify by sheer weight of numbers. Countries with smaller populations but higher incomes per capita, such as Brazil and Mexico, can also provide large enough internal markets to temper some of the demands of trade-oriented strategies. Indonesia, Nigeria, and South Korea are borderline cases. For the very large countries trade is a significantly lower share of national income and affects domestic market conditions less than in smaller countries. Strategic options, such as concentrating on one kind of manufacturing, are more limited, and balanced growth of industries and agriculture is virtually essential. Indeed any attempt to depend too heavily on trade is likely to affect world market prices and turn the terms of trade against the large country. With large internal demand it is possible to attain economies of scale, even in some producer goods industries, without establishing monopolies. The benefits of competitive, efficient industrial and agricultural development can, with good economic management, be captured within the domestic economy.

Nevertheless even with the very large countries trade can help ensure efficient, equitable growth. Imports can be used, especially in the early stages, to quell any tendency for pioneering firms to act like monopolists. Similarly, the potential for export can help fledgling firms achieve scale economies and produce more efficiently for home use as well. Any outward-looking foreign exchange regime will encourage competitive behavior, keeping prices of goods from straying very far from world market levels.

For small countries there is no way to avoid the implications of these trade strategies. With large fractions of total supply deriving from imports, the choice is either to tie the economy to world prices through outward-looking policies or to accept the costs of inward-looking, protective regimes. For the small country these costs can be very high, severe enough to retard development for long periods. Whether the small country is successful is likely to depend on its acceptance of the outside trading world more as an opportunity than as a constraint on development.

FURTHER READING In addition to the articles cited in the chapter footnotes, trade preferences for LDCs are discussed by Rachel McCulloch, "Economic and Political Issues in the New Intenational Economic Order" (International Institute for Economic Research Original Paper 22, July 1979); and Harry G. Johnson, "Trade Preferences and Developing Countries," in Robert E. Baldwin and J. David Richardson (eds.), *International Trade and Finance* (Boston: Little, Brown, 1974), pp. 246–62. Part II of the collection by Baldwin and Richardson also contains a series of articles on effective protection, nontariff barriers, and the political economy of protection from the viewpoint of American producers and consumers, which provides a good sense of the potential gains and losses to industrial countries from providing greater access to manufactures from developing countries.

The theory of static gains from customs unions was first delineated by Jacob Viner, *The Customs Unions Issue* (New York: Carnegie Endowment for Intenational Peace, 1950). Reviews of the literature on customs union theory are provided by Melvyn B. Krauss, "Recent Developments in Customs Union Theory: An Interpretive Survey," *Journal of Economic Literature* 10 (1972): 413–436; and R. G. Lipsey, "The Theory of Customs Unions: A General Survey," *The Economic Journal* 70 (1960): 496–513. For studies of specific trade arrangements among developing countries, see Joseph Grunwald, M. S. Wionczek, and Martin Carnoy, *Latin American Integration and U.S. Policy* (Washington, D.C.: Brookings Institution, 1972); Martin Carnoy, "A Welfare Analysis of Latin American Economic Union: Six Industrial Studies," *Journal of Political Economy* 78 (1970): 626–54; and W. T. Newlyn, "Gains and Losses in the East African Common Market," *Yorkshire Bulletin of Economic and Social Research* 17 (1965): 132–38.

SECTORS

Chapter 18

AGRICULTURE

Any discussion of economic development inevitably touches on agriculture. The labor surplus and neoclassical models presented in Chapter 3 dealt primarily with the nature of the relationship between the industrial and agricultural sectors. The problem of income distribution or extremes of poverty within developing nations discussed in Chapter 4 is substantially a question of how to do something about the rural poor. And nutrition, the subject of Chapter 10, is a question of food production and distribution.

Much of this book has been about *rural development,* a term that refers to all those activities which affect the well-being of rural populations: the provision of basic needs, such as food; the development of human capital in the countryside through education and nutrition programs; and efforts to improve yields by providing seed, fertilizer, and advice, or by building fertilizer plants and irrigation systems. Rather than repeat what has been said in earlier chapters, this chapter concentrates on problems that have a direct bearing on the raising of agricultural production and farmer incomes. Indirect measures treated elsewhere in this book, even ones as central as rural education, will be dealt with only in passing.

In a sense agriculture is simply one industry among many, but it is an industry with a difference. To begin with, the agricultural sector in a country at an early stage of development employs far more people than all other industries and sectors put together—60–70 percent and more of the total work force are in agriculture in many of the poorer LDCs, including China and India. By way of contrast, agriculture in developed economies typically employs less than 10 percent of the work force (only 2 percent in the United States). Second, agricultural activities have existed for thousands of years, ever since mankind gave up hunting and gathering as its main source of food. Because of this long history the rural economy is often referred to as *tradition bound.* Electric power generation or the manufacture of automobiles can only be done by means based on modern science and engineering, but crops are often grown using techniques developed hundreds or even thousands of years before the advent of modern science. And the rural society in which these traditional techniques are used often develops customs and attitudes that reinforce older ways of doing things, and thus makes change difficult.

A third characteristic of agriculture that separates it from other sectors is the crucial importance of land as a factor of production. Other sectors use and require land, but in no other sector does land play such a central role. The availability of cultivable land, whether it be relatively plentiful in relation to population, as in the Americas, or scarce, as in much of Asia, fundamentally shapes the kind of farming techniques that can be used. And closely related to the central role of land is the influence of weather. No other sector is as subject to the vagaries of the weather as is agriculture. Land, like the weather, differs from place to place so that techniques suitable in one place are often of little use elsewhere. The manufacture of steel must also adjust to differences in the quality of iron ore from place to place, and similar problems occur in other industries; but the basic techniques in much of manufacturing are similar, at least within and often between nations. In agriculture differences in soil quality, climate, and the availability of water lead to the production of different crops and different ways of raising a particular crop not only within countries but even within provinces or counties of a single country.

Finally, agriculture is the one sector that produces food. Mankind can survive without steel or coal or even electric power, but not without food. For most manufactured products, in fact, there are substitutes, but there is no substitute for food. Either food must be produced within a country or it must be imported.

Agriculture's Role in Economic Development

Agriculture's role in economic development is central because that is how most of the people in poor nations make their living. If planners are seriously concerned with the welfare of their people, the only way they can readily raise the welfare of a great majority of those people is by helping to raise their output of food and cash crops or by raising the prices they receive for those crops. Not all increases in farm output benefit the majority of rural people, of course. The creation of mechanized, large-scale farms where small peasant farms prevailed before may actually make the majority of the population worse off. We shall return to this problem later. Here, suffice it to say that while raising agricultural output is not a sufficient condition to achieve an increase in rural welfare, it is a necessary condition.

Most developing countries must rely on their own agricultural sectors to produce the food consumed by their own people. There are exceptions. Nations with large natural-resource-based exports, such as Malaysia or Saudi Arabia, have the foreign exchange necessary to import much of their food. But most developing nations cannot rely so heavily on foreign exchange earnings to feed their populations.

Farmers in developing nations must not only produce enough to feed themselves, they must produce enough to feed the urban population as well. As the share of the urban population in the total rises, therefore, the productivity of farmers must also rise. If productivity does not rise (and in the absence of food imports), the models in Chapter 3 make it clear that the terms of trade will turn sharply against the industrial sector, thus cutting into profits and eventually bringing growth to a halt.

The agricultural sector's size is the characteristic that gives agriculture such an important role in the provision of factor inputs, notably labor, to industry and to the other modern sectors. With 70 percent or more of the population in agriculture the rural sector is virtually the only source of increased labor power for the urban sector. Importation of labor is possible, and there is usually population growth within the urban sector itself, but neither of these sources is likely to be sufficient for the needs of economic growth over the long run. If there are restrictions on the movement of labor out of agriculture, economic development will be severely crippled. Serfs in Russia in the early nineteenth century, for example, were tied to their lord's land by law and hence were not free to move to the cities and into industry. Russian industry therefore did not begin to grow rapidly until after the serfs were freed. Today such feudal restrictions are increasingly rare, but heavy indebtedness by a farmer to a landlord-moneylender often has the same effect of tying an individual to the land and making him unavailable to modern industry.

The agricultural sector also can be a major source of capital for modern economic growth. Capital comes from invested savings and savings from income. However, even in the poorest countries the share of agricultural income in national product is 50 percent of gross domestic product. Half or more of national product therefore is provided by nonagricultural sectors, especially industry and commerce (services), and these sectors are often important contributors to saving and hence to investment. Furthermore, whereas imports of labor seldom provide a large portion of the domestic labor force, imports of capital, whether in the form of aid or private investment, sometimes do contribute a substantial share of domestic capital formation. Thus it is possible for a nation to achieve a high rate of capital formation without drawing on the agricultural sector at all. South Korea is a case in point where capital formation in the early years of rapid growth was provided mainly by foreign aid and in later years was paid for increasingly from the profits of the industrial sector. Still, other things being equal, capital formation is more likely to be sufficient for growth if the large agricultural sector is contributing substantially to the process. Thus agriculture made large contributions of capital for the first stage of development in China in the 1950s.

If one treats foreign exchange as a separate factor of production, agriculture has an important role to play in the supply of this factor as well. As indicated in Chapter 15, developing countries' comparative advantage usually lies with either minerals or agricultural products. In only a few cases is the export of manufactures or of services the principal source of foreign exchange for a nation in the early stages of modern economic growth. Thus unless a nation is rich in minerals such as petroleum the agricultural sector must play a key role in providing foreign exchange with which to import capital equipment that cannot be produced at home.

Finally, the farming population of a developing nation is, in some cases at least, an important market for the output of the modern urban sector. The qualification "in some cases" must be added because farm populations in some poor countries purchase very little from modern industry. This is particularly likely to be true where the distribution of income is extremely unequal, with most of the nation's income and wealth in the hands of a small urban and rural upper class. In that situation the rural population may simply pay taxes and rents to wealthy urban residents and subsist on whatever is left over. Even cheap cloth from urban factories may be beyond the means of a very poor rural population. If income is less unequally distributed, however, the rural sector can be an important source of demand for industrial products. If a large rural market exists, industries can continue to grow after they have saturated urban demand for their product without having to turn to foreign markets until they are better able to compete.[1]

Self-Sufficiency and Dwindling World Food Supplies

One important aspect of agriculture's role in development typically gets a great deal of attention from economic planers: the degree to which a nation wishes to achieve food *self-sufficiency*. Food self-sufficiency can take on several different meanings. At one extreme is the view that any dependence on foreign trade is dangerous to a nation's economic health, and dependence on food imports is simply one part of this broader danger. More common is the view that staple foods are a basic or strategic good, not unlike military weapons. If a nation is dependent on others for its staple food and hence for its very survival, the suppliers of that food will be in a position to bring the dependent nation to its knees whenever it suits the supplier nations' purposes. Others argue that population growth is rapidly eating into the world's food surpluses, and nations relying on food imports will soon find themselves paying very high prices in order to get what they need from the world's dwindling surplus.

The national defense argument for food self-sufficiency may be valid under certain specific circumstances. A discussion of these circumstances would divert us into an analysis of complex international security issues

---

1. There are a number of good studies that treat the role of agriculture in development, including John Mellor, *The New Economics of Growth* (Ithaca, N.Y.: Cornell University Press, 1976), and his earlier *The Economics of Agricultural Development* (Ithaca, N.Y.: Cornell University Press, 1966); Bruce Johnston and Peter Kilby, *Agriculture and Structural Transformation* (London: Oxford University Press, 1975); and Lloyd Reynolds, *Agriculture in Development Theory* (New Haven: Yale University Press, 1976).

not appropriate for a book on economic development. Suffice it to say that the national defense argument is frequently used to justify policies that have little relationship to a nation's real security.

The issue of a dwindling world food surplus cannot be dealt with so easily. History does not support the view that world supplies of exportable food are getting steadily smaller. Data on world grain exports are presented in Table 18–1. What these and other data indicate is that while the world grain export surplus and the corresponding size of the deficit in importing nations fluctuates, the overall surplus is growing, not declining. In 1972, for example, bad weather struck a wide part of the globe, including the Soviet Union, China, India, and Indonesia. The resulting surge in demand for grain imports drove prices up sharply in 1973, but prices fell again when production in these deficit areas recovered. The 1972–1973 "crisis" was not significantly different in magnitude from other weather-induced fluctuations of the past. After 1973 grain exports rose substantially, but prices fell from 1973 peaks.

TABLE 18–1   World Grain Exports (million metric tons)

Year	Exports
1962	85.34
1964	103.23
1966	114.11
1968	102.25
1970	113.34
1972	130.89
1974	149.05
1976	167.50
1978	191.20
1980	216.10

Source: FAO, Trade Yearbook, 1972 (p. 122), 1976 (p. 105), and 1978 (p. 109) (Rome, 1973, 1977, and 1979); International Grain and Feed Markets Forecast and Statistical Digest 1981 (London, 1981), p. 12.

Those who speak of an impeding world food crisis are implicitly or explicitly making a forecast about the future. Continued population growth is rapidly pushing people out onto the world's diminishing supply of arable land. In places like Africa's Sahel agriculture may already have developed beyond the capacity of the land to sustain it given the technologies currently used there. The real issue, however, is not whether the world is running out of surplus land—it is—but whether yields on existing arable land can be raised fast enough to meet the needs of an increasing population with rising per-capita incomes. The problem is not one of biology. Research in the plant sciences has shown that yields per acre could be higher than even those of such advanced agricultural systems as Japan. And most of the world produces food at levels per acre nowhere near those of Japan. While there is some biological limit to the capacity of the planet Earth to produce food, the planet is not remotely close to that limit today.

The real danger of a long-term food crisis arises from a different source. The nations that could, from a scientific point of view, expand food output dramatically may not do so because of internal social and economic barriers to technical progress in agriculture. At the same time the world's few food surplus nations may for economic reasons not be able to continue to expand those surpluses. The United States, for example, once held large amounts of cultivable land out of production in order to keep farm prices high. Today, however, much of that land has been put back into production, and further increases in output will not be so easily achieved. Thus it is possible that the world could face growing food deficits in importing nations that are not matched by rising surpluses in exporting nations. Under such circumstances prices of food would rise sharply, and only nations with large foreign exchange earnings could afford to continue to import sufficient food. Some of the poorest nations, including those where food imports make the difference between an adequate diet and severe malnutrition, may not have the foreign exchange earnings needed to maintain required imports. One must emphasize, however, that while the potential for a disaster of this kind is present, it is not today a reality; and many economists do not believe it ever will become a reality. A possible future world food crisis therefore is not a very sound basis for a nation's economic planners to give a high priority to the development of agriculture.[2]

The main reasons why few developing nations can afford to neglect agricultural development lie with agriculture's central role in economic development, on both the supply and the demand side. On the supply side agriculture is the only source of food, the major source of labor—at least in early stages of development—and an important source of capital and foreign exchange. On the demand side the agricultural sector is an important supplement to urban and foreign sources of demand, at least where the distribution of income is not so unequal that farmers have nothing left over after meeting their basic food requirements.

Land Tenure and Reform

Before we focus on agricultural production it is best to explore the problem of land and the way it is owned and organized. Conditions of land tenure set the context within which all efforts to raise agricultural output must operate.

Patterns of Land Tenure

The terms *land tenure* and *land tenure relations* refer to the way people own land and how they rent it to others to use if they choose not to cultivate it themselves. In the European Middle Ages, for example, a local lord

---

2. Works on the food self-sufficiency issue are numerous on both sides of the argument, including R. Barker, E. Bennagen, and Y. Hayami, "New Rice Technology and Policy Alternatives for Food Self-Sufficiency," in International Rice Research Institute, *Economic Consequences of the New Rice Technology* (Los Banos, 1978), pp. 337–61; Richard Goldman, "Staple Food Self-Sufficiency and the Distributive Impact of Malaysian Rice Policy," *Food Research Institute Studies* 14, no. 3 (1975): 251–93; Lester Brown, *By Bread Alone* (New York: Praeger, 1974).

owned a large piece of land which he allowed the local peasants to culti- vate. In exchange for cultivating that land, the peasant family not only had to deliver a part of the harvest to the lord but members of the peasant fam- ily also had to perform labor services in the lord's castle. In most cases the peasant could not freely leave the land to seek work in the cities or with another lord. Peasants did flee, but the lord had the right to force them to return if he could catch them. Serfdom, as this system is sometimes called, was only a modest step up from slavery.

Serf-like land tenure relations prevail today in only a few remote and backward areas of the globe. The patterns that do exist, however, are very diverse, as the following incomplete listing makes clear.

Large-scale modern farming or ranching usually refers to a large acreage raising crops or cattle which uses some hired labor but where many of the activities are highly mechanized. Many such farms are found in the United States, and much of Latin American agriculture is characterized by large modern farms that exist alongside small peasant plots.

Plantation agriculture is a system in which a large piece of land is used to raise a crop such as tea or rubber, usually for export. Cultivation is by hired labor who are paid wages, and the plantation is run either by the owner or more frequently by a professional manager.

Latifundia is a term used in Latin America and Europe to refer to large estates or ranches on which the hired labor still has a servile (master-ser- vant) relationship to the owner.

Family farms or *independent peasant proprietors* own (usually small and scattered) plots of land and operate them mainly or solely with their own family's labor. This type of tenure is dominant in Asia and Africa and is important in Latin America as well.

Tenancy usually refers to a situation where an individual family farms a piece or pieces of land owned by a landlord to whom the farmer pays rent. Much of Asian agriculture is made up of either individual peasant propri- etors or tenants.

Sharecropping is a form of tenancy in which the farmer shares his crops with the landlord.

Absentee landlords, who are particularly important in Asia and Latin America, tend to live in cities or other places away from the land they own. Landlords who do live near their land may have little to do with that land except to collect rents. Some resident landlords provide seeds and certain kinds of capital to tenants.

Communal farming exists today in parts of Africa, where it is still the practice for a village to own some of its land jointly. Individuals and fami- lies may farm plots on communal land, gaining access by custom or by al- location from the community's leaders. Europe in an earlier period also had such common lands that were used, among other purposes, as pasture for the village cows.

Collectivized agriculture refers to the kinds of agricultural systems found in the Soviet Union, China, and parts of Eastern Europe for the most part. Land, except for small family plots, is owned by a cooperative whose members are typically all or part of the residents of a single village. Management is by a committee elected by the villagers or appointed by government authorities, and members of the cooperative share in output on the basis of the amount of labor they contribute to it.

There are numerous variations within and between these categories, but this list gives some idea of the great range of land tenure systems that exist in the developing world. The kind of land tenure system that exists in any given country or region has an important bearing on economic development for several reasons. To begin with, prevailing land tenure arrangements have a major influence on the welfare of the farm family. A family farming only one or two acres of land that must turn over half its main crop to the landlord will not have much left over to feed itself or to invest in improvements. Such a heavy rent burden may seem harsh, but half and more of the farmers in some major countries, such as China and Korea before land reform and parts of Latin America and India today, labor under comparable conditions or worse.

A second important impact of the land tenure system is on the prevailing degree of political stability. Families that own the land they cultivate tend to feel they have a stake in the existing political order, even if they themselves are quite poor. Because they possess land they have something to lose from turmoil. Landless farm laborers and tenants who can be pushed off the land at the will of a landlord have no such stake in the existing order. The history of many nations which have large landless rural populations is often one of periodic peasant rebellions. One such rebellion played a major role in bringing the Communists to power in China. Much of the history of modern Mexico has also been shaped by revolts of the landless.

Tenure and Incentive

Land tenure systems also have a major impact on agricultural productivity. An individual proprietor who owns land knows that increased effort or skill that leads to a rise in output will also improve his income. This result does not necessarily follow if the land is owned by someone else. Under sharecropping, for example, the landlord gets a percentage share, typically a half of any increase in output. If a tenant's rent contract is only a year or two in length, a rise in output may cause the landlord to threaten eviction of the tenant so that all or much of the increase in production can be captured through a rise in the rent. In some countries landlords have had to draw up land rental contracts of many years or even a lifetime's duration, precisely because tenants otherwise would have no incentive to invest in improvements or even to maintain existing irrigation and drainage systems.

Farms with large numbers of hired laborers have an even more difficult incentive problem compounded by a management problem. Farm laborers are paid wages and typically do not benefit at all in any rise in production. One way around this difficulty is to pay on a *piece-rate basis,* that is, pay workers on the basis of the number of bushels of cotton or tea leaves they pick. But although this system works at harvest time, it is virtually impossible to pay on a piece-work basis for the cultivation of crops. A laborer can be paid by the acre for planting wheat, but it will be many months before it will be possible to tell whether the planting job was done well or carelessly. In a factory elaborate procedures can be set up by management to check on the pace and quality of work performed. But work in a factory is much easier to reduce to a routine that can be measured and supervised than is work on a farm. There are a thousand different tasks that must be performed on a typical farm; and supervision, even in the hands of a skilled manager, is seldom a good substitute for a farmer motivated by knowledge that his or her extra effort will lead directly to a rise in income.

Incentives under communal farming suffer in a different way. Because the land is owned and used in common everyone has an incentive to use the land to the maximum extent possible, but no one has much of an incentive to maintain or improve the land because the benefits of individual improvement efforts will go not mainly to the individual but to everyone who uses the land. Economists call this the *public goods* or *free rider* problem (Chapter 5). Everyone agrees that a fire department is necessary if a town is to avoid a conflagration, but few people would voluntarily pay what the fire department is worth to them. Instead they would pay little or nothing in the hope that their neighbors would pay enough to maintain the department, but of course their neighbors would not pay enough either. The usual solution to this problem is to turn payment over to the town government and allow that government to assess taxes on everyone in town on an equitable basis. Similar solutions are found in communal agriculture. Certain dates can be set aside where everyone in the village is expected to show up and work on a particular land improvement, such as repair of a fence with a neighboring village. But the incentive to work hard in a common effort relies heavily on community social pressure plus the goodwill of each individual. If farmers were saints goodwill would do the job, but for better or worse, farmers are like the rest of us.

Collectivized agriculture has some of the incentive and management problems of both plantation and communal agriculture, but with important differences. Because the land is owned in common the free rider problem is present, but its impact is modified by paying everyone "work points" on the basis of the amount of work they actually do. At the end of the year the total number of work points earned by collective members is added up and divided into the value of the collective's output, thereby determining the value of each work point. The individual therefore has a dual incentive to work hard. More work directly means more work points, and indirectly it leads to higher collective output and hence a higher value for each work point.

The incentive issue posed by collective agriculture is whether the work point system is an adequate substitute for the motivation provided on a family farm where increased output benefits a farmer's own family and only that family. The main problem with the collective system is that an individual can sometimes earn work points by saying he or she worked hard when in fact that person was off behind a tree sleeping or leaning on a hoe. The solution to the leaning on a hoe problem is to have the leadership of the collective check up on how hard each member is working, but that can introduce the supervision or management problem found in plantation labor—namely, that it is extremely difficult to supervise many agricultural activities. In general both the incentive and managerial problems get worse as the collective unit gets larger. In a unit of twenty or thirty families, the current size of the Chinese production team, families can supervise each other and penalize laggards. But in a unit of several thousand families, the size of the Chinese commune in the late 1950s, family members will have little incentive to pressure laggards to work harder because no single individual's work, however poorly done, will have much impact on the value of a neighbor's work points. If everyone in the collective thinks this way, of course, the output of the collective will fall.

From an incentive and management point of view, therefore, the family farm with an absence of tenancy would seem to be the ideal system. The analysis so far, however, has left out one very important consideration— economies of scale. In agriculture economies of scale may exist because certain kinds of machinery can be used efficiently only on large farms. On small farms tractors or combines may be badly underutilized. Such considerations help explain why many Latin Americans feel that large-scale farming is the most appropriate way to increase agricultural production and exports. Economies of scale may also exist because large collective units are better at mobilizing labor for rural construction activities than are individual family farms. We shall return to the question of scale economies later. Here all we can conclude is that the question of the most suitable types of rural land tenure system from a production point of view has not been completely resolved.

Land Reform

The reform of land tenure systems can assume many different forms. Typical measures found in many reforms, starting with the least radical, include:[3]

Reform of rent contracts ensures the tenure of a tenant farmer. Many tenants farm at the will of the landlord and can be easily removed at the end of a season. Laws requiring long-term contracts that restrict the landlord's right to remove a tenant can have a strong positive impact on the tenant's willingness to maintain and invest in the land, and will also introduce a degree of stability into the family's life.

Rent reduction typically involves a ceiling on the percentage share of the crop that a landlord can demand as rent. If the percentage share is substantially below what prevailed in the past, the impact both on tenant welfare and the tenant family's surplus available for investment can be substantial.

3. There are numerous studies of land reform. One of the best known practitioners was Wolf Ladejinsky (see Louis J. Walinsky [ed.], *Agrarian Reform as Unfinished Business: The Selected Papers of Wolf Ladejinsky* [London: Oxford University Press, 1977]).

Land to the tiller (the former tenant) *with compensation* to the landlord for loss of his land is a measure that can take on many different forms. A government can pass a law setting a ceiling on the number of acres that an individual can own, forcing that individual to sell all land over that limit. Or the reform law can state that only those who actually till the land can own it, and all other land must be sold. A key issue in this kind of reform is whether the former landlord receives full or only partial compensation for the land he has been forced to sell.

Land to the tiller without compensation involves the most radical transformation of rural relations, except for the further step of collectivization. All land not cultivated by its owner is confiscated and the former landlord receives nothing in return. Frequently in such reform the landlord may lose his life as well as his land.

While there is great diversity in the kinds of land reform that have been tried around the world, most reforms have certain features in common.

The Politics of Land Reform

The main motive for undertaking land reform is usually political, not economic.[4] The politics that leads to reform is of two types. A society with a large tenant and landless laborer population, but controlled by other classes, may find itself faced with increasing rural unrest. To keep this unrest from blowing up into a revolution, land reform bills are passed to reduce the burden on the peasantry and to give the peasantry a stake in continued stability. In the second type, land reform takes place after a revolution supported by the rural poor has already occurred. The main purpose of reform in this second case is to consolidate support for the revolution among the rural poor and to eliminate the economic base of one of the classes, the landlords, that was most opposed to the revolution.

The motive behind the Mexican land reforms of the twentieth century, for example, has been largely of the first type. Prior to the Mexican Revolution of 1911 land in Mexico had become increasingly concentrated in large haciendas ranging in size from 1000 to over 400,000 acres. While the revolution of 1911 was supported by those who had lost their land and other rural poor, those who ended up in power after the revolution were largely from upper income groups or the small middle class. This new leadership, however, had to deal with the continuing rural unrest that was often ably led by men such as Zapata. To meet the challenge of Zapata and people like him the Mexican government has periodically redistributed some arable land—most recently under the government of President Echeverría in the 1970s. Mexican land tenure relations, however, continue to be characterized by large estates existing alongside small peasant holders. Reform eliminated some of the more extreme forms of pressure for more radical change, but Mexican agriculture still includes within it a large, poor, and not very productive rural peasant class.

4. Elias Tuma, *Twenty-Six Centuries of Agrarian Reform: A Comparative Analysis* (Berkeley: University of California Press, 1965).

The Chinese land reform of the 1940s and early 1950s under the leadership of the Communist party was a reform par excellence of the second type. The Communist revolution had been built primarily on the rural poor, and the landlord class was one of the main pillars of support of the existing Kuomintang government. Prior to the reform some 40 percent of the arable land had been farmed by tenants who typically paid half of their main crop to the landlord as rent. The landlord, whether resident in the village or absentee, contributed little or nothing other than his land. After the reform (and prior to collectivization of agriculture in 1955–1956) land was owned by the tiller and the landlord received no compensation whatsoever. In fact many landlords were tried publicly in the villages and either executed or sent off to perform hard labor under harsh conditions.[5]

The Japanese land reform that followed World War II was different in important respects from the Chinese experience. Land reform in Japan was carried out by the American Occupation forces. The Occupation government believed that the landlord class had been an important supporter of the forces in Japanese society that had brought about World War II. Small peasant proprietors, in contrast, were seen as a solid basis on which to build a future democratic and stable Japan. Since the Americans had won the war, Japanese landlords were not in a position to offer resistance to reform, and a thoroughgoing reform was carried out. Compensation of landlords was provided for in the legislation, but inflation soon had the effect of reducing sharply the real value of the amounts offered in compensation. As a result Japanese land reform also amounted to confiscation of landlord land without (much) compensation.[6]

A second feature of land reform efforts is that land reform legislation is extremely difficult to enforce in the absence of a deep commitment on the part of the government to reform. Most developing countries have some kind of land reform legislation on the books, but relatively few have experienced real reform. In some cases no serious effort is made to enforce the legislation. In other cases the legislation is enforced but has little effect because of legal loopholes.

India provides examples of both kinds of problems. In the Indian state of Bihar the government has awarded substantial tracts of land to the *harijan* (former untouchable) caste. But Bihar is a state where much of the real power rests in the hands of so-called higher castes which include many landlords, and these "higher castes" have forcibly prevented the *harijans* from taking over the land the government awarded to them.

Elsewhere in India a law limiting the amount of land that can be owned by a single person has been enforced, but has had limited real effect. An individual with more land than allowed by law registers the extra land in the

5. Among the many studies on Chinese land reform are John Wong, *Land Reform in the People's Republic of China* (New York: Praeger, 1973); and William Hinton, *Fanshen* (New York: Vintage Books, 1966).
6. There are many studies of Japanese land reform, including R. P. Dore, *Land Reform in Japan* (London: Oxford University Press, 1959).

name of trusted relatives or associates. For truly enormous landholdings subterfuges of this kind may be impossible, but most landlords in India possess only several tens or a few hundreds of acres of land.

Land Reform and Productivity

The impact of land reform on agricultural productivity depends on what kind of system is being reformed as well as the content of the reform measures themselves. Land reform has the greatest positive impact on productivity where the previous system was one of small peasant farms, with high rates of insecure tenancy (for example, one-year contracts) and absentee landlords. Under such conditions reform has little impact on cultivation practices since farms are small both before and after reform. Elimination of landlords also has little effect on productivity because landlords have nothing to do with farming in the first place. On the other hand turning tenants into owners provides them with a greater incentive to invest in improvements. The Chinese, Japanese, and South Korean land reforms of the 1940s and 1950s were all essentially of this kind.

At the other extreme are reforms that break up large, highly efficient modern estates or farms and substitute small, inefficient producers. In many parts of the developing world, from Mexico to Kenya and Malaysia, large, highly mechanized estates using the most advanced techniques have grown up over time. The incentive problems inherent in the use of hired farm labor are at least partially overcome by the use of skilled professional estate managers. Often these estates are major suppliers of agricultural produce for export, and hence a crucial source of the developing country's foreign exchange. If land reform breaks up these estates and turns them over to small peasant proprietors who know little about modern techniques and lack the capital to pay for them in any case, the impact on agricultural productivity can be catastrophic. There are also examples, as in the Kenya highlands, where the breakup of large estates into small peasant holdings actually increased productivity, mainly because the small holdings are farmed much more intensively than the large estates.

In between these two extremes are a myriad of variations with different impacts on productivity, both positive and negative.

Land Reform and Income Distribution

Land reform will have a major impact on the distribution of income in rural areas only if land is taken from landlords without compensation, or at least without anything close to full compensation. If former tenants are required to pay landlords the full market value of the land received, the society's distribution of wealth will be the same as before. The tenant will receive land together with a debt exactly equal to the value of the land, and hence the change in net wealth of the former tenants will be zero. The former landlord will surrender land but will acquire an asset of equal value in the form of a loan to the former tenant. Reform with full compensation may still be desirable on productivity grounds because of the advantages of owner rather than tenant cultivation, but initially at last the new owner will be just as poor and the new landlord just as rich as before.[7]

The best known successful land reforms have commonly involved little or no compensation for confiscated assets of landlords. Such was the case not only in Russia after 1917 and China after 1949, but was also true of the Japanese and South Korean reforms after World War II.

This discussion of land tenure relations and their reform sets the scene for the discussion of agricultural production and how it can be raised. Much of the analysis that follows will deal with subjects like agricultural research or the uses of chemical fertilizer. But it must always be kept in mind that behind the use of better techniques and more inputs there must be a land tenure system that provides farmers with the incentive to introduce those techniques and inputs, and then use them efficiently.

Technology of Agricultural Production

The popular view of traditional agricultural systems is that they are made up of peasants who have been farming the same way for centuries. The implication is that traditional farmers are bound by custom and incapable of making changes that raise the productivity and efficiency of their efforts. Custom in turn is reinforced by values and beliefs often closely tied to religion. Change thus becomes doubly difficult because to make a change may involve rejection of deeply held religious beliefs. In this view only a revolution that completely overturns the traditional society and all it stood for holds out real hope for agricultural development.

Traditional Agriculture

No doubt tradition-bound societies of this sort do exist in the world, but the description does not fit the great majority of the world's peasant farmers. A great accumulation of evidence suggests that these farmers are efficient, that they have already made sensible—and sometimes complex and subtle—adaptations to their environment, and that they are willing to make further changes that increase their welfare if it is really clear that an improvement will result without an unacceptable increase in the risk of crop failure and hence starvation.[8]

When traditional agriculture is described as "efficient," the word is used in the same way as it has been used throughout this book. Given existing technology, traditional farmers get the most output they can from available inputs or get a given level of output with the smallest possible use of

---

7. If the landlord is compensated with bonds paid for out of general tax revenues, the income share of the former tenant may rise provided that the taxes to pay for this do not fall primarily on the former tenant.

8. One of the clearest statements of this point has been made by Theodore W. Schultz, *Transforming Traditional Agriculture* (New Haven: Yale University Press, 1964). A classic field study making the same point, based on the author's work in Guatemala, is Sol Tax, *Penny Capitalism* (Chicago: University of Chicago Press, 1963).

inputs. Foreign advisors, whether highly paid technicians or Peace Corps volunteers, have often had to relearn this fact, sometimes at considerable cost. With a little reflection it is hardly surprising that traditional agriculture tends to be efficient within the limits of traditional techniques. The central characteristic of traditional technology is that it changes very slowly. Farmers thus are not in a position of having constantly to respond to changing agricultural methods; they instead can experiment over long periods of time with alternative techniques until just the right method for the given technology is found. Long periods of time in this context may refer to decades or even to centuries. If a slightly deeper method of plowing or a closer planting of seeds will raise yields per acre, for example, one or two more venturesome farmers are eventually going to give such methods a try. At least they will do so if they have plows capable of deeper cultivation. If the techniques work, their neighbors will observe and eventually follow suit. Given several decades or a century all farmers in the region will be using similar methods.

This example brings out a closely related characteristic of traditional agriculture. In addition to being efficient, traditional agricultural techniques have not been stagnant; they have evolved slowly over time. That peasant farmers in a traditional setting are willing to change if benefits from a change are clearly perceived has been demonstrated over and over again. Some of the best evidence in support of this willingness to change is that provided by peasant farmer responses to changes in prices. Time and again as prices of cotton or tobacco or jute have risen, farmers even in some of the poorest nations in the world have rushed to increase the acreage planted to these crops. And the reverse has occurred when prices have fallen.

Change in traditional agriculture has involved much more than responses to fluctuations in relative prices. Through history there have been fundamental advances in all aspects of agricultural technology long before the advent of modern science and its application to farming.

Slash and Burn Cultivation

One of the most fundamental changes, of course, was the conversion of society from groups of hunters and gatherers of wild plants to groups of settled farmers who cleared and plowed the land. Initially settled farming often involved slash and burn methods of cultivation. Slash and burn agriculture refers to a technique where slashing of trees and fire are used to clear the land. Stumps of the burnt trees are left in the ground, and cultivation of the land seldom involves much more than use of a digging stick to poke holes in the earth into which to put the seeds. The original nutrients in the soil plus the nutrients from the ashes make respectable yields possible for a year or two, after which most of the nutrients are used up, weed problems increase and yields fall off drastically. Farmers then move on to slash and burn a new area, perhaps returning to the first area twenty or thirty years later when the land has regained a sufficient level of plant nutrients. Slash and burn agriculture is thus often referred to as a form of *shifting cultivation* or *forest-fallow cultivation.* Under this system it takes a large amount of land to support a small number of people. Today the system exists mainly in remote, lightly populated areas, such as in the mountains of Laos or in parts of Africa and the Amazon.

The Shortening of Fallow

The evolution from slash and burn agriculture to permanent cultivation, where a crop is grown on a piece of land at least once every year, can be thought of as a process of gradual shortening of the period that land is left fallow. The term *fallow* refers to the time that land is left idle to give the soil time to reaccumulate the nutrients essential to successful cultivation. In Europe the shortening of fallow took place gradually during and after the Middle Ages, and annual cropping did not become common until the latter part of the eighteenth century. In China the evolution to annual cropping occurred at least a thousand years earlier. In both Europe and China the driving force behind this evolution was increased population pressure on the land.[9]

The elimination of fallow did not occur automatically or easily. Farmers had to discover ways of restoring nutrients to the soil by rotating crops and by adding fertilizers such as compost and manure. Plows had to be developed that cultivate the land each year and prevent it from being taken over by grasses. Each of these changes was at least as fundamental as many that have occurred in agriculture in the twentieth century. The difference is that these earlier changes took place over centuries rather than years.

Farming Within a Fixed Technology

Once fallow had been eliminated, increases in agricultural production could be obtained either by increasing yields on annually cropped land or by expanding onto previously uncultivated land. Where population pressure was particularly severe, grain yields several centuries ago reached levels per hectare higher than those found in many parts of the world even today. In China, for example, two crops a year of rice or of rice and wheat were common by the sixteenth century or before. In both China and Japan by the mid-nineteenth century average rice paddy yields over large areas had passed 2.5 to 3 tons per hectare, while in India and Thailand as late as the 1960s average rice yields were under 1.5 tons per hectare. The main point of citing these figures is to demonstrate that traditional agriculture was capable of achieving high levels of productivity per unit of land.

What separates traditional from modern agricultural development, therefore, is not the existence of technological progress or the sophistication of the techniques used. Traditional agriculture experienced substantial techno-

9. Ester Boserup, *The Conditions of Agricultural Growth: The Economics of Agrarian Change and Population Pressure* (Chicago: Aldine, 1965); and Dwight H. Perkins, *Agricultural Development in China, 1368–1968* (Chicago: Aldine, 1969).

logical progress, and the techniques used in highly populated areas at least were as sophisticated as many so-called modern techniques found today. The difference between traditional and modern agriculture is in the pace of change and in its source. In traditional agriculture change is slow, while in modern agriculture it is rapid. And in modern agriculture it is scientific research that produces most of the new techniques used, while in traditional agriculture new techniques were sometimes the result of the tinkering of individual farmers. At other times new inputs such as improved seeds were accidents of nature that led to a variety that produced higher yields or required a shorter growing season.

The principal problem of traditional agriculture therefore was that farmers worked most of their lives within a fixed technology. They could spend their energies raising the efficiency with which they used that technology, but the gains from higher levels of efficient use of a slowly changing technique were limited. The improvements in technique that did occur happened over too long an interval of time for the improvements to have anything but a marginal impact on rural standards of living.

Modernizing Agricultural Technology

There are two levels at which one can discuss the ways in which traditional agriculture can be modernized. The first level is technological, explaining how specific inputs and techniques can be combined to produce higher agricultural production. This level deals with such issues as the role of chemical fertilizer and the relationship of fertilizer's impact to the availability of improved plant varieties and adequate supplies of water. These technological issues are the subject of this and the next section. The second level deals with how these inputs and techniques are mobilized in developing countries. How, for example, does a nation mobilize labor for rural public works or create institutes that will develop new techniques, suitable to local conditions? These issues of mobilization and organization are the subject of the following part of this chapter.

There is no such thing as a universally best technology for agriculture. All agricultural techniques must be adjusted to local soil and climatic conditions and to local factor endowments. Even in industry technology must be adapted to local conditions, but an automobile assembly plant in Ghana will look much like one of similar size in Indonesia. In agriculture local conditions are fundamental, not secondary. Students from a developing country can be sent to advanced nations to learn how to develop improved plant varieties suitable to their developing country, but only occasionally will the plant varieties in the advanced country be themselves directly transferable.

Still there are several characteristics of modern agricultural technology about which generalizations can be made. First, the technological development which occurs will differ markedly depending on whether a nation has a large area of arable land and a small declining rural population or whether a nation has a large rural population on a very limited amount of land. The problem for the former country is to get the most output possible out of its limited rural labor force. The latter nation must also raise labor productivity, but the key to success depends on also achieving rapid increases in the productivity of the land.[10] The fundamental difference between these two strategies can be illustrated with a simple diagram, Fig. 18–1. As the figure makes clear, the United States and Japan have pursued fundamentally different agricultural strategies, and most other nations fall somewhere in between. In the United States labor productivity is extremely high but yields per hectare are well below those of many nations, including more than a few in the less developed category. In Japan, in contrast, labor productivity in agriculture is only a fraction of that in the U.S. but land productivity is several times that of the U.S.

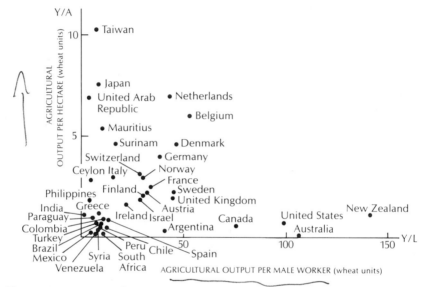

Fig. 18–1 International Comparison of Agricultural Output per Male Worker and per Hectare of Agricultural Land. Output data are 1957–1962 averages; and labor and land data are of year closest to 1960.

Source: Yujiro Hayami and Vernon W. Ruttan, *Agricultural Development: An International Perspective* (Baltimore: Johns Hopkins University Press, 1971), p. 71.

The difference between the two strategies involves basically different technologies. These different technologies are often called the mechanical package (of technologies) and the biological package. The *mechanical package* refers to the use of tractors, combines, and other forms of machinery primarily as substitutes for labor that has left the farm for the cities. The *biological package* refers to the raising of yields through the use of improved plant varieties such as hybrid corn or the new varieties of rice developed at

---

10. The point is that innovation is induced by perceived needs. See Hans P. Binswanger and Vernon W. Ruttan, *Induced Innovation: Technology, Institutions and Development* (Baltimore: Johns Hopkins University Press, 1977).

the International Rice Research Institute in the Philippines. Because of the dramatic effect on yields of some of these new varieties, the phenomenon is often referred to as the **Green Revolution.** These new varieties raise yields only if combined with adequate and timely supplies of water and increased amounts of chemical fertilizer. The basic production functions that describe these two packages therefore are fundamentally different. The isoquants of a production function representing the mechanical package indicate a high degree of substitutability (Fig. 18–2), while the isoquants for the biological package are drawn in a way to indicate a degree of complementarity (Fig. 18–3). The L-shaped isoquants in Fig. 18–3 indicate complementarity because only a limited number of fertilizer and seed combinations will produce increases in grain output. Continual increases of only one input such as fertilizer will run into diminishing returns and then, where the curve flattens out, zero returns. Even with the biological package there is some substitutability but less than in the case of the mechanical package.

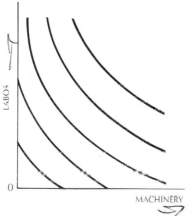

Fig. 18–2 The Mechanical Package Production Function.

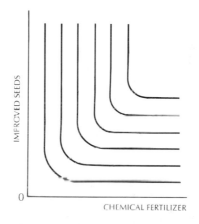

Fig. 18–3 The Biological Package Production Function.

To someone familiar with the cornfields of Iowa or the wheatfields of Nebraska and the Dakotas, mechanization means the use of large John Deere tractors and combines, metal silos with mechanical loading devices, and numerous other pieces of expensive equipment. With such equipment a single farmer with one assistant can farm hundreds of acres of land. But mechanization also can occur profitably on farms of only a few acres. As labor becomes more abundant and land less so the mechanical package becomes less important in relation to the biological package, but mechanization has a role to play even in poor labor-intensive agricultural systems.

Mechanization of agriculture in labor-abundant developing nations is primarily a substitute for labor, just as in the labor-short American Midwest. Even in nations such as China or India there are periods when the demand for labor exceeds its supply. When two crops of rice are grown each year, for example, the first crop must be harvested, fields prepared, and the second crop transplanted, all within a matter of a few weeks. Transport of the harvest to market also takes an enormous amount of labor if goods must be brought in on carts hauled by men or animals, or head loads by women, as is still the case in much of the developing world. One driver with a truck can do in a day what might otherwise take dozens of men and women several days to do. Nor can humans or animals working a hand pump or a waterwheel move much water to the fields, however hard they work. A small diesel pump can move more water to higher levels than a large number of oxen turning wheels, and oxen cost more to feed than the pump costs to fuel.

Even when labor is extremely inexpensive, therefore, it can be economical to substitute machines for labor in some operations. Over the years manufacturers in Japan and elsewhere have developed whole lines of miniaturized machinery such as hand tractors and rice transplanters to meet this need, and these machines are in widespread use in the developing world. Not all mechanization in the developing world has been economical, however. Frequently tractors and other forms of farm machinery are allowed to enter a country duty free (when other imports have high tariffs) or are subsidized in other ways. Large farmers thus sometimes find it privately profitable to buy tractors and get rid of hired labor where, in the absence of subsidies, they (and the country) would be better off economically using laborers instead. Another common motive for mechanization is land reform. There too the private and social calculation of costs and benefits differ because much land reform legislation sometimes allows a landowner to retain all land he actually farms himself. One way to farm more land oneself is to mechanize.

The Biological Package and the Green Revolution

The main impact of the biological package, as already indicated, is to raise yields. There is nothing really new about the use of improved plant varieties in combination with fertilizer and pesticides to raise yields of rice or corn. The use of modern scientific laboratories to develop the new varieties dates back a half century and more. Only in the 1960s and 1970s, however, can one speak of a worldwide effort to apply the methods found to be so successful in the industrialized countries to the developing nations. The founding of the International Maize and Wheat Improvement Center (CIMMYT)[11] in Mexico and the International Rice Research Institute (IRRI) in the Philippines marked the beginning of a truly international effort to develop high-yielding varieties of grain suitable to the tropical conditions found in so much of the developing world. National efforts preceded these international centers, and other international centers devoted to the problems of arid and semi-arid developing areas have followed. The result has been a steady stream of new, high-yielding varieties of wheat and rice that have found increasing acceptance in Asia (see Table

11. The acronym refers to the name in Spanish, Centro Internacional de Mejoramiento de Maiz y Trijo.

18–2) and Latin America and to a lesser degree in Africa. This dramatic change in biological technology is commonly referred to as the Green Revolution.

Accompanying the increased use of high-yielding and other improved varieties has been a rapid increase in the use of chemical fertilizers in the developing world (see Table 18–3). Prior to World War II modern chemical fertilizers were virtually unknown in the less developed nations of the world. By the 1970s they were in widespread use from Brazil to India. Unlike machinery, chemical fertilizer could be purchased in amounts of almost any size, and even very small amounts helped yields. Thus chemical fertilizers were within reach of even quite poor peasants. The principal limitations on the spread of chemical fertilizer use have not been the conservatism of the peasants or their poverty, but the availability of supplies and the price at which these supplies have been sold. We shall return to the price question later on in this chapter.

The third key component of the biological package is water. Improved plant varieties using more chemical fertilizer lead to dramaticaly higher yields only when there is an adequate and timely supply of water. In much of the American Midwest rainfall provides all the water required and at the right time. In many parts of the developing world rainfall is often inadequate or comes at the wrong time. In much of India the difference between

TABLE 18–2 Estimated Area Planted to High-Yielding Varieties of Wheat and Rice in Asia (in thousands of hectares)

Year	Wheat	Rice	Total
1965/66	9	49	59
1967/68	3,914	2,652	6,566
1969/70	7,771	7,558	15,329
1971/72	11,275	12,349	23,624
1973/74	14,620	18,755	33,375
1975/76	17,810	21,957	39,667

Source: Dana G. Dalrymple, *Development and Spread of High-Yielding Varieties of Wheat and Rice in the Less Developed Nations,* U.S. Department of Agriculture, Foreign Agricultural Economic Report No. 95, 1976, p. 116

TABLE 18–3 Consumption of Chemical Fertilizer in Less Developed Countries (in 1000 metric tons of nutrient)

Year	Latin America	Far East	Near East	Africa
1948/49–52/53 (annual average)	116.5	617.2	93.8	32.5
1961/62–65/66 (annual average)	609.7	1839.3	379.3	192.2
1966/67	877.5	1605.5	470.0	274.7
1969/70	1171.7	3546.3	693.9	398.5
1976/77	5410.3	6358.9	2389.0	1073.0
1979/80	6769.6	9570.5	2996.2	1210.6

Source: Food and Agricultural Organization of the United Nations, *Production Yearbook, 1970* and *Fertilizer Yearbook, 1980* (Rome: FAO, 1981), pp. 33–37. The Far East excludes Asian centrally planned economies.

a good crop and a harvest failure still depends primarily on when the monsoon rains arrive and in what amount. As a result, efforts to raise yields in the developing world have often focused on measures to extend irrigation of land so that crops are not so dependent on the vagaries of rainfall.

Extending the irrigated acreage has often been seen as primarily a financial and an engineering problem. If a nation had enough money (from aid or its own resources), it hired a group of engineers to build a dam to create a reservoir and canals to take water to the fields. As one dam project after another was completed, however, it became increasingly apparent that the irrigation potential of these systems was being badly underutilized. Engineers could build the dams and the main canals, but they could not always get the farmer to build and maintain the feeder canals to the fields. Who should do the work, and who would reap the benefits of these canals, became entangled in the conflicting interests and local politics of rural society. Irrigation extension was as much a social as an engineering and ecological question.

More than anything else it has been the increased use of inputs from this biological package that has made possible the steady, if unspectacular, expansion of agricultural output that has kept the supply of food up with or even a little bit ahead of the rise in population (see Table 18–4). Further development of improved varieties and expansion of irrigation systems, together with future rises in chemical fertilizer production, will continue to be the main path to higher yields in the future. The main function of the mechanical package, in contrast, will remain one of freeing labor from the burden of producing food so that labor can do other, hopefully more productive, things. Whether those other tasks will in fact be more productive depends on what is happening in the rest of the economy.

Mobilization of Agricultural Inputs

While the technology of increasing agricultural output is well understood except in such marginal areas as the Sahel and the Amazon, the ways in

TABLE 18–4   Food Production Per Capita in Developing Countries
(Indices, 1969–71 = 100)

Year	All developing countries[a]	Latin America	Far East[b]	Near East	Africa
1955	91	95	90	92	98
1960	95	95	95	98	102
1965	95	99	93	100	99
1970	101	102	102	99	100
1975	104	102	104	106	94
1980	108	108	105	104	89

Source: FAO, Production Yearbook (Rome, 1971, 1980, 1981).

[a] For 1955–1965 the figures are for all nations in Latin America, the Far and Near East (excluding China), and Africa.

[b] The Far East in this table does not include Asian centrally planned economies.

which the relevant inputs can be mobilized are both complex and much less well understood. Some of these problems have already been touched on, both in the discussion of difficulties in expanding irrigation and in the earlier presentation of the relationship between land tenure systems, individual incentives, and management difficulties. Here we shall discuss some of these issues further in the context of the agricultural production function. In brief the question is: What are the alternative ways a rural society can supply itself with the necessary amounts of labor, capital, and improved techniques?

Mobilizing labor to raise crops and livestock is primarily a question of individual and family incentives. The main determinant of these incentives is the land tenure system; and the way in which land tenure systems affect incentives, and hence the amount of labor supplied, has already been discussed. Mobilization of labor to create roads, irrigation systems, and other parts of the rural infrastructure, however, has not yet been touched on.

Rural Public Works Projects

Creation of a rural infrastructure (an expanding capital stock) through the mobilization of rural labor has long been the dream of economic planners in the developing world. The idea is a simple one. Labor in the off-season in the rural sectors of developing nations is unemployed or underemployed. Therefore the opportunity cost of using that labor on rural public works projects is zero or near zero (although food consumption may go up for people doing heavy construction work).

To use this labor in factories the factories must first be built, and that requires use of scarce capital equipment. Furthermore this equipment will lie idle when the rural workers return to the fields to plant and harvest their crops. No such problems exist, however, when off-season unemployed labor is used to build roads or irrigation canals. There is no need to buy bulldozers and other heavy equipment. If there is enough labor, shovels and baskets to carry dirt can accomplish much the same purpose, and farmers already have shovels and baskets or can easily make them. In the ideal situation, therefore, unemployed workers can first be put to work making crude construction tools, after which they can begin to create roads and canals. The end result is a major expansion in the rural capital stock at little or no cost to society other than the reduced leisure time of rural workers.

Attempts to apply this idea have been numerous and varied. The self-help ideas of community development programs in India and elsewhere were based in large part on a belief in the efficacy of mobilizing unemployed rural labor. Aid agencies have supported numerous public works projects based on similar principles. And perhaps most dramatic of all, the main economic justification for the Rural People's Commune of China was its capacity to mobilize labor for rural capital construction.

Effective implementation of rural public works programs using seasonally unemployed labor, however, has proved to be extremely difficult. The community development programs of India and elsewhere are widely perceived as failures. Time and again international aid agencies have started pilot public works projects, only to see the projects die quietly when aid money ran out. Of all the problems connected with the mobilization of unemployed rural labor, the most basic has been the lack of connection between those who did the work and those who reaped most of the benefits.

When an irrigation canal or a road is built, the main benefits that result take the form of higher yields on land near the canal or easier access to the market for crops grown on land near the road. Land distant from the canal or road receives fewer benefits or none at all. It follows that the people who benefit the most from a rural works project are those who own the nearby land. If these beneficiaries are also the people who did the work constructing the road or canal, then there is a direct relation between effort and reward. Unfortunately more often than not the people who do the work reap few of the rewards. The extreme case is where the land serviced by the new canal or road is owned by absentee landlords. Absentee landlords are never mobilized for rural public works projects. It is landless laborers and tenants who do all the work, while the landlords get the benefits in the form of increased rents. Workers on such projects must be paid wages, and these wages tend to be higher than what is justified by the productivity of the workers. Rural construction with crude tools is, after all, very low productivity work. If the wages paid exceed the benefits of the project, it is hardly surprising that such projects come to an end when government or aid agency subsidies run out.

Labor Mobilization in Chinese Communes   Even when land is owned by those who cultivate it there is a problem of matching effort and reward. A typical project may require the labor of an entire village or several villages, while the benefits go primarily to farmers in only one part of the village. The Chinese solution to this problem was to collectivize agriculture by forming People's Communes.[12] An entire village owned its land in common. People who participated in public works projects received work points based on the amount of effort expended just as if they had spent their time cultivating crops. When the project was completed the land in a part of the village would be more productive, but the higher productivity went not to a few individuals but to the entire village. The gap between work and reward in effect had been closed.

The Chinese commune did make possible the more or less voluntary mobilization of large amounts of underemployed rural labor. Hills were leveled to create new fields, new reservoirs dotted the countryside, and roads reached deep into the countryside where only footpaths had existed before. But the Chinese ran into the work-reward problem in a different form. As the rural works projects became larger and larger, it

12. In the beginning (1955–1957) the Chinese called their rural collectives producers' cooperatives, but to simplify the discussion we refer to them as communes.

became necessary to mobilize labor from two dozen villages, even though the benefits of the project went largely to only one or two of those villages.

The initial solution to this problem was to pool the land of all two dozen into a single commune. Then increased productivity on the land around a single village would be shared by all twenty-four villages, and workers in those villages once again had an incentive to participate in the project. This larger commune, made up of two dozen villages, however, ran immediately into all the incentive and managerial problems common to large collective units that were discussed in the section on land tenure above. The result was that despite all of the construction activity, or even because of it, Chinese agricultural output fell; and small collective units called production teams replaced the large commune as the basic agricultural management unit, although the latter continued to exist and to perform some functions.

Clearly the problem of mobilizing unemployed labor to build rural infrastructures is more difficult than economists and others first thought.[13] The problem of separation of work and reward is intimately connected to the nature of the land tenure system. Even radical changes in the nature of land tenure can alter the form taken by the work-reward problem, but they do not eliminate the problem. It is not that rural works projects using unemployed labor cannot be done. Some projects are so productive that private landowners will be willling to pay the going rural wage to get them completed. For some projects, other ways can be worked out to share the benefits equitably among those who do the work. In principle farmers could be taxed locally to pay for local projects, but that solution runs into all the problems of administering a tax system in a poor rural area. Thus the complexity of successfully sharing the benefits is such that rural public works are not the universal solution to the problem of rural development that some economists and others once thought them to be.

Rural Banks and Credit Cooperatives

A second approach to the problem of providing rural areas with sufficient capital for development is to establish rural banks or credit cooperatives that will lend to farmers. In traditional agriculture a farmer has only two sources of credit, one from members of his family, the other from the local moneylender. Since the rates of interest charged by moneylenders typically range from 30 or 40 percent to over 100 percent a year, a farmer goes to a moneylender only when desperate. Peasants do not borrow from moneylenders in order to buy more fertilizer or a new pump. Only rarely

13. For a discussion of these problems in a number of developing economies, see S. J. Burki, D. G. Davies, R. H. Hook, and J. W. Thomas, "Public Works Programs in Developing Countries: A Comparative Analysis" (World Bank Staff Working Paper No. 224, February 1976).

will such investments be productive enough to make it possible to pay off loans with such high interest charges.

There are numerous reasons why urban commercial banks do not move in and take over from moneylenders. Such banks are located in urban areas and lack the knowledge and skills necessary to effective operations in rural areas. Local moneylenders know the reliability of the people to whom they are lending and the quality of land they are putting up as collateral. Individuals without land, of course, have difficulty getting money even from local moneylenders. Women in particular may have difficulty when they farm land registered in the name of an absent husband, a frequent occurrence in Africa and elsewhere.

Credit cooperatives set up by the small farmers themselves are one potential solution to these problems. The idea is that each farmer is capable of saving a small sum, and if these sums are pooled, one or two farmers can borrow a substantial sum to buy a new thresher or pump. The next year it will be some other farmer's turn, and so on. In the meantime those who put their money in the cooperative will draw interest, thus encouraging them to save more. The problem with this approach begins with the fact that farmer savings tend to be small, and hence the co-ops tend to be financially weak. More serious is the fact that farmers in developing nations have litle experience relevant to the effective operation and management of the co-op. In addition, economic, social, and political conflicts within the village may make it impossible to decide who will get the next loan.

Because of these and other problems the establishment of rural credit institutions usually requires significant injections of both money and personnel from outside the village, usually from the government. The entry of the government, however, does not necessarily or even usually solve the underlying difficulties. A common occurrence is for a rural credit institution to be set up with funds from the central government budget. These funds are then lent out to local farmers at rates far below those charged by private credit sources. Since the rates are low and the credit institutions are run by government personnel, local farmers with political clout have both the incentive and the means to grab the lion's share of the financing available. Corrupt bank officials may also skim off some of the funds, and corrupt officials, needless to say, are seldom among the poorer elements in the village. Equally or more serious is the fact that these loans often never get paid back, so that the new credit institution must be constantly resupplied from the central budget or, more likely, go out of business. Too frequently the government personnel running the local bank or cooperative lack the will or the authority to make their clients live up to their contracts.

As with the case of mobilizing rural labor, the problems involved in setting up effective rural credit operations can be overcome. Nations with well-trained banking personnel and a strong government administration capable of drawing up sensible procedures and enforcing them are certainly able to make rural credit institutions work. The problem is that well-trained personnel and effective government administration are in short supply in a great many developing nations.

Extension Services

If one key to rapid progress in rural areas depends on the introduction of new inputs and new techniques, it follows that some of the most important rural institutions are those responsible for speeding the transfer of these new techniques to the farmers. Extension services, as these institutions are usually called, provide the key link between the research laboratories or experimental farms and the rural population that must ultimately adopt what the laboratories develop.

For an extension service to be effective, information must be able to travel unimpeded and with reasonable speed from laboratory to farm. The key to the effective flow of information is the extension worker, and the key to the effectiveness of the extension worker is the presence of contact and trust. If the extension worker has little contact with the farmer, that worker is obviously not in a position to persuade the farmer to try a new technique. Rural education helps to increase the channels of contact, because if farmers can read, contact can be made through the written as well as the spoken word. Trust is necessary, because even if there is contact the farmer may not believe what is read or heard. Trust of course depends not only on the extension worker's honesty or personality but also—and fundamentally—on his competence. There is nothing like giving a farmer bad advice that leads to crop failure to close the channels of communication. Establishment of trust and even contact is further complicated by the fact that extension workers are usually men while those doing the farming, particularly in parts of Africa, are women.

These remarks are common sense, but they get at the heart of what is wrong with extension services in developing countries that are not working. Frequently training for the extension service is seen not as a way of learning about how to help farmers but as a way of entering the government bureaucracy and escaping from the rural areas. Some extension workers are government clerks living in town and just as adverse to getting their hands dirty as their colleagues in the tax collection bureau or the post office. Even when they do visit the farmers they are supposed to be helping, they know so little about how those farmers really operate that they are incapable of pointing out new methods that would be genuinely useful. Too often the extension worker visits the village, tells the farmers what is good for them, and departs, leaving the farmers to guess as best they can whether the gain from using the new idea is worth the risk of failure.

At the other end of the spectrum are extension workers who are well trained and who live in the villages and work closely with the farmers when new techniques are being introduced. Chinese communes, for example, will send one of their own members off for training on the condition that the individual come back to work for the commune. The same can happen in villages where family farms predominate, although the absence of the authoritarian controls found in China makes it more difficult in many places to guarantee that the individual sent will return. Another variation on this theme, tried by CIMMYT among others, is for the basic research to be carried out on farmers' fields rather than in separate experimental stations.

There is much that we do not yet know about the spread of advanced technology in agriculture, but an effective extension service is only a part of the picture. Farmers to a large degree learn from their neighbors. If one local farmer owns thirty acres which he farms with a large tractor and his neighbors farm only five acres without tractors, the smaller farmers may feel they have little to learn from the experience of their larger colleague. More evidence is required, but technology appears to travel more rapidly when neighboring farms in a country or region are much alike. Extremes of inequality thus may impede technological progress as well as being undesirable on equity grounds.

This discussion of mobilization of rural labor and capital and of accelerating the rate of technical advance could readily be extended. The main point, however, has been made. Agricultural development in the less developed countries is not solely a scientific or an engineering problem. Rural development programs are fundamentally affected by the land tenure system and other sources of inequality in the countryside. They also depend on the quality of government administration at both central and local levels and on the role and status of women. It is in fact difficult to find any aspect of rural society that does not have some bearing on the effectiveness of governmental and private efforts to raise agricultural output.[14]

Markets and Prices

The Development of Rural Markets

One common theme in preceding chapters has been the importance of avoiding major distortions in the structure of prices. Nowhere is an appropriate price structure more important than in the agricultural sector. But in agriculture as in other sectors there must first be markets before there can be prices. And in the rural areas of developing countries the existence of effectively operating markets cannot be taken for granted.

There are virtually no areas of the world today where subsistence farming in its purest form still exists. All farmers specialize to some degree and trade their surplus output on some kind of market. At the most primitive level that market may be little more than a place where local farmers agree to meet once or several times a week to barter their surplus produce. These *periodic markets,* as they are called, however, are today most often tied into an elaborate network that reaches up through market towns to the major cities of the nation. Goods pass up from the farms through this network to feed the cities, and the manufactures of the cities pass down through the same network to supply the farmers.

Economic development is usually accompanied by the increasing size and sophistication of this rural marketing network, and that improved network in turn has an important impact on productivity in agriculture. The key to an increasing role for the market is specialization, and specialization

14. A major study of these issues in the African context is by Uma Lele, *The Design of Rural Development: Lessons from Africa* (Baltimore: Johns Hopkins University Press, 1975).

in turn depends on the presence of economies of scale, of low-cost transport, and of an absence of excessive risk.

Economies of scale are at the heart of specialization. If everyone could produce everything needed at the lowest possible cost, there would be no need to turn over certain tasks to others. In fact economies of scale are pervasive; and in the most advanced agricultural sectors such as the American Midwest, farmers grow only one or two crops and rely on the market for all their other needs. In developing countries the single greatest barrier to taking advantage of these economies of scale is transport costs. The absence of good roads or of trucks to run on them can mean that it can cost as much to move a bulky commodity fifty miles as to produce it in the first place. In the United States wheat is turned into flour in large mills and farmers buy bread in the local supermarket like everyone else. In developing countries only wheat destined for urban consumption is processed in large mills. In rural areas wheat is processed at home or in village mills, because to take the wheat to a large distant mill would be prohibitively expensive. In large parts of southern Sudan, to take an extreme but not uncommon example, there are no all-weather roads at all and large regions are completely cut off from the outside world during the rainy season. Needless to say regions such as this cannot readily specialize in crops for sale in the cities or for export abroad.

In large parts of the developing world, therefore, improvements in the transport system and hence in marketing can have a major impact on agricultural productivity. Construction of an all-weather road system in Korea in the 1970s, for example, made it possible for millions of Korean farmers to increase dramatically their emphasis on vegetables and cash crops destined for urban and export markets. Even the simple device of building paved bicycle paths connecting to the main road made it possible for Hong Kong farmers to expand their vegetable acreage. In the absence of refrigerated transport many vegetables spoil quickly, and hence it does not pay to raise them if too much time elapses between the harvest and their sale on the market. Furthermore enormous amounts of labor must be used if the vegetables must be carried every day on human backs across muddy fields. Therefore, the ability to move the vegetables along a paved path on the back of a bicycle can make the difference between growing vegetables or concentrating on rice, which only has to be moved to market once a year (as contrasted to daily marketing in the case of many vegetables).

Even when the transport system is adequate, farmers in developing countries may limit their dependence on the market because of the risk involved in such dependence. While cash crops can fail due to bad weather or pests, the principal risk from market dependence is that the price of the crop being raised will fall sharply by the time the farmer is ready to sell. For large farmers in advanced economies a fall in price of their main crop leads to a reduction in their income. If the fall is large enough that farmer may be forced to borrow from a local bank to tide him over until prices rise again. Or he or she may merely have to draw down the family's savings account. In developing countries a fall in the price of a cash crop, particularly if simultaneously food prices are rising, may lead to a drop in a farm family's income to a level below that necessary to survive. Credit may tide the family over, but interest rates will be so high (50 percent a year and more) that once in debt the farmer may never be able to pay off creditors and will lose the land put up as collateral. Therefore most farmers in developing countries avoid the risk of becoming solely dependent on a single cash crop and instead devote part of their land to meeting their own family's food requirements. Their average income over the long run might be higher if they planted all their land to cotton or tobacco, but they might not live to see the long run if one or two years of depressed prices wiped them out.

Governments can take measures to reduce both transport costs (by building roads) and risks (by guaranteeing prices and other similar measures) and thereby develop more efficient markets. But governments also can and often do take measures that inhibit the development of rural marketing. Governments around the world have seldom had a real understanding of the role of rural traders, of the numerous middlemen who make a marketing system work. Middlemen are seen as exploiters who get between the producer and consumer, driving the price paid to the former down and that charged to the latter up, with the middlemen reaping huge monopoly profits. In response to political pressures from farmers, therefore, governments have often moved to take over the rural marketing system in order to improve its operation and eliminate the monopoly profits.[15] The temptation for governments to take this step is particularly strong where the middlemen are of a different race from the majority of the population, as is the case in much of Southeast Asia where Chinese play a major role in marketing, and East Africa where descendants of nineteenth- and early twentieth-century Indian immigrants now control wholesale and retail trade.

While occasionally government involvement improves rural marketing, more commonly such involvement is based on a wrong diagnosis of the problem. The price at which a farm product is sold in the cities is markedly higher than the price paid to the farmer, but the difference has little to do with monopoly profits. The real cause is the high cost of transport and a generally rudimentary system of distribution and marketing. It is not that rural traders get paid so much, it is just that it takes so many of them to get the goods to market. When the government takes over it does not change this basic situation. For a high-cost, private rural trading network the government often substitutes an even higher cost bureaucratic control of the movement of goods.

Agricultural Prices

Few governments in either industrialized or developing countries have been willing to let market forces set agricultural prices for reasons that go

---

15. The problems created by too much government interference in agricultural marketing in Africa are discussed in Elliot Berg et al., *Accelerated Development in Sub-Saharan Africa* (Washington, D.C.: World Bank, 1981).

far beyond the question of political attitudes toward middlemen. The prices at which grain and other agricultural produce is bought and sold play three, and sometimes four, vital roles:[16]

1. The prices paid to farmers, and the relation of those prices to prices farmers pay for key inputs such as fertilizer, have a major impact on what and how much that farmer can produce.

2. The prices paid to farmers, together with the quantity of produce sold, are the primary determinant of farmers' cash income.

3. The prices at which agricultural products are sold in the cities are major determinants of the cost of living of urban residents in developing countries.

4. Prices of agricultural products, particularly in many African countries, are often controlled by government marketing boards which manipulate those prices to earn profits for the government, a slightly disguised form of taxation.

Prices have a profound impact on agricultural production because most farmers, even in very poor countries, are interested in maximizing their income. While some hold that peasants grow particular crops or use particular inputs because that is the way their grandfathers did it, study after study has shown that when prices change, peasant farmers respond much like any profit-maximizing businessman operating in a world fraught with uncertainty.[17] If the price of cotton rises relative to, say, wheat, farmers will grow more cotton even in very traditional societies.

The most important price relationship from the standpoint of agricultural production is that between farm outputs and purchased inputs, notably chemical fertilizer. From the point of view of the farmer it makes sense to use more chemical fertilizer so long as the additional increments of fertilizer increase the value of farm output by more than the cost of fertilizer. (This is simply a manifestation of the profit-maximizing rule that the use of a factor of production should be increased as long as the factor's marginal revenue product exceeds its marginal cost.) One of the simplest and most effective ways of raising rice yields, therefore, is either to raise the price of rice or to lower the price of chemical fertilizer, or both. As recent studies of rice production in Asia have shown, there is a clear relationship between the rice yield per acre in a country and the rice-fertilizer price ratio.[18] Other elements of course are also at work, but the role of prices is one central influence.

One of the most persistent problems facing planners and politicians in the developing world is the conflict over appropriate agricultural prices be-

16. For a full discussion of the multiple role of prices, see C. Peter Timmer, "Food Prices and Food Policy Analysis in LDCs," *Food Policy* 5, no. 3 (August 1980): 188–207.

17. The literature on farmer price responsiveness is large. See, for example, Hussein Askari and John Cummings, *Agricultural Supply Response: A Survey of the Econometric Evidence* (New York: Praeger, 1976); and Raj Krishna, "Agricultural Price Policy and Economic Development," in H. M. Southworth and B. F. Johnston (eds.), *Agricultural Development and Economic Growth* (Ithaca, N.Y.: Cornell University Press, 1967).

18. Walter Falcon and C. Peter Timmer, "The Political Economy of Rice Production and Trade in Asia," in L. Reynolds (ed.), *Agriculture in Development Theory* (New Haven: Yale University Press, 1975).

tween urban consumers and rural producers. Since food purchases account for half and more of the budget of urban consumers in most developing nations, a substantial increase in the price of food will cut sharply into the income of all but the richest urban people. Even governments indifferent to the welfare of their poorer urban residents cannot ignore the political impact of major increases in food prices. From Japan in the 1920s to Egypt in the 1970s, food price rises have triggered massive rioting that has threatened the very existence of particular regimes. (This phenomenon is closely akin to—and often part of—the politically dangerous transition from controlled to liberalized economies discussed in Chapter 17.) Because political leaders themselves live in urban areas, and because urban residents are in a better position than rural villagers to threaten governments, many nations attempt to hold food prices down even during periods of general inflationary pressure. The result is depressed prices for farmers that reduce both farm income and farm output.

In some, especially but not exclusively, developed nations the political power of the farmers is such that governments raise farm purchase prices in order to gain rural support. Democracies that still have large or politically powerful rural populations are particularly likely to respond to these pressures. The United States and Japan in the 1950s and 1960s, the European Economic Community in the 1960s, and South Korea in the late 1960s and early 1970s are examples. The result is prices that are favorable to higher yields, but the income and production benefits of the higher prices may or may not be equitably distributed. In some countries it is the richer farmers who market a high percentage of their output and hence gain most from high prices. Small subsistence farms market little and hence gain little. In other nations, however, all farmers market a high percentage of their crop and hence all gain from higher prices.

Where both urban and rural residents have considerable political influence governments have sometimes tried to maintain both low urban food prices and high farm purchase prices. Japan since World War II and South Korea and Mexico in the 1970s have pursued this dual goal. Since the government must pick up the resulting deficit arising from selling food at prices below what it cost to purchase, only governments with large resources or ones willing to forgo other high-priority goals can afford this policy. Thus there is no single right answer to how high prices to farmers should be. Ultimately the decision turns on political as well as economic judgments.

FURTHER READING   General works on agricultural development include Bruce F. Johnston and Peter Kilby, *Agriculture and Structural Transformation* (London: Oxford University Press, 1975); John Mellor, *The Economics of Agricultural Development* (Ithaca, N.Y.: Cornell University Press, 1966); Erik Thorbecke (ed.), *The Role of Agriculture in Economic Development* (New York: Columbia University Press, 1969); and T. W. Schultz, *Transforming Traditional Agriculture* (New Haven: Yale University Press, 1964). A provocative analysis of the long-term relationship between agriculture and population growth can be found in Ester Boserup, *The Conditions of Agricultural Growth* (Chicago: Aldine, 1965). The relationship between technology and agricultural development is dealt with at length in Hans P. Binswanger and Vernon W. Ruttan, *Induced Innovation: Technology, Institutions and Development* (Baltimore: Johns Hopkins University Press, 1978). An analysis of the problems entailed in designing rural development programs is in Uma Lele, *The Design of Rural Development: Lessons from Africa* (Baltimore: Johns Hopkins University Press, 1975). The political nature of most land reforms is described in Elias H. Tuma, *Twenty-six Centuries of Agrarian Reform: A Comparative Analysis* (Berkeley: University of California, 1965). Many of the best books on agricultural development are country specific, but the list of these is too long to mention here. In addition, several major journals and special publications series are devoted to agricultural topics. Three worthy of special mention are *Food Policy,* published by the Food Research Institute of Stanford University, the papers of the International Food Policy Research Institute, and those of the Overseas Development Council.

Chapter 19

ENERGY AND OTHER NONRENEWABLE RESOURCES

Nature requires almost unimaginable spans of time to build up commercial accumulations of oil and mineral resources in forms usable by humankind. Consider, for example, the complete sequence of generation of oil and gas in sedimentary basins, such as the giant fields in Alaska's Prudhoe Bay or Indonesia's Minas field in Sumatra. This sequence involves geological processes lasting between 10 and 100 million years, and the processes are so intricate that if any one of six basic necessary ingredients is missing, sizable accumulations of oil and gas are impossible. For this reason when a commercial accumulation of oil and gas does occur, it can be considered a natural anomaly. Other geological processes have, over eons, resulted in the buildup of scattered concentrations of such hard minerals as nickel, iron, copper, and tungsten. Where, as is ordinarily the case, these minerals are found in minute concentrations, they are merely rock. In the infrequent instances where these accumulations are both sizable and sufficiently concentrated, they are called *ores.*

Through such processes nature has provided a stock of **natural capital** that, from the point of view of the short history of human existence relative to that of the planet, must be considered as nonrenewable. This does not mean that the available stock of natural resources is a quantity that remains fixed from decade to decade or century to century. Rather, higher prices or technological improvements that lower extraction costs can and do convert rock into ore, and marginal sedimentary basins into commercially attractive fields that oil companies may spend billions of dollars to bring into production. But for a zinc deposit once mined, or an oilfield once depleted, the resources extracted will not be renewed by nature in the next thousand millennia, if ever. This chapter discusses the special public policy problems and opportunities presented by largesse or paucity of nonrenewable natural resources.

Ownership of Natural Resources

Systems of property rights can and do have significant effects on the way a society uses resources, including nonrenewable resources. The United States is one of the few nations in the world in which property rights in minerals can be vested in private individuals, as in all states title to surface land generally conveys title to subsoil rights as well. A private property owner in Texas or Oklahoma is also the owner of all mineral rights below the surface (unless mineral rights have been specifically reserved by a previous owner) and may dispose of any oil and gas deposits as he or she sees fit. This does not mean, however, that rights to all mineral resources are privately held in the United States. The federal government is a major landowner itself, particularly in the western states. Indeed, federal lands are thought to contain 20 percent of the nation's oil, 30 percent of its natural gas, and 40 percent of its coal. Still, most of the present known reserves of natural resources in the United States remains in private hands and in lands owned by state governments.

The situation is materially different in the overwhelming majority of developing countries. There, subsoil rights are ordinarily separate from surface rights, and the former may not be vested in individuals or private business firms. Rather, natural resource deposits in most LDCs are defined, whether by constitutional or other legal means, as part of the national patrimony, wherein the state acts as either the trustee for, or the actual owner of, all natural resource endowments. Countries in which property rights in subsoil deposits are vested entirely in the state include Bolivia, Brazil, Chile, Indonesia, Malaysia, Peru, and Thailand. In some countries, such as Colombia, Ghana, and Pakistan, limited private or tribal ownership of resource rights is allowed in certain regions, but the central government nevertheless holds property rights to most oil and mineral resources, as well as tropical forest rights.

Among other differences, the pattern of property rights in minerals in most LDCs leads to much greater direct government involvement in natural resource development than is the case in the United States. For resource exploitation projects on privately owned land in the United States the federal government is relegated to an essentially passive role. Once the landowner and/or the mineral company has satisfied environmental requirements, the only federal stake in the project is in potential federal income tax revenues. In contrast, governments play a far more active role in resource development in LDCs, functioning not only as tax collector, but as seller (or lessor) of mining or drilling rights, gatekeeper for entry of foreign firms, and often as a business partner in resource projects with private domestic and foreign firms. Indeed in many countries governments have decided to exploit their natural resource endowments directly by creating large, government-owned mineral or oil enterprises (see Chapter 21).

The nature of property rights prevailing in natural resource endowments in most LDCs also helps to explain the position of many developing countries toward property rights to seabed mineral resources. Portions of the world's seabed contain nodules having very high concentrations of valuable minerals, such as nickel and manganese. Most of these sites are hundreds and even thousands of miles distant from the nearest continental shelf. Many developed countries, and particularly the United States, with its tradition of private property rights in minerals, have taken the position that these minerals "belong" to whoever goes to the trouble and expense of finding and lifting them. The LDCs have taken the position that seabed resources are the common property of all humankind and should be exploited only under the auspices of an "internationally owned" enterprise, with profits split between all nations of the world (though not necessarily equally). Inasmuch as the technology required to exploit these deposits is confined to a very few industrial countries, the LDCs have viewed the United States position with strong misgivings. But beyond that, most LDC representatives to the several "Law of the Sea" conferences hail from countries where private property rights in natural resources are not recognized. These countries have been unwilling to accept, on an international scale, a system of property rights at odds with that of their own countries.

Natural Resources and Growth

Mineral and energy resources in the ground are, contrary to views often expressed by oil ministers, of little value to a society.[1] Only upon extraction can natural capital then be converted into capital usable by humans. We have seen in Part III that for most nations capital accumulation involves a slow, and often painful, process involving austerity in domestic consumption and/or substantial inflows of foreign savings. Many countries, however, have been favored by geological anomalies that have left sizable endowments of natural capital in the form of nonrenewable resource deposits. Some, such as the United States, Canada, and Australia in the industrial West, Kuwait and Saudi Arabia in the Mideast, and Venezuela and Chile in Latin America, have found within their borders sufficient natural capital to enable them to short-cut the usually laborious and ordinarily lengthy processes of capital accumulation. This can be done by capturing the potential surpluses from natural resource endowments and utilizing them to diversify and otherwise strengthen the economy.

Many, but by no means all, countries with significant resource endowments do have something to show from decades of extraction of nonrenewable wealth left by nature, in the form of higher stocks of physical and

1. This statement applies in almost all real-world circumstances, except during those infrequent periods (e.g., 1973–1975 and 1978–1981) when the value of a known deposit (oil) appreciates at a rate faster than the interest rate.

human capital. Over at least the period 1970–1980 several oil-producing countries outside the large Mideast oil exporters managed to secure high income growth through resource exports. These include Ecuador, Indonesia, Malaysia, and Algeria, in all of which real GDP grew at a 6 percent annual rate or better. But in general, middle-income oil-exporting LDCs grew at a slightly *slower* rate (5.5 percent) than did middle-income oil-*importing* countries (5.6 percent), even in the decade of the 1970s (see Table 19–1). Even among the high-income oil exporters of the Middle East, only Saudi Arabia showed high growth during the 1970s. And the postwar experiences of Brazil, Korea, and Spain show that rapid economic development can occur even under conditions of very limited natural resource endowments.

TABLE 19–1   Dependence on Oil Exports and Real GDP Growth, 1970–1980: OPEC Countries and Mexico

Country	Oil exports as % of total (1980)	Real GDP growth 1970–1980 (%)
Middle-income capital-importing developing OPEC countries		
Algeria	92	7.0
Ecuador	54	8.8
Gabon	95	5.5
Indonesia	62	7.6
Iran	95	2.5
Iraq	99	12.1
Nigeria	95	6.5
Venezuela	95	5.0
Mexico	39[a]	5.2
All middle-income oil exporters	(90)	(5.5)
All middle-income oil importers	(0)	(5.6)
High-income capital-surplus OPEC members		
Kuwait	92	2.5
Libya	100	2.2
Qatar	95	NA
Saudi Arabia	100	10.6
United Arab Emirates	94	NA
All high-income oil exporters	(97)	(7.0)

Source: For OPEC countries' oil exports: Organization of Petroleum Exporting Countries, *Facts and Figures: A Comparative Statistical Analysis* (Vienna, 1981), p. 17; for Mexico's oil exports and for GDP growth rates: World Bank, *World Development Report, 1982* (Washington, D.C., 1982), and Table 2.
[a] 1979.

On the other hand the postwar history of such countries as Bolivia, Zambia, and Zaire suggests that relatively rich natural resource endowments constitute no guarantee of national prosperity. This latter group of countries has encountered little success in deploying its mineral earnings in ways that foster diversified, and hence more sustainable, economic growth. In fact Table 19–2 shows that nonfuel mineral exporters tended to grow substantially more slowly than did low-income nations in general, and among middle-income, nonfuel mineral exporters, only Morocco grew as rapidly as did middle-income nations in general. But disappointing results

TABLE 19–2   Non-Fuel Minerals Exporters: Share of Mining in GDP and in Exports; GDP Growth

Country	Share of mining in GDP (1967–1975)[a]	Share of minerals in total merchandise exports (1974–1976)	Real GDP growth rates 1970–1980 (%)
Low-income countries			
Guinea	NA	70	3.3
Sierra Leone	17	11	1.6
Togo[a]	10	66	3.4
Zaire	19	97	0.1
(Average annual real growth, all low-income countries)	—	—	(4.6)
Middle-income countries			
Bolivia	12	74	4.8
Chile	9	66	2.4
Guyana	17	26	0.9
Liberia	32	70	1.7
Mauritania	28	87	1.7
Morocco	8	56	5.6
Peru	6	37	3.0
Zambia	32	97	0.7
(Average annual real growth, all middle-income countries)	—	—	(5.6)

Source: For mining and minerals: Gobind T. Nankani, "Development Problems of Nonfuel Mineral Exporting Countries," *Finance and Development* 17, no. 1 (March 1980): 7; for GDP growth rates: World Bank, *World Development Report, 1982* (Washington, D.C., 1982).
[a] 1960–1980 growth rates.

from resource-led growth is not exclusively a recent phenomenon. Chile, for example, by 1975 had little to show for nearly a century of large-scale activity in her mining sector, first in extraction of natural nitrates and later in copper, and Bolivia in the early 1980s was still one of the poorest countries in Latin America after more than three centuries as a mining country par excellence.

Tables 19–1 and 19–2 show how heavily dependent many countries are on nonrenewable resources for export earnings. Such dependence is marked in the case of major oil exporters. Table 19–1 shows that many of the relatively populous middle-income developing countries, including Algeria, Nigeria, Iran, and Venezuela, are no less dependent on petroleum earnings than are such very wealthy, thinly populated, OPEC member countries as Saudi Arabia, Libya, and Kuwait. Exporters of nonfuel minerals are listed in Table 19–2. For these nations, hard minerals have typically accounted for either a sizable share (more than 10 percent) of GDP and/or more than 50 percent of total merchandise exports.

Thus we have to reject the conventional wisdom of the 1950s and 1960s which held that countries with relatively rich natural resource endowments should ordinarily be expected to achieve higher rates of economic growth than less well-endowed nations. Neither the greater availability of foreign exchange nor the greater ease of raising tax revenues in resource-exporting countries guarantees rapid growth. The fact that LDC oil exporters have in general grown no more rapidly than oil-importing LDCs is considerably easier to explain than the relatively low growth rates experienced by mineral exporters. We defer this discussion until later in the chapter, when we consider a broader set of problems associated with resource exports.

Natural Resources: Endowments and Utilization

Although relative resource abundance furnishes no guarantees of material prosperity, countries having significant endowments of natural capital clearly enjoy advantages not available to resource-poor ones. The more accessible the natural capital is, the easier is accumulation of physical and human capital. Resource endowments often provide a basis for resource-based industrialization (see Chapter 15), particularly given the savings in transportation costs made possible by resource processing. Taxes on domestic industrial and agricultural incomes may be lower, and public spending on infrastructure and social amenities may be higher, because a nation possesses readily accessible resource deposits. Resource abundance, particularly in energy resources, may help insulate a country from unstable sources of resource supply, enabling it to continue normal growth while less fortunate countries strain to adjust to sharply higher prices for critical resource imports. Whatever problems accompany resource abundance, and there are clearly such problems, fall into the category of "good" problems, in contrast to "bad" problems such as persistent drought in the resource-poor African Sahel, about which little can soon be done.

Several of the nineteenth-century developing countries that are now classified as industrial market economies, including Canada, Australia, the United States, and Norway, have encountered and largely solved the "good" problems associated with relative resource abundance. Notwithstanding widely held perceptions, few of the more numerous countries now classed as "developing" have had sufficiently large resource endowments to be faced with the "good" problems of natural resource abundance. This is no less true of energy and mineral resources than in the case of tropical timber endowments.

Energy Reserves

Energy from nonrenewable resources includes that derived from oil, coal, natural gas, and uranium. Because nuclear power obtained from enriched uranium is an unimportant source of power for all but a very few LDCs, this energy source will not be discussed in any detail in this chapter. Other sources of *commercial* energy are renewable in nature, and in order of their relative importance in LDCs in 1980, include hydroelectric power, geothemal energy, solar power, and wind power. Of this group, only waterpower was a significant source of commercial energy in LDCs in the early 1980s, particularly in such countries as Brazil, China, Colombia, Ghana, and Zimbabwe. Indeed studies by the World Bank indicate that about 45 percent of electric power consumed in LDCs in 1980 was produced in hydro-electric plants, rather than in oil- or coal-fired generating facilities.

While virtually all energy consumed in transportation, electric power generation, and for residential and commercial use in the developed countries comes from commercial energy sources, developing countries also make substantial use of *noncommercial* energy sources, including animal dung, agricultural waste, and fuelwood. In large countries, such as India, and even OPEC member Indonesia in the mid-1970s noncommercial energy use was almost as important as commercial energy. The share of noncommercial energy in overall LDC energy utilization has, however, been declining steadily since 1960, and this decline is expected to continue as nations develop. For this reason, and because cross-country information on noncommercial energy usage is scanty, the remainder of the discussion focuses on commercial energy sources.

A *resource reserve* is an identified deposit known to be recoverable under present economic conditions with current technology. Total world *proven* recoverable reserves of any resource are merely the sum total of all known deposits that can be recovered with reasonable certainty. Reserve figures are never precise, even for a particular deposit in a particular country, and published reserve figures by country often differ significantly according to whether they are derived from industry or government sources. Further, and more significantly, reserve estimates can change abruptly as resource prices change; at higher oil prices, for example, reserves are higher, as formerly submarginal deposits are converted into commercially attractive ones.

Table 19–3 portrays the distribution of proven hydrocarbon (crude oil, natural gas, coal) energy reserves as between five groups of nations. Of these three energy resources, oil is most prized, primarily because it can be transported most easily, through pipelines on land and in tankers plying the oceans. Natural gas can be shipped across land only via pipeline, and can be shipped across oceans by tanker only when liquefied in very expensive LNG installations. Gas burns more cleanly than oil, and oil ordinarily

TABLE 19–3 World Proven Reserves of Energy in Oil, Natural Gas, and Coal, 1980

	Oil		Natural gas		Coal		Total	
	Reserves[a]	%	Reserves[a]	%	Reserves[a]	%	Reserves[a]	%
Developed market economies	58.8	9.2	80.8	17.6	1624.2	51.3	1763.8	41.3
Centrally planned economies	90.0	14.1	168.0	36.5	1229.5	38.8	1487.5	34.9
High-income OPEC nations	390.8	61.0	151.7	33.0	1.0	0.0	543.5	12.7
Developing-country oil exporters	92.1	14.4	44.7	9.7	13.5	0.1	150.3	3.5
Developing-country oil importers	8.8	1.3	14.7	0.3	297.1	9.3	320.6	6.9
Totals	640.5	100.0	459.9	100.0	3165.3	100.0	4265.7	100.0

Sources: Derived from World Bank, *Energy in the Developing Countries* (Washington, D.C., 1980), Annex II; and Committee on Interstate and Foreign Commerce, U.S. House of Representatives, *The Energy Factbook* (Washington, D.C.: U.S. Government Printing Office, November 1980), pp. 775–81.

[a] In billions of barrels of oil equivalent.

involves fewer pollution problems than coal. Coal, a resource with a high ratio of bulk to heat content, is also expensive to transport, particularly to overseas export markets.

Proven 1980 oil reserves were heavily concentrated in high-income OPEC countries, while most natural gas reserves are located in OPEC nations and in centrally planned economies. Developed market economies had respectable shares of both oil and gas reserves, but the ninety-odd oil-importing countries were virtually bereft of these energy resources. World proven coal resources were, in terms of barrels of oil equivalent (barrels of oil required to yield the same heating equivalent), over four times greater than combined oil and gas reserves, and these are very heavily concentrated in developed market economies and centrally planned economies. When coal is also considered, the energy futures of present energy-importing LDCs as a group appear somewhat brighter. Counting coal, they held almost 7 percent of total world energy reserves. Altogether, developing countries, including those non-OPEC nations that now export oil, had about 10 percent of the world's commercial energy reserves (excluding water and geothermal power).

Energy Production and Consumption

Two of the world's three largest producers of petroleum and gas are not members of OPEC, and no developing country is a major producer of coal. The world's first-ranking oil producer is the Soviet Union, followed by Saudi Arabia and the United States. Outside the broad expanses of the U.S. and USSR, the known geological anomalies that yield oil deposits have tended to occur in lightly populated countries in the Mideast, where annual production in high-income OPEC members commonly exceeded 300 barrels (bbl) per capita per year, valued at $10,200 in 1982 oil prices (see Table 19–4). For middle-income LDCs, oil riches are relatively modest, even among developing-country OPEC members. Per-capita production of oil in Canada was twice as high as in either Nigeria or Mexico, and U.S. production per capita is four times that of OPEC member Indonesia. For developing-country oil producers not included in Table 19–4, per-capita production is ordinarily less than 0.5 bbl per year, but most developing countries produce no appreciable amounts of oil or natural gas.

Over the long run improvements in living standards within a country require steady advances in labor productivity. Enhanced productivity in turn ultimately requires replacement of human and animal power by electric power obtainable from such primary energy sources as oil and gas. World consumption of commercial energy across countries is even more skewed than world reserves and world production. The 3.3 billion people in low- and middle-income developing countries (including China) constitute about three-quarters of the world's population, but use only one-third of annual world production of commercial energy. The nation with the highest per-capita consumption of energy, the United States uses nineteen times more energy per person per year than the average in low-income LDCs, and about eight times more than the average for middle-income LDCs.

TABLE 19-4 Major Producers of Crude Oil, 1980 Annual and Per-Capita Production

	Yearly production (million barrels)	Per-capita yearly production (barrels)
Soviet Union	4245.0	16.0
High-income Mideast OPEC nations		
Saudi Arabia	3467.5	385.3
Kuwait	474.5	338.9
Libya	638.7	212.9
United Arab Emirates	622.3	662.3
Middle-income OPEC LDCs		
Iraq	1204.5	91.9
Iran	803.0	20.7
Nigeria	799.3	9.2
Venezuela	746.4	50.1
Indonesia	565.8	3.9
Ecuador	91.3	11.4
Gabon	73.0	104.3
North and Central America and Europe		
United States	3197.4	14.0
Canada	507.3	21.2
Mexico	688.0	9.9
Britain	551.5	9.9
China	773.8	0.8
Other LDC Oil Exporters		
Malaysia	206.2	14.8
Trinidad-Tobago	78.5	65.4
Egypt	219.0	5.5

Source: For oil production—Committee on Interstate Commerce, U.S. House of Representatives, *Energy Factbook* (Washington, D.C.: U.S. Government Printing Office, November 1980), p. 197; for population— World Bank, *World Development Report, 1982* (Washington, D.C., 1982).

Although the U.S. is the third leading oil producer, it is one of the largest importers of oil and oil products. U.S. dependency on foreign petroleum, at 45 percent of total oil consumption in 1980, has been a source of continuing concern for reasons of national security and economic stability. However, the U.S. has diversified sources of energy in coal, natural gas, hydro and nuclear power, as imported oil and gas account for only 17 percent of total energy consumption. But there are sixty-four LDCs that depend on imported oil alone for more than 75 percent of their total commercial energy, a share that makes the U.S. energy problem seem pale in comparison.

Nonfuel Minerals and Tropical Timber

Production of nonfuel minerals is only slightly less heavily concentrated outside of developing countries than is output of nonrenewable energy resources (see Table 19-5). In the early 1980s the LDC share of annual world production exeeded 50 percent in only two metals: cobalt and tin, both of which are relatively minor items in world trade when compared to petroleum, tropical timber, or even copper. Developing countries are major producers of asbestos, bauxite, and copper, accounting for about 43 percent of

TABLE 19-5 Percentage Share of World Production of 16 Non-fuel Minerals, 1979: Developed, Developing, and Centrally Planned Countries

Mineral	Developed countries	Centrally planned countries	Developing countries
1. Asbestos	38.9	51.7	44.8
2. Bauxite	40.4	14.8	44.8
3. Chromite	37.3	37.9	25.8
4. Cobalt	15.8	13.6	70.6
5. Copper	36.0	21.1	42.9
6. Iron ore	39.2	33.8	27.0
7. Lead	46.9	31.3	21.8
8. Manganese	28.4	45.8	25.8
9. Nickel	38.0	30.0	33.1
10. Phosphate	43.2	23.7	33.1
11. Potash	55.3	41.9	2.8
12. Silver	39.0	40.0	21.0
13. Sulfur	54.6	37.0	9.4
14. Tin	7.3	24.2	68.5
15. Tungsten	28.9	45.2	25.9
16. Zinc	51.6	25.1	23.3

Source: U.S. Bureau of Mines, Minerals Yearbook, as quoted in *Engineering and Mining Journal* (November 1981), pp. 55–61.

annual world supply for the three substances, but the United States has for years been the largest producer of copper in the world.

Table 19–5 also indicates that LDCs are important producers of lead and zinc. Still, for these minerals developed nations such as the U.S., Canada, and Australia account for more than half of annual world production. Developed industrial countries are also the leading sources of world supply for six other minerals. These include potash, sulfur, chromite, phosphate, iron ore, and nickel. And for ten of the sixteen minerals in the table, centrally planned economies, principally the USSR and China, have a larger share in world population than do developing countries.

Within developing countries, production of nonfuel minerals tends to be concentrated in less than a dozen fortunate nations. Brazil is far and away the leading producer of iron ore and is an important source of manganese and asbestos. Bolivia is a leading producer of both tin and tungsten, Indonesia is the world's third-ranking producer of both tin and nickel, and Zaire and Zambia are the two principal sources of cobalt. Zambia is also, after Chile, the second leading source of copper among LDCs. Over 80 percent of LDC production of bauxite comes from four developing countries—Jamaica, Guinea, Guyana, and Surinam—but even so, developed countries produce almost as much as these four.

The years following the 1973–1974 commodity boom were not good ones for LDC hard minerals producers. Not only did real world prices of most of the minerals in Table 19–4 (particularly copper, nickel, and bauxite) decline over that period, but multinationals' search for stability (see Chapter 14) led large mining companies to shift much of their exploration efforts to developed countries, particularly the U.S., Canada, and Australia.

Plans for new mining capacity in copper were cancelled in several LDCs, and large known deposits of nickel and bauxite have remained untouched in countries as diverse as Indonesia, Brazil, and Bolivia, while copper mines in Zambia and Zaire produced at prices below extraction costs from 1978 through 1982.

Until very recently tropical timber was typically considered to be a renewable resource. But several factors have led many forest specialists to classify this resource as nonrenewable, or at best semirenewable. These factors include: (1) the long growing cycle (40–150 years) for most species of logs harvested; (2) the fragile ecology of the tropical forest; and (3) except for teak, the widespread lack of success in inducing regeneration of harvested species.

Tropical timber is the only major natural resource commodity in which developing countries heavily dominate world trade. While not all developing countries are tropical, no developed nations are so classified. Developing countries account for over 95 percent of the world's supply of short-fibered tropical logs, which are traded in markets distinct from those dealing in wood from temperate forests. But here again there is extreme imbalance in resource endowments among LDCs. In 1980 three southeast Asian countries—Malaysia, Indonesia, and the Philippines—produced almost two-thirds of the world's supply of logs and a similar share of world tropical hardwood products. Most of the rest of world production came from tropical African countries, with less than 5 percent from Latin America.

World harvests of tropical hardwood logs peaked in 1980, but since then governments in the three major producing countries have become increasingly concerned over the environmental effects of cutting on such a large scale. Indeed, at the rate of harvest prevailing in the late 1970s the spectre of a world shortage of natural tropical rain forests had arisen, even in a world with no shortage of wood. Rain forests turn out to be far more than a warehouse for wood products; large tropical timber stands are also important regulators of regional climate—particularly rainfall—and current harvesting practices can lead to irreparable damages to riverine systems and to accelerated soil erosion.

Rents and Returns in Natural Resource Projects

Resource Rents

Commercial accumulations of nonrenewable resources within the borders of any country are particularly valuable to that country because these resources involve potential surplus value over and above the costs of labor and capital used to find and extract them. In resource economics this surplus value is called *rent*. While advanced resource economics treatises show that resource rents depend on a complex set of relationships involving the time path of extraction, rate of interest, and risk considerations, we present here a more prosaic but still serviceable view of the rent concept. There are actually three types of rent associated with commercial resource deposits. First, there is a ***scarcity rent,*** defined as any return accruing to any factor of production in inelastic supply. Scarcity rents are not confined to natural resources; they can be received by sports figures blessed with extraordinary strength or speed, or by concert violinists possessing an unusual combination of musical skills and dexterity. Like natural resources, such talents are also scarce and in inelastic supply. Lacking these rare talents, the sports figures and violinists might be qualified only as security guards and music teachers. The earnings they receive in excess of salaries for security guards or teachers are called rents.

Geological processes do not produce large numbers of readily accessible anomalies. Thus resources are scarce. Indeed at any given time a given natural resource is in perfectly inelastic supply. And ignoring exploration costs to keep the presentation simple, the cost of a resource in the ground is zero, as it was left by nature at no cost to society. Because in the typical LDC situation government owns the natural resource, it may dispose of it as it sees fit. Natural resource firms will be prepared to bid for rights to extract the resource.

To understand the nature of scarcity rent, let us consider a mineral to be called monzanium. Assume initially that there is only one use for monzanium, say, in making ball bearings, and also assume that all monzanium deposits are of uniform size and quality (i.e., they are homogeneous). Then, assuming a competitive market, the demand curve for monzanium deposits (*DD* in Fig. 19-1) is the value of the marginal product schedule of monzanium in ball-bearing production. If in 1980 monzanium deposits are very plentiful and easily accessible, then (ignoring exploration costs) OD_1 deposits will be employed, and the government will receive no rents from firms that might bid for mining rights. But if monzanium is scarce relative

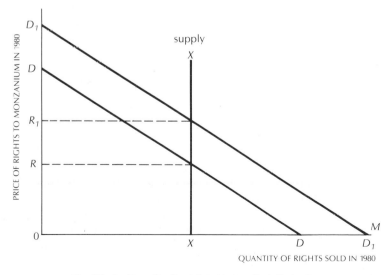

Fig. 19-1 **Scarcity Rent for Monzanium Deposits.**

to demand for it, and also in inelastic supply as shown by the supply curve in Fig. 19–1, then each of the *OX* deposits available in 1980 will earn a "scarcity" rent equal to *OR*.

In the real world, however, resource deposits are not homogeneous; some deposits are of higher quality, or can be more cheaply mined. Bidders for rights to extract monzanium will pay more for rights to the better quality deposits. Let us assume two deposit qualities, indicating demand for poorer deposits as *DD* and demand for better deposits as *DD*₁. With supply of monzanium still at *XX*, then OR_1 is the rent paid to each deposit of high quality and the lower quality deposit will receive *OR* in rent. The rent *OR* may be viewed as a scarcity rent, while the excess of OR_1 over *OR* may be called a **differential resource rent,** reflecting the differential value of the higher quality deposit.

Two types of rent—scarcity rent and differential resource rent—can therefore be associated with natural resource deposits. A third type of rent is often associated with natural resource activities: *monopoly* (or *oligopoly*) *rent*. Historically, natural resource extraction has been dominated by large multinational firms, several of which have had sufficient market power to affect world resource prices. For example, INCO of Canada until recently controlled enough of the international nickel market to set nickel prices. DuBeers of South Africa controlled virtually all the world's supply of uncut diamonds for nearly fifty years and clearly exercised monopoly power. Although the monopoly power of the natural resource multinationals has eroded in recent years, there are still enough barriers to entry in modern, highly capital-intensive mineral and petroleum extraction to generate some monopoly rents, as shown in Fig. 19–2.

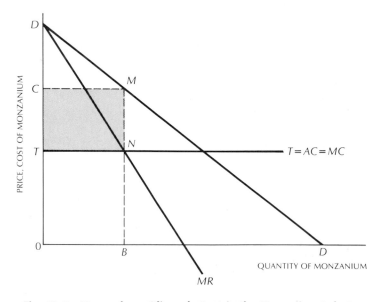

Fig. 19–2   Monopoly or Oligopoly Rent in the Monzanium Industry

Suppose that mining of monzanium is dominated by a single profit-maximizing monopoly firm, or, almost the same, by a small group of oligopolists that attempt to maximize joint profits of firms in the industry. If for a monzanium deposit in any particular country the resource can be extracted at constant marginal costs (a simplifying cost assumption), then average costs will also be constant, as represented in Fig. 19–2 by horizontal curve TT. As in any average cost curve depicted in microeconomics, included in AC is a "normal" return to capital, or simply the opportunity cost of capital.

If demand for monzanium is given as DD, we know that associated with any straight-line demand curve such as DD is a marginal revenue MR curve having exactly twice the slope of DD, which is merely an average revenue curve. Under these conditions, then, the monopolist (or the joint profit-maximizing oligopolists) will produce OB units of monzanium. This is the level of production that maximizes profit, since only at OB production does MC of producing monzanium equal MR from sales. Each unit of monzanium will sell for OC. Economic profit per unit is $OC - OT$, or the excess return over per-unit average cost inclusive of a normal return to capital. Total economic profit is the shaded rectangle $CTMN$. This is identical to monopoly rent, defined as a surplus return over and above the costs of labor and capital used to extract the resource.

Rents, whether scarcity, differential, or monopoly rents have a very special characteristic. By definition a rent is a return in excess of that required to attract factors of production to an activity. There are no laws, economic or otherwise, that can specify *who* has a "right" to rents arising from natural resources. The rents may accrue to investors in LDC resource projects; if they are multinationals, the rents will flow to stockholders abroad. Alternatively, the host LDC government may take steps to capture the rents through taxation or through direct involvement in the project. The central point, however, is that full capture of rents by the host country will not affect the behavior of the extractive firm, be it national or foreign. Only when the efforts of the government go beyond extraction of rents and impinge on the "normal" return to capital invested by the firm will the firm consider shutting down operations. That is, the government, through taxes or other devices, could appropriate 50 or 100 percent of the rents represented by the shaded area $TNMC$ in Fig. 19–2 without affecting either the price or the production of the firm.

Public Policy and Rent Capture

If capture of rents in natural resource activities in LDCs were as simple as depicted above, many resource-rich countries would be substantially wealthier than at present. In fact rents turn out to be easy to describe, difficult to identify in any given setting, and almost impossible to capture fully. They are difficult to identify with any precision for several reasons. First, modern extractive activity is a highly complex undertaking, both in an engineering and a managerial sense. Second, an accurate assessment of rent in oil and hard-mineral projects requires accurate delineation of reserves. Inasmuch as these are not always easily verifiable even with modern technology, magnitudes of potential resource rents in any project are never fully knowable. Rents are impossible to capture fully because many steps that a government may take to appropriate rents may and often do induce extractive firms to conceal them, whether by transfer pricing or other devices described in Chapter 14.

Comments of the preceding paragraph notwithstanding, there have been enough lessons from natural resource investments in enough countries in the past few decades to allow or two safe generalizations about rent and rent capture in an LDC setting, or for that matter in Alaska, or the North Sea. First, experience around the world has shown that public policy toward nonrenewable resources that is not based on an appreciation of the existence of rents is *perforce* inimical to the interests of the society owning the resource. Second, public policies purporting to secure full capture of resource rents are not to be taken seriously, owing to the very considerable difficulties involved in identifying and collecting rents in any given project.

Dozens of countries by now have learned these lessons, often only by trial and error. Over the period 1960–1980 the attitudes of LDC governments toward rent capture have evolved steadily, and this has been reflected in both the design and execution of their policies toward natural resource endowments. It is only a slight exaggeration to say that the prime objective of policy toward natural resources in most LDCs only two decades ago was a very simple one: secure for the host country at least *some* share of resource rents from exploitation of natural resources by the large multinational firms that then dominated the world resource picture. Attainment of that modest goal depended almost entirely on tax policy, given that employment, regional development, and other expected benefits from natural resource development have historically been relatively insignificant in most LDCs, owing primarily to the marked capital intensity of most extractive activity. By the end of the 1960s emphasis in many LDCs had shifted toward efforts to minimize the returns of the multinationals, and by the close of the 1970s to the much sounder objective of maximizing net host country returns, not by any means the same thing as minimizing multinationals' profits, given the type of risk considerations (both geological and market risks) always present in natural resource exploration.

Even by the mid-1970s the changes in tax policy and tax administration sketched earlier had, in a number of LDCs, converted the natural resource sectors into very significant revenue producers. Natural resources furnished between 5 and 15 percent of total central government receipts in Thailand, Colombia, Honduras, Panama, Peru, and Philippines, between 15 and 25 percent in Chile and Malaysia, in excess of 25 percent in Ecuador, Mexico, Jamaica, Liberia, Zaire, and Zambia, and well in excess of 50 percent in Bolivia, Indonesia, Gabon, the Malaysian state of Sabah, Papua New Guinea, and New Caledonia.

Recent measures for facilitating host country capture of resource rents include "windfall" or "excess" profits taxes and transfer of "free" equity shares in natural resource projects to the governments involved. The measures have met with a considerable degree of success. Except for uranium in general, and in Chile where income tax rates on new copper investments were reduced in 1980 to just under 50 percent, and in such former French colonies as Gabon, Niger, and Chad, the percentage share of host country taxes in the value of resource production or in resource profits are now typically half again—and sometimes twice—levels common in the early 1960s. This indicates a very marked tightening of terms available to investors. Rising host countries' shares have been particularly evident in the case of oil. Host countries' shares of profits in oil were never much more than 10–15 percent before 1930. But by 1980 there were numerous instances in which host countries' share of profits in crude oil extraction had long since surpassed 80 percent. Indeed by 1980 governments in even such relatively small producing countries as Malaysia had managed to capture 80 percent not only of profits, but of the value of oil production. (The Malaysian government's share in total oil profits was 98.5 percent.) Even in countries such as Colombia that do not employ windfall profits taxes or windfall royalties on oil, the government's share in the value of oil produced was by 1980 close to 70 percent, while for many other non-OPEC producers as well as OPEC member Indonesia, host countries' shares of between 75 and 85 percent of value were common.

Very substantial changes also occurred in taxation of tropical timber, but not until the latter part of the 1970s, after decades in which host governments seemed to overlook the presence of rent in timber. Tax adjustments by Indonesia and the Malaysian state of Sabah (the two dominant producers) in 1978–1980 resulted in very sizable increments in revenues. In both jurisdictions the share of taxes in gross value of timber exports doubled to 29 percent in Indonesia and to 53 percent in Sabah.

Another measure of host country benefits from natural resource projects is provided by the concept of retained value, used in several studies focusing on the division of benefits from foreign investment in hard-minerals extraction. While the measure by no means represents a perfect method of assessing host country benefits from such activity, movements in the ratio of retained value to gross natural resource exports are indicative of host country performance in capturing larger shares of resource rent over time. Simply put, *retained value* is defined as the total of all revenues from natural resource projects retained in the host country, for example in equation 19–1 below:

$$RV = W_d + C_d + DP(1 - Z) + K_d + T_d + Q_d \qquad \text{[19–1]}$$

where RV = retained value; W_d = labor income for host country workers employed in natural resource projects; C_d = proportion of income of expatriate workers spent locally; DP = domestic procurement of goods and services for natural resource projects; Z = import content of DP; K_d = capital income for domestic shareholders (including governments) in natural resource projects; T_d = taxes, royalties, and other fiscal receipts received by host country government; and Q_d = miscellaneous payments received in host country.

Retained value is itself a fraction of total proceeds (R) gained from the sale of natural resource production, where R is broken up into components as given in equation 19–2:

$$R = M + I + L + P + W_f + U + RV \qquad\qquad [19\text{--}2]$$

where M = cost of imports; I = interest cost on external loans and credits; L = loan repayments; P = profits remitted abroad; W_f = salaries of expatriates accruing abroad; U = unidentified items; and RV = retained value as defined in equation 19–1 above.

The proportion RV/R was, prior to the mid-1960s, typically less than 50 percent in many LDCs with significant foreign investment in natural resources. For example, for Peruvian copper mining in 1960–1965 retained value was but 30 percent of gross export proceeds in large projects operated by foreign enterprises. In Sierra Leone retained value in the foreign-owned mining sector in 1963–1965 was but 43 percent of R, and in Bolivia in 1973–1974 about 56 percent of gross mining revenues. In the Indonesian timber sector, retained value in the early 1970s was rarely more than 20 percent of reported gross timber export earnings. In all instances cited above foreign firms received one or more special tax incentives, usually in the form of income tax holidays of five years or more.

The capital and import intensity of modern mining generally means that the nontax components of retained value are relatively small, and that efforts to secure significant increases in retained value must of necessity focus on tax policy. Peru managed to increase substantially the ratio of retained value to total copper exports from 30 percent in 1960–1965 to 50 percent in 1966–1972, primarily through higher taxes obtained in renegotiation of its agreements with foreign firms. Indeed in the latter period taxes accounted for just over 60 percent of retained value in the largest Peruvian copper project. In both Bolivia and Sierra Leone taxes were responsible for over 45 percent of retained value, and in West African tropical forestry in the early 1970s taxes accounted for as much as 75 percent of retained value in forest projects mounted by multinationals. In Indonesian tropical timber projects mounted by foreign enterprises in the late 1970s very substantial increases in export taxes and other fiscal levies resulted in a very sharp increase in retained value, from less than 20 percent of gross timber export earnings in 1975 to perhaps 40 percent by 1980.

Exporting Taxes on Resource Exports

Many of the resource tax adjustments depicted in the foregoing section were undertaken in the belief that the burden of higher taxes on LDC natural resource exports could easily be shifted to foreign consumers. Indeed tax increases have often been seen as the preferred tool for securing the aims of the various attempts to form "commodity cartels" discussed first in

Chapter 15. Such efforts were heavily influenced by the apparent successes of OPEC in inflicting higher prices for oil on foreign consumers in the 1970s.

Taxes on nonresidents are always popular with governments everywhere. In the United States in the mid-1970s the states of New Mexico and Montana drastically increased taxes on uranium and coal, respectively, largely out of a conviction that since virtually all production of these resources was exported out-of-state, the taxes imposed on them could be fully exported as well. Virtually all of Jamaican bauxite is exported. In 1974 that government increased taxes on bauxite by 700 percent, also in the belief that "foreign consumers" would pay. To take but one more example from many such actions, both Indonesia and the Malaysian state of Sabah more than doubled taxes on timber exports in the hopes that the taxes would be passed on entirely to overseas consumers in the form of higher prices.

Clearly governments perceive measures designed to export taxes on exports to foreign consumers as in the best short-term interests of the people they represent. To what extent can expectations of tax exporting be realized? It turns out that attempts to export natural resource taxes to foreign consumers can be successful, even in the short run, only under certain rarely satisfied conditions. And even when the taxes can be fully exported to foreign consumers in the short run, this may not be in a country's long-term interests. With care, however, resource taxes may be exported to foreign stockholders and may have little effect on resource investment in the host country, provided the taxes do not go beyond full taxation of rents.

To illustrate, let us consider a hypothetical case involving the small mythical country of Binaro. This nation is a significant producer of the mineral monzanium, the value of which typically exceeds $100 million per year. All monzanium produced is exported by large multinationals operating in monzanium mining. In 1980 Binaro faced a budgetary crisis involving a projected deficit equal to 3 percent of GDP, or U.S. $5 million. The country had for years imposed a tax of $2 per pound on monzanium, which was about 1 percent of the export value. With an additional $10 tax per pound the budget deficit could be covered, provided the tax did not reduce monzanium output. The minister of finance enthusiastically recommended that the president approve the quintupling of the tax, on grounds that foreign consumers would bear the entire burden in the form of higher prices. Our task is to determine whether this expectation was justified.

Basically, five factors determine whether a country like Binaro can expect success in the short run in attempts to export taxes on monzanium, or any other resource, to foreign consumers. They are, in order of importance:

1. The share of Binaro's monzanium in the relevant export market (world or regional market), or conversely, the share of monzanium from other countries in these same markets;
2. The elasticity of supply of Binaro's monzanium;
3. The elasticity of supply of monzanium from other monzanium-producing countries;

4. The overall elasticity of supply of monzanium in the relevant market (i.e., the elasticity of supply of all producers together, including Binaro);

5. The price elasticity of demand for monzanium in the world market.

Given the relevant elasticities, we can find the fraction of Binaro's $10 per pound tax that will be exported by use of equation 19–3:

$$T_c = \frac{E_s}{E_s + E_d} \cdot \frac{ae_{st}}{ae_{st} + (1-a)e_{sn}} \qquad [19\text{--}3]$$

where T_c = the percentage share of Binaro's additional $10 per pound tax shifted forward to foreign consumers (in the form of higher prices for monzanium); E_s = overall elasticity of supply for monzanium (all producers) in the relevant market; E_d = the price elasticity of demand for monzanium in the relevant market; a = the share of Binaro's monzanium in the relevant market; $(1-a)$ = the share of other producers in the relevant market; e_{st} = the elasticity of supply of monzanium from Binaro; and e_{sn} = the elasticity of supply of monzanium from other producing nations.

Suppose that in the case at hand the relevant short-run elasticities and market shares are as follows: $E_s = 1.5$; $E_d = -0.2$; $e_{st} = 1.0$; $e_{sn} = 2.0$; $a = 25\%$; and $(1-a) = 75\%$.

The above elasticities of demand and supply are not untypical of those prevailing in recent years in markets for such resources as oil, coal, tin, and uranium, in the short term. (In determining T_c, E_d is treated as a positive number, although price elasticities of demand are conventionally given with a negative sign.)

In the case of Binaro's monzanium, only about 14 percent of the new tax of $10 per pound can be exported to foreign consumers, as indicated below.

$$T_c = \frac{1.5}{1.5 + 0.2} \cdot \frac{0.25(1.0)}{0.25(1.0) + 0.75(2.0)}$$

$$T_c - 12.6\%$$

In this case, then, Binaro would be able to shift only 13 percent of the tax to foreign consumers in the short term.[2] Nor does this result necessarily mean that the increased export tax was contrary to Binaro's interests. The portion of the tax not shifted to foreign consumers (87 percent) must be paid by someone. In fact the unshifted taxes will reduce rents received by any or all of several affected parties: (1) the owner of the deposit; (2) labor in the Binaro monzanium industry; (3) shareholders in firms extracting monzanium in Binaro.

2. Strictly speaking this result, or any result derived by use of the formula, is valid only for relatively small taxes imposed in situations where no taxes applied before. But it is indicative of the results obtained under typical real-world conditions. See Charles E. McLure, "Market Dominance and the Exporting of State Taxes," *Natural Tax Journal* 34, no. 4 (December 1981).

To the extent that any of these economic agents are not residents of Binaro, that portion of the tax not shifted to foreign consumers could also reduce their returns, thereby exporting the burden of the tax in this manner. But we have seen that in most LDCs the government itself is the owner of the property right to the resource, and in virtually all LDCs labor policies heavily favor the use of domestic, not foreign, labor. In such circumstances significant tax exporting, if it is to occur at all, must take the form of reduced returns to foreign shareholders of foreign extractive firms.

Not all countries, however, are as poorly situated to export taxes to foreign consumers as in the case of Binaro. Equation 19–3 can be used to verify that the greater the market share (a) of the taxing country, the greater the proportion of export taxes may be shifted to foreign consumers. Dominance by the taxing nation, i.e., the share of the market taken by the nation's resource, turns out to be the critical factor in exporting taxes to consumers. Even if the world market demand for monzanium were perfectly inelastic ($E_d = 0$), Binaro would still be unable to export a sizable fraction of the tax to consumers, since T_c can ordinarily never exceed (a), Binaro's market share, which is only 25 percent. This is because Binaro's market share determines the extent to which it (as opposed to all producers of monzanium) faces elastic or inelastic demand for the resource. On the other hand if elasticity of demand for monzanium were at unity, five times greater than in the first example, and Binaro's market share were at 75 percent, only three times as high, then Binaro would be able to export almost 36 percent of its export tax to foreign consumers, given the same supply elasticities as used earlier.

There are real-world examples of short-run success in exporting taxes on resources; there are not many examples of long-run success. Pakistan in the 1960s managed for a time to export substantial taxes on jute. Over time the higher prices for Pakistani jute led users to switch to synthetic substitutes and at the same time encouraged vastly expanded plantings of jute in other countries, notably Thailand. By 1970 the Pakistani jute industry was in a perilous situation, from which it has never fully recovered.

Prospects for producer cartels can be examined in the same way. Suppose a cartel were to be created consisting of Binaro plus nations having together another 55 percent of the world trade in monzanium. The cartel would then control 80 percent of the market. Now in the cartel case, e_{st} becomes the elasticity of supply in all *cartel* members, which we will take to be 1.4 (a figure between the lower elasticity in Binaro and that prevailing elsewhere). Let e_{sn} remain at 2.0, E_d at 0.2, and E_s at 1.5. If the cartel members now all enacted an additional export tax of $10 per pound, the cartel could shift 65 percent of the tax to foreign consumers, at last in the short run.

A commodity cartel able in the short run to shift as much as 65 percent of export taxes to foreign consumers would ordinarily be judged as successful. But success in exporting taxes in the short run does not always spell success in the long run. Elasticities, both of supply and demand, tend to increase over time, as both consumers and producers outside the cartel have time to adjust to the higher prices resulting from successful cartel actions. In time demand for the taxed resource may become very elastic, as consumers gradually switch to substitutes for the cartel's resources. But more important, supply from noncartel producers may become highly elastic relative to supply within the cartel, as investors rush to increase noncartel, less heavily taxed production of the resource. Both factors reduce T_c, the proportion of tax that can be shifted to foreign consumers. The second factor reduces the all-important market share of the cartel; the first reduces the ability of a given market share to foster forward shifting of taxes.

Producer cartels are price-raising commodity agreements among governments. Such cartels also use methods other than taxation to achieve cartel aims. The most common method has been that of restriction of output of producers in member countries. The aim of such restrictions is, of course, identical to that sought by cartels that rely on taxation: to increase prices paid by foreign consumers. The same factors that limit a cartel's ability to export taxes on a commodity also tend to limit the effectiveness of output restrictions. Both the International Coffee Agreement and OPEC employ output restrictions to achieve cartel aims. Several new cartels were formed in the 1970s in the wake of OPEC's success in using its power as a cartel to force up oil prices with an embargo in the fall of 1973. The new producer cartels included the International Bauxite Agreement (led by Jamaica), the Union of Banana Exporting Countries (consisting primarily of Central American exporting countries), and the Phosphate Cartel, and others were attempted in sisal, tungsten, iron ore, and other metals.

To be effective, a cartel that relies on production limits should have several characteristics. First, production must be concentrated in a few countries, as it is easier to coordinate and enforce production-limitation agreements. This implies that there should not be readily available alternative sources of supply, such as new producers who are anxious and able to take advantage of higher prices. Second, when one or two of the producers have substantially lower costs than the others, as does OPEC leader Saudi Arabia in petroleum, these countries have historically acted as "enforcers" of the agreement, discouraging others from taking advantage of the higher prices by selling more than their quotas. Third, demand must be inelastic if output restrictions are to lead to higher revenues, and this implies that there cannot be good substitutes for the product available in the short run. Thus copper faces aluminum as a good substitute in electrical uses, while it has taken several years to begin to substitute alternative forms of energy for petroleum. Finally, low concentration of imports among consuming countries also helps, because then no one or two importers have either the market power or the strong interest to break the cartel.

However much these characteristics may be met over periods of a few years, time works against cartels. In the long run elasticities of both supply and demand are greater. Producers always face a great incentive to cheat on the cartel by exporting more at high prices. As time goes on more potential producers become capable of exporting and enforcement becomes more difficult. Given time, consumers can and do adjust to higher prices by shifting to substitutes, such as coal instead of OPEC's crude oil, or by making structural changes in consumption habits, as evidenced in the U.S. by the shift, after 1975, to smaller cars which burn less fuel.

OPEC is perhaps the most outstanding example of short-term cartel success. Between early 1973 and 1980 the price of oil at the Persian Gulf increased by more than fifteen-fold, from little more than $2 per barrel to an average of $36 per barrel. But by 1982 there were signs of incipient weakness in the world oil market, and some Western observers were even predicting 1983 and 1984 prices at under $30 per barrel. Whether this will eventually result in the collapse of this influential cartel depends perhaps more on geopolitical than on economic factors.

Coping with Resource Largesse

Three populous LDCs—Nigeria, Mexico, and Indonesia—provide typical examples of what has become popularly known as "Dutch disease," an affliction (outlined earlier in Chapter 15) of the relatively affluent large- and middle-size nations exporting large quantities of oil and/or natural gas. In cases of Dutch disease the resource exports "tail" wags the "dog" of overall growth and development. Nigeria, Mexico, and Indonesia are not the only countries that suffered from Dutch disease in the 1970s and early 1980. Ivory Coast, Cameroons, Gabon, and Venezuela are other examples. In some countries with large oil exports and very small populations, the phenomenon is known as the "Kuwait effect."

Oil-Fired Development: Three Case Studies

Nigeria

Before the first oil boom in 1973–1974, Nigeria's economy was one of the most prosperous in Africa, with agriculture as the leading economic sector. The nation was the world's largest exporter of cocoa and a leading supplier of other very labor-intensive, smallholder agricultural products, such as palm oil and groundnuts. Strong export performance in these commodities and in cotton and rubber keyed major increases in rural incomes in a country that ranks seventh in population, just behind Brazil. The manufacturing sector grew rapidly as well, rising from a very small base before independence to 5 percent of GDP by 1964 and 9 percent of GDP by 1976, just after the beginning of the first oil boom. Throughout the 1960s, even through a costly civil war ending in 1969, domestic inflation was held to an average rate of less than 3 percent, and growth in governmental expenditure was held closely in check. By 1980 Nigeria's per-capita GDP, at $1010, was the fourth highest in Sub-Saharan Africa, having grown at 4.1 percent per year since 1960.

If growth in per-capita income were the only measure of improved national well-being, Nigeria's record from 1960 to 1980 would appear to be one of unmitigated prosperity. But surface appearances can be deceiving. By 1980 the labor-intensive agricultural sector lay nearly in ruins. The share of agricultural exports in total exports had fallen from 90 percent in

1960 to only 8 percent in 1980, while the share of agriculture in GDP dropped precipitously, from almost two-thirds in 1960 to one-fifth by 1980. Nigeria, a net food exporter in the 1960s, spent almost $3 billion on food imports in 1980. Inflation surged to an annual rate of 18 percent for the decade ending in 1980, as government spending grew at roughly double the rate of GDP growth, just in the period 1972–1977. Throughout the whole period, the government allowed the exchange rate to *appreciate* gradually against the dollar, as the value of the Nigerian naira rose from U.S. $1.52 in 1973 to $1.88 in 1981.

Mexico   Mexico enjoyed vibrant growth across virtually all economic sectors from 1960 to 1970, and observers began speaking of the "Mexican model" in glowing terms. Real GDP grew by over 7 percent per annum over this period because of very strong performance in both the agricultural sector (3.9 percent growth) and in industry (9.3 percent growth). By 1976 growth in Mexican GDP had slowed somewhat to 5.5 percent, and large increases in public spending had led to deficits that pushed inflation from annual rates of inflation of 4 percent in the 1960s to close to 20 percent for the period 1971–1976. These developments led to a devaluation of the peso of over 50 percent in 1976. Shortly thereafter Pemex, the state oil enterprise, confirmed rumors of truly major oil discoveries in the states of Tabasco and Chiapas, with expected 1980 production capacity in excess of 3 million barrels per day, a rate of output that would place Mexico in the elite company of such OPEC members as Venezuela and Iraq, and ahead of Nigeria and Indonesia. Thus in 1977 Mexico seemed poised to return to previous high growth, and perhaps to enter several decades of vigorous oil-fired development sufficient to propel the nation into a position as the third wealthiest in the hemisphere by the end of the century, just after the United States and Canada.

But by 1982 the bright promises of five years earlier had faded badly. The beginnings of Mexico's oil boom touched off an explosion in spending by government- and state-owned enterprises, much of which was financed not by oil export earnings but the promise of the same: Mexico's external public debt rose from $15.6 billion in 1976 (U.S. $251 per capita) to a 1982 figure reported to be as high as $80 billion (U.S. $1146 per capita), the largest amount of outstanding debt any developing country has ever incurred. Inflation, nearly tamed in 1977 and 1978, had by 1980 surpassed 30 percent and by late 1981 threatened to move well above 50 percent per annum in the subsequent year. Worse still, unemployment rose strikingly in the midst of the oil boom. According to several published reports, nearly half the labor force was either unemployed or underemployed. While unemployment figures that high seemed hardly credible among many observers, there was little disputing the presence of the greatest labor distress in modern Mexican history.

From 1976 through 1981 the exchange rate remained near 22 pesos to the dollar in spite of rapid inflation, and the current account deficit reached $13 billion, or 7 percent of GDP, in 1981. Finally, in early 1982, the government devalued the peso by 30 percent. The step turned out to be too little, too late, and in August and September the peso was devalued again. By the end of the year, between 60 and 80 pesos, depending on the transaction, were required to buy one dollar, and the government reluctantly sought emergency help from the IMF.

Indonesia in 1972 had just completed the first stages of economic re- **Indonesia** construction, following a disastrous hyperinflation from 1964 to 1967, after which almost the entire social and economic infrastructure of this densely populated, primarily rural nation lay in shambles. Economic growth, and in particular agricultural production, had rebounded smartly by 1971, and even after a 10 percent devaluation in mid-year inflation had been reduced to less than 5 percent per annum. When the first oil boom began in late 1973, following the quadrupling of oil prices by OPEC, the country appeared to be well-placed for a decade of very strong economic growth. The ensuing five years were indeed high-growth years, but as in Mexico and Nigeria, the quality of that growth was somewhat poor: the income distribution worsened and employment growth stagnated. Inflation spurted to an annual rate of 40 percent in the six months after the first oil shock, returned to a 10 percent rate after a stabilization program in April 1974, and then proceeded to roll along at a 20 percent clip through 1977.

By mid-1978 idle capacity in the manufacturing sector was widespread and manufactured exports were virtually nonexistent as rapid domestic inflation coupled with a constant nominal exchange rate from 1971 to 1978 had made exporting decidedly unattractive. The combination of inflation and a constant nominal exchange rate had even more depressive effects on the large, much more labor-intensive, agricultural export sector, particularly in rubber, the source of more employment than any other commodity except rice. Still, the country had ample foreign exchange reserves to defend the value of the rupiah, and the business community viewed devaluation as unthinkable.

Nevertheless the Indonesian rupiah was devalued by 50 percent in November 1978, not to protect a precarious foreign exchange reserve situation but primarily to encourage labor-intensive manufactured and agricultural exports. The measure had, by and large, the desired effects. Although domestic inflation remained at a relatively high 22 percent in 1979, manufactured exports enjoyed explosive growth over the subsequent two years, with some categories growing at annual rates of 300 to 500 percent, albeit from a small base. Although 1979 and 1980 saw still another oil boom, this time taking world oil prices from less than $14 to $38 per barrel, agricultural exports, including rubber, surged as well. Partly as a consequence of the devaluation, 1980 and 1981 turned out to be the most prosperous years in Indonesian history, as real GDP grew by nearly 10 percent in 1980 and close to 9 percent in 1981 amid evidence of a small reduction in income inequality. The manufacturing sector led this performance, growing by over 20 percent in 1980 alone.

Partly as a consequence of well-timed policy measures such as the 1978 devaluation, partly because of the two oil booms, and partly because of remarkable growth in rice production in this heavily rice-consuming nation, the economy grew at an unprecedented annual rate of 7.6 percent over the decade ending in 1980, while inflation dropped to an annual rate of just below world inflation in 1980 and 1981. The nation entered 1982 with a foreign debt one-third as high as that of less populous Mexico, and in a much better position to weather the effects of projected weaknesses in world oil markets in the 1980s than either Mexico or Nigeria.

An understanding of the Kuwait effect provides insights into diagnosis and treatment of Dutch disease. In Kuwait and other very small oil-exporting nations, such as Qatar, per-capita export earnings from oil, at about $14,000 in both countries, are large enough to provide every family with a high standard of living, quite apart from any income from labor and capital. In terms of Fig. 15–6 the available supply of foreign exchange from oil has been so great relative to the demand for foreign exchange that the exchange rate has steadily appreciated. In such extreme cases of oil riches a free market rate of foreign exchange (relative to, say, the U.S. dollar) would tend to be so high that almost nothing else produced in the economy could be profitably exported. Indeed in such economies practically everything tends to be imported, because the heavily appreciated exchange rate makes imports appear unusually cheap. In countries like Kuwait most of the labor force is foreign, and in Qatar 80 percent of the population consists of expatriates who have migrated to do work that Qataris find unattractive. There are clearly no employment problems for Kuwaiti or Qatari nationals, even though many of them may choose not to work.

But in more populous, diversified economies with far less oil wealth per capita, large export earnings from an "enclave" sector, such as oil or gas, can be a mixed blessing, both in developed countries like the Netherlands and in developing countries like Nigeria and Mexico. The Dutch case is particularly instructive. For virtually all of the postwar period until 1975 the Netherlands enjoyed remarkable prosperity in almost all respects. Inflation seldom exceeded 3 percent per year, GNP growth rarely dropped below 5 percent, and unemployment fluctuated around 1 percent of the labor force, very low by U.S. standards. Much of postwar Dutch prosperity was due to the fact that the traditional export sector of this very open economy was highly competitive with the rest of the world. This was particularly true of the Dutch agricultural sector, which accounted for a third of all its merchandise exports from 1950 to 1975.

In the early 1960s substantial reserves of natural gas were found in the Netherlands. By 1975 gas exports had risen to about 10 percent of total exports, and the Netherlands enjoyed a surplus (on current account) of 4 percent of GNP. By 1981 gas still accounted for 5 percent of national income, 7 percent of exports, and, more significantly, over 20 percent of government taxes. The proceeds of taxes on gas were used to fund drastically increased government spending, particularly welfare spending, but even higher taxes from gas eventually proved insufficient to finance them. One result was a surge in inflation rates, from 2 percent in 1970 to 10 percent in 1975, tapering gradually to 4 percent in 1980. From 1973 through 1978 the inflow of foreign exchange from gas exports buoyed up the exchange rate, as the Dutch guilder appreciated by about 30 percent relative to its major trading partners. As a result traditional exporters were faced with a double blow: rising domestic costs coupled with drastically lower guilder earnings from each dollar's worth of exports. Unemployment rose sharply from 1973 through 1978 as the relatively labor-intensive export sector stagnated, and GNP growth dropped from the 5 percent rates of the 1960s to 1–2 percent by the end of the decade. Clearly the gas "bonanza" brought mixed blessings to the Netherlands, just as the oil bonanza did for several large LDCs, including Mexico, Nigeria, and Indonesia.

But if there is a "Dutch disease," why is there no "Japanese disease" from equally dramatic expansion in automobile and electronic exports, or no "Singapore disease" when exports of manufactures grow at better than 30 percent for several years, as they did in the early 1970s? The answer lies partly in the "enclave" nature of oil and gas production in economies such as Nigeria, Indonesia, and Gabon, and in the Netherlands as well. But part of the answer depends on the fact that a far greater proportion of the value of oil and gas exports accrues to government treasuries than is the case for manufactured exports from Singapore or agricultural exports from The Netherlands, Indonesia, or Nigeria.

Unlike the case for "enclave" oil and gas sectors in Indonesia, Nigeria, or even in the Dutch economy, the manufacturing sectors of such important manufacturing/exporting economies as Korea, Taiwan, or Singapore are tightly linked with the rest of the economy, and with the external sector as well. If, for whatever reason, inflation in, say, Korea began to run at a rate faster than world inflation, then the exchange rate—whether fixed or freely floating—must soon adjust toward depreciation, or growth in manufactured exports will cease or turn negative because the double squeeze of higher domestic costs and constant domestic currency earnings per unit of exports will make exporting unattractive (see Chapter 17).

The situation is very different for an enclave export sector such as oil, partly because of the presence of easily taxed rents in oil and partly because of the weak linkages of most natural resource sectors with the rest of their economies. Particularly in developing countries, oil exploration, production, and processing uses very little domestic labor or materials. When, for whatever reason, inflation in economies like Indonesia or Nigeria exceeds world inflation, costs in the oil enclave are affected only very slightly. Thus while inflation of 20 percent in Taiwan, when world inflation is 10 percent, can rapidly ruin the export-oriented manufacturing sector in Taiwan unless the exchange rate is allowed to depreciate, inflation of even 30 percent in Indonesia will have little impact on the profitability of exporting oil even if the exchange rate is left untouched. International reserves then can continue to build up in an oil-exporting country, even as non-oil exporters in these countries lay off workers or close their doors in bankruptcy.

Finally, the rents in oil and gas exports make them particularly attractive sources of government revenue. Indonesia depended on oil for over two-thirds of its taxes from 1979 to 1981, Nigeria about 65 percent, Mexico about half, and The Netherlands over 20 percent, with as much as 85 percent of the value of net oil or gas exports being siphoned off as taxes. Note that such taxes do not depress household or business spending or income in the same way that higher income or sales taxes do. The deployment of a sudden flood of oil tax revenues plays the pivotal role in cases of Dutch disease. If a high proportion of oil taxes are "sterilized," that is, not spent on domestic goods, services, or transfer payments but kept in overseas deposits of the government, or are spent on additional imports to diversify the economy, the worst symptoms of Dutch disease may not appear. But increased government spending of a large proportion of oil taxes on such items as drastically increased civil service salaries or—in The Netherlands's case—on welfare payments, results in large, direct additions to the money supply that sooner or later leads to accelerated inflation. And with oil revenues propping up the value of the currency in the face of domestic inflation, the by-now-familiar signs of Dutch disease are soon manifested in higher unemployment and stagnation of the non-oil economy.

Dutch disease is not the inevitable outcome of sudden increases in oil export earnings. The foregoing discussion suggests two prophylactic measures that LDCs may take in order to avoid the problem. The first is restraint in government spending out of oil revenues, a particularly appropriate prescription for countries such as Indonesia, Qatar, or Ecuador, where depletion of present oil reserves is likely before the end of the twentieth century.

But given that virtually all governments with sizable oil income face very strong pressures to spend most of it, the second remedy is perhaps more realistic, but not materially so: a systematic policy of forced depreciation of the exchange rate, in the fashion of a "crawling peg," so that inflows of oil revenues and subsequent spending by governments are not allowed to maim or destroy other export sectors, or to artificially cheapen imports. Such a policy can best be effectuated by a series of periodic "mini-devaluations" of the domestic currency against the dollar, with intervals between mini-devaluations no longer than a year at a time. This policy allows a country to avoid the trauma of the major devaluation that is inevitable when a populous oil-exporting country goes for long periods at constant nominal exchange rates (Indonesia and Mexico), or even worse, allows the exchange rate to appreciate over time (Nigeria).

Indonesia ultimately resorted to a major devaluation to control, if not cure, Dutch disease, as did Mexico. The difference between the two countries is that Indonesia employed better timing. In 1978 it devalued by 50 percent at the very start of the second oil boom, before it was forced by acute economic distress to do so; Mexico waited until 1982 and a weak oil market, when it was forced to devalue by 30 percent. The medicine proved too weak, and another, much larger, devaluation followed within months.

The principal lesson is that maladies like Dutch disease can be contained by sensible economic management even when full remission of the disease is impossible, so that a country can enjoy more of the benefits and fewer of the problems of a generous endowment of natural capital. In particular the agricultural sector in an oil-exporting LDC need not suffer unnecessarily as a by-product of natural resource exports.

Figure 19–3 portrays the essence of policy choices involved in coping with the problems of resource largesse. Based on simulations of the economies of three Pacific Basin oil exporters (Indonesia, Malaysia, Mexico), Fig. 19–3 shows what may be expected to happen to an oil-exporting economy where oil exports are initially (year 1) 2 percent of GDP and then, after five years, rise to 4 percent of GDP as a consequence of a doubling of oil prices. Curve AA shows the predicted path of GDP per capita in the agricultural sector in the absence of the doubling of oil prices in year 5. Curve BCB shows the path of GDP per capita in the agricultural sector (GDP_{AG}) from year 5 to year 10 when the oil-exporting country *fails* to devalue the exchange rate in the face of resulting significant inflation, over and above world inflation. Curve BDE shows the path of GDP_{AG} when, before the end of the sixth year, the oil-exporting country devalues its exchange rate.

In the absence of the oil price rise agricultural GDP grows at a rate of 2.9 percent per year, a healthy rate by international standards. When oil prices double in year 5, agricultural GDP *falls* in any case, as traced by

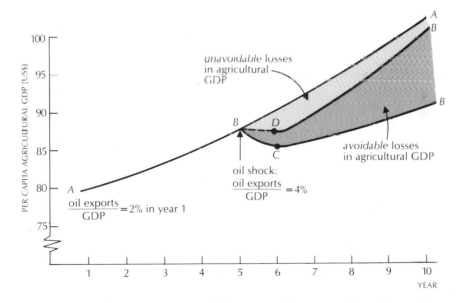

Fig. 19–3   Effects of Alternative Exchange Rate Policies on Agricultural Growth in Oil-Exporting Economies.

Source: C. Peter Timmer, "Energy and Structural Change in the Asia-Pacific Region: The Agricultural Sector, Paper prepared for the 13th Pacific Trade and Development Conference, Manila, January 24–28, 1980, Fig. 6.

curve *BDE*. But it falls *less* in the case of an immediate exchange rate devaluation than in the absence of devaluation and then grows at a more rapid rate (4.1 percent) than before the oil price increase, so that by the tenth year GDP_{AG} is nearly as high with the positive oil shock as it would have been without. But in the case where the oil-exporting country fails to devalue, the fall in GDP_{AG} is even sharper, and in the subsequent year the rate of growth is a low 1.6 percent.

The cross-hatched area under curve *AA* shows the unavoidable loss over time in agricultural GDP caused by the oil shock. The dotted area shows the *additional* and needless loss in agricultural GDP caused by avoidance of devaluation. In four years' time the needless loss reaches 2½ times the unavoidable loss. Note that the loss compounds over time, suggesting that the longer devaluation is postponed, the worse the effects for the agricultural sector.

Even for relatively oil-rich, populous nations, the type of smothering of the agricultural sector resulting from policies that yield curve *BCB* is not likely to be good for long-run development even if overall GDP growth remains high, as it is likely to lead to acute maldistribution in income distribution, accelerated rural-to-urban migration, and heightened future vulnerability to shocks in the world food market as well.

FURTHER READING Since the first "oil price shock" and the short-lived boom in other commodity prices in 1973–1974, there has been a flood of publications dealing with both the impact of resource endowments on LDCs and the impact of LDCs on world trade in nonrenewable resources. It is too early to determine whether much of this literature will have more than a transient effect on the way we think about natural resource issues, but a listing of a few of the more informative and helpful readings should prove useful to the interested student.

For developing countries, the World Bank has thus far proven to have the most comprehensive and readily available information on resource endowments and production across dozens of countries. On energy reserves and production, see especially the World Bank's publication *Energy in the Developing Countries* (Washington, D.C., August 1980), and the 1980 publication of the United States House of Representatives, Committee on Interstate Commerce, *Energy Factbook* (Washington, D.C.: U.S. Government Printing Office, November 1980). For information on nonfuel mineral endowments, see Gobind T. Nankani, "Development Problems of Non-Fuel Mineral Exporting Countries," *Finance and Development* 17, no. 1 (March 1980): 6–10. A good elementary discussion of problems in managing tropical timber endowments may be found in L. Gomez-Pompa, R. Guevara, and G. Yanes, "The Tropical Rain-Forest: A Non-Renewable Resource," *Science* 177 (1972): 762–65.

Theoretical questions in the economies of natural resources can be treated but sketchily in a textbook on development. Students with a good course in intermediate microeconomics may wish to investigate further many of the analytical issues that arise in any sensible discussion of resource economics, including the treatment of natural resource rent. Textbooks on the subject include Charles W. Howe, *Natural Resource Economics: Issues Analysis and Policy* (New York: John Wiley and Sons, 1979). An excellent but somewhat advanced compendium of articles on resource economics is contained in V. Kerry Smith (ed.), *Scarcity and Growth Reconsidered* (Baltimore: Johns Hopkins Press, 1979), an updating of the still valuable book by H. J. Barnett and C. Morse, *Scarcity and Growth: The Economics of Natural Resource Scarcity* (Baltimore: Johns Hopkins University Press, 1963). Finally, no student with any pretensions to future expertise in resource economics should miss reading several books and articles by Orris C. Herfindahl, but particularly those compiled in D. B. Brooks (ed.), *Resource Economics: Selected Works of Orris C. Herfindahl* (Baltimore: Johns Hopkins University Press, 1974).

Tax problems in LDC resource policies are discussed in a number of publications, including several by one of the authors of this textbook. For a discussion of several of these questions, and for bibliographic citations, see Malcolm Gillis, "Evolution of Natural Resource Taxes in Developing Countries," *Natural Resources Journal* 22, no. 3 (July 1982): 619–49.

Problems faced by resource-poor countries in dealing with energy and other "shocks" are discussed in Bela Belassa, "Policy Responses to External Shocks in Selected Latin American Countries," in W. Baer and M. Gillis (eds.), *Export Diversification and the New Protectionism* (Urbana: University of Illinois Press, and National Bureau of Economic Research, 1981), and in Hollis P. Chenery, "Restructuring the World Economy, Round II," *Foreign Affairs* (Summer 1981), pp. 1102–20.

As of 1982, few articles dealing with "Dutch disease" and related problems of resource largesse had found their way into print, but many were in preparation, particularly at the National Bureau of Economic Research. Two articles dealing with the impact of oil exports on agricultural sectors in large developing countries may be of particular interest to developmental specialists: C. Peter Timmer, "Energy and Structural Change in the Asia-Pacific Region: The Agricultural Sector" (Paper presented at the 13th Pacific Trade and Development Conference, Manila, January 24–28, 1983), and Lance P. Taylor, "Back to Basics: Theory for the Rhetoric in North-South Relations," *World Development* 10, no. 4 (May 1982): 327–35.

Chapter 20

INDUSTRY

The concept of development and the process of industrialization are so inextricably linked that they are often treated as synonymous. The first "developed" country is considered to have been England. The Industrial Revolution—a series of cost-saving innovations centered on steam power —enabled Britain to raise its industrial production by 400 percent over the first half of the nineteenth century.[1] From then until the present the dominant criterion for development has been the rise in per-capita income brought about largely by industrialization. Each of the major European powers, Germany and France with most success, and the United States followed Britain's example during the nineteenth century. The two most successful developers of the early twentieth century, Japan and the Soviet Union, also became world powers through industrialization.

At mid-century, as Latin America awakened to the possibilities of reduced economic dependence and European colonies in Asia and Africa won their independence, the concept of development as industrialization remained intact. The first development plans were based on it and economists built development theories upon it. You encountered these theories in earlier chapters. The debate between balanced and unbalanced growth, for example, was about the path toward industrialization (see Chapter 3). The influential two-sector models of W. Arthur Lewis, then of John Fei and Gustav Ranis, focus on the ways in which resources can be transferred from agriculture in order to develop industry (see Chapter 3). The idea behind this transfer, which is fundamental to pro-industrialization arguments, is that higher productivity in industry is the key to raising incomes for the entire population. The trade-based theories of development, described in

---

1. E. J. Hobsbawm, *The Pelican Economic History of Britain*, vol. 3, *Industry and Empire* (Baltimore: Penguin Books, 1969).

Part IV, import substitution and export substitution, are also motivated principally by the desire to industrialize.

There have always been nagging doubts about the requirement for industrialization. Countries like Denmark, Australia, and New Zealand became relatively wealthy although their economies depended on agricultural exports, and this showed that small countries do have an option if they have access to large industrial markets. Recently, a concern that industrialization has not spread the benefits of growth to the poor, especially the rural poor, has led to advocacy of alternative strategies in which rural development and the provision of basic human needs take precedence over industrialization. As earlier chapters have said, the concern is justified, although strategies focused solely on resolving it are likely to fail, as are strategies aimed solely at industrialization. Balanced priorities and strategies are needed. In any event few countries of the third world, even those most concerned about the poor, seem inclined to give up their push toward industrialization.

Because development is identified with industrialization, this text inevitably treats industry in several different contexts. This chapter emphasizes aspects not covered in depth elsewhere. The next two sections discuss the characteristics of industrial sectors in the developing countries and the features of these sectors that make industry a potential engine of growth. The third section deals with a popular variant, small-scale industry, and the last section reviews the contribution that industry has made to development in the third world and offers some conclusions.

Patterns of Industrial Development

Before going further we need to sort out a problem of terminology. The term *industry* is unfortunately an ambiguous one. In its broadest usage "industry" means a major sector of economic activity: agriculture or coffee growing, mining or copper production, manufacturing or chemical processing, services or banking, etc. The word is also used to delineate one of three broad sets of activities: "industry" covers manufacturing, construction and utilities, and sometimes mining as well, with either "agriculture" (excluding mining) or "primary production" (including mining) and "services" as the other two sectors. There is no way to tell which meaning of "industry" is intended except in the context of the discussion. *Manufacturing* is a less ambiguous term, which includes the production of all goods (not services) that require some transformation from a primary material or semifinished product, with the exception of constructed goods (buildings, roads, etc.) and goods supplied by utilities.

From Chapter 3's discussion of cross-country patterns we know that countries with higher per-capita incomes tend to have higher fractions of gross domestic product produced by industry and larger shares of the labor force employed in industry. Chenery and Syrquin found that for large countries, the average *value added share of industry* (which they define as manufacturing and construction), rises from about 18 percent for countries with incomes of about $200 in 1978 prices to over 30 percent for countries with incomes of about $1000. For small countries, those with populations of under fifteen million in 1960, the value added share rises from 13 to about 25 percent of GDP. *Industry's share of the labor force* grows from 10 to over 25 percent on average for all countries.[2] But the transition takes a long time. If a country sustains per-capita income growth of 2.5 percent a year, which would be good performance by recent historical standards, it would take sixty-five years to raise income per capita from $200 to $1000.

However, as Chapter 3 makes clear, there is nothing inevitable about the transition suggested by comparing different countries. Any one country will show different characteristics than the average and may also shift toward industry at a very different rate than indicated by cross-country averages. Figure 20–1 reproduces the regression line found by Chenery and Syrquin for the industry share of GDP in large counries (with populations over fifteen million in 1964), but also shows the positions of several large LDCs in 1977. A wide variation is evident. Countries with relatively rich natural resource endowments, such as Indonesia, Nigeria, and Iran, remain well below the average industry share, while India, the Philippines, and Taiwan (a small country, not shown in Fig. 20–1) are industrialized to a greater

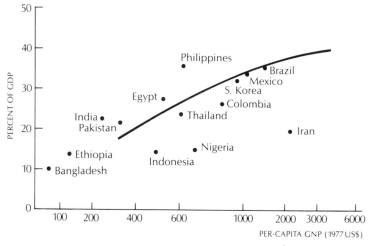

Fig. 20–1   Industry Share of Production, Large Countries, 1977, Compared to Regression Line for All Large Countries.

Sources: Hollis Chenery and Moises Syrquin, *Patterns of Development, 1950–1970* (London: Oxford University Press, 1975), p. 87 (trend line); World Bank, *World Tables 1980* (Washington, D.C., 1980), (country data for 1977).

Industry = manufacturing plus construction; large countries are defined by Chenery and Syrquin as those with populations over 15 million in 1964; regression line from Chenery and Syrquin, based on pooled cross-section and time series data, 1950–1970.

2. Hollis Chenery and Moises Syrquin, *Pattens of Development, 1950–1970* (London: Oxford University Press, 1975), pp. 50, 87, 99. As noted in Chapter 15, per-capita GNP has been multiplied by a factor of 2.0 to convert from 1964 prices to 1978 prices; this conversion factor is approximately the ratio of 1978 to 1964 prices in the United States.

extent than predicted by their income levels. And the differences between countries of similar size and endowment, such as the Philippines and Thailand, suggest that the outcome may depend on other factors, such as different development strategies.

Table 20–1 shows how the industrial sectors of several countries performed over the period from 1960 to 1979. For some, such as Kenya, Thailand, Ivory Coast, Malaysia, Korea, Taiwan, and Mexico, there has

TABLE 20–1   Characteristics of Industry, Selected Developing Countries, 1960–1980

	GNP per capita 1980 ($)	Share of GDP (%)			Growth of manu-facturing value added, 1960–1980 (% per year)
		Manufacturing		Industry[e] 1980	
		1960	1980		
Low-income countries[a]	260 (230)	12 (8)	15 (10)	35 (17)	5.0 (5.0)
Bangladesh	130	5	7	13	9.2
Ethiopia	140	6	11	16	5.0[g]
Mali	190	5[b]	6	10	NA
India	240	14	18	26	4.8
Sri Lanka	270	15	21	30	4.1
Tanzania	280	5	9[c]	13[c]	3.6[h]
Pakistan	300	12	16	25	6.7
Middle-income countries	1,410	20	20	40	6.6
Ghana	420	10	9[d]	21	2.9[h]
Kenya	420	9	13[c]	21[c]	11.4[h]
Indonesia	430	8	9	42	7.9
Senegal	450	12	19[c]	24	5.1[i]
Bolivia	570	15	14	29	5.7
Egypt	580	20	28	35[c]	6.2[i]
Thailand	670	13	20	29	11.0
Philippines	690	20	26	37	7.0
Nigeria	1,010	5	6	42	10.5
Ivory Coast	1,150	7	11[c]	22	9.5[i]
Colombia	1,180	17	22	30	6.0
Korea, South	1,520	14	28	41	17.2
Malaysia	1,620	9	23	37	11.8[j]
Brazil	2,050	26	28[c]	37	10.3[j]
Mexico	2,090	19	24[c]	38[c]	7.5
Taiwan	2,160	17	38[d]	44[d,f]	15.5[k]
High-income oil exporters	12,630	NA	4	77	9.2[i]
Saudi Arabia	11,260	NA	4	78	6.5[i]

Source: World Bank, *World Development Report 1982* (Washington, D.C., 1982), pp. 110–15.

[a] Figures in parentheses exclude China and India.
[b] 1961.
[c] 1979.
[d] 1978.
[e] Mining, manufacturing, construction, and utilities. Note that this definition inflates the share substantially for mining countries, especially for petroleum exporters.
[f] Excludes mining.
[g] 1961–1980.
[h] 1970–1979.
[i] 1960–1979.
[j] 1970–1980.
[k] 1960–1978.

been rapid industrial growth and a significant increase in the share of manufacturing in GPD. For others manufacturing was not a leading sector, or even lagged behind GDP growth. Generally, however, growth rates for manufacturing were considerably above those of GDP, as predicted by Chenery and Syrquin, with middle-income countries doing better than low-income countries.

Employment in industry has not grown as fast as value added. World Bank statistics indicate that for the low-income countries as a whole, value added in industry advanced at 5.0 percent a year from 1960 to 1980. At the same time employment in industry was growing by 4.0 percent a year. A comparison of the two rates shows that the elasticity of employment growth in manufacturing, the η of Chapter 8, was 80 percent: for every 10 percent rise in manufacturing output, manufacturing employment rose by 8 percent. The other side of the coin is that *labor productivity* in industry, the ratio of value added to employment, rose by 1 percent a year. Another implication is that since about 15 percent of the labor force in low-income countries is engaged in industry, the sector adds jobs for about 0.6 percent of the labor force each year (4.0 percent × 0.15 = 0.6 percent). With the labor force projected by the World Bank to grow at about 1.9 percent a year for the rest of the century, industry in low-income countries will be able to absorb less than one-third of those entering the work force each year (0.6 percent ÷ 1.9 percent = 0.32).[3] Clearly in these poorer countries agriculture and services must continue to bear the major burden for job creation.

Middle-income countries will not do much better, even though they employed a much higher fraction—24 percent—of their labor forces in industry in 1980. Employment in industry has been growing at 4.3 percent a year (1960–1980), enough to add jobs for 1.0 percent of the labor forces (4.3 percent × 0.24 = 1.0 percent). But with labor force projected to grow at 2.6 percent a year, this translates into new industrial jobs for only 38 percent of the new job seekers (1.0 percent ÷ 2.6 percent = 0.38).

Industry shares and growth rates do not tell the whole story, however. Industrial and developing countries are also marked by different *industrial structures*. The input-output table, described in Chapter 6, provides the most comprehensive way of seeing the difference. A glance at a detailed interindustry table for a country just beginning to industrialize will reveal many zero or small entries. There is little *backward integration,* so that many manufacturing industries acquire their inputs from abroad and there is not much flow of goods from one sector to another. In contrast, an industrial economy is highly integrated and the input-output table has entries indicating flows between most of the sectors. Lack of integration implies that developing countries manufacture finished goods more than intermediate, or producer, goods and that the process of industrialization requires a shift toward the producer goods industries, a process discussed in Chapter 16.

3. Labor force data in this and the next paragraph are from the World Bank, *World Development Report 1982* (Washington, D.C., 1982), pp. 146–47.

The progression from consumer to producer goods is evident in cross-country comparisons of the value added shares among *branches* within the manufacturing sector. The structure of manufacturing was studied by Hollis Chenery and Lance Taylor in 1968;[4] an updated version of their study is summarized in Table 20–2. It shows that by the time an "average" country has reached per-capita income of $350 (in 1978 prices) the food industries have already reached a plateau in that their GDP share will not change much with further growth, and textiles, clothing, and leather branches have already developed substantially. These can be called the "early developing" branches of manufacturing. Notice that their total shares of GDP are similar for large and small countries.

TABLE 20–2 Structure of Manufacturing: Share (%) of GDP for Manufacturing Branches at Different Levels of Income (by GNP per capita in 1978 dollars)

| | Large countries | | Small countries | | | |
| | | | Manufacturing Oriented | | Primary oriented | |
	$350	$1300	$350	$1300	$350	$1300
Branch						
1. Food	4.2	4.6	4.6	4.9	5.5	5.9
2. Textiles	2.7	2.6	2.0	2.9	1.2	1.6
3. Clothing and leather	0.8	1.4	1.1	1.8	0.6	1.0
4. Wood, paper, and printing	1.5	3.0	1.4	3.0	1.2	2.2
5. Chemicals and rubber	2.7	4.0	2.3	4.0	1.5	2.1
6. Minerals	1.0	1.6	1.1	1.7	0.7	1.0
7. Basic metals	1.2	2.5	0.3	1.6	0.3	1.0
8. Metals and misc.	8.0	7.8	2.8	6.9	1.0	3.4
Manufacturing[a]	17.0	27.0	15.3	25.5	12.1	18.0
Subtotals						
1. Simple consumer goods (early-developing) branches (1–3)	7.7	8.6	7.7	9.6	7.3	8.5
2. Producer goods and consumer durable branches (4–8)	9.4	18.9	7.9	17.2	4.7	9.7

Source: Vinod Prakash and Sherman Robinson, "A Cross-Country Analysis of Patterns of Growth" (World Bank, draft of July 1979).
[a] Estimated from a regression equation; *not* a total of the eight branches.

As development proceeds and the share of manufacturing in GDP rises, most of the above-average growth is supplied by the producer goods (and consumer durable) branches, numbered 4 through 8 in the table. These branches include the so-called basic or *heavy industries:* pulp and paper, chemicals, basic metals and metal products. The growth of these producer goods branches helps to "fill in" the input-output table. Recall from Chapter 16 the problems that protectionist import-substituting countries have in integrating backward from consumer goods industries. Obviously, "typical" countries—both large ones and small ones which tend to be or-

4. Hollis Chenery and Lance Taylor, "Development Patterns: Among Countries and Over Time," *Review of Economics and Statistics* 50 (1968): 391–418.

iented toward manufacturing[5]—are eventually able to overcome these barriers to backward integration. But the time span represented by a fourfold increase in per-capita GDP (roughly that represented in Table 20–2) is over fifty years, with 2.5 percent annual growth in per-capita GNP. In making this transition size appears to be less important than resource endowment and development strategy. Small countries oriented toward exports of manufactures—such as Chile, Kenya, Taiwan, Belgium or Norway—have characteristics very much like those of large countries at both levels of income shown in Table 20–2. Small primary-oriented countries—such as Bolivia, Ghana, Ivory Coast, Malaysia, Peru, Venezuela, Denmark, or Australia—typically industrialize more slowly.

Industry as a Leading Sector

Arguments favoring industrial investment as a development priority are based on more than the observation that industrial growth accompanies development. Industry-first advocates suggest that manufacturing is a leading sector because it stimulates investments in other sectors as well. The pattern of manufacturing development, in which consumer goods branches grow first and producer-goods-supplying industries follow, suggests that linkages within manufacturing, as well as outside it, are important to development. However, some manufactured goods are produced with decreasing costs as the scale of output grows, making it costly to start these industries, especially in small countries, where the scale of output may remain small for some time. Industry's requirements for supporting services, infrastructure, and labor markets may also stimulate rapid urban growth, another characteristic of developing countries. Finally, the growth of urban-based manufacturing creates some external diseconomies, such as pollution and congestion, that must be weighed in the scales before judging the advisability of pushing manufacturing as the engine of growth. These subjects are discussed in this section; we reserve judgment on the efficacy of industry-led development for the last section of the chapter.

Linkages

Albert Hirschman's concept of *unbalanced growth,* explained in Chapter 3, suggests that the rapid development of one or a few industries stimulates the expansion of others which are linked to the initially growing sectors. These *linkages* can be *backward* if the growth of, say, textiles leads to investment in production of cotton or dyestuffs to supply the textile industry; or *forward* if the availability of domestic textiles stimulates investment in a user industry, such as clothing, that would otherwise not have gotten started (see Chapter 3). There have been several attempts to measure Hirschman's linkages and these suggest the conclusion that if growth is to be unbalanced it should be led by manufacturing.

5. Small countries are considered "manufacturing oriented" if they export a higher fraction of manufactures than an average country of the same population and income per capita.

Among the several formulas proposed to measure linkages, those used by Pan Yotopoulos and Jeffrey Nugent seem as easy to understand and useful for our purposes as any.[6] Not surprisingly, linkage formulas depend on input-output tables, which are constructed to display linkages within an economy. A direct backward linkage for any industry, j, is measured as

$$L_{bj} = \frac{\sum\limits_i X_{ij}}{X_j} = \sum\limits_i a_{ij} \qquad [20\text{--}1]$$

where L_{bj} is the index of backward linkage, X_j is the value of the jth product, X_{ij} is the value of domestically supplied input of product (or service) i to the production of product j (the column of the input-output table), and a_{ij} is the Leontief (input-output) coefficient defined in Chapter 6. Thus a measure of backward linkage for any industry is simply the sum of its domestic input coefficients. If, for example, the textile industry adds value equal to 30 percent of its output and imports inputs equivalent to another 15 percent of output, its backward linkage index, L_b, would be 55 percent, the share of domestically purchased inputs $(100 - 30 - 15 = 55)$. The higher value added and the more inputs are imported, the lower the index and the less the industry has stimulated the development of supplying industries.

Those who recall Chapter 6 will immediately recognize that this index captures only the direct links. But if textile production stimulates cotton growing, might not cotton in turn stimulate fertilizer production? It is easy to incorporate these indirect effects in an index of total backward linkage. By analogy to equation 20–1, sum the coefficients of the Leontief inverse, designated r_{ij} in Chapter 6, to get

$$L_{tj} = \sum\limits_i r_{ij} \qquad [20\text{--}2]$$

where L_{tj} is an index of direct plus indirect (total) backward linkages from the jth industry.

There is an analogous simple measure of direct forward linkages,

$$L_{fi} = \frac{\sum\limits_j X_{ij}}{Z_i} \qquad [20\text{--}3]$$

where L_{fi} is the forward linkage index for the ith industry, X_{ij} is the output of the ith industry that is purchased by each jth user industry (the row of the input-output table), and Z_i is the sum of production of good i for both intermediate and final use.[7]

---

6. Pan A. Yotopoulos and Jeffrey B. Nugent, "A Balanced-Growth Version of the Linkage Hypothesis: A Test," *Quarterly Journal of Economics* 87 (May 1973): 157–71; reprinted in their text, *Economics of Development: Empirical Investigations* (New York: Harper & Row, 1976), pp. 299–306.

7. It is possible to define a direct-plus-indirect index for forward linkages, but it has little practical meaning.

Yotopoulos and Nugent have used input-output tables for five developing countries (Chile, Greece, Mexico, Spain, and South Korea) to measure the linkage indices for eighteen industries. The results are shown in Table 20–3. The next-to-last column tells us, for example, that for each additional $1 of leather goods produced, production of all inputs must rise by $2.39. A high index indicates that expansion of the industry will stimulate production in other sectors of the economy. Thus a strategy of unbalanced growth should start with industries enjoying high total backward linkage indices because these should give the clearest signals for subsequent investment in supplier industries and result in maximum induced growth. Manufacturing industries dominate the upper ranks of Table 20–3 whether the direct or total backward linkages are considered. Primary industries, utilities, and services are low on both lists. Hence an unbalanced growth strategy should first emphasize manufacturing, especially of consumer goods and subsequently of chemicals and metal products. Advocates of import substitution strategies clearly find sustenance in these findings.

TABLE 20–3 Sectoral Linkage Indices and Rankings in Five Less Developed Countries[a]

	Direct forward linkage index (L_f)	Rank	Direct backward linkage index (L_b)	Rank	Total backward linkage index (L_t)	Rank
Leather	0.645	4	0.683	2	2.39	1
Basic metals	0.980	1	0.632	5	2.36	2
Clothing	0.025	18	0.621	6	2.32	3
Textiles	0.590	8	0.621	7	2.24	4
Food, beverage manufactures	0.272	16	0.718	1	2.22	5
Paper	0.788	3	0.648	3	2.17	6
Chemicals and petroleum refining	0.599	7	0.637	4	2.13	7
Metal products and machinery	0.430	13	0.558	9	2.12	8
Wood, furniture	0.582	9	0.620	8	2.07	9
Construction	0.093	17	0.543	10	2.04	10
Printing	0.508	10	0.509	12	1.98	11
Other manufactures	0.362	15	0.505	13	1.94	12
Rubber	0.453	12	0.481	14	1.93	13
Minerals (nonmetalic)	0.870	2	0.517	11	1.83	14
Agriculture	0.502	11	0.368	15	1.59	15
Utilities	0.614	6	0.296	16	1.49	16
Mining	0.638	5	0.288	17	1.47	17
Services	0.378	14	0.255	18	1.41	18

Sources: P. A. Yotopoulos and J. B. Nugent, "A Balanced-Growth Version of the Linkage Hypothesis: A Test," *Quarterly Journal of Economics* 87 (1973): 163, Table 2.

[a] Chile, Greece, South Korea, Mexico, and Spain.

But what do these indices really mean? Should a country base its development strategy on them, even if rapid growth is the principal goal? The particular measurement formulas have been attacked for several reasons, many of them sound ones, but alternative (and more complicated) formulations give similar rankings anyway.[9] Note, first of all, that linkages are measured by *domestically* produced inputs and outputs. That is, a linkage index for Mexico tells us what backward or forward integration Mexico has already achieved. To discover what potential linkages Mexico might realize in the future we would have to use indices for a more industrialized country, say, Canada. The Mexican linkage indices would be guides only for a less industrialized country, say, Paraguay.

The real issue then is whether a mechanical summing up of input-output coefficients for one country really tells us anything about the dynamic processes of growth in another country. The textile industry, which ranks high in Table 20–3 according to its total backward linkage coefficient, may well require inputs of cotton and of synthetic fibers. But whether this additional demand will lead to new investment in farming and chemicals depends on many conditions, none of them reflected in the index. Can cotton be grown in the country at all, and if so at what cost? It might remain cheaper, and to the country's advantage, to import cotton and use the land to grow more profitable crops. If cotton is already being grown and exported, can output expand to accommodate the textile plant or would it simply divert exports? Reduced exports would of course cancel the backward linkage effect. In some situations home-grown cotton of high quality may fetch a premium on world markets, so it would pay to export it and import a cheaper variety that would suit the domestic textile industry. The potential linkage back to synthetic fibers raises additional issues. Petrochemical industries are subject to substantial economies of scale (see next section) and it would take a considerable expansion of the textile industry to justify the very large investment in petrochemicals. If protection is used to keep out imports of synthetic fibers the textile industry itself would suffer higher costs and perhaps lose its impetus to expand, as explained in Chapter 16. However, it is also possible that some infant supplier industries may have the potential to reduce costs over time—learning by doing—if they are given a chance.

The requirements for effective forward linkages from manufacturing are even more stringent. To continue the example, textiles have a large forward linkage index, primarily to the clothing industry. But does domestic cloth stimulate the clothing industry? It can if textiles can be produced at costs below the price of imported cloth. Otherwise the user industry is better off importing its input. If clothing manufacturers are forced, through tariffs or controls, to take more expensive domestic cloth, this would discourage rather than stimulate the forward linkage. In other words a forward linkage is effective only if the supplying industry is competitive in world markets.

The concept of forward linkage is more useful in dealing with nontraded goods, such as domestic transport, electric power and other utilities, and

---

9. One technical problem with linkage indices is that interindustry tables are not always comparable among countries, either because branches of industry are defined differently or because industries, such as "textiles," may be inherently different in two countries. Also, the value of these indices depends on the degree of disaggregation in the input-output table. See Leroy P. Jones, "The Measurement of Hirschmanian Linkages: Comment," *Quarterly Journal of Economics* 90 (1976): 323–33.

many services. Abundant and cheap supplies of these goods and services may well stimulate user industries. The opening of a new region by road or rail is the classic example of development being stimulated by infrastructure through forward linkages. But the provision of infrastructure and other services can only stimulate downstream investment if other conditions would make user industries profitable. It is better to think of these non-traded goods and services in permissive terms: they make growth of user industries possible, and their lack can constrain further investment, but they are not often leading sectors, at least not since the great openings of land in the Americas and Australia during the nineteenth and early twentieth centuries. (Brazil's Amazon may be the next example.) The static linkage indices can help direct attention to potential linkages, but detailed studies are required to consider all the relevant conditions and to pinpoint the ways in which investment in one industry will lead to investment in others. These studies may well show that some manufacturing sectors can lead growth in certain countries. But some of the case studies cited in Chapter 15 demonstrated that certain primary sectors also generate effective linkages and there is not an overwhelming case favoring manufacturing on this ground.

Economies of Scale

One factor that may retard the development of backward linkages, and help to explain the evolution of industrial structure, is *economies of scale.* It has been observed by economists at least since Adam Smith that for many kinds of production larger facilities may be able to produce at lower unit costs than small ones. For example, steel produced in a mill designed for two million tons a year might cost 15 percent less than steel produced in a mill designed for only one million tons. As the scale of output rises, the potential average cost falls. (Of course if the large mill produces only one million tons, its average cost is likely to be higher than the smaller mill, because the small one was designed for the lower output.) Readers familiar with the theory of the firm will recognize the concept of *long-run average cost,* the potential unit cost of output when plant size is variable. If the long-run average cost curve declines over a range of outputs relevant to the plant in question, there are economies of scale.

One mathematical representation of scale economies deals with *total cost, C:*

$$C = AQ^{\alpha}, \qquad\qquad [20\text{--}4]$$

where Q is total output or scale, A is a constant, and α is the *scale coefficient* or *cost elasticity*. This expression says that as output increases, total costs (for an optimally designed plant) rise less than proportionally if $\alpha < 1$. The parameter α measures the ratio of the percentage increase in total cost to the percentage increase in quantity produced (scale), or

$$\alpha = (\Delta C/C)/(\Delta Q/Q) \qquad\qquad [20\text{--}5]$$

which explains why α is also called a cost elasticity.[10] The smaller the elasticity, the less total costs rise with scale. Equation 20–4 can be transformed into a statement about average costs, c:[11]

$$c = C/Q = AQ^{\alpha-1} \qquad\qquad [20\text{--}6]$$

Since α is less than 1 for economies of scale, equation 20–6 shows (what we already know) that average cost declines with output.

Scale economies arise for a number of reasons. (1) Some costs, such as research and design efforts or start-up costs, may be fixed over a wide range of output. (2) The amount and cost of materials used in capital equipment will rise with output, but not always in proportion. For example, the capacity of a boiler is related to its volume, which for a sphere varies as the cube of its radius, while the material used to build it is related to its area, proportional to the square of the radius. (3) The amount of inventories and other working capital does not rise proportionally to output. (4) Greater scale permits greater specialization of both workers and equipment (the point emphasized by Adam Smith) which in turn permits higher productivity. (5) Larger production runs reduce the number of times equipment must be set up or readjusted for each run. For example, a plant that produces two or more products with one machine, such as metal cans of different sizes, could be run more efficiently once it has enough volume to produce each on a separate machine, reducing set-up costs. (6) Larger producers may be able to obtain quantity discounts when they procure inputs. These economies all apply to individual plants. At the level of the firm, further economies may arise in management, transport, marketing, and finance as more plants are added.

These cost savings can be quite important in manufacturing certain products. Table 20–4 presents data on the scale economies measured for several industries in the United Kingdom in 1969. The first column gives the percentage increase in average cost for a plant built and operating at half of the "minimum efficient scale." The minimum efficient scale (MES) is defined as a plant large enough so that no further economies can be gained by building a larger facility. In other words it represents the point at which the long-run average cost curve flattens out. In practice if the largest plant in existence does not exhaust potential scale economies, investigators often take that output as the MES until a larger plant is built and its costs measured. The second column gives the cost elasticity, α, of equations 20–4 and 20–6, as implied by column 1. However, although the cost function of equation 20–4 requires that average costs continue to fall indefinitely, the concept of MES implies that average costs do not fall at scales larger than the MES.

10. If $C = AQ^{\alpha}$, then $dC/dQ = \alpha AQ^{\alpha-1} = \alpha C/Q$. The cost elasticity is $(Q/C)\,(dC/dQ) = (Q/C)\,(\alpha C/Q) = \alpha$.
11. Divide equation 20–4 by Q to give $c = C/Q = AQ^{\alpha}/Q$ or $c = AQ^{\alpha-1}$

TABLE 20-4 Economies of Scale in Manufacturing, United Kingdom, 1969

Product	% increase in average cost of half the MES[a,b]	Cost elasticity (α)[c]	MES[a] as % of UK market
Bread	15	0.80	1
Beer	9	0.88	3
Footwear	2	0.97	0.2
Dyes	22	0.71	100
Sulfuric acid	1	0.99	30
Polymers	5	0.93	33
Cement	9	0.88	10
Steel (integrated)	8	0.89	80
Machine tools	5	0.93	100
Electric motors	15	0.80	60
Automobiles (one model)	6	0.92	50
Bicycles	small	—	10
Diesel engines	4	0.94	10
Domestic appliances	8	0.89	20

Source: C. F. Pratten, *Economies of Scales in Manufacturing Industries* (Cambridge: Cambridge University Press, 1971).

[a] Minimum efficient scale defined as the output beyond which average costs cease to decline (or beyond which no larger plants have been built).

[b] As a percent of the average cost of production for a plant producing at minimum economic scale.

[c] Coefficient of equations 20-4 and 20-6 in text; calculated from column 1 using equation 20-6.

Some of the cost increases in column 1 (for plants half of MES) are significant: 8 percent or more for bread, beer, dyes, cement, steel, electric motors, and domestic appliances. However, this is not very meaningful unless we know how large an MES plant is relative to the national market. In the cases of bread and beer in Britain, the third column shows that economies of scale are exhausted at outputs that are very small relative to total consumption, so it is possible to have many plants of sufficient scale. For dyes, steel, electric motors, and automobiles, however, a plant of minimum efficient scale would (in 1969) have met at least half of British demand. This suggests that as manufacturers of these products pursue profits through cost savings, output is likely to become concentrated in a very few firms, even in markets as large as Britain's.

No developing country has an internal market as large as Britain's. In 1980 the total gross national product of the largest LDC, China, was less than two-thirds that of the United Kingdom; Brazil's GNP was 55 percent of Britain's and India's only 36 percent. The largest African economy is Nigeria's, with a GNP one-fifth that of Britain; even oil-rich prerevolutionary Iran had a GNP only a third that of Britain.[12] For medium to large third world economies, then, only industries with negligible scale economies (footwear, sulfuric acid, and bicycles in the table) or with a very small MES (bread, beer, and footwear) can be accommodated efficiently in a

12. Gross national product is only a rough approximation of market size, especially for specific products. Both income per capita, which helps to indicate the per-capita demand for individual commodities, and population should be included separately in a more comprehensive measure of market size.

competitive domestic market. For the other industries in the table, large size and significant cost savings imply that plants built to serve the domestic market will eithe have no domestic competition, produce at high cost, or in many cases both.

The characteristics of these large-scale industries shed light on the industrialization process. All are producer goods or consumer durables. The industries in which small countries face the greatest disadvantages, those with large economies at large outputs, are in chemicals (dyes and, to a lesser extent, polymers), basic metals (steel), capital equipment (electric motors and, to a lesse extent, machine tools), and consumer desirables (automobiles and appliances). Thus the nondurable consumer goods industries develop early at least in part because economies of scale are not much of a barrier, xcept in the very smallest countries. And the barrier to backward integration, noted in discussing import substitution (Chapter 16) and observed in the Chenery-Taylor cross-section studies, can also be blamed in part on economies of scale.

Despite the existence of scale economies it may be efficient to build small plants in developing countries. A steel plant, for example, should be built when it can producc at a cost below the price of imported steel. This may happen long before the market grows to accommodate a steel mill of minimum efficient scale. Economic size is only one of the factors that bears on efficiency. All the others mcntioned earlier in this text—productivity, opportunity cost of capital and labor, availability of raw materials and complementary inputs, potential linkages, transport costs of competing imports or of material inputs, managerial skills, market organization also affect the outcome and may outweigh the effects of scale economies. Techniques such as project appraisal (Chapter 6) and domestic resource cost (Chapter 16) can be employed to analyze the impact of all these elements on profitability.

Moreover, the domestic market is not the only possibility. The "virtuous circle," through which export markets make it possible to attain scale economies, which in turn increase export competitiveness, was one of the forces behind Britain's Industrial Revolution. Indeed if a domestic industry in a small LDC were efficient enough to compete with foreign plants at any given output, then scale economies would not matter: the home industry could export enough to achieve any scale desired. And recently, developing countries like South Korea and Brazil have achieved scale economies, even in industries like steel and automobiles, with the help of export markets.

For small countries scale economies combined with low factor productivity may bc a formidable barrier to industrialization. For larger countries such barriers can be manageable if they can avoid high protection of the monopolies that typically result in these large-scale industries. The solution lies in moderate and declining protection, the use of imports (potential or actual) to constrain monopoly pricing, and the encouragement of exports to enter the virtuous circle. It is in these large-scale, producer goods and consumer durable industries that custom unions and other trade-promoting devices among the developing countries may be most beneficial. Groups like the Latin American Free Trade Association (LAFTA), the Andean Group, and the Association of Southeast Asian Nations (ASEAN) have promoted agreements that allocate steel, petrochemicals, fertilizer, machine tools, and other large-scale industries among members so that each can benefit from access to much larger markets and attain economies of scale (see Chapter 17).

Urbanization

Since the Industrial Revolution, urbanization and industrialization have moved in tandem. England started the nineteenth century with 30 percent of its people living in cities and ended the century with an urban population share over 70 percent.[13] That trend toward urbanization with industrial development is evident today in cross-country comparisons. As incomes per capita grow from about $200 to $1000, and on average industrial value added grows from about 18 to about 30 percent of GDP, the urban population increases its share of the total from just over 20 percent to just over 50 percent for a typical country (Fig. 20–2). Although there is considerable variation among countries at any income level, nevertheless the association between development and urbanization is unmistakable.

What causes this apparently inexorable growth of cities as industrialization proceeds? Several *external economies* (see Chapter 5) benefit manufacturing firms in urban settings. Large populations reduce the firm's cost of recruiting labor of all kinds, but especially skilled workers and technicians. Moreover, in cities workers usually find their own housing, so firms do not

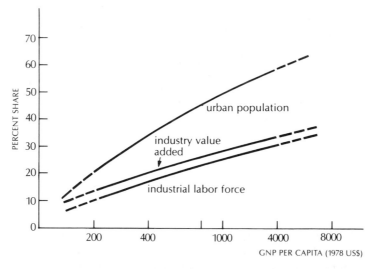

Fig. 20–2 Industrialization and Urbanization: Cross-Country Comparisons, 1965.
Source: Hollis Chenery and Moises Syrquin, *Patterns of Development, 1950–1970* (London: Oxford University Press, 1975), pp 36, 50, 55.

13. Hobsbawm, *Industry and Empire,* Fig. 13.

have to provide it, as they might in rural areas or small towns. *Infrastructure,* including industrial sites, electricity, water, sewage, roads, railroads, and in many cases ports, is provided by government in the cities at costs that reflect substantial scale economies. Health and education facilities are also more highly developed in the cities. Although some of these services could be provided by firms in remote locations, not all can and the costs would be much higher. Infrastructure is an excellent example of services with important economies of scale which can be provided relatively cheaply by government to individual users.

Each firm also benefits from the *economies of agglomeration* which result from the presence of many other firms, because a wide range of necessary inputs and services becomes available. Manufacturers can reduce transport costs and shipping delays if they locate near their suppliers. They also benefit from the proximity of repair and other industrial services. Financial markets cluster in cities where domestic and international communication facilities are available and cheap. Manufacturers need access to banks and other financial institutions. They also need the city's communications to stay in touch with distant suppliers and markets, especially export markets. When the city in question is a national capital, manufacturers may locate there to gain ready access to government officials who control investment licenses and incentives, import allocations, and a myriad of other policy and administrative devices that affect the profitability of the firm. Finally, the strong preferences of capitalists, managers, and technicians for the amenities of large cities can be a significant reason for locating there.

Once a city is established, its large market creates reinforcing attractions. Distribution costs are minimized when the firm locates near its largest market. If the costs of shipping output weigh heavily in a firm's costs, and especially if they are more important than the costs of transporting inputs, firms will be pulled toward cities. This attraction is particularly strong in developing countries where intercity and rural-urban transport networks are sparse. In developed countries, where transport networks are dense and efficient, manufacturing tends to be more footloose, seeking out advantages like cheap labor with less regard for transport costs.

There is a chicken-and-egg circularity in this reasoning. Do manufacturers locate in cities because workers, truckers, and banks are there? Or do workers, truckers, and banks move toward cities because manufacturers are there or likely to locate there? Each magnetizes the others; the attraction is mutual and leads to the markedly dualistic character of development, in which the modern sector is industrial, technologically advanced, and urban.

But urbanization has its costs as the residents of every large city in the world observe daily: overcrowding, unsanitary conditions, displacement of rural migrants, crime. These too have been features of industrialization for two centuries. During the first half of the nineteenth century, London and the other growing cities of Britain were appalling places:

> . . . smoke hung over them and filth impregnated them, . . . the elementary public services—water-supply, sanitation, street-cleaning, open spaces, and so on —could not keep pace with the mass migration of men into the cities, thus pro-

ducing, especially after 1830, epidemics of cholera, typhoid and an appalling constant toll of the two great groups of nineteenth-century urban killers—air pollution and water pollution, or respiratory and intestinal disease. . . . [N]ew city populations . . . pressed into overcrowded and bleak slums, whose very sight froze the heart of the observer.[14]

Migrants to the large cities of the third world probably do not have to put up with conditions as bad as those of early nineteenth-century London, but cities like Calcutta, Lagos, and São Paulo contain slums with many of the same kinds of problems.

Although urban infrastructure can be provided at lower cost than the alternative of providing the same services in small, scattered towns, infrastructure is still the largest direct cost of urbanization. A study of cities and towns in India conducted in 1967 estimated that the capital cost of infrastructure provided for manufacturing industry was $820 for every $1000 of incremental value added in manufacturing, or about $430 per employee in a city of one million in 1967. Only about a quarter of this is due to construction in the industrial area itself. The balance serves the residential area, so can generally be interpreted as the capital cost of supporting workers in the city. If the capital costs are amortized at 10 percent a year and maintenance costs ($200 per employee) are added, it would appear that cities provide manufacturers with annual infrastructure services costing 13 percent of the value added in manufacturing.[15]

Industrializing cities become a magnet for rural workers seeking jobs at higher wages. The pervasive third world phenomenon of rural-urban migration was explored in Chapter 8. The social cost of this migration is high. More than one migrant leaves the rural areas for each urban job created, so the opportunity cost is a multiple of that for the one worker required. Often migrants are the youngest, most energetic, and best trained of the rural population, reducing the potential for productivity increases in agriculture. And in the cities their presence in large numbers aggravates congestion, with its attendant ills: crowded and unhygienic living conditions, causing disease and malnutrition, overburdened schools, crime, social disorientation, and political unrest. Despite the risks of unemployment and the poor living conditions, urban life may still be attractive to many rural residents relative to the opportunities available at home. The costs of congestion are thus external diseconomies: each new migrant will benefit on average, but in so doing he reduces the well-being of all others, even if only slightly. The social costs are high, however, because this marginal reduction in well-being must be added up for all residents of the city.

No government feels comfortable with crowded cities and many have attempted to stem the flow of migration. Over the long run this can best be done by encouraging rural development as actively as industrialization, using the wide range of land tenure, investment, price, incentive, and other

14. Hobsbawm, *Industry and Empire,* p. 86.
15. Stanford Research Institute et al., *Costs of Urban Infrastructure for Industry as Related to City Size in Developing Countries: India Case Study* (Menlo Park, Calif., 1968). The costs per worker would be more than double in 1980 prices.

policies described in Chapter 18 and elsewhere in this text. A complementary approach is to encourage the dispersal of new industries to smaller cities through provision of infrastructure, incentives, and controls over location. Spreading investment reduces congestion. It may also dampen migration, or at least reduce its cost, by placing jobs in less glittering locations. Migrants will have shorter average distances to travel, so more of them can search for jobs without a commitment to permanent residence in cities remote from their homes. Decentralization of industry also has complementary benefits for agriculture, distributing urban markets and manufactured supplies more evenly among the populace.

Industrial dispersion does have costs, however. Infrastructure costs may be greater in small towns, which have not provided as much of the basic facilities as large cities. The study of urban infrastructure in India cited earlier (see footnote 14), showed that in a town of 50,000, infrastructure for industry costs 13 percent more than in a city of one million, allowing for both capital and recurrent costs. No measurements were made for larger cities, in which economies of scale are evidently exhausted and congestion may well raise the unit cost of infrastructure. To this must be added the higher costs of transport and other infrastructure required to connect dispersed industrial locations. Even with this wider network of transport and communications in place, private firms—and society—incur higher costs of hauling freight, both their material inputs and their final outputs, if they do not locate in the most efficient place; of communicating with suppliers, customers, and financial institutions, not to mention government officials; and of waiting with idle facilities while parts and repair specialists from distant places arrive to fix broken equipment. Whether the benefits of dispersal justify the costs will depend on the circumstances. Costs will be lower if the population is already dispersed, if several urban centers and connecting infrastructure already exist, and if the new sites have obvious advantages, such as nearby raw materials or abundant water.

Industry is guilty of another external diseconomy that has received much attention in the past decade: *pollution,* especially of urban environments. In the developed world environmental protection has been one of the important forces determining the costs and location of investment in the heavy industries (chemicals, metals) and energy-producing industries (refineries, power plants). Some have seen growing environmental concern as an opportunity for third world countries to move more rapidly into heavy industries and transform their exports of raw materials into semifinished products. Whether or not this is a real opportunity depends on two factors. First, pollution can be controlled by the installation of equipment that raises investment costs. These costs would tend to push investments toward the third world only if they outweigh the existing cost advantage of industrial countries, something that cost-benefit analysis can reveal. Second, the only way developing countries can realize any potential cost advantage conferred by anti-pollution devices is to forgo the devices and accept the pollution. Because they start with less industry, some LDC environments have been less damaged and may be better able to accept some additional pollution, at least to a point. But some LDCs have already suffered environmental damage from copper smelters, steel mills, pulp mills, fishmeal plants, and other resource-based industries. For the others the acceptance of polluting industries becomes a political choice: Is the spur to industrialization and income growth worth the reduction in the quality of life implied by pollution? It cannot be presumed that all developing countries would answer affirmatively.

Small-Scale Industry

Growing awareness of the failures and costs of industrialization has created renewed interest in an alternative path to development that has a long history: small-scale industry. Every one of today's developed market economies depended heavily on small enterprises to effect the transition from agricultural to industrial societies. As late as 1960 in the United States, the United Kingdom, and West Germany, about one fourth of manufacturing output originated in firms of fewer than 100 employees. In Japan, where small enterprises have always played a major role as subcontractors to large firms, over half of manufacturing output originated in firms with fewer than 100 workers in 1960, and a third of the workers were employed by them.[16]

Throughout the postwar era of rapid industrialization third world advocates have promoted small-scale industry as either a complementary or an alternative development. India, which has probably been the postindependence leader in planning for rapid, large-scale industrialization, has also pursued small-scale development with vigor, a legacy of Gandhi's famous advocacy of smallness. China's use of small-scale rural industry in support of local self-reliance is equally well known. Throughout the developing world there are probably very few development plans that have not paid homage to small industry. It is hoped that small workshops and factories will generate more employment than large ones; permit decentralization and reduce urban congestion; promote greater equality and participation while reducing dualism; and mobilize scarce resources, especially savings, entrepreneurship, and local raw materials.

In a moment we will assess the potential of small industry to accomplish these goals, but first we need to define "small industry." Many competing systems of classification have been suggested, and no sharp distinction between small and large is possible. For our purposes an approximate tripartite classification will do. At one extreme *traditional small-scale industry* includes handicraft industries, artisans, workshops, and household-based industry, a collection of overlapping categories sometimes fuzzily called "cottage industry." The distinguishing characteristics of these operations are their smallness—they usually employ fewer than five, or at most ten, workers—and their use of traditional techniques (hand-loom weaving, for

---

16. Eugene Staley and Richard Morse, *Modern Small Industry for Developing Countries* (New York: McGraw-Hill, 1965), p. 17.

example) to produce traditional products (cotton cloth). These are the village industries of which Gandhi spoke. Further up the hierarchy are *small, modern factories,* employing perhaps 10 to 50 or 100 workers in the manufacture of modern products, such as plastic or metal goods. The division between small and *large factories* must be elastic. In large countries or small industrial ones, a plant employing 200 would be considered small. In most developing countries it would be large. Although many countries define small industry on the basis of asset value, this seems less useful, especially for cross-country comparison in these days of rapid inflation.

How important are small firms in developing countries? One source showed that for twenty-one developing countries during the 1960s, a mean of 79 percent of all manufacturing establishments had fewer than ten employees—probably qualifying as traditional industries—and were responsible for 31 percent of the workers and 11 percent of the value added in manufacturing. Firms of up to fifty employees constituted 91 percent of the total in manufacturing for this sample, employed 52 percent of the workers, and produced 24 percent of the value added.[17] Details for selected countries are shown in Table 20–5.

TABLE 20–5 Importance of Small Industry in Manufacturing, Selected Countries, 1960s

	% share of			
	Employment in manufacturing firms employing		Value added in manufacturing firms employing	
Country (Year)	1–9	1–49	1–9	1–49
Brazil (1960)	16	35	10	26
Colombia (1968)	22	36	10	20
Iraq (1964)	37	49	25	40
South Korea (1967)	14	38	7	23
Lebanon (1964)	39	66	29	63
Malaysia (1968)	20	57	11	33
Mexico (1965)	24	37	8	20
Peru (1963)	24	43	4	15
Taiwan (1966)	13	36	14	28
Thailand (1963)	68	80	12	28
Turkey (1964)	54	60	19	28
Japan (1971)	16	41	8	26
Norway (1963)	13	38	10	31
United States (1967)	2	12	3	14

Source: Ranadev Banerji, "Small-Scale Production in Manufacturing: An International Cross-Section Overview," *Weltwirtschaftliches Archiv* 114 (1978): 67.

The case that small-scale industry can *generate more employment* than large factories is based on the observation that small firms generally use more labor and less capital per unit output. Data gathered from several studies by the World Bank generally support this conclusion.[18] In Japan,

17. Ranadev Banerji, "Small-Scale Production Units in Manufacturing: An International Cross-Section Overview," *Weltwirtschaftliches Archiv* 114 (1978): 62–82.
18. World Bank, *Employment and Development of Small Enterprises: Sector Policy Paper* (Washington, D.C., 1978), pp. 65–67.

for example, capital/labor ratios rise from an index of 30 for firms with fewer than 30 employees to over 100 for firms employing over 300. And capital productivity (as measured by the output/capital ratio) falls from an index of about 190 to around 100 (except that very small firms with fewer than ten workers have an index of only 122, indicating less efficiency than somewhat larger enterprises). The fall in output/capital ratios with firm size was also evident in India, Malaysia, Mexico, Pakistan, and the Philippines during the late 1960s.

The average indices may mask variations not only in the use of labor and capital but also in the products manufactured. Perhaps small enterprises tend to manufacture those products that are more labor-intensive, but use the same capital/output and labor/output ratios as large firms in the same industries. To sort this out we need factor ratios by product and by size of firm. Ranadev Banerji has compiled data on labor productivity for his sample of twenty-one developing countries.[19] For each of seventeen branches of manufacturing, whether we consider firms of one to nine workers or of one to forty-nine workers, labor productivity averaged across all countries is lower than in large firms in the same branch. This is consistent with the conventional wisdom that small firms use more labor-intensive techniques than large, whatever the industry. However, for some of the individual countries in Banerji's sample there are examples of higher labor productivity in small enterprises than in large ones of the same manufacturing branch, contradicting expectations. This surprising result is partially supported by detailed studies of India by Dhar and Lydall,[20] and of Ghana by William F. Steel.[21] Both found several industries in which capital productivity (the ratio of output to capital) rises for larger firms, implying reduced capital intensity and, perhaps, greater labor intensity. Dhar and Lydall offer a different explanation: traditional industries, of fewer than ten employees, may be more labor-intensive than all larger firms, but once modern methods are employed economies of scale take over and larger firms use less of *both* capital and labor.

If Dhar and Lydall are right, then employment goals can be pursued through small industry only if: (a) traditional rather than modern enterprises are encouraged, or (b) small modern factories are encouraged, but are likely to use more of both labor and capital. In either case small industry would not be a solution to the growth-versus-employment dilemma. Rather, employment would be generated at the expense of either modernization and widening consumer choice or of rising productivity and efficiency. This would be a serious indictment. But the issue is an empirical one, the available data give no clear answers, and more research is needed before we rule out the small-industry solution.

It is argued that small enterprises can lead to *decentralization* of industry

---

19. Banerji, "Small-Scale Production Units in Manufacturing," p. 80.

20. P. N. Dhar and H. F. Lydall, *The Role of Small Enterprises in Indian Economic Development* (New York: Asia Publishing House, 1961), p. 14.

21. William F. Steel, *Small-Scale Employment and Production in Developing Countries: Evidence from Ghana* (New York: Praeger, 1977), p. 107.

because they do not require large markets for their output and thus do not have to locate in big cities. An extension of the case for decentralization is that small industry can complement rural development by locating in the rural areas. Here it is important to make the distinction between traditional and modern small-scale industries. As Dhar and Lydall point out, the traditional industries are already in the rural areas. Their encouragement may help to increase rural incomes and employment, but does not draw industry away from congested cities. Furthermore the growth of rural industry must follow, not lead, agricultural growth. Modern small factories, on the other hand, are not so easily located in rural areas and cannot themselves be the moving force behind dispersion toward the smaller cities and towns. Although producers of consumer goods can find adequate markets in small urban centers, suppliers of producer goods need to locate near the large urban manufacturers they serve. Moreover, all small producers need access to material inputs, which means locations near ports and transport facilities. Perhaps more critically they need to be near the urban growth centers in which entrepreneurs and skilled workers are located. In short, with the exception of consumer goods markets, small factories depend on the same urban external economies as large manufacturers.

Rural Small Industry in China

The Chinese have done what appears to be difficult in market economies: they have established modern small factories in rural centers to supply farm inputs, equipment, and consumer goods to communes and other rural consumers.[22] Several conditions encouraged the emergence of local factories. China's rural transport and marketing system is poorly developed, isolating rural communities from urban centers of production. The central planning and control of industrial goods intensifies this isolation, because communes wanting fertilizer or trucks must apply to authorities located in urban centers, a process that entails long delays and may not be successful. It is in the communes' interest for their regions to become self-reliant in agricultural inputs to avoid these delays, and also in the planners' interests if local materials, capital, and labor can be used so that other industrial priorities are not sacrificed. Local industry has the additional advantages of bringing modern technology directly to the countryside and of helping to narrow the economic and social gap between farm and city.

Despite the success of the small-industries program, Chinese planners apparently have only limited goals in mind. The program is not conceived as a generator of off-farm employment; rather, there is concern that rural factories will draw needed workers away from the communes. Nor is rural industry expected to replace modern, urban industry. "Walking on

22. The following account is based on the report of the American Rural Small-scale Industry Delegation, *Rural Small-Scale Industry in the People's Republic of China* (Berkeley: University of California Press, 1977), Chapter 1. Dwight Perkins was chairman of the delegation.

two legs" means that both must be pursued, and self-reliance implies that rural factories must not divert resources from large-scale urban ones. Self-reliance also suggests that regional equality is not a prime goal of the program, because wealthier regions with more resources, especially savings, are likely to do better than poor ones. However, rural-urban equality is probably served by the program. Finally, it should be recognized that China is a large, densely populated country. The rural counties upon which self-reliant factories are based have populations greater than many of the countries in the third world. And the "small" factories—of 50 to 600 employees—are also large by the standards of most developing countries.

To the extent that small enterprises can generate more employment per unit and can locate in smaller cities and towns, they will *promote greater income equality* among families, among regions, and between rural and urban areas. Small firms generally pay lower wages than large ones because they use less capital per worker, are located to a greater extent in poorer regions, and are not covered by—or can easily evade—minimum-wage legislation. Hence workers in small firms earn incomes between those paid by large enterprises and those earned by workers in the informal sector and agriculture. If there are more of these workers than would otherwise be engaged in large, modern industry, the benefits of industrialization are more widely distributed. Although small firms may be quite profitable relative to capital invested, both investment and profits are small and entrepreneurs correspondingly less wealthy than the owners of large enterprises. If traditional industries are encouraged, then rural family incomes are augmented directly. Equalizing effects would be greater if small-scale manufacturing substitutes for large. Even if small industry is only additional to large, modern industries, however, and is not widely dispersed, it cannot intensify dualism and inequality, and may still promote equalization to some extent. On balance, then, small industry is a safe instrument for promoting equity. Whether it can do so extensively without reducing growth hinges on the empirical issues of employment creation and dispersal.

Small-scale manufacturing has a clear advantage in *mobilizing* two *resources:* entrepreneurship and local raw materials. Most societies have latent or actual entrepreneurs in retail trading, farming, transportation, and other small-scale activities. Small-scale manufacturing represents a feasible step for these entrepreneurs, who would be blocked from entering manufacturing if large amounts of credit and the ability to manage large-scale enterprises were essential. Small industry also permits imitation of more advanced entrants, hence requiring less innovative entrepreneurs.

Small deposits of natural resources, such as phosphates or limestone, cannot be exploited efficiently by large fertilizer or cement plants. Local small industry might be able to use these resources at competitive costs, as evidently has happened in China. But large-scale mineral exploitation usually has competitive advantages, so small units are only likely to be economic in remote regions to which transport costs are high. It is also alleged that small industry mobilizes additional savings. This has some plausibility if putative entrepreneurs would save more in order to enter small-scale manufacturing. But there is little evidence either way.

On balance, then, small industry has potential benefits in generating employment, decentralization, and equality, and in mobilizing entrepreneurs, although the empirical support of these propositions is not strong. Accepting, as most governments do, that small industries ought to be encouraged, how should this be done? Strangely enough, in this case positive measures of encouragement may not be. as important as the removal of the discouragements that plague small industrialists in most countries. The price distortions and controls described in earlier chapters generally benefit the large-scale firm at the expense of the small. Tariffs tend to favor goods produced by large producers who have the political influence to obtain protection. Import licenses for industrial inputs are most easily obtained by the same large-scale manufacturers, who have the time, and too often the money, to spend obtaining favors from officials. Controls over interest rates and credit allocations also favor the large and powerful, pushing the small firm onto the informal money market where interest rates are much higher. The only control that may help small operators is minimum wages, since they can often circumvent wage regulations and gain a competitive advantage in labor costs.

If governments aim to encourage small industries in markets where they have a competitive advantage over large firms, then a reduction of controls and a greater dependence on markets should help. It has been proposed that governments go further than this by protecting small firms from large-scale competition. This could be done by controlling large-scale output, restricting investment in big firms that would compete with small ones, applying excise taxes to large manufacturers only, or subsidizing small-scale producers. In a system with controls that discriminate against small firms these measures may have some merit as an antidote to the handicaps under which they operate. But in a liberalized regime protection of the small would introduce a new distortion that should be unnecessary if small industry really has the advantages claimed for it.

Even in a liberalized economy, however, small industry may need special help from government to overcome some of its initial handicaps, and a fairly standard package of assistance has emerged. It includes credit, made available through small industry development banks or similar institutions, but at market interest rates; technical advice, organized along the lines of an agricultural extension service; training of managers and skilled workers; help in setting up procurement and marketing channels; and industrial estates that provide sites with infrastructure and a focal point for the assistance package. The idea behind this package is to help inexperienced entrepreneurs over their early hurdles, introduce them to regular market channels, and eventually make them self-sufficient.

Nevertheless, this package can be criticized. Because it requires government agencies to make contact with individual entrepreneurs to offer assistance tailored to the needs of each, it is likely to be expensive; to draw heavily on government's limited managerial and technical resources; and to reach only a small fraction of its target firms. Thus the package is no substitute for general economic policies that benefit small operators. Nor is it clear which elements of the package are truly effective. The industrial estate in particular has little merit in promoting small industry since it affects so few firms. Rather it seems more of a convenience to the government agencies and thus likely to concentrate assistance even more. And merely providing technical assistance begs the important question of technical choice. Planners need to decide whether their aim is to promote traditional industries to emphasize rural employment and incomes, or to favor small-scale modern factories to emphasize growth, productivity, and urban employment. Once the decision has been made, then extension officers have to be trained to give consistent advice and to avoid the tendency of urban-based, college-trained experts to push for increasingly modern, capital-intensive methods.

Industry and Development Goals

This and previous chapters, which have examined industry from several perspectives, point toward a consensus on the role that industry can be expected to play in development. First, industrialization is not a panacea for underdevelopment, no cure for all the ills that afflict third world societies. One unifying theme of this book is that no single factor of production, policy, sector, or emphasis can accomplish the complex of changes that we call "development." Industry is no exception. But two of its strengths are essential for any development program. First, as suggested by the Lewis-Fei-Ranis two-sector model (Chapter 3), greater productivity in industry is a key to increased per-capita income. Second, manufacturing provides a much larger menu of possibilities for efficient import substitution and increasing exports than is possible with primary industries alone.

If industrialization is not a panacea, neither is rural development. Each requires the other, and would founder if unbalanced growth is carried too far. Industry can supply agriculture with productive inputs, especially fertilizer and simple farm equipment. If outward-looking policies have been followed and manufacturing is efficient, these inputs may be supplied more cheaply than imports. The relationship is reciprocal, because agriculture supplies raw materials for manufacturing, such as cotton and other fibers, rubber, or tobacco. Agriculture and industry also provide reciprocal consumer goods markets. If agricultural incomes grow in egalitarian fashion—which may require land reform and broad-based rural development—then manufacturing will enjoy a wide and growing market for its consumer goods, one that may enable it to achieve scale economies in both production and marketing. Similarly, the growth of urban incomes, stimulated by industrial expansion, should provide a continuing stimulus to agricultural output and productivity through increasing demand for food. The key to food demand, however, is growing employment and improved urban income distribution, rather than continuing concentration of income.

Here we encounter two of the weak links in the chain. Industry cannot by itself generate sufficient jobs to absorb the growing number of workers or to equalize income distribution, especially in the poorest countries. Liberalized economies, with reduced controls and market prices closer to scarcity values, can help to arrest the tendency toward capital intensity and inappropriate, modern technologies in manufacturing and thus to raise job creation in industry. Renewed emphasis on small industry may also help. Moreover, to the extent that intermediate or innovative technologies are needed to save capital and create more jobs relative to output, a creative, efficient capital goods industry is an essential part of a development strategy. But in the final analysis much of the burden for employment creation and income equalization will lie outside industry, in agriculture and the services.

Industry has rightly been seen as a key to another goal of many developing countries, reduced *dependence.* If a country wants the capability of doing without imports of essential commodities, it must develop both an integrated industrial structure and a productive agriculture. If it wishes to exclude foreign political and cultural influence, it must learn to operate its manufacturing plants without foreign help. Much of the discussion about reduced dependence really is about increasing autarky or self-sufficiency, implying that a country must produce everything it needs. But an alternative goal suggests the capability of producing a wide variety of goods efficiently enough to trade them on world markets, and obtaining some goods overseas when it is advantageous to do so. This of course leads to the outward-looking strategy discussed in Chapter 17.

Behind these considerations lurks a hidden development goal: industrialization for its own sake. Despite advice from many quarters to temper their protective and other industrial policies and instead to promote greater efficiency, employment, and equity, many governments continue to establish the most modern, capital-intensive industries available. This cannot be attributed entirely to misguided policy. The desire to have modern industry may be as great for a country as the desire for a radio or car can be for an individual. To the extent that modern manufacturing is a goal in itself, the best that development economists can do is to point out how much could be accomplished with alternative policies and measure the costs of industrialization in terms of other goals which remain to be achieved.

FURTHER READING

The Industrial Revolution can be a lifelong study by itself. In addition to Hobsbawm's work (footnote 1), see David S. Landes, *The Unbound Prometheus: Technological Change and Industrial Development in Western Europe from 1750 to the Present* (London: Cambridge University Press, 1969).

Among many sources on the theory and measurement of economies of scale are F. M. Scherer et al., *The Economics of Multi-Plant Operation: An International Comparisons Study* (Cambridge, Mass.: Harvard University Press, 1975); C. F. Pratten, *Economies of Scale in Manufacturing Industry* (Cambridge: Cambridge

University Press, 1971); John Haldi and David Whitcomb, "Economies of Scale in Industrial Plants," *Journal of Political Economy* 75 (1967):373–85; and Alan S. Manne (ed.), *Investments for Capacity Expansion: Size, Location and Time Phasing* (Cambridge, Mass.: M.I.T. Press, 1967).

Most of the literature on urbanization deals with the industrial countries, but Harry W. Richardson's "City Size and National Spatial Strategies in Developing Countries" (World Bank Staff Working Paper No. 252, April 1977), does an excellent job of applying the lessons of urban development to the third world. For a sample of the developed country-based literature, see John Friedman and William Alonso, *Regional Development and Planning: A Reader* (Cambridge, Mass.: MIT Press, 1964); Alonso's "Location Theory" is especially helpful in understanding how transport costs lead to urban concentrations of industry.

Articles and books assessing the role of industry in achieving development goals are legion. Some recent examples include Helen Hughes, "Industrialization and Development: A Stocktaking," *Industry and Development* 2 (1978): 1–27; Paul Streeten, "Industrialization in the Unified Development Strategy," *World Development* 3 (1975): 1–9; and Robert J. Alexander, *A New Development Strategy* (Maryknoll, N.Y.: Orbis Books, 1976). An approach to measuring the trade-offs among alternative industrial strategies is suggested in Michael Roemer et al., "The Range of Strategic Choice in Tanzanian Industry," *Journal of Development Economics* 3 (1976): 257–76.

Chapter 21

PUBLIC ENTERPRISES |

In the United States one has to look hard to find state-owned enterprises, such as municipally owned electric utilities, the Tennessee Valley Authority, Conrail, and such exotic activities as uranium-enrichment plants. The situation is very different in Europe, as we are reminded by nationalizations in France and denationalizations in England. In most developing countries, from socialist Tanzania and Cuba through such market-oriented nations as Brazil and Korea, state-owned enterprises are common, and known variously as "public enterprises" or "parastatals." In this chapter we will see that the activities of these enterprises can have far-reaching implications for development.

Concepts and Trends

Defining State-Owned Enterprise

The label "state-owned enterprise" means different things to different people. To some the label has a very broad meaning, applying to all government entities that supply goods and services to the general public. In this view entities such as disaster-relief agencies, agricultural extension services, and police and fire protection agencies would qualify as state-owned enterprises (SOEs). A far narrower view would reserve the label for government-owned entities that were created primarily for the purpose of profit-making and that, once established, were substantially free to operate in much the same fashion as purely private firms.

Neither the broad nor narrow definition is serviceable in approaching the study of modern state enterprises, whether in France, Canada, Indonesia, Brazil, or Tanzania. There is an immense variety of such enterprises; a definition is required that is broad enough to encompass this variety, but at the same time narrow enough to enable sharp focus on the major issues peculiar to the stockholder and the managers in the state-enterprise sector. For purposes of this chapter an enterprise qualifies as a state enterprise if it meets three criteria:

1. The government is the principal stockholder in the enterprise, or is otherwise able to exercise control over the broad policies followed by the enterprise, and to appoint and remove enterprise management. This does not mean that the state must necessarily be involved in the day-to-day operations of the enterprise. Nor is majority ownership essential, because the state may effectively control an enterprise with a minority share of its equity, depending on the distribution of ownership of the other shares, and on any agreements between the government and the private partners.

2. The enterprise is engaged in the production of goods or services for sale to the public, or to other enterprises, private or public.

3. As a matter of policy the revenues of the enterprise are supposed to bear some relation to its costs. State enterprises for which profit maximization is not the prime stated objective may still qualify if they are expected to pursue profitability subject to constraints implicit or explicit in social functions assigned the enterprise by the state.

In the absence of the first criterion, an enterprise qualifies as a private enterprise. In the absence of either condition 2 or 3, a governmental entity would not be viewed as a state enterprise, but as an ordinary public agency.

The Growth and Importance of SOEs

Through the first decade of the postwar period state-owned enterprises in LDCs were largely confined to the so-called natural monopoly sector (decreasing-cost public utilities), small-scale monopoly producers of sumptuary products (liquor, beer, tobacco) and basic necessities (salt, matches), transportation (railroads, airlines), and in some cases banking (Indonesia, Mexico). But except for Turkey (from 1930 onward) and China (from 1949 onward) there were few examples of significant state ownership of productive facilities extending much beyond these areas. However, in the last two decades an entirely different pattern of public enterprise involvement has emerged. The present section provides a thumbnail sketch of the extent of state enterprise participation in the economies of developing countries, while a subsequent section focuses on some of the reasons for the establishment of SOEs.

By whatever standard employed there has been a marked expansion in the relative size of state-owned enterprise sectors in LDCs. With few exceptions the reasons for this expansion have little to do with ideology. If anything the role of SOEs in such market-oriented countries as Bolivia, Brazil, Chile, Indonesia, Korea, and Taiwan was by the early 1980s no less significant than in India, Bangladesh, Sri Lanka, and Egypt, countries where interventionist traditions have historically been stronger. Unlike the pattern of the early 1900s SOEs are now common, and sometimes dominant, in manufacturing, construction, services, natural resources, and even agriculture. Although prior to 1960 public enterprises were typically small-scale undertakings in most LDCs, many are now among the largest enterprises in their countries, and some are among the largest enterprises in their fields anywhere in the world. A handful are multinational enterprises in the truest sense of that word. In 1978 of the largest 500 industrial corporations outside the United States, 34 were state enterprises from LDCs (primarily natural-resource-based industries in Brazil, Venezuela, and Korea). Of the twenty state enterprises with the highest losses worldwide in 1978, three were from LDCs.[1] By size of assets, the three largest firms in Brazil are state-owned, as are two of the three largest Mexican enterprises and the nine largest domestic firms in Indonesia. In terms of sales, twelve of the largest sixteen Korean enterprises are state-owned. Developing-country SOEs that merit the multinational label include Petrobras (oil) and CVRD (mining) in Brazil, the National Iranian Oil Company, two construction firms from Indonesia, and an Indian engineering company.

State-owned enterprises have come to dominate large segments of many LDC economies. In countries as diverse as Bangladesh, Bolivia, and Mexico, the share of SOEs in annual gross investment outside of agriculture has been upward of 75 percent, while it is close to 50 percent in India and Turkey, and has hovered between 25 percent and 33 percent in Korea and Brazil. Public enterprises have in recent years contributed about 40 percent of GDP in Bolivia, about 20 percent in Chile, 25 percent in Pakistan and Ghana, 12 percent in India, and 11 percent in Korea. In Bangladesh, Turkey, and Egypt, SOEs account for at least 60 percent of total industrial value added. In Nepal and Sri Lanka this ratio is about one-third, in India one-fifth, and Korea one-sixth. For Latin American nations the output of public enterprises is typically estimated at between 5 and 25 percent of national industrial output, depending on the country in question and the nature of the definitions applied to SOEs.[2]

Nowhere is the much-expanded role of SOEs more evident than in the natural resources industries. In hard minerals large-scale state enterprises are responsible for more than two-thirds of annual value of output in Bolivia, Chile, Guinea, Indonesia, Guyana, Guinea, Zambia, and Zaire. In hydrocarbons and energy the dominance of SOEs is complete in some countries, including Mexico and Pakistan, and nearly so in numerous others, including Bolivia, Brazil, Indonesia, Malaysia, India, Turkey, Colombia, and Iran.

While few countries have experienced growth in SOE operations as dramatic as that in Tanzania, Pakistan, and Sri Lanka, where the number of public enterprises in all fields doubled in the decade after 1964, the figures cited above provide ample indication of strong growth in government own-

1. "Directory of the 500 Largest Industrial Corporations Outside the U.S.," *Fortune,* Aug. 13, 1979, pp. 193*ff.*

2. Raymond Vernon, "The State-Owned Enterprise in Latin American Exports," in Werner Baer and Malcolm Gillis (eds.), *Trade Prospects Among the Americas* (Urbana, Ill.: National Bureau of Economic Research and University of Illinois Press, 1981), pp. 98–114.

ership of productive facilities in a wide array of fields in developing countries.

The emergence of rapidly growing LDC state enterprise sectors has important international implications as well. In a variety of fields developing country SOEs have increasingly come to represent substitutes for, or competitors to, private multinationals, certainly in the home markets of the state firms and potentially in third-country markets. This has already begun to occur in mining, steelmaking, petroleum refining, petrochemicals, and to a more limited extent in shipbuilding, textiles, and construction. To finance this expansion, state enterprises from developing countries have become major users of international credit markets. Flows of external commercial debt contracted by such firms rose by nearly 350 percent over the period 1975–1978 and accounted for nearly one-third of total LDC commercial borrowings for all purposes.[3] The expanded flows of international debt capital to SOEs was the prime factor in the buildup of large, potentially troublesome stocks of external debt in Indonesia, Brazil, Peru, Zaire, and Zambia during the 1970s.

Rationales for Establishing SOEs

It is not always easy to identify with any clarity the basic reasons why particular enterprises have been created in particular countries. In many cases the passage of time has obscured the original rationale; in other cases governments may have announced one set of justifications while intending the enterprise to serve other goals. It is often thought that most of the motives are grounded in the ideology of socialism. Among the LDCs this has been true for only a few socialist countries, such as China, Burma, Tanzania, Algeria, Cuba, and in certain periods, India. For most other developing countries the establishment of public enterprises has usually had little to do with socialist ideology, or for that matter any other ideological framework. If this were not the case it would be extremely difficult to explain the existence of very large public-enterprise sectors in such countries as Brazil, Korea, Bolivia, or Indonesia, none of which is socialist.

The taxonomy presented below breaks down rationales for the creation of public enterprises into three separate, but inextricably related, groups: primarily economic motives, primarily sociopolitical motives, and mixed motives. The compartments are by no means watertight, and many nuances are ignored.

Economic Reasons

Savings mobilization has been one of the longest standing and most frequently employed rationales for creating public enterprises. Even when decisions to establish state-owned enterprises have hinged primarily on

3. Figures on borrowing by LDC-based SOEs are computed on the basis of data presented in the World Bank, Financial Studies Division, *Borrowing in International Capital Markets* (Washington, D.C., 1978).

sociopolitical considerations, savings mobilization has often been mustered as a supplementary argument. The argument for using SOEs to generate savings runs as follows: Domestic capitalists in LDCs generate too little savings because they are conspicuous consumers. Moreover those savings that are generated by domestic capitalists are often invested abroad. Public savings cannot adequately finance capital formation because low levels of per-capita income and weak public administration make it particularly difficult to raise tax revenues. In the face of these and other difficulties in mobilizing savings, many LDC governments turned hopefully to state enterprises, whose surpluses could be used to finance investment. Earnings of SOEs would not, it was hoped, be dissipated in low-priority consumption, and since they accrue to government directly, would be more readily accessible for financing both physical and human capital formation. SOE surpluses would also reduce the need for administratively difficult and politically unpopular tax reforms.

Employment objectives have often been important in the establishment of public firms. In most instances the goal has been defined as the creation of new jobs as the economy and the firm expand. In other cases the focus has been on job preservation, as large, ailing private firms ("sinking sands" enterprises) have been taken over by the government in order to avoid the unemployment consequences of potential bankruptcies. This rationale has been present in nationalization decisions ranging from textile companies in India to cement plants and bicycle manufacturers in Bolivia.

Capital lumpiness has been an argument for public enterprise in countries where money and capital markets are not well developed, so that private domestic firms may be unable to mobilize the volumes of capital necessary to mount large, capital-intensive projects. This is particularly true in the minerals sector, where today the average size of projects around the world runs at over U.S. $200 million, and billion-dollar projects are not uncommon. In most developing countries only the state or foreign enterprises have the resources to mount such projects. And if foreign participation has been precluded, then responsibility for undertaking large projects with "lumpy" capital requirements falls to the state, which may respond by assigning the task to an existing public enterprise, as often has been the case in mining in Peru, Brazil, and Panama, or by creating an entirely new one, for example in the huge Asahan hydropower/aluminum-smelting project in Indonesia. The large scale of these projects tends to make them especially *risky*. In many LDCs private investors are highly risk-adverse, and public-sector involvement is essential if large projects are to be carried out at all.

Sociopolitical Reasons

The *"commanding heights"* is a term applied to sectors of the economy that are so strategic and generate such important linkages that they cannot, it is argued, be left in private hands, whether foreign or domestic. Rather, to guarantee socially responsible performance from these "commanding heights" of the economy it has been thought that the state must control such industries. Typically the "commanding heights" can be a rather elastic concept, but is generaly said to include basic industries, such as mineral extraction and processing, iron and steel, chemicals, electricity and railways, and crucial services such as banking. The preferred means of exercising state control over the "commanding heights" has been to turn these sectors over to government-owned enterprises. At various stages in the development of postindependence India, as well as for certain periods in Sri Lanka and under the Bhutto administration in Pakistan, the "commanding heights" rationale has been used as the prime justification for creating state enterprises in steel, shipping, coal, electric power, fertilizer, banking, and several other fields. The "commanding heights" rationale also appears to have been the basis for the largely amicable nationalization of foreign mining interests in Zaire and Zambia in the 1970s. One hears less of this argument nowadays, perhaps because of the lack of any firm evidence that the enterprises thus created could, in the absence of any stronger economic rationale, remain viable without substantial government aid over long periods of time.

Decolonialization is closely related to the "commanding heights" motive. Many countries formerly under the dominion of a colonial power have viewed the continued presence of colonial industrial interests as a bitter reminder of the past and a major impediment to development. Thus, particularly in the late 1950s and early 1960s, both socialist and nonsocialist developing countries have nationalized foreign interests. In virtually all instances the shortage both of capital and of trained indigenous managers has meant that ownership of the nationalized enterprises could not immediately pass to the domestic private sector, but rather devolved upon the state.

This rationale accounts for perhaps three-quarters of the nearly 200 central-government-owned enterprises now operating in Indonesia, primarily expropriated from Dutch interests in 1957 (and British interests in 1962); for a large number of Egyptian SOEs created in 1957 when Nasser, after the Suez War, nationalized important foreign firms; and for a significant share of public enterprises in Ghana and Algeria. This rationale has also been important in Peru, Mexico, and Chile, where nationalization was undertaken in response to what was perceived as economic neocolonialism from the United States rather than from the former colonial occupying power.

In many LDCs state-owned enterprises have been created to serve social goals; many other state-owned firms that owe their existence to other reasons have been assigned such goals. *Social goals* have been assigned to state enterprises in virtually all LDCs. These include income redistribution, correction of imbalances in regional growth, and employment creation.[4] In

---

4. For an alternative, and longer, list of such goals, see Armeane M. Choski, *State Intervention in the Industrialization of Developing Countries: Selected Issues* (Washington, D.C.: World Bank, 1979).

many countries pursuit of such objectives is second nature to public enterprise managers. In Bolivia the managers of large SOEs in mining commonly stress the "social content" of all basic enterprise decision; managers of state-owned banks in Indonesia cite the broader "development mission" to which their activities are oriented; the operations of SOEs in Bangladesh are expected to help reduce income differentials over time. Although few public enterprises owe their existence entirely to government's social or equity goals, in recent years a number of enterprises identified below have been established principally for purposes of rectifying imbalances between social groups and between regions of a country.

Mixed Reasons

At least two motives for public-enterprise establishment have had as much to do with economic as sociopolitical considerations.

Concentration of economic power in the hands of a small number of families has been significant in such countries as Pakistan, Chile, and Peru. On occasion governments have moved to reduce the scope for abuse of such power by nationalization of private domestic firms. The desire to curb drastically the influence of Pakistan's dominant "twenty-two families" was clearly a significant factor in actions taken by the Bhutto government in 1974, when many banks, insurance companies, industrial firms, and agricultural interests were nationalized. In 1971–1973 the Allende government in Chile justified seizure of a variety of textiles, banking, publishing, and industrial concerns on grounds of excessive concentration of ownership in the hands of a small number of individuals. Bolivian capitalists have long avoided rapid growth in domestic market shares for their enterprises, or the appearance of such growth, on grounds that largeness sooner or later invites expropriation.

Preferences of some foreign aid donors have reinforced the tendency to create state-owned enterprises in a number of countries. The World Bank, particularly since 1967, and the Asian, African, and Latin American development banks have preferred to channel large portions of their resources through SOEs rather than through ordinary government agencies or private enterprises in LDCs. This was not always the case. Originally the World Bank favored private enterprise in mining and manufacturing, since there were substantial reservations about the capacity of the public sector to execute projects in these sectors. But in many countries the private sector seemed too weak to undertake large projects. In addition countries such as India, Egypt, and Indonesia had decided that "strategic" or "basic" industries in any case would be in the hands of the state.[5] By the mid-1970s the World Bank's emphasis in mining and manufacturing had shifted strongly to the public sector. Independent, state-owned enterprises were favored over ordinary government agencies because the World Bank saw significant

5. The discussion on the evolution of the World Bank's attitude toward SOEs draws heavily on Berti Walstedt, "State Manufacturing Enterprises in a Mixed Economy" (unpublished manuscript; Washington, D.C., August 1978).

advantages in fostering decentralized decision-making in areas involving the production and distribution of basic industrial and agricultural goods. At the same time both the bank and many LDC officials viewed existing governmental departments as either too inefficient or too corrupt to execute large-scale projects effectively. Under this stimulus new SOEs were created and existing ones expanded to execute major projects. Examples include holding companies in shipping, investment banks, and fertilizer plants in Indonesia, development finance institutions in Colombia, a state-owned mining bank in Bolivia, and a wide variety of SOEs in several fields in African countries.

Impact on Development

Until very recently little comparative information of any kind was available on the activities of state-owned firms. Although this situation has changed for the better since the early 1970s, large gaps remain. Enough data are available, however, to permit some generalizations on savings mobilization, efficiency, employment, and a few measures of the "social" activities of the enterprises.

Savings Mobilization

While public-sector enterprises have contributed materially to overall savings mobilization efforts in a few socialist developing economies such as China and Yugoslavia, they have not performed as well in mixed LDC economies. Indeed for some avowedly socialist LDCs such as Tanzania under Nyerere, Ghana under Nkrumah, Sri Lanka under Mrs. Bandaranaike, and Indonesia under Sukarno, large state-enterprise sectors persistently ran deficits that had to be financed from general government revenues. At times even single enterprises have accumulated loses and external debt obligations large enough to cripple developmental efforts across all fields of government activity. This was the case for Comibol, the state-owned tin mining enterprise in Bolivia from 1957 to 1972, and for Pertamina, the state-owned petroleum enterprise in Indonesia from 1972 to 1976 (which accumulated over $10 billion in debt before 1976), as well as for state mining enterprises in both Zaire and Zambia from 1974 through 1978.

The severe tribulations of the Turkish economy in the 1970s, culminating in massive devaluation and debt rescheduling in 1979, were due substantially to problems originating in the debt-ridden state enterprise sector. In such countries as Argentina, Egypt, Guyana, Nicaragua, and Panama, the net saving of the consoliated state-enterprise sector was typically negative from 1970 to 1973. In other mixed LDC economies state enterprises as a group have contributed only marginally to national savings efforts. These include countries with large public-enterprise sectors, such as Bangladesh, Thailand, Bolivia, Chile, and Uruguay before 1973, as well as those with relatively small numbers of state-owned firms, such as Somalia, Jamaica, and Colombia. In all of these countries the savings of state firms in 1970–1973 accounted for less than 5 percent of investment finance.[6]

Savings-mobilization performance by LDC state enterprises has not been uniformly disappointing, however. In Korea,[7] Uruguay in 1975–1976,[8] India in 1970–1972, Pakistan in 1972–1974, and Indonesia in 1976–1978, the savings of state enterprises generated as much as 10–15 percent of gross domestic investment finance.

Why have efforts to mobilize savings through state-enterprise activities had relatively disappointing results? There are after all some reasons for expecting some state enterprises to yield larger surpluses than would be the case for business enterprise in general. First, virtually all of the largest state enterprises in developing countries are concentrated in natural resources industries and would normally be expected to generate very substantial profits from the rents present in natural resource activity (see Chapter 19), particularly from 1973 onward when prices of commodities other than copper began to surge upward. In fact some natural resource enterprises do often show sizable operating profits, but most of the others do not. Indeed three major LDC state-owned natural resource firms (Turkiye Petrolcrri of Turkey, Ecopetrol of Colombia, and Zambia Industrial and Mining) ranked, along with British Steel and ENI (hydrocarbons) of Italy, among the twenty largest money losers of all state enterprises in the world in 1978.[9]

Second, many state enterprises enjoy monopoly privileges in their respective markets, privileges not as readily available to private firms. These monopoly privileges extend well beyond those traditionally granted to state-owned producers of sumptuary items (tobacco, beer, spirits) and to public utilities (electric power, telephones). State-owned monopolies are also pervasive in other fields, from fertilizers and steel manufacture in Indonesia through distribution of refined petroleum products and domestic airline service in over thirty LDCs, to export of cocoa products in Ghana and Bolivia, peanut export in Senegal, and match manufacture in Bolivia. And where state enterprises do not enjoy full monopoly positions, they often operate in the most concentrated markets where the potential for exercise of monopoly or oligopoly power is substantial.

For example, Jones reports that for Korea in 1972 only 10 percent of value added in the public sector was marketed under competitive conditions and that public enterprises either dominated or played a leading role in all mining and manufacturing industries that might be considered strategic.[10] For Ghana, Killick observes that in 1969 state enterprises accounted for all output in six industries, and that 83 percent of total output

6. World Bank, *World Tables 1976* (Washington, D.C., 1977), pp. 424–28.

7. Leroy Jones, *Public Enterprise and Economic Development* (Seoul: Korea Development Institute, 1976), p. 83.

8. World Bank, *Economic Memorandum on Uruguay* (Washington, D.C., 1977), p. 15.

9. "Directory of the 500 Largest Industrial Corporations Outside the U.S.," *Fortune,* Aug. 13, 1979, pp. 193*ff.*

10. Jones, *Public Enterprise and Economic Development,* pp. 190–94.

of all state enterprises was produced in industries where state firms were responsible for more than 75 percent of output.[11]

Given that substantial market power is characteristically available to SOEs almost everywhere in developing countries, it might be expected that most state-owned firms would show profits and that these profits would tend to be reflected in enterprise savings. However, financial profitability is not a common characteristic of LDC state-owned firms, whether monopoly power is present or not. For some public-enterprise sectors operating losses are a chronic condition. This has been particularly true for Egypt, Somalia, Ghana, Zambia, Turkey, and to a lesser extent Bangladesh, Sri Lanka, Argentina, Sudan, and Panama. In other countries, such as Brazil, Indonesia, Chile, Uruguay, and Thailand, the results are mixed: generally more major firms show accounting profits than show losses. But the state-enterprise sectors in Korea, Taiwan, and Singapore enjoy relatively strong reputations for generating accounting profits.

This relatively poor profit and savings performance can be attributed to three factors: (1) "inefficiency" in operation, (2) government-imposed controls, particularly price controls, and often (3) the financial burden of social responsibilities assigned to SOEs.

Efficiency

Virtually everywhere the stereotypical image of state-owned firms is one of an "inefficient" economic unit. To the extent that "inefficiency" refers to a failure to minimize costs, or "X-inefficiency," state enterprises may be likely to be less efficient than private firms.

The notion of *X-inefficiency,* developed by Harvey Leibenstein, can be understood in terms of the isoquant diagram introduced in Chapters 6 and 8.[12] Figure 21-1 shows one of the production function isoquants, which were utilized in Figs. 6-5 and 8-3. The isoquant represents a single level of output, say, Q_1, and gives the different combinations of labor and capital that could be used to produce Q_1. Points along the isoquant, such as a and b, use the minimum amounts of labor and capital (L_a, K_a or L_b, K_b), so are called *technically efficient.* Points like c, to the southeast of the isoquant, are infeasible. Points like d, to the northeast of the isoquant, are feasible but inefficient because they use more of both labor *(L_d)* and capital *(K_d)* than necessary to produce Q_1.

Superimposed on the diagram are two isocost, or budget, lines, B_1B_1 and B_2B_2. Suppose, for example, that market forces determine the relative prices of labor *(P_L)* and capital *(P_K)* such that P_K/P_L represents the relative opportunity costs of the two factors (see Chapter 6), and that $P_K/P_L = 2$.

11. Tony Killick, *Development Economics in Action* (New York: St. Martins Press, 1978), pp. 220–22.

12. For a full discussion, see Harvey Leibenstein, *Beyond Economic Man* (Cambridge, Mass.: Harvard University Press, 1976). For a condensed presentation of these factors, see Leibenstein, "X-Efficiency, Intrafirm Behavior and Growth," in Schlomo Maital and Sidney Meltz (eds.), *Lagging Productivity Growth: Causes and Remedies* (Cambridge, Mass.: Ballinger Press, 1980).

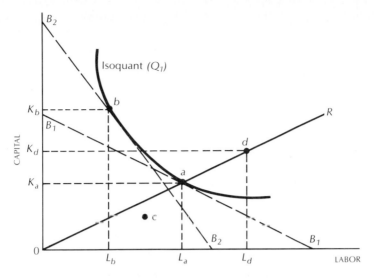

Fig. 21–1 Allocative and X-Efficiency: Production Function.

Then isocost line B_1B_1 would show the combinations of labor and capital that could be purchased for a given total cost. A producer who wants either to minimize his cost for a given output, Q_1, or to maximize his output for a given cost of inputs, B_1B_1, would produce at point a on the isoquant. Not only would the firm be producing efficiently, but because the firm's costs represent the society's opportunity costs, this would be a point of *allocative efficiency* for the society as well.

Suppose instead that the government controls interest rates to subsidize capital and enacts payroll taxes that raise labor costs. This would lower the relative price of capital and increase the slope of the isocost line, yielding a line such as B_2B_2 in Fig. 21–1. Now a profit-maximizing firm would produce at point b. Point b lies along the isoquant and is thus technically efficient. But point b is not allocatively efficient: the factor price distortions have caused the firm's factor use (L_b, K_b) to diverge from the social optimum, which remains L_a, K_a.

A firm may face a correct set of price signals, represented by B_1B_1 in the diagram, and yet not produce at an allocatively efficient point, like a in the diagram. It might, for example, produce at point d, using too much of both capital and labor to produce output Q_1 even though it is using both factors in the correct proportions (as at point a, which also lies on Ray OR, going through the origin). This depicts Leibenstein's *X-inefficiency:* even when it faces correct price signals, the firm does not minimize costs and is not allocatively efficient.

Any firm, public or private, could be X-inefficient for a variety of reasons. Managers may lack motivation to minimize costs, either because they are satisfied with less than maximum profits or because there are easier ways to earn high profits, as is true in the import substitution regimes described in Chapter 16. Or managers may be skillful and motivated but not be willing to expend the effort to adopt new productive techniques to achieve minimum costs. They may make the judgment that somewhat lower costs and higher profits are not worth the often intangible costs of convincing their peers to change, motivating middle-level managers to greater efforts, or overcoming workers' resistance. Finally, changes in method do not always lead to certain outcomes, and this risk may discourage efforts to minimize costs. Whatever the reasons, firms and their managements may be subject to "inert" regions, in Leibenstein's phrase, or gray areas in which they do not act as cost minimizers, but may accept less than optimal outcomes without taking action.

Although both private- and public-enterprise managements are subject to such inert zones, there is reason to believe that public firms, as well as private monopolies, may act less forcefully to minimize costs than do private firms facing competitors.[13] Private enterprise must eventually meet a market test or go out of business. Control of costs, if not cost minimization, is vital if the private firm is to make profits and survive in a market environment. But cost control is not nearly so essential to the survival of state-owned enterprises, for two reasons. First, governments are prone to protect their own enterprises from competition, either domestic or foreign, and thus to convey monopoly power on them.

Second, governments, the principal and often only shareholder, are loathe to permit their firms to die a natural death, to "sink beneath the sands." This is true in both industrial and developing countries: witness the loan guarantees to Lockheed and Chrysler in the United States and any number of takeovers of ailing firms by European governments (Rolls-Royce, British Leyland, etc.). This reluctance may stem from the fear of lost employment, as in the case of cement plants in Bolivia, much of the textile industry in India, the state gold mines in Ghana, and the French steel mills; the desire to preserve national prestige, as in the case of Rolls-Royce in Britain; or government's large financial stake in the firm as a result of past salvage operations, as in the cases of British Leyland and any number of SOEs in Italy. Rather than permit bankruptcy it is more common for government to pump new funds into troubled firms or, under dire circumstances, to reorganize them and change managements. Thus public-enterprise managers, with a large cushion between themselves and the demands of the market, have much less incentive than private firms to minimize costs, and there is greater scope for X-inefficiencies to go unchecked.

But X-inefficiency in SOEs is not due exclusively to any inability or unwillingness of managers to minimize costs. Pressure for X-inefficiency also arise from the external environment in which state firms operate. These include faulty incentive structures for workers and managers, such as rigid limits on compensation that are decreed by government agencies; govern-

13. For evidence that private enterprises that enjoy monopoly power (e.g., regulated electric utilities) are also susceptible to this type of inefficiency, see W. J. Primeaux, "An Assessment of X-Efficiency Gained Through Competition," *Review of Economics and Statistics* 59, no. 2 (June 1977): 516–17.

mental insistence on redundant labor, whether for patronage reasons or to relieve unemployment problems; and government-imposed materials-procurement requirements geared to realizing potential backward linkages or rewarding political favorites.

Two other common causes of poor profit performance in SOEs also have their origin in the external environment: price controls and social responsibilities. State enterprises producing items regarded as "basic necessities" or "key services" are typically subjected to rigid and infrequently adjusted price controls for their products. A major reason for the weak profit performance of many of the public enterprise monopolies cited earlier is he effect of such price controls on their revenues. In many cases the enterprises are monopolies because private firms could not survive in the presence of price controls on the regulated items. Thus in Indonesia eight of nine items subject to price controls are produced by SOEs; foodgrain and kerosene distribution are handled by state firms in Colombia, Bolivia, India, and Sri Lanka because price controls make private participation impossible; and urban bus services are operated by public enterprises in many countries because of chronicaly low government ceilings on fares.

Finally, many SOEs record low profits or continuing losses because the government-as-stockholder has decreed that the enterprises must perform certain social functions normally carried on by ordinary government agencies or otherwise handled by overall government policy instruments. These are discussed in the next three sections.

Employment

One fairly common rationale employed for establishment of SOEs has been that they would be more effective than the private sector in creating new jobs for rapidly expanding labor forces. State enterprises do employ large numbers of workers: 1.5 million in India, 0.7 million in Indonesia, and nearly 0.5 million in Bangladesh. However, in very few countries does the proportion of employment in public firms to total employment outside of agriculture reach much above 10 percent, and for most countries with important SOE sectors the share is less than 5 percent.

Since in many LDCs the state-enterprise sector's share in total investment over comparable periods has been at least 30 percent, and in some countries over 50 percent, it would appear that SOEs have not had remarkable success in creating new jobs in the past decade or so. This performance seems all the more perplexing in light of the pervasive tendency toward overstaffing of labor in state enterprises in most all developing countries.

The principal reason is traceable to one major fact: the marked capital intensity of state-enterprise investment relative to private-sector investment in the same economy. Investment in state-enterprise sectors in many LDCs has been focused on projects that involve light use of the more abundant factor of production (labor) and heavy use of the scarcer factor (capital). This pattern has been documented in a series of studies for such countries as Korea, Ghana, Brazil, India, Bolivia, Algeria, Colombia, Indonesia, and numerous others. One observer goes so far as to say that in Brazil and India "it is almost as if industries were divided between public and private enterprise according to their capital intensity," and that "public enterprise in Algeria is focused in capital intensive methods with little or no regard for chronicaly high rates of unemployment."[14] For Korea it has been demonstrated that the public-enterprise sector is more than three times as capital-intensive as the Korean economy generally.[15] Another analyst has tracked a very marked bias toward capital intensity in a wide variety of Ghananian SOEs, ranging from agricultural estates to sugar factories, footwear, fishing firms, and glass and canning factories.[16]

How does one explain an apparent anti-employment bias on the part of the public sector in countries where governmental commitments to expanded employment are written so large in national plans? Is this pattern due to ctive preference on the part of public officials and SOE managers in favor of capital-intensive investment? There is a tendency for public officials and managers to favor capital-intensive projects, but the bias is not necessarily an ctive on; rather it stems from a variety of market and nonmarket pressures toward capital intensity across a wide range of countries. The capacities, training, and orientation of governmental bureaucracies appear to operate in subtle ways that induce them to prefer capital- over labor-intensive projects.[17] There is also evidence that the terms and conditions upon which foreign aid is channeled to projects involving SOEs serve to heighten incipient biases toward capital intensity.[18]

There are a variety of other, economic considerations that help to explain why so much of SOE investment is more capital-intensive than would be the case if investment decisions were based on scarcity values for both labor and capital. First, SOEs tend to be more heavily represented in concentrated industries than their private-sector counterparts. Biases toward capital intensity in investment are stronger where monopoly or oligopoly power can be exercised, a phenomenon observed in a growing number of studies on this subject.[19] The more competitive (the less concentrated) is the environment in which firms operate, the greater are pressures for cost minimization, forcing firms to adopt more appropriate technology.

14. John B. Sheahan, "Public Enterprise in Developing Countries," in W. G. Shepherd (ed.), *Public Enterprise: Economic Analysis of Theory and Practice* (Lexington: Lexington Books, 1976), p. 211.

15. Jones, *Public Enterprise and Economic Development,* p. 123.

16. Killick, *Development Economics in Action,* pp. 228–230.

17. For a cogent discussion of such subtle biases in capital intensity in public investment, see C. Peter Timmer, "Public Policy for Improving Technology Choice" (manuscript prepared for Alternative Technology, Inc., September 1979), pp. 16–24.

18. A classic example dealing with rice milling is discussed in C. Peter Timmer, "The Choice of Technique in Indonesia," in C. Peter Timmer et al., *The Choice of Technology in Developing Countries* (Cambridge, Mass.: Harvard University Center for International Affairs, 1975), pp. 1–30.

19. For Indonesia, see Louis T. Wells, "Economic Man and Engineering Man: Choice of Technology in a Low-Wage Country," in Timmer et al., *The Choice of Technology in Developing Countries,* pp. 71–90. On Thailand, see Donald J. LeCraw, "Choice of Technology in Low-Wage Countries: A Non-Neoclassical Approach," *Quarterly Journal of Economics* 93 (November 1979): 631–54. See also R. A. McCain, "Competition, Information and Redundancy: X-Efficiency and the Cybernetics of the Firm," *Kyklos* 28 (1975): 286–308.

Second, a substantial share of SOE investment is concentrated in sectors such as mineral extraction and heavy industry that would tend in any case to be capital-intensive whether the investor is private, domestic, foreign, or government. And state enterprises dominate in other inherently capital-intensive sectors because private enterprises have been unwilling or unable to enter: activities characterized by substantial economies of scale (e.g., public utilities) and high risk.

Third, both public and private enterprises are subject to the price distortions—low interest rates, high wage rates, overvalued exchanged rates discussed in Chapters 8 and 16—that make capital cheap and labor expensive. But additional pressures for capital-intensive choices apply to SOEs. In some countries (Colombia until 1974, for example) state firms are exempt from all tax obligations, including customs duties on imported capital equipment. SOEs also tend to pay a lower price for loan capital than do their private-sector counterparts because their debt is guaranteed, explicitly or implicitly, by the parent government, therefore involving less risk of default to the lender. In countries where the banking system is also dominated by SOEs (Indonesia, Pakistan, Mexico), lower interest costs to SOE borrowers are often the result of conscious policy enforced by the parent government. Moreover SOEs often view equity capital as costless, because governments normally do not place a price on it by insisting that dividends be paid. Under such circumstances decisions by managers that involve wasteful use of capital may not reflect lack of concern for the cost of capital, but may instead reflect an accurate reading of, and rational response to, highly distorted price signals from government.

State enterprises may have had a greater impact on *preserving* jobs when private firms are about to fail, although usually at a substantial continuing cost to the government. Governments' reluctance to permit their enterprises to fail was discussed in the previous section. In many cases this reluctance can be traced to the fear that bankruptcies will lead to unemployment and its political consequences. Nowhere has this fear been more evident than in Bolivia. Under Bolivian law and tradition it is virtualy impossible for a firm to go out of business. Because it is also virtually impossible to dismiss workers, for whatever reason, many private investors over the years have, after experiencing continuing losses, merely walked away from their enterprises, leaving them, as it were, on the government's doorstep. In other cases labor groups have pressed government to assume ownership prior to this state and have met with some success. As a result perhaps half of the over fifty firms owned by the Bolivian central government belong in the "sinking sands" category, as do the majority of Indian SOEs in textiles.

Social Responsibilities

While available evidence does permit some tentative generalizations concerning the impact of SOEs on savings mobilization and employment, there is very little basis for assessing state enterprises' contribution to such common societal goals as income redistribution, provision of basic services, training of managers, rectifying long-standing societal imbalances (ethnic or otherwise), breaking of domestic monopoly power, and promotion of national independence through counterbalancing or entirely displacing the influence of multinational enterprise. Still, it is instructive to examine this set of issues briefly.

Large segments of the poor, particularly the urban poor, have direct day-to-day contact with state-owned enterprises in many lines of activity, such as food distribution, electric power transmission, water supply, and bus transportation. Given the nature and extent of this contact, and given the limited short-term effectiveness of tax and expenditure policies in reaching the poor, many economists advocate the use of the state-enterprise sector as a prime tool to advance income redistribution goals through subsidized prices for items of basic necessity.

Results from a variety of countries indicate that a well-designed system of subsidies can contribute materially to this aim, provided two conditions are met. First, items eligible for subsidy must be those which are important in the budgets of the poor, and not in the budgets of the nonpoor. If the relatively well-off are also major consumers of the item, a little redistribution may be secured at relatively great cost.[20] Second, the subsidy scheme must be structured to avoid incentives for waste and inefficiency in the operation of the affected state enterprise. Otherwise experience in a number of countries shows that the enterprise almost inevitably becomes incapable of fulfilling its social function effectively. This outcome is particularly likely to occur when the enterprise itself is required to absorb losses from the operation of the subsidy program. The public enterprise manager is then inclined to attribute all problems to the necessity of meeting its social obligations, a pattern that has been repeated in Indonesian and Bolivian SOEs in banking (subsidized loans to farmers), Pakistani SOEs in fuel distribution, and Colombian SOEs in food distribution. In such circumstances there is almost no way in which such claims can be disputed. If on the other hand the enterprise is directly reimbursed by the government for the difference between the costs of acquiring the subsidized item and the selling price, subsidy schemes directed to the poor can work reasonably well and the enterprise cannot plead extenuating circumstances in explaining large losses. Examples include rural electrification efforts in Malaysia, where the state electricity enterprise is reimbursed for the higher cost of serving distant villages, and rice distribution in Indonesia, where the cost of the subsidy is borne by the government budget and not the state firm involved.

Finally, there is one sense in which SOEs have been singularly unsuccessful in achieving income redistribution goals set by their parents. The surest method of substantially reducing income inequality has been and re-

---

20. A case from Indonesia is instructive. Kerosene is distributed by a state enterprise and is heavily subsidized primarily as a means of helping the poor. but in the case of kerosene the poorest 40 percent of the population accounts for only 20 percent of total consumption. Thus for each dollar of kerosene subsidy, 20 percent goes to the poor, 80 percent to the well-off and the relatively well-off. The subsidy program in 1978 alone cost nearly $1 billion because of the quantities involved and because subsidies on kerosene also require subsidies on diesel fuel; otherwise operators of diesel vehicles will substitute kerosene for diesel fuel.

mains that of reducing unemployment, since most of the poor are in that state because they lack good jobs. But because state enterprises have been particularly prone to capital-intensive choices in investment, opportunities have been lost for significant gains in ameliorating income disparities and for reduction of the incidence of absolute poverty through employment growth.

In recent years several governments have established enterprises that are intended to be commercial in their orientation but which have as their primary focus the achievement of a major "social" goal. Such enterprises have been created out of governmental convictions that traditional public policies by themselves would require too much time to have significant effects, and out of a recognition that existing institutions were not well equipped to deal effectively with the problem. The two prime examples of such enterprises have been those concerned with development of lagging regions within a country and those focused on expanding opportunities for economically weak groups that may not have fully benefited from past patterns of economic development and for whom "catch-up" programs are deemed essential.

Several countries have established regional development banks and regional development corporations designed to assist "lagging" regions in "catching up" with more prosperous parts of the country. Some, like the Guyana Development Corporation in Venezuela, are quite large and well endowed. Others, including several regional development corporations in Bolivia and regional development banks in Indonesia, operate on far more modest budgets. But in general these entities are typically expected to operate on commercial principles, even if they do not attempt to maximize profits. This merely reflects recognition of the fact that financially viable firms are better able to contribute to social objectives.

Malaysia and Indonesia have both established a number of public enterprises in the financial sector intended to promote greater participation by economically weak groups, largely the Malay majority (*bumipatra* or *pribumis*), in the development process. In Indonesia an enterprise has been created in order to channel more equity capital and technical assistance to economically weak entrepreneurs in the small- and medium-scale industrial sector. Another enterprise has been charged with the responsibility of providing finance for the "Indonesianization" of equity in foreign investment projects. While both SOEs were established primarily to promote a social goal, both are expected to maintain long-term commercial viability without the need for large government subsidies.

SOEs and Multinational Investments

In much of the developing world, and in particular in Latin America, public enterprises are viewed as an essential means of counterbalancing or harnessing the economic power of multinational firms based in industrial countries. Until recently this goal was generally promoted through the nationalization of the domestic operations of foreign firms and the subsequent transfer of all assets to state-owned enterprises. This approach has been particularly common in natural resources, as illustrated in Mexico, Peru, Indonesia, and Argentina in oil, and in Chile, Peru, Zambia, Zaire, and Indonesia in mining. Although in a few cases (Mexico and Peru) nationalization has been undertaken subsequent to heated domestic outbursts of nationalistic, anti-imperialist sentiment, governments have by and large selected enterprises to be nationalized with clear criteria.[21] In Chile, Zambia, Zaire, and a variety of other countries, nationalization was merely the end product of a long series of measures designed to wrest more national control over LDC natural resource endowments, coinciding with what host countries perceived to be declining national needs for foreign capital, technology, and market access.

By the late 1970s a new pattern emerged as many LDCs began to utilize state enterprises in a somewhat different fashion to counter the influence of the multinationals. New SOEs were created and existing ones rapidly expanded to move into markets previously (or still) dominated by multinationals. Examples of the former type include nearly a half dozen new firms engaged in the mining of uranium (Bolivia, Colombia, Indonesia), fishery projects (Indonesia), and natural resource processing (Bolivia, Indonesia). Among the SOEs that have undergone dramatic expansion in markets where multinationals have predominated are CVRD and Petrobras in Brazil, Ferrominera in Venezuela, and Pemex and Cananca in Mexico.

In virtually all of these countries, and in parts of Africa, a relatively new form of multinational involvement has evolved: joint ventures between the multinationals and domestic SOEs, particularly in the natural resources area. In earlier days the project undertaken would likely have been mounted exclusively by foreign private interests or, more recently, by foreign private interests in cooperation wih private domestic interests. Rising nationalism and dissatisfaction with the economic and social outcomes of direct foreign investment have curtailed the former, and disappointment with the results of earlier private joint ventures have led many governments increasingly to favor arrangements in which the state itself, through one of its public enterprises, is the joint-venture partner. Recent examples include mining projects in Brazil and Peru, fisheries and natural-resource-processing projects in Indonesia, and a host of agreements recently concluded in Latin America in uranium. All of these involved the creation of new state enterprises in the host country, or at a minimum rapid expansion of preexisting enterprises owned by the state.

Strong forces have been at work to expand the number of this new breed of public enterprise. From the point of view of foreign investors the arrangement is often very attractive, for it involves a venture in which the partner (the government) is also the dispenser of favors (tax relief, insulation from competition, etc.), and is perceived as a means of reducing political risks of operating in a foreign country. From the point of view of the government this type of arrangement is often seen as the best way to pro-

---

21. Vernon, "The State-Owned Enterprise in Latin American Exports," p. 5.

tect national interests from potential damage by commercially oriented, profit-seeking enterprises with little long-run stake in the country's future. In particular it is often viewed as a way of preventing "sophisticated" foreign investors from taking advantage of inexperienced private, domestic joint-venture investors who are thought unable to exploit their bargaining positions. And finally, the increasing reliance on state-owned joint-venture partners may in some cases represent a governmental reaction against the "sham" types of joint ventures so often concluded at the height of the "joint venture movement" of the 1960s and early 1970s in which the main domestic effect may have been to enrich small elites in the private sector without resulting in any significant transfer of technology, know-how, or meaningful managerial control to the host country.

Conclusion

Even if, as apparently has been the case, SOEs have not been particularly successful in the areas of savings mobilization and employment, one cannot conclude that the recent enlargement of their relative role in LDCs has on balance been detrimental to goals of LDC societies. Expansion of state-enterprise activities might have proceeded at a rather slower pace in the absence of pervasive and largely artificial incentives for the type of capital-intensive investment so characteristic of SOE undertakings. But SOE expansion occurred in response to very real pressures, many of them noneconomic, that no government could have afforded to overlook. These include the reaction to past colonial domination, which led to large-scale nationalizations in many countries, and protection from the feared domination of new foreign investors.

Widespread dissatisfaction with the income distributional outcomes of past growth in many LDCs, and a perception that traditional measures for rectifying inequality, such as tax policy, have had only limited impact, have also led many governments to view state-owned enterprises as possible instruments for correcting maldistribution among households. Some enterprises have also been created to deal with maldistribution between social groups, to allow segments of society to "catch up" by gaining wider participation in the development process.

Regardless of their performance as measured by standards normally applied to private firms, and whether or not they are perceived to have successfully promoted noneconomic goals of LDC societies, the role of state-owned firms in development is not likely to diminish in the foreseeable future.

FURTHER READING

One of the first systematic analyses of an entire country's state enterprise sector was that by Leroy P. Jones, *Public Enerprise and Economic Development: The Korean Case* (Seoul: KDI Press, 1975). A thoughtful survey of much of the literature on public enterprises in development through 1975 may be found in John B. Sheahan, "Public Enterprise in Developing Countries," in *Public Enterprise: Economic Analysis of Theory and Practice* edited by W. G. Shepard (Lexington, Mass.: Lexington Books, 1976). Two recent anthologies contain over two dozen articles on the role of public enterprises in economic development. They are: William J. Baumol (ed.), *Public and Private Enterprises in a Mixed Economy* (New York: St. Martins Press, 1980); and Leroy Jones, Edward Mason, and Raymond Vernon (ed.), *Public Enterprises in Developing Countries* (New York: Oxford University Press, forthcoming 1983).

INDEX

585